ETHNIC GROUPS WORLDWIDE
A Ready Reference Handbook

by
David Levinson

Oryx Press
1998

The rare Arabian oryx is believed to have inspired the myth of the unicorn. This desert antelope became virtually extinct in the early 1960s. At that time several groups of international conservationists arranged to have 9 animals sent to the Phoenix Zoo to be the nucleus of a captive breeding herd. Today the oryx population is over 1,000, and over 500 have been returned to the Middle East.

© 1998 by The Oryx Press
4041 North Central at Indian School Road
Phoenix, Arizona 85012-3397

Library of Congress Cataloging-in-Publication Data

Levinson, David, 1947–
    Ethnic groups worldwide : a ready reference handbook / by David H. Levinson.
      p. cm.
    Includes bibliographical references and index.
    ISBN 1-57356-019-7 (alk. paper)
    1. Ethnology—Handbooks, manuals, etc. 2. Ethnic groups–
–Handbooks, manuals, etc. I. Title.
GN325.L46 1998
305.8—dc21   98-13274
                                       CIP

CONTENTS

Part Two: Africa

Part Three: Asia and the Pacific

Part Four: The Americas

INTRODUCTION

The purpose of this handbook is to provide readers with an easy-to-use, accurate, up-to-date guide to ethnic groups in the contemporary world. It is being published at a time when ethnic identity, ethnic relations, ethnic conflict, and immigration are increasingly important factors in national, regional, and international affairs.

Ethnicity in the Modern World

When reading the descriptions of ethnic groups and the analyses of ethnic relations in individual nations, it is important to keep in mind the broader context—the role of ethnicity worldwide. Among the major features of ethnicity in the modern world are the following:

1. Most nations are ethnically heterogeneous; in other words, they are made up of more than one ethnic group, and no single group is completely dominant.
2. Migration of people from different ethnic groups across national boundaries and to other regions is a major component of today's global economy, and many nations have sizable populations of immigrant minorities.
3. The indigenous rights movement is a major moral, political, and legal issue in many nations that often pits the interests of indigenous peoples, such as Native Americans or Australian Aboriginals, against those who settled in the nation later but now dominate national affairs.
4. Competition between ethnic groups for power and wealth is a significant factor in

many developing nations, in some places jeopardizing national unity.
5. Political and cultural control exerted by national governments threatens the autonomy and perhaps even the survival of some ethnic minorities, leading to separatist movements in many nations.

When the information provided here about each modern state is considered within the context of these five generalities, it is obvious that, despite the underlying similarities, there are enormous differences across nations in the ethnic composition of their populations and in the nature of their ethnic relations.

In the most general sense, the ethnic composition of each nation can be described as either homogeneous or heterogeneous. Ethnically *homogeneous* nations are those whose populations are composed exclusively (or almost exclusively) of people from one ethnic group that dominates the nation culturally, economically, and politically. Such nations are in the minority, with Japan and Korea the best examples. Also falling within the homogeneous category are nations such as China and Germany, which, although heterogeneous in terms of number of groups, are more properly classified as homogeneous in that one group constitutes most of the population and is clearly dominant. For example, although China has 57 official ethnic groups, the Han are 94% of the population and dominate national affairs.

Ethnically *heterogeneous* nations—the majority of the nations of the world—have populations composed of two or more ethnic groups, none of which is completely dominant. Heterogeneous nations take a variety of forms. Some, like the United States, are made up of dozens or even hundreds of different ethnic groups, with no one group being totally dominant; all groups being united to some extent by a shared national culture and identity; and each group maintaining some degree of cultural autonomy. Other nations, such as Canada, Switzerland, and Mauritius, are officially pluralistic in that each ethnic group has considerable cultural autonomy within the national political and economic framework. Still others, such as Trinidad and Tobago, Uganda, and Kenya, are made up of two or more ethnic groups that compete for power and cultural dominance, with no group dominant in all spheres or regions, or with dominance shifting over time. And still others, such as Indonesia, are made up of many ethnic groups, with one being dominant but the others maintaining some autonomy. The key point is that heterogeneity is not simply a matter of the number of different ethnic groups in a nation, nor of the relative sizes of their populations.

As suggested above, an understanding of a national situation also requires consideration of patterns of ethnicity-based cultural, economic, and political dominance within the nation. Typically, cultural dominance means that the people of a nation speak the language, adhere to the religion, wear the style of clothing, and live the lifestyle of the dominant group. Economic dominance means that members of the dominant group control the wealth of the nation and its major commercial and industrial institutions. And political dominance means that members of the dominant group occupy the most powerful positions in the government and are able to control the political influence of other ethnic groups.

Accuracy Issues

It is important to point out for users of this work—and other works on ethnicity—a number of practical constraints that influence both the amount and trustworthiness of information on ethnic composition and ethnic relations. First, and perhaps most important, there are no definitions or criteria consistently applied to delineate ethnic groups in nations worldwide. I encountered this problem earlier in my work on the *Encyclopedia of World Cultures* and *American Immigrant Cultures: Builders of a Nation.* Thus, in this book, I have followed the same general approach taken in the previous two for choosing which ethnic groups to cover: I have been flexible in the criteria used and have considered language, religion, common history, occupational specialization, regional localization, common culture, self-identification, and identification by others as equally valid criteria for labeling a particular group an "ethnic group." In general, I have avoided strict adherence to official government lists of ethnic groups, as the compilation of such lists is often driven by political considerations. For example, if government criteria were followed, no separate ethnic groups would be listed for Turkey because the government claims that there are no ethnic minorities and that all people are simply Turks.

Related to the question of group identification is the issue of group names. Many ethnic groups around the world are identified by more than one name. For example, the group may have a name for itself, neighboring groups may label it differently, and scholarly experts might use still another name; additionally, subgroups might have separate names, the preferred name for the group may change over time, and a group may have different names in different countries. The name I have chosen to use for each group is the one most commonly used at the present time, either by the group itself or by scholarly experts who write about it. I have tried to avoid using names that are known to be insulting. For example, "Tropical Forest Foragers" is used rather than "Pygmies," although the older name is provided in parentheses, as most readers will not know that Foragers is a preferable label for groups that in the past have often been called Pygmies. In cases where there is a commonly used alternative name, it is indicated in parentheses following the more usual name.

Beyond the issue of group identification is the problem of information accuracy. I have tried to consult the most recent sources, although for some nations—such as Afghanistan—"recent" may mean 20 years old. And some ethnic groups have simply been studied more frequently, more recently, or more completely than have other groups. Data accuracy is an especially significant issue for population information. Even in nations such as the United States, where much time and money are spent on counting the population at regular 10-year intervals, experts agree that the population is undercounted by about 2%, with some ethnic minorities undercounted by even more. The situation is, of course, even less reliable for nations such as Indonesia that do not attempt to enumerate ethnic populations, nations such as Burkina Faso with large rural populations that are difficult to count, nations such as Bosnia with ongoing ethnic conflict, and nations such as Ghana in which there is much labor migration to and from other nations. Nonetheless, unless otherwise noted, the population estimates provided here give a reasonable approximation of the populations of the ethnic groups and their relative size vis-à-vis other groups in the nation.

Sources Used

In writing this volume, I have consulted a wide range of information sources: government reports; reports of regional and international governmental and nongovernmental organizations; research reports in the form of books, conference papers, and journal articles by anthropologists, sociologists, geographers, demographers, historians, and political scientists; reports by journalists; accounts by travelers; and newspaper reports. References to many of these sources are provided in the bibliographies in each of the book's four parts. In compiling this volume, I also called upon the expertise of anthropological colleagues, and I especially want to acknowledge Frank Salamone's work on the Africa section, Ronald Johnson's on northern Europe, and Frank Proschan's provision of information on Southeast Asia.

Patterns in Ethnic Relations

Most people would say that the patterns of ethnic relations in their own nation are unique. To some degree this is true, but there are also a number of features and patterns of ethnic relations that are found in many nations. As a number of these characteristics are routinely referred to in the text, they require definition here.

Two processes seem universal in the way the members of any ethnic group view the members of other groups. First, all groups are *ethnocentric* in that their members consider their own way of life—their culture—to be the "right" way and superior to other ways, and they judge other groups by their own standards. Second, people in all groups engage in *stereotyping:* both their own group and other groups are described in exaggerated or inaccurate ways that emphasize the positive features of their own group and the negative features of others.

In addition, *ethnic politics* are common in many nations. Ethnic politics is a general label for a number of behaviors and strategies in the political process, all of which involve considering ethnicity in forming governments or in governing. In some nations, ethnic politics involve open political competition, with different ethnic groups aligned with different political parties. In others, political leaders appeal to the interests of specific ethnic groups or create competition or conflict between groups to attract supporters. In some nations, ethnic diversity is publicly recognized and ethnic background is considered in selecting government officials and employees. In others, ethnic diversity is publicly disavowed and ethnic background is not permitted to be considered in selecting government officials or employees. And in some nations, the disadvantaged minority status of some ethnic groups is recognized and special affirmative action programs have been developed. Thus, ethnic politics in its various forms are a common feature of national life in many nations.

Ethnic politics reflect a more general state of ethnic relations called *ethnic competition.* Much has been written about ethnic competition by sociologists and political scientists, and some argue that ethnic groups—or at least some ethnic groups—exist as political action groups whose primary purpose is to further the political and economic interests of their members. Whether or not this view is accurate and applies across all nations, it is true that (1) ethnic competition is common across nations, (2) it tends to lead to ethnic conflict in nations with large populations of immigrants who are sometimes seen as competing with indigenous groups for jobs, and (3) it leads to conflict in recently independent nations where different groups, all previously under colonial control, compete for political power and wealth.

The final major form of ethnic relations that occurs commonly across nations is *assimilation,* the process by which one group adopts some or all of the cultural features of another group. Assimilation is a complex process and can be voluntary or forced (sometimes called *ethnocide*); can occur rapidly or over a long period of time; can be full or partial; and can involve some culture elements, such as religion, economic practices, childrearing, and political organization, but not others. Although assimilation typically involves a smaller, weaker group assimilating to a dominant group, the process is often two-way, with the dominant group also adding to its cultural inventory some elements from the weaker group.

Scope and Structure of This Volume

This handbook is divided into four parts—Europe, Africa, Asia and the Pacific, and the Americas—with each part containing an individual nation-by-nation description for that region. An introduction, a bibliography of sources, and maps are provided at the beginning of each regional part.

The nation profiles provide three categories of information. First, they list the major ethnic groups or clusters of related ethnic groups in all nations of the world in the late 1990s. Included in these lists are groups indigenous to each nation—such as Inuit in Canada or Germans in Germany—and the growing number of nonindigenous or immigrant groups (immigration is an increasingly common process around the world, and immigrants make up a substantial portion of the population in many nations). Second, the volume contains brief descriptions of the major ethnic groups or clusters of related groups in each nation. These descriptions focus on the location; population; religion; and basic economic, social, and political practices of each group. Third, for each nation, a succinct analysis is given of the current state of ethnic relations. These analyses do not necessarily cover all possible ethnic relations issues in each nation; rather, they emphasize those of greatest national importance.

In conclusion, the basic aim of this volume is to make information that is often difficult to find and analyze available to students, scholars, journalists, and other interested readers in an easy-to-use reference resource. This information is important—and often vital—because we live in an increasingly multicultural world and at a time when ethnic conflict affects many regions of the globe. Access to reliable information and analysis will allow us greater insight and understanding as we strive to cope more knowledgeably and effectively with the diverse challenges presented by ethnicity and ethnic relations.

PART ONE

Europe

EUROPE
Introduction

This section covers Europe's ethnic groups and ethnic relations in European nations. Europe is defined here to include all of continental Europe and the British Isles, Iceland, Cyprus, and the former republics of the Soviet Union in Eastern Europe, including Russia itself. The nations of Europe range from ethnically homogeneous (such as Poland) to ethnically pluralistic (such as Belgium) to ethnically heterogeneous (such as Spain and Italy). The most ethnically diverse is Russia, although that diversity is masked to some extent by the long history of Russian dominance of ethnic minorities.

Types of Ethnic Groups in Europe

European nations contain a number of different types of ethnic groups. First, many nations, such as Germany, Poland, and the Netherlands, are heavily populated by a single ethnonational group—the Germans, Poles, or Dutch. An ethnonational group is the largest ethnic group in its nation and the carrier of the national language and culture. The second kind of ethnic group in European nations is ethnonational groups from one nation living in another (Poles in Lithuania and Ukraine, for example), where they are labeled national minorities. A third type of group, really more cultural than ethnic, is defined by national culture; for example, the French and the Italians. A fourth category is ethnolinguistic minorities such as the Saami in Scandinavia or the Ladin in Italy—groups of people who have been resident in the region for a long time and have maintained some degree of cultural autonomy. Except in Russia, such groups are not a major presence in Europe. Closely related to these groups is the

fifth type, regional ethnic minorities such as the Basques and Catalans in Spain and the Bretons in France—groups with a major presence in a particular national region, differing culturally from the nation's other ethnic groups. The sixth category is immigrants from outside Europe, most of whom left their nation of origin after World War II. These include guest workers from other European and Asian nations, as well as emigrants from former European colonies in Asia, Africa, and the Americas. The seventh and final category is ethnic groups whose people are present across Europe but have no homeland there; notably, Jews and Gypsies.

Ethnic Relations in Europe

Ethnic relations take a variety of forms and have been affected by large-scale migration both within nations and across them. Across nations, ethnic relations are essentially peaceful, as reflected in the formation of the European Union and the likelihood of EU expansion of membership to Eastern European nations—and the possible inclusion of these same nations in NATO, the North Atlantic Treaty Organization. Within nations, the major conflicts are between national, regional, and ethnolinguistic minorities and the national governments, such as in Italy, Spain, and Ukraine. The conflicts involve demands by the minorities for autonomy and independence, demands that are resisted by the national governments. In some situations the conflict is peaceful, in others it is violent. In nations in Western Europe with large immigrant populations, conflict has developed in the 1990s over the number of immigrants that should be allowed and the role of these immigrants in national life. In many nations, immigrants are seen as an economic and social burden, and laws have been enacted to restrict their numbers. For their part, immigrants complain about discrimination and believe that most nations would prefer that they return to their nations of origin and that members of dominant ethnic groups be given priority in employment, housing, and education. In the post-Communist era in Eastern Europe, there has been a resurgence of anti-Semitism and anti-Gypsy feeling. Consequently, a large number of Jews have immigrated to Israel and the United States, and many Gypsies have relocated to Western Europe, although anti-Gypsy sentiments also have resurfaced there.

Europe Bibliography

Abrahamsen, Samuel. *Norway's Response to the Holocaust.* New York: Holocaust Library, 1991.

Akiner, Shirin. *Islamic Peoples of the Soviet Union: An Historical and Statistical Handbook*, 2nd ed. New York: KPI, 1986.

Ardagh, John. *Cultural Atlas of France.* New York: Facts on File, 1991.

Ardagh, John. *Germany and the Germans: An Anatomy of Society Today.* New York: Harper & Row, 1987.

Batalden, Stephen K.; and Sandra L. Batalden. *The Newly Independent States of Eurasia: Handbook of Former Soviet Republics.* Phoenix: Oryx Press, 1997.

Benet, Sula. *Abkasians: The Long-Living People of the Caucasus.* New York: Holt, Rinehart & Winston, 1974. (Georgia)

Bennett, Linda A. *Encyclopedia of World Cultures.* Volume 4: "Europe." Boston: G. K. Hall/Macmillan, 1992.

Bennigsen, Alexandre; and S. Enders Wimbush. *Muslims of the Soviet Empire.* Bloomington: Indiana University Press, 1986.

Bodega, Isabel, et al. "Recent Migrations from Morocco to Spain." *International Migration Review* 29 (1995): 794–99.

Boehm, Christopher. *Blood Revenge: The Enactment and Management of Conflict in Montenegro and Other Tribal Societies.* Philadelphia: University of Pennsylvania Press, 1986. (Yugoslavia)

Boissevain, Jeremy. *A Village in Malta.* New York: Holt, Rinehart & Winston, 1980.

Castle, Stephen; and Mark J. Miller. *The Age of Migration: International Population Movements in the Modern World.* London: Macmillan, 1993.

Coleman, David, ed. *Europe's Population in the 1990s.* Oxford: Oxford University Press, 1996.

Coleman, David; and John Salt. *The British Population: Patterns, Trends, and Processes.* Oxford: Oxford University Press, 1992.

Dima, Nicholas. *From Moldavia to Moldova: The Soviet-Romanian Territorial Dispute.* New York: Columbia University Press, 1991.

Dornberg, John. *Central and Eastern Europe.* Phoenix: Oryx Press, 1995.

Dornberg, John. *Western Europe.* Phoenix: Oryx Press, 1996.

Duncan, W. Raymond; and G. Paul Holman, Jr., eds. *Ethnic Nationalism and Regional Conflict: The Former Soviet Union and Yugoslavia.* Boulder: Westview Press, 1994.

Durrenberger, E. Paul; and Gisli Palsson, eds. *The Anthropology of Iceland.* Iowa City: University of Iowa Press, 1989.

Ehrhart, Hans-Georg; Anna Kreikemeyer; and Andrei V. Zagorski, eds. *Crisis Management in the CIS: Whither Russia?* Baden-Baden: Nomos Verlagsgesellschaft, 1995. (Armenia, Azerbaijan, Belarus, Georgia, Russia)

Fortier, David H. "Brittany: 'Breiz Atao.'" In *Nations Without a State: Ethnic Minorities in Western Europe*, Charles R. Foster, ed., 136–52. (France)

Foster, Charles R., ed. *Nations Without a State: Ethnic Minorities in Western Europe.* New York: Praeger, 1980.

Fox, Robin. *The Tory Islanders: A People of the Celtic Fringe.* Cambridge: Cambridge University Press, 1978. (Ireland)

Glenny, Michael. *The Fall of Yugoslavia: The Third Balkan War.* New York: Penguin, 1992.

Gmelch, George. *The Irish Tinkers: The Urbanization of an Itinerant People.* Prospect Heights, IL: Waveland Press, 1987.

Gurr, Ted R. *Minorities at Risk: A Global View of Ethnopolitical Conflicts.* Washington DC: United States Institute of Peace Press, 1993. (Italy, Norway, former USSR except Russia)

Hooper, John. *The Spaniards: A Portrait of the New Spain.* New York: Viking, 1988.

Horak, Stephan M. *Eastern European Ethnic Minorities, 1919–1980: A Handbook.* Littleton, CO: Libraries Unlimited, 1985. (Albania, Bulgaria, Romania)

Husband, Charles. "The Political Context of Muslim Communities' Participation in British Society." In *Muslims in Europe,* Bernard Lewis and Dominique Schnapper, eds., 79–97. (Great Britain)

Jansen, Johannes J. G. "Islam and Muslim Civil Rights in the Netherlands." In *Muslims in Europe,* Bernard Lewis and Dominique Schnapper, eds., 39–53. (Netherlands)

Jones, Trevor. *Britain's Ethnic Minorities: An Analysis of the Labour Force Survey.* London: Policy Studies Institute, 1993.

Kelly, Aidan J. D. "Ethnic Identification, Association and Redefinition: Muslim Pakistanis and Greek Cypriotes in Britain." In *New Identities in Europe*, Karmela Liebkind, ed., 77–115. (Great Britain)

Khazanov, Anatoly M. *After the USSR: Ethnicity, Nationalism, and Politics in the Commonwealth of Independent States.* Madison: University of Wisconsin Press, 1995.

Killingray, David. "Africans in the United Kingdom: An Introduction." *Immigrants and Minorities* 12 (1993): 2–27.

King, Russell, ed. *Mass Migration in Europe: The Legacy and Future.* Chichester: John Wiley and Sons, 1995.

Kipel, Vitaut. *Byelorussian Statehood.* New York: Byelorussian Central Council, 1988. (Belarus)

Krejci, Jaroslav; and Vitezslav Zelimsky. *Ethnic and Political Nations in Europe.* New York: St. Martin's Press, 1981.

Lange, Anders. "Identifications, Perceived Cultural Distance and Stereotypes in Yugoslav and Turkish Youths in Stockholm." In *New Identities in Europe,* Karmela Liebkind, ed., 169–218. (Sweden)

Levinson, David, ed. *Encyclopedia of World Cultures.* New York: G. K. Hall/Macmillan, 1991–1995.

Levinson, David. *Ethnic Relations.* Santa Barbara: ABC-CLIO, 1994.

Lewis, Bernard and Dominique Schnapper, eds. *Muslims in Europe*. London: Pinter, 1994. (France, Germany, Great Britain)

Liebkind, Karmela, ed. *New Identities in Europe*. Aldershot: Gower, 1989.

Liebkind, Karmela. "Patterns of Ethnic Identification among Finns in Sweden." In *New Identities in Europe*, Karmela Liebkind, ed., 116–39. (Sweden)

Levin, M. G.; and L. P. Potapov, eds. *The Peoples of Siberia*. Chicago: University of Chicago Press, 1964. Translated by Stephen P. Dunn and Ethel Dunn. Originally published in Russian in 1956. (Russia)

Longworth, Philip. *The Cossacks*. New York: Holt, Rinehart & Winston, 1969. (Russia)

Ludtke, Jean. *Atlantic Peaks: Ethnographic Guide to the Portuguese-Speaking Atlantic Islands*. Hanover, MA: Christopher Publishing House, 1989. (Azores, Madeira)

Magocsi, Paul R. *Our People: Carpatho-Rusyns and Their Descendants in North America*, 3rd edition. Toronto: University of Toronto Press, 1994.

Mayer, Kurt. "Ethnic Tensions in Switzerland: The Jura Conflict." In *Nations Without a State: Ethnic Minorities in Western Europe*, Charles R. Foster, ed., 189–208. (Switzerland)

McRae, Kenneth D. *Conflict and Compromise in Multilingual Societies: Switzerland*. Waterloo, Ontario: Wilfrid Laurier University Press, 1983.

Minority Rights Group. *Minorities and Autonomy in Western Europe*. London: Minority Rights Group, 1991. (Netherlands, Switzerland)

Motyl, Alexander J., ed. *The Post-Soviet Nations*. New York: Columbia University Press, 1992. (Russia)

Nauck, Bernhard. "Changes in Turkish Migrant Families in Germany." In *Muslims in Europe,* Bernard Lewis and Dominique Schnapper, eds., 130–47. (Germany)

Nielsen, Jorgen. *Muslims in Western Europe*. Edinburgh: Edinburgh University Press, 1992. (France, Great Britain, Germany)

Olcott, Martha B., ed. *The Soviet Multinational State: Readings and Documents*. Armonk, NY: M. E. Sharpe, 1990. (Armenia, Azerbaijan, Russia)

Olson, James S., ed. *An Ethnohistorical Dictionary of the Russian and Soviet Empires*. Westport, CT: Greenwood Press, 1994. (Armenia, Azerbaijan, Belarus, Moldova, Russia, Ukraine)

Peach, Ceri; and Günther Glebe. "Muslim Minorities in Western Europe." *Ethnic and Racial Studies* 18 (1995): 26–46. (France, Great Britain, Spain, Norway, Sweden, Netherlands, Germany)

Pettai, Vello A. "Shifting Relations, Shifting Identities: The Russian Minority in Estonia after Independence." *Nationalities Papers* 23 (1995): 405–11.

Pi-Sunyer, Oriol. "Dimensions of Catalan Nationalism." In *Nations Without a State: Ethnic Minorities in Western Europe*, Charles R. Foster, ed., 101–15. (Spain)

Poulton, Hugh. *The Balkans: Minorities and States in Conflict*. London: Minority Rights Group, 1993. (Albania, Bulgaria, Greece, Yugoslavia)

Pristinger, Flavia. "Ethnic Conflict and Modernization in the South Tyrol." In *Nations Without a State: Ethnic Minorities in Western Europe*, Charles R. Foster, ed., 153–88. (Italy)

Pribichevich, S. *Macedonia: Its People and History*. University Park: Pennsylvania State University Press, 1992.

Raun, Toivo U. "Ethnic Relations and Conflict in the Baltic States." In *Ethnic Nationalism and Regional Conflict*, edited by W. Raymond Duncan and G. Paul Holman, Jr., 155–82. (Estonia, Latvia, Lithuania)

Roy, Olivier. "Islam in France: Religion, Ethnic Community or Social Ghetto?" In *Muslims in Europe,* Bernard Lewis and Dominique Schnapper, eds., 54–66. (France)

Salt, John. *Migration and Population Change in Europe*. United Nations Institute for Disarmament Research, Research Paper No. 19. New York: United Nations, 1993.

Savigear, Peter. "Corsica and the French State." In *Nations Without a State: Ethnic Minorities in Western Europe*, Charles R. Foster, ed., 116–35. (France)

Schierup, Carl-Ulrik; and Aleksandra Alund. *Will They Still Be Dancing: Integration and Ethnic Transformation among Yugoslav Immigrants in Scandinavia.* Umea, Sweden: Department of Sociology, University of Umea, 1986.

Statteika, E. "Ethnic Minorities (Russians) in Lithuania." *Nationalities Papers* 23 (1995): 401–04.

Suny, Ronald G. *The Making of the Georgian Nation*. Bloomington: Indiana University Press, 1988.

Svanberg, Ingvar. "The Turkish-Speaking Ethnic Groups of Europe." *Europa Ethnica* 5 (1984): 65–73.

Sweeney, Jim; and Josef Weidenholzer, eds. *Austria: A Study in Modern Achievement.* Aldershot: 1988.

Tägil, Sven. *Ethnicity and Nation Building in the Nordic World*. London: Hurst & Company, 1995.

Taylor, Barry. *Andorra*. Oxford: ABC-CLIO, 1993.

U.S. Committee for Refugees. *1995 World Refugee Survey*. New York: U.S. Committee for Refugees, 1995.

Verdonk, Ambrose. "Young Spanish Migrants in the Netherlands and Switzerland on Their Ethnic Identity." In *New Identities in Europe*, Karmela Liebkind, ed., 140–68. (Netherlands, Switzerland)

Weekes, Richard V., ed. *Muslim Peoples: A World Ethnographic Survey*, 2nd edition. Westport, CT: Greenwood Press, 1984.

Winchester, Hillary. *Contemporary France*. New York: John Wiley & Sons, 1993.

Woolard, Kathryn A. *Double Talk: Bilingualism and the Politics of Ethnicity in Catalonia*. Stanford: Stanford University Press, 1989. (Spain)

Zaprudnik, I. A. *At a Crossroads in History*. Boulder: Westview Press, 1993. (Belarus)

Zulaika, Joseba. *Basque Violence: Metaphor and Sacrament*. Reno: University of Nevada Press, 1988. (Spain)

Albania

With a population of 3.4 million, Albania is in the Balkan region of southern Europe and is bordered by the Adriatic Sea on the west, Serbia on the north and northwest, Macedonia on the east, and Greece on the southeast. From the end of World War II to 1990, Albania was under Communist rule. From 1967 to 1990, the practice of any religion was banned by the government—it was the only officially atheistic nation in the world. Before then, Albania's population was primarily Muslim, with large minorities of Eastern Orthodox and Roman Catholic practitioners. Since the end of Communist rule in 1990, religious freedom has been restored—but the role of religion in Albania today is unclear.

Ethnic Composition

Albania is an ethnically homogeneous society. **Albanians** have for centuries been the dominant ethnic group and today constitute about 95% of the population. They call themselves **Shiptare,** number about 3.3 million in Albania, and comprise two regional subgroups, the **Ghegs** in the north and the **Tosks** in the south. Gheg culture is notable for its clan structure (rare in Europe in the 20th century), extended families, and blood feuds. Religious, cultural, and linguistic differences that separated the two groups largely disappeared during the era of Communist rule, and today Albanians are seen as a single ethnic group. Albanians may be descended, at least in part, from the Illyrians who settled in the region some 4,000 years ago, and this ancestry has served to keep them distinct from neighboring Slavic peoples who moved into the region several thousand years later. The only other sizable groups in Albania are the Greeks and Vlachs.

Greeks constitute between 2% and 5% of the population and live mainly in the south along the border with Greece. Since the reopening of the border in 1990, many have moved to Greece.

The **Vlach** population is estimated at between 35,000 and 100,000. Formerly nomadic sheepherders, the Vlachs were settled forcibly by the Communist government and are now assimilated into Albanian society. Sometimes considered Romanian because their language is similar, Vlachs are a remnant population descended from the Illyrians and Thracians who interacted with the Slavic population over the centuries in the Balkans.

Other groups in Albania include small communities of **Italians** and **Montenegrins** in the north, **Jews** in cities, **Gypsies, Slav Macedonians** in the southeast, **Armenians, Pomaks,** and **Blacks** descended from slaves brought from Africa during the rule of the Ottoman Empire.

Ethnic Relations

Albania itself is free of major ethnic conflict, with the major conflicts involving ethnic Albanians and Serbs in the Kosovo region of neighboring Serbia (*see* Yugoslavia) and Albanians and Macedonians in Macedonia (*see* Macedonia). Under Communist rule (1946–90), Greeks were the object of discrimination, manifested in restrictions on using the Greek language, a closed border with Greece, and forced relocations. Forced assimilation, including restrictions on the use of Greek names and speaking Greek in public, has lessened since 1990 and the Greeks remaining in Albania have become more politically active. However, refusal by the Greek government since 1989 to accept many Albanians seeking entry into Greece has created animosity directed at the Greek minority in Albania.

Andorra

Andorra is a small nation in the Pyrenees mountains along the border between Spain and France. It has a population of 55,000, composed of 54% **Spaniards,** 29% **Catalans,** 6% **French,** 3% **Portuguese,** and the remainder mainly from other Western European nations. About 50% of the Spaniards and most of the French are not Andorran citizens, although they live in Andorra and have work permits. Foreign immigration is limited to the Spaniards and French, who may immigrate to work in Andorra.

Andorran is a national rather than an ethnic label, and individuals classified as Andorran are ethnically **Catalan** (*see* Spain). Catalan is the official language of Andorra, although French and Spanish are also commonly spoken. Roman Catholicism is the official religion; 94% of the people are Roman Catholics, the remainder being Protestant, along with a small number of Jews. Though small and landlocked, Andorra is a prosperous nation due to its thriving international banking operations and tourism. Because of governmental controls on immigration and the prospering economy, ethnic conflict is not an issue.

Armenia

Armenia is a small nation in southeastern Europe that is bordered by Georgia on the north, Azerbaijan on the east, Iran on the south, and Turkey on the west. With a population of 3.5 million, 94% of whom are ethnic Armenians, the Republic of Armenia is one of the most ethnically homogenous nations in the world. The Armenians and an Armenian state have been a presence in the region for over 3,000 years, although borders have shifted. Armenia has been ruled by Turks, Byzantines, Persians, and Russians, and was part of the Soviet Union for much of the 20th century. The modern nation is located in what was previously called Eastern Armenia. The area once known as Western Armenia, located within the borders of modern Turkey, was emptied of Armenians through the genocide and forced relocations of the early 20th century.

Ethnic Composition

Armenia is ethnically homogeneous. **Armenians** have been a distinct ethnic group in the region for over 3,000 years and formed the first Christian nation in the world between A.D. 301 and 330. Religion, especially the Armenian Orthodox Church, remains a unifying force for Armenians both inside and outside Armenia. Other key features of Armenian culture include the large, extended family networks; the long and deep literary and artistic traditions; and ties to the homeland.

The **Khemsil,** Armenians who converted to Islam in the 18th century under Ottoman rule, live mainly in Turkey. Because of the frequent invasions of Armenia and rule imposed by other nations, many Armenians at various times over the millennia have been forced to flee their homeland, and today there is a large Armenian diaspora. Because of this diaspora, the genocide in Turkey, and the antiquity of their ethnic identity, the Armenian experience is often likened to that of the Jews.

Azerbaijani were the second largest ethnic group in Armenia (2.6% of the population) during the Soviet era, but due to ongoing conflict between Armenia and Azerbaijan, nearly all have now fled or have been expelled.

Russians numbered 51,600 in 1989, but probably fewer than that live in Armenia in 1997—many left following Armenian independence from the Soviet Union in 1991. During the Soviet era, the Armenian government was a close ally of Russia, although relations turned hostile in the late 1980s when the Soviet government failed to meet Armenian demands for the unification of the Nagorno-Karabakh region in Azerbaijan with Armenia. Still, Russians in Armenia remain influential in economic affairs, and Armenians who speak Russian remain at an advantage in dealing with the Russian government and with foreign businesses located in Russia.

Kurds in Armenia numbered 56,000 in 1989, with Armenia having the largest number of Kurds of any of the former Soviet republics. This number is, of course, only a small percentage of the 23 million Kurds in the world, who are primarily in the Middle East. Kurds are mainly Sunni Muslims, and a large segment of the community is formed by those who fled Azerbaijan in the 1920s. Relations with the Armenians are peaceful though socially distant.

Yezidis, who numbered about 52,000 in 1989, speak Kurdish and are considered by many outsiders to be Kurds although they view themselves as a distinct ethnic group and live apart from the Kurds. Their distinctiveness rests on their unique religion, based on elements drawn from Zoroastrianism, Judaism, Christianity, and Islam; their belief that they are descended from Adam alone; avoidance of commercial activities; and a social structure of three castes: laypersons, and those with special religious status called *pyir* and *sheikh*. Yezidi relations with the Armenians are peaceful.

Other groups in Armenia include several thousand **Greeks** and **Ukrainians**.

Ethnic Relations

Ethnic relations within Armenia are peaceful, with the nation's ethnic conflicts being mainly external and involving the neighboring Turkish Turks and Azerbaijani Turks—the Armenians are bitter enemies of both. The ongoing conflict with the Azerbaijanis is covered in the entry on Azerbaijan. Although tensions remain between the Russians and Armenians in Armenia, there is little threat of violent conflict.

Armenian soldiers on the move in 1993 during the war with Azerbaijan over the Nagorno-Karabakh region. Photo: Reuters/Corbis-Bettmann.

Austria

Austria, located in central Europe, is bordered by Germany and the Czech Republic on the north, Slovakia on the northeast, Hungary on the southeast, Slovenia and Italy on the south, and Switzerland on the west. Austria was created in 1918 through the unification of Vienna and the six German-speaking provinces of the defunct Austro-Hungarian Empire. In 1945, Burgenland was added. To some extent, all eight provinces—Lower Austria, Upper Austria, Steiermark, Tirol, Carinthia, Salzburg, Vorarlberg, and Burgenland—retain something of their distinct cultural traditions. Since 1945, however, all have been incorporated into the emerging Austrian national culture through governmental control of the education system and media and a conscious effort to promote an Austrian identity separate from that of Germany. Austria has a population of 7,986,000 of whom between 95% and 99% are Austrian and speak the southern dialect of German. Because Austria classifies ethnic identity on the basis of language, some non-Austrians who speak that dialect of German may be lumped in the Austrian category. "Austrian" is more a national designation than an ethnic designation, as Austrians are closely related to southern Germans in language and culture, especially to Bavarians.

Ethnic Composition

Austrians are citizens of the nation of Austria, drawn together by their language (German), religion (Roman Catholicism), values that emphasize both the rural history of the nation and its modern sophistication, and a general desire to forge an identity separate from Germans. Forces working against an Austrian identity include the growing desire for unification with Germany and the cultural traditions of the regional cultures. Especially important are local, class-based networks in which individuals spend most of their lives. Austrian society is divided into five classes—farmers, workers, bureaucrats, wealthy landowners, and nobility. About 85% of Austrians are Roman Catholic.

Most of the other ethnic groups with sizable populations in Austria fall into two categories—guest workers, and populations near the borders of their homelands. The major guest worker groups are the Serbs and Turks, most of whom live in Vienna. The **Serbs** number perhaps as many as 250,000, while the **Turks** number about 100,000. Other guest workers come from Poland, Hungary, the Czech Republic, Slovakia, and Romania.

Groups from nearby nations include the **Croats,** numbering about 20,000, who live mainly in Burgenland where they were first settled by the Hapsburgs in the 17th century; **Czechs,** who migrated to Austria in the late 1800s and early 1900s in search of employment in Vienna and other major cities and are assimilated into Austrian society; **Hungarians,** numbering about 15,000, mostly farmers who live in Burgenland on the border with Hungary, their presence in Austria the result of post–World War I negotiations that placed the province within Austria's borders; **Slovaks,** who migrated to Austria in the late 1800s and early 1900s in search of employment in Vienna and other major cities and were rapidly assimilated into Austrian society; and **Slovenes,** numbering about 20,000, mostly farmers who have lived for several thousand years in relatively isolated communities in Carinthia, and in the 20th century have been subjected to discrimination by the German-speaking majority in the region.

The **Gypsy** population is quite small, about 40,000, and both Roma and Sinti groups have lived in Austria since the 14th century. They currently live mainly in Vienna and Burgenland, where compulsory education and efforts to include them in the industrial workforce have not yet led to assimilation.

Vienna is a cosmopolitan city that draws residents from all over the world, including Iran, Russia, France, Spain, and the United States.

Ethnic Relations

Austrian law classifies the Croat, Czech, Hungarian, Slovak, and Slovene minorities as official minorities, while Jews, Gypsies, Turks, and Serbs, and others are not so classified. Although official policy protects minority rights, mass executions and assimilation pressures before and following World War II have substantially reduced the populations of all minorities. Austrian law limits the number of guest workers allowed in the country, but because they can bring spouses and children, guest workers may account for almost 10% of the population. There is considerable anti-Semitism in Austria, although Jews number less than 10,000. There also is resentment of foreign workers (who constitute about 13% of Vienna's population) and a fear of being overrun by refugees from Eastern Europe. Austria has a history of strained ethnic relations with its neighbors: with Italy, based on the treatment of Austrian Tiroleans in northern Italy; with Romania, concerning the treatment of Austrians in Transylvania; and with Croatia and Slovenia, regarding the treatment of Croats and Slovenes in Burgenland.

Belarus

Belarus (formerly called Belarussia or Byelorussia) is a small nation in Eastern Europe bordered by Latvia and Russia on the north, Russia on the east, Ukraine on the south, and Poland and Lithuania on the west. The population is 10.2 million, composed mainly of Slavic peoples—Belarusians, Russians, Ukrainians, and Poles. Ancestors of modern-day Belarusians have been settled in the region since the 9th century A.D. Once forming the core of the Grand Duchy of Lithuania, by the 16th century the region came under Polish control, and in the 17th and 18th centuries under the control of Muscovy and then Russia. Belarus was closely linked to Russia during the 20th-century Soviet era, and it remains so in the 1990s.

Ethnic Composition

Ethnically, nearly the entire population is Slavic. The largest group is the **Belarusians** (formerly called **Belarussians,** or **White Russians),** who number about 8 million, or 78% of the population. Their language is Belarusian, which is closely related to Ukrainian and Russian. Despite efforts to promote the use of Belarusian and its status as the national language since 1991, Russian is commonly spoken and remains the language of government. Since Belarus's independence from the Soviet Union in 1991, there has been an effort to begin to teach Belarusian in the schools. Nearly all Belarusians are adherents of Eastern Orthodoxy. Major distinguishing cultural features, which are now found mainly in rural areas, include distinctive red, white, and black colors in dress; an emphasis on fabric crafts; dramatic religious ceremonies; a style of folk music and song dating to pre-Christian times; and a form of Eastern Orthodoxy that combines indigenous practices such as harvest festivals with Christianity. There are large populations with Belarus ancestry in Canada, the United States, Australia, Ukraine, Russia, Poland, and Central Asia, although as immigrants, they have often been classified as Russians.

The three other Slavic peoples form about 20% of the population of Belarus, with **Poles** numbering about 418,000, or about 4% of the population (*see* Poland); **Russians** numbering about 1.4 million, or 13% of the population (*see* Russia)*;* and **Ukrainians** numbering about 300,000, or 3% of the population (*see* Ukraine).

The only non-Slavic group of significant size is the **Jews,** estimated at anywhere from 75,000 to 112,000. The easing of restrictions on emigration and an increase in anti-Semitic rhetoric has led many Belarusian Jews to leave for Israel and the United States since the late 1980s.

Ethnic Relations

Beginning in the 18th century and continuing on through the Soviet period, Belarusians were subject to a Russification campaign that restricted their political rights and language use, converted many from Roman Catholicism and indigenous religions to Eastern Orthodoxy, and made the country an economic appendage of Russia. Resistance to Russian rule emerged in the mid-1800s along with an increased sense of distinct Belarusian identity. In 1921, the territory that is now Belarus was divided among Belarus, Russia, Poland, Lithuania, and Latvia, and Russification continued, interrupted only by World War II, which devastated the nation. The Sovietization policies of the post–World War II era further Russified the population, with Russian replacing Belarusian as the primary language.

In 1991 Belarus became an independent nation, and Belarus experienced a cultural revival along with political independence. The relationship between Belarusians and the Ukrainians and Russians—associated with the old political order—is an ambivalent one. On the one hand, the groups are culturally and linguistically closely related and there is a long history of contact, although not always peaceful. On the other hand, Russian rule prevented the emergence of an autonomous Belarusian national culture and, to a large extent, replaced the Belarusian language with Russian.

The economic and political realities of the 1990s seem to have taken precedence over concerns about cultural autonomy; in 1995 and 1996, Belarus and Russia entered into agreements that made them political and economic partners. Anti-Semitism has reappeared in the post-Soviet era, which is one factor encouraging Jews to leave Belarus.

Belgium

B elgium is a small nation in northern Europe, bordered on the north by the North Sea and the Netherlands, on the east by Germany and Luxembourg, and on the south and east by France. It has a population of 10,082,000. Belgium is a modern, postindustrial society, with a highly educated population. The city of Brussels is the home of many agencies of the European Union and related institutions. Belgium became an independent nation following a revolt against the Dutch king in 1830. Although unified politically, Belgium is ethnically pluralistic and is sometimes cited by experts as a model of peaceful ethnic relations.

Ethnic Composition

Belgium is a multicultural and bilingual society, with 55% of the population classified as Flemish, 33% as Walloon, and 12% as either German, Arabs from North Africa, Turk, Greek, Italian, or Spanish.

Flemish (Flemings) are defined primarily through residence in the Flemish region and by speaking Flemish dialects of Dutch. The Flemish are descended from the original Celtic inhabitants of what are now Belgian lands and the Romans and Franks who later ruled the region. Flemish culture has been heavily influenced by its location along major trade routes—shipbuilding was once a major economic activity, and shipping and small independently owned businesses are still common. Most Flemish are Roman Catholic, although many do not participate in church activities or do so only in a limited way. Flemish art, music, dance, and literature are a well known component of Western European civilization.

Walloons are identified through their residence in Wallonia and by speaking dialects of French. They, too, are descended from the original Celtic inhabitants of the region and Romans and Franks who arrived later. Walloons are mainly Roman Catholic, although participation in church activities is declining. Wallonia was traditionally a center of industry and trade, and Walloon culture was heavily influenced by the French. While Walloons was once politically dominant, power has shifted since the 1960s to the Flemish, and the Walloons now see themselves as the weaker member of the partnership. Walloons constitute as much as 70% of the population of Brussels, although some are adopting the Dutch language in order to affiliate with the Flemish.

The major nonindigenous ethnic groups in Belgium are those formed by guest workers and their families from southern Europe, Asia, and Africa. **Greeks,** who numbered about 300,000 in 1985 but fewer in the 1990s, came as guest workers and work mainly in factories, the tourism trade, and construction. They are Greek Orthodox and live mainly in Wallonia. As most plan to return to Greece, they are little interested in, nor are they subject to, assimilation pressures.

Italians, who number fewer than 100,000, came mainly in the 1980s as guest workers in construction and industry. They are Roman Catholic, live mostly in Wallonia, and coexist peacefully with the Walloons and other European guest-worker communities.

Arabs are mainly from Morocco, with a smaller number from Algeria; they number about 150,000, and most reside in Wallonia or Brussels. They are Muslims and, along with the Turks, form the poorest population in Belgium. They live in ethnic ghettos and have little social contact with the Belgians or with other ethnic minorities.

Spaniards number about 60,000. Most came to Belgium in the 1970s and 1980s as guest workers in tourism, construction, and industry. They are Roman Catholic and live mainly in Wallonia. As most plan to return to Spain, they are little interested in, nor are they subject to, assimilation pressures.

Turks number about 100,000, with most residing in Wallonia or Brussels. They are Muslims and, along with the Arabs, form the poorest population in Belgium. They live in ethnic ghettos and have little social contact with the Belgians or with other ethnic minorities.

Germans are another major nonindigenous group in Belgium. They number about 70,000 and live in the eastern part of Wallonia, near the border with Germany. Most German speakers in the country became Belgian citizens following the redrawing of the Belgian and German border in 1919. These German speakers enjoy some degree of legal, political, and cultural autonomy.

Jews in Belgium number about 40,000 and live in major cities, where they work as merchants or professionals.

Other non–guest worker groups include **French** near the border with France and a small **Russian** community composed of the descendants of those who fled Russia after the 1917 Revolution.

Ethnic Relations

Relations between the Flemish and Walloons, while peaceful, remain distant. There are even independent Flemish and Walloon national assemblies in Belgium's government. Flemish is the national language, however, and since the 1960s the Flemish have become politically and economically dominant.

Since Belgium's independence from the Netherlands in 1830, the relative power of the Flemish and the Walloons has been a major issue in Belgium. The issue is such a concern that there has been no official attempt to measure the populations of the two language groups since 1947. In the 1980s, the Belgian constitution was revised to distinguish among three communities—Flemish-, French-, and German-speaking—and three regions—Flanders, Wallonia, and Brussels. Flemish live in the north and speak dialects of Dutch. Walloons live in the south and speak dialects of French. Brussels, a multicultural city, is officially bilingual, although the majority of its residents speak French as their primary language. Many Belgians speak not just French and Dutch, but also German and English. Although Belgium is sometimes described as a bilingual, bicultural nation, this is an oversimplification. The Flemish and Walloon groups are described by experts as "communities" rather than as ethnic groups, and individuals can move easily from one community to the other by learning to speak the other language.

Guest workers from southern Europe and North Africa were encouraged to come to Belgium in the 1970s and 1980s to fill vacancies in industry and construction, but in the 1990s concerns about the arrival of refugees from Africa and the former Yugoslavia have led to greater restrictions on settlement.

Bosnia and Herzegovina

The Republic of Bosnia and Herzegovina (also known as Bosnia-Herzegovina) is located on the Balkan Peninsula in southeastern Europe. It came into existence in 1992 as part of the demise of Yugoslavia with Yugoslavia now consisting only of Serbs and Montenegrins. From the end of World War II until the 1990s, it was a multicultural republic within Yugoslavia. Bosnia-Herzegovina is bordered by Serbia (also known as Yugoslavia) on the east and south, and by Croatia on the north and west. The war that followed Bosnia-Herzegovina's independence in 1992 and ended in late 1995—involving the Bosnian Muslims, Croats, and Serbs—drastically altered the prewar population. In 1997, Bosnia-Herzegovina is a nation partitioned into two territories occupied by Bosnian Muslims, Serbs, and Croats and governed by a coalition government representing these communities under United Nations and NATO oversight. The population in 1996 was estimated to be about 2.6 million, a decrease of almost 2 million since 1991. The war resulted in about 1.3 million people being displaced within Bosnia, about 800,000 people becoming refugees elsewhere in Europe, and over 100,000 people having been killed.

Ethnic Composition

Prior to independence and the war, Bosnia-Herzegovina was a multiethnic nation, composed of three distinct Slavic ethnic groups. Bosnian Muslims constituted 43.7% of the population, Serbs 31.5%, and Croats 17.3%. An additional 5.5% considered themselves Yugoslavians, and the remainder of the population consisted of a number of smaller groups including Vlachs, Slav Macedonians, and Gypsies.

Bosnians are a South Slavic ethnic group whose ancestors entered the region in the 6th and 7th centuries. They speak Serbo-Croatian with words added from Turkish, reflecting Ottoman rule of the region from the 15th century to the early 20th century. While Bosnia has been a distinct region in the Balkans for nearly 1,000 years, a sense of Bosnian ethnicity distinct from that of the Serbs and Croats emerged only in the 1800s and is based primarily on religious differences—Bosnians are Muslims, whereas the other groups are Eastern Orthodox and Roman Catholic. Another difference is that the Bosnians who converted to Islam were mainly urban professionals and business owners, while the Serbs and Croats were mainly rural farmers who were dominated by the Ottoman Turks and their Bosnian Muslim supporters. This pattern (Bosnians being mainly urban professionals) continues in modern times. In addition to religion, place of residence, and profession, a distinct Bosnian identity has been maintained by Bosnians marrying other Bosnian Muslims or Muslims from Turkey. Bosnian Muslims live mainly in central Bosnia. Bosnians living elsewhere were displaced during the war by Serbs and Croats.

Serbs in Bosnia are called Bosnian Serbs to distinguish them from Serbs in Serbia proper, although there is little to distinguish the groups culturally. Serbs in Serbia assisted the Serbs in Bosnia during the 1992–95 war. The Serbs live in southern, eastern, and northern Bosnia and control 49% of the territory of Bosnia.

Croats in Bosnia live mainly in the west and central regions, and through the 1994 peace agreement with the Bosnian Muslims, they are now aligned with the Muslims in opposition to the Serbs. To what extent other groups that lived in the region are still present is unclear. It is likely that many fled or were displaced.

Ethnic Relations

As part of Yugoslavia, Bosnia was a multiethnic nation of Bosnian Muslims, Serbs, and Croats. Although the three groups were generally localized in distinct regions, there was also considerable mixing, especially in the large cities. Ethnic tensions were thought to be minimal, and Bosnia was sometimes cited

Bosnian Muslims praying in a cemetery in Sarajevo in 1991.
Photo: Reuters/Corbis-Bettmann.

as a model of an ethnically pluralistic society. This notion came to an abrupt end when the Bosnian Muslims and Croats voted for and declared independence in 1992, over Bosnian Serb objections. The resulting war, which was started by the Bosnian Serbs with the support of Serbs in Yugoslavia, was the worst war in Europe since World War II. It pitted the Bosnians against the Serbs and Croats, and the Croats against the Serbs. With a superior military force and tactics of "ethnic cleansing," the Serbs by 1994 had control of 70% of Bosnia and had killed tens of thousands of Bosnian Muslims, driven nearly two million out of the country or to the Bosnian-held sectors, and had destroyed hundreds of villages. The Serb offensive also included attacks on civilians, including the bombing of major cities such as Sarajevo, Gorazde, and Bihac. International outrage directed at the Serbs led to United Nations peacekeeping forces in the region, and in 1994 the Croats and Bosnian Muslims resolved their differences and allied against the Serbs. By 1995 the Serb advance had been halted and much of the territory they had gained was returned to Bosnian or Croat control. In late 1995 a peace accord was reached; Bosnia-Herzegovina would be allowed to exist as a single nation with political power shared by a central government, a Muslim-Croat federation, and a Bosnian Serb republic. In elections held in September 1996, a three-person national presidency was elected, with one president each from the Muslim, Croat, and Serb communities, and the Bosnian president, who received the most votes, serving as chair. In the house of representatives, 28 seats are for representatives from the Muslim-Croat federation and 14 for those from the Bosnian Serb republic. In addition, the Bosnian Serb republic elects its own president and national assembly and the Muslim-Croat federation its own house of representatives.

Despite this political structure, the presence of about 40,000 foreign troops, and the indictment of former Bosnian Serb leaders for war crimes, peace is not secure. The desire of some Croat communities for unification with Croatia and fears of Serb desires for unification with Serbia raise questions about how long the multiethnic nation will survive. The Bosnian alliance with the Croats is based on the practical reality that the Bosnians require Croat support in any future war with the Serbs. Thus, the alliance is tenuous and the Croats have not been reluctant to keep Bosnians from resettling in territory now inhabited by Croats. For their part, the Serbs have refused to let Croats or Bosnians return to Serb-held territory, and attempts to do so have been met by forcible evictions.

Bulgaria

B ulgaria is in the Balkan region of southeastern Europe and is bordered by Romania on the north, the Black Sea on the east, Turkey and Greece on the south, and Macedonia and Serbia on the west. Until 1989, it was ruled by a Communist government closely aligned with the Soviet Union. Since then it has been moving toward a democratic form of government and a capitalist economy. Bulgaria has a population of about 8.7 million.

Religion (Eastern Orthodoxy, Islam, Protestantism, and Roman Catholicism), social class distinctions, and urban/rural difference are important aspects of Bulgarian social organization. Traditionally, Bulgaria was a rural nation where most people lived by farming and herding sheep and goats. The economic sector was transformed in the 20th century to one dominated by industry and commercial agriculture, and the majority of the population now lives in urban areas.

Ethnic Composition

Although ethnic Bulgarians form 85% of the population, Bulgaria is a multiethnic nation, due to the country's location at the crossroads of Asia and Europe and control of the region by the Muslim Ottoman Empire for nearly 500 years. The nation's population today is less diverse than in the past: some groups such as Albanians, Armenians, Czechs, Slovaks, Romanians, and Greeks are now remnant populations of less than 20,000 each.

Bulgarians number 7.5 million and constitute 85% of the population. They are descended from Slavic peoples who settled in the region between the 5th and 6th centuries, while the Bulgarian polity traces its roots to the Turkic peoples who entered the region in the 7th century. Most Bulgarians are Eastern Orthodox Christians, with adherence to indigenous beliefs continuing in rural areas. As the dominant group, they are subject to charges of attempting to force ethnic minorities to assimilate into Bulgarian society.

The largest minority category is **Muslims,** although there is cultural diversity within this categorization. **Turks,** nearly all of whom are Sunni Muslims, are the largest ethnic minority in Bulgaria, numbering about 750,000 or 8.5% of the population. They have lived in Bulgaria since 1396 and today live mainly in the south and northeast. The **Gagauz Turks** practice the Greek Orthodox religion, which distinguishes them from most other Turks who

are Muslims. About 12,000 live in Bulgaria, with the majority in Moldova, Ukraine, and Greece. **Pomaks,** Bulgarian Muslims who number about 280,000, live mainly in the Rhodope Mountains of southern Bulgaria. Their ancestors were converted to Islam during the period of Ottoman rule. Although they are Muslims, they speak Bulgarian and are ethnic Bulgarians.

Bulgaria has for at least 600 years had a large **Gypsy (Roma)** population, and estimates place their current number at anywhere from 260,000 to over one million. The majority live in large cities, although they are found in all regions of Bulgaria. Most work in service occupations or at low-level wage labor. The majority are Muslims, with a minority being Eastern Orthodox practitioners.

Two small remnant populations of longtime inhabitants are the Sarakatsani and the Vlachs. The **Sarakatsani** are a pastoral people located mainly in Greece, with a small number also in the border regions of southern Bulgaria. **Vlachs,** more commonly called **Karakatchans** in Bulgaria, live in the mountain regions of the north and west. Their number has been estimated at as many as 400,000, but that figure is almost certainly an overestimate. Sometimes considered Romanian because their language is similar, Vlachs are a remnant population descended from the Illyrians and Thracians who have interacted with the Slavic population over the centuries in the Balkans.

The final major group is the **Slav Macedonians,** who call themselves **Pirin Macedonians** after the southwestern region of Bulgaria where they live. Their population is approximately 200,000; their exact number is unknown, as official censuses systematically underreport them. Some segment of the group has always sought alignment with Macedonia, though the Bulgarian government has resisted such desires.

Other groups include several thousand **Albanians** and **Muslim Tatars, Circassians** closely tied to the Turks in the north, and remnant populations of **Jews (Sephardim** and **Ashkenazim), Greeks, Russians, Slovaks, Czechs, Hungarians, Germans,** and **Armenians**.

Ethnic Relations

Ethnic minorities in Bulgaria tend to live in villages in the south, although these communities are usually a mix of ethnic minorities and Bulgarians living together peacefully, for the most part. Ethnic relations with most minority ethnic groups are harmonious, save for with the Turks who are the object of both personal and official discrimination, the root of which is the Ottoman control of Bulgaria for almost 500 years beginning in 1396. During the Communist era, a largely ineffective policy of forced assimilation attempted to turn all non-Bulgarians into Bulgarians. In the post-Communist era since 1989, ethnic rivalries for power have been largely nonviolent, although the Bulgarians have been accused of using repressive tactics to silence political opponents. While concern remains about separatist interest in some groups, the harsher restrictions on ethnic groups have mostly ended since 1989.

During the rule of the Ottoman Empire from 1396 to the revolt of 1877, Turks ruled the majority of Bulgarians, who feared assimilation into Turkish culture. Since Bulgarian independence, Turks have been discriminated against, and sizable numbers were expelled or allowed to return to Turkey in the 1950s, and again in 1989. In 1984, the Bulgarian government changed all Turkish names to Bulgarian ones and attempted to close mosques and restrict the worship of Islam. The Turks responded with hunger strikes, protests, and demonstrations, which were repressed by Bulgarian forces. Following the end of Communist rule in 1989, Muslim names were restored and the repressive policies ended, although animosity toward Turks remains, and both sides continue to negotiate the role of Turks in Bulgarian society.

During the Communist era, forced assimilation—such as banning religious practice and requiring Pomaks to use Bulgarian names—was the official policy. Since 1989 these efforts have largely ended, and Pomaks freely practice Islam. Tensions remain, however, with the Bulgarian majority, in part because Pomaks tend to identify more closely with the Islamic Turks.

Compulsory education and other government programs have lifted the Gypsies' economic status, but Communist government assimilation policies sought to eradicate their identity. Although they are considered inferior and are discriminated against in daily life, their large number assures them a role in democratic Bulgaria.

Until the fall of the Communist government in 1989, Slav Macedonians often were classified as ethnic Bulgarians by the government, their political parties controlled, and their leaders imprisoned. Although the situation has relaxed since 1990, Bulgarian opinion is still firm in opposition to Macedonian independence.

Croatia

The Republic of Croatia, on the Balkan Peninsula in southeastern Europe, is bordered by Slovenia and Hungary on the north, Yugoslavia (Serbia) on the east, Bosnia-Herzegovina on the south, and the Adriatic Sea on the west. Croatia became an independent nation in June 1991 upon its withdrawal from Yugoslavia. Prior to that, it had been a unit of the Kingdom of Serbs, Croatians, and Slovenes, and then one of the republics of Yugoslavia. Since it emerged as a distinct entity in the 7th century, Croatia was ruled by the Hungarians, Austrians, Italian city-states, and the Ottoman Turks. Its location in the northern Balkans and contact with European cultures have given Croat society a strong Western European flavor. From 1991 to 1996, Croatia—along with Serbia and Bosnia-Herzegovina—was involved in the largest and most devastating war in Europe since World War II. The 1996 population was about five million, although relocations caused by the war make population estimates difficult.

Ethnic Composition

Prior to the wars in the 1990s, Croats (Croatians) accounted for 78% of the population, Serbs 12%, and a mix of other groups the remaining 10%. The wars have altered this mix, with about 190,000 Bosnians and Croats from Bosnia living as refugees in Croatia; 191,000 Croats living in different regions of Croatia than before the war; and about 100,000 Serbs living under United Nations protection in the Krajina region. In addition, some 60,000 Croats are living as refugees in other nations, a sizable percentage in Germany. Thus, it is likely that in the late 1990s, Croats form a greater percentage of the population than before independence in 1991, and Serbs a smaller percentage. Most of the Bosnian refugees in Croatia are expected to return to Bosnia eventually.

Croats are a southern Slavic people closely related to the Serbs and Bosnians. Religion (Roman Catholicism), language (the Croatian dialect of the Serbo-Croatian language), and loyalty to the Croat nation are important elements of Croat ethnic identity. In addition to these factors, Croats differ from the Serbs and Bosnians in cultural orientation—contact with western cultures has strongly influenced Croat education, science, art, and literature, while the Serbs have been more influenced by Eastern Europe and the Bosnians by the Ottoman Turks. The recent war with the Serbs resulted in the destruction of many important symbols of Croat culture including churches, public buildings, cemeteries, and museums. The Croats on the Adriatic Sea were heavily influenced by the Italian city-states of Genoa and Venice, and Croats in that region are sometimes classified as **Dalmatians** and are considered a distinct Croat subgroup. Croats primarily are a rural people, with some 20% of the population involved in agriculture. The large extended family has, in the 20th century, been replaced by smaller nuclear families. Almost all Croats are Roman Catholic, with many pre-Christian practices incorporated.

Serbs in Croatia live mainly in the Krajina region near Serbia. Following Croatia's declaration of independence in 1991, the Serbs launched a war designed to solidify Serbian control and, some experts believe, to expand the boundaries of Serbia. Using tactics labeled "ethnic cleansing," the Serbs raped, tortured, murdered, and drove off the Croats living in the Serb-dominated region. By 1995 Croatia had regained control of much of the region and they, too, were accused of using "ethnic cleansing" to drive off the Serbs. A peace treaty signed in Paris in December 1995 ended the fighting but did not completely resolve the issue of territorial control.

Prior to the war, the other ethnic minorities in Croatia were mainly from neighboring nations: **Hungarians** (234,000), **Slovenes** (234,000), and **Bosnians** (400,000). Bosnian refugees from Bosnia have increased in number. There was also a substantial **Gypsy** population before the war, which has likely decreased in size because of immigration to Western Europe.

Ethnic Relations

Ethnic relations concern almost exclusively the relations between the Croats and Serbs in Croatia and the Croats and Serbs in general. Through most of the 20th century, the two groups have been linked in an uneasy political alliance, first in the Kingdom of the Serbs, Croats, and Slovenes and then, after World War II, in Yugoslavia. The Croats have long feared and strongly resisted what they perceive as Serb attempts to gain political control in the region, to impose the use of the Serbian dialect on Croatia, and to expand the territory of Serbia by taking land from Croatia. Differences in religion also have also led to difficulties between the groups. During World War II the Croats aided the Nazis while the Serbs violently resisted, and some Serbs blame the Croats for atrocities committed by the Nazis. The Balkan wars of the 1990s were marked by ethnic cleansing by both Serbs and Croats, although it is believed that the Serbs were the chief perpetrators. In Croatia, the Serbs have been promised regional autonomy

Croatian civilians and Yugoslavian Serb soldiers face off during the 1991 conflict as Yugoslavia disintegrated. Photo: Reuters/Corbis-Bettmann.

upon the successful implementation of a peace treaty. In Bosnia, the Serbs and Croats form separate political factions and live in separate regions.

Cyprus

Located in the eastern Mediterranean Sea, Cyprus is an island nation separated since 1983 into the Republic of Cyprus (occupying the southern two-thirds of the island) and the Turkish Republic of Northern Cyprus (occupying the northern third). The Turkish Republic of Northern Cyprus is recognized only by Turkey, while the Republic of Cyprus is recognized internationally. The island population is 736,000: 78% Greek Cypriots, and 18% Turkish Cypriots, with small numbers of Maronites and Armenians.

Ethnic Composition

Greek Cypriots have lived on Cyprus since 1200 B.C. Most are members of the Greek Orthodox Church of Cyprus, which has been independent since A.D. 488. Central to Greek Cypriot identity is the concept of *enosis*—unification with Greece—which arose following the formation of the modern Greek nation in the 1830s and spread and deepened during the period of British rule of Cyprus from 1878 to 1960. Today, the influence of the Greek Orthodox Church in political affairs has diminished, the economy is expanding, and Greek Cypriots see themselves as full members of the Western European community.

Turkish Cypriots are mostly descendants of Turks who settled on the island during the period of Ottoman rule (1571–1878). They are Muslims, supported by and closely affiliated with Turkey. In opposition to the Greek goal of *enosis*, Turks have desired *taksim*—division of the island into Greek and Turkish zones—to avoid becoming an ethnic minority. Since partition, the Turkish sector has not expanded economically and is still heavily dependent on agriculture and on support from Turkey.

In addition to Greeks and Turks, the other major ethnic groups are Armenians and Maronite Christians. **Armenians** arrived on Cyprus after World War I. Numbering fewer than 3,000, they form an urban trading class in the Greek sector. **Maronites** are Arabic-speaking Christians from Lebanon and Syria who have lived as farmers on Cyprus for over 400 years. They number several thousand and nearly all live in the Greek sector.

Ethnic Relations

As a natural stopping place between Europe and the Middle East, the island has been ruled by various peoples and governments including the Greeks, Assyrians, Egyptians, Persians, Romans, Byzantines, various Mediterranean states, the Ottoman Turks, and the British, although only the Ottoman Turks had a major influence.

Since the 1960s the island has experienced continuing ethnic conflict—sometimes violent—between the Greek and Turkish communities. Underlying the conflict are strong nationalistic sentiments in Greece and Turkey, British colonial policy that emphasized ethnic differences and kept the communities apart, and economic competition as the island industrialized. Both Turkey and Greece have been involved in providing support for their co-ethnics on the island. Since the mid-1970s, the Greeks and Turks have lived separately—Greeks in the south and Turks in the north. For the previous 400 years, the groups lived in neighboring villages or side-by-side in cities across the island. A United Nations peacekeeping force has been charged with maintaining peace along the border separating the two communities since 1963. While a full Cypriot cultural identity never developed, over the centuries both Turks and Greeks on Cyprus had a sense of being different from their co-ethnics on the mainland. At the same time, differences in language and religion—and, later, allegiance to their homelands—kept the two communities on Cyprus apart.

Czech Republic

The Czech Republic, in Central Europe, is bordered by Germany and Poland on the north, Slovakia on the east, Austria on the south, and Germany on the southwest and west. It came into existence on 1 January 1993 following the division of Czechoslovakia into the two nations of the Czech Republic and Slovakia. The population is 10,940,000, 95% of whom are ethnic Czechs. The region that is now the Czech Republic enjoyed independence from the 10th to the early 17th centuries as the Bohemian Kingdom, and flourished as the cultural center of Central Europe. It was during this period that the strong and continuing literary, musical, and artistic traditions developed. Following several hundred years of decline, the Czechs became independent in 1918 with the breakup of the Austro-Hungarian Empire. Since then, the borders have been redrawn a number of times. Today, the borders are largely congruent with areas of traditional Czech settlement, and the populations of Germans and Poles, which once formed large minorities, have decreased in size.

Ethnic Composition

With Czechs forming 95% of the population, the Czech Republic is ethnically homogeneous. **Czechs** are a Slavic people whose ancestors have lived in what is now the Czech Republic since at least the 7th century. At times, the Czechs have been politically united with the Slovaks and other Slavic peoples. A distinct Czech nation and national identity have existed longer than a national ethnic identity in neighboring nations such as Germany. Czech culture can be described in a very general sense as notable for its emphasis on rational and pragmatic thinking, a long tradition of intellectual and artistic achievement, an ideology which during years of foreign rule emphasized passive resistance, the absence of religion as an organizing force, and a dichotomy between the rural/peasant culture of the small towns and the westernized culture of the larger cities. Most Czechs are Roman Catholic, Protestant, or atheist, but even for adherents, participation is limited to major holidays and rites.

The only other significant ethnic groups are Germans, Poles, and Slovaks near the borders with those nations, and Gypsies. **Germans** number approximately 150,000–200,000 and live in border regions in the north. They are a small remnant of the three million Germans who lived there before World War II, most of whom were deported across the border after the war. Germans are now classified as an ethnic minority.

Poles number about 80,000 and live in the mining region on the northern end of the border with Slovakia. Their numbers are increased substantially by workers and tourists who frequently cross the border. Fear of losing the region to Poland has led to efforts to control the political influence of Poles in the region.

Slovaks form about 3% of the population and live mainly near the Slovakia border.

Gypsies, including Rom, Sinti, and Vlach Gypsies (who are different from the Vlach of the Balkans), have been in the former Czechoslovakia for at least 600 years. Most have always lived in what is now Slovakia, and today about 165,000 live in the Czech Republic, many of whom resettled from Slovakia in the northern regions of the Czech Republic in settlements formerly occupied by Germans. The Gypsy population of the Czech Republic before World War II, long the object of persecution, was nearly annihilated by the Nazis and was the object of forced assimilation under the Communist government.

Ethnic Relations

Ethnic relations in the Czech Republic are now peaceful, although minority participation in regional and national politics is carefully monitored and controlled. During the era of Czech-Slovak unification, relations between the groups were strained though peaceful. Czechs tended to see Slovaks as poor rural folk, while Slovaks often bristled at Czech dominance of the national economy and political system. Czechs continue to worry about German expansion from the north, west, and south.

Denmark

D enmark is located on the most northerly extension of the West European Plain, which projects into Scandinavia as the peninsula of Jutland, pointing northward toward Norway and Sweden. Denmark also includes several hundred islands.

Denmark was once a larger nation. Its territory included Holstein and Schleswig to the south, taken by Germany in 1864, and the provinces of Scania, Halland, and Blekinge to the northeast, which became provinces of Sweden in 1660. Present-day Norway was part of Denmark from 1380 to 1814, and Denmark controlled Iceland from 1380 to 1918.

The Kingdom of Denmark today includes the Faroe Islands and Greenland, although both enjoy considerable freedom under a policy of home rule. Denmark is an industrialized, urbanized nation with a population of 5.2 million. Danish is the national language, but many Danes speak a second language—German was most common before World War II, and English is most common since then. Most residents (91%) are Lutherans, with Islam ranking second.

Ethnic Composition

Denmark was ethnically homogeneous prior to World War II, with the only significant non-Danish groups being other Scandinavians and, in the south, Germans. Following the war, a large labor force migrated from southern Europe to Sweden, which led to a similar government policy in Denmark. The migration to Denmark expanded over the years to include people from Asia and the Middle East, as well as refugees from Africa, Europe, and Asia. In the 1990s, 23 different non-Danish ethnic groups were living in Denmark, each with a thousand people or more. However, the population is still largely homogeneous, as non-Danes total only 153,000, or 3% of the population. People of Swedish, German, and Norwegian ancestry have a low collective profile due to rapid assimilation, while other groups, notably Muslims from the Middle East and Asia, are visible minorities who also exhibit a somewhat stronger desire to preserve their cultural traditions.

Danes make up 97% of the population of Denmark. The term "Dane" can be traced to the Middle Ages when the Old Nordic term "Danir" was in use. The current sense of Danish ethnic identity emerged in the 19th century from the rural way of life followed for centuries by Danish peasants. Prior to the 19th century, Danish culture, as reflected by the elite living in cities, was heavily influenced by Western Europe, which tended to blur their distinctiveness as Danes.

Icelanders living in Denmark numbered 3,050 in 1990. Iceland is a former Danish colony and Icelanders are culturally and linguistically very similar to Danes. Icelandic immigrants have assimilated quickly and thoroughly into Danish society.

Faroe Islanders or **Faroese** form a second native population. They are the inhabitants of the Faroe Islands in the North Atlantic Ocean, a self-governing dependency of Denmark. Faroe Islanders are descended from Nordic peoples who settled the islands since 9th century. The islands have been under Danish and Norwegian rule and were a Danish province from 1816 until 1948, at which time they became self-governing. Faroe Islanders see themselves as culturally distinct from the Danes and other Nordic peoples. Their way of life reflects a merging of traditional customs focused on fishing, sheepherding, hunting, with involvement in the modern world economy. Faroe Islanders are Lutherans within the Danish Lutheran Church. Relations with Denmark are generally harmonious, save for foreign policy disagreements resulting from Danish control of the island's foreign policy.

The "non-native" ethnic groups in Denmark can be lumped into a number of general categories—other Nordic peoples, Eastern Europeans, Western Europeans, Muslims, and southern Europeans.

Denmark is home to thousands of people of Norwegian and Swedish heritage. **Swedes** number 8,000 and are culturally and linguistically very similar to Danes, and thus are assimilated thoroughly into Danish society.

Norwegians number 10,000. Danes and Norwegians share a common history and speak dialects of the same language. Norway was a province of Denmark for over 400 years, and both were occupied by Germany during World War II. Norwegians, like Swedes, are assimilated completely into Danish society.

Eastern Europeans are mainly **Yugoslavians** and **Poles**. Immigrants of these nationalities first went to Sweden, and later to Denmark, in response to the increase in the demand for laborers following World War II. These people of Eastern European ancestry number about 14,000. Despite high levels of integration, a majority of Yugoslavians and Poles continue to harbor strong feelings of attachment to their country of origin and a desire for eventual return. Thus, these immigrants participate in two sociocultural systems—Denmark's, and that of Poland or Yugoslavia.

Bosnians number about 20,000, and most of them live in Denmark as temporary residents. While the majority are expected to return to Bosnia eventually, some are permitted to work in Denmark and may seek to be permanent residents.

The largest Western European groups in Denmark are the British, Germans, and Jews. **Britons** number about 10,000. Many are business persons or professionals, integrated but not assimilated into Danish society.

Germans number 18,000, and a large percentage live on the Jutland peninsula in Sonderjylland County, adjacent to the German border. German Danes in Sonderjylland County prefer to be identified both as part of a German minority and also as economically, socially, and politically integrated into Danish society. They are supported both by Danish and German governmental policies in their maintenance of ethnic networks, and individual Germans have the right to maintain or abandon their identification with the group.

Jews in Denmark number about 6,800. They began to arrive in Denmark as early as the 17th century and were fairly well integrated in Danish society by the beginning of World War II. In 1943 they faced deportation and extermination by the Nazis. In response, the Danes carried out a disobedience campaign against the occupying Germans to assist the Jews. It became a patriotic duty to hide Jews and help them escape to Sweden. Sweden, in turn, provided assistance and refuge to 6,000 Danish Jews who escaped over the Straits of Oresund.

Muslims, accounting for nearly 50% of the non-Danish population in Denmark, are mainly **Turks** (27,900), **Iranians** (8,400), and **Pakistanis** (6,300)—with considerably smaller numbers of **Iraqis** and **Kurds**. Most Bosnians are Muslim, too, but because they are European in appearance, they are not readily perceived as Muslim. All of these Muslim peoples tend to live in or near Copenhagen. Turks make up the single largest immigrant group in Denmark, with more than twice as many residents as any other group. Although Muslims are not a homogeneous group, they are often treated as such by those who focus solely on their adherence to Islam and ignore significant cultural differences, as well as the split between those who are Sunni and those who are Shi'ite Muslims.

Southern Europeans in Denmark are primarily **French** and **Italian** immigrants, who number almost 4,000. Most are wage laborers or fill special economic niches and are integrated into Danish society.

Other groups include small numbers of **Gypsies,** and refugees and asylum-seekers from **Ethiopia, Somalia, Sri Lanka (Tamils),** and **Palestine. Vietnamese,** refugees from the Vietnam War who were allowed to settle permanently in Denmark, now number several thousand. They are not fully assimilated, although the second generation born in Denmark is participating more fully in Danish society.

Ethnic Relations

Danish acceptance of other Nordic peoples and northern Europeans, the norm in the 20th century, has expanded to include other peoples only since World War II. Labor migrants (who began arriving in the 1950s) initially were treated favorably, but the liberal refugee policy began to be questioned in the 1980s as economic conditions deteriorated and the number and ethnic variety of refugees increased.

The earliest Muslim groups in Denmark arrived during the 1960s. Iranian immigrants, escaping the regime of the Shah, came to Denmark during the 1970s. A second wave of Iranians, trying to avoid the Iran-Iraq war, migrated during the 1980s. The Iranians have contributed to an increase in the number of Shi'ite Muslims, but the antagonism between Shi'ite and Sunni Muslims is considerably less than it is in Islamic countries. They cooperate to a certain degree and attend prayers together, although conflict between Muslim groups arises.

Political parties objecting to the admission of immigrants and refugees from non-European nations have appeared since the mid-1980s and reflect divisions in the Danish citizenry over this matter. In 1993, for example, Prime Minister Poul Schluter was forced to resign after an investigation showed that in the 1980s he had violated Danish policies by hindering the immigration to Denmark of Tamil refugees' families still in Sri Lanka. In the same year, however, new refugee and asylum policies were instituted to limit the arrival and stay of refugees and asylum-seekers. These policies led to a decrease of more than 50% from 1993 to 1994 in the number of asylum-seekers admitted. Still, in 1995, Denmark ranked fourth in the world in the ratio of refugees and asylum-seekers granted residence to the total population, with one person resettled per 139 residents.

In Denmark, as in all the Scandinavian countries, there is a split in attitudes toward Muslims, and there is much uncertainty over how to interpret Islamic culture and behavior. Most Danes do not know much about Islam and have misgivings about Muslim attitudes toward, or involvement with, radical political and religious movements. This uneasiness has been fueled in the 1990s by Kurdish terrorist attacks on Turkish targets in Denmark, and by Islamic fundamentalist protests at the Iranian mission in Copenhagen.

Estonia

E stonia is the northernmost of the three Baltic nations of Estonia, Latvia, and Lithuania. It has a population of 1,617,000 and is ethnically heterogeneous, with Estonians forming the majority of the population and Russians a large minority. Estonia has been a distinct political entity—or a conglomeration of non-unified entities—for over 1,000 years. From 1217 to 1917 and from 1940 until 1991, Estonia was under foreign rule by the Danes, Germans, Swedes, and—most recently—by the Russians. Independence came in 1991 with the demise of the Soviet Union.

Ethnic Composition

Estonians number 963,000, constituting 61.5% of the population. Most Estonians are Lutheran, with a minority of adherents of Estonian Orthodoxy. Humans have lived in the territory that is now Estonia for at least 6,000 years, and modern Estonians trace their heritage to people who lived there over 2,000 years ago.

The long period of foreign rule resulted in the settlement of large numbers of **Swedes,** Germans, and Russians in Estonian territory. Most Swedes and Germans left at the start of World War II, while the Russian presence grew after Russian annexation of Estonia in 1940.

More than 300 years of Russian domination—from 1710 to 1991—have left a deep resentment of Russia and Russians, and a strong desire to establish an independent Estonia based on Estonian culture and ethnicity. **Russians** number 474,800, or 30.3% of the population. Most are workers who arrived in the post–World War II era. In the Soviet era, Russia transformed Estonia from an agricultural to an industrial nation, made it economically dependent on Russia, and controlled the political process from Moscow. While Estonians are divided in their views as to the role of Russians in independent Estonia, changes in the language and citizenship laws, as well as preferences afforded Estonians in jobs and housing, suggest that the prevailing opinion is that the Russians either return to Russia or accept a reduced role in Estonian society.

Belarusians number 27,700, or 1.6% of the population. They are mainly urban workers settled in Estonia during the Soviet era, and as a small group, they are not a significant factor in the conflict situation. Few speak Estonian, and they tend to affiliate with the Russians.

Finns number 16,600, or 1.2% of the population. They are a largely rural people and are well assimilated into Estonian society, with some 74% speaking Estonian (41% speak it as their native language).

Ukrainians number 48,000, or 2.5% of the population. They are mainly urban workers settled in Estonia by the Russians. A small group, they are not a significant factor in the conflict situation. Few speak Estonian, and they tend to affiliate with the Russians.

Other groups include several thousand **Germans, Latvians,** and **Jews**.

Ethnic Relations

The presence of Russians is the major source of ethnic conflict in Estonia today. During the Soviet period, Russians enjoyed preferences in hiring, housing, and social programs such as healthcare and childcare. Since Estonia achieved independence in 1991, much political effort has been devoted to establishing a coherent Estonian nationalism, with an ongoing debate over the extent to which Estonia should accommodate the needs of ethnic minorities (primarily Russians). In 1989, Estonian was declared the official language, and in 1995 the citizenship law was changed to require five rather than two years of residence, as well as literacy in Estonian. The internal conflict between Estonians and Russians is complicated by tense relations between the Russian and Estonian governments. One issue concerns the presence of Russian troops in Estonia (the last departed in 1995); another is Estonian claims on 1,200 square miles of border territory, now in Russia, which Russia refuses to return.

Although many Russians in Estonia prefer to remain rather than return to Russia, most are only marginally assimilated into Estonian society, with only 15% speaking Estonian, and 13.7% of those speaking it as a second language. Russians see the changes in the language and citizenship laws as violations of their human rights and as efforts to force them to leave Estonia. Because of the protection afforded by Moscow during the Soviet era, there was little internal Russian political organization in Estonia, although since 1994 Russian interests have been represented by the United Popular Party and the Russian Party.

Finland

F inland, a Nordic nation, is bordered on the east by Russia, on the south by the Gulf of Finland and Estonia, on the west by Sweden and the Gulf of Bothnia, and on the north and northwest by Norway. Finland's archipelago in its southwestern coastal waters includes the Åland Islands. Finland's population is 5,058,000, about 94% of whom are ethnic Finns who speak Finnish. About 89% of the population is Lutheran. Over the last century, falling birthrates and heavy emigration have resulted in a very low rate of population growth. Finland underwent dramatic economic change after the 1950s, when both agriculture and the forestry industry were rapidly mechanized. As a result, many young people left the rural areas of eastern and northeastern Finland to work in the urban industrialized south. By the early 1980s, 60% of Finns lived in urban areas.

Ethnic Composition

Finland has always been ethnically homogeneous. During the 19th and 20th centuries, it has been a country of emigration, not immigration. Finland lacks the economic or political conditions that would attract large numbers of migrant workers or refugees. The total number of residents from non-Nordic nations is only about 20,000. Except for Swedes, many of those who migrate to Finland are white-collar workers attracted by commercial opportunities. Very few non-Europeans live in Finland, and only a few refugees are granted asylum. Finns have been very open about their desire to avoid admitting workers from Asia and Africa because of their concerns about racial unrest.

The **Saami (Lapps, Sami),** who number 4,400 in Finland, are the indigenous inhabitants of the nation. They are distantly related to the Finns, and both groups speak a language belonging to the Finno-Ugric language family. The Saami were gradually pushed northward by advancing Finns until they reached the northern half of the country in the 16th century, where they have remained. About 90% of the Saami live in the municipalities of Enontekio, Inari, and Utsjoki, and in the reindeer-herding area of Sodankyla. Finnish Saami speak three different dialects, but in the 1990s only a minority speak Saami as their first language.

Few Finnish Saami actually lead the nomadic life. Saami own no more than one-third of Finland's 200,000 reindeer, and only 5% have herds of 250 or more—the size necessary to support oneself by herding. Most Saami work at various jobs, including farming, construction, and in service industries such as tourism. The Saami also receive a greater portion of their income through government welfare than do Finns, as a whole. There have been various government efforts and Saami associations developed to safeguard Saami culture and to help them deal with modern society. The Society for the Promotion of Lapp Culture was formed in 1932, and in 1960 the government created the Advisory Commission on Lapp Affairs. The Saami Litto was formed by Saami in 1945, and a more aggressive organization, the Johti Sabmelazzat, was formed in 1968. The Finnish government arranged for elections every four years, beginning in 1973, to create a Saami parliament that was to advise authorities. Finnish Saami also have been involved in international organizations intended to preserve and promote Saami culture and goals. Despite these efforts, the status of the Saami people remains lower than that of ethnic Finns.

Finns are the predominant group in the country, comprising more than 99% of the population, counting Swedish-speaking Finns. Ethnic Finns comprise about 94% of the population. Finland was inhabited by Neolithic people as early as 8000 B.C., but the ancestors of today's Finns probably did not arrive until the 1st century A.D. Finland was part of Sweden from 1150 to 1809, and part of Russia until 1917. Thus, the Finns are sometimes viewed as a subject people without a culture or history of their own. The cultural awakening of the 19th century, however, established a Finnish identity based upon their language and cultural traditions.

Closely related to the Finns are the **Karelians,** a northern Finno-Ugric tribe. Their area of settlement, Karelia, is now divided by the border between Russia and Finland. There are large dialectal differences between Karelian and Finnish; Karelian in the south displays a considerable Russian influence, and in the north is more similar to Finnish. Karelians as a distinct group emerged (or re-emerged) around 1900 as part of a Finnish nationalistic movement. Romanticized images of rural, independent Karelia played an important role in the building of the Finnish nation. For some Finnish artists and scholars, Karelia became a "promised land" for Finns from Karelia. Karelia was a source for the history, religion, and mythology of the original Finns, and a literary and political inspiration for the future.

Conflicts with Russia over the Karelian area resulted in dispute settlements in which Finland lost much of Karelia (12% of Finland's total area) and hundreds of thousands of Karelians were left homeless. The displaced Karelians from the ceded areas were Finnish citizens, however, not foreign refugees, because they relocated within their own country. The large cultural and social differences between the Karelians and the Finns led many displaced Karelians to remigrate back to their old territory, which had become Soviet Karelia. Other displaced Karelians who resettled among the rest of the Finnish population lost the unity of their culture and environment in the process. In reaction to the rapid assimilation, Karelians built and maintained a Karelian organizational structure: the Karelian Union has more than 500 member organizations and about 73,000 members, which suggests that younger people are also involved in the activities. In 1977, the Karelian Union adopted a program whose main aim was to unify the Karelian culture, which also includes Karelians in Russia. In the 1980s there was a general Karelian renaissance that many regarded as a vulgarization of Karelian traditions. This attempt to create a new Karelian identity has been at least partially successful, although the process of assimilation with Finns still continues into the 1990s (*see also* Russia).

Swedish-speaking Finns number about 300,000 and constitute about 6% of the Finnish population, although assimilation makes it difficult to accurately distinguish Swedes from Finns. Swedes came to Finland during the crusades of the 12th century, and Finland was incorporated into Sweden until 1809, when it became part of Russia. Even after the takeover by Russia, Finland continued to be administered by Swedes, and the Swedish language predominated as the language of culture and government. After the Bolshevik Revolution of 1917 the Finns declared their independence, and a constitution was written that gave both Finnish and Swedish status as official languages. The Swedish-speaking population of Finland is concentrated in two areas: along the southern coast between Helsinki and Hango, and along the western coast between Pori and Jokobstad. Because both Finnish and Swedish are official languages, there has been no need for legislation to protect the Swedish minority. Municipalities are considered bilingual when the minority exceeds 8% of the population or contains at least 3,000 people from the minority, and boundaries have been drawn to make them as nearly unilingual as possible. Thus, Swedish-speaking children go to schools where the instruction is in Swedish. There were 339,000 Swedish-speaking Finns in 1920, 11% of the population. Since then, their numbers have declined precipitously. Among the reasons given are a lower birth rate, mixed marriages, and emigration.

A distinct Swedish subgroup in Finland is the **Åland Islanders.** The Åland Islands were ceded by Sweden to Russia along with Finland in 1809, and were returned to Finland by the League of Nations in 1921, despite the wishes of the Islanders for reunification with Sweden. The Finnish government agreed to respect and preserve the Islanders' Swedish language and culture, and the Swedish government withdrew its claim to sovereignty over the Islands. The Swedish character of the Islands is preserved through regulation of language, education, regional citizenship, and the acquisition of property on the Islands. Regional citizenship is attained by spending five years in residence, and only those with regional citizenship can acquire land and vote in municipal or provincial elections. Finland's treatment of the Åland Islanders is considered a model for the treatment of minority groups by a host nation.

In addition to these major groups, Finland has a few other ethnic minorities, all quite small in number and influence. These include **Americans from the United States,** who number about 1,200. Many American immigrants are actually returnees; that is, first- and second-generation emigrants to America who are now returning.

There are also about 1,200 **Britons.** Friendly relations exist between Finns and British immigrants, although the British do not enjoy the same high status as do immigrants from Nordic countries.

Danes and **Norwegians** number fewer than 1,000. Historically, movement between the Nordic countries is a centuries-old phenomenon that has taken place within a framework of extensive political cooperation. However, this is less the case with Finland because of Finland's proximity to, and ties with, Russia.

Germans number about 1,500 and are the third largest group of non-Finns in the country. Germans have trickled into Finland for centuries, and a large proportion of them have been artisans and professionals whose contributions have been welcomed. Despite some conflicts during the world wars, relations between Germans and Finns have been harmonious.

Gypsies have been present in Finland since the late 16th century. With their unique customs and dress, nomadic lifestyle, and service-based economy, Gypsies are a clearly different culture. In Finland, they have been the subject of discrimination and persecution, including special laws directed against them. There were 5,000 to 6,000 Gypsies in Finland in the late 1980s, and the population may have increased in the 1990s due to emigration of Gypsies from Eastern Europe and Russia.

Jews in Finland number about 1,000, most of whom live in Helsinki and Turku. During World War II, Finnish authorities refused to deliver Jews to the Nazis, and the Jewish community of about 2,000 survived virtually intact. Assimilation and emigration have significantly reduced the size of the community, and Finnish synagogues, schools, libraries, and other Jewish institutions barely managed to survive in the 1990s.

Russian immigrants number about 2,200. Russians migrated to Finland because of a common history and geographic proximity. Finland was part of Russia as a grand duchy from 1809 to 1917. Russia incorporated a huge portion of Finland in the 1940s and now shares Finland's entire eastern border. The Russian language is closer to Finnish than the Scandinavian languages, which also has made assimilation easier. Although there have been conflicts and tensions between the two nations in the past, primarily because of Russia's status as a world power and its imperialistic designs, relations between Finns and Russian settlers are harmonious.

Turks and other **Muslims** number about 1,000. Their nation of origin is not considered in the national census. Most live in Helsinki and are involved in commerce. Muslims first came to Finland in the middle of the 19th century, primarily from Turkey. Because of their small numbers, they are relatively "invisible" and have had difficulty maintaining the institutions needed for political participation in Finnish society.

European immigrants, other than those from northern Europe, form a significant portion of Finland's small immigrant population. However, even counted collectively, the number of those from Poland, Bulgaria, Bosnia, and Albania is insignificant compared with the often vast migrations across the borders of most other European nations. In comparison with other nations, the economic and political conditions in Finland are not attractive enough to draw other Europeans, nor is their presence desired. None of these groups is large enough to establish a strong ethnic group identity, and therefore, individuals tend to blend into the dominant Finnish culture.

Ethnic Relations

Swedish colonists and Swedish-speaking Finns, living primarily in southwestern Finland, have for centuries been the ruling elite. Finnish was considered to be a peasant language until the 19th century, when a nationalist movement made Finnish the official language of the country. Swedish is the second official language of Finland, spoken by about 6% of the population in 1990. The Swedish-speaking minority has declined in numbers over the years largely as a result of assimilation through marriage with Finnish speakers.

Linguistically, Finnish is the most distinct of the Scandinavian languages, which makes assimilation more difficult for immigrants from other Scandinavian countries. However, Danes and Norwegians assimilate very quickly, usually within a generation or two. In the last half-century, relations between the people of the Nordic countries have become even better. Relations between Danes, Norwegians, and Finns are excellent, more like intra-ethnic relations than interethnic relations (for example, there are long-range congruence of citizenship laws that give Danes and Norwegians, and other Nordic citizens, extensive rights in Finland).

Since the 1960s, measures have been taken to improve the Gypsies' standard of living, to settle them, to provide employment, and to outlaw racial discrimination. Still, Gypsies remain at the bottom of the Finnish social hierarchy.

France

F rance is located in Western Europe and is bordered on the north by the English Channel, Belgium, and Germany; on the east by Germany, Switzerland, and Italy; on the south by the Mediterranean Sea, Andorra, and Spain; and on the west by the Atlantic Ocean. It has a population of 58.1 million. About 90% of the population is classified as French, this number including several million people who are not ethnically French but are French citizens, speak French, and are assimilated into French culture. French cultural identity is the most salient feature of life in France and among French people in overseas communities around the world. It is based on a descent—real or imagined—from the Gauls, a long shared history, and a set of clearly defined French traditions and institutions. Among the most important of these are the French national values of "Liberté, Egalité, Fraternité"; the French language; French cuisine; French style; the sense of French culture and French tradition as reflected in art, music, and literature; and an humanistic-secular world view. About 90% of people in France are Roman Catholic, with the remainder being mainly Muslim (about 5 million), Protestant, or Jewish. There is a large French population dispersed around the world, with many French in neighboring nations such as Belgium, Switzerland, and Andorra, and also large French-ancestry populations in the United States and Canada. There are also many French citizens in former French colonies or French dependencies and territories in Africa, the Caribbean, and the Pacific region.

Ethnic Composition

France is an ethnically heterogeneous society, with over 100 ethnic groups from all regions of the world present. With the ethnic French constituting some 85% of the population, these other groups form only 10%, or about 8.7 million people. Included within the French majority are distinct regional cultures that some experts prefer to classify as distinct ethnic groups: the peoples of Alsace, Brittany, Burgundy, Auvergnat, Aveyronnais, Aquitaine, Occitan, and Provence. Although the traditional peoples of these regions are now integrated politically and economically into the French nation, differences in dress, food preferences, and language persist.

The two most distinctive of these groups are the Alsatians and the Bretons. **Alsatians** are the people of the two German-speaking departments of eastern France, on the border with Germany. Of the approximately 1.5 million Alsatians in France, some speak dialects of German, although the majority now also speak French. Control of the Alsace region has passed back and forth between Germany and France since the 1600s. Alsatians have a long history of resistance to both German and French rule, and when their region was con-

quered and harshly administered by the Germans early in World War II, loyalty to France increased. Since the 1970s, there has been a heightened interest among the Alsatians in reviving their German history and German elements of their culture, a trend that generally has been resisted by the French government, which stresses assimilation. Unlike the past, when some Alsatians argued for independence or joining with Germany, the current movement focuses on preserving and reestablishing Alsatian cultural traditions and continuing the use of the German dialects instead of French.

Bretons number about 3.7 million and live mainly in northwestern France. Until coming under centralized government in 1789, the Bretons' homeland—Brittany—was politically and culturally autonomous. Since then, autonomy has eroded, along with use of the Breton language, which is now the primary language of only 25% of Bretons. Bretons are a Celtic people and are culturally and linguistically related to the Cornish of southern England, the Gaels of Ireland, and the Welsh. Beginning in the 1940s, at Breton initiation, a number of economic, political, and educational reforms were implemented that have led to greater economic prosperity for Brittany and

French cultural identity is the most salient feature of life in France, and immigrant ethnic groups are expected to assimilate. Photo: Corel Corp.

a revitalization of the Breton language and culture. These changes have resulted in fewer people now believing that a separate Breton nation is likely.

In addition to these two groups, there are the **Corsicans** of Corsica, located in the Mediterranean Sea, south of northwestern Italy and about 100 miles southeast of the eastern border of France. In 1769, Corsica was taken by France from Genoa. However, Corsican resistance and effort to create a separate Corsican nation predates French control and began in the early 1700s. The population of the island is about 250,000, of whom 70% are Corsicans, with the remainder being mainly French (many of whom went there after the fall of the French Empire in Africa), Italians, and a growing number of Arabs, who fill many of the low-level jobs.

In addition to these regional cultures, there are two regional linguistic minorities, the **Catalans,** who live on the southeast border with Spain, and the **Basques,** who live on the southwest border with Spain. The majority of

the population of both of these groups are in Spain.

Another major ethnic category is Arabs and Africans, who are mainly from former French colonies. These peoples can be subdivided into North African and West African, with various national groups within each division. Arabs are primarily from the former French colonies of Algeria (620,000), Morocco (585,000), and Tunisia (208,000). In France, they are more often identified simply as **Arabs, Muslims, North Africans, Afro-Arabs,** or **Maghrebins,** rather than by nation of origin. A further distinction in France is between the Harqis and Beurs. **Harqis** are those who sided with the French in the Algerian revolution and their children; they number about 400,000 in France. Many have not assimilated into French society and are shunned by more recent arrivals from North Africa. **Beurs** are children of Muslim immigrants born in France and number about 600,000. Arabs form the poorest segment of the French population. The shanty-towns on the edge of major cities where they used to live have now disappeared, but most continue to live in low-income housing provided by the government either in the center of cities or on their peripheries.

Sub-Saharan Africans in France are mainly from the former French colonies in that region, primarily Senegal and Mali, and number about 100,000. They are Muslims. Although they form separate Muslim communities from the Arabs of North Africa, most people in France generally lump them together as a single entity, and often they are subject to the same discrimination and assimilationist policies as the Arabs of North Africa.

Asians in France now include an undetermined number of **Chinese, Japanese,** and **Vietnamese,** the presence of the latter group reflecting the French colonization of Vietnam, which ended in 1954. These Asian immigrant groups are particularly prominent in major cities, especially Paris, where they run small businesses, shops, and restaurants. The Japanese are heavily involved in finance.

Also from Asia are **Turks,** who number about 300,000. Like many Europeans, they arrived in the 1960s and 1970s under work contracts to take jobs not considered desirable by the French in tourism, construction, and industry. And—like the European contract workers—some Turks chose to stay in France, and the French population now includes a substantial number of children born to Turkish parents in France.

As the center of European diplomacy from the 17th to the mid-20th century, France attracted and continues to draw people from many other European nations. The largest European groups in France are the approximately 640,000 **Portuguese,** 254,000 **Italians,** 216,000 **Spaniards,** and smaller number of **Russians, Poles, Britons,** and **Yugoslavians.** With the exception of the Britons, most of these people are workers who came to France in the 1960s and 1970s as guest workers in the tourism and construction industries and also as domestics. Many chose to stay on in France, and the population now includes a sizable number of their children who were born in France and who have the right at the age of 18 to choose whether they want to be French citizens.

The two major non-Christian religious groups are the Muslims and the Jews. The Muslim category is composed mainly of the Arabs and Turks discussed above, and a smaller number of **Middle Eastern** peoples. Despite vast differences in culture and physical appearance, these groups are commonly lumped together as "Muslims" or "Arabs."

Jews in France number about 600,000 and include many Jews who came to southern France following the end of French rule in Algeria in the early 1960s, and Eastern European Jews who arrived at the end of World War II and their descendants. France has the fourth largest Jewish population in the world, after the United States, Israel, and Russia.

The final ethnic category is a diverse one composed of refugees and asylum-seekers. At one time, France had a liberal policy regarding refugees and asylum-seekers, but this policy became very restrictive in the 1990s. Still, there are about 200,000 refugees in France from Romania, Bosnia, Croatia, Turkey, Algeria, Zaire, Sri Lanka, China, and Somalia. Other groups in France include **U.S. Americans, Iranians,** and **Palestinians,** as well as some individuals from every other European nation.

Ethnic Relations

Ethnic relations in France are framed by the dual notions of French cultural identity and assimilation of foreigners into French society. For several centuries, the French approach to ethnic relations has been to make non-French peoples French—in culture, language, and lifestyle. The formal aspects of the French assimilation model have been centralized government control, a centralized education system, and primacy given to speaking the French language over regional languages or immigrant languages. Although there is a long history of anti-Semitism and resistance to assimilation by regional cultures such as the Bretons, adaptation has long been the pattern in France; nearly all residents, wherever their place of origin, have come to identify with French culture and regard themselves as French.

In the 1980s and 1990s, this approach to ethnic relations has worked less well than in the past. The global economic and political order has drawn France, as is the case in every other nation, into an increasingly complex web of relations with other nations and international organizations. This globalization has brought foreign products, food, ideas, investments, and culture to France, which has been seen by some as threatening the preeminence of French culture. France has initiated a number of programs to protect French culture from intrusions from elsewhere in the world, particularly the United States. Among these are a foundation to take control of and preserve various sites such as chapels, inns, and sections of countryside that are considered to be part of France's national heritage; a new law that requires French radio stations to play at least 40% French music; laws that restrict how many foreign films and foreign television programs stations may show; and restrictions on adding non-French words to the French lexicon.

A threat to France's assimilation policy has come from the Muslim community, estimated to number between four and five million. Although composed of West and North Africans,

Turks, and Arabs, these people are lumped together and defined by many French as one group—Muslims—and are viewed as resisting assimilation into French society. This resistance is manifested in the adherence to Islamic practices, which include daily prayer at mosques, fasting during Ramadan, scarves for women, and abstaining from pork and alcoholic beverages. In addition, many Arabs—who form the largest Muslim population—are distinguishable by their low socioeconomic status and are the object of economic, social, and religious discrimination. At the same time, many Muslim children have been born in France and many are citizens. Recent surveys indicate that a majority of the French believe that there are too many Muslims in France and that they threaten French cultural integrity. This view has been reflected in government actions in the 1990s designed to assimilate Muslims forcibly by repressing Islamic customs. The actions include arresting Muslims accused of supporting Islamic political movements in Africa or France, and in 1994, the banning of head scarves in schools for Muslim girls. Political action is centered in the National Front Party, which advocates deporting a majority of immigrants and giving French people priority in employment, social benefits, and housing. The underlying belief system of these policies is set forth by the National Front mayor of the southern city of Toulon: "We risk being overwhelmed by an Islamic invasion from North Africa. In France bigamy is against the law. Yet we are importing bigamous, or even polygamous, unemployed foreigners and their children. The risk is that our country—a product of its heritage and its combined genes—will be transformed" (*New York Times,* 22 November 1996, A4).

Ethnic secessionist desires in Brittany and Alsace are no longer a threat, although in both regions demands for cultural autonomy and efforts to revive the regional languages continue. Similarly, Corsican demands for autonomy continue and revolve around perennial issues such as economic development, political autonomy, a right to use the Corsican language, and a right to control the Corsican education system. Although some of those in the resistance movement are committed to an independent Corsica, there seems to be only minimal support for that position among the Corsican population.

While anti-Semitism seems less a problem in France than in some other European countries such as Germany, the 1990s has seen a revival of anti-Semitic acts, including attacks on synagogues and Jewish cemeteries. Some people blame the large Muslim population in France for these attacks, while others attribute it to French anti-Semites and perhaps to a long history of anti-Semitism in France.

Georgia

Georgia is located in southeastern Europe in the region where Asia and Europe meet. It is bordered on the north and northeast by Russia, on the southeast by Azerbaijan, on the south by Armenia and Turkey, and on the west by the Black Sea. It has a population of 5.5 million and is ethnically heterogeneous. The region has been inhabited for at least 7,000 years and has been the home of dozens of ethnic groups, most of whom merged to form new groups or were absorbed by more powerful groups over the millennia. The number of distinct ethnic groups in Georgia today is much smaller than it was even a few hundred years ago.

Ethnic Composition

Ethnic Georgians comprise about 70% of the population, the remainder being made up of six groups: the Abkhaz, Armenians, Azerbaijanis, Greeks, Ossetes, and Russians, each with a population exceeding 100,000, and several dozen other groups with populations ranging from a few thousand to 50,000. Georgia became an independent nation in 1991, and as a result of the various ethnic conflicts that developed there at that time, there has been a massive shifting of populations within Georgia. This includes the out-migration of many Russians, Ossetes, and Ukrainians, who returned to their homelands, as well as the creation of many internal refugees, mostly Abkhaz and Ossetes, who moved back to their regions, and Georgians who fled Ossetia and Abkhazia for Georgia proper. Other groups affected by independence and internal ethnic conflicts are the Greeks, Armenians, and Jews, and both the Greek and Jewish populations have been reduced markedly by the immigration of people in these groups to other countries.

Georgians number 3.8 million in Georgia and constitute 70% of the population. This percentage has increased since 1990 due to out-migration of other groups. Modern Georgians are very likely descended from some of the earliest settlers in this region. By the Middle Ages, a Georgian ethnicity had developed and a Georgian state had emerged in the region that was a powerful political force. However, in 1801, the Georgians were conquered by the Russians and came under Russian influence during the Russian Empire, an influence that continued in the Soviet era. With the demise of the Soviet Union in 1991, Georgia became an independent nation.

Included in the Georgian ethnic and national group are a number of subgroups such as the **Ajars, Khevsur,** and **Mingrelians.** These groups formerly were seen as distinct ethnic groups, but throughout the 20th century they have been absorbed into the Georgian ethnic group, speak Georgian, are Christian (with the exception of the Muslim Ajars), and are now classified by experts as Georgian. In addition to Georgians in Georgia, there are about 200,000 Georgians spread elsewhere throughout the former Soviet Union, with the majority in Russia. Georgians speak Georgian and are mainly members of the Georgian Orthodox Church, with a small number of Muslims, most of whom were formerly ethnically Ajar. Since 1991, Georgia has made a strong effort to create a single, unified Georgian nation. One part of that effort was to treat all residents of the country as Georgians. This is one factor that led to the conflict with the

Ossetes and Abkhaz, who do not define themselves as Georgian and see Georgian efforts to assimilate them as a threat to their cultural survival.

Abkhaz number about 100,000, constituting 2% of the population of Georgia. There is also a significant Abkhaz population across the border in Russia that was established in the late 1800s after an Abkhaz revolt against Russian rule in Georgia failed and the Abkhaz were forced to flee. Ancestors of the modern Abkhaz have been in the region for perhaps as long as 6,000 years and, by the 8th century A.D., various tribes in the region had joined together to form a distinct Abkhaz ethnic group. In the 10th century A.D. they came under control of the Georgian state and remained under Georgian control and influence for 700 years. Subsequently, they enjoyed relatively short periods of political freedom and were under the control of the Ottoman Empire (at which time many Georgians converted to Islam), and then under the control of the Russian Empire.

Armenians number 437,000 and constitute 8% of the population of Georgia. They live primarily in the southern region near the border with Armenia. Their neighbors in Georgia to the west are the Azerbaijani, who live across the border from their home region. The conflict that has characterized relations between Armenia and Azerbaijani since 1991 seems not to affect the communities in Georgia.

Azerbaijani number about 300,000 in Georgia and constitute about 6% of the population. As with the Armenians, they live near the border with their homeland in Azerbaijan.

Greeks in Georgia number about 120,000, or 3% of the population. They are part of a larger **Pontic Greek** population that since at least A.D. 800 has settled near and influenced the cultures around the Black Sea. The indigenous language of most of the Greeks in the Black Sea region of Russia, including Georgia, is Pontian Greek, which is derived from an Ionian dialect. However, most Greeks in Georgia today speak Russian. Greeks in Georgia traditionally were farmers, although some have moved to the cities and now are engaged in a wide range of occupations. Greeks have maintained their Greek Orthodox religion, although pressures and ties to the Russian government forced some to adopt Russian Orthodoxy instead, at least nominally. Many Greeks have returned to Greece since independence in 1991, where they felt they could have a better life and avoid the ethnic conflict that was going on in Georgia.

Kurds number 33,000 in Georgia, or about .06% of the population. This figure also includes a small number of **Yezidis,** who for census purposes are lumped with the Kurds (*see* Armenia, Turkey, Iran, and Iraq).

Ossetes live in Ossetia, a region divided into north and south zones on either side of the Russian and Georgia border in the Caucasus. They number about 400,000 in all, about 164,000 of whom are in Georgia. Relations between Russians and Ossetes on the north side of the Caucasus are friendly; however, on the south side of the border, and especially since the demise of the Soviet Union in 1991, the Ossetes and Georgians have been involved in ongoing conflict over the Ossetian desire for a unified territory in Russia. Georgians oppose this because it would mean giving up Georgian territory to Russia.

Russians, according to the 1989 census, numbered 341,000, or 6.7% of the population of Georgia. Their numbers have certainly decreased since Georgian independence in 1991, as many have returned to Russia to escape the conflicts involving the Abkhaz, the Georgians, and the Ossetes, as well as the sometimes-tense relations between the Georgians and the Russians. Russian influence since 1801, when Russia annexed Georgia, has been considerable: many people in Georgia (both Russian and Georgian) now speak Russian, especially in the cities, and Russia has had considerable influence in political and economic affairs.

Svans number about 40,000 in Georgia, or .07% of the population, with an additional 4,000 or so living in Azerbaijan. They live in a distinct region in northeastern Georgia bordering on Abkhazia where the population is mostly Svan. The Svan of today are descendants of the indigenous peoples of the Caucasus who have been there for at least 7,000 years. To a large extent, and in a way considerably different from the neighboring Abkhaz and Ossetes, the Svan have remained separate from and relatively free of influence from the Russians in the north and the Georgians in the south. Many continue to speak the Svan language, although Russian and Georgian is spoken too, and while most of them are adherents of Eastern Orthodoxy, much of the traditional religion survives as well. Additionally, the region was one of the last that the Soviets attempted to develop economically and bring into the mainstream of Soviet society. Therefore, it was not until the 1950s and 1960s that real economic change reached the region.

Other groups in Georgia include at least a few thousand people from virtually every other republic that was formerly a constituent republic of the Soviet Union; plus a small number of **Turks;** a small number of **Udi,** whose main population is in Azerbaijan; 1,500 **Laz,** who number 200,000 in Turkey; and **Jews,** who now number about 20,000.

Ethnic Relations

The framework for the current situation regarding relations in Georgia is created largely by Georgia's location on the border between Asia and Europe and between the Islamic world and the Christian world. Although the Georgian people have been a distinct ethnic entity in the region for centuries, they have been influenced by the Greeks, the Persians, the Russians, and the Turks. In addition, the region has been settled by numerous people over the millennia, and while many of those groups have disappeared or have been absorbed into the Georgian ethnic group, some of the larger ones or more localized ones, such as the Abkhaz, Ossetes, or Greeks, continue to seek ethnic autonomy or ethnic freedom.

In the 1990s, Georgia faced four major ethnic conflict situations. The first two involve the Abkhaz and Ossete separatist movements, in which these two peoples, indigenous to the regions where they live, sought to create and maintain a political and ethnic identity separate from the majority of Georgians.

In the Soviet period, the Abkhaz were subjected to both Georgian and Russian assimilation programs. One result is that many Georgians now view the Abkhaz as Georgians, although the Abkhaz continue to see themselves as a distinct group. Despite the assimilation programs, the Abkhaz were given their own territory in northwestern Georgia during the Soviet era, the Abkhazian Autonomous Republic, and that is where most continue to live, where they form approximately 20% of the population. Other major groups in the republic are Georgians, Russians, and a number of smaller minorities now largely absorbed by the Georgians or the Russians.

Following Georgian independence in 1991, Abkhaz began agitating for political independence: they desired an autonomous state or, short of that, autonomy within Russia or Georgia. Georgia resisted Abkhaz independence in any form. In 1992, the conflict became violent, and since then, over 2,000 people have died; numerous Abkhaz churches, libraries, and cultural institutions have been destroyed; and many Georgians, Russians, and Greeks have fled. In 1996, the conflict was no longer violent but remained unresolved, although the Abkhaz clearly have control of their region and the Georgians seem to have given up their efforts to simply assimilate the Abkhaz into the Georgian nation.

The situation regarding the Osscte separatist wishes is somewhat different. The Georgians would prefer that the Georgian Ossetes move north to Russia and leave their territory as part of Georgia. As of 1996, this conflict, which sometimes has been violent, was not resolved, in part because there were clear divisions in the Ossete community between those who would prefer complete independence and those who would prefer to remain in Georgia or to move to Russia.

The third major ethnic conflict concerns the relationship between the Georgians and the Russians. During the Soviet era, Russians numbered over 300,000 in Georgia, although the numbers have likely decreased since the breakup of the Soviet Union. Georgians have always resisted Russian rule. During the nearly two centuries of Russian rule, the Georgians were subject to various Russification programs including the substitution of Russian for the Georgian language in teaching and government. Since 1991, the Georgians have sought to reverse that situation and Georgian rather than Russian is now taught in schools. Today relations between Georgia and Russia remain strained because of the history of Russian rule, because of Georgian efforts to free themselves from Russian influence, and also because of Russia's role in helping the Abkhaz in their fight with the Georgians, which was seen by the Georgians as an effort to weaken the Georgian republic.

The fourth ethnic conflict situation concerns the Meskhetian Turks, who were exiled from Georgia during World War II by Joseph Stalin on the claim that, since they were Muslims, they might betray Russia during the war. Most were sent to Central Asia. With the fall of the Soviet Union in 1991, many of the 200,000 Meskhetian Turks expressed a desire to return to the region of Georgia where they lived before being deported. That region is now populated primarily by Georgians and some Russians, and those people—plus many other Georgians—are resistant to having them return.

Germany

T he Federal Republic of Germany is in Western Europe, bordered by the North Sea, Denmark, and the Baltic Sea on the north; Poland, the Czech Republic, and Austria on the east; Austria, Liechtenstein, and Switzerland on the south; and Luxembourg, France, Belgium, and the Netherlands on the west. The reunification of the independent nations of East and West Germany in 1991 produced the current nation. Germany has a population of 81.3 million and is one of the most prosperous nations in Europe and the world. Germany is a postindustrial society that stresses education, individual achievement, the rule of law, conformity, and productivity. There are a number of distinct cultural regions in Germany, including Bavaria and the Rhineland, as well as distinct patterns of speech associated with different urban centers such as Berlin, Munich, and Frankfurt. In the post–World War II years, there has been a strong effort by the government to diminish the role of regional cultures.

Ethnic Composition

About 95% of people in Germany are ethnic Germans. The second largest ethnic group is the Turks, who number about 2 million. As a large, prosperous nation, Germany has also attracted significant minorities from elsewhere in Europe, Asia, Africa, and North America.

Germans are people whose parents are German, who speak the German language, and who are citizens of Germany. There are 76 million Germans in Germany and millions of people of German ancestry living around the world. The majority of Austrians and Swiss, as well as many Dutch, are of German ancestry, although they are no longer categorized as German. The most important of these criteria is ancestry, and Germans living outside Germany are considered ethnically German. About 45% of Germans in Germany are Protestant, 37% Roman Catholic, and 3% Muslim. Protestants are more heavily concentrated in the north and Catholics in the south.

There is a large population of people who are ethnically German living outside of Germany. The majority of the population of Switzerland and Austria are German-speaking, and sizable German populations are found near the German border in Poland, France, and Denmark, and near the Austrian border in northern Italy. Many Dutch are of German ancestry. The formerly sizable German population in the Czech Republic has now mostly returned to Germany, as have many Germans in Russia and Central Asia. In the United States, people of German ancestry are the second largest ethnic group (following the British), and there also are large German populations in Canada, Argentina, Paraguay, and Bolivia.

The only significant indigenous ethnic minority are the **Sorbs** (**Wends**). They are a Slavic people identifiable as a distinct group in what is now southeastern Germany since the early 8th century. Sorbs are now bilingual in German and Sorbian due to contact with Czechs, Poles, and Germans. They number about 70,000, but the population is slowly decreasing through assimilation. At various times persecuted by their neighbors, and often seeking independence, the Sorbs are recognized as an official minority in Germany.

There are people from every European nation living in Germany. Probably the majority are guest workers from Eastern and Southern Europe. Eastern Europeans number nearly one million, the largest groups being **Bosnians** and **Poles** with smaller numbers of **Romanians, Bulgarians, Hungarians, Czechs, Slovaks, Croats, Serbs,** and **Albanians.** Most of these guest workers began arriving in Germany in the 1960s when contract labor agreements were made between their nations and Germany, and many subsequently brought their families. As the demand for labor declined in the 1970s and 1980s, the number of new arrivals decreased, but in the 1990s, many new Eastern Europeans arrived as refugees and asylumseekers. Probably because they are European, antiforeigner resentment is less often directed at them than at the Turkish guest workers.

As with the Eastern Europeans, Southern Europeans came to Germany as contract laborers in the 1960s and 1970s and now enjoy somewhat protected status as members of other European Union nations. They include about 500,000 **Italians,** 300,000 **Greeks,** 135,000 **Spaniards,** and 85,000 **Portuguese.**

Western Europeans include **Austrians** (180,000), **Dutch** (111,000), **Britons** (95,000), and **French** (80,000), most of whom are students, government officials, businesspersons, financiers, and retirees.

Danes number about 75,000 and have a different historical relationship with Germany than do other Western European groups. They live in the Schleswig-Holstein region, which was part of Denmark until it was annexed by Germany in 1863. The region is now heavily populated by Germans who settled there after World War II, and Danes currently constitute only about 8% of the regional population. Conflict over political control was settled through a series of negotiations in the 1950s and ethnic conflict is no longer a serious issue.

North Africans include about 100,000 **Tunisians** and **Moroccans,** who first arrived in the 1960s as contract workers.

The major Asian minority is **Turks,** who began arriving in Germany in substantial numbers in 1961 following an agreement between the two nations designed to allow German employers to use Turks as temporary industrial workers in German factories. Today, Turks number nearly two million and are the major non-German ethnic group in Germany. They live mainly in large industrial cities but also in many small towns, usually in their own neighborhoods with mosques, civic organizations, and stores serving their community. Many are bilingual in German and Turkish and plan to remain in Germany. While Turks were always the subject of discrimination, in the 1990s German hostility turned violent with assaults on them, and firebombings of their homes and businesses led to number of injuries and deaths. The German government has sought

A Turk mourner at the funeral of his mother, daughter, and niece who were killed in an arsonist-set fire in Hamburg in 1992. The sign says: "Children Murderer, Pigs Neo-Nazi." Photo: Reuters/Corbis-Bettmann.

to protect Turks, but many Turks fear that deep antiforeigner sentiments hinder protection efforts. Although the majority of Turks in Germany were born in Germany, fewer than 1% of them have been given citizenship.

Kurds, who number about 400,000, are not marked as a distinct group in Germany. They are generally classified as Turks because they emigrated from Turkey.

The history of **Vietnamese** settlement in Germany mirrors that of the Turks, although they number only about 100,000 and are not as often the target of antiforeigner anger. They came to East Germany as contract laborers and stayed on after German reunification. An agreement between Germany and Vietnam in 1995 to return the Vietnamese to Vietnam in exchange for German economic support has not yet led to any large-scale relocation, as Vietnam has been reluctant to accept the returnees.

The third major Asian group is **Iranians,** who number about 90,000, two-thirds of whom settled in Germany following the overthrow of the shah. Like the Turks, they are mainly Muslim.

Two groups who were numerous in Germany prior to World War II but are now much smaller are Gypsies and Jews. **Gypsies** are of unknown number in Germany because large numbers settled there recently after fleeing Eastern European nations in the 1990s, making earlier estimates of about 50,000 Gypsies no longer accurate. About 500,000 Gypsies in Europe were exterminated by the Germans during World War II. Gypsies in Germany represent a mix of groups from Eastern and Southern Europe. As elsewhere in Europe, they are now largely settled, often near cities where they provide specialized services to the urban and suburban populations.

Jews number about 40,000 and are concentrated in major cities such as Berlin and Frankfurt. The Jewish communities found in many German towns before World War II were exterminated by the Nazis. Nearly all Jews in Germany today are refugees or the children of refugees from Eastern Europe who fled to Germany after the war. They reestablished Jewish institutions such as synagogues, schools, community centers, and hospitals destroyed during the Nazi era. Despite their small numbers, anti-Semitism is persistent in Germany, and attacks on Jews and their institutions continue to occur.

U.S. Americans number 160,000 in Germany, the second largest American population in Europe after that in Great Britain. They include military personnel stationed at U.S. military bases, individuals involved in business and finance, students, expatriates, and retirees.

Ethnic Relations

Ethnic relations are complicated in Germany. Underlying the current situation are a number of related though seemingly contradictory historical events, processes, and beliefs. First, Germans have always defined being German in genetic terms; and thus, one is a German only if one's parents are German. Second, ethnic nationalism in Germany equates being German with citizenship. Thus, non-Germans are usually denied citizenship, while Germans returning from other lands are automatically granted citizenship. Third, from 1945 up to the early 1950s—save for the few Jews and Gypsies who lived, to varying degrees, apart from German society—Germany was ethnically "pure." Territorial expansion placed Germans in border regions of many neighboring nations and kept non-Germans out of Germany. Fourth, the Holocaust, for which Germany was held responsible for the murder of 6 million Jews and millions of other peoples in Europe during World War II, has made many Germans today sensitive to charges of anti-Semitism and xenophobia. Fifth, since the 1950s, Germany has entered into agreements with nations—mainly in Southern and Eastern Europe—to bring workers to Germany to take low-level jobs not considered desirable by Germans, in industry, tourism, and the service sectors. And sixth, from the 1950s until 1994, Germany had a very liberal policy regarding the acceptance of refugees and asylum-seekers. Thus, Germany continues to shelter a large population of refugees (estimated at over 400,000), over 50% of whom are Bosnians, with other groups including Croatians, Kurds, Serbs, Romanians, Afghans, Sri Lankans, Iraqis, and Iranians.

Ethnic animosity and violence directed by Germans at non-Germans became a major issue in the late 1970s. The German economy declined in the late 1970s, and in the early 1990s the unemployment rate was high. Adding to this pressure, ethnic Germans began returning from Russia and Eastern European nations following the end of Communist rule. Even so, millions of foreign workers in Germany clearly planned to stay. This situation caused some Germans, including some conservative political parties, to blame non-Germans for Germany's economic problems. Antiforeigner violence has been carried out by members of neo-Nazi organizations (which are banned in Germany). Neo-Nazism is especially prevalent in the region of the former East Germany where it is estimated that one-third of youths have neo-Nazi sympathies. One goal of the neo-Nazis is to create "foreigner-free zones" where only ethnic Germans will be allowed to live and work. Many Germans have reacted to neo-Nazism by staging mass demonstrations protesting anti-Semitism and anti-foreigner violence, and also by developing programs to teach about the Holocaust. At the same time, however, immigration policies have been made more restrictive, and some critics charge government agencies—at national, state, and local levels—with not responding quickly or harshly enough to antiforeigner violence.

A bus stop in the town of Uelfeld in southern Germany with Nazi and anti-Nazi graffiti, 1993. Photo: David Levinson.

Greece

G reece is a nation in southern Europe bordered by Albania, Macedonia, and Turkey on the north; Turkey and the Aegean Sea on the east; the Mediterranean Sea on the south; and the Ionian Sea on the west. It has a population of 10,650,000. The Greek population is now mainly urban (83%), and urban-rural differences in lifestyle are important. Although people continue to articulate their regional loyalties, actual cultural variation is now much less than in the past.

Ethnic Composition

The population is homogeneous in terms of ethnicity, religion, and language. Over 98% of the population is Greek, speaks Greek, and adheres to Greek Orthodoxy, the official religion (although religious freedom is guaranteed in the Greek constitution). Massive migrations in the 19th and 20th centuries led to the development of many large Greek communities outside Greece—mainly in the United States, Canada, the United Kingdom, Australia, Germany, and Russia—and as many people of Greek ancestry now live outside Greece as inside. There are few ethnic minorities in Greece,

A priest in Mykonos. Adherence to the Greek Orthodox faith is a key element in Greek ethnic identity. Photo: Corel Corp.

the Turks being the most cohesive group and the object of most hostility.

Greeks as a distinct ethnic group emerged about 4,000 years ago. The origins of the ancient Greeks are unclear, and modern Greek culture is an amalgam of external influences and internal change. Major features of Greek cultural identity are the Greek language, Greek Orthodoxy, immersion in a network of kin, transfer of wealth to daughters when they marry, and a long tradition of migration, both within and outside Greece. Greece was ruled by the Ottoman Empire from 1453 to 1831. The modern Greek nation emerged following the 1821–1829 war with Turkey. Since then, other wars and treaties allowed for expansion northward and east and west. Population exchanges, as Greece expanded its borders with Serbia, Bulgaria, and Turkey, have made border regions with these nations essentially Greek.

The three largest ethnic minorities in Greece are the Albanians, Slav Macedonians, and Turks. **Albanians** number perhaps 100,000 in Greece and live near the Albanian border. Most long-term residents are Greek Orthodox and are assimilated into Greek society. The end of Communist rule in Albania in 1989 led to many Greek Albanians seeking residence in Greece, a desire blocked by the Greek government. Many Greek Albanians were turned back at border crossings, and others who had managed to enter Greece were expelled. Some estimates place the number of undocumented Albanians in Greece at as many as 300,000.

Slav Macedonians live in the Macedonia region of Greece, near the modern republic of Macedonia. They number about 200,000, and are in the same ethnic group as the Slav Macedonians in Bulgaria and Macedonia (but are no relation to the ancient Macedonians, a group of much historical and symbolic importance to modern Greeks). The Greek government does not acknowledge the Slav Macedonians as a separate people, calling them **Slavophone Greeks.** Throughout much of the 20th century, they have been the object of government discrimination: they have been forced to drop Slavic names, have been removed from government positions, and some Slav businesses have been closed. Today, the population of the Macedonia region is predominately Greek. Government concern about Slav Macedonian loyalty to Greece, and efforts by the Slav Macedonians to join the Republic of Macedonia, remain issues in Greece.

Turks live mainly in western Thrace near the border with Turkey and on islands near Turkey. Their number in Greece is unknown but may be as high as 130,000; the Greek government often lumps them with Pomaks and Muslim Slav Macedonians living in the same region. The majority are Muslims, although some are Eastern Orthodox Christians. Animosity between Turks and Greeks, in both Turkey and Greece, dates to the centuries of Ottoman rule. More recently, relations have been influenced by Greek fears that Turkey will attempt to take Greek land, by the ongoing conflict between Greek and Turkish Cypriots, and by what both nations perceive as the mistreatment of their people in the other nation.

The other ethnic minorities in Greece are small. **Gagauz Turks,** a Turkish ethnic group practicing the Greek Orthodox religion, are distinguished from most other Turks, who are Muslims. About 30,000 Gagauz Turks live in Greece.

Pomaks are Bulgarian Muslims, about 30,000 of whom live in their own villages or mixed-ethnic villages near the northwestern border with Bulgaria. Greek authorities generally classify them as Turks.

Pontic refers to small communities of Pontic speakers in southern Greece. Pontic is an ancient language from Asia Minor that was brought to Greece by people who migrated there from Greek settlements near the Black Sea in the early 20th century. Pontic-speaking people are assimilated into Greek society, and their language is nearly extinct in Greece.

Since 1990 more than 100,000 Pontian Greeks from the former Soviet Union have resettled in Greece, where their Greek ancestry makes them citizens. The pressure they have put on the Greek economy has made some Greeks resistant to their settlement.

Sarakatsani are Greek-speaking people in northwestern Greece and southern Bulgaria. They number less than 100,000, are ethnically Greek, speak Greek, and are Greek Orthodox. Their traditional sheep- and goat-herding economy and transhumant settlement pattern distinguish them from the general Greek population.

Tsakonians are a Greek pastoral people of the eastern Peloponnesos. They number several thousand and speak a dialect of Greek.

Vlachs live in mountain regions of the north and number perhaps as many as 100,000. Vlachs are a remnant population descended from the Illyrians and Thracians and have interacted with the Slavic and other peoples over the centuries in the Balkans. They speak a language similar to Romanian. In Greece, they are mainly Greek Orthodox. Vlachs today enjoy relative freedom in Greece, and since the 1980s there has been a revival of traditional Vlach culture. However, the official government position still is that they are Greeks.

Gypsies in Greece include both Christian and Muslim Roma, the Muslims being found mainly in Macedonia and western Thrace. Greek laws restricting the traditional Gypsy lifestyle have made the population more sedentary, although Gypsies still tend to exist on the margins of society. Estimates place their number at about 90,000.

Ethnic Relations

In order to strengthen a sense of Greek nationalism, the Greek government attempts to minimize separate ethnic identities, and differentiates the population by language and religion, not by ethnicity. Thus, reliable census figures are not available, as anyone speaking Greek is counted as ethnically Greek. What were once significant Serb and Bulgarian populations have now largely disappeared through population exchanges in the 19th and 20th centuries. Greek relations with Turks living in northeastern Greece remain strained, and Greeks continue to deny the existence of Slav Macedonians as a distinct group. Turks are discriminated against economically, live in substandard housing, have been the object of systematic cultural and political repression, and generally believe that the Greeks desire either to remove all Turks from Greece or to assimilate them into Greek society.

Hungary

H ungary, an Eastern European nation, is bordered by Slovakia on the north; Ukraine and Romania on the east; Romania, Yugoslavia (Serbia), and Croatia on the south; and Croatia, Slovenia, and Austria on the west. It has a population of 10,318,000. As a result of loss of land to neighboring nations after World War I and population transfers after World War II, Hungary is today a much smaller nation and much more ethnically homogeneous than it has been throughout most of its history. Hungarians account for 96% of the population, with Gypsies being the largest minority at about 500,000 people. Germans, Slovenes, Slovaks, Croats, Serbs, and Romanians—who at times formed sizable groups in Hungary—are now much reduced in number and live mainly in border regions.

Ethnic Composition

Hungarians (Magyars) number nearly 10 million in Hungary and 5 million in other nations—mainly Austria, Slovakia, Romania, Ukraine, Serbia, Croatia, the United States, and Canada. About two-thirds are Roman Catholic, 25% are Protestants, and 3% are Eastern Orthodox. In all three religious groups, pre-Christian beliefs and celebrations are combined with Christian beliefs and practices. Hungarians are descended from the Magyars, one of a number of tribes that migrated from Asia in the 9th century. They speak a Finno-Ugric language unrelated to the Indo-European languages spoken in neighboring nations. This difference in ethnic origin and language is a major factor in Hungarian ethnic identity.

Gypsies, who number about 500,000, are the largest non-Hungarian ethnic group in the nation and one of the largest Gypsy populations in any European country. They are a diverse group in Hungary and include various **Rom** groups, **Sinti, Boyash,** and **Romungro** Gypsies. About 50% of Gypsies engage mainly in trade, and the other 50% are wage laborers. Most live in their own communities, often in the poorest sections of towns or villages or in urban ghettos, and 75% live below the pov-

erty level. Government efforts in the 1980s have led to the development of Gypsy advocacy organizations, but this has done little to change their status as a poor and isolated minority, considered inferior by Hungarians—as elsewhere in Europe and throughout the world.

Germans number about 250,000, only about 10% of what their population in Hungary was in the early 20th century. Germans settled in Hungary during much of the 1700s. In the cities, many were assimilated into Hungarian society and had little to do with Germans living in rural areas. Many Hungarian Germans supported Nazi Germany during World War II and, after the war, the Hungarian government deported about 250,000 of them. After 1950, the remaining Germans were treated like other ethnic minorities, although many districts that had been mainly German were settled by Hungarians.

Other European minorities are **Romanians,** who number about 30,000 and live near the Romanian border; **Slovaks,** who number about 100,000 and live in isolated communities in the mountains along the Slovakia border; **Croats, Serbs, Slovenes,** and **Bosnians,** who (combined) number about 100,000 and live in border regions or in larger cities where they have assimilated into Hungarian society; and small numbers of **Greeks** and **Carpatho-Rusyns.** Of these groups, only the Slovaks predate the Hungarians in the region.

The major religious minority is **Jews,** whose population is estimated at between 100,000 and 150,000, with most living in or near Budapest where Jewish synagogues and other institutions are maintained. About 75% of the World War II–era Jewish community, which numbered over 800,000, was exterminated by the Nazis. The remaining population has decreased since then through emigration to Israel and the United States. As in the past, Jews are mainly involved in trade and professional activities.

Ethnic Relations

Due to the homogeneity of the population today, ethnic relations in Hungary are peaceful, save for an increase in anti-Semitism following the end of Communist rule in 1989, as well as continuing discrimination against Gypsies. The Hungarian government encourages cultural freedom for ethnic minorities. This policy is motivated by a desire to encourage neighboring nations to afford Hungarian residents there the same freedoms. Most members of ethnic minorities in Hungary are bilingual in the language of their ethnic group and Hungarian, and most identify themselves as Hungarian. Most ethnic conflict concerns Hungarians, sometimes the victims of ethnicity-based discrimination, in neighboring Slovakia, Romania, and Serbia. The conflict in the former Yugoslavia has sent some Hungarians fleeing across the border into Hungary. In Romania, tension remains between the large Hungarian population in Transylvania, which was part of Hungary until 1919, and the Romanian majority.

Iceland

I celand is an island nation in the North Atlantic Ocean, 645 miles west of Norway and 837 miles northwest of Scotland. It has a population of 266,000, 99% of whom are **Icelanders**. There are only about 5,000 non-Icelanders, including **Danes, Norwegians, Britons,** and **U.S. Americans.**

Iceland was settled by Norwegians beginning in A.D. 874, and in the 10th century by smaller numbers of Irish and Scots. Iceland was under Norwegian control until 1380 when Denmark gained dominance over Norway. It gained self-rule in 1918 and became an independent nation in 1944. Icelandic cultural distinctiveness is based on use of the Icelandic language (related to Norwegian), a long although somewhat romanticized image of themselves as an independent people, the absence of surnames, and a long tradition of poetry, literary writing, and choral singing. Icelanders were converted to Lutheranism during the period of Danish rule and nearly all are members of the Icelandic State Church, another important marker of Icelandic identity. As Iceland is a homogeneous society, ethnic conflict is not an issue.

Ireland

I reland is an island nation located off the west coasts of England and Scotland. It is surrounded by the Atlantic Ocean on the west and north, the Irish Sea on the east, and the Celtic Sea on the south. A British colony from the 17th century, Ireland became a republic in 1949, but was fully autonomous in foreign and domestic affairs since 1922. Ireland has a population of 3,550,000 and is ethnically homogeneous, with about 95% of the population being Irish—although there are different categories of Irish. The population is also homogeneous in religion, with 93% being Roman Catholic and the remainder being mainly Protestant (3% Anglican) and Jewish. In addition to the Irish in Ireland, there is a substantial overseas population of people of full or partial Irish ancestry in the United States, Canada, Australia, Argentina, and the United Kingdom. Emigration from Ireland took place mainly after the potato famines beginning in the 1840s, and most overseas Irish, now third or fourth generation, are assimilated into their nations of residence. In the overseas Irish communities, however, a sense of Irish identity remains strong—many people make return visits to Ireland and some choose to retire there. In addition, in the United States, some in the Irish-American community have been strong supporters of independence for Northern Ireland.

Woman on a farm in rural Ireland. The Irish language and literary heritage are central elements of the national cultural identity. Photo: Corel Corp.

Ethnic Composition

Irish is both an ethnic and national designation in Ireland. Ethnic Irish constitute about 93% of the population of Ireland. Although Ireland has been inhabited by humans for at least 10,000 years, the modern Irish trace their ancestry to the Celts, who entered Ireland in the 1st century A.D. While the Irish prefer to stress their Celtic heritage, their culture has been influenced by the Vikings, French Normans, Anglo-Saxons, Scots, and the British. Irish identity is based on allegiance to Gaelic, the national language (although English is the language of daily life); devout adherence to Roman Catholicism, with distinctive Irish practices such as frequent pilgrimages to sacred sites; resistance to British rule and influence; and a long and continuing literary tradition, both written and oral, in Gaelic and in English. The major ethnic issue facing the Irish today is the expulsion of the British from Northern Ireland and the unification of Ireland and Northern Ireland as a single nation.

Gaels are the Irish of the Gaeltacht communities of western Ireland who continue to speak Irish Gaelic, and they are considered by many Irish to be the carriers of the traditional Irish culture. They number about 200,000, most of whom are farmers (although tourism is rapidly becoming a major source of additional revenue). Many Gaels continue to speak Irish Gaelic, although the actual number of Gaelic speakers in Ireland is unknown. Although as many as one million claim to speak Gaelic, perhaps only about 10% of these actually speak it fluently or on a regular basis. The Gaeltacht communities, located along the Atlantic coast, have land that is of poor quality, which made settlement of this area a low priority for the British colonists. Thus, people in this region escaped some of the British influences, including the imposition of the English language. Despite a century of government efforts to aid the economic development of the region and to stabilize the population, the Gaeltacht population has been declining steadily since the 1840s, and today much of the population is elderly.

Irish Travellers are ethnic Irish whose ancestors as long ago as the 5th century came to be viewed as a distinct group because of their nomadic lifestyle and occupation as metalsmiths. Although sometimes considered to be **Gypsies**—whom they resemble in lifestyle and with whom they have intermarried to a limited degree—Travellers are a distinct people of Irish ancestry. Because of their metalwork, they were known as **Tinkers,** a label now considered insulting. Travellers continue to live a primarily nomadic lifestyle, although they are now a more urban group and sell products to the settled Irish population. Travellers speak English as well as their own language, known as Cant or Shelta, and are mainly Roman Catholic. Government efforts in the 1960s to force them to live in permanent settlements have helped define the Travellers as a distinct group, and they and their advocates have resisted government interference in their lives. Travellers are found throughout the British Isles and a small number have immigrated to the United States.

The **British** in Ireland—English and Scots—account for about 3% of the population or 106,500 individuals (this number does not include Britons who identify themselves as Irish). British are mainly Anglicans and are labeled Anglo-Irish by the Irish, indicating their somewhat marginal position in Irish society. In various ways, the British in Ireland have become Irish and the Irish have become British, making generalizations about specific cultural features of the two groups and relations between the groups difficult. Relations generally are managed at the individual level, and someone of British ancestry who has married into an Irish family and converted to Roman Catholicism is more likely to be accepted as Irish than someone who is a Protestant.

Other groups consist mainly of **U.S. Americans, Canadians, Argentinians,** and **Australians** of Irish ancestry who have returned to settle in Ireland, as well as students and businesspersons of non-Irish ancestry from these and other nations. The largest of these groups are Americans, who number 30,000.

Ethnic Relations

Ethnic relations in Ireland center on the relationship between the Irish and the small British population, as well as the more general relationship between Ireland and the Irish, and England and the English. During the nearly three centuries of English rule, Irish culture was changed markedly. Most important, the English banned the use of the Irish Gaelic language and made English the national language. The English also removed Irish farmers from some of the best land and settled English and Scot Protestants in their place. As colonizers, the English also controlled the economic system and relied heavily on English and Scots managers, while the Irish were relegated to the role of laborers. The English tended to view the Irish—and in some circles continue to view them—as ignorant, fun-loving drunks, inferior to the English. One irony of this English stereotype of the Irish as inferior is that the old and deep Irish literary tradition was disrupted by English efforts to suppress the use of Gaelic. That tradition has survived, however, although Irish literature is more often produced in English. For their part, the Irish deeply resented and resisted English colonization, revolted a number of times, and sought to maintain Irish culture in the teaching of Gaelic in secret "hedge schools" and through the formation of Gaelic associations. Relations between the Irish and British in Ireland are relatively harmonious though distant in the 1990s, save for the ongoing conflict in Northern Ireland, which is discussed in the entry on the United Kingdom.

Italy

I taly, located in southern Europe, is bordered on the north by Austria and Switzerland, on the northeast by Slovenia, on the east by the Adriatic Sea, on the northwest by France, on the west by the Tyrrhenian Sea, and on the south by the Mediterranean Sea. Italy has a population of 58.2 million. About 98% of the population is Italian, speaks regional dialects of Italian, and is Roman Catholic.

Despite its surface homogeneity, Italy is culturally and ethnically complex and there is considerable regional diversity in cultural traditions and language. Italy gradually became a unified nation in the period from 1858 to 1879, and variation among the 20 regions continues to play a role in national affairs. Sicily, Val d'Aosta, Trentino-Alto Adidge, Sardinia, and Friuli-Venezia-Giuli were granted autonomous status after Italy became a democratic republic following World War II, and other regions, such as Tuscany, Piedmont, Calabria, and Lombard, have been granted limited constitutional autonomy. The traditional character of these and other regions sometimes conflicts with more general Italian national concerns and interests. Italy's national language is standard Italian, based on the Tuscan dialect and closest in pronunciation to the dialect spoken in Rome. However, there are four major regional dialects—Northern, Central, Tuscan, and Southern—and subdialects of each, not all of which are mutually intelligible. Thus, most Italians speak both standard Italian and a regional dialect or subdialect.

The north of Italy is heavily urban and industrially developed, while the south is rural and agricultural. The view that southern Italians are less urbane, less sophisticated, and poorer than northerners, held especially by some northerners, continues to define relations between the regions. In the late 1990s, the movement for a separate northern polity intensified. There is also the presence of small but vital ethnic minorities in the north, including border groups such as French and German speakers and Slovenes, as well as isolated linguistic minorities such as the Ladin and Friulians. Since 1980, migrant workers have arrived in Italy from other European nations, Asia, Africa, and the Americas at the rate of about 90,000 per year. While official counts place the foreign population at about 1.4 million, it may be double that when as-yet undocumented migrants are taken into account. Most migrant workers hold low-level jobs in construction and in the service sector.

Migration—both internal and external migration and return migration—has played an important role in Italian history, motivated mainly by economic conditions. Italian migration since unification in the mid-1800s can be divided into four periods. From the mid-1800s to the 1920s, seasonal migration to France, Switzerland, and Germany increased and millions of Italians migrated overseas, mainly to the United States, Brazil, and Argentina, with perhaps 33% eventually returning to Italy. In 1928, external migration was banned and internal migration increased, primarily from the south to the north and from rural areas to cities. After World War II, Italy, like other southern European nations, became a nation of emigration as workers moved north to work in factories in Germany, France, Switzerland, and Belgium. About 4.5 million Italian workers and their families migrated north, about 3 million of whom eventually returned to Italy. In 1972, a slowdown in emigration, the return of migrant workers, and the arrival of workers from Asia, Africa, and Eastern Europe turned Italy from a nation of emigration to one of immigration. By the 1980s and 1990s, immigration—increasingly from Asia and Africa—had increased the non-Italian population substantially.

Ethnic Composition

Italians, including Sicilians, constitute 98% of the population of Italy. Several million people of Italian ancestry live in a large Italian diaspora, primarily in northern Europe (Great Britain, Germany, Switzerland, Belgium, and France), the United States, Canada, Brazil, Argentina, Central America, and Australia. Although regional allegiances remain strong, Italian ethnic identity is based on loyalty to the Italian nation; adherence to Roman Catholicism; a shared history; appreciation of the rich Italian contribution to literature, science, and the arts; and speaking the Italian language. Important aspects of Italian culture include loyalty to and respect for the family, respect for the elderly, a strong sense of personal and family honor, and emotionality in both personal and public behavior. One indicator of the salience of Italian ethnic identity over time and place is the large number of immigrants who return to Italy. Although information on return immigration is not wholly reliable, it seems likely that about 40% of immigrants eventually return, and many descendants of those who remained overseas return regularly for vacation or to visit relatives or their ancestral villages.

Sicilians are the indigenous people of the island of Sicily, part of Italy since 1861 and an autonomous region since 1946. Sicilians in Sicily number about five million, with a large diaspora population in northern Europe, the United States, and Canada.

The island has been inhabited for at least 22,000 years, and as a stopping place between Europe and Africa, contemporary Sicilian culture is an amalgam that reflects the influences of those who have ruled the island at various times: the Greeks, Romans, Byzantines, North African Arabs, Norman French, and Bourbons. Sicilians speak Sicilian, a language based on Latin and influenced by many other languages. Speaking Sicilian is a major marker of Sicilian (as opposed to Italian) identity, although most young people also speak standard Italian. Sicily was once a largely agricultural society, but most Sicilians now live in cities along the coasts. Sicily is a poor region compared with most other parts of Italy, and many young people migrate to the cities or elsewhere in Italy in search of work.

In addition to the Italians and Sicilians, there are other small ethnic groups in Italy. **Friulians** are the largest, numbering about 600,000. They live mainly in Friuli province in the Friuli-Venezia-Giulia autonomous region of northeastern Italy near Austria and Slovenia. The Friulians are distinguished as a distinct ethnic group by the continued use of Friulian (a Rhaeto-Romansch language), their localized communities in the mountainous region, and a long history of settlement predating the arrival of the Romans. From the 10th to the 18th centuries, Friuli was politically independent; subsequently, it came under French, Austrian, and ultimately Italian control. Like their neighbors, Friulians are Roman Catholic, and although relations are peaceful, some Friulians desire complete political autonomy within Italy.

The **Ladin** are another northern minority, numbering about 35,000. They live in Bolanzo Province. Their language, Ladin (Ladino), is one of the three surviving Rhaeto-Romansch languages along with Friuli and Romansch. Their survival as a distinct culture is due to use of their language (rather than the German or Italian of the surrounding populations) and the valley location of their villages. The region was transferred from Austria to Italy after World War I, and in the interwar years, some Ladin were sent to Austria and the use of Ladin was banned. Since 1948, the right to use Ladin has been restored in most communities, but the Ladin seek political autonomy, often in concert with the neighboring German speakers, with whom they more closely identify than with the Italians.

The Greeks, Gypsies, and Jews in Italy are not indigenous, but the current populations are composed mainly of the descendants of people who arrived in Italy hundreds of years ago. People of **Greek** ancestry number between 7,500 and 15,000 and live in Puglia and Calabria in southern Italy. They are descended from Greeks who settled in the region during the era of Byzantine rule in the 6th to 10th centuries. Most are now assimilated into Italian society; the use of the Greek language is declining, although most continue to adhere to Greek Orthodoxy.

Gypsies number about 30,000, although this is a rough estimate as no official census has ever been taken of their population. Gypsies in Italy are diverse, composed of Sinti groups who have lived primarily in the north of Italy for centuries, and Rom groups in the northeast and south, most of whom arrived from Yugoslavia after the 1960s. Perhaps as many as 10,000 arrived in the 1990s, fleeing the conflict in the former Yugoslavia. Some live in settled communities, others are nomadic, and all have been the object of government programs to settle them, which have had mixed results. A small population, they live a marginalized existence separate from mainstream society.

Jews in Italy number about 40,000, the majority of whom are of Sephardic ancestry; that is, they are descended from Jews who lived in Spain before 1492, or are descended from Jews of the Middle East or North Africa. Although this small population is assimilated into Italian society economically and politically, a rise in anti-Semitism in the 1990s has led to clashes between Jews and right-wing activists, as well as to public rallies condemning anti-Semitism.

The latest immigrant groups, which have been the object of new laws designed to limit immigration and permanent settlement in Italy, are a mixed group. Africans are the largest category, numbering about 239,000 according to official counts—perhaps double that if undocumented individuals are included. It is assumed, however, that the granting of residency in the late 1980s to many Africans has substantially reduced the number of undocumented Africans in Italy. Most Africans came initially from North Africa (**Tunisians**, **Libyans**, **Moroccans**, **Egyptians**, **Somalians**, **Ethiopians**, and **Eritreans**) and more recently from West Africa (mainly **Cape Verdeans** and **Senegalese**). The majority are men migrating in search of employment. They live mainly in cities in the provinces of Latium, Sicily Lombard, Calabria, Piedmont, Campania, and Emilia-Romagna. In most locations, the population is of mixed African groups, although Tunisians are especially numerous in Sicily, where many are engaged in the fishing industry. Despite fears that they compete for scarce industrial jobs with Italians, most Africans work in low-level construction jobs and in the hotel and food industries, jobs not considered desirable by Italians. In addition, some groups specialize in specific economic activities— Senegalese as street vendors, Tunisians in fishing, and Moroccans in trading. African

immigrants are poor in comparison with the general population and live mostly in their own communities.

Asians number about 146,000 (according to official counts) and perhaps double that if estimates of undocumented individuals are included. However, as with Africans, the granting of residency permits may have reduced the undocumented population significantly. Asians, mainly **Filipinos, Sri Lankans, Vietnamese, Chinese,** and **Japanese,** live in or near Rome, with large populations also in the provinces of Lombard, Tuscany, and Umbria. Most Asian immigrants to Italy are women. Some are employed as agricultural workers and industry, but over 50% are employed in the service sector, mainly as domestics and food handlers, or do other low-level work in the hotel and food-service industries. The Japanese population includes a significant number of students, technicians, and businesspeople who do not fit the pattern of other immigrants. As with the Africans, Asian immigrants tend to live in ethnically homogeneous communities and are seen as competitors for jobs with Italians.

Eastern Europeans (other than Albanians and Slovenes) number about 100,000. They are mainly **Poles, Romanians,** and **Yugoslavians (Bosnians, Croats,** and **Serbs)** who have arrived since the late 1980s, fleeing political unrest and economic instability in their home countries and seeking jobs in Italy. About half live in or around Rome, with about 4,000 in Tuscany and 3,000 in Emilia-Romagna. Many of the Yugoslavians are of Italian ancestry and about 80,000 have been granted residency permits. While Eastern Europeans are not the victims of overt discrimination, their competition with Italians for jobs has been one factor in the rise of anti-immigration attitudes in the 1990s.

Italy also has large ethnic minority groups composed of people who live in bordering or nearby nations. The largest—and the one involved in the greatest degree of ethnic conflict—is the **South Tyroleans,** a German-speaking population that lives in northern Italy near the Austrian border. They number about 300,000, and as a result of the many Italians who have settled in the region since World War II, South Tyroleans no longer form a large majority of the regional population. Although South Tyroleans are politically, culturally, and linguistically tied to other German-speaking peoples in what is now Austria for 14 centuries, the region was placed within Italian borders at the end of World War I following the breakup of the Austro-Hungarian Empire.

Albanians number anywhere from 80,000 (those who continue to speak Albanian as their domestic language) to 250,000 (those who speak either Albanian or Italian). Albanians are the third largest ethnic minority, after the Friulians and the German speakers. The large number who speak Italian suggests considerable assimilation into Italian society, although a strong sense of Albanian identity remains. Albanians began settling in Italy in the 15th century, and they live in rural areas and cities throughout southern Italy. They are Roman Catholics. The end of Communist rule in Albania has created the opportunity for renewed ties between the Albanian community in Italy and the homeland and has created a stronger sense of ethnic identity for Albanians in Italy.

Slovenes number about 55,000 and live in the Trieste region in northeast Italy on the Slovenia border. They came under Italian control after World War II, and became part of Italy following a 1975 agreement between Italy and Yugoslavia. The division of the region also left a population of Italians now numbering about 35,000 across the border in the former Yugoslavia. The breakup of Yugoslavia has intensified demands by some groups in the Trieste region for the return of the territory to Italy. Slovenes have been concerned about their rights as an ethnic minority, and under a series of agreements dating to 1954 have been afforded various language rights by the Italian government. However, as a minority (about 10% of the population in the region), only the large community in Trieste near the Slovenian border regularly uses Slovene and maintains a vital community with its own cultural and education organizations. Slovenes are Roman Catholic.

French, numbering about 100,000, are the dominant group in the small, autonomous region of Val d'Aosta on the border with France. While Italian is the official language, French has official status as the second language of the region.

Sardinians, who number about 1.9 million, are the indigenous inhabitants of the island of Sardinia. Although they do not live on the continent, they have been linked to Italy since 1860 when the island became an autonomous region of Italy. Sardinian culture has been influenced over the millennia by cultural contact and often conquest by various other groups, including the Phoenicians, Carthaginians, Romans, Arabs, and Spaniards. Sardinians speak local dialects of Sardinian and Italian. Nearly all are Roman Catholic. The traditional Sardinian culture, which continues to some extent to resist Italian development initiatives, is found in the highlands and is based on agriculture, herding, a strong sense of personal and family honor, and the village communities. Coastal communities and cities, which are more industrialized and commercialized, are more Italian in culture, and in these areas, the Sardinian language is being replaced by Italian.

Other groups include about 7,000 **Australian** and **Oceanic** migrant workers; a small number of **Catalan** speakers on Sardinia; and about 3,000 **Croatians** in Molise in southern Italy, who have been there since the 15th century but are now assimilated. Americans number about 129,000 and include mostly individuals of Italian ancestry who have returned to Italy from the **United States, Canada, Brazil,** and **Argentina.** Some are retirees who amassed enough wealth in the Americas to retire in Italy, while others are returning with the hope of finding better jobs.

Ethnic Relations

Italians are culturally, politically, and economically dominant in Italy, although through a policy allowing slow, limited assimilation, they have granted some cultural and political autonomy to other ethnic groups of European ancestry. A major issue has been the status of the South Tyroleans in the north.

From 1922 to 1939, the Italian government sought to restrict South Tyrolean ties to Austria and to assimilate the people into Italian society. However, the settlement of Italians in the region led to conflict between the Tyroleans and Italians rather than to assimilation. A mass exodus to Austria was halted only by the start of World War II. The arrival of Italian settlers further threatened the Tyrolean sense of cultural security and reduced the German speakers of Bolzano province to about 60% of the population from 97% earlier in the century. The region remained in Italy after World War II, and from 1946 to the late 1990s, a combination of political action by the Südtiroler Volkspartei (SVP), terrorism by South Tyrolean separatists, and new laws enacted by the Italian government alleviated South Tyrolean–Italian hostility in the region and gave the South Tyroleans considerable linguistic and political autonomy.

Ethnic relations in the 1990s are driven by a combination of economic problems, including a dramatic loss of jobs in the industrial sector, migration to the north, and the political instability that has characterized Italian society since the end of World War II. Italy, long a nation of emigration, was unprepared politically, socially, and economically for the European, Asian, and African immigrants who began arriving in the 1970s.

Two laws enacted in the 1980s that were designed to stabilize the non-Italian population, by granting residency permits, resulted in 741,000 foreigners having official residence status by 1990. In the 1990s, strong resistance to uncontrolled immigration has emerged as a key political issue, fueled in part by the rise of neo-Nazi and neo-Fascist political movements, most important, the National Alliance Party. Prison statistics also reveal evidence of hostility toward non-Italians, as 11% of prisoners are non-Italians, although non-Italians form only 2% of the overall population. At the same time, it is clear that immigrant workers—and especially undocumented ones who work for low wages—have helped some sectors such as agriculture and industry. The governmental response has been the enactment of new laws to make it easier to deport undocumented immigrants, and increased efforts to halt illegal entry. There also has been an increase in anti-Semitism and anti-Gypsy activity. In 1991, many Albanians arrived as refugees but over 17,000 of about 40,000 were later deported by the government in an action criticized by the international community. A new law in 1992 made it easier to deport illegal immigrants, and in 1995 law enforcement officials increased patrols along the shore facing Albania in order to prevent Albanians from entering.

Latvia

L atvia is located between the two other Baltic nations, Estonia and Lithuania, in northeastern Europe. It has a population of 2,666,600 and is ethnically heterogeneous, with Latvians and Russians combining to form 86.5% of the population.

Ethnic Composition

The Latvians and the Russians are the two largest groups. **Latvians** number 1,388,000, or 53.7% of the population. This represents a 25% decrease in the Latvian percentage of the population since 1935, due in part to deaths during World War II and to Russian settlement after the war. Seventy-one percent of the rural population is Latvian, but Russians are the majority in the major cities. Latvians are nominally Lutheran, Roman Catholic, or Russian Orthodox, although religion is not important in daily life. During the Soviet era, Latvians were a disadvantaged majority relative to the Russian settlers, and that experience, plus the previous centuries of Russian rule, has created much hostility toward Russians. Current policies are designed to reverse the years of discrimination and to provide Latvians with better jobs and housing, as well as political control.

Russians number 906,000, or 32.8% of the population. Most are industrial workers who have settled in the major cities. They generally have resisted assimilation into Latvian society and only 22.2% speak Latvian, with 21.1% of those speaking it only as a second language. In the post-Soviet era, their power and influence has declined.

Closely related to the Russians culturally (and seen as outsiders by the Latvians) are Ukrainians and Belarusians. **Ukrainians** number 92,000, or 3.4%, and **Belarusians** 119,000, or 4.5% of the population. Like the Russians, they live mainly in cities and are identified with the large Russian minority.

The only other significant minorities are the **Lithuanians,** who number 34,600, or 1.3% of the population, and the **Poles,** who number about 60,000, or 2.3%. The Lithuanians live primarily in southern Latvia, the majority speak Latvian (which is related to Lithuanian), and relations between the groups are peaceful. In 1989, 2.4 million Latvians, Lithuanians, and Estonians formed a 400-mile chain across the three nations to protest the 40th anniversary of Soviet rule. Poles live mainly in southern Latvia, an area once under Polish control. The Poles are bilingual in Russian or Latvian, and relations with other groups are peaceful.

Other groups living in Latvia include several thousand **Germans, Jews,** and **Gypsies.**

Ethnic Relations

Latvia's history and the current ethnic relations situation is quite similar to that of Estonia. The territory that is now Latvia has been settled for thousands of years, and the ancestors of contemporary Latvians have been in the region for nearly 4,000 years. From the 13th century on, Latvia was ruled by the Germans and Poles, or contested by other peoples. In 1721, Latvia came under Russian control although there was a short period of independence from 1920 to 1940. Russian control continued from the end of World War II until 1991, when Latvia became an independent nation. While Latvia was under Russian rule, many Russians settled there, the economy was transformed from agricultural to manufacturing, and political and economic control was maintained from Moscow. Latvian religion and culture have been much influenced by Western European traditions. Latvian culture was repressed during the Soviet era, with the result being that the majority of Latvians became fluent in Russian. Beginning in the mid-1980s, Latvians became deeply concerned about Russian control, a loss of Latvian ethnic identity, and the possibility that they would become a minority in their own country. Postindependence policies that support Latvian as the official language, preferential treatment for Latvians, and strict citizenship laws are designed to produce a Latvian state based on Latvian ethnic nationalism. These new citizenship and language policies have been attacked by the Russian government in Moscow as violating the civil rights of Russians in Latvia, forcing them to leave. The Russians find the linking of the ability to read Latvian to citizenship especially onerous. Most Russians are little involved in Latvian politics and are far more concerned with economic security.

Liechtenstein

L iechtenstein is a very small, landlocked nation in Western Europe, located between Switzerland and Austria. With a per capita income of $31,000 per year (U.S. dollars), it is one of the wealthiest nations of the world. Its economy is based on a combination of light manufacturing, tourism, international finance, and banking.

Liechtensteiners speak the Allemanic dialect of German and are mainly Roman Catholic along with a small number of Protestants (10%). Liechtensteiners are a nationality, not an ethnic group, and are culturally quite similar to their Austrian and Swiss neighbors of German ancestry. The population of 28,000 includes foreign workers: **Germans** (95%) and others (5%), mainly **Italians.** There also are about 7,000 **Austrians** who work in Liechtenstein but live in Austria, along with a small number of **Swiss** who also commute across the border each day.

Lithuania

L ithuania is the southernmost of the three Baltic nations of Estonia, Latvia, and Lithuania. It is bordered by Latvia on the north, Belarus on the east, Poland and Russia on the south, and the Baltic Sea on the west. It has a population of 3.8 million. Since the 13th century, Lithuanian history has been one of frequent conflict, shifting borders, and alliances with neighboring nations, most significantly Germany, Poland, and Russia. From 1772, Russia was in control of parts of Lithuania. Germany controlled the nation during World War I, and the postwar years saw Poland and Russia vying with the Lithuanians for control. In 1940, the Soviet Union annexed the nation, and Lithuania remained under Soviet control until it declared independence in 1990. Lithuanians were not passive in the face of foreign control, and their history is marked by frequent revolts and rebellions.

Ethnic Composition

Lithuania is ethnically heterogeneous. Lithuanians form nearly 80% of the population and Poles and Russians are the two largest minority groups. The once-large **Jewish** population (about 1.5 million in the 1930s) was exterminated in World War II and now numbers only a few thousand.

Lithuanians number 2.9 million, or 79.6% of the population. The rural life of the past ended during the post–World War II era when Soviet economic reforms replaced the agricultural economy with one based on industry and manufacturing. Over 70% of Lithuanians now live in cities, an urbanization that has eroded the nation's traditional regional distinctions. Lithuanians are proud of their long literary history, and education is highly valued. Nearly all are Roman Catholics with a small Lutheran minority in regions once controlled by Germany.

Poles number 258,000, or 7% of the population, and live in close-knit communities in the Vilnius area. This area was controlled by Poland before World War II, and was annexed to Lithuania after the war. In the post-Soviet era, Lithuanians generally have ignored the Poles and the latter have aligned themselves with the Russians to protest the new Lithuanian language and citizenship laws, which they find discriminatory. Poles are not well-assimilated into Lithuanian society—only 20.5% speak Lithuanian, while 67.1% speak Russian.

Russians number 344,455, or 9.4% of the population. The majority were born in Lithuania, nearly 40% speak Lithuanian, and surveys indicate that 80% want to remain there. A majority chose to become Lithuanian citizens. Lithuanians do not consider this small group a major threat to Lithuanian control of the nation, now that Russian influence from Moscow has waned. However, some Russians feel that they are discriminated against and are worried about their future role and influence in Lithuanian society.

Often lumped with the Russians are the Belarusians and Ukrainians. **Belarusians** number 63,000, or 1.7% of the population, and **Ukrainians** number 45,000, or 1.2% of the population. Like the Russians, they live mainly in cities.

Ethnic Relations

Ethnic tensions in the 1990s are caused by the history of Lithuanian hostility toward Poland and Russia and Lithuanian efforts to form an independent nation. Lithuania and Poland signed a friendship treaty in 1994, in which they agreed to drop claims on each other's territories. However, a 1995 law making Lithuanian the official language, and a new citizenship policy with a 10-year residency requirement, trouble the Polish and Russian minorities who view these measures as discriminatory. In addition, in the post-Soviet years, Lithuanians have for the most part excluded Russians and Poles from key economic, political, and cultural positions. Although relations between the Lithuanians and the Russians and Poles are hostile, the situation has not become violent.

Luxembourg

L uxembourg is a landlocked nation bordered by Germany on the east, Belgium on the west and north, and France on the south. It is one Europe's smallest nations and the wealthiest in terms of per-capita income. Its population is 389,000, nearly 85% of whom live in cities, with nearly 30% of the population residing in the two largest cities—Luxembourg (75,000) and Esch-sur-Alzette (24,000). The economy is based on a mixture of manufacturing, banking, government (European Union offices), and tourism.

Ethnic Composition

Luxembourg is ethnically heterogeneous, with over 50% of the workforce made up of foreign workers. However, 102,000 of these 112,000 foreign workers are from Western Europe and nearly all are Roman Catholic, like the indigenous Luxembourgers.

Luxembourgers number 277,000, or 71.2% of the population. They are descended from Germans, French, Italians, Portuguese, and Belgians, who, at various times in the past, settled in or passed through what is now Luxembourg. In recent years, Luxembourgers have sought to create a separate ethnic identity based on their political autonomy and use of their traditional language, Letzeburgeshe, a local dialect of German once spoken in western Germany. However, they are more a nationality than an ethnic group. Most Luxembourgers are employed as business owners, as managers, or in senior government positions. Much of the remaining work is left to foreign workers whose admission and work conditions are carefully controlled.

Western Europeans, primarily **Portuguese** and **Italians,** make up nearly half the workforce and one-third of the population. They work in industry, construction, and the service sector. The robust economy has made for stable work conditions and harmonious relations with the Luxembourgers, although economic problems since the mid-1980s suggest a decreasing need for foreign labor.

Other groups include a small **Jewish** population, a **Mennonite** community whose members are Protestant, and a total of about 5,000 **Asian, African,** and **Latin American** foreign workers, employed in the lowest-level service jobs.

Ethnic Relations

Ethnic identity plays little role in Luxembourg affairs, and ethnic relations are harmonious.

Governmental affairs are conducted in French and business in German, although English is also widely spoken.

Macedonia

M acedonia is a small nation in the Balkan region of southeastern Europe. It is bordered on the north by Yugoslavia (Serbia), on the east by Bulgaria, on the south by Greece, and on the west by Albania. It has a population of about 2.1 million. Macedonia came into existence in 1991 following the demise of Yugoslavia. However, because of objections from the Greeks, who feared a takeover of border areas in Greece, international recognition was not given until 1993, and the United States did not recognize Macedonia until 1994. The nation of Macedonia is located in the region of Macedonia, parts of which are also within Bulgaria and Greece. From 1389 until 1912, the region was ruled by the Ottoman Empire. Following the fall of the empire, Macedonia was divided among Bulgaria, Greece, and Serbia, incorporating what is now the nation of Macedonia into the Serbian region. In 1949, it became one of the constituent republics of Yugoslavia.

Ethnic Composition

Macedonia is ethnically heterogeneous, with Slav Macedonians constituting 67% of the population; Albanians 23%; and Serbs, Turks, Vlachs, and Gypsies the remaining 10%. The Macedonians and Serbs are mainly Eastern Orthodox, and the Albanians and Turks are mainly Muslims. Macedonian, closely related to Bulgarian, is the official language, although non-Macedonians speak their own languages. Macedonia also currently shelters about 9,000 refugees, most of whom are Bosnians, with a smaller number of Croatians.

Macedonians number 1.4 million, or 67% of the population, although Albanians claim that this is an overcount designed to minimize Albanian influence. In order to distinguish the Macedonians of today from the ancient Macedonians and from the Greeks in the Greek province of Macedonia, they sometimes are called **Slav Macedonians.** Macedonians are a Slavic people closely related to the neighboring Bulgarians. A distinct sense of Macedonian identity developed after the end of Ottoman rule in 1921, at first based on residence in this region and the speaking of various regional dialects of Macedonian, a language similar to Bulgarian (claimed by Bulgarians to be a dialect of Bul-

garian). Macedonian identity was strengthened after incorporation into Yugoslavia as a republic in 1949, based on Macedonia's political status as a republic, the creation of a new Macedonian language (based on existing dialects plus words added from Serbo-Croatian and Bulgarian), and the establishment of the Macedonian Orthodox Church. However, this Church is not recognized by Eastern Orthodoxy, and many people continue to speak the regional dialects of Macedonia.

Albanians are estimated to number 483,000, or 23% of the population. Albanians, however, claim that they number about 900,000 in Macedonia. They live primarily in northwestern Macedonia near the border with Albania.

Gypsies numbered as many as two million before the demise of Yugoslavia. Due to the disruptions and massive population relocations caused by the wars involving the Serbs, Croats, and Bosnians, neither the number nor the location of Gypsies in the independent nations that formed following the breakup of Yugoslavia can be determined with any degree of accuracy. Before the wars, most Gypsies were living in settled communities and supported themselves through wage labor and such specialized economic services as entertainment or selling used vehicles. As elsewhere in Europe, Gypsies in Macedonia lived outside mainstream society, although many spoke the language of the neighboring groups and adhered to the same religions.

Turks, who number about 105,000 or 5% of the population, are a remnant population from the centuries of Ottoman rule. As elsewhere in the former Ottoman Empire, people of Turkish ancestry are a vulnerable minority subject to various discriminatory policies.

The **Vlach** population is estimated at about 6,000. Formerly nomadic sheep herders, Vlachs were settled forcibly by the Communist government and are now assimilated into Macedonian society. Sometimes considered Romanian because their language is similar, Vlachs are a remnant population descended from the Illyrians and Thracians who have interacted with the Slavic population over the centuries in the Balkans.

Ethnic Relations

Macedonia is located in a region of major political unrest and ethnic conflict. Since 1992, United Nations peacekeeping forces have been stationed there to help prevent the violence in Bosnia from spilling over, to guard against possible Serbian designs on the country, and to quell Greek fears that Macedonia will attempt to annex the Greek province of Macedonia.

The Macedonians are the dominant political group in the nation, and since independence in 1991 the government has attempted to build an economically and politically stable nation in a region of major ethnic conflict. Policies that restrict Albanian autonomy are viewed by the Macedonians as serving the larger purpose of building a unified and stable Macedonia.

The Macedonian government has closed Albanian schools, banned the use of Albanian in universities, ruled that Macedonian is the sole language of government, and attempted to close the Albanian-founded University of Tetovo. The Macedonians are motivated by a fear that the Albanians—who differ from Macedonians in culture, language, and religion—will secede from Macedonia and affiliate the northwestern region of the country with Albania. Albanians have protested these and other restrictions, and they have continued to operate their university. In 1995, the Albanian delegation to the Macedonian legislature walked out to protest restrictions on the use of Albanian. Observers fear this situation may turn into a violent ethnic conflict that might also involve Albanians in Albania and the Serbs.

Despite Greek concerns, relations with Greece have been free of open conflict.

Malta

The Republic of Malta is an island nation located in the center of the Mediterranean Sea between Sicily and Libya. It consists of the large island of Malta, the smaller, inhabited islands of Gozo and Comino, and two uninhabited islands. The population is 370,000, consisting almost entirely of **Maltese,** with small numbers of **Arabs, Britons, French,** and **Italians,** which reflects its long history of colonization. As Malta is a major tourist center, the population often increases substantially. Ninety-eight percent of the population is Roman Catholic. Maltese and English are the official languages.

Maltese trace their ancestry to their ancient Carthaginians of North Africa. The modern culture developed through the integration of elements borrowed from the Phoenicians, Carthaginians, Greeks, Romans, Muslim Arabs, Normans, Swabians, Angevins, Aragonese, Castilians, French, and finally the British, all of which ruled the islands until Malta's independence in 1964. The Maltese language is Semitic (indicating the Arab influence), with many words added from Sicilian and English. English, spoken by many Maltese, is the preferred language for education. The Roman Catholic Church is the nation's most powerful social institution, and most Maltese are devout adherents, although some proscriptions, such as the ban on contraception, are widely ignored.

Conflict in the political arena is a common feature of Maltese life, manifested in sometimes violent election campaigns involving the two major political parties. There is no significant ethnic conflict, although there remains a clear distinction between the urban and rural populations. Some ethnic tension is caused by tourists, who tend to see all Maltese as unsophisticated peasants. In particular, the British—who make up 98% of the tourists to Malta—are resented by some Maltese.

Moldova

M oldova is a nation in Eastern Europe, bordered by Ukraine on the north, east, and south, and by Romania on the west. It has an ethnically heterogeneous population of 4.35 million. The modern nation of Moldova was part of Romania until it was annexed by Russia in 1812. It became part of Romania again in 1918, and then was a Soviet republic after World War II. In order to weaken links to Romania, the Soviet government deported thousands of Moldovans to Central Asia, closed the Romanian border, encouraged Russians to settle in the nation, and restricted the use of the Romanian language, substituting Russian in its place. Moldova became an independent nation following the disintegration of the Soviet Union in 1991.

Ethnic Composition

The population is ethnically heterogeneous, composed of Romanians, Ukrainians, Russians, Gagauz Turks, Bulgarians, and others. The label Moldovan (or Moldovian) indicates nationality, as "ethnic" Moldovans are ethnically Romanian.

Romanians (Moldovans) number about three million, or 65% of the population. Romanians claim to be descended from the Geto-Dacians, the original inhabitants of the region, and the Romans who entered the region in the 1st century B.C. They also claim a continuous presence in the region since then. However, this interpretation is not accepted by all historians. The core area of the Romanian nation and culture—the Old Kingdom—is Moldovia and Wallachia, with Bessarabia and Transylvania added later. Romanians have been adherents of Eastern Orthodoxy for 1,000 years, with some converting to Uniatism in the 18th century. In rural areas, indigenous beliefs and practices have been combined with Eastern Orthodoxy. There are many differences in customs and culture—sometimes from village to village.

Russians number 562,000, or 13% of the population. They live mainly in the Trans-Dniester region, which they have declared a semi-autonomous republic.

Ukrainians number 600,000, or 14% of the population. They live in the Trans-Dniester region, where they are politically affiliated with the Russians in the separatist movement.

Gagauz Turks number 153,000 in Romania, which is about 77% of the total number of Gagauz in the former Soviet Union and a substantial percentage of the Gagauz world population. Gagauz Turks are Eastern Orthodox, distinguishing them from most other Turks, who are Muslims. The Gagauz in Moldova are mainly descendants of people who assisted the Russians in the Russo-Turkish wars of the late 18th and early 19th centuries and then emigrated to what is now southern Moldova. The Gagauz have long affiliated with the Russians and most speak Russian, rarely using Turkish. The Gagauz fear complete assimilation under Moldovan rule and have asked for an autonomous region, a possibility granted in the new Moldovan constitution ratified in 1994.

Jews number about 40,000, a number that is decreasing as many Jews are immigrating to the United States and Israel in the postindependence era.

Other groups include **Bulgarians, Gypsies, Greeks, Armenians, Poles, Germans,** and **Russian Old Believers,** together totalling about 4% of the population.

Ethnic Relations

Since its independence in 1991, Moldova has experienced considerable ethnic conflict involving the Romanian Moldovans and the Ukrainians, Russians, Jews, and Gypsies. All these conflicts—of which the dispute with the Russians and Ukrainians is the most serious—center on the rise of Moldovan ethnic nationalism. Key elements of this nationalism include the use of the Latin alphabet (instead of Cyrillic), recognition of Romanian as the national language, the requirement that all residents speak and write Romanian, the rise of Moldovan political parties, and fear on the part of the Russians and Ukrainians that Moldova eventually will affiliate with Romania. Most of the policies were enacted shortly after independence, and the Ukrainian and Russian population—heavily concentrated in the Trans-Dniester region east of the Dniester River on the Ukrainian border—reacted by forming a separatist movement which quickly turned violent. The Russian army entered the region in 1992 and remained for years, although pull-out was scheduled for the late 1990s.

In 1994, the sentiments of the Moldovan Romanian majority shifted from stressing ethnic nationalism and possible affiliation with Romania to maintaining ties with Russia and granting some freedom to all ethnic minorities, including the possibility of forming autonomous regions within the Moldovan nation. The Romanian-language laws were rescinded, and relations became more peaceful—although still tense—as Russian and Ukrainian separatists continued to press for an independent Trans-Dniester region tied to Ukraine.

Monaco

T he Principality of Monaco is the second smallest nation in the world. It is located in southern Europe along the Mediterranean Coast and is bordered by France on the west and north and by Italy on the east. It has a population of 31,500, of whom only about 7,000 are citizens. The population is ethnically diverse: **French** are the largest group, constituting 47%; **Italians** make up 16%; and native **Monegesque** number 15%. The remainder of the population is composed of other peoples from Europe and North America. French is the official language, with most Italians also speaking Italian, and English commonly used as well. The ethnic heritage of Monegesques is unclear, although Italian influence is likely. Despite the ethnic mix, ethnic identity is not a salient feature of life in Monaco, as much of the population is wealthy and shares a lifestyle that centers around tourism, recreation, the arts, and sports.

Netherlands

T he Netherlands is in north-central Europe, bordered by the North Sea on the west and north, Germany on the east, and Belgium on the south. It has a population of 15.2 million, about 1 million of whom are immigrants or the children of immigrants.

Ethnic Composition

The Netherlands is one of the most ethnically heterogeneous nations in Europe. The end of Dutch colonialism after World War II, economic expansion, and a receptiveness to political refugees brought a large number of people from other nations around the world to the Netherlands. Minorities who have arrived since World War II are called "new minorities" to distinguish them from the "old minorities" such as **Calvinists, Catholics, Jews,** and **Huguenots.**

The largest ethnic group is the **Dutch,** who number nearly 15 million. Numerically, culturally, and politically they are the dominant ethnic group. The Dutch speak a Germanic language and are descended from tribes that spoke Germanic languages who settled in the region several thousand years ago. Religion plays a major role in the daily life of this secular nation, and the marked separation of the Protestant and Catholic segments of the population has eroded in recent years. A key feature of Dutch culture in the Netherlands is "pillarization"—the tendency for different social, occupation, regional, and religious groups to form and maintain their own parallel organizations. In so densely populated a nation, this is one mechanism for reducing contact and conflict between different groups.

Culturally related to the Dutch are the **Frisians,** numbering about 730,000, with about 400,000 in Friesland Province in the northeast and the remainder living elsewhere in the country. The name Frisian derives from Mare Frisicum, the name during the Middle Ages for the North Sea, on or near whose shores most Frisians lived—and still live today. Frisians around the world speak three dialects of Frisian (West, East, and North), a language related to Dutch and English but not mutually intelligible with either. Those in the Netherlands speak West Frisian. A 2,000-year identification as a unique people, a fierce desire dating to the 14th century to remain free of external rule, their distinct language, a cultural tradition encouraging communal cooperation, and their relative isolation in an area below sea level have enabled the Frisians to retain their cultural independence while remaining citizens of the Netherlands.

The largest immigrant population is made up of a number of groups from Europe, Asia, and Africa that came to the Netherlands as guest workers in the 1960s and 1970s. Unlike other Western European nations that entered into labor agreements with other nations in order to import factory workers, the demand in the Netherlands was for workers in the service industries. While many of these workers eventually returned to their homelands, some stayed on, married women also from their homelands, and had children. The demographic shift from the original single male immigrants to these families has had major implications for Dutch society as housing, education, and employment must be made available; it is likely, also, that most children of immigrants born in the Netherlands will remain there.

The two largest groups of immigrants are **Moroccans,** numbering 195,000, and **Turks,** who number 240,000 (the Turk category includes **Syriacs, Circassians, Kurds,** and other non-Turks from Turkey). The Turks are a growing population, as spouses continue to emigrate from Turkey. Both groups are mainly **Muslim,** and they are identified as such by the Dutch, rather than by nation of origin.

The European sector of the guest-worker community is much smaller and is formed by **Italians** (32,200), **Yugoslavians** (26,600), **Spaniards** (28,600), **Portuguese** (20,100), **Greeks** (9,000), and **Cape Verdeans** (who are actually of mixed African and European ancestry), who number 14,600. Many of those people have immigrated back to their home nations, particularly during the 1980s when economic conditions and employment opportunities improved in southern Europe.

The second largest ethnic minority category is formed by immigrants from former Dutch colonies. These include the **Surinamese,** numbering 260,000. As residents of a former Dutch colony in South America, they are nearly all citizens. Most fled to the Netherlands following Surinamese independence in 1975. Many are Muslims of Indonesian ancestry (especially Javanese) who were brought to Suriname by the Dutch as indentured laborers.

Antillians are Dutch citizens from the islands of the Netherlands Antilles and Aruba in the Caribbean Sea. They number about 90,000. With the exception of Aruba, these islands remain part of the Netherlands, and the Antillians, strictly speaking, are not immigrants.

Moluccans number 40,000 and form a third distinct colonial immigrant group. They began arriving in the Netherlands in the late 1940s and early 1950s during the decline of Dutch rule in Indonesia. The majority of the early immigrants were Moluccan soldiers serving in the Dutch army who simply stayed in the Netherlands after Indonesian independence. The majority are Muslim.

The major indigenous ethnic minority is **Caravan Dwellers,** numbering about 20,000. Caravan Dwellers are ethnic Dutch who, beginning in the late 1880s, adopted a nomadic lifestyle, selling various services to the settled population.

There is also a small **Gypsy** population of about 3,000 of foreign origin who began entering the Netherlands in the early 19th century.

Ethnic Relations

Official policy in the Netherlands encourages ethnic diversity, pluralism, and equal opportunity. However, most non-Dutch residents and citizens have yet to become full and equal participants in Dutch society, although few suffer from the poverty, lack of opportunity, and discrimination against outsiders found in other Western European nations. Although unemployment rates are much higher in ethnic minority communities, the effects of unemployment are mitigated to some extent by liberal welfare policies. Perhaps the greatest discrimination is experienced by Muslims, regardless of ethnicity, due to conflicts with the Christian-based Dutch legal and political systems. Ethnic minorities are a heavily urban population, with 45% living in Amsterdam, the Hague, Rotterdam, and Utrecht, as compared with only 13% of the Dutch population. Both Gypsies and Caravan Dwellers have been, at times, the object of discrimination and genocide. Today, the official government policy is to settle them in permanent residences, a plan opposed by some Gypsies and Caravan Dwellers and their advocates.

Norway

N orway, the westernmost country on the Scandinavian peninsula of northern Europe, is 125,181 square miles in area and has a population of 4.3 million. It shares an eastern border with Sweden, Finland, and Russia, and borders the Barents Sea on the north, the Norwegian Sea on the west, and the North Sea on the south. Svalbard, a group of islands in the far north, together with 150,000 additional islands along Norway's western coastline, are part of Norwegian territory. Lutheranism has been the state religion since the 16th century, although some residents of Norway are members of other Christian churches, including Baptist and Roman Catholic. Islam ranks second to Christianity in the number of adherents.

Ethnic Composition

Norway is ethnically homogeneous, with foreign citizens numbering only about 110,000, or 2% of the population. There also is a large Finnish population, nearly all of whom are Norwegian citizens, and about 40,000 to 60,000 Saami, the indigenous people of the north. Because of its northern location, Norway drew few settlers from other parts of Europe, although small numbers of German, Dutch, English, Scots, Jewish, and Gypsy immigrants trickled into Norway over the centuries. Many were artisans and professionals and were easily integrated into Norwegian society. Third World refugees arrived in Norway in the early 1970s, and increasing numbers of refugees sought asylum in Norway in the 1980s. An important contributor to this situation was the integration of Norway into international airline networks, with direct flights between Oslo and Third World countries.

Norwegians, including Norwegian citizens of other ethnic backgrounds, number about 4.1 million, or 96% of the population. The ancestors of contemporary Norwegians settled in Norway about 12,000 years ago. The Germanic migration of A.D. 500–800 primarily affected the coastal Norwegian population. The Viking Age (A.D. 800–1100) was accompanied by political unification of Norway under a line of kings, and the arrival of Roman Catholicism. Norway was a province of Denmark from 1380 to 1814. It was then politically unified with Sweden until 1905, when it gained independence. Despite substantial cultural similarities with Sweden and Denmark, this colonial history has at times caused strained relations.

The Norwegian language is closely related to Swedish and Danish. There are two forms of standard written Norwegian: Bokmal, which is used by the urban population and the upper class, and Nynorsk, which is based on Norway's rural dialects and often is associated with "Norwegianess" and social egalitarianism.

The other indigenous group is the **Saami (Lapps, Sami)** who inhabit much of the tundra, taiga, and coastal zones north of latitude 62°. They number roughly 1% of the population, or between 40,000 and 60,000. About 7,000 Saami herd reindeer, their traditional mode of subsistence. Other Saami are engaged in farming, fishing, and entrepreneurial pursuits. Their ancestors probably entered the Scandinavian peninsula about 2,000 years ago from the east. They migrated through other areas of Scandinavia (already sparsely settled by other groups) before establishing themselves in Sapmi (Lappland), which lies in the extreme northern parts of Norway, Sweden, and Finland, and the northwest corner of Russia. Cultural and linguistic contact arose with the later northern movements of Norwegians, Swedes, Finns, and Russians.

Lapp or Saami people in Norway constitute only about 1% of the population. Photo: Corel Corp.

Norway has significant populations from the three other Nordic nations. The most complex ethnic group, the **Finns** in Norway, has a history that goes back several hundred years. Their migration can be traced northward and westward from the southern and eastern areas of Finland. Finns migrated into what was then known as Lappland in the 1600s. They reached the most northerly valleys of Norway in the 1700s, and settled on the shores of the Arctic Ocean in the 1800s. From the end of the 1500s and throughout the 1600s, the Finns of eastern Finland colonized the uninhabited western areas of central Sweden from which they migrated. The migrations of Finns were regarded positively by the Norwegians, at least until the 19th century, particularly in the context of national economic politics and, more generally, in the context of the development of the Norwegian nation.

In the middle of the 19th century, Norwegian policy regarding the Finns became part of a general assimilation policy toward minorities, and the Finns who settled in northern Norway and were less assimilated came to be known as **Kvens.** Kvens, farmers who settled the Saami areas suited for agriculture, traded with the Saami and Norwegians. In the early phases of the colonization, they enjoyed certain tax privileges through the so-called Birkarle institution. The core areas of Kven settlement are the fjords of the counties of Finnmark and Troms, an area of about 60,000 square kilometers. In 1845, Kvens made up about 13% of the population of Finnmark. By 1875, there were about 3,500 Kvens in Troms (7.6% of the population) and in Finnmark, 5,800 (24.2%). The greatest concentration of Kvens was in the district of Varanger in Eastern Finnmark near the Russia-Finland border, and in Skibotn and Nordreisa in Northern Troms.

Norwegian fears of Russia were, to some extent, transferred to the Kven and the Finns: Russia at that time controlled Finland, and the concentrations of Kvens in northern Norway were very close to Norway's borders with Finland and Russia. The perceived Russian threat was an important factor in the adoption of an assimilation policy by Norway aimed at "Norwegianizing" the minorities. Fueled by strong nationalistic feelings, this policy lasted until World War II. A key feature of this policy was instituting Norwegian as the official language. Although the Kvens were not completely assimilated, by 1945 their sense of a unique identity and cultural distinctiveness had diminished. Many Kvens came to use Norwegian in their homes, even though Finnish was their mother tongue.

The ethnicization of Norway in the 1960s and 1970s stimulated the formation of many Kven organizations and activities promoting Kven identity. The official Norwegian attitude toward the Kven, however, did not change. Norwegian policy into the 1990s did not discourage Kven or Finnish organizations, but it did little to encourage or support Kven identity. Meanwhile, the use of the Finnish language by the Kvens continued to decline.

Danes number 17,500 and have migrated to Norway for centuries. Those who have become citizens and assimilated into Norwegian society are not included in this count, so the number of people with some Danish ancestry actually is higher than the above figure. In 1954, labor permits and visa requirements for Danes, Finns, and Swedes were abolished, which further encouraged migration between the Nordic countries. Danes are the objects of "positive discrimination" in Norway (favored treatment), and Danes assimilate very quickly and totally, usually within a generation or two. In the last half-century, relations between the people of the Nordic countries have become even closer. The main basis for this integration is the sharing of language, culture, and history. Relations between Danes and Norwegians have continued to improve, despite Denmark's history of rule over Norway for 450 years. One result is the long-range congruence of citizenship laws that give Nordic citizens extensive rights in all Nordic countries.

Swedes, like Danes and Finns, have migrated to Norway for centuries. Oslo in particular has been a strong magnet for certain regions in southern and southeastern Sweden. Swedes also have assimilated very quickly in Norway. Relations between Norwegians and Swedes have improved since World War II, at which time many Norwegians disagreed with Swedish neutrality while Norway was occupied by Germany. The fact that Sweden was a close haven for escaping Norwegians during the war to some extent helped many Norwegians to overcome the resentment they felt over Swedish neutrality.

Other Western groups represented in Norway are the British and Americans. **Britons** number 12,500 and are the fourth largest non-Norwegian group. **U.S. Americans** living in Norway number 9,600. Many are returnees; that is, first- and second-generation emigrants to America who have returned to Norway.

The remaining major ethnic minorities are in Norway mainly due to the nation's liberal immigration laws. **Muslims,** primarily **Pakistanis** (11,600), **Turks** (5,000), and **Iranians** (5,000), together make up about 20% of the total non-Norwegian population. While these minorities do not form a homogeneous group, they are a Muslim minority in a predominantly Christian country.

Vietnamese number about 7,000 and arrived as refugees following the end of the Vietnam War. Norway's liberal refugee resettlement policy has enabled many to remain in Norway, where the second generation is assimilated.

Chileans number 5,300. The presence of Chilean immigrants in Norway is an indication of the extent to which Norway has become a more ethnically diverse society. The Swedish Embassy in Chile became a haven for fugitives after the Chilean coup of 1973, and this opened the door for Chilean and other Latin American refugees to immigrate to all of the Nordic countries. Chileans, like immigrants from Middle Eastern and Asian countries, are a visible minority in Norway.

Other groups include several thousand **Bosnians** and **Albanians** and several hundred **Somalis, Sri Lankans (Tamils), Iranians,** and **Iraqis** who have either been granted asylum or are awaiting asylum hearings; several thousand **Yugoslavians** and **Poles** who arrived as wage laborers; and several thousand **Dutch, Germans,** and **Asian Indians** who are primarily middle- or upper-class populations.

Ethnic Relations

Norway has a liberal policy regarding the admission of refugees and asylum-seekers, although rules have been tightened since 1993. It ranks sixth in the world, with a ratio of one refugee or asylum-seeker granted residence per 149 residents.

The recent influx of refugees and asylum-seekers put a heavy strain on Norwegian society. Immigration laws were revised and new restrictions were placed on entering the country. The refugee issue has had a polarizing effect in Norway, with protest parties formed to oppose the immigration of refugees from Third World countries. Refugees generally settle in Oslo, particularly in the older workers' districts, where they tend to live in substantial housing; the slums and ghettos that have often developed in other countries with large refugee populations are unusual in Norway.

The immigration of Muslims to Norway is a relatively new phenomenon and represents a challenge to Norwegian culture. There is a clear division in attitudes toward Muslims. The people of Norway, in general, do not know much about Islam, and they have misgivings about the Muslims' attitude toward, or involvement with, radical political and religious movements. Norway has laws that protect religious freedom, and there are no formal obstacles to the exercise of religious practices, but there have been strong local reactions against Muslim activities.

The most basic ethnic relations situation involves the Norwegians and the Saami. Prior to about 1860, Norway followed a pro-Saami policy to the extent that the Saami were allowed to live as they liked with no overt pressure to conform to the Norwegian culture and language. After 1860 the policy changed, and assimilation became the only acceptable course. The new policy necessitated teaching the Saami the Norwegian language, and "the Saami Fund," created to achieve that purpose, was a powerful instrument used to carry out the policy of Norwegianizing both the Saami and the Kvens. One of the main arguments for Norwegianizing the Saami was to "civilize" them, as they were seen as primitives still pursuing a nomadic, pre-agrarian way of life. Periods of intense missionary activity also pressured the Saami to assimilate into the dominant national culture and to use the national language.

The attitude of the Norwegian government toward the Saami culture changed dramatically after World War II. The acceptance of Saami cultural and social life was viewed as a responsibility of the state. The Norwegian government had the duty of protecting and coordinating activities centrally, while also delegating tasks to specifically Saami organizations. At the beginning of the 1990s, there was close cooperation between the Saami organizations and Norwegian authorities on all levels. The rights of the Saami as an ethnic indigenous group in Norway have been set forth in constitutional terms. The establishment in 1989 of a Saami representative body means that Norwegian authorities recognize, within limits, a form of Saami autonomy.

Poland

Poland, located in north-central Europe, is bordered by the Baltic Sea and Russia on the north; Lithuania, Belarus, and Ukraine on the east; Slovakia and the Czech Republic on the south; and Germany on the west. It has a population of 38,655,000, 98% of whom are ethnic Poles.

Ethnic Composition

Poland is one of the most ethnically homogeneous nations in the world. The population also is religiously homogeneous, with 90% being Roman Catholic. For centuries prior to World War II, shifting political borders often placed large numbers of Germans, Russians, Lithuanians, Belarusians, Ukrainians, and Jews within the Polish polity. Consolidation of borders and massive population shifts during and following World War II have left Poland the homogeneous nation it is today. Non-Poles from neighboring nations mostly live in border regions near the nations of their forebears.

Poles are descended from a people who settled in what is now Poland perhaps as long as 4,000 years ago. Polish identity today rests on residence in Poland or Polish ancestry, speaking Polish, adherence to Roman Catholicism, and a strong identification with the Polish nation-state. Although Poland is politically in Eastern Europe and geographically in central Europe, Polish urban culture has been most heavily influenced by Western European culture. Approximately 13 million Poles or individuals of Polish ancestry live outside Poland, primarily in the United States, Belarus, Ukraine, and several dozen other nations. In overseas communities, ties to the homeland remain strong, and contact has increased markedly since the end of Communist control.

Closely related to the Poles are the **Kashubians (Kashubs),** estimated at about 200,000. They speak two dialects of Polish and live in north-central Poland. They are mainly peasant farmers and choose to identify themselves as Kashubs rather than as Poles. Their religion is a mix of Christianity and their indigenous beliefs and practices.

The **Belarusian** population is estimated at from 250,000 to 500,000, and Belarusians live near the border with Belarus. They are rural farmers and are assimilated into Polish society.

Carpatho-Rusyns are a people whose traditional homeland is on the south and north slopes of the Carpathian Mountains. Under the domination of various nations over the centuries, they have been called by a number of different names. In Poland, where they number about 60,000 (of a total of 850,000), they are often called **Lemkos** or **Carpatho-Ukrainians** and are categorized as Ukrainians. Like Ukrainians, they speak an East Slavic language and are adherents of Eastern Orthodoxy, but they consider themselves a distinct group with their own dialect and religious traditions, and they seek political autonomy in Poland.

Germans live mainly in the region known as Lower Silesia along the Poland-Germany border. Their number is estimated at 1.4 million and they are called Silesians. A smaller population of Germans is concentrated in northeast Poland in what was formerly East Prussia.

The ethnic category of **Silesian** is an amorphous and shifting one that includes Germans in Poland, Poles in Germany (in Upper Silesia), and Poles in Silesia, some of whom—since the unification of East and West Germany—have claimed German Silesian identity. Silesians speak a dialect of Polish heavily influenced by German.

The **Ukrainian** population is estimated at 200,000 to 700,000. Some Ukrainians still live in northern Poland where they were forcibly relocated from the south in 1947, while others who are assimilated into Polish society live in various regions of the country.

Lithuanians number about 10,000 and live in mainly Lithuanian communities on the Poland-Lithuania border.

Other groups include small communities (less than 20,000 each) of **Russians, Slovaks,**

Greeks, Slovenes, and **Muslim and Jewish Tatars**.

The two major non-national ethnic minorities are the Gypsies and Jews. **Gypsies** number between 10,000 and 50,000 and include those who have been there for centuries and are largely settled, as well as more recent arrivals who continue to live a peripatetic lifestyle.

Jews numbered more than three million before World War II. Most either fled or were killed during the Holocaust. The population is now estimated at between 5,000 and 10,000 and consists mostly of older people living in large cities.

Ethnic Relations

Ethnic relations in Poland are generally peaceful. Following the end of Communist rule in 1990, however, some groups, such as the Silesians, have been seeking more autonomy from centralized Polish rule, and Ukrainians have been seeking compensation for mistreatment during the Communist era. In the 1990s, Poland has also seen "anti-Semitism without Jews," a phenomenon in which Jews are blamed for some of Poland's social and economic problems, even though they are few in number and without influence in Polish affairs. Gypsies are relatively few in number and there is less discrimination and violence directed at them than in other Central and East European nations.

Portugal

P ortugal, located on the Iberian Peninsula in southwestern Europe, is bordered by Spain on the east and north and by the Atlantic Ocean on the west and south. The Madeira and Azore Islands, autonomous regions of Portugal, are also covered in this entry, as is Macao, a Portuguese colony that will revert to China in 1999.

Portugal has a population of 10.5 million. The Portuguese are descended from one regional indigenous population, and the nation emerged as an autonomous political entity in 1140. Portuguese language and culture today are largely homogeneous with only small regional differences in dialect and a north-south difference in culture—the north considered to be more conservative and "Catholic."

Ethnic Composition

The overwhelming majority of the population is ethnically Portuguese and Roman Catholic. The non-Portuguese population is reported as 107,000; however, this is surely an undercount because citizens who are non-ethnic Portuguese from Portugal's former colonies are counted as Portuguese, and at least 100,000 undocumented foreigners are not included in official counts. Thus, the total number of non-Portuguese is probably 250,000 or more; about 2.5% of the population. The largest foreign group is people of African ancestry, who account for 50% or more of the non-Portuguese population.

Portuguese, the indigenous people of Portugal, constitute about 99% of the population.

They are descended from the Lusitanians who settled the region 3,000 years B.C., with later influences from the Celts, Romans, Swabians, and Moors. Included in the Portuguese population today are *retornados*, Portuguese from overseas colonies who returned to Portugal in the 1970s. The nation's culture is marked by north-south and urban-rural distinctions. In rural areas, traditional kinship, craft, religious, and medical practices are often combined with Roman Catholicism and economic and political reforms initiated in Lisbon. Parts of Portugal were farmed under the Roman *latifundia* system, in which estates were held by one family and farmed by serfs. That system has given way to a class-based society in which farming is declining and employment in the manufacturing and service sectors is growing.

Brazilians and other people from Latin America (primarily **Venezuelans**) number about 27,000. They are mainly returnees of Portuguese ancestry or people of mixed Portuguese and other ancestry. As many have easily assimilated into Portuguese society, the figure 27,000 probably represents only those who have arrived recently and are still counted as Brazilian.

Goanese number only a few thousand and are people of mixed Portuguese and Indian ancestry from the former colony of Goa on the west coast of India. Most are now assimilated into Portuguese society.

Azoreans and Madeirans are residents of Portuguese overseas departments. **Azoreans** are the residents of the Azores Archipelago in the Atlantic Ocean, first settled by the Portuguese in the mid-1400s. The modern population of 240,000 is multiethnic in origin, with Portuguese, **Italians, Germans, Britons**, **Spaniards,** *conversos* (**Jews** who converted to Roman Catholicism in the 1400s), **Moors,** and **Flemings** having settled on the islands at various times. A class system separates businessmen of foreign ancestry from the general population. Today, Azoreans are almost all Roman Catholic. The island is under Portuguese control, but the traditional, rural way of life contrasts with modern Portuguese influences. There has been a considerable amount of immigration to the United States.

Madeirans are the residents of the Madeira Archipelago in the Atlantic Ocean, first settled by the Portuguese in the early 1400s. The Madeira Archipelago is an autonomous region of Portugal with economic matters influenced by British interests. The population of about 260,000 is a mixture of the Portuguese, Britons, Spaniards, and Africans who have at various times settled on the island. Nearly all Madeirans are Roman Catholic, and the Church plays a major role in supporting Portuguese rule. There has been considerable immigration to South Africa and Canada.

Macaoans are ethnic Chinese from the colony of Macao, which is scheduled for return to China in 1999. Most are shopkeepers and more are expected to seek residence in Portugal as the deadline for the Chinese takeover of the island grows closer.

Africans number anywhere from 45,000 to well over 100,000 and came mainly from the former colonies of Angola and Mozambique, although undocumented immigrants also have come from North Africa. They are poor and live in ghettos in large cities such as Lisbon and Oporto and are the object of racial discrimination in housing, employment, and education.

Gypsies are estimated at between 20,000 and 100,000. They remain a poor, marginalized group unassimilated into Portuguese society. They, along with many Africans, occupy the bottom rung of Portuguese society.

Other groups include small numbers of **Romanians** and **Pakistanis** seeking asylum, and retirees and expatriates from the **United States** and **Canada** and from northern European nations such as **Great Britain** and **Germany**.

Ethnic Relations

From the 1950s until 1981, Portugal was a nation of emigration, with workers immigrating to Brazil, Germany, France, and the United States, and their families often following. Today there is a Portuguese diaspora of nearly four million people, with the largest populations in Brazil, France, the United States, Canada, South Africa, Venezuela, and Spain. The flow of money from these nations back to families in Portugal, as well as frequent communication, return visits, and resettlement in Portugal, has altered Portuguese culture and involved it to a greater extent in the world economy. In 1973, the flow of emigrants slowed, and some Portuguese immigrants began returning to Portugal, primarily from other European nations. Diversification of the population began in the early 1960s. The breakup of the overseas Portuguese empire resulted in the repatriation of ethnic Portuguese from these outposts and migration to Portugal by those who had supported the Portuguese regimes in Angola, Mozambique, Goa, Macao, East Timor, and Brazil. Later immigrations brought indigenous people from these nations, as well as peoples from North Africa. Initially, a significant number moved on to other nations in Europe, but in the 1980s and 1990s, many chose to remain in Portugal. This slowing of emigration and increased immigration resulted in Portugal becoming a nation of net immigration in 1981. Although still minimal, ethnic diversity in the 1990s in Portugal is greater than at any other time in its history. The government has been slow in responding to the many undocumented and documented immigrants. Not until 1993 was immigration from non-European nations limited and laws enacted to make it easier to expel undocumented immigrants, although the Portuguese population remains divided over this issue. The long history of Portuguese emigration has made the Portuguese somewhat more receptive to immigrants than are many other Europeans.

Romania

Romania, formerly called Rumania, is a nation in Eastern Europe bordered by Ukraine on the north; Moldova, Russia, and the Black Sea on the east; Bulgaria on the south; and Yugoslavia (Serbia) and Hungary on the west. It has a population of 23.5 million.

Ethnic Composition

Ethnic Romanians account for 89.1% of the population, Hungarians 8.9%, and a dozen or more other groups the remaining 2%. Prior to 1918, Romania was ethnically homogeneous, but the breakup of the Austro-Hungarian Empire and redistribution of some of its land placed large numbers of Hungarians, Germans, and Jews within the borders of modern Romania.

Romanians number 20.9 million in Romania and 3 million in neighboring Moldova, part of which has, at times, been part of Romania. Romanians claim to be descended from the Geto-Dacians, the original inhabitants of the region, and the Romans who entered the area in the 1st century B.C. They also claim to have had a continuous presence in the region since then. This interpretation is not accepted by all historians. The core area of the Romanian nation and culture—the Old Kingdom—is Moldovia and Wallachia, with Bessarabia and Transylvania added later. Romanians have been adherents of Eastern Orthodoxy for 1,000 years, with some converting to Catholic Uniatism in the 18th century. In rural areas, indigenous beliefs and practices have been combined with Christianity. Because of regional and sometimes village-to-village differences in custom, it is difficult to describe Romanian culture in any general sense. Romanian efforts to control ethnic minorities since the expansion of Romania in 1918 are largely motivated by a fear of incursions by Hungary, Russia, and the former Soviet Union and a desire to forge a strong, Romanian-based national culture.

Hungarians in Romania number over two million and as such are the largest European-nationality group in another nation. They live almost exclusively in the region known as Transylvania, which occupies the northwestern one-third of Romania. The region is multiethnic, with Romanians accounting for about 70% of the population, Hungarians 25%, and Germans, Gypsies, Jews, and others the remaining 5%. Hungarians live mainly in the eastern and central districts, and in a number of districts, they are the majority population. Two Hungarian groups—**Magyars** and **Szeklers**—entered the region as early as the 10th century. The two groups maintain separate identities today, although the Szeklers are largely assimilated into Romanian society. The Magyars are mainly Protestant and the Szeklers Roman Catholic, which tends to distinguish them from each other and also from the Romanians, who are mostly Eastern Orthodox or Uniates. Although Romanians have been the majority population since the 1600s, Hungarians ruled the region until a combination of Romanian demands for the region and the defeat of the Austro-Hungarian Empire severed Transylvania from Hungary and added it to Romania in 1918. At that time, many Hungarians fled to Hungary. Hungarians who remained in Transylvania have since been under Romanian domination.

Germans number about 200,000, and their population is declining as a pattern of immigration to Western Europe that began in the 1970s continues. The German population is composed of **Saxons** and **Swabians.** The Saxons were settled in Transylvania from the Rhineland in the 12th and 13th centuries by the Hungarians, and commerce and adherence to the Lutheran Church after the 1600s were major features of community life. The Swabians were settled in Romania by the Hapsburg Empire in the 18th century. They are mostly Roman Catholic. Reduction of the German population in Romania began after World War II (the Romanian government switched sides to the Allies in 1944), when nearly 200,000 left for Germany or were deported. Departures since the 1970s have been for better economic opportunities elsewhere and because of general repression of minorities in Romania during the Communist era.

Gypsies arrived in Romania in the 14th century and have been the objects of enslavement, persecution, ostracism, and discrimination ever since. There are no reliable estimates of their population, which is likely between one and two million. As the poorest group in Romanian society, they have been—since the end of Communist rule—the target of violence that blames them for the nation's economic problems. Many have fled to Western Europe, although some have been forcibly repatriated.

Jews today number less than 40,000, a decrease from over one million before World War II and about 250,000 after the war. The population reduction is due to extermination by the Nazis during the war and a liberal immigration policy which allowed many to leave for Israel beginning in the 1960s. The remaining population is largely assimilated into Romanian society, although anti-Semitic sentiments persist.

Other groups, numbering about 400,000 in all, include **Armenians, Carpatho- Rusyns, Ukrainians, Russians, Greeks, Tatars, Turks, Serbs, Bulgarians,** and **Croats.** Their presence is due to a combination of shifting national boundaries and the existence of major international trade routes through Romania. While some of these groups were seen as a threat to Romanian unity before World War II, their small numbers today effectively exclude them as major targets of ethnic discrimination.

Ethnic Relations

Ethnic relations are a serious problem in Romania and involve a long and continuing pattern of anti-Semitism, discrimination against Gypsies, and repression of the Hungarian population in Transylvania in the 20th century. Hungary and Romania continue to dispute ownership of the region occupied by Hungarians. The conflict centers on claims about who the region's first occupants were—Hungarians asserting that the region was uninhabited when their forebears first settled there, Romanians claiming their ancestors were living there at the time. Archaeological and linguistic evidence are insufficient to settle the dispute and, in any case, the economic and political stakes are so high that all information is interpreted by each side in a manner that supports its claim.

All ethnic minorities except Gypsies are classified as "co-inhabiting nationalities." Anti-ethnic minority sentiments in the Communist era and today are motivated in part by nationalistic sentiments and the desire for a strong, independent Romania.

Russia

R ussia is a large nation located both in Europe and Asia. European Russia lies west of the Ural Mountains, Asiatic Russia or Siberia to the east of the mountains. The population of Russia is 147 million, with ethnic Russians accounting for 81.6% of the population in 1989. This percentage has probably increased in the 1990s with the return of some ethnic Russians from former republics of the now-defunct Soviet Union and the out-migration of non-Russians. During the Soviet era, ethnic relations were relatively peaceful, as centralized government and economic control minimized ethnic differences and stressed loyalty to the Soviet nation. In the post-Soviet era (since 1991), ethnic relations among various groups—and especially between the Russians and other groups—have become tense and sometimes violent.

Ethnic Composition

Despite the numerical, economic, political, and cultural dominance of the Russians since the 12th century, Russia was and remains an ethnically heterogeneous nation, with over 100 ethnic groups. In addition to the Russians, these groups fall into a number of distinct categories:

- Indigenous Peoples of the North
- Peoples of the Caucasus
- Nationalities of the former Soviet republics
- Immigrant groups from Europe
- Peoples of Asian origin
- Other groups that do not fit into these categories
- Religious minorities

In addition, Russia is a religiously heterogeneous society, composed of large numbers of atheists, Muslims, and Russian Orthodox, as well as smaller numbers of Roman Catholics, Uniates, Jews, Old Believers, Buddhists, Protestants, and adherents of indigenous religions. Religion was repressed during the Soviet era and it is not yet clear what role religion will play in the post-Soviet era, which began in 1991.

Russians

Russians are the most numerous of the Slavic peoples, and since the 14th century they have been the dominant group in the region now known as European Russia. The label **Great**

Russians is sometimes used to distinguish Russians from Belarusians ("White Russians") and Ukrainians ("Little Russians"). Today, Russians in Russia number about 120 million, although about 145 million live in the newly independent republics of the former USSR. Russia was Christianized in A.D. 869, and Russian Orthodox Christianity was the state religion of the Russian Empire. During the period of the Russian Empire, Russian rule was extended into Eastern Europe and across Asia to the Pacific Ocean. Large numbers of ethnic Russians settled in Siberia and today form a distinct Russian subgroup called **Siberiaki**.

The history of Russian expansion and colonization is filled with wars, revolution, riots, strikes, and forced displacement involving dozens of ethnic groups in what is now Russian territory. This legacy of conflict continues to define Russian relations with other groups. Today, within the Russian Republic,

At a nationalistic rally, symbols of Russian culture are displayed.
Photo: Agence France Presse/Corbis-Bettmann.

relations with most other ethnic groups are difficult, ranging from open warfare (as with the Chechens) to peaceful conflicts over political and economic autonomy with virtually all other groups. Soviet government policies of the 1980s, which allowed far greater expression of ethnic identity, have continued in the post-Soviet era, leading to many local conflicts between Russian officials and indigenous peoples for political and economic control.

Cossacks were not an ethnic group, but rather a "military race"—mercenaries in the service of Russia, Ukraine, Lithuania, and Poland, usually fighting against the Tatars and Turks and other non-Russian groups (although the first Cossacks were actually Tatars employed by the Russians). Early Cossack settlements were located near rivers that flowed south into the Black and Caspian seas. The largest and best known was the Don Cossacks, who lived on the Don River, served the tsar, and gave rise to other Cossack groups. The second largest group was the Zaporozhe Cossacks in the Ukraine, who mainly acted as pirates, raiding ships in the Black Sea. Both groups produced men for newer Cossack groups in Russia, Ukraine, and Siberia, or served as models for these new groups. Most Cossack groups were named after a river or the region where they lived. At first these groups were composed solely of men, but in the 17th century the custom changed—most Cossacks married, and settled family life became more common. The Cossacks served the governments of Russia, Poland, and Ukraine from the 1500s until the Russian Revolution. In the 1920s and 1930s, over one million were killed by the new Russian government, and Cossack settlements were destroyed. In the post-Soviet era, the Cossacks have reemerged as a group, with some claiming special status and offering to protect Russians living in other republics.

Indigenous Peoples of the North

The term **Peoples of the North** refers to the 26 groups of indigenous peoples of northern Russia and Siberia who total about 560,000 people, a very small and widely dispersed population. Regular contact with Russians

dates to 1600s or earlier for some groups, and in all groups the contact either destroyed or seriously damaged the indigenous cultures. The traditional economy based on reindeer herding, hunting, gathering, or fishing was replaced by involvement in the fur trade and then wage labor. Traditional shamanistic religions were replaced with Russian Orthodoxy, Russian was made the language of daily life, nomadic bands were forcibly settled, and disease and forced relocations caused serious depopulation. While all groups experienced these impacts, there are differences in the degree to which traditional cultures have survived for Peoples of the North. At one extreme are

Peoples of the North in Russia

Group	Area	Population
Aleut	Pribilof and Commander Islands	600
Chukchee	Northeastern Siberia	15,180
Chuvan	Northwestern Siberia	1,510
Dolgan	North of Arctic Circle	6,000
Enets	Northwestern Siberia	200
Even	Northeastern Siberia	17,200
Evenki	Central and Southern Siberia	30,000
Itelmen	Kamchatka Peninsula	2,500
Khanty	Northeastern Siberia	22,500
Koryaks	Kamchatka Peninsula	8,000
Mansi	Northwestern Siberia	8,500
Nanai	Western Siberia	12,000
Nenets	Northwestern Siberia	32,000
Nganasan	Northwestern Siberia	1,200
Nivkh	Sakhalin Island, Southeastern Siberia	4,500
Orochi	Southeastern Siberia	900
Orok	Sakhalin Island	200
Saami (Lapps)	Kola Peninsula	1,800
Selkup	Southwestern Siberia	3,500
Tofalar	South-central Siberia	750
Udegei	Eastern Siberia	2,000
Ulchi	Southeastern Siberia	2,500
Yakut	Northeastern Siberia	382,000
Yukagir	Northeastern Siberia	1,110
Yupik (Asiatic Eskimos)	Northeastern Siberia	2,000

the smaller groups such as the **Ulchi,** who are virtually extinct as a separate group and have been absorbed by neighboring groups. At the other extreme are the **Yakut,** the largest group, who failed in an attempt to gain autonomy in the late 1980s, but nevertheless exert considerable control over Russian influence in their region, Yakutia. In 1990, the indigenous groups organized as the Association of the Peoples of the North to fight environmental destruction and economic development in Siberia and in the north and to seek restoration of lands. In the post-Soviet era there has also been an emphasis on reviving traditional languages and customs.

Peoples of the Caucasus

A second major grouping—which, like the Peoples of the North, consists mainly of groups that are indigenous to their region—is the **Peoples of the Caucasus.** These peoples live in the area around the Caucasus Mountains region of southwestern Russia and the neighboring nations of Georgia and Azerbaijan. The region has, for some 4,000 years, been a crossroads between Europe and Asia, and the Peoples of the Caucasus have been influenced by others passing through from the south, north, and east. Because the Caucasus region provides access to the Black Sea, it was contested by the Russians and the Ottoman Empire, and then by the Russians and the Turks in World War I. While Russia has generally maintained political dominance in the area, contact with the Ottoman Empire led many groups to convert to Islam. In addition to contact with outsiders such as the Greeks, Russians, and Turks, there has also been considerable interaction between some groups over the centuries, especially in the eastern district of Daghestan. In the post-Soviet era, there has been a revival of Islam, the formation of new political alliances, and calls for various degrees of autonomy from Russian control.

The following table lists the Peoples of the Caucasus who live within the Russian Republic. Some of these groups are also found in the republics of Georgia and Azerbaijan.

Peoples of the Caucasus in Russia

Group	Population
Abkhaz	33,000
Andi	15,000
Avars	500,000
Balkars	86,000
Chechens	957,000
Circassians	607,390
Dargins	366,000
Ingush	238,000
Karachay	150,000
Kumyk	290,000
Kurds	6,000
Lak	106,000
Lezgins	210,000
Nogay	75,000
Ossetes	250,000
Rutul	10,000
Tabasaran	90,000
Tats	13,000
Tsakhurs	5,000

Nationalities of the Former Soviet Republic

A third major category of non-Russians in Russia is peoples (often referred to as nationalities) from the now-independent nations that were component republics of the Soviet Union. The two largest groups are **Belarusians** and **Ukrainians,** who constitute 71% of this category. Like the Russians, they are Slavic peoples, and the three groups are culturally related. **Slavs** refers to a Central Asian people who settled in Eastern and Southern Europe from about A.D. 400 on. They have never been a unified entity, and today are classified into three categories: Eastern Slavs—Belarusians, Russians, Ukrainians; Western Slavs—Czechs, Poles, Slovaks; and Southern Slavs—Bulgarians, Croats, Macedonian Slavs, Serbs, and Slovenes.

According to the 1989 census (before the breakup of the Soviet Union), people from other Soviet republics totaled 7,842,927 in Russia, with most living either in border regions of Russia or in major Russian cities. With the demise of the Soviet Union (in 1991), some of these non-Russian peoples returned to their nations of origin, and their numbers in Russia in the mid-1990s are certainly lower than in 1989.

Non-Russian Nationalities in Russia

Group	Population
Armenian	532,675
Azerbaijani	336,908
Belarusian	1,205,887
Estonian	46,358
Georgian	130,719
Kazakh	683,083
Kyrgyz	48,083
Latvian	46,818
Lithuanian	70,386
Moldovan	172,784
Tajik	38,327
Turkmen	39,738
Ukrainian	4,363,992
Uzbek	127,169

Immigrants from Europe

A fourth major category of non-Russians is ethnic groups from elsewhere in Europe whose ancestors settled in Russia. The largest of these ethnic groups is the **Germans,** who number 842,000 in Russia and over 2 million in the former Soviet republics. They constitute Russia's largest group without an ethnic region of their own. These people of German ancestry live in particular communities—some mostly German, but many mixed—from western Russia into central Siberia and in northern Kazakhstan. Due to this dispersion, labels based on location such as Caucasus Germans or Volga Germans, or on religion such as Swiss Mennonites, are no longer commonly used. Germans came to Russia in a series of migrations beginning in the early 1700s; some in search of better farmland and others, such as Hutterites, Mennonites, and Moravians, to escape religious persecution. German-Russian relations in Russia have generally reflected German-Russian national relations. Thus, some Germans were deported to Siberia dur-

ing World War I, and the entire German- ancestry population in southwestern Russia was deported to Siberia and Central Asia during World War II. In 1955 and 1956, they were permitted to relocate, but not to their former settlements in the Volga region, which were by then settled by Russians. German desires for an autonomous region have not been granted, and as a scattered population they are concerned about the loss of ethnic identity. German ethnic organizations and schools are supported by funds from Germany and from contributions by Germans outside Russia.

Greeks have been coming to what is now Russia for at least 2,000 years, although the current population is composed primarily of people descended from Greeks who arrived since the late 1700s, most of whom were Pontic Greeks from the Pontius region of Turkey on the Black Sea. The population increased in 1948–49 when Greeks who had sided with the Communists fled after the Greek Civil War. Currently, there are about 150,000 people of Greek ancestry in Russia. The Greeks enjoyed considerable freedom in Russia until the 1917 Revolution, when 70 years of oppression began. At first they were persecuted for being business owners and traders; in the 1930s, it was because they were an ethnic minority; in the 1940s, many were deported to Siberia and Central Asia; in the 1950s, they were allowed to return to Russia but could not own property and were forced to identify themselves as Russian; and in the 1970s and early 1980s, they were denied access to some jobs and education opportunities. During these years of oppressive treatment, many Greeks were assimilated into Russian society through education, marriage, and self-identification as Russians. Since the mid-1980s, Greeks have formed a pan-Greek alliance and are lobbying for a Greek republic in Russia. At the same time, many Greeks (perhaps as many as 20,000 per year) are returning to Greece.

Gypsies are a third distinct population who came to Russia from Europe. They number about 150,000 in Russia, most of them Romani. Gypsies entered Russia from Central Europe in the early 1500s and from the Balkans after 1860. At first a peripatetic population, by the early 20th century most lived in settled communities, often separate from those of the Russians. Gypsies have always been outcasts in Russian society, except for about a dozen years following the 1917 Revolution. In the 1930s and 1940s, they were persecuted, relocated, and killed by the government, and some 30,000 were killed by the Nazis during World War II. In the post-Soviet era, they have been attacked, their houses have been destroyed, and they have been blamed by some Russians for the nation's economic problems. It is likely that many have left Russia for Western Europe. Unlike many other Russian ethnic groups, Gypsies—because of their pariah status—have retained much of their traditional culture, including maintaining their social structure based on nations, clans, and families; marrying within the group; avoiding non-Gypsies; and engaging in particular occupations such as entertaining, coppersmithing, and blacksmithing. Gypsies in Russia speak Romani and are mainly Russian Orthodox.

Poles numbered about 1.3 million in the Soviet Union before its breakup, primarily living in Russia, Ukraine, Belarus, and Lithuania. About 94,000 live in Russia. Poland was an independent nation for several centuries, then in the late 1700s, some regions were incorporated into Russia until the end of World War I, when Poland again became an independent nation. Poles who immigrated to the Soviet Union did so mainly to find employment. From the late 1930s until the mid-1980s, Poles in Russia were the subject of various assimilation and displacement programs, which resulted in a decline in their population and has left a remnant population in Siberia. Despite efforts to assimilate them, their preference for marriage to other Poles and adherence to Roman Catholicism have kept them separate from other Slavic peoples in the Soviet Union. Economic problems in the Soviet Union created hardships for Polish workers, but similar problems in Poland made return to Poland undesirable.

In addition to these major European groups, there are smaller populations of **Gauguz** (*see* Moldova), **Hungarians, Bulgarians, Serbs, Croats, Czechs,** and **Slovaks**.

Beyond the European immigrant groups, there are also **Finns** and **Karelians** living near the Finnish border who total about 200,000. They are not immigrants, but are there as a result of shifting national boundaries. Some experts consider the Karelians to be Finns who live in Russia, the majority of whom now speak Russian and are Russian Orthodox. The region of Karelia has been divided for several centuries between Sweden (and then Finland) on the west, and Novgorod, Russia (and then the Soviet Union) on the east. Although assimilated into Russian culture, the Karelians in Russia have formed a number of ethnic associations to revitalize their culture (*see also* Finland).

Peoples of Asian Ancestry

The fifth major category of non-Russians is people of Asian ancestry, some of whom have lived in what is now Russia for centuries and others who are more recent arrivals. Because of different histories and different experiences in Russia, these groups do not display general patterns of similarity as do the Peoples of the North and the Peoples of the Caucasus.

Buriats (Buryats) live in three separate locales in southern Siberia. The majority (249,000) live in the Buriat Autonomous Republic east of Lake Baikal. Although they number only 421,000 in all, their strategic location on the Mongolia border and cultural ties to Buriats in Mongolia made them major players in carrying out Russian expansion. From the mid-1600s on, although they often resisted Russian settlement and rule, they were recruited by the Russians as allies to help conquer and rule Mongolia. They are, themselves, a Mongolian people who over the centuries have assimilated individuals from neighboring groups including Tuvans, Daur, and Evenki. They follow a unique form of Buddhism that includes borrowings from Eastern Orthodox Christianity and their indigenous shamanism; repressed during the Soviet era, Buddhism is now being revived. In the post-Soviet era, Buriats are among the strongest proponents of ethnic rights and are seeking to make Buriat the official language of the region and to remove Russian influence.

Another Mongolian people are the **Kalmyks (Oirots, Western Mongols)** who number 165,000 in European Russia, with several thousand more scattered in Siberia. They live in the Republic of the Kalmykia-Khalmag Tangch, north of the Caspian Sea. They began migrating west in the late 16th century, eventually settling and coming under Russian control. In 1771, the majority of the population migrated back to China, and the remaining Kalmyk people are ancestors of the original population. Relations with the Russians were generally positive; Russians and Ukrainians settled in the Kalmykia region, and many Kalmyks became Cossacks. Under Soviet rule, Kalmyk demands for autonomy were violently repressed, and in 1943, the Kalmyks were deported to Siberia and their republic dissolved. In 1956 they began returning, although they are now a minority population in the republic. While relations with the Russians remain tense, the Kalmyks have stressed control of local mineral resources rather than political autonomy in the post-Soviet era. They are divided in religion among Lamaist Buddhism, Russian Orthodoxy, and atheism.

Tatar is a general label for people who are now adherents of Islam and/or claim to be descended from the Tatar-Mongols who invaded parts of Europe and Asia in the 13th century. In fact, most people so identified today are not direct descendants of the Mongols, but are, instead, descended from Turkic-speaking peoples who mixed with other groups and who took the name in the 16th century. The Tatars in the former Soviet Union number 6.6 million, with 5.5 million in Russia, making them the largest ethnic minority in the nation. Of the various Tatar groups, two are especially prominent—the Crimean Tatars and the Volga Tatars. Another large group, the **Siberian** Tatars, is now largely assimilated into the dominant Russian population or has mixed over the centuries with indigenous peoples in the region. **Crimean Tatars** number about 600,000 and live mainly in Central Asia. Only about 250,000 live in Crimea, which is now part of Ukraine. After several centuries of self-rule and cooperation with the Ottoman Empire, they came under Russian domination in the mid-1600s, and until they were deported to Central Asia and Siberia in 1944, Crimean Tatars were the object of Russification, Sovi-

etization, and genocidal policies. In Central Asia, they campaigned for return to Crimea. In the 1990s, the issue remains unresolved—Ukrainians and Russians in Crimea oppose their return. The **Volga Tatars,** numbering five million, live primarily in Tatarstan and Bashkirstan in Russia, but also in a number of other former Soviet republics. They are divided into three major subgroups: **Mishars, Kazanis,** and **Krjashen,** the last being Orthodox while the other two are Muslim. The Volga Tatars are descended from the Bulgars who inhabited the region during the Mongol invasions in the 14th century. Like the Crimean Tatars, they suffered from Russification and Sovietization, though not deportation. They have been among the leading advocates of ethnic rights, and with the fall of the Soviet Union, they have been demanding sovereignty for Tatarstan and surrounding republics and have been promoting a pan-Turkic movement. Their demands have been rejected by Russia, in part because of the rich oil reserves in the region and in part because of a fear of the influence of Islam in Russia.

Altai refers to a number of related groups numbering about 73,300 and who live in the Altai mountains in southern Siberia on the borders of China, Mongolia, and Kazakhstan. They are descended from Turkic and Mongolian peoples and have been a distinct group since the 6th century. Under Russification and Sovietization, they shifted from herding and hunting to agriculture, their religion was repressed although it survived in private, Russian became the official language, and Russian and Ukrainian settlers became the majority population in their region. Despite their small numbers, many Altai resisted assimilation, and since the 1980s there has been a pronounced cultural revival, focusing on their indigenous shamanistic religion.

Koreans number about 107,000 in Russia, representing about one-third of the Korean population in the former Soviet Union. At one time, all Koreans in Russia lived in the Russian Far East, but they were deported to Central Asia in 1937 and most have remained there. Many Koreans have taken Russian names and converted to Eastern Orthodoxy, so many are assimilated or identify themselves as Russians and are not counted as Koreans. In Russia, Koreans live mainly in the Caucasus and in large cities. Although once largely farmers, many Koreans in Russia have entered the professions.

Chinese (Han) in Russia number about 12,000 and live mainly in towns in eastern Siberia. The Chinese population, which approached 100,000 early in the 20th century, was reduced by often violent attacks on Chinese communities, which caused the majority to return to China.

Vietnamese number 17,000, their community in Russia dating to the arrival of Marxist Vietnamese in the 1920s. Soviet support for the Communist Vietnamese in their conflicts with the French and Americans led to the establishment of a permanent community in Russia, which is centered in Moscow since many Vietnamese who came to Russia were students, Communist party officials, and military officers.

Other Groups

The sixth category contains indigenous groups that do not fit into the other categories. One subcategory consists of distinct ethnic groups that, during the Soviet era, occupied "autonomous" administrative regions within Russia. These autonomous regions, often named for the local ethnic group, were not, in fact, autonomous. Instead, Russians and Communist leaders with ties to Moscow were the major political and economic forces in the regions, and the indigenous peoples often played a secondary role, lived in rural areas, and worked on collective farms and in government-owned factories. Despite Russian dominance and efforts to assimilate these groups culturally, some have maintained a degree of cultural autonomy, as reflected in the continued use of their native languages (although many people also speak Russian) and a sense of distinct ethnic identity.

One ethnic group that has been able to maintain some political autonomy is the **Chuvash,** who number 1.7 million, nearly 1 million of whom live in the Chuvash Republic where they constitute 68% of the popula-

tion. Russians, at 28%, are the second largest group, with some 60 other groups making up the additional 4%. The emergence of the Chuvash as a distinct group is unclear; they trace their ancestry to the ancient Bulgars. The Chuvash Republic (an internal republic within Russia) is south of Moscow in central European Russia—a location that has placed them in close contact with the Russians since the 1500s, a contact that has often involved hostility. Chuvash requests for autonomy have been regularly rejected by the Russians, and occasional revolts have been successfully put down. Still, as the largest group in the district, they have enjoyed some political influence in Soviet affairs. Forced conversion to Eastern Orthodoxy has meant that many are only nominal adherents, and Chuvash indigenous religious practices still survive. Chuvash elsewhere in Russia live in neighboring regions and Siberia.

Less successful than the Chuvash in resisting Russian control have been the other regional minorities. **Tuvans** number 207,000 in Russia, with about 198,000 living in the Tuvan autonomous region in south-central Siberia. The Tuvans emerged as a distinct group in the 18th century through the merging of various indigenous and immigrant groups in the region. They have, at times, been under Chinese, Mongolian, and Russian control. In the Soviet era, their region was mined for asbestos, which led to serious environmental and health problems. They are Buddhists, and in the post-Soviet era there have been attempts to revive the traditional culture, although Tuvans have only limited interest in political autonomy.

Udmurt (Votyak) number 750,000 and live primarily in their own internal autonomous republic in the central part of European Russia. They have been under the control of various groups since their emergence as a distinct group in the 6th century. Russian influence has been important since the 12th century although Udmurt culture did not change drastically until the industrial development and collectivization of the Soviet era. Still, the Udmurt language survives, as does the traditional religion with elements added from Russian Orthodoxy and Islam, and a long tradition of education in Udmurt culture guarantees the survival of the Udmurt culture in the post-Soviet era.

The **Bashkir,** who are Muslims, are a formerly pastoral people who now are mostly farmers or industrial workers. Most of the nearly 1.34 million Bashkirs live in Bashkirstan in west-central Russia. They constitute only 24% of the republic's population and therefore are a minority compared with the Russians (38%) and Tatars (30%). Russification and Sovietization, as well as contact with the Tatars, have altered Bashkir culture. Most Bashkir people now live in isolated farming collectives, a factor that reduces the likelihood of ethnic conflict in their multicultural region.

Maris (Cheremis) number 670,000, about 50% of whom live in the Maris Republic in central European Russia. The remainder live in neighboring regions. As nomadic hunter-gathers in the region for 1,000 years, they drew attention as a distinct ethnic group only from the late 1800s on, when they appeared to be a possible threat to Russian sovereignty. Although they are now settled farmer and industrial workers, their language and indigenous religion have been retained.

In addition to these regional groups, there are a few other distinct ethnic groups. **Kets** are a small, formerly nomadic hunter-gatherer group of western Siberia. Under Russian influence since the 17th century, they became reindeer herders and then settled farmers and herders. Their population has declined over the centuries, first due to disease and then due to intermarriage with Russians and others. They now number about 1,000. Most speak both Ket and Russian, and their religion is a mix of the indigenous belief system and Russian Orthodoxy. Due to their small size and Russian settlement, it is questionable whether they will survive as a distinct culture.

The **Khakas** formed as a distinct ethnic group over several centuries, beginning in the 17th century, from the fusing of Uighur, Kety, Tubian, Samoyed, and Shor tribal units. They gained official recognition in the 1920s. The five major regional Khakas groups are the Kacha, Kyzyl, Sagai, Beltir, and Koibal and most of them (66,000) live in Khakassia in south-central Russia. Russians, however, constitute 80% of the population in that region. Most Khakas now speak Russian and as many as 50% of younger people marry Russians. In the post-Soviet era, Khakas are seeking either an independent region or greater political power, but both of these appeals are resisted by the Russians. There is also a movement to choose a new name to replace "Khakas," which was selected by the Russians.

Komi number 336,000 in northeastern Russia and on the Kola Peninsula in western Siberia. The Komi can be divided into three groups: the Komi, Komi Permyak, and Izhmi. Contact with Russians began in the late 15th century. Due to trade routes in the region, Russian settlement, and the spread of Eastern Orthodoxy, the Komi are now largely assimilated into Russian society. An effort to expand use of the Komi language began in the late 1980s.

Mordovians number 1.1 million and live in south-central European Russia. Conquest by the Russians goes back 900 years, and over time, there has been a slow but steady assimilation into Russian society. The population has been steadily declining through assimilation in the 20th century, and few still speak Mordovinian.

Shor is a generic label used by the Soviet government for a number of small groups in southern Siberia whose total population is about 16,000. The Shor proper were known as miners and blacksmiths. Russian exploitation of the region and Shor resistance led to aggressive assimilation programs that caused a decline in the traditional language, economy, and culture. Most Shor are now wage laborers or farmers, and there is some doubt that there will be a revitalization of the traditional culture in the post-Soviet era.

Religious Minorities

Finally, in addition to these ethnic groups, there are a number of distinct religious minorities in Russia, whose members may also be regarded as ethnic groups. The most prominent are the **Jews,** who in Russia fall into three groups: Ashkenazi Jews, Karaites, and Krymchaks. **Ashkenazi Jews,** or European Jews, are Jews of Central and Eastern Europe whose ancestors first settled in Germany. Jews have had a major presence in Eastern Europe since A.D. 1500, and they came under Russian control through the expansion of the Russian Empire and through immigration to Russian territory. Ashkenazi Jews in Russia share a history with Jews in Poland, Lithuania, Belarus, and Ukraine, and all were governed under the same policies, whose effects remain today. Parts of these Eastern European nations formed the Pale of Settlement, a region where the Jews were forced to live from 1791 to 1917, although there were periods of greater tolerance when some Jews moved to cities, and in the late 1800s and early 1900s, many immigrated to North America. During the Soviet era, Jews enjoyed greater freedom, although religious practice was repressed and anti-Semitism—often in the form of blaming economic problems on Jews—remained common, especially in rural areas. Following the relaxation of emigration restrictions in the mid-1980s, hundreds of thousands left Russia for Israel and the United States (*see also* Israel).

Karaites are Jews who follow only the Five Books of the Bible and, unlike Rabbinic Jews, ignore subsequent teachings and writings. They have been present in Russia since the 13th century and today number fewer than 2,000. They are mainly scattered in large cities. The majority of Karaites in the world live in Israel.

Krymchaks number only about 1,500 in Russia and live in Crimea, on the north shore of the Black Sea in southern Russia. Although Jews have lived in Crimea for over 2,000 years, the Krymchaks emerged as a distinct group about 500 years ago, probably through the merging of groups already there with new Jewish arrivals from the Middle East and southern Europe. Following World War II and to avoid anti-Semitism, the Krymchaks claimed that they were actually descended from non-Jewish ancient peoples and had converted to Judaism. Although this claim was not widely accepted, they are now assimilated into Russian society.

Old Believers are a second major religious minority. They are people of a number of religious sects that broke from the Russian Orthodox Church in 1650 and were condemned by the Church and the Russian government in 1667 (however, the condemnation was lifted by the Church in 1971). The cause of the break was a reform of Church ritual in accord with Greek Orthodoxy, which Old Believers interpreted as a threat to Russian culture. Often the object of persecution since their break with the Church, they have become a worldwide diaspora, with about one million in Russia and other former Soviet republics. Major sects are the Belokrinitsy, Fugitive Priestly, Pomorians, Edinoverie, Chappellers, Wanderers, and Saviorites. They tend to marry within their groups, farm or work in marginal occupations, and generally remain outside mainstream Russian society, although some of the less extreme groups are permitted to hold services in public.

Assyrians number about 9,000 and live mainly in major cities such as Moscow. While their religion and language mark them as a distinct group, they are too small to be of political and economic influence and are largely ignored by Russians and other groups.

Ethnic Relations

The framework for ethnic relations within Russia today and relations between Russians and other groups in former Soviet republics were set by two processes: Russification and Sovietization. Russification, which began as early as the 14th century in European Russia, refers to the process through which Russians achieved cultural, economic, and political dominance over the ethnic groups of Russia and other lands under their control. Russification was a form of colonialism that lasted until the 1920s, when it was replaced by Sovietization, a similar process.

Key features of Russification were the settlement of Russians and other Slavs (mainly Ukrainians and Belarusians) in non-Russian regions, Russian control of the local and regional economies and political systems, centralized rule from Moscow, replacement of indigenous languages with Russian, suppression of indigenous religions, conversion of subject peoples to Russian Orthodoxy, and the forced settlement of formerly nomadic peoples. Russification altered all of the non-Russian cultures of Russia and destroyed some of them. Cultures that were drastically changed by Russification are referred to as Russified, although usually at least some traditions were maintained, and many groups are now attempting to revive their indigenous languages, reduce Russian economic and political influence, and reverse environmental destruction of their lands caused by Russian and Soviet economic development programs. However, schools, hospitals, towns, factories, farms, and even features of the associated social order established by Russians are likely to remain.

The fall of the Russian Empire and the Bolshevik Revolution ended Russification. But, by the 1920s it was replaced by Sovietization, which retained three key features of Russification: replacement of indigenous languages with Russian, Russian settlement in non-Russian areas, and Russian control of the economy. Sovietization differed, however, in that its avowed goal was not expansion of the Russian Empire. Instead, its purpose was to suppress ethnic and regional loyalties, allegedly so that all people would prosper from being members of the Soviet state. Sovietization especially emphasized economic change, and in accord with Communist principles, private property was abolished, property ownership passed to the state, and workers were organized into various forms of collectives. In addition, the Russian Orthodox religion and other religions were banned. During the rule of Josef Stalin from 1926 to 1953, persecution of non-Russian groups was especially harsh, and millions of people accused of disloyalty were killed or forcibly relocated, including entire ethnic populations. As with Russification, Sovietization not only involved peoples in Russia, but peoples in all of the republics that formed the Soviet Union. Also as part of Sovietization, a number of semi-independent ethnic republics, regions, and districts were established in Russia. In theory, the ethnic group for which the republic was named was to have a considerable measure of autonomy; in practice, many of these regions were heavily populated by Russians who exerted significant influence, and the government in Moscow maintained control.

Following the Soviet government's policy of "openness" and greater freedom for constituent republics and ethnic groups that began in the mid-1980s and the partial shift to a market economy a few years later, the Soviet Union disintegrated. By 1991, all of the former republics of the Soviet Union were independent nations, some allied as the Commonwealth of Independent States. Russia was again a single nation, not the center of an empire, although a nation with over 100 ethnic groups within its borders. In addition, millions of ethnic Russians still lived outside of Russia in the former Soviet republics, where—no longer supported by the government in Moscow—they had become an ethnic minority that the local people sought to displace.

In post-Soviet Russia, ethnic relations in the 1990s are characterized by six major trends:

- The revival of strong ethnic nationalism sentiments among most national and regional groups, which has led to many revolts against Russian rule. The longest and bloodiest of these has been the Russians' war with the Chechens in the Caucasus over Chechen independence.
- An indigenous rights movement among the Peoples of the North and other small groups who seek cultural autonomy and are attempting to revive their traditional cultures, especially their languages and religions. These peoples also seek to halt the Russian economic exploitation of natural resources in their regions, which has already caused catastrophic environmental damage in some locales.
- A revival of anti-Semitism and anti-Gypsy sentiment, despite the fact that many Jews have left and continue to leave Russia, and Gypsies are few in number. Both groups are scapegoated for Russia's economic problems.
- Ethnic conflict between rivals for economic and political control in some regions. Most rivalry involves Russians and a local ethnic group, but some is

between two non-Russian groups. This pattern is especially true in major cities, where groups such as Armenians—who have long occupied roles as merchants and traders—are blamed for post-Soviet economic woes. Another basis for these emerging ethnic conflicts is religious differences; for example, non-Christians such as Azerbaijani Muslims are discriminated against in Russian cities.

- The reemergence of religion—and especially Russian Orthodoxy and Islam—as major features of life in Russia. Islam is an especially salient and unifying force in the Caucasus, and some groups such as the Kumyk and Lak have joined the global pan-Islamic movement and are developing ties to Turkey, Azerbaijan, and Middle Eastern Islamic nations. The Russians see strong Islamic beliefs and ties to other Islamic societies as a threat to Russian control of the region.

- Continuing discrimination against immigrant groups such as Greeks and Germans who—despite generations of residence in Russia—have never fully assimilated into Russian society.

In the post-Soviet era, government controls on ethnic conflict have disappeared, and European ethnic minorities are seen by Russians as competitors for scarce jobs and economic resources. The response of these minority groups has been both to seek greater political autonomy in Russia and to return to their homelands to escape discrimination.

San Marino

T he Most Serene Republic of San Marino is a very small nation located on the northeast coast of Italy. Its population of 24,000 is almost entirely of Italian ancestry, Italian is the official language, and nearly all **Sanmarinese** are Roman Catholic. San Marino is the last survivor of the independent states that developed in the region following the fall of the Roman Empire; others were incorporated into the nation of Italy in 1861. As an ethnically homogeneous nation, ethnic relations are not an issue.

Slovakia

S lovakia is a nation in Central Europe bordered by the Czech Republic on the northwest, Poland on the north, Ukraine on the east, Hungary on the south, and Austria on the southwest. Slovakia has a population of 5,432,000. The country was ruled by the Hungarians (Magyars) from 907 until 1918, during which time most Slovaks were serfs who worked the land owned by Hungarian nobles. The current boundaries of Slovakia were established at the end of World War II, when it formed the eastern region of Czechoslovakia. Slovakia became an independent nation on January 1, 1993, following the peaceful dissolution of Czechoslovakia. The breakup was precipitated by Slovak nationalists who believed Slovakia would benefit from independence from Czech political and economic control.

Ethnic Composition

About 85% of the population is Slovak. Hungarians and Gypsies are the two major ethnic minorities. **Slovaks** are an East Slavic people who ancestors arrived in Central Europe in the 7th century or earlier. In Slovakia they number 4.6 million, with about 1 million Slovaks living elsewhere in Europe and North America.

Traditionally a rural, farming population, Slovaks continue to live mainly in villages or towns and practice farming both for subsistence and for the market. Slovak Christianity, both in Roman Catholic and Protestant forms, is syncretic with pre-Christian religious practices such as divination, the evil eye, and witchcraft, especially in rural areas.

Hungarians are the major ethnic minority and number about 600,000. They are concentrated along the border between Slovakia and Hungary. In some districts they are the majority population, and many live in exclusively Hungarian settlements. Most Hungarians in Slovakia speak Hungarian, although bilinguality with Slovak is not uncommon. Slovak resentment over Hungarian dominance during the 1,000 years of Hungarian rule, as well as fears about Hungarian annexation of Slovakian territory, have led to the repression of Hungarian language and culture.

Gypsies, including Rom, Sinti, and Vlach, have been in the former Czechoslovakia for at least 600 years. Today about 335,000 live in Slovakia, many in the eastern part of the country. Under Hungarian rule, Gypsies escaped persecution and became a settled population that provided specialized services to farm communities. Hungarian Gypsies escaped the genocide of other Gypsy groups in World War II, and under Communist assimilation policies agitated for increased rights. Today, while culturally distinct and to some extent residentially isolated, they are assimilated into the Slovakian economy.

Two smaller ethnic groups are the Carpatho-Rusyns and Poles. **Carpatho-Rusyns** are a people whose traditional homeland is on the south and north slopes of the Carpathian Mountains. When the portion of their homeland within Slovakia was given to Ukraine in 1945, the Carpatho-Rusyn population in Slokavia decreased markedly. They now number about 130,000 and are of little threat to Slovakian sovereignty.

Poles, numbering about 80,000, live in the mining region on the northern end of the border with Slovakia. Their numbers in Slovakia are increased substantially by Polish workers and tourists who frequently cross the border.

Ethnic Relations

Slovak relations with their former co-nationalists, the Czechs, are peaceful. In ethnic relations with the Hungarians, a major concern for the Slovaks is to control possible separatist or irredentist desires on the part of the large Hungarian minority. In general, relations with the Hungarians are hostile, and the government has instituted various policies such as requiring use of the Slovak language in all public places. These measures are seen by the Hungarians as an attempt either to assimilate them into Slovak society or to drive them out of the country. Hungarians have resisted such pressures, but there is no mass movement for a return to Hungary or for annexation. Similarly, Slovak fear of losing the border region where Poles live to Poland has led to efforts to control the political influence of Poles in that region.

Slovenia

T he Republic of Slovenia is a small nation in southern Europe, bordered on the north by Austria, on the east by Hungary, on the south by Croatia, and on the west by Italy. Slovenia has a population of about 2 million.

The region now called Slovenia has been inhabited by Slavic peoples, including the Slovenes, since the early 7th century. For much of their history, the Slovenes were under German control or influence, and in 1918 were joined with the Croats and Serbs in the Kingdom of the Serbs, Croats, and Slovenes, the predecessor to Yugoslavia, which was formed in 1945.

In 1991 the Slovenes declared independence from the Yugoslavian federation, quickly defeated a Serb-led military intervention, and became the Republic of Slovenia. Slovenia's status as the most economically stable of the Yugoslavian republics, the relative cultural distance from ethnic groups in other republics, the absence of a common border with Serbia, the homogeneous population of Slovenia, and ties to neighboring nations all were factors in the relatively smooth transition to independence.

Ethnic Composition

The population of Slovenia is ethnically homogeneous: 91% of the population is Slovene and 94% is Roman Catholic. The major minorities are the Croats, Serbs, Bosnians, Italians, and Gypsies, although none play major roles in Slovenian society. There are also Slovene populations across the borders in Austria, Hungary, and Italy, and an overseas community in the United States. Alleged mistreatment of Slovenes in Italy continues to be an issue for both nations. In addition to the ethnic groups listed above, Slovenia continues to give refuge to about 30,000 refugees from Bosnia and Croatia.

Slovenes number about 1.82 million. Shifting political borders have left Slovene populations in neighboring Austria, Italy, and Hungary where they total about 100,000. Slovenes are classified as Southern Slavs, and Slovene is a Slavic language although there are dozens of regional dialects, some of which are not mutually intelligible. Slovenes are Roman Catholics, and since independence the Church has assumed a greater role in Slovenian society.

Former Yugoslavians are primarily **Croats,** who number about 60,000 (3% of the population) and **Serbs,** who number about 40,000 (2% of the population). Because of Slovene-Serb and to a lesser extent Slovene-Croat differences over the structure of Yugoslavia, these groups live in an uneasy, though peaceful, relationship with the Slovenes. Since independence, and without support from their co-ethnics in Croatia and Serbia, these peoples in Slovenia have had little influence in Slovenian affairs.

Other groups include **Italians** who number about 35,000, **Austrians**, **Hungarians**, and **Gypsies**.

Ethnic Relations

Within the Yugoslavian federation before independence, Slovenes consistently argued for weak centralized authority and considerable autonomy for the constituent republics. That position created tensions between the Slovenes and the Serbs (who favored strong central control) and between the Slovenes and the Croats (who also sometimes favored central control). Because of the differing views on republic autonomy in Yugoslavia, there have often been tensions between the Slovenes and the Serbs and Croats, both within and outside Slovenia.

Spain

S pain is the larger of the two countries (the smaller being Portugal) located on the Iberian peninsula in southwestern Europe. It is bounded by Portugal on the southwest, France on the northeast, the Mediterranean Sea on the southeast, the Strait of Gibraltar on the south, the Atlantic Ocean on the northwest and the Bay of Biscay on the north. Spain also includes the Balearic Islands in the Mediterranean Sea, the Canary Islands in the Atlantic Ocean, and two urban areas in north Africa, Ceuta and Melilla. To some extent isolated from mainstream European affairs for some centuries, Spain remained neutral during both World War I and World War II. During the rule of Generalissimo Francisco Franco, Spain was essentially ostracized from much of Europe because of Franco's Fascist ties and dictatorial rule. Following Franco's death in 1975, Spain established closer ties with Western Europe and the United States and became recognized as a democratic society.

Spain has a population of 39.5 million and is ethnically heterogeneous. Castilian Spanish is the official language, but an estimated 25% of Spanish citizens use another language in their homes. The 1978 constitution allows Catalan, Valencian, Euskera (the Basque language), Galician, and Majorcan to be considered co-official with Castilian Spanish.

Ethnic Composition

While the overwhelming majority of the residents of Spain identify themselves as Spaniards, there are also a number of distinct regional minorities and linguistic minorities, and in recent years, an increasing number of foreign workers. Among the regional and linguistic minorities, the Basques are the only group actively engaged in an ethnic separatist movement, while the Catalans continue to press the government for greater regional autonomy. Other regional groups, including the Andalusians, Castilians, Galicians, and Leonese, are largely integrated into Spanish society. In addition, Spain has a growing population of immigrants from other parts of the world who choose to live there because of employment opportunities, low costs, and the favorable climate. Official estimates suggest that there are about 400,000 individuals from other nations currently in Spain. This is probably an undercount, especially in regard to people who immigrate there from North Africa. Immigration to Spain, particularly from elsewhere in Europe and the Americas, was motivated by the low housing costs from the 1960s on and by the opportunities provided for business development by economic expansion in Spain. During most of that period, however, Spain was also a country of emigration, as many Spaniards left for countries in western and northern Europe to work in the tourism, construction, and other industries. Since the 1980s, some of them have returned to Spain, while others have immigrated with their families and have evidently chosen to stay in these other nations, such as Switzerland, Belgium, the Netherlands, and France.

Spain has a number of native populations. In addition to the Spaniards, there are the Andalusians, Basques, Catalans, Galicians, Canarians, Leonese, and Herders of the North. **Spaniard** is a national cultural designation rather than a name for a specific ethnic group.

Spain was settled over a period of thousands of years by Iberians, Goths, and Celtic peoples, and the Moors ruled part or virtually all of the Iberian peninsula from A.D. 711 to 1429, when Spain was unified under the Crown of Castile. Modern Spain and the modern Spanish people reflect all of these ancient influences, integrated with influences from the various regional cultures, including the Catalans, Leonese, Andalusians, and Galicians. Because of its political domination, modern Spain strongly reflects Castilian cultural influences, including Roman Catholicism (to which 95% of the population adheres), and the use of the Castilian dialect of Spanish as the official language. The Castilian influence is felt most in overseas Spanish communities and former colonies, particularly in the New World.

The four major regional groups that continue to maintain some degree of cultural autonomy are the Basques, Canarians, Catalans, and Galicians.

Basques live in northern Spain on both sides of the border between Spain and France. They number approximately 3 million in that region, 90% of whom live in Spain. The Basques refer to the region as Euskadi, meaning Country of the Basque. The origins of the Basque people are unknown, and their language is unrelated to any other language of Europe. Nevertheless, they have been a known population in the region for 1,000 years and have successfully resisted rule by various groups, including the Romans, Moors, French, and Castiles. The Basque region is one of the fastest growing and most rapidly developing regions of Spain. It is considered a highly desirable region in which to live and do business, and there has been a major influx of Spaniards into the region. The Basques are now a minority in Euskadi. The unique sense of Basque identity is based on a number of factors, including their long residence in the region; their resistance to outside rule; the

Basque language (although it is now the primary language of only a minority of Basques), adherence to Roman Catholicism; a focus on strong nuclear family units; and indigenous arts, recreational activities, games, and sports, such as jailai.

Canarians are inhabitants of the Canary Islands, which has been an autonomous division of Spain since 1982. There are approximately 1.7 million Canarians in the Canary Islands and there is a very large immigrant population, especially in the Americas, with substantial Canarian communities in the United States, Cuba, and Venezuela. Canarians are descended from African peoples, primarily Berbers, who initially settled the islands and then intermarried with the Spanish after Spanish colonization. Culturally, the islands also reflect influences from France, Portugal, the United States, and Great Britain. Canarians are Spaniards in the sense that they speak Spanish, are mainly Roman Catholic, and are administratively part of Spain. On the other hand, they see themselves (and are generally perceived by others) as being a distinct ethnic group. Over the centuries, they have developed their own traditions, their own dialect of Spanish, and their own form of Roman Catholicism, which reflects indigenous beliefs and practices. Canarians make a clear distinction between themselves and other Spaniards, whom they call *Peninsulares.*

Catalans are the people of Catalonia, which is in eastern Spain. Catalan populations also live across the border in France, on the Balearic Islands in the Mediterranean Sea, in Andorra, and in Sardinia. In all, there are about 6.5 million Catalans in the world, of whom about 5.7 million live in Catalonia. Although there are a number of markers of Catalan identity such as residence in Catalonia and having Catalan parents, the most important is speaking the Catalan language. It is estimated that about 80% of the people of Catalonia speak Catalan as their domestic language, although most also speak Castilian Spanish. Catalonia, beginning in the Middle Ages, was an independent political unit, one of a number of such units on the Mediterranean Sea. In 1714 it was conquered by the Castilians and absorbed into the Spanish state.

Galicians are the residents of Galicia, a section of Spain located in the northwest and bordered on the south by Portugal. Galicians are of Celtic ancestry and, therefore, are related to the Celtic peoples of Brittany in France, Cornwall in England, and the Gaels of Ireland. About 80% of Galicians speak their native language, although all also speak Castilian Spanish. Nearly all are Roman Catholic. Galicia is a poor agricultural region of Spain that has been late to develop economically, although since the 1980s tourism has developed there and property near the coast is considered highly desirable. There is no major separatist or autonomy movement in Galicia, although some Galicians are lobbying the government for greater autonomy.

Herders of Northern Spain is a general label for a number of culturally related peoples, all together numbering perhaps 10,000 to 15,000, who live in the Cantabrian mountain range of northern Spain. Included in this category are groups such as the **Pasiegos,** the **Maragotos,** the **Vacaros de el Zada,** and the **Santandar.** While all are clearly related to the other people of Spanish ancestry in Spain, in the 20th century their ethnohistory has been redefined by outsiders and they are sometimes described as being non-Spanish. They speak an ancient dialect of Spanish, have traditionally lived by raising and breeding cattle in the mountains, and are Roman Catholic. Rather than being a distinct ethnic group, it seems more likely that they are a Spanish subgroup that—because of residence in the mountains, a focus on herding as a livelihood, and relative isolation from the rest of Spanish society—has been seen as a completely different group.

Like the Herders, **Gypsies** also occupy a unique position in Spanish society, with their identity defined by location, occupation, and ancestry. Gypsies in Spain number anywhere between 50,000 and 500,000, or even more. In Spain there are two general Gypsy populations. The first are **Gitanos,** who live primarily in southern Spain, where they work in the tourism industry and in entertainment. To a large extent, Gitanos are assimilated into Spanish society, even though they continue to occupy particular economic niches. The second major Gypsy population is called **Hungaros.** They are Central European Rom Gypsies who evidently migrated to Spain from Hungary and now live primarily in northern Spain. Their experience resembles more closely that of European Gypsies, and they suffer continual discrimination. In the past, Hungaros were largely nomadic, but they are now more settled and work in low-level jobs while living outside of mainstream Spanish society.

From the 15th century to the 19th century, Spain was a major colonial power, and that history is reflected to some extent in the current population. **North and South Americans** in Spain include 32,000 people from North and Central America and 48,750 from South America. They constitute 19.7% of the foreign population of Spain. The largest number are **Argentinians**, numbering almost 18,000, a substantial portion of these being ethnic Spaniards who had settled in Argentina but returned to Spain because of the Argentinian political and economic unrest of the 1980s. **People from the United States** number 16,000; **Venezuelans** 9,300; and **Cubans** 5,100.

Ceuta and Melilla are two Spanish colonies on the north coast of Morocco, with a total population of about 120,000. The population is composed of **Spaniards, African Moroccans,** and people of mixed ancestry. Spanish control of Ceuta and Melilla is contested by the Moroccan government, which clearly wishes for the Spaniards to leave so that Morocco could take control of the two communities. The Spanish government, however, has refused to relinquish control, even though there has been political and ethnic violence in both communities directed at getting the Spanish to leave. On the other hand, a significant portion of the Muslims in both communities prefer that the Spanish remain in control so that they can continue to benefit from the tourist trade. At the same time, they realize that they are second-class citizens in comparison with the Spaniards who live there, and they have petitioned the government for new laws that will protect their religious, language, and cultural rights.

Spanish colonization in North Africa and the region's proximity to the continent are factors in the growing number of **Africans** in Spain, who come primarily from North Africa and West Africa. The number of Africans in Spain is officially estimated to be 26,000, but unofficial figures suggest that in the 1990s there are over 100,000, most of them Moroccans. They have been entering Spain because of the job opportunities, particularly in tourism, construction, and industry. Of all the immigrant groups in Spain, it is the Africans who suffer the most discrimination. African immigrants and their advocates have argued that the Foreigner Law of 1985 has been applied inconsistently—that they are denied fair access to jobs and that other non-African groups are given preference in hiring.

Europeans number 270,000 in Spain, making this the largest non-Spanish population group in the country. Of these, 18% are **Britons;** 11% are **Germans;** 8% are **Portuguese;** and 7% are **French.** Smaller numbers of **Dutch, Italians,** and **Belgians** also live in Spain. Many Europeans in Spain live on the Mediterranean coast and are retired or have established businesses there to take advantage of the relatively low living costs that persisted in Spain up until the 1990s.

Asians are a very small group in Spain. They number only 29,000, the largest groups being Filipinos (7,400) and Chinese (4,100). In both of these groups, a large number of individuals work in low-level jobs in tourism and industry.

Ethnic Relations

While Spain is, in general, free of ethnic strife, there are three major ongoing ethnic conflicts, one of which has caused major disruptions in some parts of the country. The primary ethnic conflict involves the Basque separatist movement in the north. This movement began early in the 20th century when Spanish workers moved into the Basque region. Since then, this ethnic conflict has resulted in nearly 1,000 deaths, has involved terrorist bombings and attacks on Spanish citizens and government officials, and has led to the presence of the paramilitary civil guard in the region to control violence. The movement has also caused splits in the Basque community over whether they want separatism and a separate nation or to be an autonomous region within Spain. In 1996, the conflict was still unresolved. Terrorist attacks by the Basques and oppression of Basques by the Spanish government continue. On the French side of the border where only about 300,000 Basques live, there is no major separatism movement, although the French government has cracked down on separatists there in response to claims by the Spanish government that the French Basque separatists were hiding Spanish Basque leaders.

Demands for autonomy by the Catalans in Eastern Spain have generally been nonviolent. Under the Franco regime in the 20th century, efforts were made to end Catalonian linguistic and cultural independence, and Catalonian-language presses were shut down, Castilian Spanish was imposed as the official language, Catalan people were deported and executed, and various social and cultural activities that were defined as Catalan were banned. In 1975, at the end of Franco's rule, Catalonia slowly emerged as a semi-autonomous political unit within Spain, and since that time, Catalan has been recognized as a co-official language in Spain. The region has become economically developed, and many Castilian speakers have immigrated there, making the native Catalans a minority. However, unlike the Basque region, there is little call for Catalan separatism.

The third conflict focuses on the increasing number of immigrants coming from Africa, particularly Morocco, who are perceived as taking jobs that Spaniards want. The new African immigrants also include a large number who are undocumented. New laws and harsher enforcement of existing laws have apparently slowed the flow of immigrants from North Africa. Part of Spain's difficulty in dealing with foreign immigrants is that it was traditionally not a country that foreigners immigrated to, and until 1985 there was no legislation dealing with the status, rights, and freedoms of non-Spaniards living in Spain. Legislation enacted in 1985, commonly referred to as the "Foreigners Law," was designed to correct this situation and to regulate the management of immigrants. While it has been successful to some degree in standardizing policy, it has also been criticized by some as being applied in a discriminatory manner to Africans, with immigrants from other parts of the world given preference in jobs and housing.

Sweden

S weden is a Nordic nation located on the Scandinavian peninsula in northwestern Europe. It is bordered by the three other Nordic nations—Norway to the west, Finland to the northeast, and Denmark to the southwest. The Gulf of Bothnia is to the east, the Baltic Sea to the southeast, and the North Sea to the southwest. The main regions of Sweden are Norrland, which consists of the northern mountain and lake region; Svealand, which is the lowlands region of central Sweden; and the low Smaland highlands and the plains of Skane, which are in Gotaland. About 15% of the country lies within the Arctic Circle, and climatic differences are substantial. Sweden has a population of 8,821,700.

Ethnic Composition

About 89% of the people in Sweden are ethnic Swedes; the other 11% consists of people from 166 different nations and an even greater number of ethnic groups. Thus, while Sweden is essentially homogeneous ethnically, it is also ethnically diverse. Liberal social values and policies have ensured that many minority groups have been able to maintain their cultural traditions while also enjoying the benefits of Swedish citizenship.

The ethnic complexity of Swedish society today is a recent development—prior to World War II, Sweden was extremely homogeneous in language and ethnic composition. The nation had a nationalistic, antiforeigner bias that was reflected in restrictive policies directed at non-Nordic immigrants. The belief underlying these policies was set forth in a 1927 bill before the Swedish Parliament, which stated that "the population of Sweden consists of an unusually unitary and blended race . . . the value of this can hardly be overestimated." Other than Nordic immigrants, only a trickle of German, Walloon, Dutch, and Scottish immigrants found their way to Sweden from the Middle Ages on.

During World War II, Sweden was a neutral nation, and thousands of refugees fled to Sweden, primarily from Denmark, Norway, and Finland but also from Estonia, Latvia, and Lithuania. Sweden's immigration policy changed, and migration to Sweden increased dramatically after the war. Population losses in many countries and lower birth rates combined with economic reconstruction programs created a demand for labor in Western Europe that could not be met within the countries themselves. Sweden, because of its neutral status during the war, was more prepared for postwar economic expansion than most other European countries, and along with Switzerland, was the first to open its gates to foreign labor. As a center of migration, it attracted streams of migrations from the Baltic area (1944–45), Poland (the years around 1945), Hungary (1956), and Yugoslavia.

Although labor migration ended in 1972, family members of earlier migrants have continued to arrive since then, and their children make up about 20% of the non-Swedish population. Sweden's liberal immigration and refugee policies, its willingness to grant citizenship to non-Swedes, and its acceptance of non-Swedish cultures have encouraged immigrants, refugees, and asylum-seekers to come to Sweden and settle there. About 50% of the non-Swedes living in the country are citizens, and Sweden ranks first in the world in the acceptance of refugees, with a ratio of one person settled or granted asylum per 47 residents of the nation.

Swedes number 7.85 million and constitute 89% of the population of Sweden. They are descended from reindeer hunters who followed the herds from Central Europe to Sweden about 14,000 years ago. Although Sweden is traditionally an agrarian country, agriculture has virtually disappeared as a livelihood and has been replaced by manufacturing and services.

In addition to the Swedes, the **Saami (Lapps)** form another indigenous population. The Saami are the indigenous people of the tundra, taiga, and coastal zones north of latitude 62°. They number roughly 17,000, the majority of whom live in northern Sweden, although a large number also live in Stockholm. Their traditional mode of subsistence is reindeer herding, but they are also engaged in farming, fishing, and entrepreneurial pursuits. Early contacts between Saami and Swedes came through traders and tax collectors. Initially, Swedish authorities viewed the Saami simply as reindeer herders, and a policy emerged that was aimed at economic and ethnic segregation. The Swedish government introduced "agricultural borders" *(odlingsgransen)* in 1867 so that different peoples could exploit different features of the environment. The mountain plateaus did not suit the needs of the Swedish farmer, but they did accommodate the wide-ranging economic activities of the Saami, particularly their reindeer herding. By the end of the 19th century, the Swedish policy toward the Saami could be summed up as "let the Saami be Saami."

The attitude of Swedish authorities to Saami culture has changed dramatically since World War II. An integral part of the new policy has been the acceptance of Saami cultural and social life as a responsibility of the state. The Swedish government coordinates activities centrally and delegates tasks to specifically Saami organizations. While traces of paternalism may still be present in Swedish policy, the Saami enjoy the freedom to pursue their own interests as a distinct ethnic group.

Sweden also has a sizable population of people from the three other Nordic nations. **Danes** are the fifth largest non-Swedish group, numbering 278,000. Danes, as well as Finns and Norwegians, have migrated to Sweden for centuries within a framework of extensive political cooperation. In 1954, work permits and visa requirements for Danes, Finns, and Norwegians were abolished, which further encouraged migration between the Nordic countries. Danes, like other Nordic immigrants to Sweden, experience "positive discrimination" (favored treatment) and can count on easy access to jobs and housing. Danes have assimilated readily, usually within a generation or two, and traces of their ancestral culture essentially disappear by the third generation. In the last half-century, relations between the people of the Nordic countries have become even closer. The main basis for this integration is their shared language, culture, and history. Relations between Danes and Swedes are excellent, more like intra-ethnic relations than interethnic relations. There is, for example, long-range congruence of citizenship laws that give Danes, and other Nordic citizens, extensive rights in Sweden.

Finns are the largest non-Swedish ethnic group in Sweden, numbering between 250,000 and 380,000, depending on whether those who have become Swedish citizens are counted. They live primarily in the north. Finns in Sweden have a history that goes back several hundred years. Their migration into Sweden can be traced from the southern and eastern areas of Finland in the 1600s. From the 1600s on, the Finns colonized the uninhabited western areas of central Sweden. After 1945, the flow of immigrants from Finland to Sweden was the largest of all inter-Nordic migrations—as large as the mass emigrations from Finland to America in the late 19th and early 20th centuries, and reached a climax around 1970. The pattern of Finnish immigration to Sweden after World War II was largely dictated by Sweden's large demand for labor, which shifted from agriculture to industry, and Finnish settlement shifted from rural to urban. Language was another strong selection factor—many of the Finns who migrated to Sweden spoke Swedish. The relations between Swedes and the Finnish minority have historically been harmonious. However, Finland's ties to Russia generated feelings of distrust among Swedes, which, in turn, affected immigration policies and the treatment of Finns.

This began changing in the 1950s, and in 1958 the prohibition against speaking Finnish at school was abolished. In 1970, experiments using Finnish as the first language began. In 1987, Finns in the Torne Valley of Sweden were given partial minority status, reflecting their preference for living in Finnish communities and the number of Finnish associations that had developed.

Norwegians in Sweden number 38,000, making them the nation's fourth largest non-Swedish ethnic group. A Norwegian refugee community developed in Sweden when Norway was occupied by Germany during World War II, and nearly 45,000 Norwegians found temporary refuge there. Norwegians, like Danes and Finns, enjoy high social status in Sweden and are readily assimilated into Swedish society.

Sweden also has significant populations from Western and Eastern Europe. The major Western European groups are the Germans and British. **Germans** in Sweden number 13,000. They have made their way to Sweden over the centuries, and a large proportion of them have been artisans and professionals whose contributions have been welcomed. **British** settlers number about 10,000.

Jews in Sweden number about 15,000. In 1938–40, Jews who fled Germany were not considered political refugees, and their chances of entering Sweden were minimal. In 1943, Sweden provided assistance and refuge to 6,000 Danish Jews who escaped over the Straits of Oresund. The Swedish government was well aware that this act would be considered a "good deed" in the eyes of the world and also in the eyes of the potential victors. Sweden also saw this as a way to demonstrate sympathy with the Danes and Denmark. The Swedish rescue action paved the way for a more positive stance towards the victims of the war and may have set the course for Sweden's subsequent immigration and ethnic policies.

Eastern Europeans came to Sweden, and later to other Scandinavian countries, following an increase in the demand for labor following World War II. **Poles** number about 16,000. When they first arrived in the 1940s and 1950s, Swedes expected them to become

Swedes, adopt Swedish manners and customs, and become integrated into Swedish society. After the reforms of the 1980s, Swedish expectations changed. Despite high levels of integration, a majority of Polish migrants continue to harbor strong feelings of attachment to their country of origin and a desire for eventual return. This means that these immigrants participate in two sociocultural systems—Swedish and Polish.

Yugoslavians arrived in the 1960s and they now number about 41,000. About 50% are **Serbs,** 20% **Croats,** 15% **Bosnians,** and 10% each **Slovenes** and **Macedonians.** When they first arrived in the 1940s and 1950s, Swedes expected them to become Swedes, adopt Swedish manners and customs, and become integrated into Swedish society—or return to Yugoslavia. However, less than 20% returned to Yugoslavia, and of those who stayed in Sweden, only a small percentage applied for citizenship. They live primarily in the cities of Stockholm, Malmö, and Götenberg and many are industrial workers. The Serbs and Macedonians are mainly Eastern Orthodox, the Croat and Slovenes are Roman Catholic, and the Bosnians are Muslims. Yugoslavian and Polish patterns of integration, therefore, can be described as ranging from almost complete assimilation into Swedish life to the formation of relatively isolated ethnic enclaves.

Chileans living in Sweden number 20,000. Many are expatriates who fled Chile after the 1973 coup. Swedish diplomats were active in Santiago after the Chilean coup, and the Swedish embassy there became a haven for those at odds with the regime.

Latin Americans arrived in the years following 1973. After the arrival of Chileans, a chain migration started from South America to Sweden, especially from Bolivia, Brazil, Peru, Cuba, and Argentina. While Chileans remain the largest group, there are several thousand from each of these nations, all of whom have sought to preserve cultural traditions from their home countries. One effect is that these groups have come together and built a Latin American community with a pan–Latin American culture and have maintained ties to their home communities not typical of other groups.

These immigrants' visible display of their Latin heritage and resistance to assimilation trouble some in the Swedish community.

Also in Sweden from the New World are **U.S. Americans,** who number about 7,500. Many of those classified as Americans are return immigrants; that is, first- and second-generation emigrants from Sweden to the United States who have returned to Sweden.

Perhaps the most visible minority in Sweden is the **Muslims,** who number about 75,000—about 15% of the nation's total immigrant population. Most are **Iranians** (39,000) or **Turks** (26,000). Included in the Turk category are non-Turkish people from Turkey including **Kurds** and **Assyrians,** who actually outnumber the ethnic Turks. There are also small populations of Muslim **Afghans, Iraqis,** and **Bosnians.** Although these groups are not culturally homogeneous, they are unified by their adherence to Islam and are often perceived as a single group in this predominantly Christian country. The immigration of Muslims to Sweden is a relatively new phenomenon. The earliest groups arrived among the labor immigrants from Yugoslavia and Turkey during the 1960s. Iranian immigrants, escaping the regime of the shah, came to Sweden during the 1970s. A second wave of Iranians, trying to avoid the Iran-Iraq war, migrated during the 1980s. Most Turks are poor, live in ethnic communities, and associate mainly with other Turks. The Iranians are more middle class and are fuller participants in Swedish society. The Iranians also have contributed to an increase in the number of Shi'ite Muslims, but the antagonism between Shi'ite and Sunni Muslims is considerably less in Sweden than in Islamic countries. The two sects cooperate to a certain degree and pray together. Animosity between Muslim groups, however, is one reason why a mosque planned for Stockholm was not built.

Other groups include several thousand **Czechs, Serbs, Russians, Romanians, Hungarians, Somalians,** and **Eritreans,** and smaller groups of **Bulgarians** and **Albanians,** many of whom are refugees or asylum-seekers.

Ethnic Relations

Prior to World War II, Swedes were nationalistic and displayed prejudiced attitudes toward non-Swedes. For example, there was talk about preserving pure Swedish stock, and one popular slogan promoted "Sweden for Swedes." This resulted in restrictive policies directed at non-Nordic ethnic groups and immigrants in Sweden. As noted above, however, these attitudes have largely changed since World War II. Swedes now are one of the most ethnically tolerant people in the world, as demonstrated by their acceptance of the rights of immigrants and ethnic groups to preserve their cultural traditions. Treatment of non-Europeans has, however, raised the possibility that this tolerance is not as deep for non-Europeans.

Many reforms were initiated in the 1980s designed to support immigrants' desires to preserve their cultures. Integration into Swedish society was encouraged into a policy of "equality, freedom of choice, and cooperation" (*jamlikhet, valfrihet, samverkan*). Equality was understood to mean parity between non-Swedes and Swedes in terms of rights, duties, and opportunities. Immigrants have the right to choose whether to retain the culture of their homeland, to "become Swedes," or to blend cultural traits from the homeland and Sweden. The cooperation goal was intended to bring harmony between majority and minority populations. The implementation of these goals has not always been successful, and since the mid-1980s, economic problems and the lack of affordable housing have created a small anti-immigrant movement, directed especially toward non-Nordic peoples and non-Western Europeans. Particular targets are refugees from the Middle East, Africa, and Latin America, and there have been attacks on refugee centers and neo-Nazi demonstrations, although the overwhelming majority of Swedes do not support such actions. Nonetheless, the government has tightened restrictions on the acceptance of refugees, and in 1994 the number of refugees admitted declined by over 50% from the previous year. Economic problems have also impacted the non-Swedish labor force, where the unemployment rate is two times that of Swedes and other Scandinavians. In general, however, ethnic relations in Sweden are harmonious, and ethnic conflict is less a problem than in any other European nation.

In Sweden, as in all the Scandinavian countries, there is much uncertainty over how to interpret Islamic culture and behavior. Most Swedes do not know much about Islam and have misgivings about Muslim attitudes toward, or involvement with, radical political and religious movements. There are no formal obstacles to the exercise of religious freedom, but there have been strong local reactions against plans to build mosques.

Switzerland

S witzerland is a small, landlocked nation in Western Europe with a multicultural population of 7,085,000. The major ethnolinguistic groups are the German, French, and Italian speakers, reflecting Switzerland's location with Germany on the north, Austria on the east, Italy on the east and south, and France on the west. Switzerland emerged as a confederation of three cantons in 1291. German was the official language until 1798. Today, it is a confederation of 20 full cantons, and 6 half-cantons. German, French, Italian, and Romansch are the official languages, with the first three used in government and business. Switzerland is an officially neutral nation, has not engaged in a foreign war since 1515, and is not a member of the United Nations, although many UN agencies are headquartered there.

Ethnic Composition

As noted above, Switzerland's three major ethnic groups are the Germans, Italians, and French. **German Swiss** number about 4.6 million, or 65% of the population. They are the most numerous ethnolinguistic group in 19 of the cantons. As the largest group—and because of their dominance in banking, insurance, and industry—the German Swiss are capable of controlling some aspects of Swiss life. For example, hostility to non-Swiss is seen by some as reflecting German rather than general Swiss sentiments. The German Swiss population is about one-half Roman Catholic and one-half Protestant. German Swiss generally speak English, the language of global commerce, as a second language.

Italian Swiss number about 700,000, or 10% of the population, and live almost exclusively in two cantons in the south on the border with Italy. Agriculture has been replaced by banking, tourism, and industry, and cultural ties to Italy (especially to Milan) are stronger than those to other peoples in Switzerland. At various times, the Italian Swiss were under German domination, so various policies have been developed to protect Italian Swiss ownership of land and to revive traditional arts and crafts. Most are Roman Catholic with an overlay of local beliefs and practices. The Italian Swiss are citizens, which distinguishes them from Italian guest workers, although relations between the communities are close and they jointly support Italian Swiss schools, churches, and organizations.

French Swiss number about 1.2 million, or 18% of the population. They live mainly in western Switzerland near the French border. They speak French, are mainly Roman Catholic, and culturally are tied to Paris. There is some resentment of German hegemony, but they enjoy peaceful relations with the other major groups.

Jurassians, who number about 70,000, are the Catholic, French-speaking residents of Jura Canton, established in 1975 following ethnic conflict between Catholic French speakers and Protestant German speakers in Bern Canton dating to the early 1800s. The conflict was notable in the 20th century for the use of violence. Relations are now peaceful, but some Jurassians would prefer to have the canton enlarged to include Protestant French speakers in Bern.

Romansch are speakers of the Romansch language and live in the Canton of Graubunden (Grisons) in southern Switzerland. Number-

ing only 65,000, they are full members of the Swiss Confederation, although their language is slowly disappearing and the group is assimilating into the German Swiss and Italian Swiss communities as young people are drawn into urban Swiss society.

Additionally, there are substantial numbers of guest workers in Switzerland, along with small numbers of people from many other nations who either are wealthy or have arrived as refugees or asylum-seekers. **Spanish** guest workers began arriving in the early 1970s. They now number about 300,000 and include many children born in Switzerland. They work in unskilled jobs in tourism, industry, and construction, and as domestics. Chain migration, marriage within the community, Swiss hostility, and the presence of some 175 Spanish organizations suggest a strong ethnic identity.

Italians, in contrast to Italian Swiss, are guest workers who are dispersed throughout Switzerland and work in low-paid jobs in tourism, industry, and construction. They number about 400,000 and many now live in the Italian Swiss cantons in the south where industry has developed. Some are permanent residents while others cross the border daily to work in German Swiss–owned factories. They maintain ties both to Italy and the Italian Swiss community.

Austrians number 29,000, all of whom are native speakers of German and came to Switzerland to obtain skilled or professional employment.

Tibetan refugees fleeing Chinese rule in Tibet now number about 2,000. They have settled in Switzerland since 1960 with the aid of the Swiss Red Cross.

Ethnic Relations

Relations among the three main Swiss groups are peaceful, despite differences in language and religion, and residential isolation in different cantons. Among factors promoting harmony are a world view that sees outsiders as hostile to the Swiss; a political system that places power in the local districts, cantons, and individual citizens; hostility to foreign residents; and a high standard of living. Relations are less friendly with guest workers, who constitute about 8% of the population, and refugees. While the Swiss have encouraged guest workers from Spain and Italy to work in Switzerland since the 1970s, their presence is a major social issue, and since the 1970s various campaigns have been mounted to reduce their numbers. Today, Swiss laws carefully control immigration, with non-Swiss admitted only if their presence benefits the Swiss economy. In recent years, the Swiss have also become more restrictive about admitting refugees, although several thousand Sri Lankan, Angolan, Somalian, and Turkish refugees and asylum-seekers are living in Switzerland, awaiting disposition of their requests for asylum. Switzerland has been almost entirely free of ethnic or linguistic conflict, with disputes over religion (Roman Catholicism versus Protestantism) and economic matters more common. While Swiss see their nation as egalitarian, it is clear that the Germans are the wealthiest group and Italians the poorest.

Ukraine

U kraine is a nation in Eastern Europe. Formerly a republic of the Soviet Union, it became independent in 1991, although it retains strong economic and political ties to other former republics such as Russia and Belarus. Ukraine is bordered by Belarus and Russia on the north; Russia on the east, the Black Sea on the south, and Moldova, Romania, Hungary, Slovakia, and Poland on the west. Ukraine is a large nation—the second largest in Europe—and much of its territory is fertile farmland, which has led it to be labeled the land of black soil (*chernozem*) and the "breadbasket of Europe" or the "breadbasket of the Soviet Union." Ukraine is located along major trade and migration routes between Asia and Europe, which has contributed to its considerable ethnic complexity. The population is 52.2 million.

Ethnic Composition

Ukraine is a multiethnic nation. About 73% of the population is Ukrainian, 22% Russian, and the remaining 5% composed of nine different groups, with populations exceeding 100,000 and at least a dozen smaller groups. The nation is also heterogeneous in religion, with the Ukrainian population split mainly between Ukrainian Orthodoxy and Uniate Catholicism; Russian Orthodoxy, Islam, Protestantism, and Judaism are also represented. The ethnic diversity of Ukraine is the result of a number of historical factors. First, the region has been inhabited for at least 30,000 years and continuously settled for 6,000 years. Second, its strategic location has meant that many different peoples have passed through and settled in the region over the millennia, often mixing with the populations already living there. Third, the territory or part of the territory that is now Ukraine has been at various times under the control of neighboring nations such as Russia and Poland, or empires such as the Austro-Hungarian Empire. Only since 1939 has Ukraine existed in its current form. Finally, Ukraine has experienced several centuries of Russification, which accounts for the large number of Russians and Belarusians living there.

Ukrainians number about 40 million in Ukraine. There is also a large diaspora population of nearly 12 million, with about 4.5 million in Russia, 2 million in other former Soviet republics such as Kazakhstan and Belarus, and sizable communities in the United States and Canada. Ukrainian ethnicity is a complex topic and subject to various interpretations. Although some Ukrainians trace their ancestry to peoples who have lived in the region for at least 6,000 years, the mixture of various peoples over the millennia means that modern Ukrainians derive their ancestry from numerous peoples. The most significant of these are the Slavs, who moved into Eastern Europe from Asia by about A.D. 400. Ukrainians, with the Belarusians and Russians, form the eastern Slavic group, and following the

Russians, the Ukrainians are the second largest Slavic group in Europe. These Slavs mixed with other peoples from the Mediterranean region (Greeks and Romans), Central Europe, and Northern Europe over the centuries. Modern Ukrainians trace their Ukrainian identity and the notion of a distinct Ukrainian nation to the Kingdom of Rus' that emerged with Kiev as its capital in the 6th century, became a major military and political force in the 9th century, and then was vanquished by the Mongols in the 13th century. This view contradicts the Russian version of Ukrainian history, in which Ukrainians are seen as an offshoot of the Russians.

Modern Ukrainians can be divided into three regional groups: (1) The southeastern region is centered on Kiev and stresses ties to the ancient Rus' polity. The eastern portion of that region has been under Russian influence for centuries. (2) The northern region is associated with Belarus and Russia and was the home of a number of distinct Ukrainian subgroups who have now been assimilated into Ukrainian society. One group that had continued to survive is the **Polishchuk**, who live in the swampy area near and across the border with Belarus. (3) The western region has been strongly influenced over the centuries by neighboring groups to the west, such as Hungarians and Poles, and Ukrainians in this region are mainly Uniate Catholics rather than Ukrainian Orthodox.

Because of geographic isolation, regional cultural variation, and ties to other nations, the Ukrainian ethnic category traditionally contained a number of distinct and localized subgroups. These included the **Gutsuls, Lemks, Boyks, Litvins, Kalakuts, Volokhs, Opolyans, Nistrovyans,** and **Sotaks,** all of whom are now assimilated into Ukrainian society.

Up until the end of World War II, Ukraine was an agricultural nation and the majority of Ukrainians were rural farmers. A combination of collectivization, urbanization, and industrialization changed this, and Ukraine is now an urban, industrial nation, although mechanized agriculture remains a major economic activity. To a large extent, modern Ukrainian ethnic identity is based on the rural culture of the past, with use of the Ukrainian language, religious beliefs combining pre-Christian and Orthodox belief and practices, Ukrainian epics, and Ukrainian artistic traditions (embroidery, pottery, Easter egg decorating, and wood carving) being important components of this ethnic identity.

Russians form the second largest ethnic group and number about 11.5 million. Russians live mainly in eastern Ukraine, in major cities. Crimea, on the Black Sea, is also heavily populated by Russians. The Russians and Ukrainians, as Eastern Slavic peoples, are closely related culturally and linguistically. In addition, because Ukraine was a major supplier of food and other materials to Russia and the Soviet Union, the two entities have long been linked economically and politically. The major feature of this Russian-Ukrainian interaction was Russian dominance, which continues to influence relations between the groups.

The major indigenous ethnic minority is the **Carpatho-Rusyns,** who number about 650,000 out of their total worldwide population of about 850,000. Most non-Ukrainian Carpatho-Rusyns live in nations bordering Ukraine, such as Slovakia and Poland. The Carpatho-Rusyns live in the Carpathian Mountains and their ethnic identity is subject to various interpretations. Although many see themselves as a distinct group, outsiders often classify them as Ukrainians because they speak dialects of Ukrainian. Under Russian influence, many Carpatho-Rusyns were forced to convert from Uniate and Greek Catholicism to Russian Orthodoxy and were officially classified as Ukrainians. In the post-Soviet era, a sense of Carpatho-Rusyn identity has reemerged in Ukraine and Slovakia.

In addition, Ukraine contains seven other ethnic groups with populations over 100,000: **Belarusians** (440,000), **Bulgarians** (234,000), **Hungarians** (163,000), **Moldovans** (325,000), **Poles** (215,000), and **Romanians** (135,000). **Jews** numbered 486,000 in 1989, but immigration to Western Europe, Israel, and the United States since the late 1980s reduced the population to 375,000 by 1992, and it is certainly less than that in the late 1990s.

The 1989 Soviet census indicates that Ukraine is the home of peoples from all other former Soviet republics in addition to Russia, Moldova, and Belarus: **Uzbeks** (27,753), **Kazakhs** (37,318), **Azerbaijani** (59,149), **Armenians** (60,047), **Tajiks** (25,514), **Georgians** (23,689), **Lithuanians** (11,385), **Turkmen** (3,990), **Kyrgyz** (3,881), **Latvians** (7,169), and **Estonians** (4,208). In the post-Soviet era, it likely that some of these peoples have returned to their home nations, while Ukrainians in those nations have returned to Ukraine.

Ukraine also contains a number of smaller ethnic groups. **Crimean Tatars** (*see* Russia) number about 50,000, with the majority now living elsewhere in the former Soviet Union in places to which they were forcibly relocated during the Stalin era. An undetermined number of **Gypsies** live in Ukraine. **Crimeans,** people who trace their ancestry to the French, Venetian, and Genoese who first settled in the Crimea in the 1200s, number about 1,300. There is also a sizable **Greek** population, mainly in Crimea, although a combination of assimilation and return to Greece in the post-Soviet years has certainly reduced the population substantially from the 109,000 enumerated in the 1970s.

Ethnic Relations

Ethnic relations in the post-Soviet era are mainly peaceful, although a major conflict between the Ukrainians and the Russians in Crimea remains unresolved. Crimea is a peninsula of southern Ukraine that extends into the Black Sea. It was a part of Russia until 1954 when it was ceded to Ukraine to celebrate 300 years of friendship between the two countries. About 70% of the population is Russian, Russian is the primary language, and it is the headquarters for the Russian fleet in the Black Sea. With support from the Russian government, Russians in Crimea see it as an autonomous region within Ukraine and prefer self-rule. In 1994, they enacted their own constitution, a measure rejected by the Ukrainian government, which fears that the Russian Crimeans as well as the large Russian population in eastern Ukraine seeks reunification with Russia. In 1995, the conflict eased as proseparatist Russians lost power in the Crimea and the Ukrainian government expressed a willingness to grant Crimea limited autonomy. The uneasy relations between Ukrainians and Russians are also seen in a dispute over control of the Orthodox Church in Ukraine. Russians prefer that their churches be affiliated with the Russian Orthodox Church while Ukrainians prefer affiliation with the Ukrainian Orthodox Church. The influence of the Russian Orthodox Church is seen by some as a sign of continuing Russian dominance, and those who prefer Ukrainian independence have affiliated with the Ukrainian churches.

In addition to the Russian-Ukrainian dispute in Crimea, the Crimean Tatar population has also agitated for autonomy from both Ukrainian and Russian rule. As a small group, they have been effectively excluded from any real political power in the region, and the Ukrainian government continues to resist efforts by Crimean Tatars in Central Asia to return to Crimea.

Relations between the Ukrainians and the other ethnic minorities such as the Poles, Hungarians, and Romanians are peaceful, reflecting, in part, a desire by the Ukrainians to build economic and political ties to nations in Eastern and Central Europe.

United Kingdom

T he United Kingdom encompasses the peoples of England, Scotland, Wales, and Northern Ireland. Although often used synonymously with "United Kingdom," Great Britain refers only to England, Scotland, and Wales. The United Kingdom is located off the northwest coast of continental Europe and has a population of 58.5 million. The population is heavily concentrated in England, with 2.9 million in Wales, 5.1 million in Scotland, and 1.6 million in Northern Ireland. The Scots and Welsh are descended from the early Celtic inhabitants while the English trace their ancestry from the Anglo-Saxons who conquered the region in the 6th and 7th centuries. However, there has been considerable mixture among these groups and with others such as the Danes. Wales came under English control in 1536, Ireland in the 1600s, and Scotland in the 1700s. When Ireland achieved full independence in 1949, England retained control of Northern Ireland. Unity across the political entities is achieved in large part by the use of the English language, adherence to Protestantism, and centralized rule from London.

Ethnic Composition

Prior to World War II, the United Kingdom was an ethnically homogeneous society, with less than 1% of the population not of English, Irish, Scottish, or Welsh origin. Although for centuries people from Western Europe had settled in England, they had been quickly assimilated, and distinct ethnic communities, other than those formed by Jews, were rare. Similarly, Africans brought to the U.K. as slaves or servants, or those sent from British colonies for education in the early 20th century, did not form large ethnic communities. However, this situation changed within 25 years of the end of World War II as the British worldwide colonial empire disintegrated and hundreds of thousands of people of non-British ethnicity poured into England. Although non-British account for only 5% of the population, they are a major presence in many large cities, and the country's ethnic composition—in England especially—now mirrors that of its former empire.

The British census classifies the population into the following categories:

- English, Welsh, Scots, or Irish
- Other European
- West Indian or Guyanese
- African
- Indian
- Pakistani
- Bangladeshi
- Arab
- Chinese
- Any other racial or ethnic group, or of mixed racial or ethnic descent

While this system does allow the identification of major ethnic groups in the U.K., it does not account for the full range of ethnicity found there. A more comprehensive system includes the following major groups, although it should be kept in mind that the U.K. has members of virtually every national ethnic group and many smaller groups living within its borders.

British (Subjects of the United Kingdom)
    English
    Scots (Highland and Lowland)
    Welsh
    Northern Irish Protestants

Linguistic Minorities
    Gael
    Cornish
    Manx

Africans
    West Africans
    East Africans
    South Africans
    Afro-Caribbeans

Asians
    Indians (Sikhs, Punjabis, Gujaratis)
    Pakistanis
    Bangladeshis
    Asians from Africa

Turkish Cypriots
Chinese

Middle Easterners
Iraqis
Iranians

Europeans
Greeks
Poles
Italians
Irish

Other Groups
Australians
Americans

Religious Minorities
Jews
Muslims
Sikhs
Roman Catholics

British

Of the British groups, the **English** is the largest and accounts for nearly 85% of the population of the United Kingdom. The English are also the dominant group, as their language, their religion (the Church of England), and their political and legal systems form the backbone of British society. English identity is based on English parentage, support for the monarchy, the English language and its literary and scholarly traditions, the aristocracy, Parliament, a reserved public manner, adherence to the rules of etiquette, and rationality and control in dealing with life. Most English are members of the Church of England and are also called Anglicans, and about 9% are Roman Catholics. An important distinction in English society is between those from the south (the "home counties" encircling London) and those from the north. Northerners are considered to be more "earthy" and less cosmopolitan than southerners. Many English are also fiercely loyal to their home communities, whether they are from a county, such as Yorkshire, or a community, such as Camberwell in London. The English are sometimes stereotyped by others in the U.K. as aloof, arrogant, and emotionally repressed.

The **Welsh** are descendants of the Celtic peoples who settled in Wales in about 300 B.C.

Cymraeg is the native language, although its use has declined under English rule, and most Welsh now speak English. Nearly all Welsh are Protestants, although the majority belong to non-Anglican churches. Wales was traditionally a rural farming society composed of numerous small towns. In the 19th century, coal mining became an important activity in the south, and in the 20th century, the region along the English border has experienced considerable industrial development. Wales has been under English control since the 13th century, and until the 1500s the Welsh often revolted and sought independence. In the 20th century, there has been a revival of Welsh nationalism and an attempt to revive or preserve the Welsh language and literature. There is also a small political movement that seeks complete separation from England. The Welsh, who are found in significant numbers in England as well as Wales, are sometimes stereotyped by others in the U.K. as fun-loving, musical, and irresponsible.

Scots are the people of Scotland, located north of England in the British Isles. Scots emerged as a distinct people in the 11th century following nearly 10 centuries of mixing among the Picts, Scots, Britons, and Angles in what is now southern or lowland Scotland. Following centuries of alliances and wars with England, Scotland was unified with England in 1707 and English became the official language. Scots in lowland Scotland speak a variant of English called Scots or Northern English. The language is an important cultural marker for the Scots, as is their long literary and musical tradition of ballads, folk songs, poetry, and native sports and dances. The history and culture of northern or highland Scotland, which is the home of about 20% of Scots, is somewhat different from those of the lowland. Highlanders traditionally spoke Gaelic, which has now been replaced by English except in a few isolated communities, and they resisted English rule into the latter half of the 18th century. The highlands were the home of the Scot clans, the small-farm crofting system, and the raising of sheep to produce wool for clothing manufacture. The Highlands experienced much out-migration in the 20th century, and today most of the small farms are no longer viable. Efforts to revitalize the region have attempted to retain elements of the traditional culture and economy. The Scots are stereotyped by others in the U.K. as being extremely frugal and overconcerned with education and learning.

In the United Kingdom, the designation Irish refers to four groups: the **Irish** proper (*see* Ireland); **Irish immigrants** in England, Scotland, and Wales; the **Irish Catholics** of Northern Ireland; and the **Irish Protestants** of Northern Ireland. About 560,000 Irish live in the United Kingdom, not including those who have become British citizens. English control of Ireland meant that many Irish came to England in search of work, a pattern that escalated following the Irish potato famines of the mid-19th century. The Irish continue to come to England, mainly to find work at higher pay than in Ireland, and a significant proportion are employed in the construction trades. The Irish are Roman Catholic and live mainly in cities. The British stereotype the Irish as heavy drinkers, and ethnic jokes commonly portray them as fools.

There are 1.6 million people living in Northern Ireland: Catholics are 40% of the population and Protestants are 58%. The Irish Catholics are Irish of Ireland, while the Irish Protestants are descendants of English and Scottish settlers who came during the period of British rule. Northern Ireland is the scene of one of the country's longest and most violent ethnic conflicts, as discussed below.

Linguistic Minorities

In addition to these British groups, the U.K. has three populations that are descended from the Celtic peoples who began settling the islands about 400 B.C. These are the **Gaelic Scots** in the highlands of Scotland and the off-islands mentioned above, the Manx, and the Cornish.

The **Manx** number about 50,000 and live on the Isle of Man in the Irish Sea. The remainder of the island population of 70,000 is English, Scottish, and Irish. Although Manx is an extinct Celtic language and all Manx speak English, there are attempts to revive the language, and the Manx have a strong sense of identity separate from that of other U.K. residents. The large influx of tourists and wealthy English and Scottish second-home owners has created ethnic tension on the island and has strengthened the resolve of the Manx to remain free of British rule. Most Manx are Protestants.

The **Cornish** live in Cornwall in southwestern England and are closely related to the Welsh and to the Bretons across the English Channel in France. The Cornish language died out 200 years ago, and the Cornish speak English, are mostly Protestants, and are now assimilated into English society. However, they continue to be seen as distinct group: they are concentrated in Cornwall, other British stereotype them as being good-looking and having darker complexions, and some Cornish are attempting to revive the language.

Africans

People of African ancestry in the U.K. come from former British colonies in Africa and the Caribbean. The total from Africa is estimated at 207,000, with the majority from West and East African nations such as Ghana, Nigeria, Kenya, Somalia, and Uganda. A number of distinct African ethnic groups such as the Asante, Ga, Luo, and Edo are in the U.K., and they tend to live in the same neighborhoods and participate in ethnic voluntary associations with ties to their home countries.

The majority of Africans are **Afro-Caribbeans,** who number about 1.2 million and are from former British colonies in the Caribbean, especially Jamaica, from which 50% originated. Afro-Caribbeans live mainly African neighborhoods in London, Bradford, and other large cities. Although public policy and laws prohibit racism and ensure minority rights, Africans are frequently the targets of prejudice, are poorer and show less upward economic mobility than other groups, and work mainly in service professions.

Within the general African community in the U.K., a distinction is made between those from Africa and those from Africa via the Caribbean. Africans, who often arrive in the U.K. better educated than those from the Caribbean, tend to look down on Afro-Caribbeans, whom they often stereotype as lazy.

Asians

Asians are a diverse group. The majority come from the former British colonies in South Asia. The largest group is **Indians,** with about 841,000 people, of whom about 168,000 are Muslims, the remainder being Hindus and Sikhs. The largest Indian ethnic groups within this Indian population are the **Gujaratis** and the **Punjabis.** The heaviest concentrations are in London, where many Indians are owners of small businesses. Although Indians are the object of prejudice, there is less hostility directed at them than at Pakistanis or Afro-Caribbeans.

Second in size is the **Pakistanis** group, containing about 475,000 people. Pakistanis are heavily concentrated in northern cities such as Bradford and Manchester, although the largest concentration is in London. Although Pakistanis have settled in Great Britain since the 1800s, most arrived since the 1950s, including a large group that came from the north of Pakistan and others who were expelled from former English colonies in Africa such as Uganda in the 1960s and 1970s. Although Pakistanis work in all areas of the economy, they are often identified with small shop ownership, and as members of the "Black" minority, they are subject to various forms of discrimination.

Bangladeshis number about 160,000, and like the Pakistanis, nearly all are Muslims. The majority live in the poorest neighborhoods of London.

Other Asian groups with populations exceeding 20,000 are the **Turks** (mainly from Cyprus), **Sri Lankans, Malaysians,** and **Chinese** from Hong Kong, along with smaller numbers of **Vietnamese, Japanese, Filipinos,** and people from most other Asian nations.

Middle Easterners

People from the Middle East total about 150,000. The majority are **Iraqis,** who number about 80,000, a significant percentage of whom are refugees who fled from the Hussein regime, and **Palestinians** (Muslim and Christian) who fled or were displaced by the Israeli-Arab wars in the Middle East. Many Palestinians express a desire to return home when peace is achieved. Also in England are about 30,000 **Iranians.** They are Persians, not Arabs, but are Muslims like most other Middle Easterners. Arabs live mainly in London, and there are numerous voluntary organizations and newspapers serving the community.

Europeans

The U.K. is home to some 375,000 citizens of other European nations, not including Ireland. About 315,000 are from Western Europe and 58,000 from Eastern Europe. The largest group is the **Italians,** who number about 77,000; most arrived after World War II seeking employment. Their population has decreased since the 1960s as Italian migrants have gone to other European nations with better employment opportunities. Other European groups with populations over 20,000 are the **French, Germans,** and **Spanish.**

Other Groups

Other groups include peoples from the Americas, Australians, and New Zealanders. The largest group is **U.S. Americans,** who number 110,000. They are drawn to the U.K. for education, employment, or the experience of living in a foreign nation that is not too different from their homeland. There is much intermarriage between U.S. Americans and the British, and most Americans eventually return to the United States.

There is also a population of undetermined size of **Gypsies** and **Travellers** in the U.K. Most now lived settled lives.

Religious Groups

In addition to ethnicity, U.K. society can be categorized in terms of religion, although the two categories overlap to some degree. All major religions are practiced in the U.K. The British are mainly **Protestants,** mostly Anglican (members of the Church of England). About 9% are **Roman Catholics** (not including the Irish). Many British Roman Catholics are upper class and are descended from families that resisted conversion to Protestantism during the Reformation. They tend to marry one another but are full participants in British society.

Jews form the major religious minority. Jews have lived in the U.K. for over 1,000 years. They were expelled in 1290, and although a small number returned in the 1600s, most arrived after 1880. The current population is about 350,000 and is heavily concentrated in London. All branches of Judaism—Orthodox, Conservative, and Reform— are represented. The overwhelming majority are Eastern European Jews, although there is a thriving Sephardic community as well.

Black youths tossing stones at police during race riots in the Brixton section of London in 1981. Ethnically homogeneous before 1945, the United Kingdom is now a multicultural society. Photo: UPI/Corbis-Bettmann.

As Pakistanis, Bangladeshis, Arabs, and some Indians are **Muslims,** there are over one million Muslims in the U.K., making Islam the third largest religious group. However, their identity as Muslims is a less salient feature to the general population than their identity as Asians or Arabs.

Ethnic Relations

In the 1990s, the U.K. is often described as resembling the United States both in ethnic composition and ethnic relations. There are major differences between the two nations, but one similarity is the treatment of the "Black" population. In Great Britain, all non-Europeans, whether African, Arab, Afro-Caribbean, Indian, or South Asian are commonly lumped as Blacks, although Asians are sometimes treated as a separate category. But, even then, there is lumping—all South Asians are regarded as "Pakistanis." Although official policy and laws are opposed to racial and ethnic discrimination, and programs have been funded to support minority cultures and languages, prejudice and discrimination remain a serious problem in British society. From the perspective of the White British, non-Europeans in the

U.K. are ranked on a scale of discrimination starting with the Pakistanis at the top, who experience the greatest persecution. Following the Pakistanis are Afro-Caribbeans, Africans, Arabs, and then Asian Indians. Although Indians are subject to less discrimination than other groups, they are often classified as Pakistanis and are treated accordingly. As a group, these "Blacks" form the lowest level of British society, live in the poorest inner-city neighborhoods, hold the lowest-paying jobs, are more likely to be unemployed, and have the least education. While minority groups have established ethnic organizations to represent their interests, they have little influence at the national level. White British see these newcomers as competition for scarce jobs in a changing economy and as placing a financial burden on British society through use of public-supported housing, education, and health care.

The failure of the U.K. in 1995 to support a European Union initiative to develop a common antiracism policy has led to charges by other nations that Britain is a racist society. Adding weight to these charges were new British policies in 1995 regarding asylum-seekers, designed to make it more difficult for them to remain in the U.K. At the same time, however, the U.K. has—since immigrants began flowing in from its former colonies—enacted a number of laws to combat ethnic discrimination. These include the Race Relations Act of 1976, which supports earlier laws that make discrimination illegal; the Public Order Act of 1986, which bans racial violence; and the establishment of a Commission for Racial Equality in 1976.

Another key feature of ethnic relations in the U.K. is the dominance of certain groups in specific economic activities. For example, many taxicab drivers in London are Afro-Caribbeans and Africans; Greeks run small food shops; Pakistanis have taken over many news stands, candy shops, and grocery shops; and Indians run grocery shops and restaurants.

An important marker of ethnic separatism in any society is the frequency of marriage across ethnic group boundaries. Such intermarriage accounts for only about 1% of marriages in the U.K., with marriages between Afro-Caribbean and African men and White women being the most common. There is also a small population of people of mixed African and Asian ancestry. Intermarriage by Asians is unusual.

In addition to ethnic discrimination aimed at recent immigrants to the U.K., there is continuing resentment among the Scots and Welsh over English rule. Although the national union seems firm, in fall of 1997 both Scotland and Wales passed devolution resolutions, creating a parliament for Scotland and an assembly for Wales, allowing each more control over local legislation.

Far more significant is the ethnic conflict in Northern Ireland, in which violence in the form of bombings has spilled over into England. The U.K. retained control of Northern Ireland after Ireland gained full independence in 1949, and since then, there has been a movement for independence and affiliation with Ireland by the Catholic Northern Irish—a movement that has been resisted by the Protestant Northern Irish and the British. The conflict in Northern Ireland has its roots in the 400 years of British rule and Britain's policy of settling Scots and English Protestants in Northern Ireland where they became competitors for jobs and political control with the Irish. Although a violent ethnic separatism movement has existed since the 1920s, the current conflict escalated in the 1960s, and in 1972 the British government renewed its direct control of Northern Ireland. The independence movement is led by the Irish Republican Army (IRA) and the resistance is led by the British army and the mainly Protestant Ulster Defense Association. The conflict has been marked by violence on both sides, including vigilante killings, assaults, and terrorist bombings. Talks that began in 1993 have failed to resolve the conflict, and in 1998, the violence continues.

Vatican City

T he state of Vatican City (The Holy See) is located within the city of Rome in western Italy. Both in size (108.7 acres) and in population (about 800), it is the smallest nation in the world. Since the early centuries of Christianity, the Vatican has been the seat of the Pope and the center of first the Christian and then the Roman Catholic Church. The Vatican is a multicultural nation in the sense that its small population includes nuns, priests, bishops, archbishops, and cardinals who come from many different nations (although a sizable percentage are Italians). Also present in the Vatican are the Swiss Guards. All are in Vatican City to serve the Church. The daytime population can more than double due to Italian workers who work in the Vatican but live outside it. The official language is Italian although important church matters are communicated in Latin.

Yugoslavia

Y ugoslavia (Serbia), a nation in the Balkans region of Europe, is bounded by Hungary on the north, Romania and Bulgaria on the east, Macedonia and Albania on the south, and on the west by Bosnia-Herzegovina and Croatia. In 1996, Yugoslavia was made up of the republics of Serbia and Montenegro. Prior to 1992, Yugoslavia also contained Croatia, Slovenia, Macedonia, and Bosnia-Herzegovina, each of which is now an independent nation.

Ethnic Composition

The label **Yugoslavian** or **Yugoslav** is a national rather than an ethnic identifier. However, outside Yugoslavia (past and present) it is sometimes used as a label for anyone from Yugoslavia.

The nation's dominant ethnic group—in terms of size and political control—is the Serbs, who number about 8 million in the national population of about 11 million. The Serb population includes several hundred thousand Serbs who fled Croatia and Bosnia-Herzegovina in the wars of the 1990s. The resolution of the fighting in Bosnia has left a large Bosnian Serb population occupying about one-third of the nation. Because of the wars involving the Serbs, Croats, and Bosnians, it impossible to accurately measure the current population of Yugoslavia (Serbia). The largest ethnic minorities are the Albanians and Montenegrins in the south and the Hungarians in the north.

Serbs are an ancient Iranian people who in the 4th–6th centuries merged with Slavic peoples in the region. They are mainly Eastern Orthodox and speak the Serbo-Croatian language, which they write using the Cyrillic alphabet.

Montenegrins are ethnic Serbs, but they see themselves as culturally distinct in some ways. They number about 400,000 and live in southwestern Yugoslavia. Distinctions include speaking a particular dialect of Serbo-Croatian, looking to different culture heroes for inspiration, knowing a different set of folk epics, residing in a separate region, and sharing a history of 400 years of armed resistance to Turkish rule. Like the main population of Serbs, they write Serbo-Croatian in the Cyrillic alphabet and are adherents of Eastern Orthodoxy.

Vlachs are estimated at about 25,000. Formerly nomadic sheep herders, the Vlachs were forcibly settled by the Communist government and are now assimilated into Serbian society. Sometimes considered Romanian because their languages are similar, Vlachs are a remnant population descended from the Illyrians and Thracians who have interacted with the Slavic population over the centuries in the Balkans.

The other major groups in Yugoslavia have been involved in ethnic conflict or have had their communities disrupted by the armed conflicts of the mid-1990s. **Albanians** number about two million and live in the Kosovo Province, which borders Albania. The wars of the 1990s have overshadowed the Albanian-Serb conflict in the region, which centers on conflicting claims to the territory and Albanian demands for autonomy.

Hungarians numbered about 450,000 in Yugoslavia in 1991, nearly all in the Vojvodina region of Serbia along the border with Hungary. They are in Yugoslavia because shifting national boundaries resulted in territory that was once part of Hungary ending up as part of Yugoslavia. In 1991, following the outbreak of the wars with the Croats and Bosnians, many Serb refugees from Bosnian and Croat regions were resettled in Vojvodina, creating conflict with the Hungarians whose special minority status (which had afforded them various cultural, linguistic, and political freedoms) was revoked by the government. However, to avoid drawing Hungary into the conflict, the Hungarians were not subjected to the "ethnic cleansing" that characterized much of the fighting elsewhere. Nevertheless, to escape the economic pressures caused by the refugees and the restrictions on their minority rights, many Hungarians resettled across the border in Hungary.

Before the breakup of Yugoslavia, **Gypsies** numbered as many as two million in the nation. Due to the disruptions and massive population relocations caused by the wars involving the Serbs, Croats, and Bosnians, neither the number nor location of Gypsies in the newly independent nations can be determined with any degree of accuracy. Before the wars, most Gypsies were living in settled communities and supporting themselves through wage labor and by specialized services such as selling used vehicles or providing entertainment. As elsewhere in Europe, Gypsies lived outside mainstream society, although many spoke the language of the neighboring groups (usually Serbo-Croatian) and were adherents of the same religions.

Other groups include immigrant **Carpatho-Rusyns** and **Romanians** in the Vojvodina region, a small number of **Jews**, and undetermined numbers of **Bosnians** and **Croats.** Croats formerly constituted some 12% of the population of Serbia, but relocation to Croatia has drastically reduced the size of the community.

Ethnic Relations

Ethnic relations in Yugoslavia since 1991 have been among the most difficult of any nation in the world. Since Croatia and Slovenia declared their independence from Yugoslavia in June 1991, the Serbs have been involved in some of the most devastating ethnic conflicts of the 1990s. These conflicts—involving the Serbs, Serb-dominated Yugoslavian army, Croats, and Bosnians—have been costly in the over 100,000 lives lost, over two million refugees created, and the mass destruction of irreplaceable property, including mosques, churches, and cultural institutions. These wars have made "ethnic cleansing" a household phrase around the world, as a major tactic used by all groups in this conflict was to forcibly remove people of the other ethnic groups from the territory the aggressor wanted to control. For all participants, the goals were the same—establishing or protecting boundaries for territory to be controlled by their group. For the Serbs, this meant expansion into regions with large Serb populations in Croatia and Bosnia and solidifying control over minority regions in Serbia. For the Croats and Bosnians, their involvement was more defensive—maintaining control of land in their borders. The Croat-Serb war ended in 1994 with considerable shifts of population and the establishment of international borders. The Bosnia war involving all three groups— as well as United Nations peacekeeping forces—ended in 1995 and resulted in a single nation of Bosnia-Herzegovina, composed of Bosnian Muslims, Bosnian Serbs, and Croats, with all represented in the new government elected in 1996.

Ethnically, there is little to separate the Serbs, Croats, and Bosnian Muslims, although they each see themselves as distinct peoples with the right to control their ancestral territory. In addition to concerns about territory, the current conflicts are fueled by older issues including Bosnian dominance of Serbian peasants, Albanian adherence to Islam, and Croatian support for the Nazis in World War II while atrocities were committed against the Serbs who resisted Nazi rule.

Like the other disputes in the region, the Serb-Albanian dispute goes back centuries and centers on different versions of the settlement history of the region, with both groups claiming the territory. The current conflict dates to 1989 and renewed calls for autonomy by the Albanians. The Serb-dominated Yugoslavian government refused and instead instituted direct rule with restrictions placed on the political freedoms of the Albanians. The Albanians have responded by creating their own government, schools, hospitals, and other institutions, and partly because of the wars, the Serbs have not attempted in any significant way to intervene. Some experts fear that with the end of the wars, the Serbs will soon turn their attention to an "ethnic cleansing" of the Kosovo region.

PART TWO
Africa

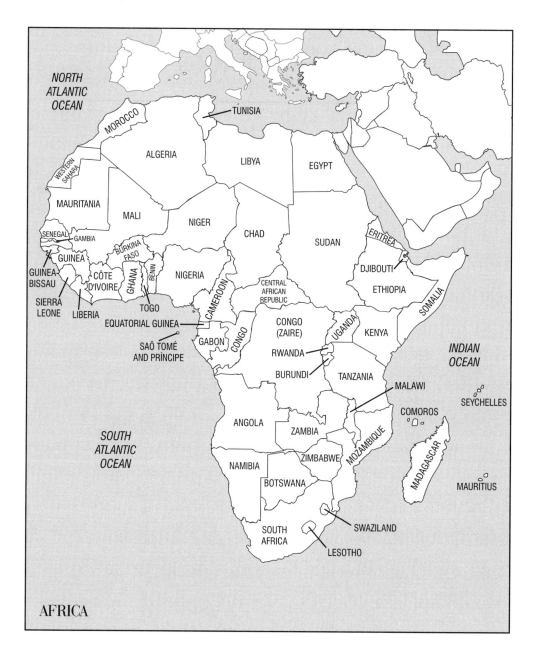

AFRICA

AFRICA
Introduction

The continent of Africa is conventionally divided into two regions—North Africa and Sub-Saharan Africa.

North Africa

North Africa consists of the nations of

Algeria
Chad
Egypt
Eritrea
Libya
Mauritania's northern reaches
Morocco
Sudan
Tunisia
Western Sahara

Because North Africa has been influenced by the Arab and Muslim Middle East for over 1,000 years, it is usually classified culturally as part of the Muslim or Arab world.

Sub-Saharan Africa

Sub-Saharan Africa, formerly labeled Black Africa in reference to the skin color of the region's indigenous people, is conventionally subdivided into West Africa, Central Africa, East Africa, and Southern Africa.

West Africa
  Benin
  Burkina Faso
  Cameroon
  Cape Verde
  Côte d'Ivoire
  Equatorial Guinea
  Gabon
  Gambia
  Ghana
  Guinea
  Guinea-Bissau
  Liberia
  Mali
  Mauritania
  Niger
  Nigeria
  São Tomé and Príncipe
  Senegal
  Sierra Leone
  Togo

Central Africa
  Burundi
  Central African Republic
  Congo (formerly Zaire)
  Congo, Republic of
  Malawi
  Rwanda
  Uganda
  Zambia
  Zimbabwe

East Africa
  Comoros
  Djibouti
  Ethiopia
  Kenya
  Madagascar
  Mozambique
  Seychelles

Somalia

Tanzania

Southern Africa

Angola

Botswana

Lesotho

Namibia

South Africa

Swaziland

The island nations off the east coast of Africa are culturally aligned with Southeast Asia as they were settled by and are much influenced by peoples from Indonesia and India. However, Madagascar and the Comoros, which have become politically tied to Africa since their independence in 1960 and 1975, respectively, are covered in this section.

Africa is an ethnically complex continent. Nearly all nations are ethnically heterogeneous, and developing or maintaining peaceful ethnic relations has been a major issue in much of Africa, as nations seek to achieve political stability and economic development in the postindependence era that began for many of them in the 1960s.

Settlement, colonization, and control of the continent, with their long-term implications for ethnic relations, began with the Muslim Arabs in the 8th century. These Arabs eventually converted most of the population of North Africa to Islam, which then spread south into West Africa. Portugal began intensive and extensive colonization of the continent in the 15th century, although most colonization of Africa took place during the 19th century. The major European colonial powers were Great Britain and France with Belgium, Portugal, the Netherlands, Spain, Germany, and Italy controlling smaller regions. Except in the north and in South Africa, colonial settlement was limited, as the hot and humid climate and various diseases made the region largely unappealing to Europeans. The European strategy was, instead, to control a colony's possessions and to extract minerals and other resources, including human beings for the slave trade, using as few Europeans as possible. Part of this strategy involved the management of ethnicity and ethnic relations in the colonies. The colonists often gave special favored treatment to one se-

lected ethnic group, which then assisted the colonists in gaining control over other groups. Some of these groups were already dominant in their region, while others achieved dominance with European support. In some nations, this colonial divide-and-conquer policy led to prolonged ethnic conflicts and rivalries for political power after independence, with the groups that were favored by the colonial powers possessing a number of advantages, such as living in the capital city, and having literacy and modern education. Another colonial strategy that led to long-term ethnic problems was the establishment of national boundaries without consideration of the traditional territories of regional ethnic groups. This policy has created many multiethnic nations and forced some groups to straddle two or more nations, producing conditions that are hardly conducive to political stability.

Religion was also an important component of the colonial strategy for control of indigenous populations. Africa has been the target of missionary activity for over 1,000 years. Although there was a Muslim presence in North Africa, East Africa, and the northern nations of West Africa, most other missionary activity was by Christians as part of the European colonization of the continent. Many Africans today are at least nominal Christians, although indigenous religions remain strong in many ethnic groups, and Christianity has often been molded to conform to indigenous practices and beliefs.

It is important to note, however, that European colonization is not the whole story of the complex ethnic mix and ethnic situation in modern Africa. Numerous African kingdoms and empires existed prior to European arrival, trade was common among various groups across the continent, and major population migrations took place (such as the movement of Bantu-speaking peoples into the south for about 2,000 years). All of these had an impact on the ethnic composition of, and ethnic relations in, the modern nations of Africa.

The majority of people in Africa are Africans—that is, people who can trace their ancestry to people indigenous to the continent. Many anthropologists now believe that human beings evolved in Africa and that the rest of the world was settled by peoples who migrated out of Africa, perhaps approximately 100,000 to 200,000 years ago. The non-African population of Africa is small and consists primarily of Arabs in the North and small populations of Europeans, South Asians, and Chinese in some other nations.

Most modern Africans live in rural areas and subsist by farming or cattle herding. Crops such as cassava and corn (introduced from the New World), along with crops such as yams and millet, are of considerable importance. In some regions, mining and other industries begun by the European colonists remain economically important. The hunters/gatherers of the interior rain forests and southern deserts, although the focus of considerable outside attention, constitute only a very small percentage of the population. Historically, most Africans lived in small villages (as they do today) and were organized politically into tribes ruled by chiefs or kingdoms ruled by monarchs. Integration of these traditional forms of government into the modern nations of Africa has been difficult.

By and large, most African nations are poor and politically unstable. Political coups are common, and religious conflicts in the North and ethnic and wealth-related conflicts elsewhere are a continual source of instability.

At the time of this writing, the history and anthropology of Africa are undergoing considerable debate and revision. Much of the revision is being done by African historians and anthropologists who question both the accuracy and interpretations of European social scientists, whose work is seen—consciously or unconsciously—as reflecting the viewpoints of the colonial nations who controlled much of Africa into the 1960s.

Africa Bibliography

Adegbola, E. A. Ade, ed. *Traditional Religion in West Africa*. Nairobi: Uzima Press, 1983.

Afigbo, A. E., et al., eds. *The Making of Modern Africa*. New York: Longman, 1986.

Africa Since 1914: A Historical Bibliography. Santa Barbara, CA: ABC-CLIO, 1985.

African Studies Association. *The Arts of Africa: An Annotated Bibliography*. Atlanta, GA: African Studies Association, 1986.

Appiah, Kwame Anthony, and Henry Lewis Gates Jr., eds. *The Dictionary of Global Culture*. New York: Alfred A. Knopf, 1996.

Baldick, Julian. *Mystical Islam*. NY: New York University Press, 1989.

Barnes, James F. *Gabon: Beyond the Colonial Legacy*. Boulder, CO: Westview Press, 1992.

Bates, R. H. *Markets and States in Tropical Africa*. Berkeley: University of California Press, 1981.

Bender, M. Lionel. *Peoples and Cultures of the Ethio-Sudan Borderlands*. East Lansing: African Studies Center, Michigan State University, 1981.

Bernard, Allan. *Hunters and Herders of Southern Africa: A Comparative Ethnography of the Khoisan Peoples*. Cambridge: Cambridge University Press, 1992.

Bever, Edward. *Africa*. Phoenix, AZ: The Oryx Press, 1996.

Biebuyck, Daniel P. *The Arts of Central Africa*. Boston: G. K. Hall, 1987.

Bohannan, Paul, and Philip Curtin. *Africa and the Africans*, 3rd ed. Prospect Heights, IL: Waveland Press, 1988.

Bourdillon, M. F. C. *The Shona Peoples*, 3rd edition. Gweru: Mambo Press, 1987. (Zimbabwe)

Byrnes, Rita M., ed. *Uganda: A Country Study*. Washington, DC: Government Printing Office, 1990.

Colello, Thomas, ed. *Chad: A Country Study*, 2nd ed. Washington, DC: Government Printing Office, 1990.

Covell, Maureen. *Historical Dictionary of Madagascar*. Latham, MD: The Scarecrow Press, 1995.

Davidson, Basil. *African Civilization Revisited: From Antiquity to Modern Times*. Trenton, NJ: Africa World Press, 1991.

Decalo, Samuel. *Historical Dictionary of Benin,* 2nd ed. Metuchen, NJ: The Scarecrow Press, 1988.

DeLancey, Mark W. *Cameroon: Dependence and Independence*. Boulder, CO: Westview Press, 1989.

Destexhe, Alain. *Rwanda and Genocide in the Twentieth Century*. New York: New York University Press, 1995. Translated from the French by Alison Marschener.

Eades, S. *Strangers and Traders*. Trenton, NJ: Africa World Press, 1995.

Eades, J. S., ed. *Migrants, Workers, and the Social Order*. London: Tavistock, 1987.

Englebert, Pierre. *Burkina Faso: Unsteady Statehood in West Africa*. Boulder, CO: Westview Press, 1996.

Fenton, Thomas P., and Mary J. Heffron, eds. *Africa: A Directory of Resources*. Maryknoll, NY: Orbis Books, 1987.

Fowler, Ian, and David Zeitlyn, eds. *African Crossroads: Intersections between History and Anthropology in Cameroon*. Providence, RI: Berghahn Books, 1996.

General History of Africa, 8 vols. UNESCO International Scientific Committee for the Drafting of a General History of Africa. London: Heinemann, 1981–1992.

Gilliland, Dean S. *African Religion Meets Islam*. Lanham, MD: University Press of America, 1987.

Greenberg, Joseph H. *The Languages of Africa*. The Hague: Mouton, 1963.

Gunatilleke, Godfrey. *Migration to the Arab World: Experience of Returning Migrants*. Tokyo: United Nations University Press, 1991.

Hackett, Rosalind I. J., ed. *New Religious Movements in Nigeria*. Lewiston, NY: Edwin Mellen Press, 1987.

Hansen, Holger B., and Michael Twaddle, eds. *Changing Uganda: The Dilemmas of Structural Adjustment and Revolutionary Change*. London: James Currey, 1991.

Hart, David M. *The Aith Waryaghar of the Moroccan Rif: An Ethnography and History*. Viking Fund Publications in Anthropology, no. 55. Tucson: University of Arizona Press, 1976.

Hildebrandt, Jonathan. *History of the Church in Africa*. Achimota, Ghana: Africa Christian Press, 1990.

Kent, Susan, ed. *Cultural Diversity among Twentieth-Century African Foragers*. Cambridge: Cambridge University Press, 1996.

Kottak, Conrad P., J. A. Rakotoarisoa, Aidan Southall, and P. Vérin. *Madagascar: Society and History*. Durham, NC: Carolina Academic Press, 1986.

Latham, A. J. H., ed. *Africa, Asia and South America since 1800: A Bibliographical Guide*. Manchester: Manchester University Press, 1995.

Levtzion, Nehemia, and Humphrey J. Fisher, eds. *Rural and Urban Islam in West Africa*. Boulder, CO: Lynne Rienner Publishers, 1989.

Liniger-Goumaz, Max. *Small Is Not Always Beautiful: The Story of Equatorial Guinea*. Totowa, NJ: Barnes and Noble Books, 1989. Translated from the French by John Wood.

Lloyd, Peter C. *Africa in Social Change*. New York: Praeger, 1968.

Lobban, Richard, and Soshua Forrest. *Historical Dictionary of the Republic of Guinea-Bissau*, 2nd ed. Metuchen, NJ: The Scarecrow Press, 1988.

Martin, Phyllis M., and Patrick O' Meara, eds. *Africa*, 2nd ed. Bloomington: Indiana University Press, 1986.

Mbiti, John. *African Religions and Philosophy*. London: Heinemann, 1969.

Metz, Helen C., ed. *Sudan: A Country Study*, 4th ed. Washington, DC: Library of Congress, 1992.

Middleton, John, and Amal Rassam, eds. *Encyclopedia of World Cultures, Volume 9: Africa and the Middle East.* New York: G. K. Hall/Macmillan, 1995.

Miller, Joseph Calder. *Slavery and Slaving in World History: A Bibliography, 1900–1991.* Millwood, NY: Kraus International, 1993.

Mostert, Noel. *Frontiers: The Epic of South Africa's Creation and the Tragedy of the Xhosa People.* New York: Knopf, 1992.

Musiker, Naomi, and Reuben Musike. *South African History: A Bibliographical Guide with Special Reference to Territorial Expansion and Colonization, Volume 5: Themes in European Expansion: Exploration, Colonization, and the Impact of Empire.* New York: Garland Publishing, 1984.

Oliver, Roland, and J. D. Fage, eds. *Cambridge History of Africa*, 8 vols. London: Cambridge University Press, 1975–1986.

O'Toole, Thomas. *The Central African Republic: The Continent's Hidden Heart.* Boulder, CO: Westview Press, 1986.

Peil, M. *African Urban Society.* Chichester: Wiley, 1984.

Quinn, Charlotte A. *Mandingo Kingdoms of the Senegambia.* Evanston: Northwestern University Press, 1972.

Shack, William A. *The Central Ethiopians: Amhara, Tigriña, and Related Peoples.* London: International African Institute, 1975.

Soliday, Gerald L., et al., eds. *History of the Family and Kinship: A Select International Bibliography.* Millwood, NY: Kraus International, 1980.

Trimingham, J. Spencer. *The Influence of Islam Upon Africa.* New York: Frederick A. Praeger, 1968.

U.S. Committee for Refugees. *1995 World Refugee Survey.* New York: U.S. Committee for Refugees, 1995.

U.S. Department of State. *Country Reports.* Issued Annually.

U.S. Department of State. *Human Rights Reports.* Issued Annually.

Vennerier, Pierre, ed. *Atlas de la Côte d'Ivoire*, 2nd edition. Paris, 1983.

Weber, Alain. "Les Tsiganes d'Egypte." *Études Tsiganes* 35 (1989): 47–59.

Weekes, Richard V., ed. *Muslim Peoples: A World Ethnographic Survey.* Westport, CT: Greenwood Press, 1984.

Yeager, Rodger. *Tanzania: An African Experiment.* Boulder, CO: Westview Press, 1982.

Algeria

T he Democratic and Popular Republic of Algeria is located in North Africa and is bordered by Tunisia and Libya on the east; Niger, Mali, and Mauritania on the south; Morocco on the west; and the Mediterranean Sea on the north. Beginning in the 8th century B.C., Algeria as part of the northern region of Africa came under the control of various nations and empires, including the Carthaginians, Romans, Vandals, Byzantines, Arabs, Moroccans, Ottoman Turks, and Spaniards. France controlled the country from 1830 until 1962, when Algeria achieved independence following an eight-year war. During its period of dominance, France sought to make Algeria culturally part of France through the use of the French language, French education, and Roman Catholicism. Since independence, French influence has declined rapidly, and many Algerians who were affiliated with the French government or French businesses have fled to France. Their numbers were increased by subsequent migrations; nearly one million Algerians now live in France.

Algeria has a population of 29.2 million, which is concentrated in the north. Arabic is the official language, and French, which was the language of the elite during the years of French rule, is declining in use. Islam is the official religion, and, except for the remaining European minority, nearly all Algerians are Sunni Muslims.

Ethnic Composition and Ethnic Relations

Algeria is an ethnically homogeneous society; over 80% of Algerians are classified as Arabs. Classification as an Arab is more cultural than ethnic, as most Arabs in Algeria are of mixed Arab and Berber ancestry, dating to the arrival of the Arabs in A.D. 637. Despite this common ancestry, an ethnic split between Berbers and Arabs remains in Algerian society, especially in rural areas where Berbers are more likely to retain their traditional language and culture.

Arabs are an ethnic group indigenous to the Middle East and are the majority population of 15 nations in the Middle East and North Africa, including Algeria. The history of the emergence of Arabs as a distinct group in the Middle East is unclear, but as early as 853 B.C., the Arabic language was in use. Although being an "Arab" has different meanings in different nations, a shared Arab identity is based on a number of key elements. These include use of the Arabic language in its classical form in religion and literature, along with use in daily life of one of the varieties of colloquial Arabic; a personal identity with Arab culture, history, and the Arab community; a value placed on children and family life; a clear division of labor based on sex; and adherence to Islam (about 93% of Arabs around the world follow Islam). Arabs in Algeria live mainly in the north and are politically dominant to the point that, in that part of Algeria, Berbers are no longer enumerated by the government as a separate ethnic group. **Bedouin** Arabs in the desert regions were traditionally nomadic herders, but government initiatives have sought to settle them in villages and weaken ties to tribes that the government fears will interfere with their loyalty to the Algerian nation.

A Muslim woman standing in front of a pro-Islamic fundamentalism slogan in Algeria. Photo: Agence France Presse/Corbis-Bettmann.

Berbers are the indigenous people of North Africa. Although details about their origins and where they came from are unclear, ancestors of the contemporary Berbers have lived in North Africa for at least 5,000 years. The Berbers across North Africa are collectively referred to as **Imazighen** ("free men"), although the names for regional groups within nations and identification with specific settlements are more salient markers of identity. Berbers constitute about 20% of the population of North Africa. There are four major Berber groups: the **Kabyles** of the mountains in the northwest, the **Chaouia** of the northeast, the **Mzab** of the northern Sahara, and the **Tuareg** of the east, near Libya. In each of these groups there are a number of distinct Berber tribes, with family and tribal affiliation based on descent through the male line. Some Berbers initially resisted conversion to Islam, all eventually did not convert and some were then involved in holy wars launched against kingdoms in West Africa. Some Berbers in Algeria live in mixed Arab-Berber villages while others live in exclusively Berber communities, speak dialects of the Berber language, and have resisted assimilation into Arab Algerian society. Some of these groups are strongly opposed to Islamic fundamentalism, fearing it will end their independence.

The formerly large population of **French** people in Algeria has been reduced to less than 50,000 by the war of independence from 1954 to 1962 as well as by the conflict between the government and Islamic fundamentalists since the 1970s. Similarly, the large community of **Jews** has disappeared through immigration to southern France and Israel.

The major conflict in Algerian society is not ethnic but religious. Islamic fundamentalism emerged in the late 1970s as a potent political movement in Algeria, and since then, the government and Islamic fundamentalists have been involved in a sometimes violent conflict for political control of the nation. The fundamentalists have relied on terrorism—aimed at both other Algerians and foreigners, as well as at the political process—while the government has used repression, including mass arrests and rigid control of the political system, to maintain power. Key issues for Islamic fundamentalists are a society based on the tenets of Islam, a loosening of ties to Western nations, and a strengthening of ties to other Islamic Middle Eastern and North African nations. In the first five years of the 1990s, over 30,000 people were killed in fighting over this issue.

Angola

The Republic of Angola is located on the southwestern coast of Africa. It is bordered on the north and northeast by the Congo (formerly Zaire), on the southeast by Zambia, and on the south by Namibia. The Atlantic Ocean forms its western boundary. Angola was first visited by the Portuguese in 1482. Colonization of the coastal region began at that time, with the interior not coming under Portuguese control until the early 20th century. A revolt against Portuguese rule began in 1961, and in 1974 the Portuguese government was overthrown, with Angola achieving full independence in 1975. The postindependence era has been marked by almost continuous political unrest that at times has escalated into civil war, sometimes involving outside forces from Cuba and South Africa, support from the United States and the Soviet Union for different factions, and United Nations intervention.

The estimated population of Angola is 11.5 million. The official language is Portuguese, although many indigenous languages are spoken across the nation. Currently, traditional religions are giving way to Christianity and syncretic Afro-Christian sects; a majority of Angolan Christians are Roman Catholics.

Ethnic Composition

Although there have been a number of population migrations within Africa, the most important migration in historic times has been that of the Bantu-speaking peoples, whose population explosion led to their spread over most of Africa south of the equator. The original inhabitants of what is now Angola were probably Khoisan-speaking hunter-gatherers. During the first thousand years of the current era, large-scale Bantu-speaking migrations brought about major changes in the region. The aboriginal peoples of Angola were consolidated into the migrating populations, and cereal cultivation and technologically advanced iron work were introduced. Gradually, the Bantu-speaking groups became the dominant group of southern Africa. By 1600, they had thoroughly occupied Angola.

Currently, most of Angola's population is made up of Bantu-speaking peoples, who form a number of distinct ethnic groups. Because a census by ethnic group has not been conducted for some years, the exact population of each group is not known. The two largest groups that collectively make up about 60% of the Angolan population are the Umbandu and Mbundu, both of which live in western Angola. The **Umbandu** have undergone considerable change in the 20th century, first through involvement in the coffee-growing industry, then as workers in industrial plants begun by the Portuguese colonists, and finally through leadership of the revolution that ended Portuguese rule. The **Mbundu,** most of whom live north of the Umbandu, now consist of two social categories—those who continue to farm in the rural areas and those who have settled in cities and live a more Portuguese lifestyle, acquired through education and through military and government service.

Other major groups of Angola are the **Kongo, Lunda,** and **Chokwe,** who live mainly in neighboring Congo (formerly Zaire), and the **Ngangela.** Most of these peoples are farmers. The Khoisan-speaking **San (Bushmen)** are traditionally hunter-gatherers and are mainly scattered in isolated refuge areas in southeastern Angola. The people of southern Angola—the **Ambo, Nyaneka, Herero,** and several other smaller groups—are mainly cattle herders. The term **Mestico** is used in Angola to refer to people of mixed Portuguese and African ancestry. Mesticos constitute about 1% of the population and are a mostly urban group who were assimilated in some ways into colonial Portuguese society. Many of them worked as low-level officials. Mesticos living in rural communities are more likely to affiliate with their African-ancestry group. The 300,000 or so Portuguese in Angola left the nation in 1974 following the overthrow of the Portuguese government.

Ethnic Relations

When Portuguese explorers reached Angola in the 15th century, they began to Christianize the ruling family of the Kongo and engage in trade and missionary work. There were always far fewer Portuguese in Angola and Mozambique than there were European settlers in other colonies. Despite Portuguese claims of equality for all, there was often a clear distinction between "pure" Portuguese and the indigenous population or people of mixed ancestry. The Portuguese settlers were favored and had superior status and prestige—if not always greater power—in Angola. The expansion of Portuguese power and the use of African land for plantations were resisted, and Portuguese attempts to expand their colonial nucleus led to a series of wars with African peoples that was followed by famine and epidemics. When Portugal finally withdrew from Angola in 1975, more than 300,000 Portuguese nationals and other Whites fled. During the ensuing civil war in which the former independence movements fought one another, there were large-scale relocations of the population and a general movement from the cities to rural areas.

Benin

The Republic of Benin is located in West Africa and is bordered by Togo on the west, Burkina Faso and Niger on the north, and Nigeria on the east. Traditional agriculture is extremely important to Benin's economy, and the vast majority of Benin's population is engaged in farming on family farms. Benin, once part of French West Africa, gained independence in 1960. Its law is based on French civil law and customary law. The population is 5.7 million and over 60% live in rural areas. Indigenous religions account for 70% of the population and Islam and Christianity each account for 15%, but traditional African beliefs remain strong among Christians and Muslims. French is the official language of Benin but is only one of many languages spoken there. Fon and Yoruba are the most common vernaculars in the south. There are six major tribal languages in the north—Fulani (or Fulfulde), spoken as a first language by about 225,000 people, is foremost among these. Ditmari (spoken by 136,000 people), Kotokoli (spoken by 46,000 people), and Ayizo-Gbe (spoken by over 200,000 people) are also important northern Benin languages.

Ethnic Composition

Indigenous Africans form 99% of the population, distributed among 42 ethnic groups. There are also about 5,500 Europeans in Benin. The eight major African groups and their percentages of the total population are the **Fon** (47%), **Adja** (12%), **Bariba** (10%), **Yoruba** (**Nagot**) (9%), **Aizo** (5%), **Somba** (5%), **Fulani** (4%), and the **Dendi** (2%). The Fon and the related Adja live in the south and are primarily farmers and civil servants. The Fon were the core ethnic group of the regional Dahomey Kingdom, which was active from the early 1600s until about 1900, and the Fon are still sometimes labeled **Dahomeans.** The Aizo are also farmers in the south. The Bariba are Muslim agriculturalists and are the major group in the north. They are also found in Nigeria. The Yoruba (*see* Nigeria) are farmers and urban residents in the east and include Christians, Muslims, and traditionalists. It is a general Yoruba practice to have representatives of various religions within the same family. The Fulani are found in a number of West African countries and are generally also Muslims. They are pastoral nomads in Benin. The Somba are herders of the northwest and the Dendi are an influential group in the northeast and are mainly an urban group of Muslim traders.

Ethnic Relations

There is a long history of ethnic regional rivalries, with the north and northern ethnic groups such as the Bariba and Somba often pitted against the south and southern groups such as the Fon. These regional and ethnic differences were exploited by regional political leaders in the first decade of independence, although they are now somewhat less salient. Although southerners dominate the government's senior ranks, northerners dominate the military. The south is more economically advanced and more westernized. It also has a larger population, and beginning with the French has traditionally held a favored status. In the 1996 elections, however, a northerner was elected president. Benin's policy toward transhumance allows migratory Fulani herdsmen in the region to have open access to land in Benin, although the government does enforce the use of designated entry points. In recent years, there has been friction between native farmers and itinerant foreign herders, sometimes leading to violence.

Botswana

The Republic of Botswana is a landlocked nation in southern Africa bordered by Namibia on the north and west, Zimbabwe on the northeast, and South Africa on the southeast and south. Botswana's history is closely tied to that of neighboring South Africa and Namibia. Though coveted for its diamonds and other mineral sources by the Dutch Boers in South Africa and the Germans in Namibia, the region came under British control in 1886 and remained so until it gained independence in 1966. Botswana's current population is 1.48 million. Although most Botswanans were traditionally rural, a five-year drought in the 1980s forced many to migrate to cities or large towns. Setswana and English are the official languages, with the former being the language of most people. About half the population adheres to indigenous religions while the other half is Christian, although many Botswana Christians also follow indigenous practices.

Ethnic Composition and Ethnic Relations

Although Botswana is sometimes described as an ethnically heterogeneous nation because the population is composed of a number of ethnic groups, this characterization is misleading, as the majority of people (there has been no ethnic census since 1946) are Tswana (Botswana). The most visible minorities are the Khoisan peoples and the Herero.

The **Tswana (Botswana)** are a rural people who live in large, permanent villages located near water sources and controlled by local chiefs. Outside the villages, often miles away, they herd cattle and farm corn, grains, cotton, and peanuts. Although mining—especially for diamonds—is an important national economic activity, it employs few Tswana. More Tswana live in the northern part of South Africa than live in Botswana. Traditionally, the Tswana were not a unified people but were composed of a number of distinct tribes that competed for farm and grazing land and control of regional trade routes. Under British control, tribal rivalries declined, but they have reappeared since independence in the form of competition for political power. Some Tswana were also actively involved in the anti-apartheid movement in South Africa.

The **Khoisan** peoples (speakers of the Khoi and San languages) are thought by some experts to be the indigenous people of southwestern Africa and include the **Khoi** groups who live mainly in South Africa and the **San** groups who live in Namibia, Angola, and Botswana. In Botswana, the Khoisan number about 45,000 and are herders and farmers. The hunter-gatherer way of life associated with the San groups had mostly disappeared before European colonization began.

The **Herero** in Botswana arrived in the region in 1904 as refugees from a failed war with the German colonists in what is now Namibia. They number about 8,000 and live in the western part of the nation. Most continue the cattle-herding lifeway they brought with them from Namibia, although there is much contact—through trade and marriage—with people from other groups.

Other smaller groups include the **Kalanga, Yei, Subiya, Kgalagadi,** and **Mbukushu,** as well as several thousand **British, Asian Indians,** and **Afrikaners** (*see* South Africa).

Ethnic relations are generally peaceful, given the dominance of the Tswana and the relative isolation and small size of the ethnic minorities.

Burkina Faso

B urkina Faso is in West Africa and is bordered by Mali on the west and north; Niger on the east; and Benin, Togo, Ghana, and Côte d'Ivoire on the south. Burkina Faso is the locale of the former Mossi states, which ruled the region beginning perhaps as early as the 14th century and continuing into the 19th century. The French ruled the region from 1896 until independence in 1960. The population is about 10.6 million, 80% of which is rural. French is the official language, although over 50% of the people speak Moré, the Mossi language, as well as regional languages. Statistics about religion are unreliable, with Muslims placed at anywhere from 30% to 50% of the population, 10% said to be Christian, and the remainder practicing indigenous religions.

Ethnic Composition

Burkina Faso has an ethnically heterogeneous population estimated to include some 40 different groups. The groups can be classified by language into three categories—Voltaic, Mande, and West Atlantic—or politically into the Mossi and non-Mossi.

The **Mossi** are the largest ethnic group in Burkina Faso, constituting slightly more than 50% of the population and living primarily in the central region of the nation. Because of economic opportunities, there are also large Mossi populations in Ghana and Côte d'Ivoire. During the 500 years that Mossi states ruled the region and expanded the territory under their control, many other smaller groups were assimilated into the Mossi states. Like most people in Burkina Faso, most Mossi are farmers, with millet, sorghum, and cotton their primary crops. During the French colonial era, Mossi kings lost their power, and although the position of King still exists, since independence the government has prevented the restoration of their power. The Mossi initially resisted conversion to Islam, although now perhaps 50% of the population is Muslim.

Related to the Mossi in terms of language are other groups in Burkina Faso including the **Bwa, Gurmanche, Dagara, Lobi, Senufo,** and **Gurunsi.** Like the Mossi, they are primarily farmers—although most did not have the centralized government of the pre-colonial Mossi.

The major non-Mossi groups are the Muslim **Fulani (Peul)** herders in the northeast, who form about 10% of the population, and small border populations of **Berbers** and **Songhay** in the extreme northeast. The Mande speakers who form a number of distinct groups live primarily in the west and include the **Bobo, Samo, Marka, Bissa,** and **Dioula.** The Bobo are the largest of these groups and constitute about 7% of the national population while the Bissa constitute about 5%.

Ethnic Relations

The key feature of ethnic relations in Burkina Faso is that the Mossi have for centuries been the largest group, the most highly organized, and the most politically powerful. However, other groups participate in the government, and since Burkina Faso's independence, the government—whether led by a Mossi or not—has routinely acted in ways designed to limit the authority of traditional kings and chiefs, a policy that has most affected the Mossi. Mossi dominance is as much cultural as it is political, as can be seen in the history of their absorption of other groups, as well as the current spread of Mossi into the southwest and their influence there on non-Mossi peoples.

Although Burkina Faso is poor and the government has not always been stable, it is free of the violent ethnic conflict that is found in many other African nations. Four factors are cited as accounting for this somewhat unusual situation. First, there is a general similarity among Voltaic and other ethnic groups, due to assimilation to the Mossi model. Second, government efforts have controlled and limited ethnicity-based politics. Third, the relative poverty of the nation means that there is little wealth for which to compete (in fact, economic conditions prompt many people to immigrate to neighboring nations). And fourth, some eth-nic groups in Burkina Faso focus on family and village ties, which are more important than association with the ethnic group as a whole.

Burundi

The Republic of Burundi is a small, landlocked nation in Central Africa. It is bordered by Rwanda on the north, Tanzania on the east and south, and Congo (formerly Zaire) on the west. Occupied for centuries by the two major ethnic groups that still form almost the entire population—the Hutu and Tutsi—the region came under German control as German East Africa in the late 1800s until, following the defeat of Germany in World War I, it was placed under Belgian administration. What are now the two nations of Burundi and Rwanda were under Belgian rule as the single administrative unit of Ruanda-Urundi. Under United Nations supervision, Burundi became an independent nation in 1962. Since independence, the nation has experienced long periods of civil war involving the Hutu and Tutsi, and fighting has continued through most of the 1990s. The population is estimated at 5.9 million, although the civil war and the hundreds of thousands of refugees in Congo (formerly Zaire) and Tanzania make such estimates unreliable. French, which was introduced by the Belgians, is the official language but is spoken only by a small minority. Kirundi is spoken by the majority of the population. About 70% of the current population can be described as Christian, although many continue also to adhere to indigenous beliefs.

Ethnic Composition and Ethnic Relations

The two major ethnic groups are the **Hutu** and the **Tutsi.** Before the massive population relocations of the 1990s, the Hutu constituted about 83% of the population and the Tutsi constituted about 13%. The remaining 1% percent of the population is made up of the **Twa,** a former hunter-gatherer people who were politically and economically tied to the Tutsi, and small numbers of **Asian** traders and **Europeans.**

The Hutu and Tutsi have a long history of interaction in the region, and some experts consider them to be two socioeconomic divisions of the same group. The Hutu first entered the region during the 7th century A.D. and were firmly established by the 10th century. The Tutsi migrated to the area, probably from Ethiopia, in the 16th century. The Hutu were primarily farmers of peas, beans, corn, and other crops. The Tutsi were nomadic cattle herders and warriors. The groups also differed in physical appearance, as the Tutsi were tall and thin and the Hutu short and stout. There was considerable interaction between the two groups, and also with the less numerous Twa. A state structure emerged with the Tutsi forming the ruling class and the Hutu the farming, herding, and agricultural class. The Tutsi considered the Hutu socially inferior, although the relationship between the groups entailed Tutsi rulers protecting their Hutu subjects from attacks by other Tutsi rulers. Many Tutsi men took Hutu women as concubines, and the children from these relationships were often considered to be Tutsi. Through this process, the marked physical differences between the groups lessened somewhat, as did cultural differences, with the two groups eventually speaking the same language, sharing a common social system, and following the same religious beliefs. Under Belgian rule, the system continued, with the Belgians favoring the Tutsi and ruling through them, the Hutu having even less influence than when they were under Tutsi dominance.

Both before and following independence in 1962, the Hutu majority began agitating for increased rights and participation in the political process, a possibility that became more likely with independence and a move toward democratic government. In 1972 a Hutu revolt failed to remove the Tutsi government, and the Tutsi retaliated by killing the Hutu leadership and educated elite and driving some 150,000 into exile in Congo (formerly Zaire), Rwanda, and Tanzania. The Tutsi strategy of removing the Hutu leadership and thereby ending Hutu resistance was successful, and as many as 100,000 Hutu were killed over the next decade. In the early 1990s, the Tutsi government faced the reality of Hutu numerical dominance and initiated reforms designed to form a bicultural government and programs to allow Hutu exiles to return. However, the Tutsi continued to control the military, and a military coup in 1993 overthrew the civilian government. Open warfare between the Tutsi and Hutu followed, with tens of thousands killed and hundreds of thousands of Tutsi fleeing to Rwanda and Zaire. Although more international attention in the late 1990s has been drawn to the Hutu-Tutsi conflict in Rwanda to the north, the situation in Burundi remains unresolved.

Cameroon

The Republic of Cameroon is in West Africa. It is bordered by the Atlantic Ocean and Nigeria on the west; Chad on the north and northeast; the Central African Republic on the east; and Congo (formerly Zaire), Gabon, and Equatorial Guinea on the south. The region was exploited by the Portuguese beginning in the 15th century, and was a German colony from 1884 until the end of World War I, when it came under British and French control. Cameroon gained independence from the French in 1960. Cameroon is one of the most prosperous African nations, with an economy based on agriculture. Cacao, cotton, coffee, bananas, and palm oil are the major crops. Agriculture is supplemented by oil refining and mineral extraction. The population is about 14.3 million. English and French are the official languages, with French used more often and indigenous languages and pidgin languages such as Wes Cos used in daily life by most people. Information on religion is not reliable, but some authorities report that the majority of Cameroonians adhere to indigenous religions, about 30% are Christian, and 15% are Muslim.

Ethnic Composition

With more than 200 ethnic groups and 200 languages and dialects, Cameroon appears to be one of the most ethnically diverse nations in the world. However, most of the ethnic groups are small and many are similar culturally. Cameroon's ethnic groups can be divided into those of the north, the south, and the western highlands regions.

The north is the most ethnically diverse of the three cultural regions. For several centuries, it has been dominated by the **Fulani (Fulbe, Peul),** a Muslim people who are spread widely throughout West Africa and adjacent areas of North and Central Africa. They constitute about 10% of the national population and at least one-third of the population in the north. Although the Fulani are nomadic herders in most nations, in Cameroon they are mainly settled and raise livestock; oversee their farms; are craftsmen, traders, and merchants; and work for the government. They are also active spreaders of Islam in the region.

The other groups in the north are, to a large extent, defined in terms of their relationship to the Fulani. The label **Kirdi,** which is the Fulani term for "pagan," is applied to some two dozen small groups who fled the Fulani advance and refused to convert to Islam. They live in the hills and are mainly farmers, living at a subsistence level. Among the major Kirdi groups are the **Fali, Matakam,** and **Manadra.**

Peoples who resisted Fulani rule and refused to convert to Islam but remained in their traditional territory are labeled **Plains Kirdi** and form the third major ethnic cluster in the north. Major Plains Kirdi groups are the **Guidar, Guiziga, Daba, Moundang,** and **Mboum;** they are primarily farmers and, to varying degrees, continue to resist Fulani control. The two Kirdi groupings are believed to constitute about 11% of the nation's population.

The other major groups in the north are **Arabs** in the far north, who herd cattle, and peoples of the floodplains in the northeast, who have a variety of economic adaptations including fishing, farming, and cattle raising. Their relative isolation made it easier to avoid Fulani incursions, although some have converted to Islam. The largest and best-known of these groups is the **Toubouri.**

The western highlands region is dominated by the **Bamiléké,** the largest group in Cameroon, who constitute about 25% of the national population and at least two-thirds of the regional population. The Bamiléké is not one unified political entity but is composed of over 100 semi-autonomous chiefdoms. Although the power of the chiefs has eroded, they still play a major role in local and some regional matters. People in rural areas are mainly farmers, and for over 100 years, Bamiléké men have regularly migrated to work on plantations or in cities. The Bamiléké are heterogeneous in religion: some maintain indigenous beliefs, others are Christian converts, and still others combine Christian and indigenous beliefs.

Other peoples of the western highlands are the **Tikar, Widekum,** and **Bamoun,** who in various ways are related culturally to the Bamiléké but have long been adversaries, both before and following the end of colonial rule.

The peoples of southern Cameroon, the least populated of the three regions, are mainly forest peoples. The major groups are the **Pahouin, Baloundou-Mbo, Bassa, Kpe, Baboute,** and several thousand **Tropical Forest Foragers (Pygmies).** They subsist by growing vegetables, hunting, gathering, and fishing.

Ethnic Relations

Since independence, governmental interest in ethnic relations has centered on the need to mitigate and control north-south, Muslim-Christian, and English-French differences, as well as to control conflict between the Fulani and other peoples in the north and between the Bamiléké and other peoples in the highlands. Hostilities that predate colonial rule in the latter two regions still partially define ethnic relations in the post-colonial era. The government has sought to control ethnic conflict tied to competition for political influence by reserving set numbers of ministerial seats and legislative seats for representatives of major ethnic groups, although order has been maintained more successfully by a single-party political system, economic development, and control of the national wealth by a small segment of society.

A mission school in Cameroon. In Africa, Christian missionaries have been involved in education since the 1800s. Photo: Corbis-Bettmann.

Cape Verde

C ape Verde is an archipelago in the Atlantic Ocean, approximately 385 miles west of Senegal. Its islands are divided into two groups, Barlavento in the north and Sotavento in the south. There is a long history of contact with Guinea-Bisssau. *See* Guinea-Bissau.

Central African Republic

The Central African Republic is in Central Africa and is bordered by Chad on the north, Sudan on the east, Congo (formerly Zaire) and Republic of the Congo on the south, and Cameroon on the west. In 1960, the nation gained independence from French rule, which began in the late 19th century. Since independence, the country has suffered from considerable political unrest, although some stability has been achieved in the mid-1990s. The population is about 3.3 million and is about 80% rural. French is the official language, with Sangho, the language of one ethnic group, the language that is spoken by most people. While estimates suggest that 50% of the population is Christian (Roman Catholic and Protestant), most people adhere to indigenous religions.

Ethnic Composition

It is clear that the Central African Republic is an ethnically heterogeneous nation, with as many as 80 ethnic groups, but experts do not agree on how the population should be categorized. The French divided the population into eight ethnic groups, with French political considerations being perhaps the major criteria. Some experts have classified the population on the basis of region or language while others have argued that ethnic variation is especially hard to measure in the country because of the frequent mixing and contact between people from different groups. Two unifying similarities across the ethnic groups of the Central African Republic are that most people are farmers and most speak or are familiar with the same language, Sangho.

On the basis of language, the population can be divided into two major ethnic clusters and a few other groups that do not fit into these two categories. The first are speakers of Central Sudanic languages who live in the north and east. The largest of these groups is the **Sara,** who constitute about 90% of the national population. The Sara are composed of a number of subgroups including the **Kaba, Sar, Gulay,** and **Mbay.** Most Sara are farmers who grow grains, cassava, and other crops through slash-and-burn methods. Some are also involved in the growing of cotton for sale. Most Sara are Protestants, although many indigenous beliefs are followed as well.

The second major linguistic category is the **Ubangians,** who live in the central, southern, and western regions and comprise about 82% of the regional population. The major groups are the **Baya (Gbaya)** (34%), **Banda** (27%), and **Manja (Mandjia)** (21%). Smaller groups include the **Mbum, Banziri, Sango, Yakoma,** and the **Mbaka.** Ubangians, too, are primarily farmers who use slash-and-burn methods to grow cassava, yams, corn, and other crops for their own use, and cotton and coffee for export.

The other groups, which for linguistic or cultural reasons do not fit into either of these categories, are the **Zande** (*see* Sudan), **Tropical Forest Foragers (Pygmies)** (*see* Congo [formerly Zaire]), and **Hausa,** who are Muslims and traders (*see* Nigeria). The label "Muslim" is sometimes used in the Central African Republic as a general label, although it actually refers to peoples of various ethnic groups whose only commonality is that they are Muslims.

Ethnic Relations

Ethnic relations in the Central African Republic are characterized by the relative isolation of the various ethnic groups. Each group tends to live primarily in its own villages in its own region, and in towns and cities, people live mainly in ethnic neighborhoods and maintain ties with their home villages.

Chad

The Republic of Chad is in north-central Africa and is bordered by Libya on the north; Sudan on the east; the Central African Republic on the south; and Cameroon, Nigeria, and Niger on the west. Contemporary Chad society and the ethnic composition of the nation has been heavily influenced by the spread of Islam, by the arrival of peoples into the region from Sudan and Nigeria, and by French colonial rule from about 1900 to independence in 1960. From 1965 until 1993, the nation experienced a civil war that pitted peoples of the north against those of the south, along with political unrest and conflict with neighboring Libya. The population is estimated at about 6.9 million. French and Arabic are the official languages, although over 100 other languages are spoken. Arabic is spoken mainly in the north. About 50% of the population is Muslim, 25% Christian, and 25% adherents of indigenous religions.

Ethnic Composition

It is estimated that Chad is home to some 200 ethnic groups that can be classified into two or three very general categories. First, the population can be divided on the basis of region and religion into the northerners (who are Muslims) and the southerners (who are Christians or followers of traditional religions); however, this dichotomy masks ethnic diversity in the north. It is more meaningful to divide the population of Chad into three ethnic categories: Muslim herders of the north, Arabs, and African peoples of the south. It is important to note that although it is possible to place names on the different ethnic groups of Chad, ethnic identity has been fluid and has changed over time in Chad. Much of this change has been the result of east-west and north-south trade routes that over the centuries brought new peoples to Chad and also enabled the Chad groups to migrate elsewhere.

The people of northern Chad are primarily nomadic or seminomadic herders, with the **Tebu (Toubou)** and **Daza**—each containing a number of subgroups—being the major northern ethnic groups. All together, these constitute about 5% of the national population. The primary herd animals are camels, goats, donkeys, sheep, and horses. Before European influence ended slavery, the Tebu and Daza enslaved agricultural peoples who supplied them with vegetables. Conversion to Islam began for some groups as early as the 8th century, and all are now Muslims. Although the pastoral peoples of the north traditionally avoided involvement in national affairs, they were involved in the postindependence civil war designed to end southern control of the national government.

Arabs, who began arriving in Chad in the 8th century, constitute about 15% of the population and are the nation's second largest ethnic group. Arabs live mainly in the Sahel region south of the Sahara Desert. Arabs in Chad speak some 30 dialects of Arabic with Turku or Chadian Arabic serving as the lingua franca. Although some Arabs live in towns and some are farmers, most are nomadic or seminomadic herders of camels, cattle, sheep, and goats. The different herding or grazing requirements of their primary livestock have produced different lifestyles among the Arab groups. Politically, Arabs in Chad are divided into three tribes—**Juhayna, Hassuna,** and **Awlad Sulayman**—and each tribe comprises numerous clans. As with nomadic Arabs elsewhere, ties to one's clan and tribe are important. In addition to the Tebu, Daza, and Arabs, there are other small Muslim groups—pastoralists and farmers—scattered throughout the Sahel and the north. The larger groups are the **Maba, Dadjo, Sungor,** and **Tama,** as well as the **Fulani,** who immigrated from Nigeria in the 19th century.

While the peoples of the Sahel have been influenced by Arab and Muslim culture, those in the south are of African origin and the major outside influence has been European, primarily that of the French colonists. Most people in the south live in the extreme south and are horticulturists, growing cassava and grains for food and cotton as a commercial crop. The **Sara** are the largest southern group and the largest ethnic group in Chad, constituting about 25% of the national population. Favored by the French government, many Sara were installed in government positions during French rule. French presence also altered the local economy, adding cash cropping and wage labor to the local economy. Other significant groups in the south are the **Toubouri** and **Moundan.** People in the south follow either their indigenous religions or are Christians, mainly Protestants.

Ethnic Relations

Chad has never been a unified political entity with all ethnic groups active and full partici-pants in national society. In addition, no single language is spoken by all Chadians. This situation existed prior to the colonial era but was reinforced by the French, who established local districts along what they took to be boundaries between ethnic groups. The French preferred the southern farmers over the northern herders and placed these southerners in positions of authority. This pattern of southern control of the government continued after independence and continues to define ethnic relations in Chad. The civil war that raged from 1965 until 1993 (when an uneasy peace was reached) focused on northern resentment of southern rule. Although the new government is seeking to establish governmental authority and more representation for all groups, tensions remain between the north and south.

Comoros

The Federal Islamic Republic of the Comoros is an island nation located in the Mozambique Channel off the east coast of Africa. It lies between northern Mozambique and Madagascar and consists of the three main islands of Nzwani, Mwali, and Njazídja and several smaller islands. A fourth major island in that group, Mayotte, is an overseas territory of France, although it is also claimed by the Comoros. The islands were settled about 2,000 years ago by peoples from East Africa, Malaysia, Indonesia, and several hundred years later by Arabs from the Middle East. The islands were under Arab Muslim control until 1886 when they came under French control, which lasted until independence in 1975. Contact with France remains important and in 1995 French troops ended a coup. The population of about 570,000 is 99% Sunni Muslim. Arabic and French are the official languages, although most people speak Comoran, a language based on Swahili and Arabic.

Ethnic Composition and Ethnic Relations

The Comoros is an ethnically and religiously homogeneous nation. All **Comorians** are of mixed African, Southeast Asian, and Arab ancestry, and virtually all are Muslims. Most Comorians are farmers who grow cassava, rice, bananas, and sweet potatoes for local use, and vanilla, perfume oil, cloves, and copra (coconut flesh) for export. The retail and wholesale trade industries are largely controlled by the small population of **Asian Indians, French, and Malagasy** from Madagascar. The approximately 70,000 Comorians who live on Mayotte are ethnically like other Comorians although most are Roman Catholics and have greater involvement with French culture.

Congo, Republic of the

The Republic of the Congo is located on the border of the East and Central Africa geographic/culture regions. It is bordered by Cameroon and the Central African Republic on the north, Congo (formerly Zaire) on the east, Congo (formerly Zaire) and Angola on the south, and the Atlantic Ocean and Gabon on the west. Formerly the locale of two major kingdoms, the region came under French control in 1885. The Republic of the Congo became an independent nation in 1960 although economic ties to France have remained strong. The population is about 2.5 million and is 58% urban, with nearly one million people living in the capital city of Brazzaville. French is the official language although outside government and commerce, people speak their indigenous languages. Most people in cities are bilingual or trilingual. About 50% of the population is Christian (mainly Roman Catholic), 48% practice indigenous religions, and 2% are Muslims. In 1992, a democratically elected government came to power; since then, the nation has been experiencing political and ethnic violence as different groups compete for power.

Ethnic Composition

The Republic of the Congo has an ethnically diverse population of over 40 ethnic groups that can be grouped into four major ethnic categories: Kongo, Teke, Mboshi, and Sangha.

The **Kongo** live in the southwestern part of the nation, in the region from Brazzaville to the Atlantic Ocean. They constitute nearly 50% of the country's population and also live in Angola and Congo (formerly Zaire). People labeled today as Kongo are those who formed the core or were associated with the Kongo Empire, which dominated the region from the 15th century into the 18th century. The major Kongo subgroups are the **Vili, Yombe, Sundi, Lali, Kougni, Bembe, Kamba,** and **Dondo.** Today, nearly all are Christians, mainly Roman Catholic.

Living north of the Kongo are the **Teke,** who constitute about 17% of the population. At one time they were primarily hunters and gatherers, then they became traders and miners, and now most are farmers who grow cassava and bananas.

Living in the northwest are the **Mboshi (Boubangi)** who constitute about 12% of the population and are also made up of a number of subgroups including the **Makoua, Kouyou, Likouala, Banagal,** and **Bonga.** The Mboshi

are traders, farmers, and fishermen; additionally, Mboshi men have for years migrated to Brazzaville where they comprise a sizable percentage of the government workforce.

The fourth major group, the **Sangha,** lives in the northeast and are farmers and fisherman on the edge of the rain forest. They trade with the **Tropical Forest Foragers (Pygmies)** of the rain forest. It is estimated that there are about 12,000 Tropical Forest Foragers in the Republic of the Congo (*see* Congo [formerly Zaire]).

Ethnic Relations

Distrust and hostility between groups in the north and the Kongo in the south are a major source of political unrest in the Republic of the Congo. Distrust between northern and southern groups has a long history that dates to a time when the groups competed for access to trade routes through the region. Ethnic rivalry decreased under French rule, and the establishment of cities and subsequent migration from rural areas led to substantial mixing and contact between Mboshi peoples from the north, who worked for the government, and Kongo peoples from the south, where the capital city is located. Some experts believe that many urban residents today have a more cosmopolitan attitude and that relations are usually harmonious among people of different ethnic groups in the cities.

Following independence, the Republic of the Congo was ruled as a one-party state and ethnic rivalries continued to remain muted. However, in 1992, democratic elections were held and ethnic conflict broke out—mainly involving the Mboshi and Lali. Conflict has often been violent and has involved riots, insurrections directed at the government, arson, and murders. It has also destabilized the government: the military and the government are staffed and backed by different ethnic groups, and the two have often been in conflict, with the former not supporting the latter. Ethnic conflict also has been fueled, in part, by politicians who sought to establish political parties by appealing to ethnic and regional loyalties.

Congo (formerly Zaire)

Congo (formerly Zaire) is in Central Africa. It is bordered by the Republic of the Congo on the west; the Central African Republic and Sudan on the north; Uganda, Rwanda, Burundi, and Tanzania on the east; and Zambia and Angola on the south. Initially exploited by Europeans for its mineral wealth and slaves, Congo came under the direct rule of King Leopold II of Belgium in 1885 and then under Belgian rule in 1908. It gained independence in 1960. Since then it has experienced considerable political unrest including a civil war from 1961 to 1963, problems arising from the arrival of millions of refugees from neighboring nations in the 1980s and 1990s, and economic decline in the 1990s. In the late 1990s, its economy and political system are in turmoil and the central government barely exerts control over the nation.

Congo has a population of about 46.5 million. French is the official language, although indigenous languages are spoken by most people. About 50% of the people are Roman Catholics, 20% are Protestants, 10% are Muslims, and the remainder are adherents of indigenous religions.

Ethnic Composition

Congo (formerly Zaire) is an ethnically heterogeneous nation with approximately 200 different ethnic groups. However, many of these groups are small and localized, and are either subgroups of a larger group or are but one of a number of related groups who form a larger ethnic cluster. Persisting political unrest has meant that there are no reliable population figures for the ethnic composition of the nation. The overwhelming majority of Congo's peoples are classified as Bantu speakers, meaning that they speak related Bantu languages—as do many people in Africa south of Cameroon.

Since labeling people Bantu speakers does little to describe ethnic variation in Congo, it is more useful to categorize groups regionally. In the northeast are border populations of **Lugbara** and **Zande,** non–Bantu speakers who are also found in neighboring Sudan and Uganda. The primary group in the region is the **Mangbetu,** who are mainly farmers and number about 650,000. The Mangbetu were the dominant kingdom in the region until their rule and influence were ended by the Belgians.

Also living in the north—and in the other Central African nations of Uganda, Rwanda, Burundi, Central African Republic, Cameroon, Equatorial Guinea, Gabon, and the Repubic of the Congo—are the people once collectively referred to as **"Pygmies."** Although this term is now considered insulting, no other general name for this group has replaced it, although anthropologists use **"Tropical Foragers"** or **"Tropical Forest Foragers."** Tropical Foragers in Central Africa are not a unified group, politically, geographically, or culturally. Rather, they are a number of independent groups including the **Efe, Aka, Bofi, Kola, Mbuti, Baka,** and **Twa.** In total, across the nine nations where they live, they number about 90,000. In the past, Tropical Foragers were nomadic hunters and gatherers of the tropical rain forest, and to varying degrees, this remains their livelihood today. They also maintain trade ties to farming groups on the edge of the forest, who supply grains and root crops in return for meat and forest products.

In the north-central part of the country is a region known as the *cuvette,* home to a large number of groups, nearly all of whom are considered members of the **Mongo** ethnic cluster. They number about three million in total and are primarily rural farmers, although involvement with Belgian colonial society brought many into the wage-labor market and most converted to Roman Catholicism.

In the eastern forest and plains are a number of other groups including the **Metoko, Lengola,** and **Lega,** who are now much assimilated into the cultures of the Sudanic speakers to the north or into those the Bantu groups to the west and south.

Farther south are a number of smaller groups including the **Shi** and **Furiiru,** who are related to Bantu speakers in Rwanda, Burundi, and Tanzania and are mainly farmers and herders.

The southern savanna region of Congo is one of considerable ethnic diversity. Parts of the south were ruled by different kingdoms until the 20th century. The region also contained important trade routes linking central and east Africa. The rule of the kingdoms and traders passing through the region increased contact among groups and led to considerable mixing among the peoples of the region, resulting in both ethnic diversity and similarity, and also the mixing of peoples in many communities. Major ethnic clusters are the **Bemba,** who number about 1.8 million in Zambia, Tanzania, and Congo (*see* Zambia), the **Hemba**, and the **Haut of Shaba.** Virtually all groups in the western section of the south are classified as **Lunda** and were part of a powerful trading empire that ruled the region for three centuries beginning about A.D. 1600. The empire dissolved under colonial rule. The Lunda groups number about 1.5 million, with about 750,000 in Congo and the remainder in Angola and Zambia. Many are now Christians, al-

though indigenous beliefs have been incorporated into the Christian practices. A Lunda group that has drawn special attention because of its resistance to Lunda control is the **Chokwe,** who also live in Angola and Zambia. Also in the south are the **Luba** peoples. Luba is another general category which includes the **Luba of Shaba,** the **Eastern Luba,** and the **Western Luba.** These groupings include a number of groups including the **Kaniok, Lalundwe, Luntu, Binji, Mputu, Kete, Songye, Bangu,** and the **Hemba.** While most groups are farmers and speak related languages, there are significant variations in kinship organization and in political organization that are, to some extent, the result of different experiences with other African groups in the region, with Muslims, and with European colonists. All together, they number about two million.

In western Congo, south and east of the capital of Kinshasa, live several dozen groups who fall into a number of general cultural groupings including the **Tio** (composed of people formerly of that kingdom), **Boma-Sakata, Yans-Mbun,** and **Kuba.** Other clusters of groups in the region—all of whom are related to the Kongo to the west—are the **Yaka, Mbala,** and **Pende.**

The most politically active and at some times the most influential group in Congo is the **Kongo,** who live in the extreme western region and also in Angola and the Republic of the Congo. People labeled today as "Kongo" are those who formed the core of the Kongo Empire (or were associated with it), which dominated the region from the 15th into the 18th century. They number about four million, with about one million in Congo. In part because of their involvement with the Portuguese in Angola and the Belgians in Congo, the Kongo differ in significant ways from other ethnic groups in the nation. Their orientation in modern times is urban, and many live in Kinshasa, where they form 50% of the population, or in towns. Those who live in rural areas are farmers, but they grow food mainly for sale and are involved in the regional economy. Nearly all are Christians, primarily Roman Catholic.

Congo at one time had a population of some 200,000 **Belgians, Asian Indians, Lebanese,** and **Greeks.** Most have now left the country.

Ethnic Relations

Because of the severe economic and political problems facing Congo in the 1990s, any attempt to analyze ethnic relations is overshadowed by the greater attention given to, and more information about, the nation's widespread poverty, disease, and political unrest. Even in the past when problems were not as severe, both before and following independence, ethnic relations were complex and varied from region to region and even within regions. Ethnic relations were influenced by a number of factors including the traditional relations between the groups, relations during the colonial era, and competition for political power and wealth following independence. The most serious political crisis before the 1990s was the civil war from 1961 to 1963, which centered on an attempt by the Lunda in Katanga (now Shaba)—with Belgian support—to secede from the new nation. With United Nations involvement, the effort ended in failure, but it left a legacy of resentment between the Lunda and other groups who resisted Lunda efforts to secede. Relations in the west center on the Kongo, who controlled or influenced many other groups in the region and were the most active group politically following independence.

Côte d'Ivoire

Côte d'Ivoire, or the Republic of the Ivory Coast, is in West Africa. It is bordered by Liberia and Guinea on the west, Mali and Burkina Faso on the north, Ghana on the east, and the Atlantic Ocean on the south. It was under French control from 1842 until independence in 1960. Côte d'Ivoire is one of the more economically prosperous nations of Africa, with an economy based on oil refining; the growing and export of cacao, coffee, and palm oil; and a growing industrial sector. The population is about 14.8 million, of which about 50% is urban. French is the official language, although many people speak their indigenous languages. About 25% of the population is Muslim, 12% is Christian, and the remainder are followers of indigenous religions.

Ethnic Composition

The population is ethnically heterogeneous both in terms of the variety of African groups indigenous to Côte d'Ivoire and the immigrants from neighboring nations. The indigenous population, which is composed of as many as 80 different ethnic groups, can be classified into four regional cultural clusters: (1) East Atlantic—mainly Akan and related peoples; (2) West Atlantic—Kruan speakers; (3) Northwest—Mande speakers; and (4) Northeast—Voltaic peoples.

The **Akan** label covers a number of different peoples who live in southern and central Ghana and in the southeastern area of Côte d'Ivoire. There are about 6 million Akan people who share a common language, Twi, but had distinct kingdoms in the past. About 2.8 million live in Côte d'Ivoire, where the major groups are the **Agni** and **Baoulé,** the latter numbering about 2 million, making it the largest ethnic group in the nation. Smaller groups are the **Abron, Abouré,** and **Nzima.** Most of the Akan peoples are forest dwellers and horticulturists. They have also been famous as gold traders in the past. They are proud of their illustrious history, which includes the powerful Ashante and Fante kingdoms. Most Akan peoples are Christian, although their rulers have kept up the indigenous religious traditions.

Related to the Akan (probably through assimilation by Akan kingdoms) are a number of small groups along the southeastern coast known collectively as **Lagoon Cultures.** They constitute about 5% of the population and are primarily farmers. Despite living near the national capital of Abidjan, they do not play a significant role in national politics.

The major groups in the southwest are the **Kruan speakers,** also labeled the **Krou,** who form about 12% of the national population. They are culturally the same as the Kruan speakers in Liberia. The major Kruan group in Côte d'Ivoire is the **Bété,** with the smaller groups of **Dida, Guéré,** and **Wobé** also living in the southwest. Most Kruan peoples are farmers who grow crops both for subsistence and sale, supplemented by hunting or fishing, depending on the environment. Most Kruan have converted to Christianity. Related to the Kruan culturally are the **Dan, Gouro,** and other groups of the west-central region, although they speak Mande languages.

The northwestern region is dominated by peoples who speak Mande languages and constitute about 17% of the national population. The major **Mande** groups—who speak related languages but vary culturally from one another—are the **Malinké, Bambara,** and **Juula.** As with all other major ethnic groups in Côte d'Ivoire, there are also sizable numbers of these peoples in neighboring nations. The Mande groups are primarily farmers, although some also raise cattle. The Juula are known as traders and Muslim scholars. There is a mix of religions in the region, with the Juula being mainly Muslim, the Bambara adhering to indigenous beliefs, and the Malinké combining Islam and indigenous beliefs.

The fourth major culture cluster is the **Voltaic** peoples of the northeast, who form about 11% of the national population. The major Voltaic groups are the **Sénoufo** and **Lobi.** They are mainly farmers, with the former being mainly Muslim and the latter living in relative isolation from other groups in the region. Côte d'Ivoire also has about one million immigrant Mossi (another Voltaic group) from Burkina Faso.

As an economically prosperous nation, Côte d'Ivoire has attracted, for at least five decades, labor migrants from neighboring nations. They are estimated to form about 20% of the national population, although their numbers fluctuate in relation to the availability of jobs. The majority of immigrants are men who work in industry in the cities or as agricultural workers on the plantations. The major ethnic groups represented in this migrant population are the **Mossi, Kru, Fanti, Hausa, Fulani,** and **Dogon**.

The major non-African groups are the **Lebanese** and **Syrians** who number as many as 200,000 and are widely dispersed throughout the nation as retail-store owners and traders. The formerly large **French** population has now decreased to about 30,000 individuals, most of whom are involved in commerce and business.

Ethnic Relations

Ethnic relations in Côte d'Ivoire are difficult to characterize. The nation is made up of a number of different ethnic groups, some of which—such as the Baoulé, Agni, and Lobi—are protective of their ethnic identities and resist assimilation to an Ivorian identity. The nation is also religiously diverse, with Muslims, Christians, and followers of indigenous religions, and freedom of religion is protected in the national constitution. In addition, there are sizable populations of all major ethnic groups in neighboring nations, and many people maintain relationships with co-ethnics across the borders. At the same time, however, it is clear that the Baoulé are politically dominant, and the national government has moved to control ethnic conflict and to promote a sense of Ivorian identity that exists alongside the various ethnic identities. To some extent, this national identity has been built on an "us" (indigenous ethnic groups) versus "them" (French and immigrant workers) ideology. Thus, there is considerable resistance to affording immigrants equal rights, which has caused concern among the segment of the immigrant community that has lived in Côte d'Ivoire for many years and sees the nation as its home.

Djibouti

The Republic of Djibouti is a small nation in northeastern Africa. It is bordered by Ethiopia on the south, west, and northwest; Eritrea on the north; the Gulf of Aden on the east; and Somalia on the southeast. It was a French colony from 1862 to 1977, when it gained independence. Both Ethiopia and Somalia have claimed the region, although it has remained an independent nation with economic ties to France and some Middle Eastern Arab nations. Although most inhabitants of what is now Djibouti are the decendants of herders, the present population is heavily urbanized, with about 85% living in cities or towns. Famine and fighting in the region since the 1970s have led to considerable population movement both across and within national boundaries. The current population is estimated at 428,000. Both French and Arabic are the official languages. About 94% of the population is Muslim, and 6% is Christian.

Ethnic Composition

Despite its small size and small population, Djibouti is an ethnically heterogeneous nation. All ethnic groups in Djibouti also are present, often in larger numbers, in the three neighboring nations of Eritrea, Somalia, and Ethiopia. The two largest groups are the Afar (Danakil) and the Issas.

The **Issas** comprise about one-third of the population and live in the southern region of Djibouti. They are a subgroup of the **Somali** (the major ethnic group of Somalia), speak a dialect of the Somali language, and are Muslims. There is also a sizable Issas population in Ethiopia and a smaller one in Somalia. Like other Somali groups, the Issas are socially and politically divided into clans and subclans, with clan membership continuing to take precedence over any strong sense of national identity.

In addition to the Issas, two other Somali subgroups, the **Gadaboursis** and **Issaks,** together constitute about 28% of Djibouti's population. Both live mainly in the capital city of Djibouti City.

The **Afar (Danakil)** occupy the northern two-thirds of Djibouti, as well as neighboring sections of Ethiopia and Eritrea, a region known as the Afar triangle—the traditional homeland of the Afar people. The Afar constitute about 20% of the Djibouti population. Like the Issas, they were traditionally herders and are Muslims, although their version of Islam incorporates traditional beliefs that are not

followed by the Issas. The Afar were organized into a number of independent sultanates before European rule and distinct social classes, and allegiance to these groups continues to be important.

In addition to these major groups, about 6% of the population of Djibouti is comprised of **Arabs,** mainly workers from Yemen, and there are several thousand **Europeans** (mainly **French**) involved in commerce.

Ethnic Relations

Tensions and conflicts between the Afar and Issas (and Ethiopia and Somalia) date to the period of French rule, when the Issas resented French favoritism for the minority Afar. The Issas, along with supporters in Somalia, favored and led the independence movement, while the Afar, who feared dominance by the more numerous Issas, preferred French rule. After independence, the Afar resisted rule by the Issas-dominated government, and there was fighting between the two groups. The new government sought to promote national unity by making both French and Arabic the national languages, although both Afar and Somali were more commonly spoken. In 1991, some Afars, in the Front for the Restoration of Unity and Democracy (FRUD), revolted against the government. Although FRUD captured some territory in the north, French- and Issas-dominated Djibouti forces controlled the revolt, and a settlement was reached in 1994. Since then, the Djibouti government has tried to increase Afar participation in the political system by appointing FRUD leaders to government posts, and in 1996 FRUD was recognized as a politi- cal party. Nonetheless, both the Afar and Issas, as small groups in a small nation, continue to be caught in the middle of both Ethiopian and Somali desires for control of Djibouti.

Egypt

E gypt is in northeast Africa, and in terms of ethnicity, religion, and politics is classified as being in the Middle East. It is bordered by Israel and the Red Sea on the east, the Mediter- ranean Sea on the north, Libya on the west, and Sudan on the south. Egypt has existed as a discrete political unit for 5,000 years. Continuous and extensive contact with southern Europe, the Islamic Middle East, and sub-Saharan Africa has produced a modern Egyptian people, soci- ety, and culture that reflects influences from Europe (especially Greece and Rome), Persia, Turkey, the Arab nations to the east, Islamic states, Great Britain, and other African cultures. Claims that the ancient Egyptian civilization was heavily influenced by African cultures to the south are not supported by archaeological or historical research. While Egypt was under British control from 1882 to 1920, and then British influence for some 30 years, Egyptian society was ruled by a small, wealthy, urban, European-influenced elite while the majority of the population remained rural and poor. Since the military coup of 1952, this pattern has changed in some ways, with the ruling elite now being Islamic and Middle Eastern in cultural and political orientation, rather than European. A large urban middle class has emerged, and women play a greater role in life outside the home. Egypt has a population of 62.3 million, which is heavily concentrated in the major cities: Cairo (6.8 million), Alexandria (3.4 million), El-Giza (2.2 million), and seven other cities with populations exceeding 300,000. Arabic is the official language, although English and French are also used in major cities in the north.

Ethnic Composition

The ethnic composition of Egypt is relatively homogeneous. Ninety percent of the popula- tion are Eastern Hamitic Arabs, and 94% are Muslims, mainly of the Sunni rite. The term "Egyptian" indicates nationality, not ethnicity or religion.

Arabs, not including Bedouins and Berbers, constitute 90% of the population of Egypt. Arab culture came to Egypt from the Arabian Peninsula shortly after the founding of Islam in the 7th century. Due to contact with ancient Greece and other European nations, Arabs in Egypt, as in other North African na- tions, differ in some ways from Arabs in the Middle East and from Bedouin Arabs. The use of English, Western-style dress, repression of Islamic fundamentalism, and urbanization are some signs of Western influence. Still, a strong sense of Arab identity is reflected in Egyptian Arabs in the speaking of Arabic, adherence to Islam, and involvement in political and eco- nomic issues of importance to other Arab na- tions, although strong ties to the West and Egypt's peace accord with Israel point to con- tinuing European influence. Major divisions within Egypt are between urban and rural Ar- abs (to some extent, northerners and southerners) and the violent conflict (280 deaths in 1994) involving a minority of Islamic fundamentalists. Because Egypt is a relatively poor nation in comparison with the oil-rich na- tions of the Arabian Peninsula, Egypt has been, since the mid-1970s, a source of labor mi- grants, who are temporary residents of nations such as Kuwait and Saudi Arabia.

The **Bedouin** are traditional Arab nomadic herders and number anywhere from 500,000 to one million in Egypt. They live mainly in the deserts of the east and west and on the Sinai Peninsula. They are Muslims, although some pre-Islamic religious elements survive. Bedouins throughout North Africa and the

Bedouin camel camp. Bedouins throughout North Africa and the Middle East are seen as the bearers of traditional Arab culture. Photo: Corel Corp.

Middle East are seen as the bearers of the traditional Arab culture exemplified by a reverence for the family, resistance to outside influence, independence, and a strong sense of honor and equality within the Muslim community. For much of the 20th century, Egyptian governments have sought to settle the Bedouins and have forced many to switch to agriculture and wage labor in place of cattle herding. The result has been a drastic reduction over the last century in the portion of the population identified as Bedouin, although this is largely due to assimilation of Bedouin people into Egyptian society, with many Bedouins now identified as Egyptian Arabs. Additionally, overcrowded Bedouin communities have led to conflict between different family groups, and restricted grazing land has led to conflict with Egyptian farmers.

The three indigenous peoples of Egypt are the Copts, Berbers, and Nubians. **Copts** (Orthodox Coptic Christians) number about six million in Egypt, with substantial immigrant communities living in Sudan, the United States, and Great Britain. The population estimate is an approximation, as both government census counts and Copt estimates are believed to be inaccurate. Copts trace their ancestry to the ancient Egyptians. They are a religious minority and are adherents of Coptic Christianity, which developed out of a number of Christian sects active in Alexandria in the first three centuries A.D. Distinguishing features of the Coptic religion are the Monophysite interpretation of Christ (in which God and Christ

are believed to be essentially the same), the celebration of martyrs, a monastic order, and a patriarch who heads the church. Church liturgy is in the ancient Coptic language, although Copts in Egypt speak Arabic as their domestic language. The Coptic religion, marriage rules that effectively prohibit marriage to non-Copts, settlement in Copt communities, and relative affluence have set Copts apart from other Egyptians. The Copt history is one of periodic persecution at the hands of the Byzantines, Muslims, and—in the 1980s, after some years of peaceful coexistence—the Egyptian government and Muslim fundamentalists. In response to Muslim extremists who have attacked Copt communities, the Egyptian government has restricted Copt political participation and sought to control religious activities. As has been their tradition, the Copts have reacted peacefully, although some in the community seek separation from Egypt and want political autonomy.

Berbers, who called themselves **Imazighen** ("free men"), is the generic name given to the indigenous people of North Africa who speak non-Arabic languages and are today almost all Muslims. Many Arabs in Egypt and North Africa are descended from Berber peoples, although Berber tribes have always been, and continue to be, identified as a distinct group. Of a total Berber population of roughly 20 million, only about 6,000 live in Egypt, mainly in the desert near the border with Libya (*see* Algeria, Libya, Morocco).

Nubians number about 160,000 in Egypt, with a large population in Sudan. They are non-Arab Muslims descended from Egyptians who mixed with people migrating north from central and western Africa about 4,000 years ago. Thus, they resemble Black Africans more closely than Arab Egyptians. Until 1963 and 1964, most lived in villages in Nubia, a region in southern Egypt and northern Sudan, but the Egyptian government relocated 50,000 of them farther north because their land and villages were to come under flood waters after the construction of the Aswan Dam. Since then, some have remained in these villages or have started new ones, while many have settled in Cairo, Alexandria, and other northern cities. Although many Nubians remain farmers, settlement in cities has involved many in wage labor and in small businesses. As Muslims, Nubians are not subject to overt discrimination, although their different physical appearance and long residence in the south has led to a relatively low level of political participation. In addition, their forced relocation—despite the government provision of new land and housing—caused lingering resentment and a disruption of traditional family and village forms of social organization.

Ties to Europe have created distinctive Armenian and Greek communities in Egypt. **Armenians** came to Egypt as part of the Armenian diaspora over the centuries and now number about 12,000. They live mainly in Alexandria and Cairo where many are engaged in commerce and trade. Most Armenians are Eastern Orthodox Christians. The population has declined steadily since 1952 due to emigration to Armenia or other Armenian communities, following the coup in that year and concerns about the independence of the Armenian community.

Greeks number 350,000 and are the largest non-Arab minority in Egypt. Greeks have lived in Egypt for several thousand years, and most now live in Alexandria (founded by Alexander the Great), with a sizable community in Cairo, as well. They are engaged mainly in small businesses, are adherents of Greek Orthodoxy, have maintained a distinct cultural identity, and continue to use the Greek language.

In addition to the Greeks and Armenians, there are several hundred **French** and **Italians** who live in the cities of the north and a distinct, though small, **Albanian** community.

Egypt is also home to peoples from neighboring nations. **Palestinians** number about 4,000 and live mainly in camps near the Gaza Strip. Most are awaiting repatriation to settlements in Gaza, a process that is speeding up with the return of Gaza to Palestinian rule in 1995.

Sudanese number as many as four million following a series of migrations north through-

out the 20th century. They live mainly in rural communities in southern Egypt near the Sudan border. They are poor and live largely outside Egyptian society, although legally they have full rights in Egypt, including the right to own land, following a 1978 agreement between Egypt and Sudan. Because of these rights, they are not classified as refugees and thus are not entitled to receive aid from either Egypt or the United Nations, a situation that has led to protests in the 1990s.

Other groups residing in Egypt include 6,000 documented refugees from **Somalia** and several thousand refugees from **Eritrea** and **Ethiopia.** An unknown number of undocumented refugees from these nations are also in Egypt. All live in poor conditions on the margins of Egyptian society, and most will likely return to their home nations when conditions permit or will seek asylum in European nations.

Gypsies include at a least a dozen small groups with a total population of several thousand. Most are now settled, speak Arabic, and are Muslims. But, as they are scattered

A Muslim fundamentalist couple walking on a street in Cairo. Their identity is marked by their clothing.
Photo: Reuters/Corbis-Bettmann.

throughout Egypt and without a shared identity or political organization, Gypsies live outside mainstream society.

The once-substantial **Jewish** community in Egypt has been reduced to less than 1,000 people through immigration to Israel.

Ethnic Relations

Current relations with minority groups reflect Egyptian Arab concerns about maintaining power and order in Egyptian society. Formerly nomadic Bedouin Arabs have been settled, Copts have faced political and economic discrimination, and Nubians have been relocated to make way for economic development projects. The major conflict of the 1990s involves fundamentalist Muslims who seek to replace the secular government with an Islamic state. Muslim violence has been directed at the government, civic leaders, Coptic Christians, and tourists, and has been met with harsh government responses including mass arrests and executions that have been criticized by international human rights organizations.

Equatorial Guinea

The Republic of Equatorial Guinea is a small nation in West Africa. It consists of the continental province of Rio Muni and two chains of islands in the Gulf of Guinea. The major islands are Fernando Po and Annobon. Rio Muni is bordered by Cameroon on the north and Gabon on the east and south. The region was under Portuguese control beginning in the 15th century and then was ceded to Spain in 1778. It became an independent nation in 1968, and since the early 1970s it has experienced considerable political unrest and economic instability. The population is about 431,000. Spanish is the official language, although many people speak Fang and other African languages. The majority of the population is at least nominally Roman Catholic.

Ethnic Composition

Equatorial Guinea has an ethnically diverse population consisting of five major ethnic groups. The **Tropical Forest Foragers (Pygmies),** found throughout nine nations in Central Africa and bordering West Africa, are believed to be the first inhabitants of Equatorial Guinea. They now number a few thousand and live in the southeast; (*see* Congo [formerly Zaire]).

The **Fang** total about two million in Equatorial Guinea, Cameroon, Gabon, and the Republic of the Congo. In Equatorial Guinea, they constitute about 80% of the population and are the dominant group on the mainland. The Fang are mainly slash-and-burn farmers. They strongly resisted foreign rule, and although missionaries converted a large number of Fang to Roman Catholicism, many indigenous beliefs are still followed. Also intact is their highly structured form of social organization based on clans and marriage between clans.

The **Ndowe** live mainly along the coast and were already living there when the Fang began arriving from the east in the 1600s. They are subdivided into two major subgroups, the **Bumba** in the north and the **Bongue** in the south, with each further subdivided into even smaller groups. They are primarily farmers of cassava, yams, and plantains, and their farming livelihood is supplemented in many villages by fishing. Unlike the Fang, who resisted Spanish rule, many Ndowe served as laborers on Spanish plantations. Most are Christians.

The **Bubi** are the people of the island of Fernando Po. They are evidently descended from mainland peoples who began migrating to the island about 700 years ago. Like the mainlanders, they are primarily farmers and grow mainly yams. Although some were assimilated into Spanish colonial society, most resisted assimilation and maintained a separate identity into modern times.

The **Creoles** are people of mixed African, European (mainly British), and American ancestry who came to the capital city of Santa Isabel from Liberia, Nigeria, and Sierra Leone. Prior to independence, although numbering only about 3,000, they dominated the economy. Their numbers have declined since then, as has their role in the economy.

Ethnic Relations

A major concern for many in Equatorial Guinea is the possibility of Fang unification and the creation of a Fang state from territory now in Equatorial Guinea, Cameroon, Gabon, and the Republic of the Congo. An effort by the Fang in this direction in the mid-20th century did not succeed but other groups continue to be concerned about future efforts. The concern is fueled in part by the fact that since independence, one extended Fang family from one clan has controlled the government. However, the ruling family and clan is not entirely pro-Fang, and at times has had political opponents massacred.

Eritrea

The state of Eritrea is in northeastern Africa and is bordered by Sudan on the west, the Red Sea on the east, and Ethiopia and Djibouti on the south. What is now Eritrea was formerly part of the Aksum Kingdom, the precursor of modern Ethiopia. From 1890 to 1941, it was an Italian colony, then it came under British administration in 1941 until 1952, when it was appended to Ethiopia. In 1962, Ethiopia made Eritrea a province, an act that led to a civil war that resulted in Eritrean independence in 1993. The population of Eritrea is now about 3.9 million, 83% of which is rural. About half the population (mainly in the north) is Christian, and about half (mainly in the south) is Muslim. Nine different languages are spoken, although English is gaining prominence as the language of education and business. Eritrea has suffered much political, economic, and social unrest since independence, and the process of building a nation has been ongoing. The revolution also created nearly one million Eritrean refugees in Ethiopia, Somalia, Sudan, and Djibouti who have been returning to Eritrea since 1994.

Ethnic Composition

The **Tigray** are one of the largest ethnic groups of northeastern Africa, numbering about two million. They live mainly in northeastern Ethiopia and neighboring Eritrea and speak the Tigrinya language. Some estimates suggest that they constitute nearly 50% of the Eritrean population. Political unrest and population shifts make exact counts of the number of Tigray in either Eritrea or Ethiopia impossible. In both nations, the Tigray are primarily rural farmers who for centuries have grown a variety of grains, including wheat and barley. They have lived in the region for over 2,000 years, although there has been much mixing with the Amhara in Ethiopia, and in Eritrea, there has been considerable Italian influence from the Italian colonial period. The Tigray began converting to Christianity in the 4th century and are members of the Ethiopian Eastern Orthodox Church, which is affiliated with the Coptic Church in Egypt. The Tigray also were the leaders of the independence movement that created the nation of Eritrea.

About 40% of the population of Eritrea is formed by two other ethnic groups: the **Tigre** and **Kunama.** The Tigre live in the lowlands of south-central Eritrea and the Kunama live in the southwest. Both groups are herders. The Tigre are Muslims, while some Kunama were converted to Roman Catholicism by the Italian colonists. The cultural orientation of these and other southern peoples is Middle Eastern. Other ethnic groups, who in total constitute about 10% of the population, are the **Afar** (*see* Djibouti); the **Saho,** who live along the coast; and small numbers of **Arabs** and **Europeans.**

Ethnic Relations

As noted above, there is a basic division in Eritrea based on region (north/south), ethnicity (Tigray/Tigre), religion (Christianity/Islam), and economy (farming/herding). Whether a national government can develop and maintain a unified nation remains to be seen. During the 30 years of war with Ethiopia, there was both cooperation and conflict among the ethnic groups. The Eritrean Liberation Front (ELF), which led the revolution in its early years, was composed of both Tigray and Tigre groups, although the different ethnic/religious/ regional groups operated separately. The Ethiopian People's Liberation Front (EPLF), which joined the fight in 1970, was also multi-ethnic, but its groups were usually composed of an ethnic and religious mix. After three years of fighting between the two parties, the EPLF was victorious in 1981 and the post-independence government has continued to promote a policy of ethnic cooperation, fearing that the emergence of ethnic-, religion-, or region-based political parties will cause the nation to disintegrate.

Ethiopia

The Federal Democratic Republic of Ethiopia is in northeastern Africa and is bordered by Eritrea, Djibouti, and Somalia on the north; Somalia on the east and southeast; Kenya on the south; and Sudan on the west. Paleontological research indicates that the first human beings evolved in what is now Ethiopia some three million to four million years ago.

Ethiopia has had a long and complex history. From the 2nd century to the 12th century, the northern highlands area was the center of the Aksum Kingdom, which had trade and other ties to the Mediterranean and Arab worlds. The kingdom adopted Christianity in the 4th century, and from the 7th century on was under pressure from the Muslims to convert to Islam. After the decline of the Aksum Kingdom, Ethiopia experienced centuries of decline. In the late 1800s, the region was again unified, and independence was achieved following the defeat of the Italians in 1913. During the 20th century, modernization programs were enacted and one ethnic group, the Amhara, enjoyed much political power until the Emperor Haile Selassie was dethroned in 1974. Since then, Ethiopia has experienced several severe famines; conflict with Sudan and Somalia; internal political unrest; and the Eritrean revolt, which led to Eritrean independence in 1993. The population is estimated at 57.2 million. Amharic is the official language, although most people speak other languages.

Ethnic Composition

Ethiopia is an ethnically heterogeneous nation, with some 70 to 80 different ethnic groups living within its borders. However, the majority of the population is composed of people from only four groups—Oromo, Amhara, Tigray, and Somali. Other groups in Ethiopia are small, and some—such as the **Tigre, Saho, Afar, Nuer,** and **Anuak**—are also found in the neighboring nations of Eritrea, Djibouti, and Sudan. The nation is also religiously diverse, with about 45%–50% of the population (mainly in the south) Muslim, about 35%–40% Ethiopian Eastern Orthodox, and the remainder other Christian denominations or adherents of indigenous religions. Ethiopia also has about 250,000 refugees, mainly from Somalia and the Sudan, and there are about 200,000 Ethiopian refugees in other nations, most of them in Sudan.

The **Oromo (Galla)** are the largest ethnic group, estimated to constitute about 40% of the national population. The Oromo were at one time concentrated in the southern highlands but have now spread to other regions. The "Oromo" ethnic category is composed of a number of linguistically related groups including the **Boran, Shewa,** and **Welega.** The Oromo are not unified politically and there are important differences in social organization, religion, and economy across the groups: most are farmers, though some are herders; some are Muslims, others are Christians, and still others adhere to indigenous religions.

The **Amhara** live in the western highlands and constitute perhaps as much as 30% of the Ethiopian population. The Amhara, along with the Tigray and Tigre, trace their ancestry to a merging of Semitic and African peoples in the region several thousand years ago. Amhara culture was later influenced by the Greeks and Egyptians and was the center of the Aksum Kingdom. The Amhara also were dominant in the 19th century and parts of the 20th century, although since the 1960s other groups have sought to end Amhara dominance. Most Amhara are farmers and nearly all are Ethiopian Eastern Orthodox Christians. A basic distinction within the Amhara groups is between those who claim ancestry from the Aksum Kingdom and those who do not.

The **Tigray** are one of the larger ethnic groups of northeastern Africa, numbering about two million. They were the leaders of the independence movement that led to the creation of the nation of Eritrea. The Tigray live mainly in northeastern Ethiopia and neighboring Eritrea. Some estimates suggest they constitute nearly 50% of the Eritrean population and about 14% of the population of Ethiopia, but political unrest in the region and population shifts make exact counts impossible. The Tigray speak the Tigrinya language. In both nations, they are primarily rural farmers who for centuries have grown a variety of grains including wheat and barley. The Tigray have lived in the region for over 2,000 years although there has been much mixing with the Amhara in Ethiopia, and the two groups are now sometimes lumped together. The Tigray began converting to Christianity in the 4th century and most are members of the Ethiopian Eastern Orthodox Church, which is affiliated with the Coptic Church in Egypt.

The **Somali** live in the southeast and are the same people as the Somali across the border in Somalia. They are Muslims. Because of massive population shifts caused by political conflict and fighting in both nations, the Somali population in Ethiopia is impossible to

estimate but probably numbers about two million or more.

Other Ethiopian Ethnic Groups

Group	Area	Population
Beja (Beni Amir)	North	1 million (also in Egypt, Sudan, Eritrea)
Tigre	North	120,000
Bilen	North	120,000
Kunema	North	70,000
Nara	North	25,000
Saho	Northeast	120,000 (most in Eritrea)
Afar	Northeast	300,000 (mainly in Eritrea)
Qimant	Northwest	20,000
Beta Israel (Falasha)	Northwest	2,000 (most in Israel)
Kamtanga	Central	5,000
Kunfel	West	5,000
Gumuz	West	unknown
Awi	West	50,000
Berta	West	50,000
Argobba	Central	3,000
Harari	East	90,000
Gurage	South-Central	750,000
Sidamo	South-Central	2 million
Kefa and Mocha	South-Central	200,000
Welamo	South-Central	500,000
Gamo and Gofa	South-Central	300,000
Konso	South	60,000
Nuer	Southwest	500,000 (also in Sudan)
Anuak	Southwest	50,000 (also in Sudan)

All together, the remaining ethnic groups in Ethiopia constitute about 10% of the national population. Like the major groups, most people in these smaller groups are farmers. Some are Muslims while others are Eastern Orthodox Christians. The groups that deviate from this pattern are the **Harari,** who are mainly merchants and live in the city of Harar, and the **Nuer,** who herd cattle and other livestock in addition to farming. Most groups are located in the north or the south-central region. The list above includes both major ethnic group clusters such as the **Sidamo** (which includes the **Sidama, Hadya, Libido, Kembata, Timbaro, Alaba,** and **Deresa,** all of whom speak related Sidamo languages), as well as specific groups such as **Tigre.**

Ethnic Relations

Ethiopia is unique among the nations of the world in that the government dealt with the potential problem of ethnic conflict by creating nine ethnic states in 1994. The states, most of which are dominated by one ethnic group, are: Tigre; Afar; Amhara; Oromia; Somalia; Benshangul-Gumaz; Gambela Peoples; Harari People; and Southern Nations, Nationalities, and Peoples. Within a state, each ethnic group has the right to withdraw from the state and form its own state or even withdraw from Ethiopia. Proponents of this plan see it as a means to recognize explicitly the ethnic heterogeneity of Ethiopia's peoples and also, through local government agencies, to give each major ethnic group control over its own region. Additionally, vesting authority in the local ethnic groups weakens Amhara dominance, which many other groups resent.

Proponents also point out that Ethiopia is already politically fragmented into a number of ethnic-based political parties. Additionally, as it is a largely rural society, there has been relatively little contact among many ethnic groups. Critics argue that in the absence of any strong unifying forces such as religion or language at the national level, dividing Ethiopia ethnically risks the possibility of the country fragmenting into a number of smaller nations—or disappearing entirely if groups choose to join neighboring nations. In the late 1990s, the region deemed most likely to secede is the Ogaden region in the south, which is heavily populated by Somalis who also live across the border in Somalia. However, continuing political unrest in Somalia makes it unlikely that Somalia can annex the neighboring region of Ethiopia by force. There are also concerns among the Christian minority in Ethiopia about the influence of Islamic fundamentalism, and there has been conflict between Sudan and the Ethiopian government over Sudan's alleged support of Islamic fundamentalists. Sudan, which has an Islamic fundamentalist government, is seen by many experts as a major supporter of terrorist activity in the region (*see also* Egypt).

Gabon

The Gabonese Republic is in West Africa and is bordered by the Atlantic Ocean on the west, Equatorial Guinea and Cameroon on the north, and the Republic of the Congo on the east and south. Gabon was under French rule from about 1849 until independence in 1960. Since a drop in oil prices in 1986 damaged the already weakening economy, Gabon has experienced political and economic upheaval. Prior to then, it was considered one of the more prosperous nations in sub-Saharan Africa. The population is about 1.2 million. French is the official language, although indigenous languages are more commonly used. The population is primarily Christian (with Roman Catholics more numerous than Protestants), along with significant Muslim and indigenous minorities.

Ethnic Composition

Gabon is an ethnically heterogeneous nation with about 50 different ethnic groups. However, there is considerable similarity across groups: most groups are speakers of Bantu languages, and the people in most groups are farmers who grow cassava, bananas, and rice and live in small villages. Those who live near the ocean or rivers also fish. Many Gabonese are also involved in the growing of coffee and cacao for export, and some are involved in the oil and mineral industries.

The largest ethnic group in Gabon is the **Fang,** who live in the north and constitute from 30% to 35% of the population. Although they are not politically dominant, they pose a threat to other, smaller groups and are heavily involved in the prosperous regional agricultural economy.

The other major groups are the **Myéné, Mbete, Duma, Tsogo, Kota, Teke,** and **Puna-Eshira.** Each of these is actually an ethnolinguistic category with a number of subgroups who speak related languages or dialects. The Myéné live south and west of the Fang and are their major rivals for political power. The Puna-Eshira peoples live in the southwest along the coast and inland. The Kota groups live in the northeast and south-central regions and those in the northeast are involved in the mineral industry. The Teke are located in the far southeast and are related to peoples across the border in the Republic of the Congo.

About 1,000 **Europeans,** mainly French, live in Gabon. There are also groups of **Tropical Forest Foragers (Pygmies)** in the central and southwestern regions (*see* Congo [formerly Zaire]).

Ethnic Relations

Since Gabon's independence, ethnic relations have been relatively harmonious at the national level due to the regional isolation of different groups, single-party rule, and economic prosperity. In the 1990s, as economic problems developed and political unrest tied to forming a multi-party state emerged, ethnic identity has become more salient and more politicized. Today, ethnic, regional, and religious affiliations play a greater role in politics than in the past. Although persons from all major ethnic groups continue to occupy positions in government, in the military services, and in the private sector, reports suggest that ethnic favoritism in hiring and promotion is pervasive.

Ethnic conflict in Gabon centers primarily on the relationship between the Gabonese and workers from ethnic groups of other African nations who have been drawn to Gabon by its prosperous economy. While these workers are tolerated in good times, they are not especially welcome and they are provided less government services than are the Gabonese. For example, children of non-Gabonese have far less access to education and health care than do children of Gabonese, and they are sometimes victims of child labor abuses.

In times of economic hardship, the non-Gabonese are seen as competitors for jobs and as an economic drain. Thus, beginning in the late 1970s, the government has sometimes expelled foreign workers. In the mid-1990s, this practice has resumed and tens of thousands were forced to leave when the government required foreign workers to purchase work permits that cost as much as $1,200 (U.S. dollars). The government has been charged with discrimination against poor African workers as French technicians are charged only $100 for their permits. In addition to forced expulsion, foreign workers have also been subject to mass arrests and detention and have been the targets in riots.

Gambia

The Republic of Gambia is on the west coast of Africa between Senegal and the North Atlantic Ocean. It is almost an enclave of Senegal and is the smallest country in Africa. Its population is 1.2 million. The Gambia gained its independence from the United Kingdom in 1965, and the Gambia and Senegal signed an agreement in 1981 that called for the creation of a loose confederation to be known as "Senegambia." However, this federation dissolved in 1989. Currently, the Gambia is governed by a military dictatorship, which came to power through a coup d'état in 1994, deposing the democratically elected government. In the Gambia, 90% of the people are Muslims, 9% are Christian, and the rest follow indigenous faiths. As in other African countries, indigenous beliefs influence followers of both Christianity and Islam. At least 20 languages are recognized in the Gambia. English is the official language, and Mandinka, Wolof, Fula, and other indigenous vernaculars are widely spoken. Most Gambians are subsistence farmers.

Ethnic Composition

The Gambia has at least 20 separate ethnic groups. Its major groups are the **Mandinka** (42% of the population), **Fula** (18%), **Wolof** (16%), **Jola** (10%), and **Serahuli** (9%). The Mandinka group (also known as the **Mande**) includes a number of distinct subgroups. Nearly all Mandinka are farmers and many are subsistence farmers. Rice is a major staple crop and many towns are surrounded by family fields and women's garden plots. The Mandinka are generally Muslims, and villages are under the leadership of an *iman*, an Islamic religious leader.

The **Fula,** or **Fulani,** are pastoral groups and are Muslim.

The **Wolof,** also Muslim, are found in Senegal, the Gambia, and Mauritania. The Wolof are farmers, traders, and skilled crafts workers.

The **Jola** are primarily farmers who earlier were much involved in the Atlantic slave trade, both as slaves and as slave traders. One of the first groups to settle in the region, they strongly resisted Mandinka aggression and most have also resisted Islam and adhere to their traditional religion.

The **Serahuli** are a Mande-speaking group closely aligned with the Mandinka, whom they formerly served as traders and mercenaries.

Other groups comprise about 4% of the population, and non-Gambians make up a further 1%. Other groups (with available population estimates) are the following: **Bainouk, Bambara** (4,200), **Bayot, Jahanka, Diola** (45,000–51,000), **Kalanke** (1,000), **Kassonke, Krio** (6,600), **Mandyak** (14,100), **Mankanya** (1,200), **Mansoanka, Serrer** (21,000), and the **Sonninke** (51,000). Many of the "non-Gambians" are refugees. Recent conflicts in Liberia and Sierra Leone have affected many West African countries. The Gambia hosts around 2,000 **Senegalese** refugees from the Casamance region, and hundreds of **Liberian** and **Sierra Leonean** refugees. An attack on the military barracks near the border with Senegal recently caused the Gambia to reevaluate the status of many of the refugees from Liberia and Sierra Leone.

Ethnic Relations

Until the 1993 coup, the Gambia was a model of internal ethnic harmony. Since the coup, problems with neighboring Senegal, some of which have an ethnic basis, have emerged as a serious issue for both nations. The coup was aimed at President Dawda Jerawa's close ties with Western and other West African countries and was led by those who stressed Gambian autonomy. One major ethnic factor is that Gambian president Yahya Jammeh is an ethnic Jola, and Jola people are related to the Diola people in the Casamance region of southern Senegal. The Senegal government is concerned that the ties between the two ethnic groups will further encourage an already growing secessionist movement in the region, with the Casamance becoming part of the Gambia. One approach to preventing secession has been to attempt to form a union between Senegal and the Gambia. However, all attempts have so far failed to create a union. The most recent attempt, in 1991, failed because the then-ruling Mandinka-dominated Gambia political party feared that the Gambia would lose its identity in a union dominated by the Wolof Senegalese ruling elites.

Ghana

The Republic of Ghana is located in the middle of the countries along the Gulf of Guinea in West Africa. It is bordered on the east, west, and north by the Republics of Togo, Côte d'Ivoire, and Burkina Faso. The Atlantic Ocean is Ghana's southern border. Ghana's population is about 17.7 million. A little over half of the population live in rural areas and are farmers.

Prior to European colonization, Ghana was part of an African kingdom that included present-day Mali. It was named after the ancient kingdom of Ghana, which occupied a different location in Africa from present-day Ghana. European colonialists named present-day Ghana "The Gold Coast," and it was settled by a number of European countries who desired gold, ivory, and slaves. By the middle of the 19th century, Ghana was a crown colony of Britain. After World War II, Ghanaians sought political independence, and in 1957, Ghana became the first sub-Saharan African country to achieve it. Ghana's first president was Kwame Nkrumah, a charismatic leader who sought to impose African socialism on the country.

Ghana's major languages are English, Twi, Mossi-Dagomba, Ewe, and Ga. Its chief religions are Islam, Christianity, and traditional ones.

Ethnic Composition

Ghana is an ethnically heterogeneous nation, with some 100 different ethnic groups who speak an equal number of languages and dialects. These groups fall into five general ethnolinguistic categories: Akan, Ewe, MoleDagbane, Guan, and Ga-Adangbe.

The **Akan** label is used to designate a number of different peoples who live in southern and central Ghana. There are about six million Akan people who share a common language, Twi, although they had distinct, regional kingdoms in the past. Most of the Akan peoples are forest dwellers and farmers. They were formerly famous as gold traders. They are proud of their illustrious history, which includes the glories of the Ashante and Fante kingdoms. Most Akan peoples are Christian, although their rulers have kept up indigenous religious traditions. Akan peoples are also found in large numbers in Nigeria, and Ewe peoples in Togo and in Benin, where they are called **Fon.**

Ewe is a generic label for a number of related groups who speak variants of the same language and live in southeastern Ghana. Major Ewe subgroups are the **Anlo, Be, Gen, Peki, Ho, Kpando, Tori,** and **Ave.** They practice farming and fishing, and Ewe women are famous for trading in the market. There are many Christians among the Ewe. In fact, Ewe

were among the first Christian converts in Ghana. However, the traditional voudon religion still holds great influence.

The **Guan** live in west-central Ghana, with a few groups farther north. Major subgroups are the **Anum-Boso, Larteh,** and **Kyerepong.** Many Guan groups have mixed with and have been assimilated to some extent by the neighboring Akan, Ewe, and Ga-Adangbe. The Guan are farmers with some men earning additional income as migrant farmers.

MoleDagbane is a subfamily of languages in the Gur language family. Speakers of MoleDagbane languages form about 15% of the national population in Ghana and are the largest ethnic category in the north. Major subgroups are the **Mamumba, Dagomba, Mamprusi, Talensi,** and **Kusase.** Other major groups in the north are **speakers of Gurma and Grusi** languages, which are related to MoleDagbane, and small numbers of Guan, Akan, and **Mande speakers** in the extreme northeast. They are primarily farmers, and adherence to indigenous religions remains strong.

The **Ga-Adangbe** are clusters of related peoples who live in southern Ghana, both in the capital city of Accra, along the adjacent coast, and in the surrounding plains. The Ga live to the west and the Adangbe to the east of Accra. A major Ga subgroup is the **Ga-Mashpie** who live in their own neighborhoods in Accra. The major Adangbe subgroups are the **Sahi, La, Ningo, Krobob, Ada,** and **Gbugble.** Many of these peoples were fishers in the past, although many are now involved in the commercial society that has developed in and around Accra.

Ghana has a liberal policy of accepting refugees from other West African nations and thus has a large refugee population including some 94,000 **Togolese** who fled to Ghana in 1993 and an estimated 20,000 **Liberians.**

Ethnic Relations

Ethnic conflict is a serious issue in Ghana. One major, ongoing problem has been a war between the Konkomba and Dagomba (two Gur-speaking groups in the north) for the last few years. The Konkomba are largely traditionalist and live in scattered communities lacking central political control, while the Dagomba, about 400,000 in number, are centralized Muslim farmers. The primary issue between these two groups—as among many groups in the north—is control of land. Since March 1994, many Konkomba have fled to Togo as a result of ethnic conflict in the north. This and other ethnic conflicts in the north from 1994 through 1996 have left about 20,000

people dead and some 100,000 injured. The government has not been able to end the conflicts, although it has created a permanent negotiating team composed of religious leaders, NGOs, Council of State members, and other interested parties. The presence of troops in the region has also made it easier for traders from one group to travel to markets by protecting them from attacks by other groups.

Another major ethnic issue is the role of the Ewe in controlling senior government positions, although some officials are from other ethnic groups. Political opponents from other groups often make Ewe ethnicity a political issue. A major issue involving some Ewe groups is their custom of "trokosi." Trokosi is a traditional practice found among the Ewe in the Volta region, in which a girl—usually less than 10 years of age—is bound to a traditional shrine for offenses allegedly committed by a family member. The Ewe believe that unless this atonement is made for its crimes, family members will die. This violation of the rights of women and children has come under great criticism in Ghana.

There have also been conflicts between religious groups, particularly among Islamic sects, and also between Christians and Muslims near the city of Tamale.

Guinea

The Republic of Guinea is a West African nation, bordered on the north by Guinea-Bissau, Senegal, and Mali; on the east and southeast by the Côte d'Ivoire; on the south by Liberia and Sierra Leone, and on the west by the Atlantic Ocean. Guinea has a population of about 7.4 million, 70% of whom live in rural areas.

Hunting and gathering populations first occupied the area at least 30,000 years ago, and farming has been practiced there for about 3,000 years. Roughly 1,000 years ago, Susu (Saussou) and Malinke (Maninka) people began to move into Guinea from the east, pressing into the territory of the Baga, Koniagi (Coniagui), and Nalu (Nalou) populations. The people of the north and east parts of modern Guinea were part of the Mali and Songhai empires from the 13th century on. The Mandingo elite converted to Islam and employed Islamic legal principles in organizing their kingdoms after the 15th century. The Torobde clan of the Fulani acted as missionaries for the new religion and spread it throughout the region.

The Portuguese entered Guinea's history in the 15th century, engaging in the slave trade, which influenced Guinea until the mid-19th century. French influence began in the 1880s and some Guineans resisted until about 1920. In 1958, Guinea rejected membership in the French Union and chose independence.

The major religion of Guinea is Islam, the religion of 85% of the population. The remainder are chiefly traditionalists with a few Christians. Traditional religions, however, still have great influence among Christians and Muslims.

Ethnic Composition

Guinea's ethnic diversity is reflected in its languages. French is the official language, but there are eight national languages—Malinke, Susu, Fulani, Kissi, Basari, Loma, Koniasi, and Kpelle.

Guinea is composed of a number of ethnic groups. **Fulani (Fulbe, Fula,** or **Peul)** of the Fouta Djallon tend to live in small hillside hamlets of 75 to 95 persons each, with the lower classes occupying the valleys. In the heart of the highlands, the countryside is thickly settled with hamlets every few miles, while in the east the land is less settled. In Lower Guinea, villages are grouped together at the bases of hills, in the open plain, or in a valley floor. Village solidarity is more marked in this area than in the highlands, and each village contains between 100 and 200 people. The Fulani, who are Muslims, comprise about 35% of Guinea's population.

Mande people of Upper Guinea live in moderately large villages of about 1,000 inhabitants located near permanent water sources, the adjacent soils of which are used for cultivation. The villages are tightly grouped; these were empty brush areas in which farming was unprofitable. The Mande are divided into the **Malinke** in the east (30% of the population) and the **Susu** along the coast (20% of the population). The Malinke are Muslim farmers, and the Susu, who are largely Christian, are cultivators, traders, and fishers along the coast.

There are also 500,000–600,000 refugees from Liberia and Sierra Leone in Guinea.

Among the people who lived on the Sierra Leone and Liberian borders, rice was grown on most hillsides and in every low-lying and swampy area. Villages in this area tended to be small and rarely contained more than 150 people; they were often tucked inside groves of kola, mango, and coffee trees. Farther east among the **Kpelle** people (*see* Liberia), fire-cleared land was used to plant vegetables and rice. Larger villages were usually located on remote hillside terraces that were often surrounded by secondary forest growth.

Ethnic Relations

Within Guinea, ethnic identification is strong. It is not unusual for members of different ethnic groups to suspect one another of wrongdoing or discrimination against other ethnic groups in almost every aspect of public life. Within the government, promotions to senior government positions and the highest military ranks below the president carefully include people of all three major ethnic groups. The Cabinet also includes representatives of all major ethnic groups. However, a lopsided number of the senior-ranking military officers are Susu, President Conte's own ethnic group. So explosive is the ethnic factor that the penal code forbids any meeting that has an ethnic or racial character or any gathering "whose nature threatens national unity."

Religious differences within the Islamic community are also a cause of recent conflict. The government and the quasi-governmental National Islamic League have spoken out against the increase of Shi'ite sects that they claimed were promulgating new ideas and threatening the cohesion of Islam in Guinea.

Guinea's record with ethnic groups outside its country is generally good. In 1996 it provided first asylum to over 600,000 Liberian and Sierra Leonean refugees. There have been no reports of people being forcibly returned to a country where they feared persecution. Guinea has been generous in providing access to school buildings, local medical facilities, and land for farming to assist those denoted refugees.

Guinea-Bissau

The Republic of Guinea-Bissau is in West Africa and is bordered by Senegal on the north, Guinea on the west and south, and the Atlantic Ocean on the east. The Portuguese made the European discovery of the region in the 16th century, and from then until independence in 1974 they controlled the region. Guinea-Bissau has a population of 1.2 million. Portuguese is the official language, although Crioulo, a language based on Portuguese and African languages, serves as the lingua franca throughout most of the nation. A majority of the people are adherents of traditional religion, with about 35% Muslims and the remainder (less than 10%) Christians.

Ethnic Composition

Guinea-Bissau is an ethnically heterogeneous nation with about two dozen ethnic groups forming its population. There are more similarities than differences among many of these groups, and they are conventionally lumped together into three general categories: Senegambians, Fulani, and Mande.

The **Senegambians** constitute about 60% of the national population and the major groups within this category are the **Diola, Balanta, Nalu, Bissago, Papel, Serer, Landuma, Banhun, Baga,** and **Beafada.** They all speak West Atlantic languages and most are farmers, with rice, corn, millet, and sorghum the major crops, and nuts and coconuts grown for sale. Most Senegambians have retained their traditional religions.

The **Mande** peoples, who are dispersed throughout this region of West Africa, include in Guinea-Bissau the **Mandingo, Conhaque, Dialonke,** and **Soninke.** They form about 20% of the national population. Many are farmers, but they also have a long tradition of involvement in trade flowing from the interior of Africa to the Atlantic coast, and some continue to be involved in trade.

The **Fulani** are pastoral nomads of eastern Guinea-Bissau, and live as well in other nations in the region. They form about 20% of the population and are Muslims.

The major non-African minority is the **Cape Verdeans,** people of mixed African and Portuguese ancestry from the Cape Verde Islands off the coast of West Africa. There is a long history of contact between the Cape Verde Islands and Guinea-Bissau, and the two were one nation from 1974 until Cape Verde became independent in 1975. The population of the islands is about 450,000. Cape Verdeans worked on Portuguese plantations on the islands and were involved in the Atlantic slave trade. In Guinea-Bissau, Cape Verdeans were involved in establishing plantations in the north. They now constitute about 2% of the national population and nearly all are Roman Catholics.

There is also a population of people of mixed African and Portuguese ancestry native to Guinea-Bissau who are labeled **Mesticos.** There have been traditionally close ties between Mesticos and Cape Verdeans.

The other minorities are small numbers of **French** and **Portuguese** who are involved in commerce and economic development, and **Syrians** and **Lebanese** who are involved in retail trade.

Ethnic Relations

As in neighboring Guinea, there is considerable mistrust and limited contact among the different ethnic groups in Guinea-Bissau. The primary ethnic issue in Guinea-Bissau is the role of the Cape Verdeans. What was perceived as disproportionate Cape Verdean political and economic influence was a major factor in the separation of Cape Verde from Guinea-Bissau in 1975 and in the overthrow of the Mestico-led government in that same year. Both Mesticos and Cape Verdeans had closer ties to the Portuguese than did the African majority, and resentment over their role during Portuguese rule and the exploitation of African laborers on the plantations persist in the postindependence period. Ethnicity also plays a role in Guinea-Bissau politics, and the 1991 constitution, which legalized a multiparty system, led to the establishment of a number of ethnic-based parties, including one representing Muslims.

Kenya

The Republic of Kenya is on the east coast of Africa and is bordered on the east by Somalia and the Indian Ocean, on the south by Tanzania, on the west by Uganda, and on the north by Sudan and Ethiopia. The region that is now Kenya was settled by several waves of immigration from the north and west, which eventually produced a population composed of a number of different ethnic groups. Contact with Arab traders dates to at least the 8th century when Islam was introduced to the region. Continual European contact began in the 15th century with the British taking control in 1887. Following a four-year war known as the Mau Mau Rebellion, Kenya became an independent nation in 1963.

The population of Kenya is 28.2 million and is largely (73%) rural. Swahili and English are the official languages, with the latter being used as the language of business and government. Swahili is the native language of only a small percentage of the population, but it has become the lingua franca for many people who continue to speak their indigenous languages. The people of Kenya were the object of considerable missionary activity, and about 75% of the population is now Christian, about 28% being Roman Catholic and 47% Protestant. As elsewhere in Africa, many people continue to follow their traditional beliefs along with Christianity. Twenty-five percent of Kenyans either follow traditional religions (19%) or Islam (6%).

Ethnic Composition

Kenya has an ethnically diverse population of over 100 African ethnic groups, as well as Arab, Asian, and European peoples. Nearly all the African groups can be classified into nine major groups or clusters of groups, based on language. In Kenya, where politics are to some extent based on ethnicity, identification with a large ethnic group is important when a group is seeking to influence the political process.

The largest ethnic group is the **Kikuyu,** who number about 4.5 million and live mainly in central Kenya. Jomo Kenyatta, the leader of Kenya's independence movement and its first president, was a Kikuyu. Often lumped with the Kikuyu are a number of much smaller groups, such as the **Kamba, Embu, Mbere, Tharaka,** and **Meru,** who share a common history with the Kikuyu. These groups are known collectively as the **Thagicu,** and all migrated into the region between the 12th century and 14th century. The Kikuyu are mainly farmers of crops such as yams, bananas, millet, and sweet potatoes. Because of their location, Kikuyu culture was significantly affected by the British colonials, who settled mainly in the east. Much farmland was taken by the British, a large number of Kikuyu were converted to Christianity, and many were drawn into the colonial economy as laborers.

The next largest group is the **Luyia (Lhuya),** who live in the west and number about 3.5 million in Kenya. There are another 1.5 million across the border in Uganda. The Luyia category is composed of 17 subgroups in Kenya and at least 3 more in Uganda, all of whom speak dialects of the Luyia language. Most are farmers who grow a wide variety of crops for their own use and for sale in the regional markets. Nearly all are Christians, although traditional beliefs remain important.

Third in size are the **Luo,** who live in the southwest near Lake Victoria. They number about 3.2 million with several hundred thousand living across the border in Tanzania. Unlike the Kikuyu and Luyia, they are cattle herders, although they also farm to provide food for their own use. Conversion to Christianity has reached most Luo, although many continue to follow traditional practices.

Fourth in population are the **Kalenjin,** an ethnic category composed of eight groups—**Endo (Keiyo), Kipsigis, Marrakwet, Nandi, Pokot (Suk), Sebei, Terik,** and **Tugen**—who live in western Kenya. The current Kenyan president, Daniel Moi, is Kalenjin. Most Kalenjin groups combine cattle herding with farming. Farming provides most of their food as well as surplus for sale, while cattle herding, which is identified with the traditional Kalenjin way of life, is an important marker of ethnic identity. As with other groups, Christianity has won many converts among the Kalejin, although it has not completely replaced traditional beliefs and practices.

The fifth largest group, and the only other one with a population exceeding one million, is the **Gusii,** who number about 1.3 million and live in the west. They are primarily farmers who grow grains and vegetables for their own use and for trade with other groups. There have also been substantial migrations of Gusii to cities because their rapid population growth has meant the land can no longer support the entire population.

The other major African groups in Kenya are the Swahili, Mijikenda, Turkana, and Maasai. The **Swahili,** who number about 400,000, are one of the best-known groups of East Africa. Through contact with Muslim traders, their language has become the lingua franca for much of the region. They live along the coast from southern Somalia through Kenya and Tanzania into northern Mozambique. The Swahili are Muslims, which sets them apart from other Kenyan Africans, as does their historic role as traders of raw materials and slaves. Today, some are merchants while others are laborers, especially in the smaller towns.

The **Mijikenda,** who number about 800,000, are a cluster of nine linguistically related groups—**Chonyi, Digo, Duruma, Giriama, Kamabe, Kauma, Jibana, Rabai,** and **Ribe.** The two largest groups, the Giriama

and Duruma, constitute about 75% of the Mijikenda. The Mijikenda live along the coast and subsist by growing fruits, grains, and vegetables, with coconut oil being their major export crop.

The **Turkana,** who number about 200,000 and live in the northwest, and the **Maasai,** who number about 250,000 and live in the south and in Tanzania, are the major pastoral peoples of Kenya. The Turkana, who are divided into two major subgroups, herd camels, cattle, and goats, and many continue to live a nomadic lifestyle as they move about the region in search of food and grazing land. Because they live in a remote and arid region and in nomadic

Maasai cattle herders in Kenya. The Maasai are losing valuable herding land to the government and developers. Photo: UPI/Corbis-Bettmann.

camps, they have been able to maintain much of their traditional culture. The Maasai herd cattle, along with sheep and goats, though the latter two are less important and less prestigious. The Maasai are not one unified group but rather a cluster of herding groups who live in the same region and speak the same language. Much of their traditional culture survives, and the Maasai are of considerable interest to non-Africans because of their unique cultural practices including a social class system based on age and a distinct class of warriors.

In addition to these groups centered in Kenya, there are also small populations of **Somali** and **Oromo** near the Somalia border, **Iteseo** near the Uganda border, and **Fulani** (*see* Nigeria). In addition, Kenya houses about

260,000 refugees from Somalia (220,000), Sudan (25,000), and Ethiopia (10,000).

The major non-African ethnic groups in Kenya are the Asians, Arabs, and Europeans. Asians are primarily **Indians** who arrived during the period of British rule to work as laborers, low-level government officials, and traders. They were a diverse group and included **Goans, Punjabis, Sikhs, Jains, Parsis,** and **Gujaratis.** Differences in language, religion, region, and caste that had been important in India remained so in Kenya, and the Indian population was never unified. They numbered about 150,000 at the time of independence, and about half left in the next few years. The population has continued to decline, with only a minority of Indians being Kenyan citizens. Most Indians in Kenya today are Hindus, although there is a Muslim minority. Indians remain a visible minority. Their skin color, style of dress, cuisine, languages, and houses of worship continue to set them apart from the African majority.

At the time of independence, **Europeans,** who were mainly **British,** numbered about 40,000. Like the Indians, their numbers quickly declined, and Whites classified as Kenyan citizens now number about 10,000. Others are temporary residents who work for the government.

The **Arab** population falls into three groups—those who trace their ancestry to Arabs who arrived before the arrival of the Portuguese in the 15th century, Arabs who arrived in the 19th century, and those who have come recently from nations such as Yemen in search of work. As there was much mixing of Arabs and Africans, many Arabs are of mixed ancestry and have, since independence, claimed to be Africans for political purposes. Like the other non-African minorities, they live mainly in cities and are mostly involved in commerce and the retail trade.

Ethnic Relations

Ethnic relations are a serious matter in Kenya; so serious that ethnic conflict is a continual problem and some experts fear that ethnic conflict may lead to civil war. Kenya has long been an ethnically divided society, but open conflict tended to be rare when each group controlled its own region and interaction between groups was mainly for trade. This pattern was disrupted first by the Arabs, who used the Swahili as slave traders, and then by the British, who took land from the Kikuyu and the Maasai. Resentment of the Swahili because of their role as slave traders remains an issue in Kenya. Continuing resentment of Indians by the Africans centers on the preferential treatment afforded the Indians by the British.

In the 1990s, the primary and most threatening ethnic conflict involves the Kalenjin, who control the government, and the Maasai on one side versus the Kikuyu and other groups including the Luo. Since 1991, the Kalenjin and Maasai fighting against the Kikuyu has led to over 1,500 deaths and over 200,000 Kenyans being driven from their homes. Most of the victims have been Kikuyu. Most experts believe that the violence represents the policy of President Moi, who retains his dictatorial rule after elections in late 1997. In 1993, he was criticized by the Africa Watch human rights organization for encouraging attacks on the Kikuyu and for not using government forces to end the fighting. While this is the major ethnic conflict, there are also conflicts between different groups living in urban slums; attacks by backers of the president on members of the White Safina Party and its leader, paleontologist Richard Leakey; and resentment of the continuing presence of Somali refugees.

Lesotho

The Kingdom of Lesotho is in southeastern Africa and is entirely surrounded by South Africa. Lesotho was previously called Basutoland, and in 1868, it came under British control when Lesotho's king sought protection from the Boers (South Africans of primarily Dutch ancestry) who had designs on Lesotho territory. Lesotho became an independent nation in 1966. Although politically independent, Lesotho is economically tied to South Africa as some 38% of Lesotho men work in mines and on farms in South Africa.

Lesotho is ethnically homogeneous: about 98% of the population of 2 million is **Basotho.** Over 100,000 Basotho also live in South Africa. Those Basotho who do not earn income by working in South Africa mainly farm or raise cattle. The Basotho speak seSotho, with English also serving as an official language, although few people speak it. Nearly all Basotho are at least nominally Christian, although—as elsewhere in the region—traditional practices are often combined with Christianity and many people belong to distinctively African Christian churches.

The 2% of the population that is not Basotho is made up of **Europeans (Afrikaners** and **Britons),** a few hundred **Asians,** and **Zulus.** As an ethnically homogeneous nation, Lesotho is free of ethnic conflict, although several dozen Basotho have been killed in the fighting between the Xhosa and Zulu in South Africa.

Liberia

The Republic of Liberia is in West Africa and is bordered by the South Atlantic on the west, Sierra Leone and Guinea on the north, and Côte d'Ivoire on the east. Liberia was founded in 1822 by freed African slaves from the United States. Liberia became an independent nation in 1847. From then until 1980, when the government was overthrown, Americo-Liberians dominated and ruled the country. Since 1980, the nation has been experiencing a civil war that has devastated the economy and political system and has forced about 50% of the population to relocate internally or flee the country.

Liberia has a population of 2.1 million. English is the official language, although most Liberians speak indigenous languages. It is estimated that about 70% of Liberians are adherents of indigenous religions (including those who are nominal Christians), 20% are Muslims, and 10% are Christians.

Ethnic Composition

Liberia is an ethnically heterogeneous nation, with the number of different ethnic groups in the country placed between 16 and 28. Efforts by the government to identify and list the ethnic groups have been criticized by experts who see political concerns rather than cultural variation as underlying the designations. The ethnic groups of Liberia fall into three general categories: indigenous Africans, nonindigenous Africans, and non-Africans.

Most indigenous African ethnic groups fall into two general categories, based on language: the Mande-speakers in the north and west, and the Kruan-speakers in the east and southeast. The indigenous African groups constitute about 90% of the national population. Most indigenous peoples are horticulturists who grow rice, cassava, and other crops by means of slash-and-burn horticulture. The growing of coffee, cacao, and palm nuts for export has been disrupted by the civil war.

The **Mande** category includes the **Kpelle** (the largest group in Liberia, accounting for about 20% of the population), **Mende, Loma,** and **Mano.** The major **Kruan** groups are the **Kru, Bassa, Krahn,** and **Grebo.** Most Kruan groups are farmers, with fishing also important for the Kru living along the coast. Other African groups who live in the north are the **Vai** (also in Sierra Leone), **Dey,** and **Bandi.**

The two major nonindigenous African ethnic groups are the Fante and Mandingo. The **Fante** are indigenous to Ghana, and in Liberia live mainly along the coast, especially in and around the capital city of Monrovia. Many are employed in low-level white collar jobs. The **Mandingo** have been immigrating to Liberia from neighboring nations for several centuries. They were primarily traders, and as such, spread across much of the nation, with some being assimilated into indigenous ethnic groups and others maintaining their Mandingo identity. Some are still traders while others are now farmers. Most are Muslims.

The major non-African groups are the **Americo-Liberians,** who form about 5% of the population, and several thousand **Lebanese** and **Syrians,** who are dispersed throughout the nation, working as traders and owners of retail shops. Americo-Liberians are the descendants of the freed slaves from the United States who founded Liberia. Although dominant politically and economically for most of the nation's history, they have always been only a small minority of the population and live mainly in the northwest, in and around Monrovia. Americo-Liberians fall into two groups. First are the very small minority who have formed the national elite, speak English, and are Christian. Second are the majority of the group who are poor and to some extent have been absorbed by the African population. The Americo-Liberian population also includes people called **Congoes**—the descendants of slaves taken from slave ships in the early to mid-1800s, who were then assimilated into Americo-Liberian society. Americo-Liberians have traditionally been influenced by Western culture as reflected in their dress, food preferences, and architecture. In the last several decades, as other groups have resisted Americo-Liberian dominance, some Americo-Liberians have been identifying more closely with the African Liberian culture.

Ethnic Relations

From the founding of Liberia, ethnic relations centered on the relationship between the Americo-Liberian ruling elite and the Africans. The freed slaves who established Liberia as an independent nation were well-assimilated into—although not a part of—White American society. They spoke English, were Protestants, believed in formal education, dressed in Western-style clothing, and lived in cities. The Americo-Liberians saw themselves as civilized and the indigenous peoples as primitive. Like their White supporters, they viewed the indigenous Africans as socially inferior and ranked them at the bottom of the Liberian social ladder. The economic ties of the Americo-Liberians were to financial interests in the United States, and African laborers were used on the plantations, to extract rubber, and in the mines. To a large extent, the two populations lived in separate worlds, with contact occurring primarily through government officials who collected taxes or recruited laborers from the indigenous population. Even after 1944, when the government sought to bring indigenous peoples into mainstream society, the two populations still continued to live in two different worlds. Even in the capital city of Monrovia, different ethnic groups lived in their own neighborhoods and interacted mostly with co-ethnics.

At the time of the coup that toppled the Americo-Liberian government in 1980, Liberia was controlled by no more than 2,000 Americo-Liberians, all of whom lived in their own exclusive world apart from the rest of the population. The coup placed a Krahn at the head of the government, and although reforms were promised, the Krahn banned the political opposition. This led to coup attempts by other ethnic groups, and by 1989, open warfare had broken out between the Krahn and other ethnic groups including the Gio and Mano. Despite intervention by other nations and four peace agreements, the civil war continues.

Libya

The Socialist People's Libyan Arab Jamahiriya is in North Africa and is bordered by Egypt on the east, Chad and Niger on the south, Algeria and Tunisia on the west, and the Mediterranean Sea on the north. Because of its strategic location, Libya has a long history of contact with other nations. Beginning in the 7th century B.C., coastal Libya has been settled or ruled by the Greeks, Carthaginians, Romans, Vandals, Byzantines, Egyptians, Arabs, European Crusaders, Ottoman Turks, and Italians. It became an independent nation in 1951. Libya has benefited from oil discovered in 1959, but for the last several decades, it has been embroiled in various disputes with neighboring countries and other nations that have charged the Libyan government with meddling in their affairs or with supporting international terrorism. Libya has a population of 5.5 million, which is heavily concentrated in the north. Arabic is the official language and Islam the official religion.

Ethnic Composition and Ethnic Relations

Like that of most other North African nations, Libya's population is composed mainly of people of Arab or Berber descent. Because of extensive intermarriage between the two groups, and because both are mainly Sunni Muslims (97%) and speak Arabic, the ethnic composition of Libya is usually described as Arab-Berber.

Arabs are an ethnic group indigenous to the Middle East. They are the majority population in 15 nations in the Middle East and North Africa. Arabs first arrived in Libya in the early 8th century, and within two centuries had converted most Berbers to Islam. Although Arabs never formed more than 10% of the Libyan population, their cultural dominance and the assimilation of many Berbers have made Libya an Arab nation. The history of the emergence of Arabs as a distinct group in the Middle East is unclear, but as early as 853 B.C., the Arabic language was in use. Although being an "Arab" has different meanings in different nations, a shared Arab identity is based on a number of key elements. These include the Arabic language in its classical form used in religion and literature and the varieties of colloquial Arabic used in daily life; a personal identity with Arab culture, history, and the Arab community; a strong value placed on children and family life; a clear division of labor based on sex; and adherence to Islam. About 93% of Arabs around the world follow

Islam, with Arabs in Libya being Sunni Muslims. Arabs live mainly in the north in the regions of Cyrenaica and Tripolitania. Nomadic Arabs, called **Bedouin,** live in the desert regions and are mainly herders. Once a sizable percentage of the Arab population, they are declining in number through government programs to settle them in permanent communities. Family and tribal affiliations are somewhat more important for the Bedouin than for other Libyan Arabs.

Berbers are the indigenous people of North Africa. Although details about their origins are unclear, ancestors of the contemporary Berbers have lived in North Africa for at least 5,000 years. The Berbers across North Africa are collectively referred to as **Imazighen,** although the names for regional groups within nations and identification with specific settlements are more salient markers of identity for most rural Berbers. About 5% of the population continue to be identified as Berbers, and they are found mainly in the northwest. They live in largely Berber communities, speak the Berber language, and subsist through a combination of farming and herding. Although some Berbers resisted conversion to Islam initially, all eventually did convert. They are Sunni Muslims like the Libyan Arabs, but most subscribe to a different school of Islamic law than do the Arabs. A distinct Berber community are the **Tuareg,** who number about 10,000 and live in the west on the border with Algeria.

In the south there are several thousand **Tebu** and other Africans, whose main populations are across the border in Chad and Niger. Libya also has a large immigrant population, although population estimates are uncertain and range anywhere from as low as 500,000 to as high as 2 million. **Egyptians** are the largest immigrant group, but there are also **Palestinians, Tunisians,** and Asians including **Filipinos, Vietnamese, Thais,** and **South Koreans.** Immigrants were first drawn to Libya for work in the oil industry but now work mainly in low-level jobs in industry and agriculture, or in the service sector. Their status in Libya is always uncertain, and at various times the government has deported hundreds of thousands for political reasons or because their work was deemed no longer necessary. There are also about 25,000 **Europeans** in Libya—mainly **Italians** and **Britons**—who hold professional and managerial positions. In addition, small communities of **Greeks, Maltese,** and **Armenians** continue to live in the large cities. The large Italian and **Jewish** communities that were once part of Libya have now all but disappeared through immigration to Italy and Israel.

Madagascar

The Republic of Madagascar is an island nation located off the coast of East Africa, with Mozambique being the closest nation on the continent. Although the settlement history of the island is not completely known, it was most likely first permanently settled about 2,000 years ago by peoples migrating west from the islands of Southeast Asia, most likely from Indonesia. It was also settled by Africans and Arabs. In 1885, it came under French control from which it gained its independence in 1960. The population is about 13.7 million, 74% of which is rural. Malagasy and French are the official languages, with all people speaking one of the Malagasy dialects. A majority of people adhere to indigenous religions, with the remainder being Muslim or Christian.

Ethnic Composition

Experts are divided on whether Madagascar should be considered an ethnically homogeneous or an ethnically heterogeneous nation. Those who argue that it is homogeneous consider all indigenous residents as **Malagasy** and point out that all share a mixed Southeast Asian and African ancestry; all speak dialects of the Malagasy language; many share common customs in regard to dress, religion, social organization, and other matters; and that some groups identified as distinct groups do not actually share a sense of cultural identity. Those who argue that it is heterogeneous suggest that there are as many as 20 different ethnic groups in Madagascar that view themselves as distinct social groups, some of which are aligned with specific political parties.

The largest ethnic groups are the Merina (25%), Betsimisaraka (18%), Betsileo (12%), Tsimihety (7%), Sakalava (5%), Tandroy (Antandroy) (3%), Antaisaka (4%), Antaimoro (3%), Antansoy (2%), Bara (2%), and Tanala.

The **Merina** are the largest and most widely dispersed of the groups. While their homeland is the central highlands, the spread of the Merina Kingdom from 1810 until 1895 has left Merina people employed in many occupations across Madagascar.

The **Betsileo, Tanala, Antaiska,** and **Antaimoro** live in the south. Betsileo and Tanala are primarily farmers, while the Antaiska and Antaimoro are herders of cattle. There is a pattern of migration by southern peoples to the north in search of work, and the Betsileo are now distributed in the north, as well.

The **Bara** live in the south-central region where they farm and herd.

A good stretch of the east coast is the homeland of the **Betsimisaraka,** who are mainly farmers.

The **Sakalava** live in the west and the **Tsimihety** in the northwest, and both herd cattle. Of all the groups, the three largest—Merina, Betsimisaraka, and Betsileo—are most often employed by the government and many senior officials, although not all, come from these groups.

The non-Malagasy population numbers about 70,000 and consists of about 20,000 **Comorians,** who are of the same mixed ethnic ancestry as the Malagasy, about 20,000 **Indians** and **Pakistanis,** about 15,000 **French,** and about 10,000 **Chinese.** All of these groups are primarily urban and are engaged in retail trade and commerce.

Ethnic Relations

Ethnic identity in Madagascar is highly politicized. There are some 30 political parties representing various regions, ethnic groups, and issues, and some Malagasy look to ethnic-based political ties as a means of achieving power or influence at the national level. Perhaps the single overriding issue is resistance to Merina dominance. There are still harsh feelings about the period of Merina rule in the 1800s that ended with the arrival of the French. Some groups were assimilated or influenced by the Merina, while others such as the Bara resisted. In the postindependence period, all groups stressed their ethnic identities both to weaken Merina dominance and to enhance their own political influence. An especially prominent issue has been the use of the written form of the Merina dialect of Malagasy as the national language, which other groups have resisted.

To some extent the continuing pattern of migration from the south to the north is weakening the solidarity of some groups and enhancing the national Malagasy identity.

Malawi

The Republic of Malawi is a small, landlocked nation in southeastern Africa. It is bordered by Zambia on the northwest; Tanzania on the northeast; and Mozambique on the southeast, south, and southwest. Lake Malawi runs north to south along the eastern borders with Tanzania and Mozambique. The present African population is derived mainly from Bantu-speaking groups who migrated to the region from the north beginning in the 16th century and other groups who arrived later. The region was involved in the Arab slave trade, which led to the conversion of some people to Islam. European contact began with the Portuguese, then the British took control in 1891 and named the region Nyasaland. Malawi became an independent nation in 1964. Malawi has a population of 9.4 million, over 85% of whom live in rural areas. English and Chichewa are the official languages, with most people speaking their indigenous languages. About 75% of Malawians are classified as Christian, 20% are Muslim, and 5% practice indigenous religions.

Ethnic Composition

Malawi is an ethnically heterogeneous nation, with most of the population affiliated with the seven major ethnic groups. About 1% of the population is non-African and consists of **Britons, Portuguese,** and **Asian Indians** who are mainly urban and involved in business and trade. Although the nation is ethnically diverse, the different groups are much alike. Most people are farmers who grow corn, cassava, beans, and other crops for their own or local use, and raise tobacco for export. Most communities are organized matrilineally, meaning that people trace their ancestry through their mother's line and that property is inherited and controlled through the female line. This does not mean, however, that women have more power than men, as it is the senior men in the female line who often lead the families and villages. Nonetheless, a common experience for many Malawians is the female-headed household, because men frequently emigrate to work and may live for years in Zambia, Zimbabwe, or South Africa.

Malawi ethnic groups can be divided into those of the indigenous peoples of Malawi and those of people who arrived in the last half of the 19th century. The major indigenous groups are the Chewa, and closely related Nyanja, Tumbuka, and Tonga. The major immigrant groups are the Lomwe, Ngoni, and Yao.

The **Chewa** and **Nyanja** constitute about 50% of the population and live in central and southern Malawi. They have lived in the region for about 500 years and have seen themselves as separate groups for some 200 years. They were called the **Maravi** by the early Portuguese in the region. The two groups are similar culturally and both speak the Chichewa language. The Chewa are concentrated in central Malawi while the Nyanja are in the south where they often live amongst other ethnic groups. Two other groups that have lived in Malawi for hundreds of years are the **Tumbuka** and the closely related **Tonga.** Both groups were conquered by the Ngoni, but reasserted their ethnic identities when British rule ended Ngoni rule in the early 20th century.

The **Ngoni** migrated north into Malawi in the mid-1800s and conquered various peoples living in Malawi including the Tumbuka and Tonga. The Ngoni were cattle herders with a large and powerful military that conquered all of the peoples they encountered in Malawi except for the Yao. The Ngoni assimilated many of the peoples they conquered; thus, when they arrived in Malawi, they were already composed of people from at least six ethnic groups including the **Suto** and **Kalanga.** The British refused to support Ngoni rule, and in the first several decades of the 20th century, Ngoni power declined and some conquered peoples such as the Tumbuka and Tonga reasserted their own ethnic identities. Today, the Ngoni are a relatively small group in Malawi, with only about 1% of the population speaking the Ngoni language. They are found throughout Malawi but are concentrated in the south.

The **Lomwe** have been migrating to Malawi from Mozambique since the late 1800s and have settled peacefully among the Yao and Nyanja in southern Malawi. Although they speak a different language, the groups are similar culturally and intermarriage is common. They constitute about 15%–20% of the national population.

The **Yao** began entering Malawi from the east in the mid-19th century and their influence on the Nyanja already living in southern Malawi has been considerable. The Yao were traders of slaves, gunpowder, weapons, and other items, and for centuries had been associated with Arab traders along the coast of the Indian Ocean. They had largely adopted Arab culture, many had converted to Islam before their spread into Malawi, and they brought Islam with them. Although not conquerors, the Yao nonetheless enjoyed superior wealth and political organization and they dominated the Nyanja and later the Lomwe, some of whom converted to Islam. The Yao continue to live among these other groups and some continue to be involved in trade while others have become part of the general pattern of migration to Zimbabwe and South Africa to work in mines or on plantations. Along with the Ngoni, the Yao constitute about 15% of the national population.

The most recent arrivals in Malawi are the **Sena,** a generic term for a number of related groups in eastern Malawi that began arriving from Mozambique in the early 20th century. In some regions, there is a question of whether they are a distinct group or are related to the Nyanja. A major cultural difference is that they are patrilineal, meaning that they trace their ancestry through the male line. In northern Malawi there is also a small **Ngonde** population related to the Ngonde across the border in Tanzania.

Ethnic Relations

Compared with most other nations in the region, ethnic relations in Malawi are peaceful and cooperative. Many Malawians identify more strongly with the nation or with their home region (north, central, and south) than they do with their ethnic group. Thus, ethnicity is not a major factor in politics or in political party membership, and ethnicity is usually not considered in selecting government officials.

This relative ethnic harmony is the result of a number of factors. Perhaps most important is the similarity among the major ethnic groups of Malawi. Most are organized matrilineally and have economies based on farming, and people's lives center on the small villages where they live. Second, because of the assimilation policies of the Ngoni as they conquered other groups, and also because of labor migration by men, marriages across ethnic groups are not uncommon. Thus, some communities become linked through ties of marriage. Third, the migration of men for work both outside and within the country has led to considerable contact between men from different groups.

Mali

The Republic of Mali is a land-locked country in the middle of West Africa. It is bordered on the north by Algeria, on the south by Guinea and Côte d'Ivoire, by Burkina Faso and Niger on the east, and by Mauritania on the west.

Under French colonial rule, Mali was part of the French Sudan. It gained its independence in 1960. Mali's population is about 9.7 million. It is an extremely poor country; 65% of its land area is either desert or semidesert. Economic activity takes place mostly in the area irrigated by the Niger River. About 10% of the population is nomadic and some 80% of the labor force is engaged in agriculture and fishing. Industrial activity is centered on the processing of farm products. Ninety percent of Mali's people are Muslims, 9% practice local religions, and 1% are Christians. Although only a small percentage of the population are "animists," followers of traditional religions, animism has a great influence on those who identify themselves as Muslims or Christians.

Ethnic Composition

Mali has been inhabited since the Paleolithic period and its current population diversity has a long history. Although French is the official language, most people speak African languages of two major language families. The first family includes Niger-Congo languages and its divisions, such as Mandingo, Malinke, Bozo, and others. Other subgroups of this family include West Atlantic languages, represented by Fulani, and Voltaic languages, represented by Bobo, Minianka, and Noufo. The second major family includes the Arabic of the Moors and similar tongues.

Mali's ethnic composition breaks down in the following manner: **Mande (Bambara, Malinke, Sarakole)** 50%, **Fulani (Peul)** 17%, **Voltaic** 12%, **Songhai** 6%, **Tuareg** and **Moor** 10%, and other 5%. The Malinke are Muslim farmers. The Peul, or Fulani, are Muslim pastoral nomads. The Tuareg are also Muslim nomads who engage in trade and are skilled crafts workers. The Songhai are found in a number of West African countries. They are farmers and fishers. They are nominally Muslims but generally carry on the practice of their traditional religion.

Ethnic Relations

The government has sought to encourage peaceful ethnic relations by generally adhering to constitutional provisions that protect freedom of speech, press, assembly, association, and religion. Mali is a secular state with freedom of religion and does not discriminate on religious grounds. There are, however, legal restrictions on the Baha'i faith, although the government does not enforce them. There is also representation of different ethnic groups in the government, with, for example, the Tuareg serving in both the cabinet and National Assembly while the president of the Assembly is a Fulani.

This has not entirely ended ethnic conflict, with the major recent problems involving the Tuareg and Moors in the north. The Tuareg are a Berber people related to other Berbers across the border in Algeria, while the Moors are the same people as the Moors in Mauritania. In January 1995, the government reached an agreement with the majority of the Tuareg and Moor rebel groups in the north, ending several years of a rebellion and the threat of secession. All parties have honored the agreement and there have been no major breaches of the peace.

Mauritania

The Islamic Republic of Mauritania is in West Africa and has a population of about 2.3 million people. It is about 80% desert, with most of its good farmland in the south, in the Senegal River Valley. Mauritania borders Western Sahara and the Atlantic Ocean on the west, Algeria on the north, Mali on the east and south, and Senegal on the south. In this geographical position it straddles the Arab and Black African worlds, a situation that has caused great internal conflicts within Mauritania and has focused the attention of human rights organizations on its policies. Mauritania has been influenced by Muslim Arabs and Arabized Berbers from the north and east since the 9th century A.D. European powers have also left their mark. Mauritania became a French protectorate in 1903 and gained independence in 1960. Islam is the official religion, and Arabic and Wolof are the official languages, although use of the latter is discouraged by the government.

Mauritania's mixed economy of herding, subsistence agriculture, and mining for export permits little interaction between modern and traditional economic spheres. The majority of Mauritania's citizens engage in subsistence herding and farming. People supplement their incomes by occasionally working as laborers or by selling in local markets. Most agriculture is limited to the north bank of the Senegal River, where millet, sorghum, rice, and other cereals are grown.

Ethnic Composition

Mauritania has six distinct ethnic groups. The largest group is the **Moors (Maures),** a people of mixed Arab and Berber ancestry, and—to a lesser extent—Black African ancestry. Moors also live in southern Morocco, Senegal, Gambia, and Mali, but the largest concentration is in Mauritania, where they form about 80% of the population. Moors are Muslims, speak dialects of Arabic, and many are nomadic or seminomadic herders. Internally, the Moors are divided into a number of ranked subgroups on the basis of ancestry and occupation. At the top of the social hierarchy are those of the warrior and religious leader groups, although the former are now mainly herders, merchants, and government workers. Also near the top are the descendants of the former nobility who served the two upper classes. These three groups are collectively labeled "White Moors," which emphasizes their Arab and Berber ancestry. Most other Moors are herders, crafts workers, or artisans. At the bottom of the hierarchy are the so-called "Black Moors," who were formerly servants and slaves. They continue to be looked down upon because of the group's former occupational status and because they more often intermarried with Black Africans than did the White Moors. Although slavery was outlawed by the government in 1960 and banned again in 1980, some Black Moors continue to live in slavery under the control of White Moors.

The other five ethnic groups in Mauritania are **Black African** groups, consisting mainly of farmers in the Senegal River Valley in the south. They constitute about 20% of the population, although they claim that this number is too low and is a deliberate underestimate by the Moor-dominated government. All of these groups are non-Arab, non-Berber, and non-Moor, although they are mainly Muslims. The largest group is the **Toucouleur,** followed by the **Fulbe (Fulani),** who unlike the others are mainly herders. The **Soninke, Wolof,** and **Bambara** are fewer in number. As with the Moors, all five African groups are internally differentiated on the basis of occupation and ancestry into ranked classes ranging from the nobility down to former slaves. Black African groups in Mauritania prefer to speak their own languages, which has become a major ethnic issue as the government promotes the use of Arabic as the national language.

Ethnic Relations

Since independence, Mauritania has struggled with the problem of creating a unified nation from a population that was traditionally divided by ethnicity, language, skin color, and social status. Although the major division in Mauritania is between the Arab-Berber population and the African population, there are also important divisions within each of these two categories, and divisions within every ethnic group based on family and occupation. Also

important in ethnic relations is the division between the Arab-Berber conquerors and the people whom they enslaved, whether Black, White, or a combination. Nonetheless, those who cannot claim ties to the Arab-Berbers are considered to be at the bottom of society. For example, a Black Moor who is descended from slaves claims a higher social position than a free Black Wolof.

Since independence, the Moors have sought to increase their control of the government (which under French rule had employed many Black African civil servants), have tried to make Arabic the de facto national language, and have attempted to create a stronger sense of unity among the large Moor population. These policies have led to conflicts with the African population in the south who found themselves losing government jobs, control of the education system, and land to Moor developers. Matters came to a head in 1989. Clashes erupted between Arabic-speaking Moors and Africans in both Senegal and Mauritania. The immediate cause of the conflict was a dispute over grazing rights, but the deeper cause was the Moors' sense of superiority over the Senegalese, whom they had enslaved for centuries.

Morocco

The Kingdom of Morocco is in western North Africa and is bordered by Algeria on the east and southeast, Western Sahara (which is occupied by Morocco) on the south, the Atlantic Ocean on the west and northwest, and the Mediterranean Sea on the northeast. The Arabs invaded and brought Islam to the region in the early 8th century. The population today is entirely Sunni Muslim, with the exception of a small population of Christian Europeans—mainly French and Spanish.

Morocco's proximity to Europe led to heavy Spanish, German, and French control or influence since the middle of the 19th century. In 1956, French rule ended and Morocco became an independent nation. Morocco has a population of 29.8 million, with a large overseas population numbering over 1 million; the majority of these Moroccans are guest workers in Western European nations such as France, Germany, and Belgium.

Ethnic Composition and Ethnic Relations

Morocco's population is composed of two major ethnic groups, the Berbers and the Ar-

abs. However, mixing between the two groups since the arrival of the Arabs in the early 8th century has made the Berber/Arab dichotomy largely meaningless in many communities. Today, Berbers and Arabs often live and work side-by-side, both groups being Sunni Muslims and both speaking a North African dialect of Arabic, which is the national language. In addition, because there were many marriages between Arab men and Berber women in the first centuries of Arab rule, many Arabs in Morocco today are of partial Berber ancestry.

Assuming that it is actually possible to separate Arabs from Berbers in Morocco, **Arabs** are believed to constitute about 66% of the Moroccan population, although this figure also includes people of mixed Arab and Berber descent. Arabs are an ethnic group indigenous to the Middle East and are the majority population in 15 nations in the Middle East and North Africa. The history of the emergence of Arabs as a distinct group in the Middle East is unclear, but as early as 853 B.C., the Arabic language was in use. Although being an "Arab" has different meanings in different nations, a shared Arab identity is based on a number of key elements. These include knowledge of the Arabic language, both in its classical form (used in religion and literature) and in the varieties of colloquial Arabic used in daily life, which are usually called Moroccan Arabic; a personal identity with Arab culture, history, and the Arab community; a strong value placed on children and family life; a clear division of labor based on sex; and adherence to Islam. About 93% of Arabs around the world follow Islam. Arabs in Morocco live mainly in the plains and the major cities.

Berbers are the indigenous people of North Africa. Although details about their origins are unclear, ancestors of the contemporary Berbers have lived in North Africa for at least 5,000 years. The Berbers across North Africa are collectively referred to as **Imazighen,** although for most rural Berbers, the names of regional groups within nations and of specific settlements are more salient markers of identity. During the initial Arab invasion, Berbers in Morocco fled into the mountains and to the interior, and most rural Berbers continue to live in small farming communities or herding camps in three regional groupings—the **Rif** of the north, the **Tamazight** of the Middle Atlas mountains, and the **Tashilhit** of the High Atlas. Each region includes a number of distinct Berber tribes, with family and tribal affiliation based on descent through the male line. Although some Berbers resisted conversion to Islam initially, all eventually did convert, and some were involved in "holy wars" launched against kingdoms in West Africa. Although Berbers are Sunni Muslims like their Arab neighbors, some elements of their traditional religion have been retained, and Berbers afford a special status to individuals who can claim descent from Muhammad, the prophet and founder of Islam in the 7th century in Arabia.

In addition to the Arabs and Berbers, a **French** community remains in Morocco that has been estimated to number as many as 100,000.

Ethnic relations between the Arabs and Berbers are peaceful, despite efforts by the French in the early 20th century to divide the groups by affording the Berbers preferential treatment. Social distinctions in Morocco are based more on wealth and status than on ethnicity. Morocco has also experienced less internal strife from Islamic fundamentalism than other North African nations.

Mozambique

The Republic of Mozambique, situated on the southeastern coast of Africa, has an elongated shape. It is bordered on the north by Tanzania, and on the west by Malawi, Zambia, Zimbabwe, South Africa, and Swaziland. Its entire eastern boundary is the Mozambique Channel of the Indian Ocean. The earliest inhabitants of Mozambique were probably Bantu-speaking peoples who settled in the region around A.D. 200. Around A.D. 700, Arab traders established settlements that became city-states, competing for coastal trade. By the 1300s, the Arabs controlled the coast politically and economically. In the 16th century they moved inland, establishing two trading settlements. In 1544, they founded a post on the coast at Quelimane. Their hegemony was challenged by the Portuguese in the 17th century, and by the 20th century the Portuguese had control of the area. Independence was gained in 1975, after a 10-year war with the Portuguese. Since then, Mozambique has experienced considerable political instability, civil war, drought, and famine, with about 10% of the population becoming refugees in the neighboring nations of Malawi and Zambia. The restoration of order in the 1990s led to the return of most refugees by 1995.

Mozambique's population is estimated at about 17.8 million. Portuguese is the official language, although indigenous languages are spoken by most people. Religion in Mozambique is divided among traditionalists, Christians, and Muslims. Approximately half its population are traditionalists (animists). Islam is practiced mainly in the north, and Christianity mainly in the south. Traditional beliefs, however, are still strong among both Christians and Muslims.

Ethnic Composition

The Bantu migration into the southern part of Africa has left its mark on the population composition of Mozambique. Virtually all its people are Bantu speakers. Nevertheless, there are differences between the various ethnic groups in Mozambique. The groups north of the Zambezi River, notably the **Makua-Lomwe** (35% of the population), practice slash-and-burn cultivation and are distinguished from groups to the south by their matrilineal form of kinship organization; that is, they trace their descent through the female or the mother's line.

The Muslim **Yao** (2%), also northerners, were intermediaries in the slave trade between the Arabs and interior tribes during the 18th century and 19th century. They are the only interior group that is entirely Muslim.

Groups south of the Zambezi River trace their descent patrilineally (through the male or father's line) and subsist by raising cattle and by farming. The **Tsongaa** (25%) predominate in the south and also constitute the majority of Mozambique's migrant labor force in nearby South Africa. Two smaller groups related to the Tsongaa, the **Tonga** and **Chopi,** are also involved in the labor migration to South African mines. The **Swahili** (2%), **Shona** (9%), and **Nguni** (1%) are other Mozambican groups who also live in other nations in the region. The Swahili were active as slave traders in the past.

While most **Portuguese** left the country after independence, a small population remains in cities along with about 15,000 **Asian Indi-ans** and people of mixed Portuguese and African ancestry.

Ethnic Relations

Mozambique is well known for its cultural diversity. In addition to differences based on region, kinship practices, and economy, some groups are noted for their distinctive artistic traditions. Among the best-known artworks from Mozambique are the carved wood sculptures of the Makonde in the north and the orchestral music of the Chopi.

Slavery has had a profound impact on Mozambique's development as well as on ethnic relations. By the 18th century, the slave trade was an integral part of the economy. Yao traders managed extensive slave-trading networks, while interior peoples sold gold and slaves to Portuguese merchants. The Tsongaa—ivory traders who developed trade routes from the Transvaal and Zimbabwe plateau to the coastal ports—were also involved in the slave trade. Even though slave trading was made illegal in the middle of the 19th century, illegal trade continued into the 20th century. The trade was furthered by the presence of various small political states in the interior who were often at war with one another. The various roles of different groups in the slave trade continue to impact ethnic relations, with those peoples in the interior who were enslaved continuing to resent the role of Yao and Swahili who served as agents of the Arab and European traders.

Namibia

The Republic of Namibia is in southwestern Africa and is bordered by the Atlantic Ocean on the west, Angola on the north, Botswana on the east, and South Africa on the southeast and south. Namibia was under German control from 1890 until 1915 when it was taken by South Africa. The Namibians resisted both German and South African rule, and a combination of armed resistance, support by other nations, and intervention by the United Nations finally resulted in Namibia becoming an independent republic in 1990. The population is 1.7 million, 68% of which is rural, with the capital, Windhoek, being the only major city. English is the official language, although a significant percentage of the White population speaks German or Afrikaans, while most Africans speak their native languages. Missionary activity was especially heavy during the German period, and about 50% of the population is Lutheran, 30% adhere to other Christian denominations, and the remainder practice traditional religions.

Ethnic Composition

Namibia is an ethnically heterogeneous society. In the broad sense, there are two primary ethnic categories—Africans and Whites—with a number of distinct ethnic groups within each.

The major African groups are the Ovambo, Kavango, Herero, and the Khoisan peoples. The **Ovambo** are the largest ethnic group in Namibia and number over 800,000, about 50% of the national population. They live primarily in the north and also across the border in Angola where they are called the **Ovimbundu.** In both nations, they were actively involved and were often the leaders of the fight for independence, and since independence, they have been much involved in the national government.

The **Kavango** live in the northeast in one of few regions where farming is possible. They number about 150,000 and have been involved in economic development programs that seek to bring commercial agriculture to their region.

The **Herero (Damara),** cattle-herding people of western Namibia, were decimated by the Germans. Although the number of Herero in Namibia today is estimated at about 120,000, they have been assimilated into Ovambo-influenced society since the early 20th century, and it is the much smaller Herero population in Botswana that retains the traditional way of life.

The **Khoisan** peoples (speakers of the Khoi and San languages) are thought by some experts to be the indigenous people of southwestern Africa and include the **Khoi** groups, who live mainly in South Africa and were herders, and **San** groups, who live in Namibia, Angola, and Botswana. In Namibia, the Khoisan number about 25,000 and are herders and farmers. The hunter-gatherer way of life associated with the San groups had mostly disappeared before European colonization began.

People of full or partial European ancestry are believed to account for about 6% of the population, or about 100,000 people. However, population relocations to South Africa since independence make this figure uncertain, and the European population may now range from 50,000 to 80,000. In terms of long-term cultural significance, the **Germans,** who now number about 25,000, are the most important. Lutheranism, German models of town planning, German beer, and continuing use of the German language in German communities have survived the end of German rule over 80 years ago. The other major European groups are the **Britons,** who number fewer than 5,000, and the **Afrikaners** and **Cape Coloureds** (*see* South Africa), whose presence is a result of South African rule during most of the 20th century. Europeans live mainly in Windhoek and in southern Namibia. Those not involved in commerce and business are primarily cattle herders and farmers.

Ethnic Relations

During the colonial period of both German and South African rule, ethnic relations were marked by African-White distinctions and conflics. For example, the Germans wanted some of the African-controlled land, and in the early 1900s, in one of the worst cases of genocide in African history, they killed over 65,000 Herero to obtain it. The South Africans—many of whom were Afrikaners— sought to establish apartheid in Namibia although their efforts were partially thwarted by the nationalism movement led by the Ovambo. During the 1970s and 1980s, a variety of political parties emerged, with some representing regional and/ or ethnic interests. The Ovambo, Herero, Coloureds, Kavango, Afrikaners, and Whites are each represented by one or more political parties. In 1992, SWAPO (the South West Africa People's Organization), composed mainly of Ovambo, came to power through elections. Since the elections, the government has moved to control the influence of ethnic-based parties and also sought to ease tensions between the majority African population and the Europeans who live mainly in the capital city of Windhoek and who control the commercial sector of the economy.

Niger

The Republic of Niger is a landlocked nation at the northern and eastern extremes of West Africa. It is bordered by Algeria and Libya on the north, Chad on the east, Nigeria and Benin on the south, and Burkina Faso and Mali on the west. Archaeological evidence shows that about 600,000 years ago, humans inhabited the area that is now the Sahara of northern Niger. Niger has long been an important commercial crossroads and was a prize for many empires. At one time or another, the empires of Songhai, Mali, Gao, Kanem, and Bornu, as well as a number of Hausa states, have claimed control over it. Contact with the West began in the 19th century when European explorers, mainly Mungo Park (British) and Heinrich Barth (German), were searching for the mouth of the Niger River. The French attempted to control the region long before 1900; however, groups such as the desert Tuareg were not "pacified" until 1922, the year Niger became a French colony.

The French ruled their territories, including Niger, under a policy of direct rule. This led to greater centralization of colonial government, and Niger was ruled from Senegal (also a French colony). The peoples of Niger were given rights in the French Empire, and those who had "evolved" were considered full French citizens. The Republic of Niger became independent in 1960, and since that time, it has had a series of military governments and is still awaiting a promised return to democracy.

In spite of a large uranium reserve, Niger is one of the poorest countries in the world. Agriculture and livestock raising are the main occupations of about 85% of Niger's population of 9,113,000. Approximately 21 languages are spoken in Niger. French is the official language, but Hausa and Djerma are spoken by large numbers of its population, with Hausa being nearly universal. Islam is Niger's dominant religion, and 80% of its population is Sunni Muslim. The remainder of its people follow indigenous beliefs or are Christians.

Ethnic Composition and Ethnic Relations

Niger is ethnically diverse, although two ethnic groups account for over 75% of the population. The different ethnic groups in Niger reflect the nation's location: Niger has groups that are found in North African Arab nations, as well as groups found in West African nations.

The **Hausa** are the largest ethnic group, making up 56% of the population, followed by the **Djerma** at 22%. Smaller groups are the **Fula (Fulani)** (8.5%); **Tuareg** (8%); **Beri Beri (Kanouri)** (4.3%); **Arabs, Toubou,** and **Gourmantche** (1.2%); and about 4,000 **French** expatriates.

The Hausa are sedentary farmers. In addition to being Niger's largest ethnic group, they are the largest ethnic group in the northern part of Nigeria. The Djerma live in Mali as well as in Niger. The Hausa and Djerma live in the fertile southern area. The rest of the Nigerois are nomadic or seminomadic livestock-raising peoples. The Fula or Fulani are Muslim pastoral nomads. The Tuareg are also Muslim nomads who engage in trade and are skilled artisans. The Beri Beri are often allied with the Hausa and are Muslims. There has been much competition between the sedentary and nomadic peoples due to Niger's fast-growing population and the resulting competition for scarce natural resources.

The Tuareg, Arabs, Toubou, and Beri Beri have had problems with the Hausa-dominated government and have sought independence. These groups argue that the far more numerous Hausa and Djerma ethnic groups, which dominate the government and commerce, discriminate against them. Plans to develop the northern regions, which are lacking in basic services and are behind the southern areas of the country, have not yet been implemented— which has led to complaints from Niger's minority ethnic groups. The government has been striving to control ethnic violence and to enter into agreements with groups that might secede because of perceived discrimination. However, there are credible reports of police or military personnel beating and otherwise abusing political leaders and their supporters. These people tend to represent ethnic groups other than those in control. Thus, ethnic conflict remains a major threat to national unity.

Nigeria

The Federal Republic of Nigeria is in West Africa on the Gulf of Guinea. Benin borders it on the west, Cameroon on the east and southeast, Niger on the north, and Chad on the northeast. Nigeria was not a political entity until it was created by the British in 1900. The hundreds of ethnic groups contained within the borders of the new state created an extremely complex mix of peoples and religions that continues to cause serious problems in Nigerian society.

Nigeria became an independent nation in 1960. It has a population of 103.2 million, 84% of whom live in rural areas, mainly in small villages and towns or on farms. Nigeria has great religious diversity; simply put, it is 50% Muslim, 40% Christian, and 10% adherents to indigenous beliefs. In reality, however, each of these categories is further subdivided, and the mixtures of beliefs are often bewildering to outsiders. Additionally, no single area is totally associated with a given religion. Thus, although a majority of the northern peoples are Muslim, and most of the southern peoples are Christian, there are also Christian northerners and Muslim southerners. The peoples in the middle part of the nation, known as the "Middle Belt," tend to be of mixed faiths. It is not uncommon for people to have both Christian and Muslim adherents in their families; indeed, the Yoruba—who are noted for their religious combinations—have a blend of both called Chrislam. Christian denominations include Anglican, Roman Catholic, Methodist, Baptist, and African independent churches, including the famous Aerobe Aladura churches.

Ethnic Composition

Nigeria has between 250 and 400 ethnic groups, depending on how ethnicity is defined. It has more ethnic groups than any other African nation, and it ranks among the most ethnically complex nations in the world. However, most ethnic groups are small and localized, and only a few play a central role in Nigerian society. These major groups are the Hausa, Fulani, Yoruba, and Igbo (Ibo). These groups comprise 65% of the population. Other groups of significant size and importance are the Kanuri, Ibibio, Tiv, Ijaw, Nupe, Anang, Efik, and Kalabari. Each of these groups has its own language but members may speak either English—Nigeria's official language—or Yoruba, Igbo, or Hausa, which serve as lingua francas, or market languages.

Each of Nigeria's regions has significant subdivisions based on a mix of ethnicity, geography, and history. The south has a western Yoruba region and an eastern Igbo region. Additionally there is a grouping of peoples labeled **Niger Delta peoples** in the eastern and central coastal area. The north is home to the Hausa groups and the Kanuri in the northeast, along with a range of other peoples including the Fulani pastoralists. Nigeria's Middle Belt has a number of different peoples.

The north is dominated by **Hausa** and **Hausa-allied peoples.** Often the language and the people are confused with one another, and it is difficult to know which an author is discussing. Their main settlement area is in the north and northwest of Nigeria's northern states. Here are found the core groups of the Hausa people and the Islamic states that originally formed a linked set of centralized states that still remain politically and commercially important.

The Hausa are found as traders throughout the Sahara and Sahel region. They are also skilled farmers. These expatriate Hausa maintain close ties with their home areas, further complicating ethnic relations in the region in general, and in Nigeria in particular. Their spread has made Hausa a general market language throughout the region.

The **Fulani** cattle-raising nomads have spread inexorably westward into the area. Many of the Fulani settled in villages and towns. The general relationship between the Fulani and settled farmers was symbiotic. However, conflicts did erupt, and at the beginning of the 19th century, the Fulani led a holy war, or *jihad*, that resulted in the founding of the Sokoto Caliphate. The Fulani took over the Hausa states and intermarried with their former rulers, assimilating Hausa culture in the process. Hence, the rulers of these states and the people are generally referred to as **Hausa-Fulani.** There are, however, a number of "pure Hausa" who resent the term—just as there are "pure Fulani" who prefer to be called simply "Fulani," even among the settled Fulani of the region.

The **Kanuri** form another major group in the north. They came into what is present-day Nigeria in the 15th century. They absorbed the indigenous Chadic-speaking peoples into their kingdom. In the 16th century, their empire often included some Hausa states and a large area of the central Sahara. In the 19th century, they battled the Fulani and managed to resist their advance. The Kanuri share many cultural traits with the Hausa, including the Islamic faith, Islamic law and governmental structure, extended patrilineal and patrilocal households, and the distinction between rural and urban life. They maintain, however, their own history and sense of identity, as indicated by their preference for a U-shaped town design, distinctive female hairstyles, food choices, and epics of past rulers. Kanuri cultural independence, nevertheless, is being threatened through peaceful assimilation into Hausa-Fulani culture as Hausa influence spreads into the Kanuri major city of Maiduguri.

The Middle Belt area divides northern and southern peoples. It consists of the area from the Cameroon Highlands in the east to the Niger River valley on the west. In this area, there are from 50 to 100 separate languages spoken and separate ethnic groups. The Nupe and Tiv, with about 500,000 people each, are the largest groups, while some groups in the Jos area, such as the **Afusare,** are relatively small. In the east, the Chadic languages of the Niger-Congo prevail, while in the west there are ties to Mende-speaking peoples.

There are three types of ethnic organization found in the Middle Belt. The first is that of the **Nupe,** a large centralized group. The Nupe, under the prodding of the colonial government, became rulers of Hausa-styled states governed by a ruler called an emir. The **Tiv** follow a segmentary lineage variety of social organization. A strong patrilineage links large parts of the group into named segments. All political life, land tenure, law, and other aspects of life were related to this organization. The third and most common form of social organization consists of small villages and households that were once autonomous. During the colonial period these small units were absorbed into wider administrative units. Hausaization has spread into the area, especially in the north, and exerted great influence on the people. Missionary and British influence has also effected changes in the cultural life of the people.

The southern region of Nigeria has a number of different peoples. The Igbo and Yoruba, better viewed as linguistic communities than single ethnic entities, dominate the area. The pressures of competition in the nation-state have led to their self-identification as ethnic groups, blurring differences, including some that to led to wars among their sub-units.

The **Yoruba** area includes most of the southwestern area of Nigeria. There are 20 to 30 million people in this region. There were seven separate Yoruba kingdoms in the area, often fighting among themselves for dominance. The Yoruba language, which has many dialects, is part of the Kwa group of the Niger-Congo family. It is related to Idoma and Igala, southern Middle Belt languages based south of the Benue River. The state of Ilorin is an Islamic one and forms a bridge between north and south. The Yoruba have had the longest contact with the outside world. In the 19th century, returned slaves from Brazil brought a style of architecture that still marks Yoruba housing. It is a region that is highly westernized: It had Nigeria's first university, the University of Ibadan (1948); first publishing house; first radio and television stations; a Nobel Prize laureate (Wole Soyinke); and in many other ways led the nation in its "modern" orientation. About half of Yoruba are Christians and half are Muslims.

The **Igbo (Ibo)** are located mainly in the southeastern section of Nigeria although they have spread throughout Nigeria. Their language is a Kwa language of the Niger-Congo language family. The Igbo are mainly Christian. Severe land shortages in the region, combined with a high achievement motivation, have led Igbo to excel in contemporary Nigeria. Igbo success is also attributable to their openness to outside influence. Unlike many other Nigerian groups, the Igbo place great emphasis on individual achievement, and children are encouraged by their parents to succeed. This emphasis on success and eagerness to get ahead often irritates other Nigerians, who term the Igbo "pushy." Competition with

members of other ethnic groups has increased the Igbo sense of ethnic unity, while encouraging similar feelings in those who compete with them.

The Atlantic Coast and Niger River Delta regions contain people who are linguistically and culturally related to the Igbo. However, these peoples maintain separate identities, and many of them resisted the Igbo attempt at secession during the Civil War. They include **Ijaw, Ibibio, Anang,** and **Efik.** The peoples of the western bank of the Niger River, particularly the **Bini** and the **Urhobo,** are culturally close to the Yoruba. However, they maintain a separate sense of identity, and the Bini, in particular, use the glory of the former Benin Kingdom as an anchor for their ethnic identity.

Ethnic Relations

Nigeria was a colonial creation. Before it was unified by the British in 1900, there was never a single political entity in the area now known as Nigeria. The British relocated various groups and initiated a divide-and-conquer policy that led to strong ethnic rivalries among Nigeria's numerous ethnic groups. In fact, it has been argued that British policies led to the creation of many of Nigeria's ethnic groups, as some of these groups did not have a shared sense of ethnic identity prior to British rule.

Ethnic rivalry did not end with Nigeria's independence in 1960. Independence led to an increase in rivalry for economic and political positions among Nigeria's major ethnic groups, the Hausa-Fulani alliance, Igbo, and Yoruba. In 1966, the first of Nigeria's many military coups took place. It was led by General Ironsi, an Igbo, and became widely regarded as "an Igbo coup." The Northern Nigerian groups under the Hausa-Fulani led a counterattack, and as many as 50,000 Igbo were killed in northern Nigeria. This civil war was perceived by many as a genocidal war, the goal of which was to slaughter the Igbo. In 1970, the Igbo and their allies surrendered, and a slaughter was prevented by the new national government.

At the present time, ethnic relations remain a significant problem in Nigeria. For most Nigerians, social life unfolds within an ethnic context, and this tie to one's group is manifested in a proliferation of ethnic states, political parties, demands for teaching in local languages, and various other ethnic cultural organizations. It is perpetuated by marriage customs, as well, with over 90% of all marriages occurring within ethnic groups, even in cosmopolitan settings.

Nigeria's rich petroleum resources have served to increase ethnic rivalries rather than reduce them. The acknowledged widespread corruption and misuse of funds have led Nigeria to be a poor country with most wealth in the hands of only a few. The continued control of the government by northern politicians and military rulers, along with the government's control of petroleum reserves, has ensured that interethnic conflicts will continue in Nigeria for many years to come.

The Nigerian government has attempted to combat ethnic rivalries, at least those in the form of outbreaks of violence. However, ethnic conflict is a real part of everyday life for most Nigerians.

The current political organization—in which there is one federal territory, Abuja, and 30 states—is an attempt to lessen ethnic tensions. The idea is that each major ethnic group will have its own area to control. In fact, the multiplication of states has led to even further demands for more states from minority ethnic groups who argue that they are kept from sharing fairly in the public largesse.

Rwanda

The Republic of Rwanda is a small, landlocked nation in Central Africa. It is bordered by Uganda on the north, Tanzania on the east, Burundi on the south, and Zaire on the west. Occupied for centuries by the two major ethnic groups that still form almost the entire population—the Hutu and Tutsi—the region came under German control as German East Africa in the late 1800s, and following the defeat of Germany in World War I, it was placed under Belgian administration. What are now the two nations of Burundi and Rwanda were the single administrative unit of Ruanda-Urundi. Under United Nations supervision, Burundi became an independent nation in 1962. Since independence, the nation has experienced long periods of civil war involving the Hutu and Tutsi. The population is estimated at 6.8 million, although the civil war and the hundreds of thousands of Rwandans who have become refugees in Zaire and Tanzania make such estimates highly unreliable. French (introduced by the Belgians, but spoken only by a minority of the people) is the official language, along with Kinyarwanda, which is widely spoken. While missionary activity has led to about 75% of the population being described as Christian, many continue also to adhere to indigenous beliefs.

Ethnic Composition and Ethnic Relations

The two major ethnic groups in Rwanda are the **Hutu,** who constituted about 90% of the population, and **Tutsi,** who constituted about 9%, before the massive population relocations that have been part of the civil war during the 1990s. The remaining 1% of the population was made up of the **Twa,** a former hunter-gatherer people who were politically and economically tied to the Tutsi, and small numbers of **Asian** traders and **Europeans.**

The Hutu and Tutsi have a long history of interaction in the region, and some experts consider them to be two socioeconomic divisions of the same group. The Hutu first entered the region during the 7th century A.D. and were firmly established by the 10th century. The Tutsi migrated to the area, probably from Ethiopia, in the 16th century. The Hutu were primarily farmers of peas, beans, corn, and other crops. The Tutsi were nomadic cattle herders and warriors. The groups also differed in physical appearance, as the Tutsi were tall and thin and the Hutu short and stout. There

Rwandan refugees on their way back to Rwanda from Zaire, 1996. Photo: Agence France Presse/Corbis-Bettmann.

Both before and following independence in 1962, the Hutu majority began agitating for increased rights and participation in the political process. A civil war in 1959 ended Tutsi rule, with many Tutsi fleeing to Congo (formerly Zaire). In 1963, a Tutsi force invaded and was defeated. The Hutu have ruled Rwanda since then and have refused to allow to allow Tutsi exiles to return. In 1990, the Tutsi-led Rwandan Patriotic Front invaded from Uganda and a bloody civil war broke out, leading to more deaths and refugees, but also peace talks that produced an agreement to form a bicultural government. The process was disrupted in 1994 when the presidents of Rwanda and Burundi (both nations being involved in the Hutu-Tutsi conflict) died in a plane crash, and uncontrolled violence resulted, with over 500,000 (mostly Tutsi) being killed and over 2 million Tutsi and Hutu fleeing to Congo (formerly Zaire) and other nations. The situation, while in general terms involved Hutu attacks on the Tutsi, also involved the reverse—Hutu fleeing in fear of Tutsi reprisals, and Hutu killing other Hutu accused of aiding Tutsi. Under French and United Nations supervision, peace was restored and a Hutu-led government with Tutsi participation came to power. In 1996, hundreds of thousands of refugees began returning from Congo (formerly Zaire), some voluntarily, others forced out by rebel forces in Congo.

was considerable interaction between the two groups, and also with the less numerous Twa, and a state structure emerged with the Tutsi forming the ruling class and the Hutu the farming, herding, and agricultural class. The Tutsi considered the Hutu socially inferior, although the relationship between the groups entailed Tutsi rulers protecting their Hutu subjects from attacks by other Tutsi rulers. Many Tutsi men took Hutu women as concubines, and the children from these relationships were often considered to be Tutsi. Through this process, the marked physical differences between the groups lessened somewhat, as did cultural differences, with the two groups eventually speaking the same language, sharing a common social system, and following the same religious beliefs. Under Belgian rule, the system continued, with the Belgians favoring the Tutsi and ruling through them, with the Hutu having even less influence than when they were under Tutsi dominance.

São Tomé and Príncipe

The Democratic Republic of São Tomé and Príncipe is a small island nation located in the Atlantic Ocean off the coast of Gabon in West Africa. The islands were claimed by the Portuguese in 1471 and colonization began in 1485. It is not clear whether the islands were inhabited at the time of Portuguese arrival. As a Portuguese colony, the islands were developed for sugar plantations and also became a key port for the slave trade. The islands became an independent nation in 1975. The population is 144,000. Nearly the entire population is Christian, mostly Roman Catholic. Although Portuguese is the official language and the language of written communication, most people speak one of three related island Creole languages (based on African languages and Portuguese) as their domestic language. The relative isolation of the islands, and the mixing of the African and Portuguese cultures, produced a unique island culture that remains vital in the 1990s. The islands have a rich tradition of folklore, poetry, drama, music, and dance.

Ethnic Composition and Ethnic Relations

The Portuguese settled São Tomé and Príncipe with people from Portugal, as well as slaves from the what are now the nations of Zaire, southern Nigeria, and Benin. There was considerable mixing between the Portuguese and Africans, producing a population of mixed ancestry known as **Mesticos,** who eventually became the primary ethnic group. A much smaller though distinct group are the **Angolars** in southern São Tomé, who claim to be descendants of survivors of a slave ship that sank off the coast in 1540. Others suggest that the Angolars may have been the indigenous inhabitants of the island who were already there when the Portuguese arrived. They lived in the hills and outside the plantation society of the colonial era.

Senegal

The Republic of Senegal is in West Africa and is bordered by Mauritania on the north, Mali on the east, Guinea and Guinea-Bissau on the south, and the Atlantic Ocean on the west. It completely surrounds the nation of the Gambia, which is located within southern Senegal. The Gambia and Senegal signed an agreement in 1981 that called for the creation of a loose confederation to be known as Senegambia. However, the federation dissolved in 1989. The ethnic composition of the two nations is quite similar. Prior to European arrival, the region was under the rule of a number of West African kingdoms including the Tekrur, Ghana, Mali, and Jolof. The coastal area of Senegal was exploited by the Portuguese and Dutch and then the British and French until the French established control in the late 19th century. It became an independent nation in 1960. Senegal has a population of about 9.1 million and is one of the most urban nations in Africa, with 43% of the population living in cities. The capital of Dakar has a population of 1.7 million. French is the official language, although Wolof is spoken by over 70% of the people and other indigenous languages are used, as well. About 93% of the population is Muslim and 6% is Christian.

Ethnic Composition

Senegal is an ethnically heterogeneous nation composed of two general categories of ethnic groups. First are the larger and more prominent groups whose members live primarily in Senegal but are also found in smaller numbers in neighboring nations such as Mali, Mauritania, and Guinea. Second are smaller groups, mainly in the interior, whose members live primarily in other West African nations. Despite this ethnic diversity, there is considerable similarity among the major ethnic groups of Senegal—most are Muslims and are farmers, and both rural and urban Senegalese speak dialects of Wolof, dress similarly, and are organized internally into rigid social classes based on wealth and status.

The six major ethnic groups are the Wolof (40%), Serer (15%), Fulani (Peul) (17%), Toucouleur (Tukulor) (9%), Diola (9%), and Mande (5%). The **Wolof** are the largest group; they live in the northwest and are politically and culturally dominant. Most Wolof are rural farmers of millet, cassava, and other crops grown primarily for sale, but they are also well represented in all major cities. The Wolof are Muslims and are divided into a number of Sufi brotherhoods.

Related to the Wolof are the **Serer,** who live in north-central Senegal. They are also mainly farmers who grow rice, millet, or peanuts as their primary crops. In the past, some Serer were assimilated by the Wolof though others maintained their cultural autonomy. The modern Serer population is composed of those who avoided assimilation and also rejected conversion to Islam. However, some eventually did become Muslims or Christians, but many also retain their indigenous beliefs.

The **Fulani (Peul)** are Muslim pastoral nomads found widely throughout West Africa.

The **Toucouleur (Tukulor),** who live in the northeast, are strong adherents of Islam and played a role in spreading Islam to other peoples of the region. They, too, are farmers but as many as 25% live in cities where they go in search of work.

The **Diola** live in southern Senegal, are farmers, and in comparison with other groups, are relatively isolated from national affairs. The nation of the Gambia physically separates them from the peoples and cities of the north.

Mande is a general label for a number of peoples who speak related languages and live throughout West Africa, including southeast Senegal. They are primarily farmers but have traditionally been involved in regional trade networks, which remains true today.

The rest of Senegal's population is composed of people from a number of small African groups and non-Africans. The African groups include Mande subgroups such as the **Bambara;** those with specialized economic adaptation such as the **Lebou** in the west, who fish, and the **Diankhanke,** who were traders; the **Soninke,** who are descendants of the people who formed the Ghana Empire; border populations near Guinea and Guinea-Bissau such as the **Balante** and **Bassari;** the **Moors,** who are the major group in neighboring Mauritania; and **Cape Verdeans** (*see* Guinea-Bissau). The primary non-African groups, which make up about 1.8% of the population, are **Europeans** (primarily French) who are involved in commerce and industry and **Lebanese** who are involved in retail trade.

Ethnic Relations

Ethnic relations in Senegal are described as among the most peaceful in Africa. A number of factors are cited as accounting for this state of affairs. First, most groups live in, and have lived in, their own territories. Second, when there has been migration in recent times, it has been peaceful and has often involved assimilation of smaller groups into larger ones, such as the Wolof and Toucouleur. Third, there is much cultural unity across Senegal created by the widespread use of the Wolof language and by adherence to Islam. However, in many groups in Senegal, adherence to Islam also involves membership in brotherhoods, some of which are organized along ethnic lines, while others cross ethnic boundaries. Fourth, some groups have long had trade or other relationships with one another. And, fifth, people from many ethnic groups mix in the cities and towns, and people living in urban areas have developed a sense of Senegalese identity that may take precedence over their ethnic identity.

All this does not mean that Senegal is entirely free of ethnic conflict. Both during the colonial era and since, relations between the Africans and non-Africans have been distant and at times strained. To a large extent, the French and Lebanese continue to live apart from African Senegalese society, with their primary involvement in the country being economic. People living in the southwest below the Gambian border are relatively isolated from national life, and since 1982, some have supported a secessionist movement and affiliation with the Gambia. This conflict, which has involved riots, terrorism, and military action by the Senegalese army, is more regional than ethnic and it has also led to strained relations between Senegal and the Gambia.

Seychelles

The Republic of the Seychelles is a small island nation in the western Indian Ocean off the east coast of Africa. It consists of over 100 small islands, most of which are inhabited. The islands were colonized in 1776 by the French, who imported slaves from Africa to work on the plantations and in the logging industry. The islands were taken by the British in 1794 and controlled by Great Britain until they were granted independence in 1976. Seychelles has a population of 77,500 and is ethnically homogeneous: over 99% of the population is of mixed **French, African,** and **Asian Indian** ancestry. The rest of the population is **British, Chinese,** and **Indian.** About 90% of the population is Roman Catholic, 6% Protestant, and the remainder a mix of other faiths including Islam, Buddhism, and Hinduism. Seychellois speak a Creole language based on French and African languages, with French and English also serving as official languages. As an ethnically homogeneous society, ethnic relations are not an issue.

Sierra Leone

The Republic of Sierra Leone is in West Africa and is bordered on the north and east by Guinea, on the southeast by Liberia, and on the west by the Atlantic Ocean. Freetown, the capital of Sierra Leone, was established as a colony for freed slaves by the British in 1787. Sierra Leone became an independent nation in 1961. Since the late 1960s, the nation has been plagued by either political instability or economic disruptions, and in the 1990s has experienced considerable political turmoil. The population is about five million. About 52% of the people are adherents of traditional religions, 8% are Christian, and 40% are Muslim. The majority of Muslims are from the Temne ethnic group. The languages in Sierra Leone are English (the official language whose regular use is limited to the literate minority); Mende, the principal vernacular in the south; Temne, the principal vernacular in the north; and Krio, the language of the resettled ex-slave population of the Freetown area and the lingua franca of Sierra Leone.

Ethnic Composition

There are 18 indigenous ethnic groups in Sierra Leone. The Mende in the south, the Temne in the north, and the Krio in Freetown are the largest. There are also about 11,000 Lebanese, 500 **Indians,** and 2,000 **Europeans** who live mainly in Freetown.

The **Temne (Timmannee),** about 30% of Sierra Leone's population, are found in Sierra Leone's Northern Province. They are now farmers and use the swidden or slash-and-burn method of farming. The Temne migrated from the northeast, probably from Guinea, and were present in Sierra Leone during the 1460s when the Portuguese arrived. When Europeans came to Africa, the Temne expanded their trade in slaves, gold, ivory, and food with the Portuguese, the British, and other Europeans. When Freetown was established, the Temne established trade relations with it. Although the majority of Temne are Muslims, traditional beliefs are still important.

The **Mende,** comprising about 29% of the population, inhabit the southern third of Sierra Leone. They came into the area in the 16th century from the south as invaders. They live in small villages of 70 to 250 people, which are from about one to three miles apart. The Mende are primarily farmers and work is divided by gender. Households are typically composed of brothers and their wives. The eldest brother is the household head. Mende culture borrows from Muslims, Christians, and neighboring peoples, and there is no single Mende culture. Their religion is also a blend of traditional elements, Islam, and Christianity.

The **Krio (Creoles, Crioulo),** forming less than 2% of the population, are Christian descendants of the freed slaves who were brought to Sierra Leone from the New World or from slave ships stopped by the British. Until recently, they controlled the government of Sierra Leone and formed the educated elite.

Some other groups—none of which comprise 10% of the population and most of which are less than 5%—are the **Limba, Kono, Koranko, Sherbo, Susu, Loko, Mandingo, Kissi, Krim,** and **Vai.** Most of these peoples are farmers.

Ethnic Relations

During the era of British rule, indigenous peoples attempted to end Creole dominance and overthrow the British on a number of occasions. However, once the British established control by the end of the 19th century, general peace reigned. The 20th century was largely peaceful and independence was achieved with no violence, although there was (and still is) lingering resentment over the influence of the Creoles, who number only about 60,000 and live almost exclusively in the west in and around Freetown. Although ethnic identity is an important feature of life in Sierra Leone, it has not been a primary factor in the political and economic unrest dating to the 1980s that has seriously damaged the vitality of the nation.

Somalia

S omalia is on the Horn of Africa and is bordered by Kenya, Ethiopia, and Djibouti on the west; the Gulf of Aden on the north; and the Indian Ocean on the east and south. From the 19th century until World War II, Somalia was under British and Italian control. It became an independent nation in 1960. Since then, a war with Ethiopia (over southern Ethiopia, which is occupied by ethnic Somalis), droughts, famines, and economic crises have contributed to political instability that, in the 1990s, resulted in United States and United Nations intervention to deliver relief supplies and restore order. The U.S. withdrew in 1994 and the UN in 1995 and there has been no effective central government since. The population is about 9.7 million, 74% of which is rural. Somali is the official language and most Somali are Sunni Muslims.

Ethnic Composition and Ethnic Relations

Unlike the ethnically diverse nations throughout most of Africa, Somalia is ethnically homogeneous. Nearly all people in Somalia are **Somali.** There are also sizable Somali populations in the border regions of Kenya, Ethiopia, and Djibouti. Somali identity is based on speaking Somali, adherence to Islam (most

Somali are Sunni Muslims), and most importantly, membership in one of the six Somali clans that trace their ancestry to the Quaraysh lineage of the Prophet Muhammad, the founder of Islam in 7th-century Arabia. These six regional clans are: **Daarood, Isaaq, Hawiye, Dir, Rahanwayn,** and **Digil.** The first four clans live in the central and northern regions and are herders of camels, cattle, sheep, and goats, with camels considered the most prestigious. They have traditionally lived a nomadic or seminomadic lifestyle. These four clans, collectively labeled **Samaal,** see themselves as superior to the two southern farming clans. They are also more numerous, accounting for about 70% of the national population. The two groups in the south herd but also farm grains, vegetables, and fruit and live a more sedentary lifestyle. Conflicts between different clans and between lineages within clans, especially over land and matters of personal honor, were common during the pre-independence period. Such conflicts reappeared in the 1980s as the national government weakened and then collapsed. In the 1990s, Somalia lacks central governmental authority, and the various regions of the country are again ruled by clans or lineages.

Living alongside the Somali—but outside Somali society—are occupational castes such as potters, blacksmiths, leather workers, and barbers, who provide these services for the Somali but are considered socially inferior. Whether they are Somali in origin or are descendants of the indigenous inhabitants of the region is not clear.

About 2% of the population are **non-Somalis** who live in farming and fishing communities along the southern coast. They are descended from Arabs, Persians, Indians, and African peoples from Kenya and are called **Habash** by the Somalis.

South Africa

S outh Africa lies at the southern tip of Africa. It is bounded on the north by Namibia, Botswana, Zimbabwe, and Mozambique. The Atlantic Ocean is to the west and the Indian Ocean to the east and south. The nations of Lesotho and Swaziland lie within its borders. South Africa is the most industrially developed country in Africa. Almost one-third of the world's gold comes from South Africa, and it is also a major producer of diamonds, manganese, chromium, and vanadium.

Although ancestral humans lived in South Africa some 3 million years ago, the ancestors of the modern people of the nation go back only about 3,000 years to the Khoisan hunter-gatherers. They were followed by peoples migrating from the north about 700 years ago.

In 1652, the Dutch settled near the Cape of Good Hope. They encountered Khokhoi, or Hottentots, pastoralists. Eventually additional French and Dutch Huguenots and Calvinistic settlers arrived. They had taken most of the Hottentot cattle herds by the 18th century. By the early 1700s, the Cape had become a center of East Indian trade, further stimulating Dutch settlement. By the 1770s, Dutch (Boer) settlers advancing into the interior to herd and farm met up with the culmination of 2,000 years of Bantu migration southward into South Africa. The Nguni had settled between the Drakensberg Mountains and the ocean. The Sotho had settled north of the Cape Colony by the early 19th century. The struggle for land led to a number of clashes between the Boers and Bantu as well as conflict between different Bantu tribes. In the early 19th century there were wars among Bantu peoples that led to the death of hundreds of thousands of people. This period is referred to as the *mfecane.* Eventually, the survivors formed a number of centralized states; among them, the Zulu, Swazi, Sotho, and Xhosa who today are among the major ethnic groups of the region.

The British became interested in South Africa and from 1795 to 1806 the British occupied the Cape to protect the route to India. In 1814 they purchased the Cape from the Dutch. The Boers objected to British rule and they left on the first of their Great Treks into the interior. Along the way north they defeated the Ndebele and Zulu. Other clashes broke out periodically between the Dutch and British. The discovery of gold and diamonds led to British incursions into Boer territory. In the South African or Boer War from 1899 to 1902 Britain defeated the Boers and created the Union of South Africa in 1910. Soon the practice known as apartheid, or separation of Blacks and Whites with complete White dominance, began. It came into more complete use in 1948 and prevailed until world opinion and the ability of Nelson Mandela and other African leaders ended it in 1994. In that year, Mandela and his African Nationalist Party won the election and proclaimed the "Rainbow Nation," the Black Africans taking political power.

South Africa has a population of about 45 million. South Africa's major religion is Christianity, although Islam, Hinduism, and Judaism have sizable followings as well. Traditional beliefs still exist and many who practice major world religions also follow traditional practices. Many Christian Africans belong to churches that are uniquely South African in their merging of Christianity with traditional beliefs. There are 11 official languages in South Africa: Afrikaans, English, Ndebele, Pedi, Sotho, Swazi, Tsonga, Tswana, Venda, Xhosa, and Zulu. These languages reflect South Africa's major ethnic groups.

Ethnic Composition

South Africa is ethnically heterogeneous. The population can be classified into four general categories: Africans (76.1%), people of European ancestry (12.8%), Coloureds (8.5%), and Asians (2.6%).

Africans in South Africa are the numerically dominant group, and since 1994 they have been politically dominant as well. They consist of a number of major groups and dozens of subgroups. To some extent, the major groups are localized regionally, although there is considerable mixing of groups in major cities.

The indigenous people of South Africa are collectively labeled the **Khoi** or **Khoikhoi.** The labels **Hottentot** and **Hotnot** were used by early European settlers but those names are now considered to be derogatory. At the time of European arrival (and for centuries before then) the Khoi lived by herding cattle, although prior to European arrival, they had begun to be displaced by Bantu-speaking groups migrating into the region from the north. The Bantu, and then the Europeans, succeeded in pushing the Khoi off the best land and into the most arid and remote regions, and today Khoi live in isolated reserves in South Africa and Namibia. The reserves were usually located near old mission stations where the fleeing Khoi seeking protection were converted to Christianity. Khoi herders traditionally spoke

one of a number of mutually understandable Khoikhoi languages, which are now disappearing from use—physical displacement has been replaced by linguistic displacement, and even on the reserves, Afrikaans is replacing the traditional language. The Khoi-Afrikaner contact was not entirely conflictual: some Afrikaner men and Khoi women parented a mixed-ancestry population called **Bastars,** meaning "bastards." Because they spoke Dutch and were Christians, and Khoi-Afrikaner contact and intermixing diminished over time, the offspring of some Bastars were absorbed into Afrikaner society. Others, however, maintained a distinct identity and formed independent political communities including the **Grigua,** several Bastar groups of Little Namaqualand, and the **Rehoboth Bastars** of Namibia.

From the contemporary political perspective, the two major African groups are the Xhosa and Zulu. **Xhosa** is an umbrella term for a number of related groups in South Africa, including the **Mpondo, Bomvana, Bhaca, Thembu, Mopndomise, Xesibe, Mfengu, Hlubi,** and the Xhosa proper. These Xhosa, or **Southern Nguni** peoples, share a common language, Isixhosa, and are culturally very similar. They were cattle herders and farmers, and their lives centered on cattle, which played an important part in their religious system. Currently, many Xhosa are Christians. The Xhosa have had contact with many other peoples over the centuries and were much influenced by the Dutch and British during the colonial period. Thus, it is not accurate to refer to a distinctive Xhosa culture, as their culture is a mix of elements combined from various groups. The Transkei, with 3.5 million Xhosa, and Ciskei, with about 1 million Xhosa, are their home areas. In addition, many Xhosa live in the cities of Cape Town, Port Elizabeth, and East London, and on farms outside Transkei and Ciskei. All together, there are about six million Xhosa in South Africa, and they are much involved in political affairs and the postapartheid government.

The **Zulu** live mainly in kwaZulu (Zululand), part of the province of Natal in the southeast. There are about six million in South Africa. The Zulu were originally one of a number of clans of the Nguni people. Shaka, the grandson of the Zulu clan founder, came to power in 1815 and organized a powerful army that united the northern Nguni clans into the group now known as the Zulu. As a result of the Zulu War of 1879–80, one of the most famous wars in British colonial history, the British achieved dominance over the Zulu. More than half the population is Christian, although the Zulu combine Christianity with traditional beliefs in distinctly Zulu churches. Zulu wealth was traditionally counted in cattle: cattle provided many of the necessities of life, such as meat, milk, clothing, shields, and a means of acquiring further wealth through bride-price. Most modern Zulu depend on agriculture, and many are poor. To add to their family income, men often migrate elsewhere for wage labor.

The end of White rule and the beginning of African rule stirred up political rivalries and led to violent conflict between the Zulu and other African groups, most importantly the politically powerful Xhosa. The Zulu National Cultural Liberation Movement (Inkatha Ye Sizwe), also known as Inkatha or the Inkatha party, is the political body that represents Zulu interests.

The **Ndebele** number over 400,000, most of whom live in the Eastern Transvaal Province. They are basically cattle or goat herders, although in current South Africa many are also agriculturists. Although the Ndebele resisted Christianity throughout the 19th century, to-

day most are members of the Zion Christian Church. In the late 1500s, the Ndebele split into two main tribal units, **Ndzundza** and **Manala.** The larger of the two groups, Ndzundza, migrated to KwaSimkhulu, about 200 kilometers east of what is now Pretoria. The smaller group, Manala, occupied the areas of Ezotshaneni, KoNonduna, and Embilameni, which include what are today the eastern suburbs of Pretoria. Under apartheid, which kept Blacks and Whites apart, the Ndebele (both Manala and Ndzundza) were allowed to settle only in a homeland called KwaNdebele.

In addition to these groups, South Africa is home to several million other Africans from groups that are centered in neighboring nations. These include several hundred thousand **Sotho** and nearly one million **Swazi.** The Sotho and Swazi are associated with the independent nation of Lesotho, which is entirely surrounded by South Africa, and Swaziland, which is bordered by South Africa on three sides. **Northern Sotho** (formerly **Pedi**) is the generic label for a large number of groups, all of whom speak dialects of Sotho and live in the northern Transvaal in the east. These groups include the **Tau, Kone, Roka, Ntwane, Mphahlele, Th-wene, Mathabathe, Kone (Matlala), Dikgale, Batlokwa, Gananwa (Mmalebogo), Mmamabolo, Molet-e, Lobedu, Narene, Phalaborwa, Mogoboya, Kgakga, Pulana, Pai,** and **Kutswe.** There are also about two million **Tswana** in South Africa and another 1.4 million in their home nation of Botswana. Many Tswana work in South Africa's mines while attempting to maintain their farms as well. Thus, the term "peasant-proletarians" has been applied to them.

The South African population of **European** ancestry is split roughly 60-40 between Afrikaners (who are primarily of Dutch descent) and those of British descent. The **Afrikaners** (or **Boers**) have been called "the White tribe of Africa" and are the descendants of the Dutch and French Huguenots who settled in southern Africa. Boer means "farmer" in the Afrikaans language. Driven inland by later British settlers and consequently isolated from European influences, they developed their own culture and now see themselves as African rather than as European. The Afrikaners are White, speak the Afrikaans language, are of Western European descent, were mainly politically aligned with the National Party, belong to the Dutch reformed church (NGK), and share a common cultural heritage with other Afrikaners—which distinguishes them from all other peoples of South Africa. In addition to skin color, language is probably the most important marker of Afrikaner identity. Afrikaans is based on the Dutch of the early Dutch settlers, with words added from English, French, German, and various African languages. Afrikaans is also widely spoken by people classified as Coloureds, who are of mixed White and other ancestry. The Afrikaners founded the National Party in 1914, and they and the party played a central role in developing and enforcing apartheid. The end of apartheid and the election of African political leaders have led to a major decline in Afrikaner political power, which—coupled with their residence mainly in the interior—has left them isolated from what is now mainstream South African society. Some Afrikaners prefer separation from South Africa to African rule.

South Africans of **British** descent, who live mainly in the major cities and are involved in commerce, are a much less visible minority than the Afrikaners, despite South Africa's ties to Britain.

A significant minority within the European category is **Jews,** who number about 175,000. Jews from Europe have settled in South Africa since the late 19th century, with a sizable influx of refugees after World War II. South Africa's Jews live mainly in cities and are involved in businesses and the professions.

Asians are the largest nonindigenous minority. About 90% are **Asian Indians** who were brought to South Africa by the British as indentured laborers in the late 19th century. These laborers were followed by Indian traders who established a strong Indian presence in the merchant class. Nearly all Asian Indians in South Africa today were born in South Africa have only minimal ties to India. Nearly all Indians live in cities and are active participants in the South African economy and wealth-based social-class system. Although the Indian community was once divided on the basis of caste distinctions brought from India, as well as occupation (laborers versus merchants), social class distinctions are far more important in the 1990s. The community includes both Hindus and Muslims. A small percentage are very wealthy, a larger number are in the middle class, and the greatest percentage are involved in retail sales, clerical work, and service occupations. Under apartheid, Asians were in the middle—between the Whites at the top and Africans at the bottom. The end of apartheid means greater freedom for Asians in South Africa, but also more competition from Africans for education and jobs. The other significant Asian population is the **Chinese,** who number about 10,000.

Cape Coloureds is the label conventionally used to refer to people whose European ancestors settled in Cape Town or in the Cape Colony province and who mixed with the indigenous African population. Their descendants are now widely distributed throughout South Africa and the neighboring nations of Namibia, Botswana, Lesotho, Swaziland, and Zimbabwe. Today, the label Coloureds is used more broadly to mean anyone of mixed ancestry, which might be various combinations of European, African, and Asian forebears. Beginning in 1950 under apartheid, the Coloureds were designated a distinct category with fewer rights than Whites and more than Africans. Seven arbitrary subcategories of Coloureds were officially listed—**Cape Coloured, Malay, Grigua, Chinese, Indian, other Asiatic,** and **other Coloured.** The Coloured population in South Africa is about three million, about 75% of whom live in cities, mainly in the south. Most Coloureds speak Afrikaans and only about 10% speak English. Because of pre- and apartheid era discrimination, most Coloureds are skilled or semiskilled laborers and farm workers, although some of Malay descent have enjoyed economic success that was built on their traditional position as artisans, professional fishers, and commodity producers in colonial society. The Coloureds became active in the anti-apartheid movement in the 1950s.

Ethnic Relations

Under colonial domination and during the nearly 50 years of apartheid, South Africa was a divided society. Whites and Africans lived separate lives, with Whites controlling of all aspects of South African society. When apartheid came to an end in 1994, about half of all African adults were unemployed. Africans who were impoverished during decades of political repression had high expectations of Nelson Mandela, the newly elected African leader who sought to create national unity despite opposition from the National Party as well as the Zulu-based Inkatha Freedom Party. Although the political situation remains volatile, Mandela has had success in obtaining foreign investments in South Africa, and he has generated much political goodwill toward the newly formed democracy.

South Africa has continued the democratic change launched by the historic 1994 national elections. The Government of National Unity is made up of ministers from the African National Congress (ANC), the National Party (NP), and the Inkatha Freedom Party (IFP). In addition to the three major parties, the 400-member National Assembly includes the Democratic Party (DP), the Freedom Front (FF), the Pan Africanist Congress (PAC), and the African Christian Democratic Party (ACDP). Nonetheless, the inequities of apartheid continue to cause problems for the African population, including illiteracy, a high unemployment rate, and a lack of health care.

South Africa is attempting to control unemployment through economic development, but the effects of apartheid will remain a ma-

In post-apartheid South Africa, White, Black, and Coloured children can mix. Photo: Reuters/Corbis-Bettmann.

jor economic and social problem for generations. In another initiative to resolve apartheid issues, the government has established a Truth and Reconciliation Commission (TRC), to investigate apartheid-era human rights abuses and to compensate victims.

Politically motivated ethnic conflict continues to be a problem, although there has been a decrease in politically motivated killings in KwaZulu/Natal.

Sudan

The Republic of Sudan is in northeastern Africa. It is the largest nation in Africa in terms of size and is bordered by Egypt on the north; the Red Sea, Eritrea, and Ethiopia on the east; Kenya, Uganda, and Congo (formerly Zaire) on the south; and the Central African Republic, Chad, and Libya on the west. Sudan was settled by African peoples migrating east and north, peoples from Egypt migrating south, and Muslims migrating from Arabia: the result is an ethnically diverse population. From the 1820s until independence in 1956, Sudan was under Egyptian control and relations between the two nations remain strained. Sudan today has an Islamic fundamentalist government and continues to experience several major problems including periodic famines and separatist movements in the south, a limited number of allied nations, and condemnation by international human rights organizations that criticize the treatment of non-Muslims and political opponents. The population is about 31 million and is 73% rural. Islam is the official religion and about 70% of Sudanese are Muslims, 25% adhere to indigenous beliefs, and 5% are Christians. Arabic is the official language, although most African peoples in the south speak their own languages.

Ethnic Composition

Sudan is believed to be the home of over 600 ethnic groups whose members speak over 400 different languages, making it one of the most ethnically heterogeneous nations in the world. However, most of these ethnic groups are small, and most of the languages are spoken by only a few hundred or a few thousand people. In addition, population migrations and secessionist movements in the south have both reduced the populations of some already small groups and led to the demise of others. Thus, while Sudan is ethnically diverse, only a few large groups actually play a significant role in Sudanese society. Some experts suggest that Sudanese ethnic and religious groups can be lumped into three general categories: (1) peoples of the north, who are mostly Muslims; (2) African peoples of the south; and (3) West Africans who have migrated to southern Sudan. While this classification is not perfect and masks some variation within the groupings, it does serve to make for easier discussion of ethnicity in the Sudan.

The major Muslim group in the north—and the largest group in Sudan—is the **Arabs,** who form about 40% of the national population and a majority of the population in the north. The Arabs in Sudan include those living in cities and towns, nomadic **(Bedouin) Arabs** (called **Juhayna** in Sudan), the cattle-herding **Baggara Arabs** of central Sudan, and people of mixed Arab and African or other ancestry. Identity as an Arab is based on Arab ancestry, speaking one of the three major dialects of Arabic spoken in Sudan, and adherence to Islam. Sudanese Arabs are Sunni Arabs, although many are members of Sufi sects, which have their origin in Shi'ite Islam. As elsewhere in North Africa, many Arabs in Sudan feel primary allegiance to their clan and tribe rather than to the Arab ethnic category in general.

Muslim Arabs are the dominant group in Sudan; government service has been restricted to Muslims, most of whom are Arabs.

The second largest Muslim group is the **Nubians,** who number several million in Sudan and about 160,000 in Egypt. They are non- Arab Muslims descended from Egyptians who mixed with people migrating north from central and western Africa some 4,000 years ago. Thus, they more closely resemble Black Africans than Arab Sudanese. Until the mid-1960s, most lived in villages in Nubia, a region in southern Egypt and northern Sudan, but the Egyptian government relocated 50,000 of them further north because their land and villages were flooded by the reservoir created by the building of the Aswan Dam. While many Nubians remain farmers, settlement in cities has involved many in wage labor and in small businesses. As Muslims, Nubians are not subject to overt discrimination in Sudan.

The other Muslim peoples in Sudan are smaller ethnic groups or clusters of related groups in the northeast and northwest who either lived in the region prior to the arrival of the Arabs in the 7th century or arrived later but lived outside Arab Muslim society. These include the **Beja** groups along the Red Sea and the **Fur, Zaghawa, Masalit, Daju,** and **Beti** in the northwest. Most of these groups subsist by herding or through a combination of farming and herding.

Southern Sudan is the home of several hundred African ethnic groups who are physically, culturally, linguistically, and historically distinct from the Arab and other Muslim populations to the north. Few southerners are Muslim; most are adherents of their traditional religions and a minority were converted to a number of Christian denominations by missionaries. The major groups are the **Dinka, Nuer, Shilluk, Zande,** and **Nuba.** Smaller group are the

Ndogo, Bviri, Bongo, Baka, Moru, Avukaya, Mandari, Bari, Madi, Kuku, Didinga, Acholi, Anuak, and Suri.

The **Dinka** are the largest, most widely distributed, and most politically significant African ethnic group in the nation. They number over 3 million and constitute about 40% of the African population of Sudan. The Dinka are not a unified political entity but are composed of at least 25 related subgroups widely distributed across the northern region of southern Sudan. The Dinka have long been herders of cattle, a livelihood that is supplemented by horticulture and fishing.

Next in size is the **Nuer,** whose members number about 600,000. They live in the central region of southern Sudan, often in close proximity to the Dinka. Although the Nuer and Dinka are culturally related and are very likely descended from the same ancestors, the two groups have often fought over land in Sudan, a pattern ended by British intervention in the 1800s. Like the Dinka, the Nuer are cattle herders and horticulturists, and most continue to practice their indigenous religion.

Living north of the Nuer are the **Shilluk (Collo),** who number about 150,000. The Shilluk, Nuer, Dinka, and other regional groups are often labeled **Nilotes** or Nilotic-speaking peoples as they all speak related Nilotic languages and it is likely that they share a common ancestry. Unlike the Nuer and Dinka, the Shilluk are mainly settled farmers, although they also keep some cattle.

The fourth major Nilotic group is the **Zande (Azande),** who number about one million and live in Sudan, Congo (formerly Zaire), and the Central African Republic. Their population in southwestern Sudan is probably declining as people move to Congo to escape control by the Arabs and conflict with the Dinka. The Zande are a mix of peoples who were politically unified and became culturally similar under the rule of expanding Zande kingdoms beginning in the 18th century. The influence of the kingdoms ended under British and French colonial rule in the late 19th century. Most Zande today are farmers, and many are involved in the commercial growing of coffee and other crops for export.

The most visible non-Nilotic people in the south are the **Nuba,** who live in the Nuba Mountains in the northern reaches of the southern region. Most are farmers. Unlike the other groups in the southern part of Sudan who are physically distant from large Muslim populations, the Nuba live close to Muslims. Despite this proximity, most have resisted conversion and few speak Arabic.

West Africans in Sudan, primarily **Fulani** and **Hausa** people from Nigeria, live mainly in central Sudan and number about one million. They are Muslims who have arrived mainly since the 1960s to escape political domination by other groups in Nigeria and to search for jobs or establish farms. Although there has been friction with Arab farmers already established in the Sudan, and they are seen as a clearly distinct population by other Sudanese, their settlement in Sudan has been relatively conflict free.

Ethnic Relations

The major ethnic relations issue in Sudan, though not the only issue, concerns relations between the Arab Muslim north and the African south. Hostility between these two large population groups predates the modern and even the colonial era and goes back several centuries to when Arabs raided southern Sudan for slaves. The southern Africans in Sudan continue to distrust Arabs, and the Arabs continue to see the Africans as social inferiors who should be converted to Islam and incorporated into Arab society, although the Africans prefer to maintain their indigenous cultural traditions. In the 1960s until a cease-fire was arranged in 1972, and again from 1983 until the present, southern Sudan has been the location of continuous fighting between northern troops and southern groups, with the Dinka being the most prominent. Southern resistance has been hampered to some extent by conflict between the major Nilote groups, with other groups resisting Dinka control of local government. According to the *World Refugee Survey* (1995:76): "The protracted war has created a cycle of displacement and malnourishment among the civilian population, has flooded neighboring countries with refugees, created enormous squatter and displacement camps, and has caused a chronic humanitarian emergency that has remained one of the UN's most expensive operations."

The war in the south, though the most destructive and visible, is not the only ethnic relations issue in Sudan. Since the early 1970s, there has been considerable migration from rural areas to towns and to the country's two major cities, and there has also been increased use of laborers from different ethnic groups on major construction projects. The result has been a greater mixing of people from different ethnic groups than in the past. However, ethnic rivalries, the absence of a central unifying force in Sudan (other than Islam for some), and scarce resources (including jobs) have tended to reinforce ethnic identity and thus distance between ethnic groups is maintained even in multiethnic communities.

In the north, the primary ethnic conflict involves the Fur and the Arabs in the northwest, where competition for political control of the region and control of the slowly developing oil industry has led the Fur to attempt to take political control away from the more numerous Arabs. Other groups in the north also resent Arab control, but Arab numerical dominance makes resistance largely ineffective.

Swaziland

The Kingdom of Swaziland is a landlocked nation in southeastern Africa. It is bordered by South Africa on three sides and by Mozambique on the north. It has a population of 998,000. Swaziland is a kingdom that dates back to the 1600s and thus is one of the last surviving ancient dynasties of sub-Saharan Africa. It is named after the **Swazi,** the major ethnic group in the nation. Swazi people also live in smaller numbers in South Africa and Mozambique. In addition to the Swazi, there are about 15,000 **Zulu** (*see* South Africa) and a few thousand **Europeans** (mainly **British**) in Swaziland. The region became distinctly Swazi in the 1820s when the Swazi were driven into it by the Zulu. They then came under British protection and eventually gained independence in 1968. Although Swaziland was granted independence as a constitutional monarchy, the king took control in 1972 and it has remained a monarchy ever since. Swazis speak siSwazi, and some also speak English. Most people in Swaziland live in rural homesteads where farming is the principal activity. Since independence, economic development has created localized employment hubs, and there has been some population relocation to these centers. As it is for some other groups in East Africa, cattle herding is an important component of traditional Swazi life: in addition to providing material benefits such as food and clothing, ownership of cattle is an important source of wealth and prestige. Although most Swazi are nominally Christian, traditional beliefs remain strong and most Swazis prefer churches that allow incorporation of traditional beliefs and practices into Christianity. As an ethnically homogeneous nation, there is no ethnic conflict, although in the past, there were conflicts between the British and Zulu over land. Today, most conflict is between individuals and often concerns employment opportunities, or is between different socioeconomic groups, as a social-class system is forming in Swaziland based on education and wealth.

Tanzania

The United Republic of Tanzania is in East Africa and is bordered by Uganda and Kenya on the north; the Indian Ocean on the east; Mozambique, Malawi, and Zambia on the south; and Congo (formerly Zaire), Burundi, and Rwanda on the west. It consists of the former

Tanganyika and Zanzibar. The island of Zanzibar came under Arab Muslim influence in the 12th century, then Portuguese influence in the 17th century and 18th century, then Islamic control, and finally British control from 1890 until the island's independence in 1961. Tanganyika followed the same general pattern of external control, but was also under German control from 1885 until World War I, at which time it, too, came under British control. The population of Tanzania is about 29 million. Its official languages are Swahili and English.

Ethnic Composition

Tanzania is an ethnically heterogeneous nation of about 125 ethnic groups. About 99% of the population is African, with the remaining 1% being of Asian, European, and Arab origin. The religious composition of the mainland is 40% Christian, 33% Muslim, and the remainder traditionalist. The island of Zanzibar is almost 100% Muslim. There is a strong Arab influence on the coast and on the islands of Pemba and Zanzibar, and strong Asian influence on the economy, with about 40% of private enterprises owned by South Asians from India and Pakistan.

The population of Tanzania consists mostly of members of about 120 Black African groups, about 95% of which speak a Bantu language and many of which are culturally similar to one another. The largest ethnic groups are the **Sukuma, Makonde, Chagga, Haya** and the **Nyamwezi.** The Sukuma are estimated to account for from 13% to 20% of the population, with no other group accounting for more than 5%. Other groups of significant size include the **Ngonde, Gogo, Ha, Hehe, Nyakyusa, Nyika, Ngoni** (*see* South Africa), **Swahili, Yao, Luo,** and **Maasai** (*see* Kenya). The population also includes people of **Asian Indian, Pakistani,** and **Goan** origin, and small **Arab** and **European** communities. Three-quarters of the people live in rural areas. About one-third of the population follow traditional religions. Islam is the religion of about one-third of the people and is dominant on Zanzibar. Roman Catholicism is the largest Christian denomination of Tanzania, with some six million adherents. Swahili and English are the official languages of Tanzania, but many people continue to use the language of their ethnic group.

The **Sukuma,** the largest group, live in the north, south of Lake Victoria. They are not unified politically, and village and kinship ties remain strong. Many are farmers and a sizable percentage are involved in the cotton-growing industry.

The **Makonde** live in the southeast and are subsistence farmers who until recently were relatively isolated from Tanzanian society.

The **Chagga** live in the north on the southern slopes of Mt. Kilimanjaro and are the third largest group, with a population of about one million. The Chagga are farmers who are much involved in the coffee industry. Many have converted to Christianity.

The **Haya** live next to the Chagga and have also been involved in the coffee industry. Both the Chagga and Haya were favored by the British and were afforded more education than other groups, were more readily converted to Christianity, and were employed in government positions.

The **Nyamwezi** live in central Tanzania and are primarily farmers. There are about 1.5 million Nyamwezi. They are closely related to the Sukuma, who are their neighbors, and Sukuma, Tusi, and Sumbwa people often live in Nyamwezi villages. However, Sukuma villages tend to be more ethnically homogeneous.

Occupying a somewhat unique position in Tanzanian society are the **Swahili,** who number about 200,000 and live along the East African coast and on Zanzibar, Pemba, and Mafia islands. They are also found on the Aomoro Islands and northwestern Madagascar. Their settlements are urban. Their language, KiSwahili, is a lingua franca for eastern Africa. The word Swahili means "coast." The Swahili are Muslims and feel themselves distinct from the majority peoples of the nations of southern East Africa. Moreover, they were once heavily engaged in the slave trade and wish to distinguish themselves from their fellow Africans who were taken as slaves. In turn, they are remembered as slave traders by these people. Swahili trading, a lifeway that has almost ended, lasted for 2,000 years. Ivory, slaves, gold, grain, and mangrove poles were traded for textiles, beads, weapons, and porcelain. The Swahili are Sunni Muslims with traditional beliefs combined with Islam.

Ethnic Relations

Ethnic relations are generally peaceful, and few religious- and ethnic-based disputes have disrupted national life since independence. Ethnic conflict is controlled in the national assembly by broad ethnic representation in the national legislature. Groups tend to be localized, meaning that people from the major group in each district tend to represent the district. In addition, ethnic competition tends to occur at the local level, especially when different groups find themselves competing for jobs, a share of the agricultural market, or educational opportunities. Groups such as the Chagga, who have had more of these opportunities in the past than other groups, are sometimes the object of jealousy and resentment. As elsewhere in the region, there is also resentment of the Swahili for their role in the slave trade.

Togo

The Republic of Togo is in West Africa and is bordered on the south by the Gulf of Guinea, on the east by Benin, on the north by Burkina Faso, and on the west by Ghana. More than two-thirds of Togolese are farmers, most of whom are engaged in subsistence farming.

The region was a major slave-trading center for the Atlantic slave trade. It was under German control beginning the 1800s and then was split between French and British control in the twentieth century. The French-controlled region became the independent nation of Togo in 1960.

Togo's population is 4,570,000. French is its official language, but in addition, there are many indigenous languages. A Voltaic language called Gur, a branch of the Niger-Congo family of languages, is spoken in northern Togo, and about 70% of Togolese people speak Ewe, a language of the Kwa branch of the Niger-Congo language family. Chadic languages are also spoken in Togo, the most important of which is Hausa, which is used as a second language for both literary and trade functions throughout West Africa.

Although Christianity has profoundly influenced the country, more than half of the people in Togo adhere to traditional beliefs, and there is an expanding Islamic community in the north. In the south, many Togolese still participate in traditional rituals. The main Protestant (Calvinistic) church has been governed for many years by Togolese ministers, and there has been a Togolese Roman Catholic archbishop since independence.

Ethnic Composition

Togo has about 30 ethnic groups. The largest group—and the major group in the south—is the **Ewe,** who constitute about 40% of the national population and are closely related (some experts consider them to be the same) to the **Fon,** the major group across the border in Benin. Ewe is a general label for not one particular group but a number of related groups including the **Adja, Oatchi, Peda, Anlo, Abutia, Be,** and **Ho.** The Ewe are mainly farmers, fishers along the coast, and women are often traders and shopkeepers. The Ewe are also employed in many government positions, by businesses, and in all sectors of the market economy, which is centered in southern Togo. Many Ewe have converted to Christianity, although traditional beliefs and practices remain in use.

Northern Togo is home to a number of smaller groups, none of which is as large as or has the national influence of the Ewe in the south. The major northern groups are the

Gurma, Losso, and **Kabre,** while smaller groups include the **Konkomba, Basrai, Moba,** and **Temba.** They are primarily farmers and adherents of indigenous religions. Their contact with Europeans has been of shorter duration and less intense than is the case with Ewe peoples in the south. There are also nomadic cattle-herding **Fulani** (*see* Nigeria) in northern Togo and **Hausa** (*see* Nigeria) are distributed throughout the country.

Most of Togo's non-Africans live in Lome. These people are mainly **French,** but they also include a few **Mulattos** of Brazilian, German, and French ancestry, as well as **Brazilians,** or **Portuguese** of Brazilian birth. They constituted the original trading settlement in Togo. Today Brazilian Mulattos are closely associated with economic and political development.

Ethnic Relations

The major ethnic issue in Togo in the postcolonial era is competition between the economically undeveloped groups in the north and the more advanced Ewe in the south for economic and political power. Since the mid-1960s the nation has been ruled by northerners, although they have been careful to make sure that southern groups are represented in the government. Nonetheless, there has been Ewe opposition to rule by northerners, which at times has included bombings in Lome. Rampant corruption and economic problems have contributed to dissatisfaction with the government and have provided the Ewe with substantive issues that go beyond ethnic rivalries for power. In addition to giving ethnic groups representation in the government, the government has also sought to build a sense of national identity by promoting the publication of literature and plays in Togo languages and also by forming the African Ballet of Togo to promote Togo ethnic dance forms.

Tunisia

T he Republic of Tunisia is in North Africa and is bordered by the Mediterranean Sea on the north and east, Libya on the southeast, and Algeria on the west. Northern Tunisia was the center of the Carthaginian Empire, which was established by people who migrated west from the region that is now Lebanon in the 9th century B.C. After Carthage fell to the Romans, it became the African hub of the Roman Empire and then came under the control of the Vandals, Byzantines, Arabs, various local and regional Muslim dynasties, and then the Ottoman Turks. Desired by both Italy and France, it came under French control in 1883 and remained so until achieving independence in 1955. Since then, Arab culture and Islam have become dominant and French influence has faded. Tunisia has a population of nine million. Arabic is the official language, and the entire population—except for a small number of Europeans—are Sunni Muslims.

Ethnic Composition and Ethnic Relations

Tunisia, like its neighbors, has a population that is almost entirely of Arab and Berber ancestry. The two groups have mixed to a large extent over the centuries, both are Sunni Muslims, and both speak Arabic; thus, Tunisians are commonly referred to as Arab-Berbers rather than as one group or the other. The Berbers are less prominent in Tunisia than in Algeria and Morocco.

Arabs are an ethnic group indigenous to the Middle East and are the majority population in 15 nations in the Middle East and North Africa. The history of the emergence of Arabs as a distinct group in the Middle East is unclear, but as early as 853 B.C., the Arabic language was in use. Although being an "Arab" has different meanings in different nations, a

Elders in Kairorun, Tunisia. Arabs and Berbers in Tunisia have mixed to a large extent over the centuries, and Tunisians are commonly referred to as Arab-Berbers. Photo: Corel Corp.

shared Arab identity is based on a number of key elements. These include knowledge of the Arabic language, both in its classical form (used in religion and literature) and in the colloquial Arabic used in daily life, which is called Moroccan Arabic; a personal identity with Arab culture, history, and the Arab community; a strong value placed on children and family life; a clear division of labor based on sex; and adherence to Islam. About 93% of Arabs around the world follow Islam. Arabs in Tunisia live mainly in the north.

Berbers are the indigenous people of North Africa. Although details about their origins are unclear, ancestors of the contemporary Berbers have lived in North Africa for at least 5,000 years. The Berbers across North Africa are collectively referred to as **Imazighen,** although the names for regional groups within nations and identification with specific settlements are more salient markers of identity for most rural Berbers.

Tunisia is relatively free of ethnic conflict, and the government has been able to control the Islamic fundamentalist movement that has been active across North Africa.

Uganda

The Republic of Uganda is in Central Africa and is bordered by Sudan on the north, Kenya on the east, Tanzania and Rwanda on the south, and Congo (formerly Zaire) on the west. Prior to British rule, which began in 1894, southern Uganda was the locale of a number of African kingdoms including the Buganda, the most powerful, which lost power under the British. Uganda gained independence from Britain in 1962, and since then has experienced considerable political turmoil including periods of civil war. The national government banned Uganda's former kingdoms in 1967. In the late 1990s, new efforts are underway to create a stable national government. Uganda has a population of about 20.2 million. English is the official language, although indigenous languages are widely spoken. Through the efforts of Christian missionaries, about 66% of the population is considered Christian, the remainder consisting of Muslims and adherents of traditional religions.

Ethnic Composition

Uganda is an ethnically diverse nation with a population composed of 40 different African ethnic groups, 16 of which can be considered major regional groups. There are also about one million Rwandans (**Hutu** and **Tutsi**) in southern Uganda and about 10,000 Asians. **Asians (Indians** and **Pakistanis)** arrived during the British period and at one time numbered perhaps as many as 100,000. After independence, the government nationalized many businesses, which hurt the Asian businesspersons financially and prompted some to leave Uganda. In 1972, the remaining 70,000 or so were expelled by the government of Idi Amin. About 10,000 have subsequently returned.

The ethnic groups of Uganda are conventionally classified by language into five language groupings: **Eastern Lacustrine Bantu, Western Lacustrine Bantu, Eastern Nilotes, Western Nilotes,** and **Central Sudanic.**

The Eastern Lacustrine Bantu live in southeastern Uganda north of Lake Victoria and include the Ganda, Basoga, and Bagisu. The **Ganda** are the largest ethnic group in Uganda and the nation is named after them. Their population is estimated (Uganda does not conduct an ethnic census) at from 10% to 17% of the national population. Prior to the arrival of the British colonials, they were a powerful kingdom that frequently engaged in war with rival kingdoms and used slave labor and migrant laborers from the north. They were—as many Ganda still are—farmers, with bananas and yams being the primary crops. Their kingdom was permitted to remain in place during the British period, and the Ganda often served the British as government officials. Nearly all Ganda are Christian, with a small minority being Muslim.

The **Basoga** were another kingdom in precolonial times, located north and east of the Ganda. However, unlike the Ganda, the Basoga never had political unification under a single ruler, but were ruled instead by a number of smaller kingdoms. They, like the Ganda, are mainly farmers but they also keep livestock. They constitute about 8% of the national population.

Moving farther east and north we find the third major Eastern Lacustrine Bantu group, the **Bagisu (Gisu)** who constitute about 5% of the national population. They, too, are farmers, but living in an especially fertile region, they also grow coffee for export and are important contributors to the national economy, which affords them some political autonomy.

The Western Lacustrine Bantu also speak Bantu languages but live in southwestern Uganda. The major groups are the **Banyoro, Batoro,** and **Banyankole.** They are culturally related and all are believed to be descended from agricultural and herding peoples in the region. In each group, a distinction continues to be made between people descended from herders and those descended from farmers, with the former enjoying higher prestige. Status difference aside, herders and farmers were often linked by economic and social arrangements that made each group dependent on the other. The three groups had independent kingdoms, and each continues to exist today as a distinct ethnic group.

The people of northeastern Uganda are mainly cattle herders, most of whom immigrated to the region from neighboring Kenya. Linguistically, they are labeled Eastern Nilotes. Most groups in the region fall under the general ethnic label **Karamojong,** which includes a number of subgroups including the **Jie** and **Dodoz.** The Karamojong number about 300,000 in all. They are a pastoral people with a culture centered on the herding of cattle, which are used for their milk and blood. Some Karamojong also live in villages where they farm, although farming is considered less prestigious than herding.

The largest Eastern Nilote group is the **Iteso,** who form about 9% of the national population. They are primarily farmers who, in the 20th century, have become much involved in the commercial agriculture of coffee and other crops. This has brought them some economic security, but it has also involved them in the national economic and political systems. In addition, the Iteso have a long history of their men traveling to other regions of the nation to work, leading to considerable contact with other ethnic groups. Thus, in comparison with other groups in Uganda, the Iteso are cosmopolitan and worldly. Some experts suggest that much of their traditional culture has disappeared and that Iteso culture is now a mix of elements drawn from other cultures.

Smaller groups in the Eastern Nilote grouping include the **Teuso, Tepeth, Labwor,** and **Kumam,** all of whom are now assimilated into neighboring groups. Also classified as Eastern Nilotes, although they live in the northwest among speakers of other languages, are the **Kakwa,** who constitute less than 1% of the national population. They are mainly farmers.

The fourth major ethnic category are the speakers of Western Nilote languages who live in north and north-central Uganda. The category consists of a number of larger and smaller groups who all together constitute about 15% of the national population. The three largest groups—**Acholi, Langi,** and **Alur**—make up about 7% of the national population. Western Nilote groups speak Luo, the language spoken by the people of that name in Kenya. As with other Nilote groups, it is likely that they migrated into the region from the east. Most are farmers, with the growing of millet, cassava, and other crops supplemented by trade, fishing, and the keeping of livestock. Most people are now at least nominally Christian, although many indigenous beliefs and practices have been merged with Christianity, and in the 1980s and 1990s, the region has been the locale of a number of religious-based social movements.

The Central Sudanic peoples live in the northwest and constitute about 6% of the national population. The **Lugbara** and closely related **Madi** are the two largest groups and together constitute about 5% of the national population. They are mainly farmers, although in the postindependence period their economy has been transformed from one based on subsistence farming to one based on commercial farming for export. As with Nilote groups to the east, Christian missionaries have won many converts, but most in name only.

Ethnic Relations

Upon achieving independence in 1962, Uganda faced the same political issue faced by many other former colonies—how to build a unified nation with authority vested in the central government from a mix of ethnic groups that had never been unified politically and whose relations ranged from friendly to distant to hostile. Since then, the government has adopted various approaches to dealing with ethnic diversity. Initially, the region's ethnic structure remained in place, the king of the Ganda becoming the first leader of Uganda. However, the government chose not to enumerate the population by ethnic group in order to downplay group differences, and in 1967, when the first government was overthrown, the new government outlawed the kingdoms. During the period from 1971 to 1979 when Uganda was ruled as a dictatorship by Idi Amin, some groups such as the Lugbara were seen as getting favors, such as government employment, while others were ignored. From 1979 to 1985, the situation continued to deteriorate under unstable governments as groups believed to support or benefit from Amin's rule (such as the Lugbara and Western Nilote groups) were repressed, and some people were killed or fled. In the 1990s, problems based on ethnic diversity persist. One is the continuing Karamojong separatist movement and another is the religious movement among Western Nilote groups. To deal with these issues, the new 1995 constitution created a non-party government for five years in order to remove ethnic factors from politics.

Western Sahara

W estern Sahara—north of Mauritania and southwest of Morocco—has been occupied by Morocco since the 1970s. Its status as a nation is under discussion. *See* Morocco.

Zambia

The Republic of Zambia is located in south-central Africa and is bordered by Congo (formerly Zaire) on the north, Tanzania on the northeast, Malawi on the east, Mozambique on the southeast, Zimbabwe and Namibia on the south, and Angola on the west. From 1889 until 1924, what is now Zambia was under the control of the British South Africa Company, which was interested in exploiting copper and other mineral resources. Britain ruled the region directly from 1924 until independence in 1964. Zambia has a population of 9.2 million. English remains the official language, although most people speak indigenous Bantu languages. About 75% of the population adheres to indigenous religions or syncretic religions that combine the Christianity brought by Protestant missionaries with indigenous beliefs and practices. The other 25% are Christians.

Ethnic Composition

With the departure of most Europeans following independence in 1964, Zambia became an almost exclusively African nation, with over 99% of the population belonging to one of 75 different African ethnic groups. The non-African population, which numbers about 60,000, consists of about 20,000 **Europeans** (most of whom are **British**) and 40,000 **Asian Indians** and **Coloureds** (people of mixed African and European or Asian ancestry). Like the Europeans, the Indians and Coloureds live mainly in cities. Zambia also hosts over 100,000 refugees, mainly from Angola and Congo (formerly Zaire).

Although Zambia is ethnically heterogeneous, almost all groups speak Bantu languages, and many groups are considered subgroups within larger ethnic categories. Population estimates for individual ethnic groups in Zambia are unreliable and can vary by as much as several hundred thousand for a given group. Thus, the figures given below should be considered rough estimates.

The largest ethnic group is the **Bemba,** who live in the northeast (Northern Province) and in smaller numbers across the border in Congo and Tanzania. Estimates place their population at anywhere from 18% to 37% of the national population. The Bemba category contains some 18 closely related groups whose unity is maintained by their allegiance to the Bemba chief, speaking the Cibemba language, tracing descent through the female line, subsistence based on agricultural, and relative geographical isolation from other groups. Bemba men were—and to some extent continue to be—heavily involved in mining and are often away from their home villages for long periods of time.

Located to the east and south of the Bemba is another ethnic cluster known as the **Nyanja,** who also live across the border in Malawi where they are called the **Chewa.** Associated with and often classified with the Nyanja are the **Nsenga** and **Ngoni.** One estimate suggests that the Nyanja constitute about 11% of the Zambian population. Nyanja groups were among the first to be reached by British officials and missionaries and were favored by the colonial government in which many Nyanja served in the military and held low-level government jobs. This pattern has continued since independence: the Nyanja are heavily represented in the capital city of Lusaka and in government.

The major ethnic group in the south is the **Tonga** who constitute from 8% to 19% of the national population, with a smaller population across the border in Zimbabwe. Like the other major groups, Tonga is actually an ethnic category that consists of a number of groups who speak dialects of the CeTonga language and live in the same region. Their sense of ethnic identity today is also defined in terms of difference from other regional ethnic groups. The Tonga have undergone considerable change in the 20th century, and most are now involved in commercial agriculture, manufacturing, and trade. Their religious beliefs are a complex mix based on various Christian denominations and indigenous beliefs and practices. Socially, ties to kin traced through the female line remain important, although the influx of cash into the region has led to the emergence of social-class status based on wealth and education.

Located to the west of the Tonga in the south are the **Lozi,** who constitute from 3% to 7% of the national population, with smaller numbers living in Mozambique and Zimbabwe. The Lozi proper are descendants of the people of the Barotese Kingdom, which ruled the region from the 1600s until the British established control in the early 20th century. The Lozi today include at least a dozen other groups who had been under the control of the Empire and now all speak the Lozi language and are culturally similar to one another. The Lozi are mainly farmers but many also raise cattle, fish, and hunt to supplement their diet. The Lozi kingship has declined in power throughout the 20th century, and today most of its authority has been transferred to the Zambian government.

The primary group in the northwest is the **Lunda,** who form anywhere from less than 1% to 12% of the national population with other Lunda groups in Angola and Congo (formerly Zaire). The 12% estimate for Zambia is probably reasonably accurate if it includes all Lunda subgroups in the nation. Lunda is a generic label for several hundred groups in Central Africa who, from the 1600s on, were affiliated with the Lunda trading empire that remained powerful and influential into the 19th century. Europeans eventually displaced the Lunda as international traders, and most Lunda today are farmers who grow their own food, as well as crops such as corn and cassava for export. Life for the Lunda in Angola was disrupted by the civil war in that nation, and many Lunda refugees fled into Zambia.

Ethnic Relations

Compared to most other newly independent nations in Africa and elsewhere, Zambia is relatively free of ethnic conflict. This seems to be the case because—both traditionally and during the colonial era—major ethnic groups had little contact with one another. In addition, with the major exception of the Tonga, affiliation to an ethnic group (such as Bemba, Nyanja, or Lozi) is often weak, as people's major ties are to their family, kin group, village, and ethnic subgroup. In modern Zambia, social class, based on wealth, education, and type of employment (manual versus professional), has emerged as a more important factor in the social order than ethnicity. This does not mean, however, that ethnicity does not matter, as people generally prefer to associate with others from their own group.

Zimbabwe

The Republic of Zimbabwe is in southeastern Africa and is bordered by Zambia on the north, Mozambique on the northeast and east, South Africa on the south, and Botswana on the west. Parts of Zimbabwe came under British influence in 1897 when the British South Africa Company took control of the region, which it called Rhodesia, in order to exploit mineral resources. In 1923, the British government took control and Zimbabwe became a colony of Great Britain. In 1965, the White-controlled government declared independence, a move rejected by Great Britain and other nations, which eventually led to international sanctions and a civil war that pitted Africans against the White government. Independence was achieved in 1980.

Zimbabwe has a population of 11.3 million people, 77% of which live in rural areas. Although English is the official language, most people speak their indigenous languages. Missionary activity had some influence on indigenous beliefs, and about 25% of the population is now considered Christian, 25% are considered to be adherents of their traditional religions, and 50% follow a mix of Christian and indigenous beliefs.

Ethnic Composition

Although Zimbabwe is considered an ethnically heterogeneous nation, it is also important to note that nearly the entire population is African; nearly all people speak Bantu languages; and two groups, the Shona and Ndebele, account for at least 87% of the population—with the Shona alone constituting at least 70%. As with other nations in the region, Zimbabwe's population can be categorized into four ethnic categories: Africans, Whites or Europeans, Coloureds, and Asians.

The major African group, the **Shona,** is estimated to account for 70% to 80% of Zimbabwe's population, with a sizable Shona population also living across the border in Mozambique. "Shona" includes a number of groups, all of whom speak related Shona languages, though they have never been unified as a single cultural or political entity. The major Shona subgroups are the **Korekore** in the north, the **Manyika** and **Ndau** in the east, the **Karanga** in the south, the **Kalanga** in the west, the **Zezuru** in the center of the nation, and the **Rozvi,** who are spread across the Shona regions. The Shona are mostly farmers and miners who have long migrated to South Africa to work in the mines. Those in the cities are engaged in a full range of occupations and professions. Traditionally, and to a large extent today, the Shona affiliate primarily with people who speak their language, and those from their regions, their chiefdoms, and their local communities. Communication across groups is aided by speaking *chilapalapa*, a contact language based on Zulu and Afrikaans. Most Shona remain adherents of indigenous religions.

The **Ndebele** live in a region running north to south through western Zimbabwe. The Ndebele were formed as a distinct group in Zimbabwe (as distinguished from the Ndebele of South Africa) in the 19th century by the invading Nguni, who incorporated Shona, Sotho, and other peoples into their military empire. Ndebele are primarily farmers, and despite their much smaller population, they are active competitors with the Shona for political power.

The other African groups in Zimbabwe are the **Tonga** in the northwest, the **Venda** and **Sotho** in the south, and small numbers of **Khoisan** in the west. All together, these groups constitute less than 5% of the national population, and most are found in greater numbers in neighboring nations.

The label **Whites** in Zimbabwe refers to anyone of European ancestry, including people of **British, Dutch,** and **German** ancestry, as well as **Afrikaners** who moved into the region from what is now South Africa. Before independence, Whites were the politically and economically dominant group in Zimbabwe (Rhodesia), although they numbered only about 300,000 and lived apart from Africans. Their political dominance has ended and their population has declined steadily since independence, and they now number only about 100,000. Whites live almost entirely in cities; speak English or Afrikaans; are Christian; and own businesses, land, mines, or are engaged in commerce.

The **Coloureds,** who number about 25,000, are people of mixed African and European ancestry. The category includes both descendants of Afrikaner-African unions (primarily **Khoisan** peoples) from the 19th century and later unions between British men and African women in the early 20th century. Coloureds live almost entirely in cities, and during the colonial era they identified with White society.

Asians in Zimbabwe number about 10,000 and are **Asian Indians** imported by the British. They now live mainly in cities and are involved in industry and trade. Due to restrictions on emigration from India, most Indians in Zimbabwe were born there and were much involved in British-dominated colonial society.

Ethnic Relations

It has been usual to cite ethnicity as a major factor in postindependence Zimbabwean politics, with the central ethnic factor being competition between the Ndebele and the Shona, who had formed rival political organizations during the struggle for independence. Some experts also see the Shona/Ndebele split as having its genesis in resentment by the Shona over the Ndebele conquest of part of the region in the 19th century and the Ndebele attitude of superiority that resulted from that experience.

More recently, authorities have been suggesting that the importance of ethnicity in Zimbabwe has been exaggerated and that regionalism is perhaps more significant. Some experts suggest that cultural variations based on language and region, and strong affiliations to traditional tribes and local communities, are more important to most Shona than a general sense of Shona ethnic unity or a unified sense of opposition to the Ndebele. Some Shona groups have distant relations, with Ndebele communities; others have peaceful relations or none at all. While not as heterogeneous, the Ndebele also lack a strong sense of unified ethnic identity.

This lack of strong ethnic identity in both major ethnic groups in Zimbabwe leads some experts to suggest that ethnicity is not a major factor in national politics after all. Additionally, Zimbabwean political leaders have tended not to appeal to ethnicity in attracting followers, and allegiance to political parties seems to rest more on the attractiveness of its leaders.

Zimbabwe's Whites—and the Asians and Coloureds who identified with them in the colonial era—have lost virtually all power to the indigenous Africans and are now to some extent outside the political system, as were the Africans during the colonial era. The national constitution, however, bans discrimination on the basis of race. Nonetheless, White farmers continue to control much of the best farmland, and in 1997, in response to rising prices for food, protests have sometimes turned into beatings of Whites who are blamed for the situation.

PART THREE
Asia and the Pacific

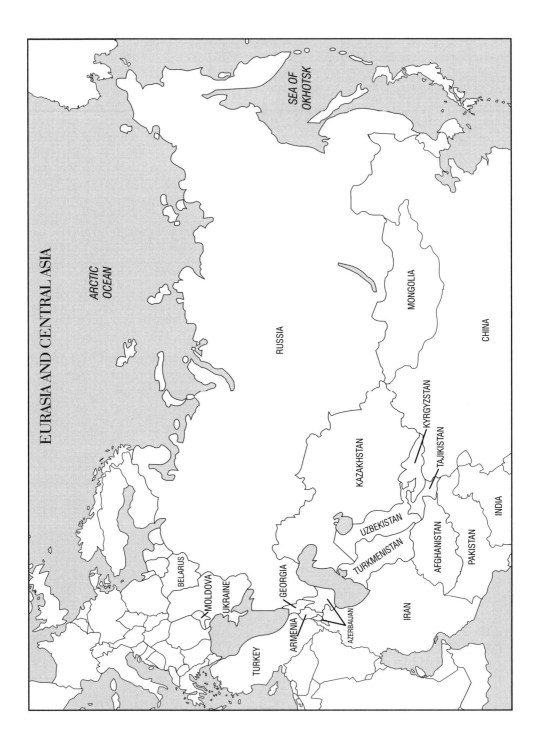

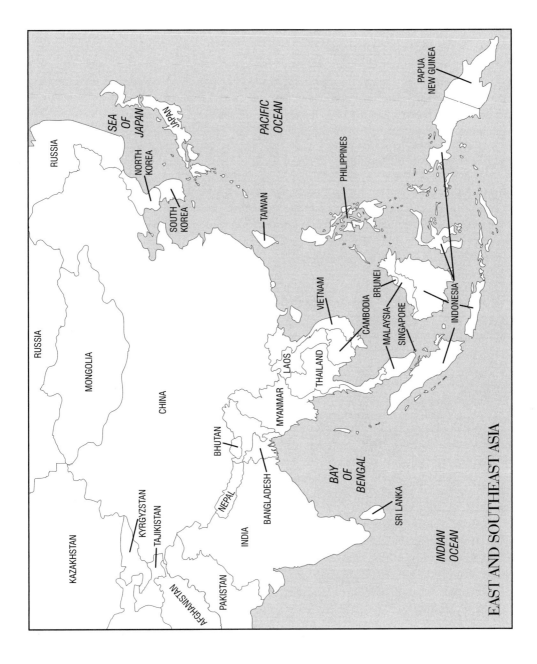

EAST AND SOUTHEAST ASIA

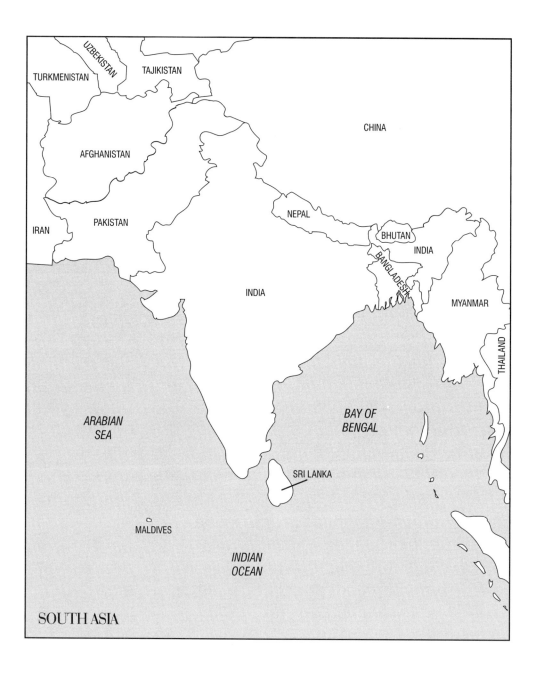

TURKMENISTAN
UZBEKISTAN
TAJIKISTAN

AFGHANISTAN

IRAN

PAKISTAN

CHINA

NEPAL

BHUTAN

BANGLADESH

INDIA

INDIA

MYANMAR

THAILAND

*ARABIAN
SEA*

*BAY OF
BENGAL*

SRI LANKA

MALDIVES

*INDIAN
OCEAN*

SOUTH ASIA

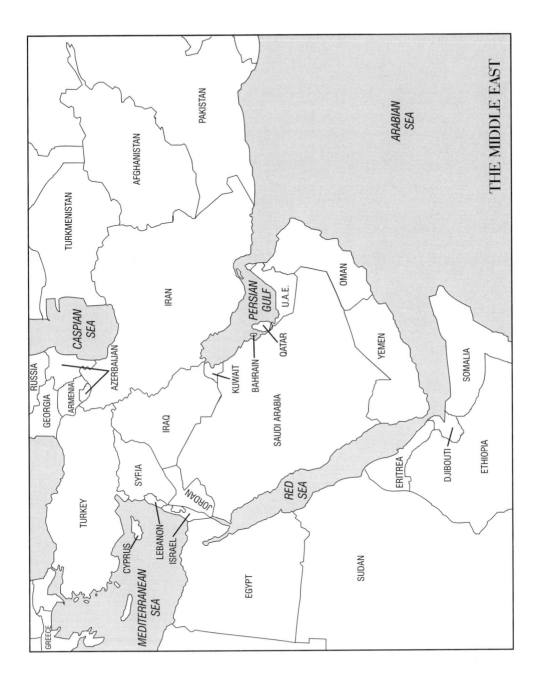

THE MIDDLE EAST

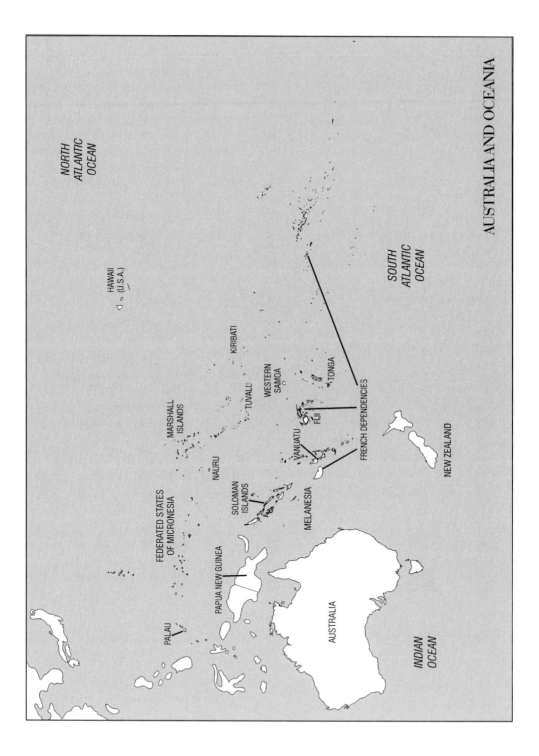

ASIA

AND

THE PACIFIC
Introduction

Asia is a large geographical region with enormous ethnic and religious diversity. Not unified in any broad sense, Asia consists of a number of distinct subregions, which are themselves quite diverse.

Central or Inner Asia
    Afghanistan
    Kazakhstan
    Kyrgyzstan
    Mongolia
    Tajikistan
    Turkmenistan
    Uzbekistan

Middle East or West Asia
    Azerbaijan
    Bahrain
    Iran
    Iraq
    Israel
    Jordan
    Kuwait
    Lebanon
    Oman
    Qatar
    Saudi Arabia
    Syria
    Turkey
    United Arab Emirates
    Yemen

East Asia
    China
    Japan
    North Korea
    South Korea
    Taiwan

South Asia
    Bangladesh
    Bhutan
    India
    Mauritius
    Maldives
    Myanmar
    Nepal
    Pakistan
    Sri Lanka

Southeast Asia
    Brunei
    Cambodia
    Indonesia
    Laos
    Malaysia
    Philippines
    Singapore

Thailand
Vietnam

Oceania or the Pacific
Australia
Federated States of Micronesia
Fiji
French Pacific Dependencies
Kiribati
Marshall Islands
Nauru
New Zealand
Palau
Papua New Guinea
Solomon Islands
Vanuatu
Tonga
Tuvalu
Western Samoa

This classification system is somewhat arbitrary because nations such as Pakistan and Afghanistan fall into two or more subregions, and others such as Australia and New Zealand are culturally European due to their colonization by Great Britain.

Asia's diversity can be seen in a number of ways. It contains the two most populous nations in the world—China and India—as well as two of the smallest—Kiribati and Nauru. Nearly all of the world's major religions—Judaism, Roman Catholicism, Protestantism, Hinduism, Islam, Buddhism, Taoism, and Shinto—are represented in Asia, and each is the dominant religion in at least one Asian nation. Asia includes countries such as Indonesia and South Korea that actively work to increase their participation in the world economy and others such as Iran and Iraq that do not seek broad economic expansion. Asia contains nations with high standards of living such as Japan, Israel, Saudi Arabia, and South Korea, as well as some of the poorest nations in the world such as North Korea and Bangladesh. Asia is home to nations that are very old such as China and Egypt and to some whose current boundaries are 20th-century in-

ventions such as Lebanon and the Marshall Islands.

The ethnic composition of Asia is equally diverse, and few generalizations are possible. Some nations are ethnically homogeneous in that almost the entire population belongs to one ethnic group (for example, Japan, China, Nauru, and Bangladesh). Other nations are homogeneous in that one group is dominant even though ethnic minorities are present (for example, Israel, Iran, Vietnam, and Australia). Yet other nations in the region, such as Pakistan, Afghanistan, and Papua New Guinea, display considerable ethnic heterogeneity. In general, however, one ethnic group or one religious group prevails in most Asian nations.

The dominance of one group—or one religion or cultural tradition—in many nations of Asia yields the most common pattern of ethnic relationship in the region. Perhaps because of such a pattern of dominance, many Asian nations suffer from ethnic-based conflict. Much of this conflict takes the form of minority groups fighting for their rights or for political autonomy, as in Israel, India, and the Philippines. In some regions, particularly in the Arab Middle East, religious differences lead to conflict between rival groups. In other nations, particularly in Central Asia, conflict takes the form of hostility directed at a former colonial power (the Russians). In Australia and New Zealand, indigenous inhabitants are pitted against the colonizers. And in a few nations such as Fiji, ethnic conflict centers on competition between groups for power. Although most nations in Asia face the reality of ethnic conflict, in only a few is it a major disruptive force. Asian nations are not consumed with ethnic conflict. The focus is more often on economic development and on Asia's expanding role in the global economy and global politics. However, ethnic relations often lurks as a political issue, for in some nations ethnic diversity is seen as an impediment to these economic goals, while in others it is seen as irrelevant or even as a national resource.

Asia and the Pacific Bibliography

Abu Bakar, Noor Laily bt. Dato', et al. *Ethnicity and Fertility in Malaysia.* Research Notes and Discussion Paper no. 52. Singapore: Institute of Southeast Asian Studies, 1985.

Ahmed, Akbar. *Pukhtun Economy and Society: Traditional Structure and Economic Development in a Tribal Society.* London: Routledge & Kegan Paul, 1980. (Pakistan)

Allen, M. R., ed. *Vanuatu: Politics, Economics, and Ritual in Island Melanesia.* Sydney: Academic Press, 1981.

Allworth, Edward, ed. *Central Asia: 130 Years of Russian Dominance*, 3rd ed. Durham, NC: Duke University Press, 1994. (Kazakhstan, Kyrgyzstan, Tajikistan, Turkmenistan, Uzbekistan)

Ashkenazi, M., and A. Weingrod. *Ethiopian Jews and Israel.* New Brunswick: Transaction Books, 1987.

Baloch, Inayatullah. *The Problem of Greater Baluchistan: A Study of Baluch Nationalism.* Stuttgart: Steiner Verlag Wiesbaden, 1987. (Pakistan, Afghanistan)

Batalden, Stephen K.; and Sandra L. Batalden. *The Newly Independent States of Eurasia: Handbook of Former Soviet Republics.* Phoenix: Oryx Press, 1997. (Azerbaijan, Kazakhstan, Kyrgyzstan, Tajikistan, Turkmenistan)

Benchley, Peter. "French Polynesia." *National Geographic* 191, no. 6 (June 1997): 2–29.

Brass, Paul R. *Caste, Faction and Party in Indian Politics, Volume 1: Faction and Party.* Delhi: Chanakya Publications, 1983.

Brass, Paul R. *Caste, Faction and Party in Indian Politics: Volume 2: Election Studies.* Delhi: Chanakya Publications, 1985.

Brown, Paula. *Highland Peoples of New Guinea.* Cambridge: Cambridge University Press, 1978.

"Burma: A Cry for Freedom." Special issue of *The New Internationalist,* no. 280 (June 1996).

Canfield, Robert L. *Turko-Persia in Historical Perspective.* Cambridge: Cambridge University Press, 1991. (Afghanistan, Pakistan, Iran)

Chiao Chin, and Nicolas Tapp. *Ethnicity and Ethnic Groups in China.* New Territories: Chinese University of Hong Kong, 1989.

Colarusso, John. "Circassian Repatriation." *The World and I* 11 (November 1991): 656–69.

Connell, John. *New Caledonia or Kanaky? The Political History of a French Colony.* Canberra: Australian National University, National Center for Development Studies. (French Pacific Dependencies)

Dani, A. H., and V. M. Masson, eds. *History of Civilizations of Central Asia, Volume 1: The Dawn of Civilization: Earliest Times to 700 B.C.* Paris: UNESCO Publishing, 1992.

DeVos, George A. William O. Wetherall, and Kaye Stearmen. *Japan's Minorities: Burakumin, Koreans, Ainu and Okinawans.* London: Minority Rights Group, 1983.

Dupree, Louis. *Afghanistan.* Princeton, NJ: Princeton University Press, 1980.

Ebihara, May, Carol A. Mortland, and Judy Ledgerwood, eds. *Cambodian Culture Since 1975: Homeland and Exile.* Ithaca, NY: Cornell University Press, 1994.

Eickelman, Dale F. *The Middle East: An Anthropological Approach.* Englewood Cliffs, NJ: Prentice Hall, 1989.

Eriksen, Thomas H. "Containing Conflict and Transcending Ethnicity in Mauritius." In *Internal Conflict and Governance*, edited by Kumar Rupesimghe, 103–29, 1992.

Fänge, Anders. "Afghanistan after April 1992: A Struggle for State and Ethnicity." *Central Asian Survey* 14 (1995): 17–24.

Friedrich, Paul, and Norma Diamond, eds. *Encyclopedia of World Cultures, Volume 6: Russia/Eurasia and China.* New York: G. K. Hall, 1994.

Gastardo-Conaco Ma, Cecilia, and Pilar Ramos-Jimenez. *Ethnicity and Fertility in the Philippines.* Singapore: Institute of Southeast Asian Studies, 1986.

Griffiths, John C. *Afghanistan: Key to a Continent.* Boulder, CO: Westview Press, 1981.

Harmatta, Janos, ed. *History of Civilizations of Central Asia, Volume 2: The Development of Sedentary and Nomadic Civilizations: 700 B.C. to A.D. 250.* Paris: UNESCO Publishing, 1994.

Jackson, Keith, and Alan McRobie. *Historical Dictionary of New Zealand.* Lanham, MD: The Scarecrow Press, 1996.

Jawad, Nassim. *Afghanistan: A Nation of Minorities.* London: Minority Rights Group, 1992.

Hays, Terence E., ed. *Encyclopedia of World Cultures, Volume 2: Oceania.* Boston: G. K. Hall, 1991.

Hickey, Gerald C. *Village in Vietnam.* New Haven, CT: Yale University Press, 1964.

Hockings, Paul, ed. *Encyclopedia of World Cultures, Volume 3: South Asia.* Boston: G.K. Hall, 1992.

Hockings, Paul, ed. *Encyclopedia of World Cultures, Volume 5: East and Southeast Asia.* Boston: G. K. Hall, 1993.

Hong, Evelyne. *Natives of Sarawak: Survival on Borneo's Vanishing Forest.* Palau Pinang, Malaysia: Institut Masyarakat, 1987.

Hook, Brian, ed. *The Cambridge Encyclopedia of China.* London and New York: Cambridge University Press, 1982.

Hopkirk, Kathleen. *Central Asia: A Traveller's Companion.* London: John Murray, Ltd., 1993.

Keyes, Charles F., ed. *Ethnic Adaptation and Identity: The Karen on the Thai Frontier with Burma.* Philadelphia: Institute for the Study of Human Issues, 1979.

Khan, Zillur R. "Minorities in Bangladesh." In *Bengal: Studies in Literature, Society and History,* edited by Marvin Davis, East Lansing: Asian Studies Center, Michigan State University, 1976: 101–13.

Khazanov, Anatoly M. *After the USSR: Ethnicity, Nationalism, and Politics in the Commonwealth of Independent States.* Madison: University of Wisconsin Press, 1995. (Kazakhstan)

Khazanov, Anatoly M. "The Ethnic Problems of Contemporary Kazakhstan." *Central Asia Survey* 14 (1995): 243–64.

Khoo, Siew-Ean, Kee Pookong, Trevor Dang, and Jing Shu. "Asian Immigrant Settlement and Adjustment in Australia." *Asian and Pacific Migration Journal* 3 (1994): 339–72.

Knauft, Bruce M., ed. *South Coast New Guinea Cultures: History, Comparison, Dialectic.* Cambridge: Cambridge University Press, 1993.

Koentjaraningrat, R. M. *Introduction to the Peoples and Cultures of Indonesia and Malaysia.* Menlo Park, CA: Cummings Publishing Company, 1975.

Kozlov, Viktor. *The Peoples of the Soviet Union.* Bloomington, IN: Indiana University Press, 1988. Translated by Pauline M. Tiffen.

Kunstadter, Peter, ed. *Southeast Asian Tribes, Minorities, and Nations.* Princeton: Princeton University Press, 1967.

Kurdish Studies, An International Journal 5 (1992).

Leake, David Jr. *Brunei: The Modern Southeast-Asian Islamic Sultanate.* Jefferson, NC: McFarland & Company, 1989.

LeBar, Frank M., Gerald C. Hickey, and John K. Musgrave, eds. *Ethnic Groups of Mainland Southeast Asia.* New Haven, CT: Human Relations Area Files Press. (Vietnam, Cambodia, Laos, Thailand)

Levinson, David. *Ethnic Relations: A Cross-Cultural Encyclopedia.* Santa Barbara: ABC-CLIO, 1994.

Levy, Robert I. *Tahitians: Mind and Experience in the Society Islands.* Chicago: University of Chicago Press, 1973. (French Pacific Dependencies)

Lewis, Paul, and Elaine Lewis. *Peoples of the Golden Triangle: Six Tribes of Thailand.* London: Thames & Hudson, 1986.

Ma Yin, ed. *China's National Minorities.* Beijing: Foreign Languages Press, 1989.

Magnarella, Paul J. "Diversity in Turkey's Eastern Black Sea Region." *World Today* April 1987.

Malik, Iftikhar H. *State and Civil Society in Pakistan: Politics of Authority, Ideology and Ethnicity.* New York: St. Martin's Press, 1997.

Mandelbaum, Michael, ed. *Central Asia and the World: Kazakhstan, Uzbekistan, Tajikistan, Kyrgyzstan, and Turkmenistan.* New York: Council on Foreign Relations Press, 1994.

Maring, Joel M., and Ester G. Maring. *Historical and Cultural Dictionary of Burma.* Metuchen, NJ: Scarecrow Press, 1973.

Mason, Philip, ed. *India and Ceylon: Unity and Diversity.* London: Oxford University Press, 1967.

McDowall, David. *Lebanon: A Conflict of Minorities.* London: Minority Rights Group, 1983.

Middleton, John, and Amal Rassam, eds. *Encyclopedia of World Cultures, Volume 9: Africa and the Middle East.* New York: G. K. Hall/Macmillan, 1995.

Min, Pyong Gap. "A Comparison of the Korean Minorities in China and Japan." *International Migration Review* 26 (1982): 4–21.

Ministry of Information and Broadcasting. *India 1995: A Reference Annual.* Government of India, 1996.

Minority Rights Group. *World Directory of Minorities.* London: Minority Rights Group, 1994.

Misra, P. K., and K. C. Malhotra, eds. *Nomads in India.* Calcutta: Anthropological Survey of India, 1982.

Morris, Barry. *Domesticating Resistance: The Dhan-Gadi Aborigines and the Australian State.* Oxford: Berg, 1989.

Muller, Kal. *East of Bali from Lombok to Timor.* Lincolnwood, IL: Passport Books, 1995. (Indonesia)

Nagata, Judith. *Malaysian Mosaic: Perspectives from a Poly-Ethnic Society.* Vancouver: University of British Columbia Press, 1979.

Nayagam, James. "Migrant Labor Absorption in Malaysia." *Asian and Pacific Migration Journal* 1 (1992): 477–94.

Nissan, Mordechai. *Minorities in the Middle East: A History of Struggle and Self-Expression.* Jefferson, NC: McFarland & Co.

Nydell, Margaret K. *Understanding Arabs: A Guide for Westerners.* Yarmouth, ME: Intercultural Press, 1987.

Olcott, Martha Brill. *The Kazakhs.* Stanford, CA: Hoover Institution Press, 1987.

Oliver, Douglas. *Oceania: The Native Cultures of Australia and the Pacific Islands.* 2 vols. Honolulu: University of Hawaii Press, 1989.

Olson, James S. *An Ethnohistorical Dictionary of the Russian and Soviet Empires.* Westport, CT: Greenwood Press, 1994. (Kazakhstan, Kyrgyzstan, Tajikistan, Turkmenistan, Uzbekistan)

Peacock, James L. *Indonesia: An Anthropological Perspective.* Pacific Palisades, CA: Goodyear Publishing Company, 1973.

Pookong, Kee, Jing Shu, Trevor Dang, and Siew-Ean Khoo. "People Movements between Australia and Asian-Pacific Nations: Trends, Issues and Prospects." *Asian and Pacific Migration Journal* 3 (1994): 311–37. (Australia)

Proschan, Frank. *Lao People's Democratic Republic 1995 Classification of Ethnic Groups Compared with Previous Classifications,* Unpublished Manuscript, 1994.

Sandhu, K. S., and A. Mani, eds. *Indian Communities in Southeast Asia.* Singapore: Times Academic Press, 1993. (Brunei)

Schwartz, Henry G. *The Minorities of Northern China.* Bellingham: Western Washington University Press, 1984.

Sinclair, Kevin. *The Forgotten Tribes of China.* Missisauga, Canada: Cupress, 1987.

Smith, Christopher J. *China: People and Places in the Land of One Billion.* Boulder, CO: Westview Press, 1991.

Smith, Martin. *Ethnic Groups in Burma.* London: Zed Books, 1994.

Speake, Graham. *Atlas of the Jewish World.* New York: Facts on File, 1984.

Tindale, Norman B. *Aboriginal Tribes of Australia: Their Terrain, Environmental Controls, Distribution, Limits, and Proper Names.* 2 vols. Berkeley: University of California Press, 1974.

U.S. Committee for Refugees. *World Refugee Survey.* New York: Immigration and Refugee Services of America, 1995.

Weekes, Richard V., ed. *Muslim Peoples: A World Ethnographic Survey*, 2nd edition. Westport, CT: Greenwood Press, 1984.

Whitaker, Ben. *The Biharis in Bangladesh.* London: Minority Rights Group, 1982.

Wirsing, Robert G. *The Baluchis and Pathans.* London: Minority Rights Group, 1981.

Zenner, Walter, and Shlomo Deshen, eds. *Jewish Societies in the Middle East.* Lanham, MD: University Press of America, 1982.

Afghanistan

Located at the crossroads of Central Asia, the Middle East, and South Asia, the Islamic state of Afghanistan is bordered by Turkmenistan, Uzbekistan, and Tajikistan on the north; a tiny portion of China on the east; Pakistan on the southeast; and Iran on the west. The people living in the area have been influenced by a large number of nations, empires, and peoples, including the Persians, Greeks, Arab Muslims, and Turkic tribes of Central Asia. Not until the mid-18th century under Iranian (Persian) rule did Afghanistan become a political entity, although strong ties to tribes and ethnic groups have prevented political unity from being realized. In the mid-19th century, Afghanistan was caught between Russian expansion from the north and British incursion from India in the south, and by 1880 the government was under British control. The 20th century has been marked by gradual separation from British domination, frequent political unrest, and conflict with Pakistan. Since 1978, Afghanistan has been consumed by an internal war that has prevented any long-term political stability, has caused more than two million deaths, and has created as many as six million Afghan refugees who have fled to neighboring Iran and Pakistan. From 1979 until 1989, Afghanistan was occupied by Soviet troops, who supported the government against rebels, mainly Central Asian peoples in the north and Shi'ite Muslims. After the withdrawal of the Soviet forces, the internal war continued. In the mid-1990s, the Taliban political-religious-military movement, led by Islamic fundamentalist Pashtuns, took power and conquered most of the nation, save for parts of the north where Uzbeks and Tajiks, as well as Shi'ite Muslims, continue to resist. Afghanistan's population is estimated at 22.6 million. Decades of unrest, mass killings, and flight to other nations, have made it impossible, however, to accurately estimate the population or status of any of the constituent ethnic or regional groups. Both Pashto and Dari Persian are Afghanistan's official languages, and virtually the entire population is Muslim.

Ethnic Composition and Ethnic Relations

Afghanistan is an ethnically heterogeneous nation with two major religious groups—the Sunni Muslims (who are the majority) and the Shi'ite Muslims—(who form a small minority) along with and several other Muslim sects.

Pashtuns (Pakhtuns, Pathan) are the largest and currently the politically dominant ethnic group in Afghanistan. The labels Afghan and Pashtun are often used synonymously, although Afghan also applies to all citizens of the nation, regardless of ethnic identity. The Pashtuns in Afghanistan number about 8.5 million and live mainly in the south-central and eastern regions, with a larger population across the border in the North-West Frontier Province of Pakistan, where they number about 10 million. There are also about 1.2 million Pashtun refugees from Afghanistan in Pakistan. The Pashtuns are divided into a number of distinct tribes and speak different dialects of the Pashto language, resulting in considerable cultural diversity within the population. There is also a strong sense of Pashtun identity, based on the Pashto language, adherence to Sunni Islam, belief in descent from a common ancestor, a strong sense of male honor, and—in the 1990s—support for the Taliban movement. The Pashtuns are a traditional tribal society in which the primary social units are regional tribes composed of clans founded on lineages of related people who trace their family ties through their fathers' lines. In the 1990s, the Pashtuns have emerged as the most politically powerful ethnic group in Afghanistan. As the primary supporters of the Taliban movement, they are involved in an internal war with the Tajiks and Uzbeks who are resisting Taliban dominance of the north.

Northern Afghanistan has traditionally been the home of Central Asian peoples whose primary population centers are in the independent Central Asian republics that were formerly part of the Soviet Union. Going from west to east, these peoples are the Turkmen, Uzbeks, Tajiks, and Kyrgyz. Of the four, the **Tajiks** are the largest and number about 5.5 million. The other groups are considerably smaller, and regular population movement across the borders makes accurate enumeration impossible. Tajiks (called **Dari speakers** in Afghanistan) have an ethnic identity based on the Tajik language (which comprises a number of closely related dialects of Farsi, the Persian language spoken in Iran), a traditional way of life based on farming and living in permanent villages, and adherence to Islam. The number of Tajiks in the world is estimated at about nine million. They are descended from a mix of Iranian peoples from the south and Turkic peoples from the north, who passed through or settled in the region several thousand years ago. Tajiks speak some 19 dialects of the Tajik language. The majority are Sunni Muslims.

Related to the Tajiks in Tajikistan are the **Pamir** peoples of the Pamir Mountains. Although classified as Tajiks by the Soviets, the Pamir prefer to label themselves **Pamirian Tajiks** to mark their distinctiveness from the Tajiks. There are about 120,000 Pamirian Tajiks, to whom regional affiliations have traditionally been more important than any unified sense of Pamirian or Tajik identity. Pamirians speak dialects related to Tajik and are mainly farmers and herders. Their relative isolation in the high mountains of the region has kept them somewhat free of Soviet influence. Pamirians are Muslims, but most are adherents of the Ismaili sect, which separates them from other Tajiks and Muslims. As a result of the civil war in Tajikistan, about 50% of the Pamirian population fled into Afghanistan, although most later returned home.

Turkmen are descendants of the Oghuz people who migrated from Inner Asia to Central Asia between the 9th and 10th centuries A.D. Modern Turkmen trace their ancestry to the Oghuz khan who first ruled the region. Craft production, especially the weaving of carpets, is an important economic activity. For Turkmen—perhaps more so than for any other Central Asian people—loyalty to one's lineage (a family unit traced through the paternal line) and one's tribe remains a major feature of individual identity. A distinct Turkmen subgroup is the **Owland,** an in-marrying group of religious specialists who trace their ancestry to the earliest leaders of the Muslim empire in the 7th century. The Turkmen are Sunni Muslims.

The **Uzbeks** emerged from the clans and tribes that inhabited and vied for control of Central Asia between the 12th and the 15th centuries. Although the Uzbeks are politically unified today as the nation of Uzbekistan, their clan, tribal, and regional ties have always been important and may at times compete with their national loyalty. More important than nationality in creating Uzbek unity has been adherence to Islam.

The **Kyrgyz** are the smallest of the Central Asian groups and live in the northeast fingerlike extension of Afghanistan near the Chinese border.

The other major ethnic minorities (with 1980 population estimates) are **Persians** in the west (600,000) (*see* Iran); **Arabs** in the northwest; small communities of **Qizilbash,** Shi'ite Muslims living in cities; **Baluch** (*see* Iran and Pakistan) in the west; **Aimaq** (800,000) and **Hazara** (870,000) in the center of the nation; **Nuristanis** in the east; and **Pashai** (108,000) in the northeast. All of these groups are Muslims, although the Persians and Hazara are mainly Shi'ite Muslims. In the mainly Sunni Muslim nation of Afghanistan, the latter were considered inferior to the other ethnic groups. The Persians are related to the Persians in Iran, the Arabs are mainly seminomadic herders, the Nuristani are farmers and herders, and the Aimaq are primarily herders. The Hazara, Nuristanis, and Shi'ite Muslims were heavily involved in the anti-Soviet resistance but may now be under the control of the Pashtun-backed Taliban government. These groups have not been carefully studied since the early 1970s, and little is known about their current status, although those who resist Islamic fundamentalism are subject to Taliban persecution.

Australia

S outh of Asia lies the continent of Australia. Together with the island of Tasmania to the south and small islands to the north, it forms the nation of Australia. Nearby countries are Indonesia and Papua New Guinea to the north and New Zealand to the southeast. Australia has a population of 18.3 million, heavily concentrated in the cities along the east, south, and southwest coasts. Sparsely populated in the interior and the north, Australia has one of the lowest population densities (two persons per square mile) of any nation in the world. Australia was settled about 40,000 years ago by peoples from Asia, whose present-day descendants are called Aboriginals. In modern times, Australia was colonized by the British, beginning in 1788. Since then, Australia has been largely a European society, and English is spoken by almost everyone. At least 80% of the population adheres to a Christian religion—27% Roman Catholic, 26% Anglican, 24% other Protestant, 3% Eastern Orthodox, and 12% professing no religion. The remainder are Jews, Muslims, and Hindus. With the arrival of significant populations from Asian nations in the 1970s, Australia has become a more ethnically diverse society in which the rights of the Aboriginal people have become a major political issue.

Ethnic Composition

Until the 1970s, Australia was by design a "White" society. Immigration by non-Europeans was restricted, and most Australians, with the exception of several hundred thousand Aboriginals, were of British descent. The end of immigration restrictions has made Australia a multicultural nation, or, as a recent prime minister labeled it, a "Wok" society. Still, about 94% of Australians are of European ancestry, 4.5% are of Asian or Pacific Islander background, and 1.5% are Aboriginals.

The term **White Australians** refers to Australians of European ancestry. About 76% of this population comes from Great Britain (England, Wales, Northern Ireland, and Scotland) and Ireland and 18% of it derives from other European nations. Despite the number of Asians settling in Australia, Europe continues to provide a substantial number of immigrants. According to the 1991 census, 2,051,518 Europeans living in Australia were immigrants born in Europe.

In addition, there are smaller numbers of **Romanians, Swedes, Danes, Norwegians, Jews** of European origin (88,000), and U.S. Americans (69,000). There are also about 300,000 **New Zealanders** in Australia, nearly all of European—primarily British or Irish—ancestry. Although non-British and non-Irish Europeans arrived during the 1800s and early 1900s, heavy European settlement came mainly during the post–World War II period, when immigration to Australia was encouraged by a government concerned about the economic consequences of the small Australian population.

Although some elements of traditional European cultures survive in Australia, such as food preferences and religious observances, Europeans have generally assimilated rather quickly into mainstream "White" Australian society. In spite of its British origin and English language, a unique Australian culture has developed. Key elements of this cultural identity include the speaking of an Australian dialect of English; the identification with uniquely Australian art, music, literature, and education; a strong sense of independence; the reality of

European Immigrants in Australia

Country of Origin	Population
United Kingdom and Ireland	1,174,843
Italy	254,780
Yugoslavia/Bosnia, Croatia, Macedonia, Slovenia	161,076
Greece	136,627
Germany	114,915
Netherlands	95,818
Poland	68,931
Soviet Union/N.I.S.	44,528

an ethnocentrism in which Australian culture is seen as superior to Aboriginal or Asian cultures; and an admiration for the "cowboy" culture of the rural outback, where sheep and cattle ranchers are admired for their bravery, self-reliance, and ability to live in the harsh environment.

Aboriginal Australians (Aborigines, Black Australians) are the indigenous people of Australia. Although Australia was first settled by humans as long as 100,000 years ago, that early population evidently died off and was eventually replaced by the ancestors of the contemporary Aboriginals, who arrived about 40,000 years ago. These

Australians demonstrating for Aboriginal rights in the 1970s. In recent years, Australia has begun to reverse the results of over two centuries of genocide and discrimination. Photo: UPI/ Corbis-Bettmann.

people migrated from Southeast Asia across water that was much shallower than it is today. A great deal is known about the Aboriginal tribes that have survived into the 20th century, but information about them during the 150 years following British settlement in 1788 is far less certain. There are two major reasons for this gap in our knowledge. First, the British had come to settle Australia, and their interest in the Aboriginals was simply to displace them from desirable land. Second, the structure of Aboriginal tribes was very different from that of British society. Even those newcomers interested in understanding the Aboriginals tended to confuse clans (kinship groups) with tribes, misnamed tribes, confused languages and dialects, and did not fully comprehend the patterned nature of Aboriginal nomadism. The best estimates suggest that at the time the British arrived, there were some 300,000 Aboriginals making up from 300 to 600 tribes. Tribes were organized along kinship lines and consisted of people related to one another through a common ancestor on either their mother's or father's side. Spouses always came from other clans. Each tribe occupied a specific territory marked by sacred sites and natural features. Nearly all Aboriginal groups were nomadic hunter-gatherers who moved about in seasonal patterns to search for food. Those who lived near the coasts tended to be less nomadic because they also fished and collected shellfish. An important feature of Aboriginal life—then and now—is what is

called "the Dreamtime" or "Dreaming." The concept, which does not easily translate into English, refers in a general sense to the time long ago when the ancestors of the Aboriginals first appeared.

The 1991 census counted 238,590 Aboriginals, with the greatest numbers in New South Wales (26.4%), Queensland (26.4%), Western Australia (15.7%), and the Northern Territory (15%). Although some tribes in the interior avoided interaction with White Australians well into the 20th century, all Aboriginal groups have now had extensive contact with—and have been influenced by—White society. As a result, many Aboriginal people have moved to cities and to the outskirts of White settlements in the interior. Urban Aboriginal communities are often poor ghettos or shantytowns. Nonetheless, urban Aboriginals have played a major role in the Aboriginal rights movement of the 1980s and 1990s and have been the leaders of an international resurgence of interest in Aboriginal art, music, dance, and sports. Aboriginals remain third-class citizens in their homeland and, as a population, experience more unemployment, poorer housing, lower life expectancy, higher infant mortality rates, and greater levels of government assistance than do other groups.

Related to the Aboriginals are the **Torres Straits Islanders,** who live on the islands of the same name off the north coast of Queensland. In the 1991 census, they numbered 26,902. About half of them live on the islands, and the other half live on the Australian mainland. They are thought to be descended from a mix of Aboriginals and peoples from Papua New Guinea. In the centuries prior to European arrival, they were involved in an extensive trade network in the region.

Major Aboriginal Groups in Australia

Queensland

Wik Mungkan	Workia
Yir Yoront	Wakelbura

New South Wales

Dhan-Gadi	Wuradjeri
Kumbaingeri	Wongaibon
Kamilaroi	Narinyeri
Kameraigal	Wurunjerri

Northern Territory

Tiwi	Gurindji
Gunwinggu	Walpiri
Murngin	Ngalia
Nunggubuyu	Pintubi
Mara	Aranda
Mudbara	

South Australia

Andingari	Kamilaroi
Dieri	Gaurna
Pitjantatjara	

Western Australia

Wunambal	Kariera
Mardudjara	Karadjeri
Djaru	Njangomada
Walmadjeri	Yungar
Mandjildjara	Ngatatjara
Whadjuk	

Asians and **Pacific Islanders** number 740,000, according to the 1991 census. The number is probably considerably higher now, given the continuing stream of Asians who have arrived in Australia in the 1990s. Asian Australians vary both in their reasons for immigrating to Australia and in their subsequent adjustment patterns. Asians come to Australia to be reunited with family members already there, to find jobs commensurate with their training, to work in business or commerce, to attend secondary school and universities, and

Asians and Pacific Islanders in Australia

Group	Population
East Asians	
Chinese	147,736
Japanese	18,441
Koreans	20,338
Southeast Asians	
Burmans	8,260
Bruneians	1,651
Cambodians	17,555
Indonesians	32,688
Lao	9,537
Malaysians	71,665
Filipinos	73,144
Singaporeans	24,021
Thai	13,756
Vietnamese	121,813
South Asians	
Afghans	2,674
Bangladeshis	2,289
Indians	60,958
Pakistanis	5,806
Sri Lankans	37,263
Other Asians	2,454
Pacific Islanders	
Papuans and New Guineans	23,716
Fijians	30,558
Samoans	2,983
Tongans	4,476
Others	9,183

to seek a new life as refugees. Those who come from former British colonies such as India, Sri Lanka, or Malaysia often speak English and find employment quickly. Those who come as refugees from such places as Vietnam, Cambodia, and Laos have a more difficult time adjusting to Australian society, and unemployment and poverty are often problems for the first generation of these immigrants. Japanese arrivals tend to do well in the commercial sector but are less likely than others to become permanent residents. Many Chinese from Taiwan come as students. The history of Asians in Australia may be divided into three periods: 1788–1973, when Asians were banned from permanent residence and immigration was restricted; 1973–95, when Asian immigration was encouraged; and 1995 to the present, when a backlash has emerged against Asian immigration.

Ethnic Relations

Ethnic relations in Australia have two major foci: relations between White Australians and Aboriginals and relations between White Australians and Asians. Because of the harsh treatment of Aboriginals and the restrictions on settlement by Asians, White Australia has sometimes been labeled a racist society. The recent return of rights to Aboriginals and the occurrence of Asian settlement suggest, however, that the situation is complicated, and that not all White Australians view Aboriginals and Asians in the same way.

White-Aboriginal relations—from the time of first contact in 1788 until 1992—were based on the principle of *terra nullis*, in which land in Australia is viewed as belonging to no one. It could therefore be taken by the British without treaty or compensation to the Aboriginals living on or using the land. The British often took the land by killing the Aboriginals or by driving them inland, where tens of thousands of these peoples then died from European diseases such as influenza, measles, and smallpox. Killing remained a common practice until the late 1800s, and Aboriginal resistance was harshly suppressed. The most extreme example of this policy happened on Tasmania, where over 5,000 Tasmanians were pushed inland and then killed. The entire population disappeared, and Tasmanian culture was entirely destroyed in less than 100 years. At some point during the 19th century, however, an assimilation policy was advocated, and efforts were made to educate Aboriginals and to convert them to Christianity. Although Aboriginals were seen as the "other," sexual relations between White men and Aboriginal women were not uncommon. As a result, from the mid-19th century on, many people of mixed ancestry were born. By the early 1920s, the combination of these British policies had reduced the Aboriginal population to about 60,000.

When the Aboriginals no longer posed a threat to European colonization and settlement, government policy in the early 20th century shifted to protection, with reserves established and White use of reserve land limited. Although the Aboriginal population began to expand, they remained a poor, rural minority, and in the 1960s an assimilation policy, which stressed relocation to towns and cities, was introduced. The relocations did not markedly improve the situation but did bring Aboriginals into regular contact with White society. In 1967, Aboriginals were granted citizenship by White voters, and, in the early 1970s, the assimilation policy was replaced by a policy of self-determination. In accord with this policy in 1976, Aboriginals were given the right to reserve land in the Northern Territory. In 1977, the National Aboriginal Conference emerged as a major advocacy group for Aboriginal rights. The most important change in relations between Aboriginals and Whites came in 1992, when the High Court of Australia ruled in the Mabo case that Torres Straits Islanders had a right to their land, thereby establishing pre-European Aboriginal ownership of land. Following this decision, the government enacted in 1993 the Native Title Act, which permits Aboriginals to claim land to which they can prove "a direct and continuing association." The Act was upheld by the High Court in 1995 in response to a challenge from Western Australia, where Aboriginals had filed claims for 40% of the land. Thus, by the 1990s Aboriginals began to reverse the results of over two centuries of genocide and discrimination.

Although Asians from Indonesian islands, and perhaps from China, traded with Aboriginals in northern Australia prior to British settlement, the British colonization pursued a policy of "Whites only" until 1973. Enforced less through restrictive immigration laws and more through customary government procedures that severely restricted immigration to Australia by Asians and banned their permanent settlement there, Australia remained a White nation, except for the Aboriginals. In 1973 the policy changed, in part because Australia sought to increase its population and in part because some Australians began to see

Australia as a European society in Asia and recognized the future importance of trade relations with Asian nations. The new policy encouraged Asian immigration and led to the varied Asian population described above.

Although many Australians no longer see Australia as a White society, a backlash has developed in the 1990s to the Aboriginal rights movement and associated land claims, and to the arrival of Asians. The backlash's center is the One Nation Movement, which claims that White Australians are suffering from the "new religion of internationalism, or anti-White racialism, multiculturalism, feminism, and Asianization." The movement seeks to ban Asian immigration, to end Aboriginal land rights claims, and to limit trade relations with Asian nations. The movement's support comes from rural and working-class White Australians. In 1994, the government announced plans to restrict the flow of Chinese refugees, who are arriving illegally in Australia and asking for political asylum. In the future, they will be detained and returned to China more quickly.

Azerbaijan

The Azerbaijan Republic, located in the Caucasus region of Eurasia, is bordered by Russia on the north, Georgia on the northwest, Armenia on the west, Iran on the south, and the Caspian Sea on the east. It has a population of 7.6 million. The Azerbaijani region includes both the republic itself and the northernmost provinces of Iran to the south. The Azerbaijani population in Iran is estimated at about 12 million. Formerly a constituent republic of the Soviet Union, Azerbaijan became an independent nation in 1991.

Ethnic Composition

Azerbaijan is a multiethnic nation, about 85% of the population being ethnic Azerbaijanis. The Azerbaijani percentage of the population has increased since the 1960s due to the high Azerbaijani birth rate, the emigration of ethnic Armenians from the Nagorno-Karabagh region, and the resettlement of Azerbaijanis from Armenia in Azerbaijan. In the Azerbaijan Republic, Russians and Armenians are the only other large ethnic groups, although there are a number of smaller groups, especially in the mountainous regions bordering Dagestan in the north. These peoples are sometimes referred to as Peoples of the Caucasus, which also includes peoples in Dagestan and in Georgia.

Azerbaijanis (also called **Azeris** or **Azerbaijani Turks**) number about 18 million worldwide, of which about 6 million live in Azerbaijan. Having a high birth rate and a low median age, the Azerbaijanis are a rapidly expanding group. The Azerbaijanis speak a dialect of Turkish and are Muslims, about 75% being Shi'ite and 25% Sunni. The culture is a mix of Turkish and Iranian traditions. Despite efforts to eradicate Islam during the period of Russian and Soviet rule, it remains vital today, as reflected in regional architecture, art, music, and religion.

For centuries, the Azerbaijanis have been involved with both Russians and Armenians, their neighbors to the north and west. **Russians** in Azerbaijan numbered 392,000 in 1989, but many have recently migrated to Russia, especially since Azerbaijan's independence in 1991.

The Azerbaijanis have been at war with their Armenian neighbors over the past few years. **Armenians** number about 150,000 and constitute about 80% of the population of the Nagorno-Karabagh autonomous district, located within the borders of Azerbaijan, near its border with Armenia. Predominantly Christian Armenians claim this district as their homeland, a position disputed by the Islamic Azerbaijanis, who maintain that it belongs to

Azerbaijan. Relations that have long been strained between the two groups erupted in 1988 into open warfare over control of the district. Although the dispute remains unresolved, the Armenians are currently in control.

The term Peoples of the Caucasus refers to the indigenous peoples of the Caucasus region of southern Europe and western Asia. Many of these peoples live in the mountainous regions of northwestern Azerbaijan and the bordering Dagestan region of Russia. Located on the crossroads between Asia and Europe, the area has been inhabited for at least 7,000 years, and it has been under the control of Greeks, Byzantines, Arabs, Ottoman Turks, and Russians. Arabs have had the greatest long-term influence in the region because they converted many of the indigenous groups to Islam. Adherence to Islam, however, led to conflicts with the Russians, who feared Azerbaijani aid to the Turks in the ongoing battle between Russian and Turkey from the 18th century on for control of the region. The major Peoples of the Caucasus in Azerbaijan are as follows.

Aghuls are an indigenous herding and farming people of the southern, mountainous region of Dagestan in Russia, a small number of whom live across the border in Azerbaijan.

Avars are an indigenous people of the southern mountains of Dagestan, a small number of whom live across the border in Azerbaijan.

Lezgins are an indigenous people of the southern Caucasus and number about 420,000, of whom about 50% live in Dagestan and 41% in Azerbaijan. In Azerbaijan, many Lezgins now reside in cities, have converted to Islam, and are assimilated into Azerbaijani society. An ethnic revival movement dating to the 1980s seeks to unify the two population centers separated by the Russia-Azerbaijan border.

Rutuls are an indigenous people of the southern mountains of Dagestan, a small number of whom live across the border in Azerbaijan.

Shah Dagh is a general term used to refer to a cluster of small, now largely assimilated, ethnic groups living in several mountain villages in Azerbaijan near Dagestan. These groups include the **Khinalughs, Dzheks,** and **Budugs,** all of whom are Muslims.

Tabasarans are an indigenous people of the southern mountains of Dagestan, several thousand of whom live in Azerbaijan.

Talysh are an agricultural, Muslim people of southern Azerbaijan and northern Iran, of whom 22,000 live in Azerbaijan. They are descended from the earliest inhabitants of the Caucasus, and though most have been assimilated into Azerbaijani and Russian society, some speak only Talysh, wear traditional dress, and affiliate with kin-based tribal groups.

Tsakhurs are an indigenous people of the Caucasus. Five thousand live in Dagestan and 13,500 in Azerbaijan. They are Muslims, and those in Dagestan are primarily sheep herders, while those in Azerbaijan are agriculturalists.

Although not indigenous to the region, **Jews** in Azerbaijan and Dagestan to the north are culturally similar to their neighbors in the Caucasus and form a distinctive Jewish subgroup known as **Mountain Jews.** Their origin is unclear, although some may have settled in the region as early as 700 B.C. They speak Tat dialects, and many have left for Israel or the United States in recent years. The remainder have largely assimilated into the surrounding Christian and Muslim populations. Their number is unknown; many identify themselves as Tats (who are Muslim) in order to avoid anti-Semitic discrimination.

The other major ethnic group in northeastern Azerbaijan are the **Tats,** who number 23,000 in the former Soviet Union, 10,000 in Azerbaijan, and 13,000 in neighboring Dagestan. Tats are descendants of people forced to leave Persia in the 5th and 6th centuries. Muslim Tats have assimilated into Azerbaijani society, and the smaller group of Christian Tats has blended into Armenian communities.

The border with Georgia has placed two Georgian ethnic groups within Azerbaijan. The **Udis** number about 9,000, of whom all, except a small group in Georgia, live in Azerbaijan. There are three distinct groups: Armeno-Gregorian Christians, a remnant population of Muslim Udis (most having previously assimilated into Azerbaijani society), and a small Russian Orthodox group in Georgia. The **Ingilos** are a Georgian ethnic group numbering about 5,000, who live in the Sainglo region of Azerbaijan, bordering Georgia. They speak a dialect of Georgian, are culturally similar to other Georgian and Caucasian groups, and may be either Muslim or Christian. The inclusion of their territory in Azerbaijan is a result of Soviet settlement policies.

Also living in Azerbaijan are the formerly Georgian-based **Meskhetians.** They are an Islamic people from southern Georgia and northern Armenia deported to Central Asia in 1944 by the Soviets. Their name is derived from the Meshki Turks, another of the deported populations. Only in the 1960s did they emerge as a united group, largely in reaction to the deportation and to virtual captivity in Central Asia. Having been subjected to discrimination and violence, including two murders in 1989, Meskhetians are leaving Central Asia. They number about 160,000–260,000 in Azerbaijan, 14,000 in central Russia, and an undetermined number in the Central Asian republics. Their requests to immigrate to Turkey or to resettle in Georgia have been refused by the two governments. The Azerbaijanis settled them in the Nagorno-Karabagh region where they were displaced by the Armenians. Relocated to the Lezgin region of northern Azerbaijan, they are now in conflict with the Lezgins.

On the border of the region known as Kurdistan, which cuts across the nations of Turkey, Iraq, Iran, and Syria, Azerbaijan also has a small **Kurd** population that numbered 12,000 in 1989. This number is, of course, only a small percentage of the 23 million Kurds in the world, most of whom live in the Middle East. Mainly Sunni Muslims, the Kurdish community in Azerbaijan was considerably diminished in the 1920s when many Kurds moved to Armenia. Contacts with the Azerbaijanis are peaceful though formal. Related to the Kurds are the **Yezidis,** who speak Kurdish and are considered by many outsiders to be Kurds. Yezidis view themselves, however, as a distinct ethnic group and live apart from the Kurds. A small number live in western Azerbaijan.

Ethnic Relations

The Muslim peoples of Azerbaijan have experienced a long and difficult relationship with the Russians to the north. Beginning in the 18th century, Russians attempted to expand their empire to the south and were met by Turks, Persians, and others who fought to halt this Russian expansion. Parts or all of Azerbaijan had been under Russian or Soviet control from the early 19th century until the demise of the Soviet Union in 1991. The Russian conquerors used military force to end local revolts, to suppress Islam, to initiate Russification programs designed to eradicate Azerbaijani culture, and to extract minerals and other resources. With the end of the Soviet Union, Russian influence has waned.

Ethnic relations among Azerbaijani ethnic groups are generally peaceful, and the smaller groups are generally assimilating into Azerbaijani society. A commonality among many of these groups is their adherence to Islam and the memory of their repression during the Soviet era. Since Azerbaijan's independence in 1991, ethnic groups such as the Talysh and Lezgins have been campaigning for rights denied them during the Soviet era, and some groups have been looking to form closer ties to Islamic nations in the Middle East. The only major ethnic conflict remaining is the ongoing dispute between the Azerbaijanis and the Armenians regarding the Nagorno-Karabagh region.

Bahrain

B ahrain is a small island nation located on the Persian Gulf. Its population is 575,000. The majority of Bahrainis live in the cities of Manama and Al Muharraq. Bahrain is an ethnically homogeneous society in which all citizens are Muslim Arabs. However, about 37% of the population are not citizens. This includes Palestinians, Arabs from other Middle East nations, Persians from Iran, and Urdu speakers from India, all of whom are in Bahrain as guest workers. Most live in Manama.

Ethnic Composition and Ethnic Relations

Bahraini is a national rather than an ethnic designation, but since virtually all Bahraini citizens are Arabs, the terms Arab and Bahraini are essentially synonymous. Bahrainis number 362,000 and constitute 63% of the population. They are primarily Shi'ite Muslims, although Sunni Muslims form a distinct minority. Due to oil income, the standard of living is very high. **Arabs** other than Bahrainis number about 57,000 and are mainly guest workers from other Middle Eastern nations. **Palestinians,** who are also Arabs, also work in Bahrain.

Indians number about 75,000 and are mainly Urdu speakers from northwestern India who work in the construction and oil industries, and as domestics. They live separately from the Bahrainis and are subject to deportation at any time. **Persians (Iranians)** number about 46,000 and work mainly in the oil industry. They speak Farsi and live mainly in Manama.

Bahrain is free of ethnic unrest, due in part to the tight control maintained by the government. Since 1994, however, there have been riots, protests, and government crackdowns involving Muslim fundamentalists and others who seek a return to democratic rule.

Bangladesh

B angladesh is a nation in Southeast Asia bordered by India on the west, north, and east; Myanmar (Burma) on the extreme southeast; and the Bay of Bengal on the south. It has a population of 125 million, over 99% of whom are Bengalis or, as they now often call themselves, Bangladeshis. Formerly known as East Pakistan, Bangladesh became an independent nation following the 1971 civil war with West Pakistan (now Pakistan). Bangladesh is a nation of impoverished farmers and is one of the poorest nations in the world.

Ethnic Composition and Ethnic Relations

Bangladesh is an ethnically homogeneous nation, and the 1% of the population that is not Bengali is composed mainly of "tribal" groups near the India and Myanmar borders. These groups see themselves as second-class citizens compared to the numerically and politically dominant Bengalis. **Bengalis (Bangladeshis)** occupy the Bengal region of South Asia, with

sizable overseas communities in Canada, the United States, and Great Britain. In Bangladesh they number about 123 million, of whom about 85% are Muslim, 14% Hindu, and 1% Christian. In the neighboring West Bengal state of India, Bengalis number about 50 million, and there are about 8 million in other Indian states, about 75% of whom are Hindus. Bengalis speak Bangla, with a number of regional dialects, and they have a strong literary tradition that is a source of considerable pride. Most Bengalis are family farmers who live in small rural villages in the southern delta region of the country. Although the delta has especially rich soil, the region is subject to frequent devastating hurricanes that periodically destroy thousands of farms and homes. Bengali Hindus are organized into occupational castes (as are Muslims, though to a lesser extent) and provide services and products for the farmers.

Children transporting water during the dry season. Bangladesh is one of the poorest nations in the world. Photo: Robert Bailey/Corbis-Bettmann.

The major ethnic minority is the **Biharis,** who number about 600,000 in Bangladesh, about 85 million in the neighboring Indian state of Bihar, and about 200,000 in Pakistan. Prior to independence, Biharis in Bangladesh held important government and business positions. They supported West Pakistan in the 1971 war, and when Bangladesh achieved independence, many were killed or forced to flee to India or Pakistan.

The second largest minority is the **Chakma,** who call themselves **Changma** and live in southeastern Bangladesh. They are mainly Buddhists. Numbering over 200,000, the Chakma are the largest non-Bengali group in southern Bangladesh, although the Bengalis are the majority population in the region. They speak Bengali and are in many ways assimilated into Bengali society, although as rural farmers, they have resisted attempts by the government to develop industrial projects in the region.

Two other distinct minorities are the **Marmas (Magh),** an agricultural, Buddhist tribal group numbering about 20,000, who are now much assimilated into Bengali society, and the **Tripura (Mro, Moorang, Tippera),** who are horticulturists numbering about 250,000 in Tripura, India, and Bangladesh. Other groups include small numbers of **Santals, Khasis, Garos,** and **Khajons,** who live in border areas; and small numbers of **Anglo-Bengalis, Chinese,** and **low-caste Hindu** tea pickers who, despite the shared Hindu religion, remain a group distinct from the Hindu Bengalis.

Bhutan

B hutan is a small nation located in the Himalayan region of northern South Asia. It is bordered by the Tibet Province of China on the north, India on the east and south, and India and China on the west. Bhutan has a population (1,822,625) that is entirely rural, and there are no cities. Most residents are farmers who grow rice, wheat, and corn. The official language is Dzongkha, a dialect of Tibetan. Bumthangkkha is spoken by people in the central region and Sharchopkha by people in the east. The Nepalese in Bhutan speak Nepali. About 70% of Bhutanese are Buddhists and follow Tibetan Lamaist Buddhism. Another 20% are Hindus, and the remaining 5% practice indigenous religions. Buddhism is the nation's official religion.

Ethnic Composition and Ethnic Relations

Bhutan is an ethnically heterogeneous nation composed of two major populations—the Bhutanese and the Nepalese. **Bhutanese** is a national rather than an ethnic designation, and those people who consider themselves Bhutanese come from three major ethnic groupings. The dominant group, which lives mainly in the north and west, is commonly labeled **Bhote** or **Ngalop.** They are closely related to the Tibetans to the north and practice Buddhism. A major Bhote subgroup in the west is the **Drukpa,** who control the government. The largest group in terms of population is the **Sharchop** in the east, who moved into the region hundreds of years ago from India and Myanmar. Although their indigenous language remains in use, they have been much assimilated into Bhote society. The third major ethnic grouping consists of a number of smaller groups such as the **Rai, Lepcha, Limbu,** and **Gurung,** who live mainly in central Bhutan, and also in other Himalayan nations. As with the other ethnic groups in Bhutan, they are mainly Buddhist farmers and live in small villages.

Nepalese make up about 25% of the population of Bhutan. Forbidden by the government to settle in the north, they occupy the southern half of the nation where they constitute the majority population. The Nepalese arrived in Bhutan between the late 1880s and early 1900s, when the region was under the control of British India. They speak Nepali and most are Hindus, although some have converted to Buddhism. Like other residents of the nation, the Nepalese are farmers, but some also work in the logging industry and participate in trade with Indian companies. As a group, they are economically better off than most Bhutanese.

Ethnic relations center on the desire of the Bhutanese government to maintain traditional Bhutanese culture and to resist possible cultural or political influences from China, Tibet, India, and Nepal. The government carefully controls all aspects of cultural life and has imposed a dress code, requires that houses conform to government-approved plans, and is attempting to make Dzongkha the language of daily life throughout the nation. Some critics of the government suggest that these policies have less to do with maintaining cultural "purity" and more to do with controlling a democracy movement that began in the 1980s. The Nepalese are seen by the Bhutanese as outsiders and as a threat to the nation's cultural unity. Bhutanese believe that the Nepalese have taken over Sikkim to the west, and they want to avoid the same fate. During the 1990s, the government has followed a policy of ethnic cleansing, including the removal of Nepalese from government employment, arrests, imprisonment, torture, and the destruction of villages. They have also, since 1991, forcibly deported over 85,000 Nepalese to Nepal and about 15,000 to India. The Nepalese refugees in Nepal have been placed in refugee camps where hundreds have died from disease and starvation. Since 1995, the Nepal and Bhutan governments have been negotiating the repatriation of some refugees to Bhutan, although the government has so far refused to accept returnees.

Brunei

The State of Brunei Darussalam is a small nation located on the north coast of the island of Borneo. It is bordered by the South China Sea on the north and the Malaysian province of Sarawak on the east, south, and west. Brunei was a Malaysian sultanate from the 15th through the 19th century and came under British control in 1888. In 1984 it became an independent nation. The discovery of oil in the 1930s transformed Brunei society, and it became one of the wealthiest nations in the world. Although the oil wealth is concentrated in the ruling family, all citizens benefit through full employment and liberal social services. Brunei has a population of 300,000. Malay is the official language and Islam the official religion.

Ethnic Composition and Ethnic Relations

Brunei is an ethnically heterogeneous society, and about 64% of the population are Malay. Approximately 20% are Chinese, and the remainder is made up of indigenous peoples of Borneo and Europeans, as well as immigrants from Indonesia and Malaysia, most of whom are ethnic Malays. Thus, its ethnic composition is quite similar to that of the Malaysian province of Sarawak.

Malays number about 200,000 and live mainly in the cities and near the coast. At one time mainly rice farmers, most now work for the government, in the oil industry, and in related services and industries. The Malays speak Malay and are Muslims, although Islam in Brunei exists alongside many surviving elements of the traditional religion, including magic and both evil and helpful spirits. Although much of the traditional culture disappeared as Brunei became a modern nation, the government has actively promoted the revival of crafts such as silversmithing and cloth weaving. The two major Malay subgroups are the royal family and Malays who consider themselves to be the nobility because they can trace their ancestry to sultans who ruled in the past. While being a noble may increase one's status in certain social situations, it has no economic benefits.

Chinese, who number about 60,000, are the second largest group in Brunei. Like the Malays, they were formerly rice farmers, but nearly all now work as professionals, technicians, or store owners. Most Chinese are Buddhists or Taoists, or a combination of the two, although in recent decades a significant minority have converted to Christianity and a small minority to Islam. Despite their dominance in the commercial sector, only about 10% of the Chinese are citizens, and Brunei's citizenship laws, which require a detailed knowledge of Brunei history to became naturalized, are seen as an attempt to prevent the Chinese from achieving citizenship. In the 1980s, this led to a considerable departure of Chinese for Canada and Australia.

The second largest non-Malay or nonindigenous group is the **Asian Indians,** who number about 6,000. Mainly Hindus, they speak a number of different Indian languages and work primarily in the service sector, especially the hotel and restaurant business. A wealthy nation with many employment opportunities, Brunei has also attracted small numbers of immigrants from other Asian nations, such as Taiwan, Pakistan, Nepal, Sri Lanka, Bangladesh, and the Philippines.

The indigenous people of Brunei include a number of the same groups as are found in Sarawak, and they are often lumped together under a general label, **Dayak.** The largest of these groups is the **Kedayans,** who number about 15,000. They traditionally served the sultans as rice farmers and over the centuries have become assimilated into Malay society through intermarriage. Most now speak Malay and are Muslims. The other indigenous groups are the **Bisaya, Penan, Murat,** and **Iban,** who, all together, number about 15,000. In Brunei, the Bisaya and Murat have been largely assimilated by Malays and the Iban. The Penan are a small group of former hunter-gatherers in the interior. Only the Iban have retained their traditional culture, and as in Sarawak, they live in long-house communities and subsist primarily by growing rice.

Cambodia

The Kingdom of Cambodia, located in Southeast Asia, is bordered by Thailand and Laos on the north, Vietnam on the east and southeast, the Gulf of Thailand on the southwest, and Thailand on the west. Cambodia was settled by the ancestors of the modern Khmer people (the primary ethnic group in Cambodia) over 2,000 years ago, and the Khmer empire ruled the region—including Thailand, Laos, and southern Vietnam—from the beginning of the 9th century to the early 15th century. Thailand and Vietnam then took territory from the Khmer empire, and much of the region including Cambodia came under French control in 1863. Cambodia became an independent nation in 1953. Early influence on the Khmer civilization came from India, but the Khmer population eventually became Buddhists. Since the early 1960s, Cambodia has experienced considerable political instability and internal violence. The period between 1975 and 1993 is seen as an especially dark one in Cambodian history. The mass killings and population relocations, the economic decline under a Communist (Khmer Rouge) regime, the invasion by Vietnam in 1978, and subsequent formation of a Vietnam-supported government in 1979 all took a terrible toll on the Cambodian people. Partial restoration of democratic rule in 1993 under United Nations direction temporarily alleviated the situation, although it cannot be called stable. Because of these three decades of disruption, information about the ethnic composition of Cambodia in the 1990s is unreliable. The population is estimated at 10.8 million in 1997, although some experts believe it may be as low as 8 million due to the more than 1 million deaths during the period of Khmer rule, as well as the settlement of over 200,000 Cambodians in other nations, such as the United States and Canada. Most Cambodians who took refuge in Thailand have now returned home. Khmer is the national language. French, which had been the language of the elite, has declined in importance. Most non-Khmer speak their own languages. Theravada Buddhism, the state religion since the 15th century, was repressed by the Khmer Rouge but became the state religion again in 1989. About 95% of the population is Buddhist; the remainder are Muslim, Christian, or adherents of traditional religions.

Ethnic Composition

Cambodia's population may be divided into three major ethnic categories: the Khmer, the hill tribes, and ethnic minorities of foreign origin. The **Khmer** constitute about 90% of the population of Cambodia. Although the names Khmer and Cambodian are sometimes used synonymously, Cambodian also pertains to all citizens of Cambodia regardless of ethnic identity. The Khmer have been the largest and the dominant ethnic group for some 2,000 years. They have been Theravada Buddhists since the 15th century, although their version of Buddhism differs from that of neighboring nations because of the survival of Hindu beliefs and the incorporation of indigenous beliefs. Most Khmer live in small villages and grow wet rice and other crops, both for their own use and for sale. Many also work as wage laborers and run craft businesses to earn cash income. It is likely that close to one million Khmer died during the unrest of the 1970s and 1980s, and many more fled the country or were forcibly relocated under the Communist deurbanization policy. To what extent village life has recovered is not yet clear, and political unrest continues in the late 1990s.

As with other Southeast Asian nations, Cambodia has a number of relatively small ethnic minorities collectively classified as hill tribes. In Cambodia, these tribes are called **Khmer Loeu** meaning Upland or Hill Khmer, although most are not culturally or linguistically related to the Khmer. They live primarily in the northeast on the Vietnam and Laos borders (with populations across the borders as well), in the north, and in the west. As with other hill tribes, the Hill Khmer reside in small villages or in family settlements and subsist mainly by growing dry rice in semipermanent fields cleared by the slash-and-burn method. Hunting, gathering, and fishing techniques have supplemented the growing of rice and other crops. After Cambodia became independent in 1953, the various governments sought to assimilate these tribes into Khmer society. Government programs—which stressed literacy in Khmer, resettlement in permanent villages, and official supervision of village life—along with the civil disruptions in the 1970s and 1980s have very likely destroyed much of the traditional culture. The killings of the 1970s and 1980s also reduced the population and it is now believed that the hill tribes constitute from 5% to 10% of the national population, in contrast to an estimated 15% in the 1950s. The hill tribes, with population estimates, are as follows:

Hill Tribes of Cambodia

Group	Population
Brao	10,000–15,000, also in Laos
Jarai	10,000, also in Vietnam
Kuy	160,000, also in Thailand
Mnong	25,000, also in Vietnam
Pear	10,000, also in Thailand
Rhade (Rade)	15,000, also in Vietnam
Stieng	20,000, also in Vietnam

Prior to the 1970s, the major non-Khmer ethnic groups in Cambodia were those of foreign origin—the Chinese, the Vietnamese, and the Cham. At that time, the **Chinese** numbered nearly half a million; today there are less than 60,000. As elsewhere in the Chinese Southeast Asian diaspora, the Chinese came mainly from southern China, they spoke various Chinese languages, and many intermarried with the local population (usually the Khmer), forming a distinct Sino-Khmer minority. The Chinese lived mainly in cities and towns and were involved in commerce, trade, and moneylending. Under the Khmer Rouge regime, ethnic Chinese were defined as enemies of the Communist state. Those in cities were relocated, just as Cambodians were, and over 75% of the population was either killed or fled—to Thailand, China, or various Western nations. Vietnamese hostility toward the Chinese in Vietnam carried over into Cambodia during the more recent period of Vietnamese rule, and the Chinese became a small minority population.

Unlike Chinese-Khmer relations, which were generally friendly, relations between the **Vietnamese** and Khmer have for centuries been characterized by animosity and periods of warfare. Although the Khmer at one time ruled southern Vietnam, the Vietnamese eventually displaced them and began settling in southern Cambodia. Cambodian concerns about Vietnamese expansion, as well as cultural and linguistic differences between the two groups (including the belief by both sides that each was more civilized than the other), have resulted in less than friendly relations since the early 19th century. During the 1960s and 1970s, the conflict intensified because Vietnam used Cambodia as a staging area in its war with the United States, and the United States consequently bombed Cambodia. When the Khmer Rouge came to power, anti-Vietnam rhetoric was part of the agenda, and many Vietnamese were killed or driven out. Although the Vietnamese took control of Cambodia in the 1980s, the Vietnamese population had declined from nearly 300,000 to about 60,000. Anti-Vietnamese political factions in Cambodia, however, continue to claim a much larger Vietnamese presence and influence.

The third major foreign minority is the **Cham,** who are also called the **Muslim Cham, Khmer Islam,** or **Cham-Malays,** in reference to the fact that many of them are Muslims. They live mainly in farming communities along rivers in central Cambodia, where they established settlements after the Champa Kingdom in Vietnam was conquered by the Vietnamese in 1471. There is also a sizable Cham community in Vietnam. Like the Vietnamese, the Cham were considered enemies of the state by the Khmer Rouge, and many were killed or driven out. Their population is unknown but is very likely less than 10,000.

The only other significant minority in Cambodia is several thousand **Asian Indians,** who are involved primarily in commerce.

Ethnic Relations

Traditional patterns of ethnic relations have been severely—perhaps permanently—altered by the political unrest and fighting of the last three decades. The major effect of the conflict has been a decrease in the population of all ethnic groups, although the size of the Khmer majority actually increased as a percentage of the population. In addition to being less numerous, the Cham, Vietnamese, and Chinese have ceased to function as significant communities. Similarly, disruptions to the lives of the hill tribes have eroded the traditional ways of life that were already under pressure from government assimilation programs, and it is likely that they will disappear as distinct groups in Cambodia.

China, People's Republic of

Also known as China or Mainland China, the People's Republic of China is the largest nation in Asia, both in physical size and in population. China is bordered by Mongolia and Russia on the north; North Korea, the East China Sea, and the South China Sea on the east; Vietnam, Laos, Myanmar, India, Bhutan, and Nepal on the south; and India, Pakistan, Afghanistan, Tajikistan, Kyrgyzstan, and Kazakhstan on the west. It has an estimated population of 1.15 billion.

Traditionally, Confucianism, Buddhism, Taoism, and Chinese folk religions (which focus on ancestor worship) were the primary religions, although considerable regional variation existed, and many people adhered to the tenets of more than one religion. The Communist government banned all religious activity in 1949 and then in 1972 allowed religious bodies to operate again. Mandarin and Cantonese are two major forms of the Chinese language used in China, with a number of regional dialects of each commonly spoken. Many minority groups continue to speak their indigenous languages, although use of Chinese is becoming more common in all groups.

Ethnic Composition

While not ethnically homogeneous, China is dominated by the **Han Chinese,** who account in general for 92% of the population but comprise an even higher percentage of the population in the densely populated eastern provinces and cities. Han number about 1.05 billion and are the dominant ethnic group in the nation. There is significant variation within the Han, and important distinctions are based on region (north or south), residence (urban or rural), and dialects of the Chinese language (Gan, Hakka, Mandarin or Pei, Min Nan or Hokkien, Min Pei, Wu, Xiang or Hunan, Yue or Cantonese). Experts disagree whether the speakers of the Hakka and Hokkien dialects should be classified as Han or as distinct groups. The Han are the culturally, politically,

The Han Chinese are the culturally, politically, and economically dominant ethnic group in China. Photo: Corel Corp.

and economically dominant group in China. While minority groups are not forced to assimilate to Han culture, they are nonetheless dominated by the Han and must conform to the Communist ideology of the nation. The major ethnic conflict in China involves the Tibetans, who seek autonomy. A large "overseas" Chinese population is present in nations such as Thailand, Vietnam, Indonesia, the Philippines, Singapore, Malaysia, Canada, Great Britain, the United States, and the West Indies. Most of these Chinese have emigrated from southern China and are speakers of Cantonese or Hakka Chinese. Overseas Chinese were often engaged in specialized occupations such as trading and operating general stores or laundries. Today, especially in Western nations, they are engaged in a far wider range of economic activities.

Other than the Han Chinese, all ethnic groups in China are designated by the government as "national minorities." There are 55 of these official national minorities, having a combined population of about 75 million. Most minority groups are located in southern, western, north-central, and northeast China; some are also found in neighboring nations such as Myanmar, Laos, Thailand, and Vietnam. Many of these minorities are indigenous peoples, others are groups who have migrated to their current locales over the centuries, and still others have formed through intermarriage between members of different groups. Minorities are relatively few in number in eastern China, where the Han are heavily concentrated. Minority groups speak some 52 different languages from 10 different language families. Official classification as a national minority means that members of the group may be subject to laws different from those of the Han Chinese. For example, while members of national minority groups are generally not restricted to one child per family as are the Han, they may not move or settle anywhere they choose in China unless they have government approval. In general, the efforts made during the Cultural Revolution era (1966–76) to eradicate the non-Han cultures have ended, and groups are now free to engage in their traditional ways of life.

Achang number 27,000 and are wet-rice agriculturalists located mainly in Yunnan province. Having lived there for at least 700 years, they are dominated by the Han and Dai but were converted to Theravada Buddhism by the latter.

Bai (Baizu) number 1.6 million and live mainly in Yunnan province. They were incorporated into the Chinese state in 221 B.C. Through their work in Han-directed local industries and tourism, as well as their speaking of the Han language, the Bai have been drawn into Han-dominated society. Many, however, remain adherents of their traditional religion, a mix of indigenous beliefs and practices with Taoism.

Blang number 82,000 and live in the mountains of southwestern Yunnan province. Most Blang are agriculturalists. A small group with no written language of their own, they were long dominated by the Dai (who converted them to Theravada Buddhism) and more recently by the Han.

Bonan, a very small group numbering only 12,000, live in several communities in Gansu province. Probably a remnant population from the time of Mongol rule, they are Muslims, who under communist rule have been drawn into the national economy as the producers of cash crops.

Bouyei number 2.5 million and live in Guizhou province. They are primarily farmers, but also engage in various crafts. Many Bouyei speak Han, and intermarriage with Han

is common, suggesting considerable assimilation into Han society. At the same time, however, traditional religious practices—focusing on ancestor worship—remain strong.

Dai number 1.5 million and live in southern Yunnan province, mainly near the Myanmar border. Dai have lived in the region for over 2,000 years, and from the 10th century, as rulers of the region, they dominated the small ethnic groups who also lived there. From the 14th century until the Communist Revolution, the Dai ruled with the support of the Han, although Han settlement of the region created local conflict. The Dai subsist through wet-rice cultivation and the production of cash crops and craft items. The population is divided into a number of local subgroups, of which the **Dailü** and **Daina** are the two largest. They are Theravada and Hinayana Buddhists, and they have converted a number of smaller groups in southern Yunnan province to Buddhism.

Daur number 122,000 and live in northern China, in Inner Mongolia, and in Heilongjiang province. Most Daur are bilingual in Daur (a Mongolian language) and the language of neighboring groups such as Mongolian or Kazakh. Their economy is a mix of farming and animal raising. The polytheistic, shamanistic religion of the Daur remains strong.

De'ang (Benglong) number 16,000 and live in scattered communities along the China-Myanmar border. One of the first groups to emerge in the region, the De'ang are wet-rice farmers who for centuries were dominated by the Dai and then the Han. They were converted to Theravada Buddhism by the former.

Dong number 2.5 million and live in hillside villages in Hunan, Guizhou, and Guangxi provinces. Their economy is based on farming, selling of wood and other forest products, and working in factories. Their traditional polytheistic religion remains strong.

Dongxiang number 374,000 and live in Gansu and Xinjiang provinces. They are descendants of Mongol warriors who mixed with local peoples. They are Muslims and devotion to the faith remains strong.

Drung number about 6,000 and live near the Myanmar border in northwestern Yunnan province. A small group of horticulturalists, they have been particularly influenced by Han culture. Many of their traditional customs, such as facial tattooing and distinctive dress, have given way to Han practices and to participation in agricultural collectives. Some Drung continue indigenous religious practices while others are Christians, having been converted in the 1930s.

Evenk, who number 26,000 in Inner Mongolia and Heilongjiang province and about 30,000 in Russia, are an indigenous hunter-gatherer and pastoral people of southeast Siberia. Under centuries of Manchu, Russian, Soviet, and Han control, their traditional culture has essentially disappeared.

Gelao number 438,000 and live in numerous villages in Guizhou province. Whether they are descended from Han settlers or were conquered by the Han is unclear. Although they are somewhat assimilated into Han society, much of their traditional culture, such as music, religious ceremonies, and marriage customs, survive.

Hakka who number over 38 million in China and over 75 million elsewhere, are not classified as a minority but are considered a Han subgroup. Hakka culture developed in north-central China, and over the centuries Hakka migrated and settled throughout much of China and later Southeast Asia. Recently Hakka have emigrated to many nations of the world. At times the Hakka have been treated as an inferior minority by other Han groups, a fact that explains the large number who have left China.

Hani (Akha) number 1.3 million in mountain villages in southern Yunnan province. They also live in Vietnam, Laos, Thailand, and Myanmar. Under Chinese control since the 8th century, Hani have been drawn into the Communist economic system, although traditional customs remain important, including their indigenous religion.

Hezhen number 4,200 in Heilongjiang province, where they live among the Han, Koreans, and other groups. Many Hezhen were killed by the Japanese in World War II, and, due to their small number and to intermarriage, they have now been assimilated into Han society (*see also* Nanai in Russia).

Hui, numbering 8.7 million, are the largest and most geographically dispersed Muslim group in China. Although found in greatest numbers in the northwestern and central provinces, Hui are present in all provinces and cities of China. They are descended from Persian, Arab, and Turkish Muslims who settled in China between the 7th and 14th centuries and married Han women. Thus, while Hui are Muslims and speak Chinese, they differ in physical appearance from the Han.

Jing number 19,000 and live on the China-Vietnam border and on three islands in the Gulf of Tonkin.

Jingpo number 119,000 and represent about 10% of the **Kachin** (as they are called in Myanmar) population. Most of them live in Myanmar and in mountain villages of southern Yunnan province (*see* Myanmar).

Jino number 18,000 and live in mountain villages in Yunnan province. Long under Dai domination, they were recognized as a distinct minority by the government in 1979.

Kazakh number 1.2 million in China and 8.1 million in Kazakhstan (*see* Kazakhstan).

Koreans number 1.6 million and live in northeastern China bordering North Korea. Most came in the late 1800s or early 1900s, first to escape poverty and then the Japanese domination of Korea. The Koreans have maintained ethnic autonomy in the region and control the local political system. They also provide Korean language education for their children and marry mostly within their own group.

Kyrgyz number 142,000 in China and 2.5 million in Kyrgyzstan (*see* Kyrgyzstan).

Lahu number 411,000 in Yunnan province. Whether under the control of the Dai or Han, or affiliated with other small ethnic groups in the region, the Lahu have been drawn into Dai and Han society only in recent years. The mix of religions including indigenous beliefs, Mahayana Buddhism, Roman Catholicism, and Protestantism reflects the centuries of contact with other peoples.

Lhoba are the smallest ethnic minority, numbering only 2,300 and living in southern Tibet. Treated as inferior by the Tibetans, they remain a separate group.

Li number 1.1 million and have lived on Hainan Island for at least 3,000 years. For the past 1,400 years they have been dominated by the Han, although traditional customs—such as the 12-day week and ancestor worship—survive.

Lisu number 575,000 in Yunnan and Sichuan provinces, with smaller numbers living in Myanmar and Thailand. Having arrived in the region in the 16th century, they have had much contact with other minorities and with the Dai and Han.

Manchu number 9.8 million and live mainly in northeast China. They ruled China during the Qing Dynasty (1644–1911). In that period, they were much influenced by Han culture and today are like the Han in many ways, even including the use of the Chinese language. For centuries, most Manchu have been farmers.

Maonan number 72,000 and live in northern Guangxi province. They live in scattered villages among other minorities and the Han, and they are much assimilated into Han society.

Miao, who number 7.4 million in a number of provinces in southeast China, are called **Hmnong** in other nations of Southeast Asia. The label Miao refers to related groups who differ widely in their religious, language, and economic practices. Han treatment of the Miao, who have joined a number of revolts, has ranged from assimilation to extermination. In the 1990s, Miao traditional music, dance, and dress have been encouraged as a tourist attraction.

Moinba number 7,500 in southern Tibet and are essentially assimilated into Tibetan society.

Mongols are descended from the hordes of the Mongol empire of the 13th and 14th centuries. Mongols live mainly in three nations—Russia (580,000), the Mongolian People's Republic (1.8 million), and China (2.6 million)—and only in the Mongolian People's Republic are they the numerically dominant group. Major Mongol subgroups are the **Buriats, Kalmyks, Daur, Khalka,** and **Oirats**. Most Mongols are Lamaist Buddhists.

Mulam number 159,000 and live in Guangxi province, where they are mainly farmers. While influenced by government economic and political policies, they retain their family-based social organization and traditional religion, which is a mix of ancestor worship, Taoism, and Confucianism.

Muslims number about 19 million in China in 10 groups: **Hui** (8.7 million), **Uighur** (7.3 million), **Kazakhs** (1.1 million), **Dongxiang** (374,000), **Kirghiz** (142,000), **Salars** (88,000), **Tajiks** (34,000), **Bonan** (12,000), **Uzbek** (15,000), and **Tatars** (5,000). The Hui, Salars, Dongxiang, and Bonan live mainly in north-central China, the others in western China. Once subject to religious persecution, Muslims today enjoy greater freedom. The end of Soviet rule in the former Soviet Union has also made it easier to establish and maintain contact with Muslims in the Central Asian republics.

Naxi number 278,000 in Northwestern Province. The indigenous culture, influenced by the Tibetans and Han, is reflected in Naxi religion, which incorporates features from Taoism, Buddhism (Chinese and Tibetan), and native beliefs.

Nu number 27,000 in northern Yunnan province. They are farmers but are one of the poorest groups in China. Although they consider themselves distinct from other local minorities, they may be culturally related to them and have been much assimilated into Han society. A majority are nominal Christians, due to missionary activity in the 19th and early 20th centuries.

Oroqen were a nomadic hunting people who fled from Russian expansion and settled in what is now Heilongjiang province in the 1600s. Numbering about 7,000, they have become settled farmers but are on the verge of cultural extinction.

Pumi, who number 30,000, live in Yunnan and Sichuan provinces. Communist rule ended their traditional stratified social organization, and the Pumi participate in the economy as farmers and industrial workers. They are Buddhists.

The term Qiang, although used to designate a distinct minority in China, actually refers to a number of groups who speak Qiang languages. In China these groups number over 500,000. The two major peoples are **Qiang**

(220,000) and **Jiarong** (180,000). Some other Qiang groups, such as the Pumi, are classified as distinct minorities and are enumerated separately. The Jiarong live in Sichuan and Yunnan provinces. Both groups have been influenced by the Tibetans and Han but have been largely assimilated into the latter. A distinctive feature of traditional Qiang culture was the relative equality of men and women.

Russians number about 9,700, and they serve primarily as advisors to the Chinese government. Their number varies according to the nature of Russian-Chinese relations.

Salar number 88,000 and live mainly in Qinghai province, with a minority in Gansu province. They are Muslims and are descended from Turkmen tribes that entered the region before the 14th century.

She number 630,000 and live mainly in Zhejiang and Fujian provinces, primarily in their own communities. Despite this residential isolation, long contact with the Han (dating to the 14th century) and current Communist rule have drawn them into Han society. Their religion is a mix of both indigenous and Han practices.

Shui number 246,000 in southern Guizhou province. Although heavily Sinicized, some traditional customs persist, including Shui polytheistic religion.

Tajiks in China number 34,000, with a worldwide population of about nine million (*see* Afghanistan, Tajikistan, and Uzbekistan).

Tatars, who number only 5,000, are descendants of Turkic peoples who settled in China and intermarried with local groups. They are Muslims.

Tibetans number about 4.5 million in southwestern China, mainly in the Tibet Autonomous Region and adjacent provinces. There is a large refugee population in India (100,000), Nepal, Bhutan, and in the United States and Great Britain. These Tibetan refugees fled following a failed revolt in 1959. Tibetans commonly identify themselves in terms of their region of residence or their specific Tibetan subgroup. Devout Buddhists, Tibetans have for much of their history been a theocracy, ruled by the Dalai Lama. They are now under the control of the Chinese government.

Much of Tibetan culture is centered around Tibetan Buddhism. This monk is attending to his duties in the Lhasa Cave Temple. Photo: Corel Corp.

Tu number 192,000 in Quinghai province. Descended from local peoples who intermarried with Mongols after the 1300s, Tu refer to themselves as Mongolians, although their distinctively bright clothing and Buddhist religion distinguish them from other groups.

Tujia number 5.7 million and are the largest minority in south-central China (Hunan, Sichuan, and Hubei provinces). Some experts believe that Tujia are the indigenous inhabitants of the region, while others see them as having emerged from groups already resident there. Centuries of contact with the Miao and Han have influenced Tujia culture, and the majority of Tujia now speak Miao or Han.

Uighur number 7.3 million and live in Xinjiang province. The Uighur emerged as a distinct people in the 8th century. At times Buddhist or Christian, since the 15th century they have been devout Muslims, the key marker of their identity today.

Uzbeks in China number 15,000, while 14 million live in neighboring Uzbekistan (*see* Uzbekistan).

Vietnamese refugees numbering about 285,000 live in southern China. Most are ethnic Chinese who fled discrimination in postwar Vietnam. Due to their Chinese heritage, they are assimilated into Chinese society, although they are not citizens.

Wa number 352,000 and live in the mountains of Yunnan province on the Myanmar border. They have maintained a considerable degree of cultural autonomy including the preservation of their own language, use of private property, traditional farming techniques, and their indigenous religion, which combines animism and ancestor worship.

Xibe number 173,000 and live in Liaoning and Xinjiang provinces. Those in Liaoning province have been much influenced by the Kazakhs, Uighurs, and Han, while those in Xinjiang province have retained more of their traditional culture, including distinctive walled villages and cremation funerary practices for certain categories of people.

Yao number 2.1 million, the majority living in Guangxi province and the remainder in neighboring provinces. Settled farmers, they have had a long relationship with the Zhuang and Han, although regional variations in Yao culture have resulted in resistance to wholesale assimilation.

Yi number 6.6 million in Yunnan and Sichuan provinces. Like other groups in the area, they probably emerged several thousand years ago from another group in the region. Prior to 1949 they were landowners and had become the dominant group in a number of locales. This dominance has since given way to the Han, although in areas with small Han populations, traditional kinship and religious practices survive.

Yugur number 13,000 in Gansu province. They are a remnant of the Uigur, who fled a Kyrgyz attack in the 9th century and then came under Tibetan influence. They are primarily herders and Lamaist Buddhists.

Zhuang number 15.5 million, speak a Tai language, and constitute the largest ethnic minority. They are concentrated in southeastern China along the border with Vietnam. Han influence in the region dates to 211 B.C. Since then, the Zhuang have been gradually assimilated into Han society and today are mainly wet-rice farmers.

The classification system used by the Chinese government to identify a group as a national minority is somewhat arbitrary, and some ethnic groups are not so identified. They may be lumped together with other groups who are actually quite different culturally and who speak different languages. The total number of ethnic groups in China is unknown; it may be as high as 400. Some of these groups are indigenous to China, while others are found mainly in neighboring nations such as Myanmar, Vietnam, Laos, and Nepal, with only small populations living in the border regions of China. Ethnic groups in China not listed separately in the official list of national minorities are: **Abor** (450,000), **Angku, Atsi** (50,000), **Atuence** (520,000), **Aini** (5,000), **Ching** (4,000), **Chona, Dianbo, Hu** (1,000), **Kadu, Kang, Bhotia** (1,000), **Laka** (6,000), **Lama** (3,000), **Lashi** (55,000), **Lati, Lawa, Lhomi, Tai Lu** (200,000), **Mahei, Mang** (600), **Manmit** (900), **Maru, Menghua, Mun, Nhang, Nung** (100,000), **Ongbe** (300,000), **Panag, Puman, Punu** (220,000), **Purik Bhotia, Qienjiang, Riang, Rumai, Sanei, Sansu, Sotatipo, Black Tai, White Tai, Shan** (200,000), **T'en, Tay, Tseku, U,** and **Zhongjia.**

Ethnic Relations

Although ethnic minority groups are able to maintain some degree of cultural independence, Han political, cultural, and economic dominance has become so great that the three largest ethnic minority groups—the Zhuang, Manchu, and Hui—are heavily Sinicized, as evidenced by their primary or exclusive use of the Chinese language. During the Communist era, from 1949 to the mid-1990s, ethnic conflict was not a major problem in China. Peaceful relations resulted from Han dominance, Sinicization of the non-Han population, and the physical separation of some groups. Sinicization is reflected in the use of Chinese in the schools and public life; the overall control exerted by Han officials; and the replacement of traditional forms of social, political, and economic organization with those advocated by the state. The major ethnic conflict has concerned the Tibetans, who have long sought political autonomy. An ongoing campaign for autonomy is being waged by Tibetan refugees outside China and by some Tibetans in Tibet, although the settlement of many Han in the region and the Sinicization of the area have placed Tibet firmly under Chinese control.

In the mid-1990s, ethnic conflict developed in the far western provinces that had large Muslim populations. The major conflict involves the Uighurs, who seek an autonomous republic and have turned to bombings and demonstrations to achieve that goal. The Chinese government has responded by stationing troops in the region to put down any revolts. The movement for autonomy among the Uighur and other western Muslim groups such as the Kyrgyz has been stimulated by the demise of the Soviet Union and the emergence of the Muslim Central Asian republics as independent nations in which people can adhere to Islam openly. The Chinese government has made it clear that it will not grant any of these regions autonomy and will continue to enforce policies designed to assimilate all minorities into Chinese society.

Fiji

T he Republic of Fiji is an island nation located in the Polynesia region of the South Pacific Ocean. It contains 322 islands, 106 of which are inhabited. Over 50% of the population of 764,000 lives on Viti Levu, the largest island. In the post-colonial period, Fiji has become a major political, economic, and cultural center in the Pacific region. Its capital city of Suva has emerged as the center of commerce for the area. This has affected the ethnic composition of the nation by attracting people from other islands and ethnic groups.

Ethnic Composition and Ethnic Relations

Fiji is a bicultural nation, with 49% of the population Fijian and 46% Indo-Fijian. Fiji was a British colony from 1874 to 1970, and during that time Indians were brought to the islands as contract laborers. Ethnic conflict developed between the two groups and has been a feature of Fijian life since 1987, when the democratically elected government was replaced by a military coup. Since then, the Fijian-dominated government has sought additional political and economic power at the expense of the Indo-Fijians. Preferential treatment for Fijians and attacks on Indo-Fijian culture have caused some Indo-Fijians to flee and have made them a numerical minority in a nation where they had been a clear majority.

Fijians are the indigenous inhabitants of the islands; their ancestors arrived as long as 3,500 years ago. Prior to British rule, Fiji was politically divided into a number of island con-

A pottery maker in Fiji, which was a British colony until 1970. Photo: Corel Corp.

federacies ruled by chiefs such as the Bau, Lau, and Rewa confederacies. Generally ignored by the British colonists, these confederacies and their chiefs have emerged as powerful political forces since independence was achieved in 1968. For economic reasons, a sizable number of younger Fijians have been leaving the nation for opportunities elsewhere, especially in New Zealand. Culturally related to the Fijians are the **Rotumans,** who inhabit Rotuma Island, about 250 miles north of Fiji. Only a minority of the 12,000 Rotumans live on Rotuma, the majority having migrated over the past 30 years to Fiji, New Zealand, Australia, and the United States.

Indo-Fijians are Asian Indians whose ancestors the British brought from India between 1874 and 1920 to work on the sugar and coconut plantations. The majority of Indo-Fijians are Hindus, with a minority being Muslims and Sikhs. Nearly all Indo-Fijians were born in Fiji and consider it their homeland. Active participants in the bicultural political process following independence, Indo-Fijians have come to see themselves as reduced to second-class citizens by the dominant Fijian political parties.

The major ethnic minority is the **Chinese,** who constitute less than 1% of the population and are mainly shopkeepers. Fiji is a large nation in the region, the population includes people from other islands such as **Samoa, Kiribati,** and **Tuvalu** who have emigrated in search of employment or education.

French Dependencies

Three sets of islands in the Pacific Ocean remain under the control of France. They are: (1) French Polynesia, consisting of the administrative departments of the Marquesas Islands, the Tuamotu Archipelago, the Society Islands (which include Tahiti), the Gambier Islands, and the Austral Islands; (2) Wallis and Futuna Islands; and (3) New Caledonia. French Polynesia is located in the central Pacific Ocean, between the equator and the Tropic of Capricorn and has a population of about 220,000. Wallis and Futuna are located farther to the west in the South Pacific Ocean northeast of Fiji and have a population of about 15,000. New Caledonia is located in Melanesia to the east of Australia and southwest of Fiji. It has a population of 188,000.

Although most of the over 120 islands that form these French overseas territories were discovered by other colonial nations—Britain, the Netherlands, and Spain—all the islands eventually became French colonies. Between the 1840s and 1900, French control was established. After World War II, the status of the islands was changed from that of colonies to overseas territories or departments. They remain under French political and economic control, but have a greater degree of local government autonomy than in the past. The standard of living is relatively high on the islands, largely due to financial assistance from the French government. Most inhabitants are Christians, either Protestant or Roman Catholic, although on many islands some elements of the indigenous religion survive alongside Christianity or are integrated with it.

Ethnic Composition

The indigenous people of French Polynesia are classified as **Polynesians.** They number 172,000 and constitute about 78% of the population. Polynesian is a term developed by anthropologists as a general label for all peoples of this region of the Pacific Ocean.

The people do not tend to think of themselves as Polynesians, but rather identify with specific island societies such as Tahiti, Magareva, Raroia, and Rapa. Or, when under French control, they might have identified with one of the five districts, such as the Marquesas Islands or Austral Islands. Identification with one specific island or district also involves stereotyping the people of other islands or districts, with some described as stupid, others as drunkards, or rustics, and dangerous.

The Polynesian classification indicates that traditional cultures of different island groups shared a number of general features such as a village life, a social structure based on kinship ties, rule by hereditary chiefs, and an economic system based on horticulture and, sometimes, fishing. Under French control, much of traditional Polynesian culture has disappeared, including the central role played by the chiefs and the reliance of the Polynesians on the growing of food. About 50% of French Polynesians are employed by the government, and tourism has emerged as a major economic activity. The islands have also served as the major locale for French nuclear testing. Such testing in 1995–96 led to opposition and riots, and the end of testing has led to unemployment. French is the official language although many of the indigenous island languages are spoken as well.

In addition to the indigenous Polynesians (some of whom are of mixed Polynesian, French, British, German, or Chinese ancestry) there are about 26,000 **Chinese,** 20,000 **Europeans** (mainly **French** but also **British** and **German**), and several thousand people from other islands in the region who live in French Polynesia. The Chinese are mainly involved in retail trade, Europeans in government and commerce, and other islanders come to the French Dependencies in a search for employment.

Wallis (Uvea) and Futuna were discovered by the Dutch and British but came under French control in 1887. They became French colonies in 1913 and an overseas territory in 1961. Small islands with minor populations, they have not drawn the same level of colonial attention as the other French dependencies. Nearly the entire population is composed of the indigenous **Futunans** and **Uveans,** most of whom subsist by growing yams, taro, bananas, and manioc for their own use. They also fish and produce copra (dried coconut meat used for coconut oil) for sale. Nearly all Futunans and Uveans are Roman Catholic and

speak French as well as their own languages. A substantial overseas population of at least 5,000 lives in Fiji and on New Caledonia where employment and education is available. The major nonindigenous group are the French administrators and teachers.

New Caledonia, unlike Wallis and Futuna, is located in Melanesia. It is a relatively large island, already occupied by a number of different groups when it was encountered by the French in 1768. The island has been inhabited

Melanesian nuns in Noumea, New Caledonia. Residents of the French Pacific Dependencies are debating whether to continue association with France or to seek independence. Photo: Corel Corp.

for some 6,000 years; the first inhabitants were people who migrated from Southeast Asia. Although language and other differences remain among the indigenous groups, they now refer to themselves as **Kanaks.** This not only marks them as the indigenous people of the island but also differentiates them from other ethnic groups now resident there. Kanaks number about 85,000 and constitute 45% of the island population.

Closely related to the Kanaks are the 22,000 people of the Loyalty Islands, located to the east of New Caledonia. Under French rule, plantation agriculture, logging, and fishing became important economic activities and cost the Kanaks much of their land. In the 20th century, mining and mineral processing have been added as major economic activities. The employment opportunities provided by these industries have attracted people from other Pacific Islands such as the **Tahitians,**

Vanuatuans, and **Uveans,** who number about 24,000 (12% of the population), and **Indonesians** and **Vietnamese,** who total about 10,000 (5% of the population). The other 34% of the population is European (mainly French) and is involved in government, commerce, business management, and the professions.

Ethnic Relations

The primary issue in the French dependencies is the question of whether to continue association with France or to seek independence. The French Polynesians are divided on the issue. Those who work for the French government—about 50% of the labor force—have traditionally favored ongoing ties with France for personal economic reasons. Those who live a more traditional lifestyle and are less dependent on France prefer independence. The former have so far prevailed in referendums on this issue.

In the late 1990s, with the cessation of nuclear testing and the consequent loss of jobs, independence has again become a key issue. The French have begun providing economic assistance to control the loss of income caused by the end of nuclear testing.

Independence from France is also a major issue for the Kanaks of New Caledonia. By 1900, the French were in firm control of the island, and the Kanaks were placed on reserves, which constituted only a small percentage of the island's land formerly owned by the Kanaks. The Kanaks were forced to work on the coffee plantations and then in logging operations. After World War II, the French relaxed their control a bit, ended forced labor, and allowed some Kanaks to vote. After nearly 50 years of disadvantage, however, the Kanaks had become the poorest and least influential people on the island. In the 1970s, a loss of jobs in the mineral processing industry and crowded living conditions on the reserves led some Kanak leaders to question the value of continued association with France. By the 1980s, Kanak demands for independence had become a major issue, and in 1984 they boycotted the elections and formed their own government. In 1988, a compromise regarding independence was reached with the French in the form of the Matignon Accords. These accords established a 10-year period during which France will assist with economic development and set 1998 as the year the Kanaks will vote on their future. The large French population and the dependence of some Kanaks on French-supplied jobs and government assistance mean that a vote for independence cannot be taken for granted, despite the large Kanak population. The division over this issue on New Caledonia is apparent in the fact that one provincial assembly is controlled by those supporting independence and the other by those supporting affiliation with France.

India

The Republic of India is located in South Asia and occupies most of the Indian subcontinent. It is bordered by the Arabian Sea and Pakistan on the west; China, Nepal, and Bhutan on the north; Myanmar and the Bay of Bengal on the east; and the Indian Ocean on the south. The territory of the nation of Bangladesh lies entirely within eastern India, and Sri Lanka lies just off the southeast coast. India has a long and rich history. One of the world's great civilizations—the ancient Indus civilization—developed in the Indus Valley of northwest India about 5,000 years ago. Modern Indian development began about 3,500 years ago, when peoples called Aryans moved into the region from Central Asia and mixed with or displaced peoples already living there. Hinduism, which remains a unifying force in India and provides the religious and social framework for Indian society, emerged there about 3,000 years ago. Buddhism developed in northern India in the 6th century B.C. but eventually spread north and east, and today there are few Buddhists in India. Islam arrived in approximately 1200, and by the 17th century virtually all of India was under Muslim rule. Most people remained Hindus, however, and conversion to Islam occurred mainly in the north. The Portuguese were the first Europeans to settle in India, followed by the French and British, the latter ruling from the mid-1800s until India achieved independence in 1947. Pakistan and East Pakistan (now Bangladesh) split off from India at that time and established a separate nation. Since independence, India has moved rapidly toward industrial development and modernization, efforts that have been hampered by wars with Pakistan, border conflicts with China, and the considerable diversity in the Indian population. According to the 1991 census, India had a population of 846,302,688 and was the second most populous nation in the world after China. In 1997, the population is estimated as having increased to 952 million. About 60% of the population is rural and most are farmers.

Ethnic Composition

India is home to probably the most diverse population of any nation in the world. The five sources of this diversity are: (1) religions; (2) languages and regions; (3) tribes; (4) castes; and (5) social classes and power. These sources of diversity do not operate independently but rather overlap and interact to provide an incredibly diverse mix of peoples.

Religion

Not only is India the birthplace of two world religions—**Hinduism and Buddhism**—but also the site of **Muslim** rule for over two cen-

Hindu women celebrating at a festival in New Delhi. Such festivals, some of which involve only women, are celebrated often throughout India. Photo: Reuters/Corbis-Bettmann.

turies. India is, in addition, the original home of two smaller major religions—**Sikhism** and **Jainism.** When one adds to these groups the nearly 20 million **Christians,** the small **Jewish** communities, and other groups such as the **Parsi (Zoroastrians**—members of a religion of ancient Persia)—it is clear that India has had at one time or another sizable populations of adherents of nearly all the major world religions, save those indigenous to East Asia. Additionally, hundreds of tribal peoples of India continue to practice their own religions as well as Hinduism, a complex religion with thousands of village variants and numerous specialized sects. According to the 1981 census, the Indian population was distributed by religion as follows.

Distribution of the Population of India by Religion

Group	Population
Hindus	672,600,000
Muslims	95,200,000
Christians	18,900,000
Sikhs	16,300,000
Buddhists	6,300,000
Jains	3,400,000

Languages and Regions

The second major source of ethnic diversity in India is language and region. These are closely tied together in India, because in 1956 the boundaries of the states were realigned so that the linguistic borders of the major languages would conform to the new state political boundaries. Thus, most people in Tamil Nadu speak Tamil, most in Kerala speak Malayalam, most in Orissa speak Oriya, most in Gujarat speak Gujarati, and so on.

The people of India speak some 1,500 different languages, of which the 14 listed below are considered the major languages, recognized as "official." In addition, many educated Indians speak English.

Percentage of the Population of India Speaking the Major Languages

Group	Percentage
Hindi	42.9
Bengali	8.3
Telugu	8.2
Marathi	8.0
Tamil	6.0
Urdu	5.7
Gujarati	5.4
Malayalam	4.2
Kannada	4.2
Oriya	3.7
Punjabi	3.2
Kashmiri	0.5
Sindhi	0.3
Assamese	0.01

Although some 43% speak Hindi, no language is spoken by the majority of Indians as their first language, and there is no national movement to make Hindi or any other language the sole official language. Instead, Indians accept the regional variation in language and see it as the normal state of affairs. Language diversity is closely related, of course, to cultural diversity, and there are major variations in dress, food, patterns of kinship relations, marriage practices, and other customs among the major language/regional groups. These differences are most obvious when rural regional groups are compared, and they tend to disappear in cities, where people adopt a more Western lifestyle and where Hindi and English are the major languages.

Tribes

The third major source of diversity in India is the presence of hundreds of tribes *(adivasis)*. No one knows how many tribes exist, partly because of difficulties in differentiating tribes from subtribes and also because some tribes have become castes. It is likely, though, that there are still at least 500 tribes in India.

In India, a tribe is a group of people, usually localized in one community or region, who have traditionally lived outside the Indian caste system, and continue to do so. Some tribes already were present in India before the arrival of the Aryans and the subsequent emergence of Hinduism and the caste system, others arrived later from the north, and still others may have developed from Hindu castes. Regardless of how they coalesced, the key feature of tribes is that they live outside Hindu society.

Since the advent of British rule, tribal peoples have owned little or no land and live at a subsistence level as farmers, isolated from Hindu society because they rarely marry outsiders. Most continue to practice their indigenous religions, although some have converted to Hinduism, Islam, Christianity, or Buddhism, and in large groups a number of different religions may now be followed. After independence, programs introduced by the government to increase the status of tribal peoples have eroded adherence to traditional culture, and some tribes are actively resisting such interference in their affairs.

The tribal peoples of India live in three major regions—the northeast, a number of localized regions across the center of India, and on the western side of the Ghats mountains in southwestern India. According to the 1981 census, there were 51.6 million tribal people in India, constituting 7.8% of the population. The largest numbers are concentrated in the states of Madhya Pradesh, Bihar, Maharashtra, Orissa, and Rajasthan. Tribes form over 50% of the population in six states and union territories: Arunachal Pradesh, Meghalaya, Mizoram, Nagaland, Dadra and Nagar Haveli, and Lakshadweep.

Estimated Populations of Major Tribes or Tribal Clusters

Area/Group	Population
Northeast Tribal Areas	
Abor	5,000
Garo	400,000
Khasi	500,000
Lakher	15,000
Mikir	230,000
Mizo	500,000
Nagas	1,500,000
Thadou	130,000
Central Tribal Areas	
Bhuiya	1,500,000
Bhil	5,200,000
Gond	5,000,000
Korku	300,000
Oraon	2,000,000
Santal	4,000,000
Southern Tribal Areas	
Badaga	145,000
Irulu	90,000
Kota	1,500
Kurumba	5,000
Malayali	160,000
Pandaram	2,000
Toda	1,100

Castes

The term "caste" comes from a Portuguese word, *casta,* and was the name given by Portuguese explorers in the 15th century to the system of social organization they found in India. Of all aspects of Indian society, castes and the caste system have drawn the most attention. A caste is not the same as an ethnic group, although there are commonalities, including birth into the group, lifelong membership, individual status based on group status, marriage within the group, and certain occupations associated with the group.

Caste refers to three different indigenous concepts used by the people of Hindu India. First, it refers to the several-thousand-year-old overarching varna system, in which all individuals and groups in Hindu society are classified into four ranked categories, Brahman, Kshatriya, Vaisya, and Sudra.

Brahman is the highest caste category or varna, and the highest caste group in any locale. Brahmans are traditionally priests and serve in that role for their village or, more commonly, for specific families within the village. Brahmans are also teachers, government workers, and landowners. In recent times, many Brahmans have moved to the cities and entered professions, while continuing to control rural property as absentee landowners. The Brahmans' high status derives from their ritual purity, as evidenced by their vegetarianism, their ability to read Sanskrit (the sacred language of Hinduism), and their knowledge of Hindu ritual. There are hundreds of Brahman castes in South Asia and Southeast Asia.

Kshatriya is the second highest caste category, located mainly in northern India, with many of the castes claiming descent from warrior castes of the past. Kshatriyas eat meat (but not beef) and were traditionally defenders of both the caste system and the supremacy of the Brahmans. Today, they are primarily landowners and professionals.

Vaisya, the third-ranked caste category, is composed of a large number of castes in northern India. Vaisya traditionally engaged in trading, farming, and money lending, and they still play a central role in the village economies.

Sudra, the lowest of the four caste categories, is composed of hundreds of castes throughout India. Sudra traditionally work small farms, although in the cities they may be found in all occupations. Those originally classified as Sudras several thousand years ago may have been aboriginal peoples of darker skin color than the Indo-Aryan settlers who formed the three higher varna.

A fifth category, although not considered as such in the original varna system, is the **Untouchables** (also known as **Panchamas, Pariahs, Harijans, Adi-Dravida).** Untouchables are those groups that exist outside the caste system and are considered inferior even to the lowest Sudra castes. Both the number of Untouchable castes and the actual count of former Untouchables are unknown (the category of Untouchables and discriminatory practices directed at its members is now illegal in India), although according to the 1981 census, members of Scheduled Castes, mainly Untouchables, numbered 104 million or nearly 16% of the national population. Untouchables are most heavily concentrated in the states of Uttar Pradesh, West Bengal, Bihar, Tamil Nadu, and Madhya Pradesh and form over 20% of the population of the states of Himachal Pradesh, Punjab, Uttar Pradesh, and West Bengal.

While the four-tier caste system is associated with Hindus in India, the social organization of non-Hindu groups in South Asia such as Muslims, Jains, and Jews has been influenced by it and is also characterized by an overarching caste structure. For example, while Islam in general has no caste structure and no such structure exists in Arab Muslim groups of the Middle East, the Muslims of South Asia recognize four caste-like categories: those who trace their ancestry to the Middle East—the Sayyid, Shaikh, Mughal, and Pathan; the Rajputs; various occupational castes; and sweepers.

The second indigenous use of the term caste is in reference to jati. Jati are hereditary occupational castes or clusters of castes whose numbers traditionally perform specific tasks within a village or region. Although there have been attempts to list all the jati of India, no list is complete and estimates place their number at between 3,000 and 5,000. Many retain their traditional names although they no longer perform their traditional tasks. Each jati, of course, is classified in one of the four varna, or in the Untouchable category. In the rural villages where most Indians have lived, the jatis were linked through the jajmani system. In the jajmani system, occupational castes or families provided services for other castes or families. Traditionally, the caste was paid through reciprocal service or with food, although modernization has brought payment in money as the most common form of compensation. For example, in one northern Indian village there are 12 jati. One of these, the Khati (carpenters), repairs agricultural tools for the Brahman (priests), Baniya (traders), Nai (barbers), and Jat (farmers) castes and receives services from seven other castes. In addition to this structured economic relationship, the jajmani system also provides many social rules that reinforce the hierarchical nature of the caste system by restricting contact between higher- and lower-ranked castes. The strict rules of endogamous marriage and life-long caste membership ensure the vitality of the system. And, because the jajmani system has persisted for hundreds of years, it remains in some villages the primary mechanism of social and economic cohesion.

The third indigenous use of the term caste refers to gotra, kinship groups within a jati, whose members marry members of other gotra within the same jati, and may live in the same village or region and own property jointly.

An individual's caste position in Hindu India is determined by one's *karma*; that is, behavior in a previous life. An individual's future caste position is determined by *dharma*; that is, behavior in the current life. Thus, acting in ways prescribed by caste status is the only way an individual can achieve a higher caste rank in the next life. Relations between castes and individuals are governed by the notions of ritual purity, pollution, and obligatory service. The caste hierarchy is based on the degree of purity exhibited by each varna and is maintained by rules that prohibit contact with lower (less "pure") castes, which would pollute the higher castes. In addition, higher castes do not engage in activities that are considered polluting, such as leather working.

In addition to being part of the Hindu religious system, the caste structure is maintained by:

- Marriage within the caste.
- Eating and drinking only with members of the same or equal castes.
- Membership for life in the caste of one's birth.
- Occupational specialization with each caste engaged in only one calling.
- Hierarchical arrangement on the basis of pollution and purity.

While no individual can enter a higher caste, castes themselves can move into a higher varna category. One way of doing this is for a caste to take on a ritually purer occupation. A second and more common way is for the caste to emulate the behavior of a higher caste by using Sanskrit in prayer, retaining Brahman priests, adopting a vegetarian diet, and following other purer ritual behaviors. This process, widespread throughout India, is known as Sanskritization.

Social Classes and Power

The fifth major source of diversity in Indian society is based on wealth, status, and power. Under the British system, some high-ranking caste groups, as well as certain individuals, had greater wealth and status than did others. Those favored by the British were provided a full English education, lived in the cities, were given jobs in the government or military, and enjoyed much greater wealth than the typical Indian farmer.

With the end of British rule and the coming of independence, this arrangement has gradually withered, and speaking English is no longer a requirement for success in life. Business now provides more opportunity for upward mobility than does government or military service, and new laws have opened education and employment opportunities to virtually all members of society. Nonetheless, a wide gap remains between the small number of people who control Indian national and regional society and the majority of poor, rural farmers and laborers.

Non-Indian Groups

India is home to people from many other nations and backgrounds. There are about five million Indians of **European** (mainly **British, Portuguese,** and **French**) or mixed European and Indian ancestry.

India also has several hundred peripatetic **(Gypsy or Roma)** groups, mainly occupational caste groups who differ from other jati in that they travel about a particular region or state or series of villages as entertainers, traders, and providers of specialized services. As with other jati, specific peripatetic groups are in-marrying and often have economic relations with other caste groups. While the number of groups is unknown, the number of individuals may approach 10 million.

Finally, India is the home of nearly 400,000 refugees, including several hundred thousand from Sri Lanka and smaller numbers from Bangladesh, Tibet, Nepal, Bhutan, and Afghanistan.

Ethnic Relations

As one would expect in a nation with such ethnic, cultural, and religious diversity, especially one that has experienced rapid economic growth and modernization over the last 50 years, ethnic relations are complicated, and a number of ethnic conflicts are causing considerable disruption to Indian society. One might expect that in the face of this diversity, India would have a major problem creating and maintaining any semblance of national identity and national cohesion. This is not the case, however, and except for some regional separatist movements, India is seen by experts as not being in any danger of fragmentation into the dozen or more separate "nations" that reflect its language and cultural variation.

National cohesion is supported by a number of factors, including the relatively autonomous state governments, the mixed ethnic populations of many states, the open political process with its many competing factions and parties, a long and rich common history, the legacy of Hinduism, and an acceptance of language diversity in Indian society. Hostile relations with the neighboring nations of Pakistan, China, and Bangladesh have also contributed to creating a unified India.

Despite the general sense of national unity, India does face a number of serious problems arising from the relationships among various religious, ethnic, and caste groups. When India achieved independence, a significant percentage of its population—perhaps as much as 20%—lived outside mainstream Hindu society. These outsiders were the Untouchables and the tribes. Being outside the system meant that they had little or no opportunity for upward social mobility, save moving to a city where they might be able to shed their Untouchable or tribal status. It also meant that many were poor and did not own land—an important determinant of wealth in rural India. Furthermore, marriage restrictions meant that an individual could not improve his or her status by marrying into one of the four major caste categories. There has been increasing concern about the fate of the Untouchables, and the Indian Constitution of 1949 banned discrimination against them. In addition, the new government created policies, laws, and an administrative structure to help improve opportunities for the former Untouchables and tribal peoples. Three categories of disadvantaged Indians were established: (1) Scheduled Castes consisting of the former Untouchable castes; (2) Scheduled Tribes consisting of the tribes; and (3) Backward Classes consisting of other groups who considered themselves disadvantaged. Lists of the groups in each category were compiled and routinely updated as a group's status changed. Groups fought hard to maintain their special status because it brought them the right to special "affirmative action" programs. Individual members of the Scheduled Castes, Scheduled Tribes, and Backward Classes were eligible for special education programs, seats were reserved for them in Indian universities, they were given hiring preferences, and their representation in the legislature was guaranteed. Although the program was only meant to last 20 years, it remains in place, and its preferential treatment aspect has led to a backlash, especially among members of Sudra castes, who are also poor but do not enjoy any special privileges. Some individuals have gone so far as to label themselves members of Scheduled Castes in order to gain university positions or jobs. What especially troubles some critics of the program is that individual wealth or status is not considered in awarding privileges. All one needs to be is a member of a given caste or tribe.

While individual Untouchables and tribe members have used the program to improve their situation, entire formerly Untouchable castes have also sought to improve their group status by becoming castes within the four-tier varna system, by becoming Buddhists or Christians, by inventing a higher status past for their group, or by participating in politics. Some castes are so large that different castes in the same varna may share similar concerns about their role in society and, thus, political participation has become a route to power and wealth for some castes. In 1995, for example, a low-caste woman in Uttar Pradesh, who was the leader of a small caste-based political party allied with the ruling party was named the state's chief minister. And in 1996, the traditionally powerful Congress Party suffered a major legislative defeat when blocs of caste votes it had depended on disappeared because some castes chose to vote instead for representatives they believed would better represent their regional interests. In the new Parliament, farmers held the majority of seats and members of Scheduled or Backward Castes held 23.3% of the seats. Thus, castes have become a powerful political force. In addition, the government took strong steps in the 1996 elections to end efforts by higher castes to restrict the voting of lower castes. It also banned the use of divisive religious or caste slogans in political campaigns. Most observers believe that elections in India are now more open than ever before, but despite the use of new approaches to upward social mobility, former Untouchables remain the poorest segment of Indian society.

The situation of the tribes is more complicated. Although some of the tribes are large and form a significant portion of the population in certain regions, they are even more outside Hindu society than the Untouchables; they speak languages other than Hindu; they practice different religions; and under British rule many lost much of the land they had used for hunting, gathering, fishing, and farming. A key issue for many tribes is land. Especially among groups in the northeast, such as the Nagas, the recovery of land taken by the British for plantations and the continuing settlement of nontribal peoples in traditionally tribal regions have led to campaigns both for the return of land and for political autonomy. Sometimes these campaigns have turned violent because the tribal rebels employed terrorism, and the government responded with military force. As tribal peoples become more involved in the political process, the issue of how much control they will be granted over their traditional territories remains a major concern in the northeast and central tribal regions.

At the time of independence, British India (now the nations of India, Pakistan, and Bangladesh) was the home of over 200 million Muslims, who formed a large minority in the region as a whole and a majority in some areas of the north. Although sharing the same ethnic ancestry as their Hindu neighbors, the Muslims in what is now India had converted to Islam during the centuries of Muslim rule and therefore enjoyed favored status. The British divide-and-conquer policy was designed to maintain antagonistic relations between the Muslims and Hindus to prevent any mass revolt. Largely because the Muslims feared discrimination as a minority in Hindu India, Pakistan and India were partitioned at the time of independence and Pakistan was established as an Islamic nation. Massive population relocations followed; Muslims moved to Pakistan and Hindus went to India. Nonetheless, a sizable Muslim population remained in north India, although the Hindus were now the majority in the region, and Sikhs predominated in the northwest Punjab state.

Hindu-Muslim relations remain a major stress point in Indian society. Although Muslims account for less than 10% of India's total population, they still number nearly 100 million and are heavily concentrated. Thus, contact between Hindus and Muslims is a fact of daily life in the north. To better understand Hindu-Muslim relations, one must consider the history of Muslim dominance in India, the hostile relations and three wars between India and Pakistan, and the Hindu nationalist movement of the Bharatiya Janata Party (BJP), which calls for India to become an officially Hindu nation. In the 1980s and 1990s, relations between Muslims and Hindus were tense, with incidents including riots, terrorism, destruction of holy places, and mass arrests. In the late 1990s, the BJP and smaller nationalist parties have lost influence in the face of corruption charges, and the government has actively sought to control religious violence and Muslim-Hindu conflict. Muslim-Hindu relations remain an issue in the Kashmir region, where Muslims supported by Pakistan seek separation from India. The region is claimed by both nations. Talks to resolve the conflict began in 1997.

The major separatist threat to India comes from the Sikhs in the agricultural Punjab region of the northwest. Sikhs constitute about 60% of the area's population. The religion of Sikhism emerged in the 15th century as an alternative to Hinduism. Since the 1880s, the Sikhs have feared assimilation into Hindu society and have stressed their unique identity as reflected in their dress, religious beliefs and practices, and close-knit community. In the late 1970s, the Sikhs began to show concern about government designs on Sikh land, about the movement of Hindus into the region, about possible repression of their religion, and about discrimination in employment. To protect their culture and autonomy, some Sikhs want to establish an independent Sikh nation, to be called Khalistan. Since 1984, the Sikhs have participated in a sometimes violent conflict with the Indian government over this issue. As a result, thousands have died, and the Indian military has come to control the region.

Indonesia

The Republic of Indonesia is a Southeast Asian island nation consisting of over 13,000 islands. Although over 6,000 of these islands are inhabited, the population is concentrated on several dozen islands or island groups. The most heavily populated islands are Java and Sumatra in the west. In fact, the island of Java is one of the most heavily populated areas of the world, and the government has encouraged residents to move to other, less populated islands to the east. Other major islands of Indonesia are Sunda Islands, Flores, Timor, the Moluccas, the Kalimantan region of Borneo, Sulawesi, and Irian Jaya in western New Guinea. The only nations directly bordering Indonesian territory are Malaysia and Brunei on the Island of Borneo and Papua New Guinea on the island of New Guinea. Indonesia was first settled by peoples migrating from the Malay peninsula. Hinduism and Buddhism arrived from India about 2,000 years ago, and Javanese culture, which is often portrayed as Indonesian culture, was influenced by both traditions. Islam came in the 15th century, spread by traders from Arabia, and most people eventually converted. The Portuguese entered the region in the 16th century but were replaced by the Dutch two centuries later. Indonesia became an independent nation in 1949 and has moved rapidly toward modernization and industrialization; it is now a major supplier of raw materials and labor to the developed nations of the world. The population of Indonesia is 206.6 million. About 87% of Indonesians are Muslims, although in many communities traditional indigenous religious beliefs exist alongside Islam, differentiating Indonesian Islam from Islam elsewhere in the world. The remainder of the population is Christian, Buddhist, or Hindu. Bahasa Indonesian, based on Malaya, is the official language, although it is the first language of only about 7% of the population. It is used in government, education, and the media. It is the government's hope that it will eventually become the first language of all Indonesians. English, Dutch, Chinese, and over 600 indigenous languages are also spoken.

Ethnic Composition

The ethnic composition of Indonesia is unclear due to the government's practice of not enumerating the population by ethnicity. The government wants to build a strong national identity, in part by weakening existing ethnic identities. Thus, the label "Indonesian" is not an ethnic one, because it refers to all citizens of the nation.

Indonesians generally differentiate between those of indigenous Indonesian ancestry *(pribumi)* and those from elsewhere *(keturunan asing);* most of the latter are Chinese. Experts generally place the number of indigenous ethnic groups in Indonesia at between 200 and 300. Some experts believe that as many as 700 languages are spoken across Indonesia, although it is likely that many of these are actually dialects of a smaller number of languages. All groups in the archipelago speak Austronesian languages, although the peoples in Irian Jaya speak Papuan languages.

Irian Jaya was not a part of Indonesia until it was handed over by the United Nations in 1963, following the end of Dutch rule. The ethnic groups there are small, and many initially resisted Indonesian rule. These groups have now been displaced by several hundred thousand Javanese, encouraged to settle there by the government.

Indonesia's ethnic groups vary in size from the Javanese, numbering about 70 million, to others, such as the **Penan** on Borneo, who number only a few thousand. Ethnic identity is marked by location (a specific island or region of a large island), language, dress, cuisine, and other customs (called *adat* in Indonesia). Thus, each distinct group has customs that differ from those of other groups and from the national culture, called *kebudayaan Indonesia,* in reference to Javanese culture and civilization.

The largest and the dominant ethnic group is the **Javanese,** who constitute about 45% of the population and are the only group spread across the entire archipelago. Closely related to the Javanese are the **Sudanese** in west Java, who comprise about 15% of the population, and the **Balinese** on Bali to the east, who make up about 1% of the population. Thus, the Javanese ethnic cluster accounts for about 61% of the population. Numbering some 125 mil-

A procession of villagers in Bali. There is no central unifying force for the many ethnic groups of Indonesia, and people often identify more strongly with their village than with the nation. Photo: Corel Corp.

Major Ethnic Groups of Major Indonesian Islands

Sumatra and Neighboring Islands

Acehnese	Kubu
Batak	Mentaweian
Gayo	Minangkabau
Kalagan	Nias
Kerentji	

Java and Lesser Sunda Islands

Badui	Madurese
Bali	Sasak
Baweanese	Sundanese
Javanese	Tenggarese

Sumba-Flores-Timor

Alorese	Makassar
Ata Sikka	Manggarai
Ata Tana 'Ai	Ndaonese
Atoni	Palu'e
Endenese	Rotinese
Kedang	Tetum
Lamaholot	

Borneo

Dayaks	Modang
Kenyah	Penan
Malays	Tidong

Sulawesi

Balantak	Saluan
Banggai	Toala
Bolaang Mongondow	Tomini
Bonerate	Toradja
Bugis	Halmahera and the Moluccas
Butonese	Ambonese
Gorontalese	Tanimbarese
Laki	Ternatan
Minahasans	Tidorese
Muna	Tobelorese

Irian Jaya

Asmat	Mejbrat
Dani	Muyu
Eipo	Ningerum
Kapauku	Tor
Marind-Anim	Waropen
Mimika	

lion, they are one of the largest ethnic groups in the world, and the third largest Islamic group in the world (after the Arabs and Bengalis).

A distinct Javanese state has existed for at least 1,200 years. The Javanese have been influenced by Hindus and Buddhists from India and, beginning in the 15th century, by Muslims from Arabia. These multiple cultural influences are reflected by the devout adherence of some Javanese to traditional Islam, while others follow a form of Islam that incorporates beliefs and practices from Hinduism and Buddhism.

Although 75% of Javanese live in villages on Java, the island is so densely populated that in many areas, villages are strung together. Most Javanese identify strongly with their village, although those living in cities or involved in government or the national economy are likely to identify more strongly with the Indonesian nation. Many Javanese speak Bahasa Indonesian as a second language while Javanese is their native tongue. Traditionally, Javanese have been wet-rice farmers and build elaborate rice field terraces to cope with land shortages. In the modern era, however, the Javanese have been much involved in commerce, trade, and industrial development. The Javanese are known for their music, literature, highly stylized dance forms, shadow plays, and textile arts, which are seen by many Indonesians as forming the core of Indonesian civilization.

On the island of Sumatra (west of Java), there are several large ethnic groups. These are the Achenese, Batak, and Minangkabau. The **Achenese** number about 3.5 million and are devout Muslims. Many have relocated to islands in the east in search of employment. Batak is a general label for a number of related groups that live in the hills and plains of northwestern Sumatra and number about three million. Most are rice farmers, although in the modern era many have moved to towns or cities for wage labor. The **Batak** population includes Muslims and Christians, although both retain elements of their traditional religions. To some extent, the Batak have resisted assimilation into the national culture by stressing village identity and by maintaining kinship ties, even after moving to the city. The

Minangkabau live in western Sumatra, and number about 3.5 million. They subsist as rice farmers, by growing other crops for export, and by trading. There is considerable out-migration to towns and cities. The Minangkabau are known as a society in which women have much prestige and influence and in which individuals trace kinship ties through their mother's line.

The largest nonindigenous ethnic group is the **Chinese.** A distinction is made between the **Peranakan** and the **Totok,** the former being Chinese born in Indonesia mainly of mixed Indonesian and Chinese ancestry, and the latter being born in China, having come to Indonesia more recently. The Chinese number about six million, although the number of people of mixed ancestry—who may not be labeled Chinese—may be significantly higher. Concentrated in cities and towns throughout the archipelago, the Chinese are engaged in commerce and retail trade. Totok Chinese usually speak Chinese, with Bahasa Indonesian used as a second language, while the Peranakan are likely to speak regional or local languages as well as Bahasa Indonesian. Resentful of Chinese dominance in the commercial sector, other Indonesians destroyed Chinese property during anti-Chinese riots in the 1970s and 1980s. In 1998, as the Indonesian economy worsens, anti-Chinese feelings are resurfacing. Seeking to assimilate the Chinese into Indonesian society, the government notes that over 95% of the Chinese are citizens of Indonesia. At the same time, the government has attempted to repress Chinese culture by banning Chinese-language publications and schools.

In addition to the Chinese, there are also several thousand **Asian Indians, Europeans,** and **North Americans** involved in commerce, trade, and industry, as well as several hundred thousand other Asian immigrants, who have come to Indonesia seeking employment.

Anthropologists have traditionally divided Indonesian ethnic groups into four categories.

1. Groups subsisting mainly by growing yams, taro, and other roots crops, and being generally not influenced by Islam or other major religions.

2. Groups living in the interior, growing rice and other crops, and inhabiting villages partially under governmental control.
3. Groups living in villages on the coast, subsisting by growing rice and by trading and being much influenced by Javanese, Malay, and other cultures.
4. Groups living in the interior, subsisting by growing wet (irrigated) rice, and being integrated into the national culture.

In the modern era, this classification system has become obsolete. Most Indonesians are now much influenced by decisions made by the national government. Distinctions based on wealth and status (social class) have become an important marker of intergroup variation.

Ethnic Relations

Building and maintaining a strong sense of national or Indonesian identity in the face of ethnic diversity and the wide geographical distribution of the population are the major ethnic relations issues in Indonesia. There is no central unifying force across all the ethnic groups. Although most groups grow and eat rice as their staple food, and most are Muslim, variations exist. In addition, rice farming has declined in importance as Indonesia modernizes, and many people now earn their income working outside the home. Islam, because it varies according to the adat of different groups, is not the unifying force in Indonesian society that it is in other nations. Other possible unifying forces are the widely played sport of badminton, the keeping of dogs and cocks as pets, and the generally high status afforded women in Indonesian society. But not all groups follow the same pattern. At the same time, these groups have similarities that encourage a sense of national unity. These similarities also serve to distinguish between indigenous Indonesians and those who came from elsewhere.

Nonetheless, the natural forces that might create and maintain a national culture and identity are weak, and the government has supported policies designed to foster unity. One of these is the national saying "Unity in Diversity." Another is the citizenship policy that has made it easy for nonnatives such as Chinese to become citizens. The decline of the Indonesian economy and resulting high unemployment among native Indonesians beginning in late 1997 produced a revival of anti-Chinese sentiment and some violence. As in the past, the Chinese are resented by some Indonesians for their economic success. A third is the language policy that requires children to learn Bahasa Indonesian in school and makes it necessary for adults to learn it in order to participate in politics and business. Although most people still speak their indigenous language at home, Bahasa Indonesian has now become the contact language for all groups, especially for Chinese merchants and their non-Chinese customers. A fourth initiative is the development of the national economy and the encouraging of foreign firms to build factories and assembly plants in Indonesia. Government support, low wages, and employer-friendly labor laws have made this initiative successful, and millions of Indonesians now produce goods for sale in the developed world. A fifth government effort, a transmigration program that began in the 1950s, seeks to reduce the crowded living conditions on Java by encouraging Javanese to move to other islands. Another purpose is to spread Javanese culture to these islands and at the same time to weaken the local adat systems. So far, some six million Javanese have

relocated, primarily to Kalimantan, Sumatra, Sulawesi, and Irian Jaya. Initially, most were rice farmers, but many of them moved into other occupations. Their presence has often led to conflict with local groups that are concerned about losing land to the newcomers and potentially becoming a minority group in their own region or on their home island. The relocations have also caused damage to the environment and the program has been condemned by environmental and human rights groups. In addition, some Javanese also object when they find the living conditions and economic opportunities far less desirable than promised by the government. Nonetheless, the program continues, with population reduction on Java cited as its main goal.

The conflict in East Timor has brought the most international attention to Indonesia. East Timor, where the local population is mainly Roman Catholic, has had to defend itself against the national government and its military. Until 1975, East Timor was a Portuguese colony. When East Timor declared independence, Indonesia almost immediately invaded, and the ensuing war has raged ever since, pitting the Timorese independence forces against government troops and resulting in thousands of deaths and the condemnation of Indonesia by human rights organizations and the United Nations.

Iran

The Islamic Republic of Iran is located in the Middle East. Iran is bordered by Armenia, Azerbaijan, the Caspian Sea, and Turkmenistan on the north; Afghanistan and Pakistan on the east; the Persian Gulf and the Gulf of Oman on the south; and Iraq on the west. The region has been settled for 12,000 years. Through a series of wars and alliances, the Persian Empire emerged and ruled the area from the 6th century B.C. until the Persian Empire was conquered by the Muslim Arabs over 1,000 years later in the 7th century. Persian culture, however, has survived and, along with Shi'ite Islam, remains an important unifying force for the Persians in Iran today. The population of Iran is 66 million. About 99% of the population is Muslim; 95% are Shi'ites and 4% are Sunnis. The remaining 1% of the population (about 700,000 people) includes Zoroastrians (followers of the religion of the ancient Persians), as well as Baha'is and Christians, including Nestorians and Chaldeans, believers in two ancient eastern Christian religions.

Ethnic Composition

Iran is an ethnically heterogeneous nation, although Persians comprise 51% of the population and are culturally, politically, and economically dominant. Because of its location at the crossroads of Asia and Europe and the arbitrary nature of current political boundaries, Iran finds within its borders sizable populations of people culturally aligned with the populations of neighboring nations. These include **Baluch** in the southeast (who also live in southwest Pakistan); **Aimaq** in the northeast (most of whom live in Afghanistan); **Armenians** and **Azerbaijani** in the north (who also live in Azerbaijan); and **Uzbeks, Turkmen, Karakalpaks,** and **Tajiks,** who are Central Asian Muslim peoples. Of these groups only the Azerbaijani are a significant population in Iran, because they number about 16 million and comprise 24% of the population. In addition, there are a number of distinct ethnic minorities located mainly in the eastern part of Iran.

Persians number about 34 million. They live mainly in the large cities of eastern and central Iran and in the central plains. Persians speak dialects of Farsi, the national language and the second language of many non-Persians. "Persian" and "Iranian" refer to the same people, although Iranian can also be used for all citizens of Iran. Persian art, music, and literature have survived from ancient times to become the dominant cultural forms in modern Iran. Persians also predominate in the government; in the leadership of the Shi'ite Muslim community; and in the military, commerce, and industry. Those Persians who continue to adhere to Zoroastrianism or Baha'i, and who number less than 500,000 even when combined with the Sunni Muslims, continue to be the object of persecution and discrimination. Many have fled the country in the last 20 years.

In the 7th century, Persia was conquered by Arab Muslims, and conversion to Islam began. About 500,000 **Arabs** now live in Iran. They reside almost exclusively in the west, in Khuzestan, and farther south along the coast. The majority are Shi'ite Muslims, although those on the coast are more often Sunni Muslims. In comparison to the Persians, the Arabs are a poor group. Many work in the oil industry, in factories, or as farmers or herders. Tribal affiliations remain strong.

In addition to the Arab enclaves in the west, there is a large Kurd population in the northwest. **Kurds** are the indigenous people of the region known as Kurdistan, located in southeastern Turkey, northern Syria, northeastern Iraq, and western Iran. Never politically unified under Kurd control, Kurdistan is nonetheless claimed by the Kurds as their homeland. The total population of Kurds is about 26 million, but 13.7 million of them live in Turkey, 6.6 million in Iran, 4.4 million in Iraq, and 1.3 million in Syria. Kurds speak various dialects of Kurdish, a language related to the Persian spoken in neighboring Iran. Mainly Muslims, Kurds belong to the Sunni branch of Islam. Traditionally, Kurds were a mountain people who lived by herding and farming. Kurdish culture has become more varied, and today several million Kurds live in cities. The Kurds have never been politically unified and are organized into a number of tribes and confederacies. Politically, they are now represented by a number of different political parties.

In addition to Arabs, Kurds, and Armenians, who number about 250,000, the mountainous western region of Iran is home to other distinct ethnic groups. The largest such group is the **Lur,** an amalgam of tribes with a membership of about 500,000. The majority of the Lur live in the Zagros Mountains of northwestern Iran, and there are smaller populations elsewhere in the nation. The Lur are Shi'ite Muslims who were traditionally herders. Under a government policy that lasted from 1925 to 1979, the Lur were forced to live in settled communities, learn Farsi in the schools, and farm rather than herd. The Lur are organized into distinct tribes, of which wealthier tribes traditionally exerted considerable economic and political control over the poorer tribes. This structure was disrupted in the 20th century, and it is not clear if it recovered after the end of secular dictatorial rule and the beginning of Muslim rule in 1979.

Living between the two major Lur population centers are the **Bakhtiari,** who number about 250,000. They are culturally and linguistically related to the Lur. A significant percentage of Bakhtiari, however, moved to the cities in the 20th century and became part of an urban, educated elite that assimilated into Persian society.

Farther south in the west are the **Qashqa'i,** who also number about 250,000. Traditionally herders who were forced to become settled farmers in the 20th century, they are Shi'ite Muslims but speak a Turkic language and are often labeled **Turks.**

Other Turkic groups are located in the northwest. The largest group is the **Shahsevan (Ilsaven),** who number about 100,000. Their history and modern culture are much the same as that of the other minority populations in Iran.

In addition to these groups, there are, in the northwest, about 20,000 **Assyrians** and several dozen other Turkic-speaking tribes, who are often classified as **Azerbaijanis, Shahsevan,** or as Turks.

Iran is also home to a sizable refugee population including about 1.6 million **Afghans** and 600,000 **Iraqis,** as well as **Kurds,** and **Azerbaijanis** from Azerbaijan.

Ethnic Relations

Due to the closed nature of Iranian society after the overthrow of Shah Reza Pahlavi in 1979 and the subsequent establishment of a Shi'ite Muslim government, little is known about the current ethnic relations situation in Iran. It is likely that government schemes to settle the nomadic herders in the west have been curtailed, and that these peoples have enjoyed greater freedom as Shi'ite Muslims. Iraq has charged that Arabs and Sunni Muslims have been persecuted in Iran, but whether this is true is not known. The Kurds have revolted at various times since the 1940s, although the region of Kurdistan is now under government control, and there are no major separatist movements like those in Iraq and Turkey.

Iraq

The Republic of Iraq is located in the Middle East. Iraq is bordered by Turkey on the north, Iran on the east, Saudi Arabia on the south, and Jordan and Syria on the west. In modern Iraq lies the Tigris-Euphrates Valley, site of ancient Mesopotamia, where early city-states such as Sumer, Babylon, and Assyria developed and flourished. In the 8th century and 9th century, the region came under Arab control and was the center of the Arab Muslim Empire. From the 13th century to the early 20th century, the Ottoman Empire ruled over all of this Middle Eastern area. Following World War I and a period of British control, Iraq became an independent nation in 1932. Iraq's recent history was marked by the war with Iran from 1980 to 1988, the invasion of Kuwait and subsequent defeat by United States–led United Nations forces in the 1991 Gulf War, and the long-standing on-again/off-again internal conflict with the Kurds. Iraq has a population of 21,422,000. Arabic is the official language, and Islam is the official religion. The majority of Iraqis are Shi'ite Muslims, making Iraq distinct from other Muslim nations where the majority of Muslims are Sunni. In Iraq, Sunni Muslims constitute only 15% of the population.

Ethnic Composition

The population of Iraq is composed of two major ethnic groups: Arabs and Kurds. A number of small minorities—Christians, Turkmen, and Assyrians—also inhabit Iraq. **Arabs,** an ethnic group indigenous to the Middle East, are the majority population in 15 nations of the Middle East and North Africa. In Iraq, Arabs constitute from 70% to 75% of the population and dominate political affairs. The emergence of Arabs as a distinct group in the region dates to at least 853 B.C. when the Arabic language was already in use. Although being an "Arab" has different meanings in different nations, a shared Arab identity is based on a number of key elements. These include the Arabic language, both the classical form used in religion and literature as well as the varieties of colloquial Arabic used in daily life; a personal identity with Arab culture, history, and community; a priority placed on children and family life; a clear division of labor based on gender; and adherence to Islam. Arabs in Iraq speak a dialect of Arabic related to that spoken in Syria and Jordan. The Arabs in Iraq include **Bedouins** whose traditional way of life in the deserts of the west is based on camel herding and regional tribal organization. The major division among Arabs in Iraq is based on religion. The majority—about 65%—are Shi'ite Muslims, and about 35% are Sunni Muslims. The basic difference between the two groups dates to a 7th-century disagreement among the earliest adherents of Islam as to how to pick the successor to Muhammad—the prophet and founder of the Islamic religious community. Shi'ites believe that the leader should be a direct descendant of Muhammad, whereas Sunnis believe the leader need only come from Muhammad's tribe. In Iraq, Shi'ites live mainly in the south and are sometimes called **Marsh Arabs,** in reference to the environment.

Kurds are the indigenous people of the region known as Kurdistan, located in an area that includes southeastern Turkey, northern Syria, northeastern Iraq, and western Iran. Although never politically unified under Kurd control, Kurdistan is claimed by the Kurds as their homeland. Kurds number about 26 million, of which 13.7 million are in Turkey, 6.6 million in Iran, 4.4 million in Iraq, and 1.3 million in Syria. Kurds speak various dialects of Kurdish, a language related to the Persian spoken in neighboring Iran. They are mainly Sunni Muslims. Traditionally, the Kurds were a mountain people who lived by herding and farming. Kurdish culture is today more varied. Several million Kurds live in cities and although not politically unified, they are organized into a number of tribes and confederacies represented by a number of different political parties. In Iraq, as elsewhere in the Kurdistan region, the Kurds continue to desire a separate Kurdish state. Since the 1920s, conflict has been a common feature of the relations between the Kurds and any government under which they live.

Iraq's two major ethnic minorities are Turkmen and Assyrians. The **Turkmen** number about 400,000 and comprise 2% of the population. They live mainly in the northeast, where they were settled by the Ottoman Empire in an attempt to separate the Kurd and Arab regions. Turkmen are Sunni Muslims and speak Turkmen, a Turkic language. They are being rapidly assimilated into Arab society.

Assyrians are descendants of the people of the Assyrian Empire, which ruled the region in the 9th century and 8th century B.C. Because of assimilation into Arab society, the number of Assyrians is unknown. Estimates range from as low as 133,000 to as high as 750,000. There are probably about one million Assyrians in the world, the greatest number being in the United States, and smaller populations in Iraq, Iran, Turkey, and Syria. In Iraq, Assyrians live mainly in the northeast and are part of middle-class professional and business world. Most Assyrians are Nestorian Christians, Jacobite Christians, or Roman Catholics.

In addition, there are also small numbers of **Armenians** and **Yezidis** in Iraq (*see* Armenia).

Ethnic Relations

Throughout the 20th century, ethnic relations in Iraq have been characterized by conflict between the Kurds and the government. Beginning in the 1920s, the Kurds launched a number of unsuccessful revolts—1922–23, 1930–31, 1932, 1963–64, 1965–66, 1974–75, and 1987–89. All of these were repressed by the government, often with substantial loss of life and property. Because Kurds live in four different nations, revolts in Iraq have sometimes taken place in a regional context. The revolt in 1987–89 happened during the Iran-Iraq War and ended in defeat for the Kurds, when Iran stopped supporting them and made peace with Iraq. Following the Gulf War in 1992, Iraqi forces attacked Kurd settlements and many Kurds fled into Turkey. Turkey, in its own war with the Kurds in southeast Turkey, continues to attack Kurd settlements in Iraq. In the 1990s, the Kurd separatist movement has suffered from a lack of internal political unity, with two major political parties—the Kurdistan Democratic Party and the Patriotic Union of Kurdistan—battling each other.

The other major conflict in Iraq is not ethnic but religious and pits the majority Shi'ite Muslims against the minority Sunni Muslims. Although the Shi'ites are the dominant group, the Sunnis have not been entirely excluded from national affairs. Those in the south, however, were attacked by Iraqi forces after the Gulf War and are now protected by a United Nations–enforced no-fly zone. The Iraqi government, secular in its ideology, fears a revolt by Islamic fundamentalists, as has occurred in other Middle Eastern and North African nations.

Israel

I srael is a small nation located in the Middle East. It is bordered by the Mediterranean Sea and Egypt on the west, Lebanon and Syria on the north, and Jordan on the east and south. It has a population of 5,143,000. Founded in 1947, it is officially a Jewish state, although freedom of religion is guaranteed for other groups. Israel is considered by both Jews and Palestinians to be their ancestral home.

Ethnic Composition

Israel is largely a nation of Jewish immigrants who come from over 103 nations and speak 70 different languages. Since the mid-1970s, however, native-born **Israelis (Sabras)** have been in the majority, even though most of them are children of immigrants. Hebrew and Arabic are the official languages of Israel, and about 83% of the population is Jewish, the remainder being mostly Muslim.

While Israel is often described as a Jewish state, and it is true that Jewish religious leaders and organizations strongly influence government policy, the ethnic composition of the country is far more complex. First, the Jewish population itself is divided into two ethnic-religious populations, Ashkenazim (European) and Sephardim/Oriental (Afro-Asian), as well as a number of subgroups; and second, the Jewish population differs in the depth of its adherence to Judaism—be they ultra-Orthodox, Orthodox, Conservative, or secular. The whole issue of Jewish identity is further complicated by the fact that 70% of Israeli Jews are not observant. A lively debate continues over the question of who is a Jew and to whom should apply the Law of Return, which affords all Jews the right to settlement and immediate citizenship in Israel. In addition to place of origin, language, and religious practice, there are socioeconomic and class differences between the Ashkenazic and Oriental communi-

Jewish man. Israel is largely a nation of Jewish settlers who have emigrated from more than 100 different nations. Photo: Corel Corp.

ties, the former being mainly middle and upper class and the latter working class.

Ashkenazi (European) Jews are of European or North American ancestry. They formed the majority of the Israeli population in 1947 but are now outnumbered by Oriental Jews. Ashkenazi Jews speak Hebrew, and many in the older generation also speak their native language, such as Russian or German. Younger people often speak English as a second language. Religious belief ranges from those who are ultra-Orthodox and live in secluded communities to those who are Orthodox, Conservative, secular, or even nonbelieving.

Oriental (Afro-Asian) Jews migrated to Israel after 1947 and now form a majority of the population. They came from nations in the Middle East and North Africa that had substantial Jewish communities, some dating back thousands of years. Nations of origin include Algeria, Morocco, Tunisia, Egypt, Iran, Yemen, Syria, Jordan, Turkey, and the Kurdistan region. Although Hebrew is becoming the preferred language, most also speak Arabic. Oriental Jews are usually **Sephardic Jews,** that is, their form of Judaism derived from the Judaism that developed among the Jews of Spain and Portugal. The Sephardic and Ashkenazic traditions differ in liturgy, language, and interpretation of some religious laws, but both groups consider the other to be Jews.

In addition to these two major categories of Israeli Jews, there are others who defy easy classification. **Falasha (Ethiopian Jews, Beta Esrael)** are the Jews of Ethiopia, some 60,000 of whom now live in Israel. These Jews migrated in the 1970s and 1980s through a series of airlifts arranged by the Ethiopian and Israeli governments. Their origin as a distinct group (in Ethiopia) is unknown. Despite claims of having arrived during the rule of King Solomon in Israel, reliable information dates their presence in Ethiopia only to the 14th century. They lived in the Ethiopian highlands, due in part to their religion and in part to their low-class status as potters, blacksmiths, and peasant farmers. Falasha speak Amharic and Tegrenna; in Israel they speak Hebrew. Because Falashas practice a pre-Rabbinic form of Judaism, they were required to "convert" to

Judaism before being accepted under the Law of Return. They remain unassimilated into Israeli society, living in isolated housing and engaged in mostly unskilled labor. The Falashas' low status was reinforced in 1996 when it was disclosed that their donations of blood over the last 15 years had been routinely discarded by Israeli authorities due to a fear of HIV contamination.

Indian Jews refers to **Cochin Jews** and **Bene Israel,** two Jewish groups from India, most of whose members immigrated to Israel in the late 1940s and early 1950s. Today they number about 35,000 in Israel, with remnant populations in India. Cochin Jews, about 5,000 in Israel, come from communities along India's Malabar Coast. Bene Israel, about 30,000 in Israel, lived in Bombay and villages to its south. The origins of both groups are uncertain, though Bene Israel claim to have arrived in India in the 1st century and 2nd century. For several centuries they have been linked to mainstream Judaism, and they follow Rabbinic traditions merged with customs such as a division into castes borrowed from their Hindu neighbors. In Israel, while their South Asian identity remains, they are largely integrated into Israeli society.

Karaites are a Jewish religious minority who number between 8,000 and 25,000. Most immigrated to Israel from Egypt in the 1950s, and a small number came from Eastern Europe. They are distinguished from other Jews in Israel by their adherence to a pre-Rabbinic form of Judaism in which only the Bible is considered of divine origin. Rabbinic Jews, in contrast, also follow post-Biblical rabbinic teachings and interpretations. In Israel, Karaites speak Hebrew and Arabic, maintain their own congregations and communities, and are generally part of the working class.

Russian Jews is the label used in Israel for Jews from the Soviet Union who immigrated to Israel beginning in the 1970s. Prior to that time, immigration was restricted by the Soviet government. Large numbers of Jews have also arrived from **Belarus, Ukraine,** and the **Central Asian** republics of the former USSR. These Russian Jews number about 550,000 in Israel, or 10% of the national population. Although freely admitted under the Law of Return, their assimilation has been slowed by a number of factors—very few speak Hebrew, they received little education on or exposure to Judaism in the Soviet Union, most are professionals essentially underemployed in Israel, many are housed temporarily in communities that are ethnically homogeneous, and other Jews have come to resent the drain this resettlement has caused on the Israeli economy.

Sometimes counted as Russian Jews and at other times as Oriental Jews are the small number who have emigrated from the Caucasus region and Central Asia. **Samaritans,** who number only several hundred, live in two communities, one in Israel and the other on the West Bank. They trace their descent from the Samaritans who lived in the region in the first millennium B.C. Samaritans practice a mix of pre-Rabbinic and Rabbinic Judaism. While keeping socially separate, they are integrated into Israeli society economically.

The second major division in Israeli society is between Jews and **Arabs** (Palestinians, Bedouin, Druze). Arabs in Israel are further

Cave of the Patriarchs, in Hebron. Both Jews and Muslims regard this ancient burial place as sacred. In 1994, a Jewish extremist killed 29 Muslims worshippers at the site; the Israeli Army has taken extraordinary security measures to prevent future violent incidents. Photo: Reuters/Corbis-Bettmann.

divided by religion; about two-thirds are Muslim and one-third are Christian. **Druze** are a distinct Arab group that emerged in the 11th century as a Muslim religious minority. By adhering to their unique form of Islam, living in close-knit communities, fighting for autonomy, and accommodating the demands of peoples they have lived among, the Druze have

managed to survive as a distinct ethnoreligious group. There are about 350,000 Druze in the world, 70,000 of whom live in Israel and the Israeli-occupied Golan Heights region of Syria. At times, Druze have been persecuted by both Arab Christian groups and Muslims. In Israel, they are citizens and supporters of Israeli nationhood. Poorer than the Jewish population, younger Druze are demanding full rights and benefits of Israeli citizenship. **Palestinians** were the majority Arab population when Israel became a nation in 1947. Most fled or were expelled during the 1948 war between Israel and the neighboring Arab nations. Worldwide, Palestinians number 3.1 million. They are now the largest refugee population in the world, with 800,000 in Israel, 644,000 in Gaza, and 504,000 on the West Bank. About two-thirds of these Palestinians are Muslim, and one-third are Christian. Relations between the two groups are generally peaceful. Palestinians speak Arabic, and some speak Hebrew as well. The **Bedouin** speak Arabic and were, until several decades ago, nomadic pastoralists of the deserts of Arabia and North Africa. In Israel they live mainly in Galilee and the Negev Desert in settled communities. Since 1947, they have lost control of the lands they once used for herding. They number about 130,000. Bedouins are citizens, are generally seen as loyal to Israel by the government, and thus serve in the military. Although Bedouins believe their interests are aligned with those of the Palestinians, they are not fully accepted into the group.

Other ethnic minorities include small numbers of **Armenians** and **Baha'is,** as well as **Circassians** (about 15,000) who live in two villages near the Golan Heights where they serve Israel as border guards (*see* Russia). The largest immigrant group is **U.S. Americans,** who number about 125,000, including both those who have chosen to remain in Israel, and those who expect to return to the United States. They are mainly Jews of Ashkenazi ancestry.

Other ethnic groups in Israel are composed of men who are there as contract laborers

(100,000), or as illegal immigrants (150,000). Their numbers include **Thais, Ghanaians, Nigerians, Arabs from Egypt and Jordan, Romanians,** and **South Americans.** They work primarily in construction, agriculture, and domestic service. Palestinians formerly did much of the agricultural and construction work, but on-again/off-again restrictions on their travel in Israel have made them an unreliable labor pool. Thus, despite government concerns about immigration of non-Jews, many businesses prefer to hire foreign nationals. They are an almost exclusively male population, forced to live in substandard housing, mainly in Tel Aviv.

Ethnic Relations

The conflict between Jewish Israelis and the Palestinians in Israel over territory controlled by Israel has been a major feature of life in the region since 1947. Israeli-Arab tensions have also been strong during this period. Peace agreements made with Egypt in 1979; with the Palestine Liberation Organization in 1993, 1994, and 1995 (although conflict and violence continue); and with Jordan in 1994 eased the situation somewhat, although the election of a more conservative Israeli government in 1996 is seen as slowing the peace process by some experts. With the implementation of the Israel-Palestine Liberation Agreement of 1993 in 1994 and 1995, Palestinians in Gaza and in some locations on the West Bank are now under self-rule. At the same time, as tensions continue between the two sides, Palestinians in Israel remain under Israeli political and economic control and factions on both sides (who

oppose the agreement) continue to use violence to disrupt the process.

Relations between Ashkenazi and Oriental Jews are not without their tensions as well. Ashkenazi Jews are the dominant ethnoreligious group in Israel. They occupy the majority of professional positions and dominate the government. As a group, the Ashkenazi are better educated, live in better housing, and have smaller families than do the Oriental Jews, Palestinians, and other groups. Ethnic-based class rivalry continues between the Ashkenazi and Oriental communities partly because some Orthodox Ashkenazi do not consider the non-Rabbinic Karaites, Falasha, and Indian Jews to be legitimate. Views concerning Palestinian-Israeli relations range from those who desire peaceful coexistence to those who see no place for Palestinians in Israel. The key distinction between Oriental and Ashkenazi Jews today is socioeconomic. Most Oriental Jews are employed in low-paying, blue-collar jobs, whereas those who move up the socioeconomic ladder identify with the better-off Ashkenazi community.

Tensions in Israel also exist between the Orthodox Jewish religious community on the one hand and the Conservative and Reform communities on the other. Although a numerical minority, Orthodox Jews are the governing religious force in Israel, and Judaism there is based primarily on Orthodox traditions, even though those traditions are not followed by many Israelis. For Orthodox Jews in Israel, Conservative and Reform Judaism are not valid forms of authentic Judaism.

Japan

J apan is an island nation located off the east coast of Asia. An urban, highly industrialized country, Japan has a social system in which people are differentiated on the basis of gender, age, status, and kinship. Shinto is the indigenous religion of Japan. Buddhism was introduced from China in the 6th century. Many Japanese today classify themselves as adherents of both Shinto and Buddhism. The ancestors of the modern Japanese have been in Japan for over 2,000 years and Japanese culture has been influenced by contact with China, Korea, and, most recently, the Western world.

Ethnic Composition

In Japan, one of the most ethnically homogeneous nations in the world, 99.5% of the population of 125 million is Japanese. Restrictive immigration laws and criteria for citizenship ensure that it will remain ethnically homogeneous. In 1994, Japan tightened restrictions on asylum-seekers, although it provides major financial support for refugee programs elsewhere.

Japanese identity is based on having Japanese parents, being born in Japan, speaking Japanese, and bearing allegiance to the nation of Japan. Also of importance is Japan's unique cultural heritage and the institutions associated with that heritage, such things as extended family groups, simplicity in artistic design, respect for authority, cooperative work and play groups, and decision-making by consensus. There is a substantial Japanese diaspora, with large populations in the United States, Canada, Latin America (Peru's president is of Japanese ancestry), and Mexico.

Three non-mainstream Japanese groups in Japan are viewed by some Japanese as inferior. **Burakumin** (formerly called **Eta**) are ethnic Japanese descended from low-class groups from about the 8th century. These groups engaged in ritually impure occupations such as leather working, burying the dead, butchering, and street-sweeping. Burakumin number about two to three million and live in some 6,000 communities separate from mainstream Japanese neighborhoods. Although discrimination against Burakumin is illegal, most continue to live in poor, segregated neighborhoods, hold low-paying jobs, and marry within the group. Some Burakumin seek to hide their identity, but are exposed when their place of birth or current residence is discovered.

The **Ainu** are the indigenous hunter-gatherer people of Japan. In the past, they lived on the northern island of Hokkaido, on northern Honshu Island, on Sakhalin Peninsula, and on the Kurile Islands. The Ainu are physically and culturally related to the indigenous peoples of Siberia. Today, they number about 18,000 and live only on Hokkaido. Under pressure for 1,000 years from the Mongols, Chinese, Russians, and Japanese, Ainu resistance effectively

An Ainu elder in Hokkaido. The Ainu are a small ethnic minority in Japan, although their forebears were the indigenous people of several of the northern islands. Photo: Corel Corp.

ended in the 1600s, and their traditional culture has since been altered to the point of extinction.

Koreans are the largest ethnic minority in Japan. They number about 700,000, 75% of whom were born in Japan and speak only Japanese. Most are classified as "resident aliens" and are denied citizenship. Although contact between Korea and Japan dates to the 7th century, Koreans in Japan today are mainly children or grandchildren of Korean laborers forced to move to Japan in the early 20th century.

In addition to these three major minorities, there are two other distinct minority groups. **Okinawans** are residents of the Ryukyu Islands south of Japan. Okinawa is the largest of the islands and home to a majority of the population. Okinawans are ethnically Japanese, speak a dialect of Japanese, and since 1972 have been part of Japan. United States control of Okinawa from 1945 to 1972 altered the traditional agricultural way of life, and incorporation into modern Japan has turned the island into a modern, industrial region. Although Okinawa is a poor region of Japan, some Okinawans have petitioned unsuccessfully for independence. A small number of Okinawans of mixed Okinawan and U.S. parentage are discriminated against.

Vietnamese number about 8,000, nearly all of whom are "boat people" living under temporary residence status in poor neighborhoods of large cities. Whether they will be allowed to settle in Japan permanently is unclear.

Other groups include several hundred asylum-seekers and refugees from **Laos, Cambodia,** and **Myanmar.**

Ethnic Relations

Ethnic relations in Japan are marked by a clear sense of Japanese superiority and a marginal role for people of non-Japanese ancestry. Animosity between Koreans and Japanese is a central feature of the relationship between the two groups. The mistreatment of Koreans during the Japanese occupation of Korea in the 20th century is a major issue for the Koreans. It led many to immigrate to Japan to escape poverty in Korea. The Korean minority in Japan is generally denied both citizenship and access to government employment. Those who support North Korea (about 300,000) are identified by the Japanese as North Korean citizens and are denied any rights of Japanese citizenship. Despite their classification as second-class residents, most Koreans speak only Japanese and live in communities dispersed throughout the country, two factors that have caused the Korean community to lose much of its distinct identity. As a small minority, Koreans have increasingly attempted to become Japanese by attending Japanese schools, taking Japanese surnames, marrying Japanese (often Burakumin), and trying to pass as Japanese.

Jordan

J ordan, a nation in the Middle East, is bordered by Syria on the north, Iraq on the northeast, Saudi Arabia on the east and south, and Israel on the west. Jordan has a population of 4.2 million. Arabic is the official language, and Islam is the official religion although religious freedom is guaranteed to others. From the 7th century until 1920, Jordan was part of the broader Islamic Middle East; Jordan did not exist as a separate political entity. The region was first part of the Islamic Empire and then under the control of the Ottoman Empire. Following the demise of the Ottoman Empire in World War I, Jordan came under British control and was established as a separate political unit with territory that included modern Jordan and much of Palestine (now Israel). In the 1967 war, Jordan lost both the West Bank region and East Jerusalem to Israel. In 1974, Jordan gave up claims to the West Bank, essentially turning the territory over to the Palestinians, the major occupants of the region. In 1995, Jordan and Israel entered into a peace treaty that ended the hostilities between the two nations.

Ethnic Composition and Ethnic Relations

Jordan is an Arab nation; 98% of the population is Arab. The only significant minorities are Armenians and Circassians.

Arabs are an ethnic group indigenous to the Middle East and constitute the majority population in 15 nations in the Middle East and North Africa. The history of the emergence of Arabs as a distinct group in the region is unclear, but as early as 853 B.C., the Arabic language was written, according to documents dating from that time. A shared Arab identity is based on a number of key elements. These include use of the Arabic language both in the classical form found in religion and literature and in the varieties of colloquial Arabic spoken in daily life; identification with Arab culture, history, and the Arab community; a value placed on children and family life; a division of labor based on gender; and adherence to Islam. About 93% of Arabs around the world follow Islam. However, not all Muslims are Arabs, and the largest Muslim populations are found in the non-Arab nations of Bangladesh, Indonesia, and India.

Although nearly all Jordanians are Arabs, there is considerable diversity within the Arab population. Traditionally, there was a division between those who lived a settled lifestyle, often in cities, and those nomadic or seminomadic **Bedouin** herders who were organized into tribes and tribal confederations in the desert. However, over the last several decades, nomadic herding has declined in importance and most Bedouins have settled in towns and cities. While many Bedouins maintain their Bedouin identity, their lifestyle is now much the same as other Jordanian Arabs.

Another distinction in the Arab population is between the 92% of Arabs who are Muslims and the 8% who are Christians. Because the groups are both Arab and Jordanian, a sense of shared identity exists. However, due to the difference in religion, social interaction is limited and intermarriage between the groups is rare. With the rise of Islamic fundamentalism in the Middle East, the status of **Christian Arabs** remains uncertain.

The third and most significant variation in the Arab population is between those native to Jordan proper—that is, Jordan east of the Jordan River—and the **Palestinians.** Palestinians are Arabs who are indigenous to Palestine—the region that is now essentially Israel—and to the West Bank. Over 50% of Arabs in Jordan are Palestinians. The population was formed by Palestinians who came to Jordan when much of Palestine was part of Jordan, by Palestinians who settled in Jordan after Israel was established in 1947, and by Palestinians who lived on the West Bank. The political and legal status of Palestinians in Jordan is complex and is determined, in part, by Jordanian-Israeli and Palestinian-Israeli rela-

tions. Technically, the approximately 500,000 Palestinians on the West Bank are neither Jordanians nor refugees because the region is no longer part of Jordan. The West Bank remains under Israeli control, although some communities are moving toward autonomy in accord with the Israel-Palestinian peace accords of the 1990s. Of the over 2 million Palestinians in Jordan, 1.2 million are refugees. Unlike most other refugees, however, they do enjoy full citizenship rights (except for those from the Gaza strip, a region that has never been part of Jordan). Palestinian refugees live mainly around Amman and in the north; about 25% live in refugee camps. Many live outside the mainstream economy. Politically, Palestinians, especially those who have arrived since 1947, have posed a problem for the ruling Hashemite government, traditionally supported by the Bedouin. Many Palestinians seek their own homeland outside Jordan and have formed political organizations to further this goal. This has created political problems for the government, which wants the support of the large Palestinian population but also must consider its relations with Israel and with other Arab nations.

The two major ethnic minority groups—although both are small—are the Circassians and Armenians. The **Circassians,** whose population is estimated at from 20,000 to 100,000, live in and around Amman. The original community was established by those fleeing Russian conquest of the Circassian region in the Caucasus in 1864. Most are wealthy, partly from having control of the electric and power industry.

Armenians, who number about 40,000 and live mainly in the cities of Irbid and Amman, are Christians and are employed mainly in trade.

In addition, there are several thousand **Chechens** (*see* Russia) also from the Caucasus region who are also Muslims like the Circassians, and smaller numbers **Druze** (*see* Israel and Syria), **Kurds** (*see* Iraq and Turkey), and **Iraqi** refugees.

Kazakhstan

K azakhstan, a nation located in Central Asia, is bordered by the Caspian Sea and Russia on the west; Russia on the north and northeast; China on the southeast; and Kyrgyzstan, Uzbekistan, and Turkmenistan on the south. Formerly a republic of the Soviet Union, it became an independent nation in 1991 when the Soviet Union dissolved. It has a population of 17,376,000.

Ethnic Composition

Kazakhstan is a multicultural nation. The population in 1989 numbered 39.7% Kazakh, 37.8% Russian, and 22.5% from a dozen different ethnic groups. The number of Russians, Ukrainians, Belarusians, and Germans has decreased since then. The region has been inhabited for some 5,000 years, although the ethnic groups found there today emerged as distinct entities only in the past 500 years.

Kazakhs, who number 6,535,000, emerged as a distinct group from an amalgam of tribal peoples in the 15th century. Kazakh identity was based on nomadic pastoralism. Kazakhs herded sheep, cattle, horses, and camels across large seasonal pastures. Kazakhs were organized into tribes and cooperative family work groups; they lived in yurts. Since the 15th century, they have been Muslims, although religious worship was repressed in the Soviet era. Russian and Soviet rule destroyed much of the traditional culture, and the Kazakhs were transformed into a settled, largely urban people who lived mainly by working in factories or on collective farms. Since the end of Soviet rule, there has been a reemergence of Islam and of traditional crafts, music, and art as an expression of ethnic identity. The Kazakh population is split between those who favor ethnic nationalism and the removal or displacement of non-Kazakh peoples, and those who wish only for Kazakh dominance in this multicultural nation.

The largest ethnic grouping in Kazakhstan is that of the Slavic peoples—Russians, Ukrainians, and Belarusians. **Russians** numbered 6,228,000 in 1989, or 37.8% of the population. In reaction to Kazakh efforts since 1989 to become the dominant group, several hundred thousand Russians have moved to Russia. Dominant in northern Kazakhstan for 200 years and a majority in the capital city of Alma-Ata, Russians now face the possibility of becoming a numerical and ethnic minority. Kazakh initiatives to make Kazakh the official language, to resettle Kazakhs in northern Kazakhstan, to establish employment preferences for Kazakhs, and to take control of the political system all pose threats to Russians resident in Kazakhstan. The Russians have responded by seeking laws of protection for ethnic rights and also have broached the possibility of a separate Russian region. After centuries of Russian rule, most Kazakhs are not receptive to such requests.

Ukrainians number 896,000, or 5.4% of the population. Their settlement history and current situation in Kazakhstan mirrors those of the Russians. From the viewpoint of Kazakh nationalists, the Ukrainians are considered Russians.

Belarusians number 183,000, or 1.11% of the population, They came to Kazakhstan during the era of Russian settlement and are mainly middle-class workers and professionals living in the north. Generally lumped together with the Russians by the Kazakhs, Belarusians are subject to the same hostility.

Another major ethnic minority of European origin is the **Germans,** who numbered 956,000 in 1989, or 5.8% of the population. At least 200,000 have voluntarily returned to Germany since then. Germans had originally settled in northern Kazakhstan in the 1800s as farmers, craftsmen, and government workers. In 1941 and 1942, a large population of Germans, deported from Russia for fear of collaboration with the enemy, was resettled in Siberia and Kazakhstan. As with other Europeans, the Germans settled mainly in the north, often forming homogeneous ethnic communities. While some Kazakhs would prefer to see the Germans leave, relations are not as strained as those between Kazakhs and Russians. Also, the emigration of many Germans has opened up jobs and housing for Kazakhs migrating to the north.

Like the Germans who arrived in the 20th century, there are additional ethnic groups whose settlement in Kazakhstan and other Central Asian republics was forced by the Soviet government in the 1930s and 1940s. **Koreans** (103,000) make up .6% of the population. They are descendants of Koreans who first settled in eastern Siberia in the 1860s and then in 1937 were forcibly relocated to Central Asia. The survivors of this relocation were farmers, but now Koreans are mainly urban professionals, a sizable number of whom have joined the Communist Party and speak Russian. At the same time, a strong Korean identity is maintained through clubs, newspapers, language schools for children, and marriage within the group. Adherence to Confucianism, Buddhism, and Korean folk religions, however, has eroded in Kazakhstan, and most Koreans are nonbelievers. The Koreans enjoy peaceful relations with the Kazakhs and other groups.

Meskhetians are Islamic peoples from a region that is part of southern Georgia and northern Armenia. In 1944, they were deported by Stalin to Kazakhstan, Uzbekistan, and Kyrgyzia. The name is derived from the Meshki Turks, one of the deported populations. Only in the 1960s did they emerge as a united group, largely in reaction to their deportation and virtual captivity in Central Asia. The object of discrimination and violence, including two murders in 1989, they are all trying to leave Central Asia. They number about 160,000–260,000 in Azerbaijan, 14,000 in central Russia, and an undetermined number in the Central Asian republics. The Meskhetians' request to immigrate to Turkey or resettle in Georgia has been refused by each of the two governments.

Poles number about 60,000 and are mainly descendants of Poles forcibly resettled in Central Asia in the 1930s and 1940s. A small group in comparison to the Russians and Germans, their conflict with the Kazakhs is less pronounced.

Tatars number 328,000, or 2% of the population. Tatar is an imprecise label, which in the most general sense refers to people of Muslim or Turkic ancestry who have been present in Russia, Siberia, and Central Asia since the 13th century. Most Tatars in Kazakhstan are **Crimean Tatars,** forcibly resettled in Central Asia during World War II. Their total population in the Soviet Union was 6.7 million. Tatar adherence to Islam and the small number of Tatars in Kazakhstan make for peaceful relations between Kazakhs and Tatars. There is no Tatar movement for autonomy in Kazakhstan as there is in some other regions where Tatars live.

There are a number of other Muslim groups in addition to the Kazakhs and Tatars. The **Dungans** (about 22,000) live in southeastern Kazakhstan. They are descendants of Chinese Muslims (Hui) who fled persecution by both the Manchu and Chinese in China in the 1880s. Their settlement in Central Asia was encouraged by the Russians who wanted to displace Kazakhs and obtain allies against the Chinese. The Muslim Dungans manage their own farming communities, and consider themselves a distinct, non-Chinese ethnic group. Relations with the Russians and Kazakhs are distant, though peaceful.

Uighurs in Kazakhstan number 185,000, or 1.1% of the population. In the nations of former Soviet Central Asia, they number about 300,000 and in China 7 million. Uighurs live mainly in an autonomous region in southeastern Kazakhstan where they have been highly successful farmers in a desert environment. Living on the Chinese border, they have at times been caught in the middle of Soviet-China border disputes. As devout Muslims with little traditional culture surviving, they maintain ties to the wider Islamic community in the Middle East.

Uzbeks number 332,000, or 2% of the population, and live mainly near the Uzbekistan border (*see* Uzbekistan).

Other groups include several thousand **Jews, Kyrgyz, Tajiks, Turkmens, Greeks, Kurds, Turks,** and **Mordvins.**

Ethnic Relations

In the early 1700s, some Kazakh tribes turned to Russia for help in warding off invaders.

Since that time, Russians and other Slavic peoples have been a major presence in the region, and Kazakh-Russian relations have varied from strained to violent. Beginning in the mid-1700s, the Russians began moving Russian, Ukrainian, and other settlers into northern Kazakh territory, eventually displacing Kazakh nomadic herders and forcing them to relocate to the south. Herding was difficult there, and many had to switch to farming. A revolt against the Russians in 1916, the Russian Revolution of 1917, and the famine of 1921–22 took hundreds of thousands of lives and drastically reduced the Kazakh population, further strengthening Russian influence. From the 1930s on, the Soviet government displaced, resettled, and collectivized the Kazakhs. At the same time, more Slavs were brought into the region, pasturage was converted to agricultural use, and factories were built. In the 1940s, various ethnic groups in the USSR thought by Stalin to be disloyal to Russia were forcibly deported to Kazakhstan and other Central Asian republics. All of these developments resulted in a decrease in the ethnic Kazakh population and an increase in the size of other groups. By 1959 the Kazakhs constituted only 30% of the population.

Russian emerged as the lingua franca for the region and a two-tier division of labor developed, with Russians and other Slavs holding middle-class administrative and skilled jobs, while the Kazakhs formed the working class. At the same time, Kazakhs maintained control of the political structure, especially in the south where Russians were less numerous. The breakup of the Soviet Union beginning in the late 1980s unleashed considerable ethnic conflict in Kazakhstan. While some hostility was directed at small groups such as the Chechens, most was aimed at the Russians, as Kazakh leaders sought to take control of the nation. A new language law made Kazakh the official language, although few Russians could speak it. Preferences in housing and employment were awarded to Kazakhs, and Germans and other ethnic groups were made to feel unwelcome. Kazakh political parties emerged, and hundreds of thousands of Russians, Ukrainians, and Germans left for their homelands. The attitude of many Kazakhs was summed up in the saying: "We bid farewell to Germans and shake hands with them; we turn Russians out by kicking their backs." At this point, the basic issue is whether Kazakhstan will remain a multiethnic nation or will become essentially Kazakh.

Kiribati

K iribati, formerly known as the Gilbert Islands, is a small island nation composed of 16 inhabited islands in the Micronesian region of the Pacific Ocean. Under British control from 1892 to 1940, Kiribati was controlled by Japan during World War II. It became an independent nation in 1979. The population of the nation is almost 100% Kiribati.

Kiribati number 81,000 on the islands. The ancestors of the current residents arrived at least 1,400 years ago from Melanesia to the south. Kiribati speak and write Gilbertese, and many are fluent in English as well. The economy is based mainly on fishing, and many Kiribati men are trained as seamen and work in the German shipping industry. The remittances they send home are an important contribution to the economy. About 53% are Roman Catholics, 41% are Protestant, and the remainder are Seventh-Day Adventists, Baha'i, Church of God, or Mormon.

Banabans, who number several thousand, inhabit Banaba, an island part of the nation to the west of Kiribati. The Banabans are culturally quite similar to the Kiribati but consider themselves as a separate political unit. Banabans have moved in great numbers to Fiji.

Kuwait

K uwait, located at the northern end of the Persian Gulf, is bordered by Iraq on the north and Saudi Arabia on the west. The nation's territory consists of the mainland and nine offshore islands. Kuwait has a population of 1.2 million. The official language is Arabic. Kuwait is heavily dependent on oil exports, and the citizens of Kuwait enjoy a high quality of life based on oil revenues. In 1990, Kuwait became the center of international attention when it was occupied by troops from Iraq, which claimed sovereignty over the region. In the Gulf War of 1991, a coalition of forces led by the United States expelled the Iraqis.

Ethnic Composition and Ethnic Relations

Like its neighbors, Kuwait is a multiethnic state. About 45% of the population are **Arab Kuwaitis,** 35% are Arabs from other nations of the Middle East, and the remainder are foreign workers from Asia, Europe, and North America. These figures are only estimates, because the Gulf War and efforts by the government to end its dependence on foreign labor have altered the ethnic composition of the population in the 1990s.

Arabs, an ethnic group indigenous to the Middle East, are the majority population in 15 nations of the Middle East and North Africa. The emergence of Arabs as a distinct group in the region dates to at least 853 B.C. when the Arabic language was already in use. Although being an "Arab" has different meanings in different nations, a shared Arab identity is based on a number of key elements. These include the Arabic language, both the classical form found in religion and literature, as well as the varieties of colloquial Arabic spoken in daily life; personal identification with Arab culture, history, and the Arab community; value placed on children and family life; division of labor based on gender; and adherence to Islam. About 93% of Arabs around the world follow Islam. However, not all Muslims are Arabs, and the largest Muslim populations are found in the non-Arab nations of Bangladesh, Indonesia, and India.

Arabs native to Kuwait share a strong sense of **Kuwaiti** identity. At the same time, there are important divisions within the Arab population. About 80% are **Sunni Muslims** and 20% are **Shi'ite Muslims.** Some Shi'ite groups

maintain ties to the Iraqi Shi'ite minority across the border in southern Iraq. Other Shi'ites are not actually Arabs but Persians from Iran, who maintain ties to the Shi'ite community in Iran. The tensions between the two populations are now overshadowed by tensions resulting from the rise of Islamic fundamentalism.

The discovery of oil in 1938, and the post–World War II development of the oil industry, created a need for managers, technicians, and workers, both in the oil industry and in the growing government bureaucracy, in educational institutions, and in commerce and associated industries. Because the native population was small, uneducated, and unskilled, and because women were not permitted to work outside the home, the government turned to foreign workers—managers and technicians from **Europe** and **the United States** and workers from other Arab nations **(Jordan, Syria, Palestine, Lebanon,** and **Egypt).** Until 1991, the majority of the imported personnel were Palestinians, who numbered as many as 350,000, and Egyptians. The Iraqi invasion and the Gulf War, however, caused most foreign workers to flee, and, because the Palestinians sided with Iraq, most have not returned. In the 1980s, to limit the number of non-Kuwaiti Arabs in the country, Kuwait began to encourage the immigration of laborers from Asia, mainly from **India** and **Pakistan.** They now form the majority of the guest-worker population.

Foreign workers are not citizens of Kuwait. It is virtually impossible for a non-Arab to become a citizen. Foreign workers are expected to return home after their labor contract expires. Because they are not citizens, they cannot vote, own land, or join labor unions. The relationship between Kuwaitis and foreign workers is one of hostility. The workers resent their second-class status, while the Kuwaitis are concerned about the sizable number of these workers and the pressures they place on the social welfare system. Although development of the school system has produced an educated population, many Kuwaitis do not yet have the skills for technical positions or the experience for managerial positions, much less the desire for manual labor. Thus, Kuwait has been unable to reduce its dependency on foreign labor.

Kyrgyzstan

The Republic of Kyrgyzstan is a Central Asian nation bordered by Kazakhstan on the north, China on the east, Tajikistan on the south, and Uzbekistan on the west. It has a population of 4.5 million. Kyrgyz is the official language, although Russian continues to be used, especially in business and foreign commerce. About 75% of the population is Muslim, and the remainder are Christians or nonbelievers. Kyrgyzstan was conquered by Russia in 1864, became a Soviet republic in 1926, and achieved independence in 1991 following the demise of the Soviet Union.

Ethnic Composition

Kyrgyzstan is an ethnically heterogeneous nation. The Kyrgyz are the numerical majority, although minority groups constitute almost 50% of the population. In the post-Soviet era, the Kyrgyz percentage of the population has increased while the percentage of non-Kyrgyz is decreasing due to the emigration of the Slavic population. Russians continue to constitute the major minority. Other Central Asian Muslim groups form much of the remainder of the non-Kyrgyz population.

Kyrgyz (Khirgiz, Khirghiz) numbered 2,228,482 in the 1989 census, or about 50% of the population. There are also several hundred thousand Kyrgyz in Afghanistan, Pakistan, and China. The Kyrgyz entered the region in the 16th century, probably from Mongolia. Through wars with neighboring Turkic tribes, especially the Uzbeks, the modern boundaries of Kyrgyzstan were established. The Kyrgyz remain to some extent a nomadic, pastoral people who raise sheep, goats, horses, and cattle. Today, they are divided culturally into the northern and southern groups. The northern Kyrgyz, sheltered from outside control by the high mountains in the region, have continued to maintain the nomadic pastoral culture far longer than the Kyrgyz in the south. Even after the Russians and Soviets altered the economy and forced many Kyrgyz to live in settled communities and work on collective farms, those in the north continued for at least part of the year to live the traditional lifestyle. Kyrgyz in the south live in the fertile farming region of the Farghona Valley and in the cities of Bishek and Osh where less of the traditional way of life survives. Many there speak Russian, while Kyrgyz remains the major language in the north. Russians and Uzbeks live in the south as well. Islam came to the region in the 9th century, and, despite Russian and Soviet efforts to repress it, Islam remains a major force in Kyrgyz life. The southern Kyrgyz area was an important center of Islam in the past, and the Throne of Sulieman remains a major pilgrimage site for Central Asian Muslims, second only to Mecca itself. Although Kyrgyz in the north are now adherents of Islam, they converted later and many traditional religious practices, including shamanistic healing, coexist alongside Islam.

Like other nations in the area, Kyrgyzstan has a significant population of Central Asian ethnic groups. The major national groups are **Uzbeks** (550,095), **Kazakhs** (37,318), and **Tajiks** (33,842). These peoples are also Muslims and lived under Russian control for 150 years. Nationalist movements have developed in all these groups in the post-Soviet era. Two Central Asian Muslim groups that do not have an ethnic homeland in Kyrgyzstan are the Dungans and Uighurs.

The **Dungans** number about 27,000. They are descendants of Chinese Muslims (Hui) who fled persecution by the Manchu and Chinese in China in the 1880s. Dungan settlement was encouraged by the Russians, who wanted to displace Kyrgyz and obtain allies against the Chinese. The Muslim Dungans manage their own farming communities and consider themselves a distinct, non-Chinese ethnic group.

Uighurs number about 100,000 in Kyrgyzstan, about 200,000 in other Central Asian nations, and about seven million in China. As they live on the border, they were at times caught in the middle of Soviet-China border disputes. As devout Muslims and with little of the traditional culture surviving in some regions, they maintain ties to the wider Islamic community in the Middle East.

One other major Muslim group is the **Tatars,** who number 70,000 in Kyrgyzstan. Tatar is an imprecise label, which in the most general sense refers to people of Muslim or Turkic ancestry who have been present in the region since the 13th century. Some Tatars in Kyrgyzstan are **Crimean Tatars,** forcibly resettled in Central Asia during World War II. Their total population in the former Soviet Union is 6.7 million. Their adherence to Islam and small numbers make for relatively easy ethnic relations, although those from Europe are seen as being culturally different.

There are also about 16,000 **Azerbaijanis** in Kyrgyzstan.

In addition to other Central Asian Muslim groups, Kyrgyz territory has been inhabited by a sizable European minority dating from the Russian conquest in the 19th century. The largest group is the **Russians,** who numbered 916,500, or 22% of the population, in 1989. Their number has been decreasing, however, because many are returning to Russia following the demise of the Soviet Union. The Russians are primarily an urban population, heavily involved in business, government, and industry. They speak Russian (not Kyrgyz), attend Russian schools, and identify with Russian Orthodoxy if they are believers. Few made any effort to assimilate into Kyrgyz society,

resulting in hardships in the now independent nation.

Smaller populations from the European regions of the former Soviet Union are the **Ukrainians** (108,800), **Belarusians** (9,200), **Armenians** (3,975), and **Moldovans** (1,875). Their lives too are now uncertain in the independent Kyrgyzstan, and many are returning to their homelands.

Another European minority is the **Germans,** who now number less than 100,000, many having immigrated to Germany or Russia. Germans first settled in southern Kyrgyzstan in the 1800s as farmers, craftsmen, and government workers. In 1941 and 1942, a large population of ethnic Germans was deported from Russia, for fear of their collaboration with Hitler's invading Germans, and this groups was resettled in Central Asia. Most went to Kazakhstan, but some came to Kyrgyzstan as well. The voluntary departure of these Germans has opened up jobs and housing for the Kyrgyz.

Ethnic Relations

Ethnic relations in Kyrgyzstan, as in the rest of Central Asia, reflect long-standing ethnic conflict among the region's major national groups, particularly in light of the history of Russian domination there since the mid-19th century. Although Islam creates some sense of unity across national boundaries, the end of Soviet control has raised concerns about conflict between the nations over both borderlands and political sovereignty. Although no major wars have yet occurred, ethnic tensions have led to violence between national majorities and ethnic minorities across Central Asia. In Kyrgyzstan, this has involved violence between ethnic Kyrgyz and the Uzbeks in southern Kyrgyzstan, a region rich in valuable farmland but suffering from high unemployment and substandard housing. The mix of the two large Kyrgyz and Uzbek populations in the region is considered by some experts a situation ripe for continuing ethnic violence.

During the period of Russian (and later Soviet) rule, the Kyrgyz were subject to the full range of Russification and Sovietization—repression of Islam, substitution of the Russian language for Kyrgyz, rewriting of Kyrgyz history to reflect Communist ideology, collectivization of farming and herding, and Moscow-based control of the government. Beginning in the late 1980s and continuing since independence in 1991, Kyrgyz leaders have moved to end Russian domination and to develop a stronger sense of Kyrgyz national identity. Kyrgyz is now the national language,

Kyrgyz literature has been revived, the name of the capital has been changed from Frunze to Bishkek, and many Russians have returned to Russia. While the majority of Kyrgyz favor an Islamic state with greater rights for the Kyrgyz, there is a strong minority political movement that continues to work for ethnic equality and to protect the rights of all minorities.

Laos

T he Lao People's Democratic Republic is a landlocked nation in Southeast Asia, bordered by Myanmar and China on the north, Vietnam on the east, Cambodia on the south, and Thailand on the west. Laos was first settled by tribal peoples later displaced or absorbed by the Lao, who came as part of a larger migration of Tai-speaking peoples from the north in the 8th century. By the 14th century, the region had emerged as a distinct political entity. During the 18th century, it came under the control of Thailand and in the 19th century under the control of France, as part of French Indochina. After Japan took the region from France in World War II, Laos slowly moved toward independence, which was achieved in 1954. Since then, the government has experienced considerable instability, and economic development has lagged behind that of its neighbors. Laos now remains one of the poorest nations in the world. Since 1975, it has been ruled by a Communist government closely aligned with Vietnam, although ties to the West have increased since the late 1980s. The population of Laos is 4,975,000, a sizable increase from the 3,571,616 reported in the 1985 census. Lao is the official language, and about 85% of the population are Theravada Buddhists.

Ethnic Composition

According to official counts, 48 ethnic groups exist in Laos, although some experts suggest there are as many as 68 different groups. This difference in count is due to disagreements about whether some small groups are distinct groups or are subgroups of larger groups. The 48 names used below were adopted in 1995, although the population figures come from the 1985 census. Based on language, these 48 groups can be divided into three general categories. The **Lao Loum** category includes those who speak Lao-Tai languages and constitutes 67% of the national population. The largest and most important Lao Loum group is the Lao. The Lao and Thai peoples are culturally closely related, and there is actually a larger Lao population in Thailand, where they are called the Lao Isan, than there is in Laos. The label "Lao Loum" is also used for the low-

land peoples of Laos, who are mainly Lao speakers and live by growing wet rice in the Mekong and other river valleys. They are Theravada Buddhists.

Lao Loum Groups

Group	Population
Lao	1,804,101
Phou Thay (Phu Tai)	441,497
Leu (Lue)	102,760
Nyouan (Nhuon)	33,940
Yang	3,447
Xèk (Saek)	2,459

The second major linguistic-based category is the **Lao Theung,** who constitute 23% of the population of Laos. The Lao Theung groups are mostly tribal peoples who lived in Southeast Asia prior to the arrival of the Thai, Lao, and Vietnamese who absorbed or displaced them. Many Lao Theung groups are found in Vietnam, Thailand, and southern China, as well as in Laos. They speak Mon-Khmer languages and have lived largely apart from mainstream Lao society, which is centered in the lowlands. Considered "backward" by the Lao, many subsist by dry-rice cultivation in semipermanent fields. They live in small village communities while continuing to practice their traditional religions. Some have been involved in the opium trade.

Lao Theung Groups

Group	Population
Kam Mou (Khmu)	389,964
Ka Tang (Katang)	72,391
Ma Kong (Makong)	70,382
Xouay (Souei)	49,059
La Ven (Laven)	28,057
Ta Oy (Ta-oi)	24,577
Ta Liang (Taliang)	23,665
Try (Chli)	20,902
Phong	18,165
La Vè (Lavae)	16,433
Ka Tou (Katu)	14,676
La Met (Lamet)	14,355
Thin (Htin)	13,977
A Lak (Alak)	13,217
Pa Ko (Pakoh)	12,923
Oy (Oi)	11,194
Ngè (Ngae)	8,971
Cheng	4,540
Nya Heun (Nhaheun)	3,960
Yè (Yae)	3,376
Sam Tao (Samtao)	2,359
Xing Moun (Singmun)	2,164
Toum (Tum)	2,042
Mon	2,022
Bit	1,530
Ngouan	988
La Vy (Lavi)	584
Sa Dang (Sadang)	520
Kha Mè (Khmer)	169
Kry (Kri)	31
Yumbri	24

The third major linguistic category is the **Lao Sung,** composed of groups in the north, who speak languages also spoken in neighboring Myanmar and China. Lao Sung are the most recent arrivals in Laos, having migrated south only about 200 years ago. Like their hill tribe neighbors, they are primarily dry rice farmers and have maintained their traditional beliefs.

Lao Sung Groups

Group	Population
Mong (Hmong)	231,168
Ko (Kaw, Akha)	58,500
Phou Noy (Phu Noi)	23,618
Yao (Mien)	18,091
Mou Xoe (Museu)	9,200
Kuy (Lahu)	6,493
Ho (Haw, Chinese)	6,361
Sy La (Sila)	1,518
Lo Lo (Lolo)	842
Ha Nhy (Ha-nhi)	727

In addition to these three major categories, Laos also has about 10,000 **Chinese,** mainly traders living in cities and towns, and a **Vietnamese** population.

Ethnic Relations

Little is known about the nature of ethnic relations in Laos. In the 1990s, the government is trying to establish a definitive list of the ethnic groups in the nation as well as objective criteria for distinguishing among these groups. A basic division, as elsewhere in Southeast Asia, is between the numerically dominant lowlanders—the Lao—and the hill tribes. It is the Lao, involved in national politics and economic development, with whom Westerners come in contact. The hill tribes—perhaps more so than in other South Asian nations—continue to live in relative isolation because of Laos's slow economic development.

Lebanon

Lebanon is located in the Middle East. It is bordered by Syria on the north and east, Israel on the south, and the Mediterranean Sea on the west. Until it became an independent nation in 1920, Lebanon was often affiliated with Syria, having also been a part of the Roman, Byzantine, Mongol, and Ottoman empires in the past. From 1920 to 1941, Lebanon was administered by France. For 15 years, beginning in 1975, Lebanon was devastated by a civil war that pitted various religious and political groups against one another. Israel and Syria were heavily involved in this conflict. Although relative peace was restored in 1991, the Christian minority now perceives itself to be discriminated against by the Muslim majority. Israel occupies a buffer zone in southern Lebanon, from where some Palestinian refugees continue to launch terrorist attacks against Israel. Lebanon's government is largely controlled by the Syrian government. Thus, Lebanon continues to experience considerable political and social unrest. Lebanon has a population of about 3.8 million. Arabic and French are the official languages.

Ethnic Composition

Lebanon is an ethnically homogeneous nation, Arabs forming 95% of the population. Deep divisions along religious, tribal, and political lines, however, make this ethnic homogeneity irrelevant to group relations in Lebanon. In the most general sense, Lebanese society can be divided into two major religious groupings— Muslim and Christian—with Arabs the majority in both populations. There has been no census of ethnic or religious groups since 1932, although it is now believed that Muslims form about 70% of the population and Christians 30%. For many Muslims and Christians, family ties through lineages, clans, and tribes are more salient markers of their identity than are religion or Lebanese national identity.

The Muslim population numbers about 2.7 million, if the 70% estimate is correct. It is made up of three major religious groups: Shi'ites, Sunnis, and Druze. **Shi'ite Muslims** believe that the leader of Islam should be a direct descendant of the founder of Islam, Muhammad the prophet, through his son-in-law Ali. In Lebanon, Shi'ites form about 60% of the Muslim population and 40% of the general population. Despite their numerical superiority, they have long been the poorest and least influential of the major groups. Most live in the south or in Beirut, where many fled during the civil war.

Sunni Muslims differ from Shi'ites in their beliefs about the proper leaders of Islam. Although Sunnis constitute the majority of Muslims in the world, they make up only about 30% of the Muslim population in Lebanon. They live mainly in the cities of Beirut and Sidon and are active in commerce, business, and government.

The **Druze** (*see* Israel) are a distinct Islamic sect, not accepted by Shi'ite and Sunni Muslims as true Muslims. They constitute about 10% of the Muslim population in Lebanon and maintain a close-knit community centered on the leadership of two prominent Druze families.

Other Muslim groups include small populations of **Kurds, Alawites,** and **Ismailis.**

Christians now form about 30% of the population of Lebanon. This is a marked decrease from the 50% figure earlier in the century. It is the result of both a higher birth rate among Muslims, and emigration by Christians. Most Christians are Arabs, the largest non-Arab group being the Armenians. The most politically and economically significant Christian group is the **Maronites,** about 75% of the Christian population. Maronites are a Christian sect that split from the Eastern Christians of the Byzantine Empire in the 5th century. They managed to preserve their community from both Byzantine and Muslim influence by taking refuge in the mountainous region of Mt. Lebanon. Some Maronites became formally linked to the Roman Catholic church in Rome in 1736, although ties between the groups date from the 12th century. The Maronites have been closely aligned with the French, and many adopted the French language and culture. Although a largely rural people, Maronites were the dominant political and economic group until the civil war of 1975. In the 1990s, their numbers having been reduced, they see themselves as unable to compete politically with the Muslims.

The second largest Christian group is the **Greek Orthodox,** a branch of the Eastern Orthodox Church. They number about 100,000. Greek Orthodox families are members of Lebanon's business elite. They stress their Arab identity and maintain ties with other Greek Orthodox populations in the Middle East.

The third major Christian group is the **Greek Catholics,** who separated from the Greek Orthodox Church in the 18th century and affiliated with the Roman Catholic Church. Mainly a rural population, they number about 75,000. Despite their tie to Rome, many of the Greek Catholic rites remain similar to those of the Greek Orthodox community. The Greek Catholics also stress their Arab identity.

Other Christian groups in Lebanon are the **Roman Catholics** (whose population in the past was primarily European), **Protestants,** and adherents of the Jacobite, Chaldean, and Nestorian sects. The major non-Arab Christian group is the **Armenians,** numbering nearly 175,000 earlier in the century but now far less because of immigration to Armenia. Armenians arrived in Lebanon as refugees from Turkey during and after World War I. Involved in business activities in Beirut and northern Lebanon, they have been able to avoid deep involvement in the civil war. They are members of the Armenian Apostolic Church, founded in the early 4th century.

In addition to these religious groups, the other prominent group in Lebanon is the **Palestinians.** Palestinians are an indigenous people of Palestine (now Israel). Most current residents came to Lebanon around the time of the 1948 Israel-Arab war or were born in Lebanon. Others have arrived in Lebanon since 1948 from other Middle Eastern nations. Official estimates place their population at 328,000, although they may number over 400,000. Most Palestinians lived in refugee camps and settlements in the south of Lebanon. Destruction caused by the civil war, Israeli raids, and Palestinian factional disputes have led many of them to move north, and they now make up a large, poor minority in and around Beirut. The Palestinians are split into a number of political factions, including those who support the Palestine Liberation Organization (PLO), those aligned with Syria, and those with ties to Iran.

Ethnic Relations

When Lebanon became an independent nation, a pluralistic society—with all major religious groups represented in government—was envisioned. This idea prevailed even after the end of the civil war in 1990. Christians and Muslims each held 50% of the legislative seats; the president was bound by the constitution to be a Maronite and the prime minister was required to be a Muslim. However, constitutional changes have given the prime minister more power and lessened the role of the president, thereby increasing Muslim power and weakening that of the Christians. These developments, coupled with the decreasing number of Christians and burgeoning number of Muslims, have led many Christians to see themselves as a politically weak minority in a nation they view as their homeland, and which they once controlled. Although the causes of the civil war are complex, the loss of power in the Christian communities was certainly one factor. The civil war also destroyed the considerable mixing of groups—in neighborhoods, villages, and business—that was a characteristic of Lebanese society. Instead, in the 1990s, most groups live in their own urban neighborhoods or villages. The Palestinians are regarded by many Lebanese—both Christian and Muslim—as outsiders, and the hope is that they will eventually leave Lebanon and move elsewhere. Not surprisingly, the Palestinians believe themselves a victimized minority.

Malaysia

M alaysia, located in Southeast Asia, is physically divided into two regions. Peninsular, or Western, Malaysia is located at the southern tip of mainland Southeast Asia and is bordered by Thailand on the north, the South China Sea on the east, and the Straits of Malacca on the west and south. The island of Sumatra, which is part of Indonesia, lies off the west coast. The Malaysian provinces of Sabah and Sarawak occupy the northern section of the island of Borneo to the east of Peninsular Malaysia. The remainder of Borneo belongs to Indonesia and Brunei. From the early 16th century on, what is now Malaysia was successively under Portuguese, Dutch, and British control and did not become independent until 1963. Malaysia has a population of 19.95 million. Bahasa Malaysian is the official language and the lingua franca for the nation; Chinese, English, and various indigenous languages are spoken as well. Malays began converting to Islam in the 15th century through contact with Muslim traders from Arabia. Today Islam is the official religion, although other religions including Hinduism, Confucianism, Buddhism, and Christianity are practiced as well.

Ethnic Composition

Malaysia is an ethnically heterogeneous nation. This heterogeneity is largely the result of British colonial policies dating from 1874 that encouraged emigration from South Asia and China, thus adding large numbers of Indians and Chinese to a population already composed of Malays, Chinese, and indigenous peoples. The current population may be divided into six major ethnic categories: (1) Malays; (2) Chinese; (3) South Asians; (4) indigenous peoples of Peninsular Malaysia; (5) indigenous peoples of Sabah and Sarawak; and (6) recent immigrants.

Malays number about 11.7 million and constitute from 59% to 62% of the population. Malays consider themselves, and the indigenous peoples already present when the Malays arrived, to be the indigenous population of Malaysia, in contrast to the Chinese and South Asians who arrived later. At one time Malays were called **Bumiputra,** meaning sons of the soil, although the label is no longer commonly used. The Malays began migrating from south-central Asia about 2,000 years ago and settled much of southern Southeast Asia, insular Southeast Asia, and islands in the Pacific. Malays in the interior were primarily farmers, while those on the coast were involved in trade, primarily with the Chinese and Arabs. A number of distinct Malay-ruled states developed and then succumbed to Portuguese, Dutch, and

British rule. The Malays resisted forced labor on the rubber plantations and in the tin mines, leading the British to import laborers from China and India. In the 15th century, Muslim traders brought Islam to Malaysia and today virtually all Malays are Sunni Muslims. Al-

Muslims praying at the Jamek Mosque, the oldest mosque in Kuala Lumpur, Malaysia. Photo: Reuters/Corbis-Bettmann.

though many Malays are involved in commerce, industry, and government, they remain a largely rural people and subsist by growing rice for sale and by fishing. In addition to the urban-rural distinction, other important markers of Malay subgroup identity are place of birth—Malays from some states, such as Kelantan, consider themselves a distinct subgroup—social class, and descent from the traditional Malay aristocracy, which ruled the states prior to European colonization.

Chinese in Malaysia number about six million and constitute from 30% to 32% of the population. Chinese have been coming to Malaysia for as long as, if not longer than, the Malays. However, prior to the late 19th century they were a small population mainly involved in the regional trade network. Many of the early Chinese settlers assimilated into Malay society and their descendants are considered a distinct Chinese subgroup called the **Baba Chinese.** Most Chinese settlers came in the late 1800s under British auspices to work on the plantations and in the tin mines. Although they came mainly from southern China, they formed a diverse population in which at least six different Chinese languages were spoken and ties to family and community remained more important than any sense of pan-Chinese identity. In the last half of the 20th century, Mandarin Chinese has become the lingua franca for the Chinese in Malaysia, and intermarriage across language groups has become more common. Thus, the Chinese in Malaysia are now a more unified ethnic group than in the past. Most Chinese continue to practice a mix of Confucianism, Buddhism, and ancestor worship. The major division within the population is based on social class, with middle- and upper-class Chinese tending to affiliate with Malays and Indians of the same class, rather than with working-class Chinese.

South Asians number about 1.5 million and constitute about 8% or 9% of the population. The majority (about 70%) are Hindu Tamils from Tamil Nadu State in southeastern India. There are also communities of Sikhs from the Punjab region of northwestern India, Pakistanis and Bangladeshis who are Muslims, and Sri Lankans. Most South Asians arrived in the late 19th century and early 20th century, re-

cruited by the British to work on plantations and construction projects, and in low-level government positions because they arrived speaking English. Indians continue to hold many government jobs and are also found in the professions, the communications industry, and commerce.

The indigenous peoples of Peninsular Malaysia are collectively labeled the **Orang Asli,** meaning "original people." They live mainly in the rain forests of the interior region and in southern Thailand. They were more widely distributed before the arrival of Malays, who pushed them into the interior. The Orang Asli category includes a number of distinct cultural groups including the **Semang, Semai, Senoi, Temiar, Jah Hut, Che Wong, Semalai,** and **Btsisi.** They number about 70,000 in total. These peoples traditionally lived in small villages and subsisted through hunting and gathering, fishing, or slash-and-burn growing of cassava, rice, and other crops, or some combination of these three subsistence activities. As discussed below, the groups have come under pressure from the government and developers in recent years and now vary widely in the degree to which their traditional cultures survive.

The indigenous peoples of Sarawak are defined in the constitution of Malaysia as the **Bidayuh, Bukitan, Bisayah, Dusun, Iban, Kedayan, Kelabit, Kanyan, Kenyah, Kajang, Lugat, Lisum, Malay, Melanau, Murut, Penan, Sian, Tagal, Tabun,** and **Ukit.** They are often lumped together under the general label **Dayak,** with a further division into those living near the coast—Malays and Melanau—and those living in the interior. In total, they number (not including the Malays) about 550,000 and constitute about 40% of the regional population; the Chinese, Malays, and Indians comprising the other 60%. Although there is variation across the groups, they are similar in their growing of rice, their residence in long houses (with each house forming a community of families), and their adherence to *adat,* the traditional law and customs now under attack by the forces of economic and political change that seek to exploit the rich natural resources of their homeland.

A girl of the Iban tribe. The Iban are one of a number of ethnic groups indigenous to Sarawak that are feeling the impact of Malaysian economic growth.
Photo: Corel Corp.

Recent immigrants, most of whom are in Malaysia illegally, are primarily **Thais, Filipinos,** and **Indonesians.** Their number is unknown, but estimates run as high as one million. They are attracted to Malaysia by the growing economy and the resulting opportunity for employment. Most work in construction, on plantations, or as domestics. The Indonesians tend to live throughout Malaysia, the Thais near Thailand, and the Filipinos in the south and on Borneo. Due to similarities in religion (the Filipinos and Indonesians are Muslims), language, and culture, the immigrants from all three groups fit easily into Malaysian society.

In addition to these groups, Malaysia has other, small ethnic populations. These include **Javanese** and **Bugis** from Indonesia; **Europeans** and **North Americans** involved in commerce, industry, and trade; and a few thousand **Sea People (Orang Laut),** who traditionally lived on boats in the seas off the coasts of Malaysia and Thailand but in recent decades have been forced to live in settled communities.

Ethnic Relations

Ethnic relations in Malaysia center on two issues. First, Malaysians desire to create a single nation from a multiethnic society that had been under European influence for hundreds of years. Second, they want to balance the needs of the indigenous peoples on the peninsula and on Borneo with the desire for rapid economic growth through the exploitation of natural resources.

The Malaysian society that existed at the time of independence in 1963 was largely a British creation. The two major nonindigenous groups—the Chinese and Indians—had been imported by the British and fulfilled a British-created social order in which each group lived in a different place and worked in different sections of the economy. In order to control widespread revolts, the British made no attempt to create a unified nation and instead fostered ethnic hostility by promulgating ethnic stereotypes, which survive to this day—Malays are labeled as lazy and Chinese are said to be money-hungry. The fact that Malays, as rural farmers, were poorer than the Chinese and Indians made many fear that widespread ethnic conflict might erupt when independence was achieved. Although there was violence between Malays and Chinese in Singapore (then part of Malaysia) in 1963 and riots in the capital city of Kuala Lumpur in 1969, ethnic conflict did not become a serious problem. This was due in part to the provisions of the 1957 constitution, in which leaders of the Malay and Chinese communities promoted both Malay identity and Malay cultural autonomy, while protecting the rights of the Chinese and other minorities. Thus, Malays are given preference in education and government employment to raise their economic status, Islam is the official religion but other religions are allowed, and Bahasa Malaysian is the national language but other languages are allowed to be taught. To open the economy to Malays, an economic plan was instituted in 1971 designed to increase the role of Malays as business owners and managers. These political and economic initiatives have tended to control the potential conflict between the Malays and Chinese.

The constitution of 1957 also sought to protect the rights and cultures of the indigenous peoples, but in this case economic development has come into conflict with political goals since the early 1980s. A primary objective of political and business leaders is rapid economic growth, based at least in part on the exploitation of natural resources such as timber, natural gas, and oil. Many of these resources lie in the interior forests of the peninsula and on Sarawak, where many indigenous peoples live. To exploit the resources, roads must be built, rivers dammed, and power plants erected. This economic development, plus the long-held view among Malays that the indigenous peoples are inferior, has led to the rapid destruction of the indigenous cultures, especially in the last two decades. Many groups have been driven from their land, placed in settlements, forced to practice agriculture, and now are compelled to have their educational and health needs administered by government agencies. In addition, the Malays on the peninsula have long sought to convert the indigenous peoples to Islam. Although their efforts have not yet been successful, some groups on Borneo have converted.

Maldives

The Republic of the Maldives, an island nation located south of India in the Indian Ocean, consists of over 1,200 islands, of which 201 are inhabited. It has a population of about 270,000. The islands are located on the maritime trade route from Africa and the Middle East to India and Southeast Asia and the modern nation shows influences from the numerous peoples who have stopped there over the past 2,000 years. Despite the mix of ethnic groups in the past, the Maldives today is an ethnically homogeneous society, whose population is almost entirely composed of **Divehis,** as Maldivians call themselves. Divehis are descended from Sinhalese from Sri Lanka, and Tamils and Malayali from Kerala in India, as well as Arabs and Africans. At one time, many residents were Buddhists, but in the 12th century, Islam was brought by Muslim traders, and today the entire population is Muslim. Non-Muslims are not allowed to become permanent residents. Divehis speak Divehi, a language based on Sinhala with added vocabulary from South Indian languages and Arabic. The only permanent ethnic minority is the **Giravaru,** a small group that may represent the earliest inhabitants of the island. The Giravaru view themselves as a distinct group. They are viewed as socially inferior by Divehis.

Marshall Islands

The Republic of the Marshall Islands, located in the west-central Pacific Ocean, consists of 29 atolls and 5 islands aligned in the Ratak and Ralik chains. It has a population of 58,000. Controlled in the 20th century by Germany, Japan, and the United States, it became an independent nation in 1991. Prior to American control, the islanders shared no sense of cultural or political unity and instead identified with their atoll or island community. The islands, used for the testing of atomic and nuclear weapons and missiles by the United States, were transformed by these and related activities. The populations of some atolls, such as Bikini, were forced to move elsewhere, a wage-based economy developed, and some atoll and island residents were compensated for the use of their land. This led to large income differentials whereby some people lived on their compensation payments and others continued their traditional lifestyle of fishing, collecting wild plants, and horticulture. Although people are now to a large degree integrated into the Marshalese nation and share a common political identity, the right to own land on one's native atoll or island remains an important marker of personal and group identity.

Ethnic Composition and Ethnic Relations

Nearly the entire population is **Marshalese.** The primary ethnic minorities are **Kosrae,** who are from the Federated States of Micronesia and work in the Marshall Islands; **Filipinos;** and **Americans.** Marshalese speak three dialects of Marshalese, plus English and Japanese as secondary languages. Although residents of the Marshall Islands are integrated into a wage-based economy, affiliation with one's local community remains strong, and the social system continues to be based on ties created by tracing kinship lines through one's mother. Most Marshalese are Protestants, with elements of the indigenous religions integrated into Christian belief and practice.

Mauritius

Mauritius is located east of Madagascar in the south Indian Ocean (*see* Africa map). The main island, also named Mauritius; a smaller island called Rodrigues; and several even smaller islands make up this nation. All but about 40,000 out of a population of 1.1 million live on the main island of Mauritius.

Ethnic Composition and Ethnic Relations

Mauritius has no indigenous population and is today a multiethnic society composed of Creoles, Asian Indians, Chinese, and small numbers of French and British. Mauritius is perhaps the only pluralistic nation in the world, with 4 major ethnic groups, 14 languages, 3 major religions (Hinduism, Roman Catholicism, and Islam), a social-class system, and peaceful ethnic relations (since 1968). Members of all ethnic groups participate in the institutions of Mauritian society. Conflict is mitigated by avoidance in social situations, tolerance, and compromise. Rapid economic growth has benefited all Mauritians. English is the official language and French is the literary language. However, the majority of Mauritians speak Kreol, a contact language based on French.

Creoles are people of African descent whose ancestors were brought to the islands during the period of French rule between 1715 and 1830. They constitute 27% of the population.

Asian Indians (Indo-Mauritians) are a diverse group and include Hindus from northern and southern India and Muslims. Asian Indians were brought to the islands during the period of British rule, beginning in 1814. Today they make up 67% of the population.

Chinese (Sino-Mauritians) constitute 3% of the population and are mainly merchants.

Mulattoes are people of mixed ancestry, comprising 2% of the population.

The **French (Franco-Mauritians)** and **Britons** constitute 2% of the population. The French remain economically and culturally dominant.

Micronesia, Federated States of

The Federated States of Micronesia is a nation located north of Papua New Guinea in the South Pacific Ocean. Formerly the Caroline Islands, the nation consists of the islands or island clusters of Kosrae, Pohnpei, Truk, Yap, and a few inhabited smaller islands. Some of the islands are high or volcanic islands while others are atolls. Beginning in the first half of the 19th century, the islands came under Spanish, German, Japanese, and U.S. control, until becoming independent in 1991. English is the official language, although indigenous languages are still spoken. Nearly the entire population is Christian, about half Roman Catholic and half Protestant. The national population is 125,377. Truk has the largest population of the constituent islands (over 60,000), followed by Pohnpei (over 30,000), Yap (about 15,000), and Kosrae (8,000).

Ethnic Composition and Ethnic Relations

The Federated States of Micronesia are composed of eight cultural groups: **Kapingamarangi, Kosrae, Nomoi, Pohnpei, Trukese, Ulithi, Wolea,** and the **Yap.** All but the Kapingamarangi, considered Polynesian, are classified as Micronesians. Although there are similarities in language and culture across the islands, each group—and in some cases each subgroup—continues to maintain a distinctive ethnic identity. Traditionally, the islanders have subsisted through a combination of fishing and small-scale farming with breadfruit, coconuts, and taro the primary crops. Social organization was based on family groups with authority vested in chiefs. In the late 20th century, farming and fishing remain important, but some people are now earning wages in small-scale industrial developments or are working for the government. While traditional forms of self-rule remain in place on most islands, elected leaders at the local and national level are gaining prominence. The islanders were converted by Protestant and Catholic missionaries. Religion and the local church are of major importance in community life. Separated by large differences but having a democratic form of government, the islands seem to have little ethnic conflict. Because of post–World War II ties to the Allies, there has been some migration to the United States by young people in search of education.

Mongolia

The Mongolian People's Republic is located in Asia. It is bordered by Russia on the north and China on the south. It is a distinct political entity from Inner Mongolia to the south, which is a part of China. In the 13th century, Mongolia emerged as major political power under the rule of Genghis Khan and his successors, who extended Mongol rule into China, Central Asia, the Middle East, and eastern Europe. Mongolia subsequently came under Chinese and Soviet rule. It has a population of 2.5 million.

Ethnic Composition and Ethnic Relations

Mongolia is ethnically homogeneous. About 90% of the population is composed of **Mongols** who speak the Mongol language. The largest ethnic minority in Mongolia is the **Kazakhs** followed by the **Russians** and **Chinese.** Although Mongols were Lamaist Buddhists from the 16th century on, Soviet anti-religion campaigns of the 1920s and 1930s effectively eradicated Buddhism, and most Mongols are now unaffiliated with any religion. Ethnic Mongols in Mongolia fall into three subcategories: Khalkas, Buriats, and Kalmyks. **Khalka Mongols** form about two-thirds of the Mongol population, and their dialect of the Mongol language has become the national standard. They are mainly rural people who live by herding and farming. The remaining one-third of the Mongol population is composed of **Buriats (Buryats)** and **Kalmyks (Oirots, Western Mongols).** The majority populations of both of these groups live across the border in Russia. They speak dialects closely related to Khalka Mongol and relations among all three groups are peaceful.

Kazakhs, the major ethnic minority, live in western Mongolia, near the Kazakh populations in China and Kazakhstan. Their population in Mongolia has been estimated at 4% to 6% of the total Mongolian population. Following the establishment of independent Kazakhstan in 1991, many of these Kazakhs may have migrated there. During the Soviet era, contact between Kazakh communities in Mongolia and Kazakhstan was close. Kazakhs are Muslims, many are bilingual in Kazakh and Mongolian, and many work for the government or as coal miners. Although Kazakhs in Mongolia were seen as a potential source of conflict by the government of the former Soviet Union, Kazakhs and Mongols in Kazakhstan enjoyed harmonious relations.

The number of Russians and Chinese in Mongolia is estimated at 2% each of the total population, although this estimate may not be reliable, given the ambiguous status of these groups in Mongolia. Both are mainly urban groups, involved in commerce and industry. There are also communities of Russians and Chinese along Mongolia's borders with Russia and China. Neither group is especially welcome in Mongolia, given Mongolia's long history of conflict with and rule by China and Russia. While resenting the Russian presence, Mongolia fears a takeover by China and thus sees its ties to Russia as protective. There is much hostility between Mongolians and Han Chinese in Inner Mongolia, which is part of China. There are small populations of **Tuvans, Uigurs,** and **Uzbeks** in Mongolia.

Myanmar (Burma)

M yanmar, located in Southeast Asia, is bordered on the west by the Bay of Bengal, Bangladesh, and India; on the north by Tibet; on the east by Laos and China; and on the south by Thailand. There has been no reliable census for decades; the population in 1996 was estimated at 47.5 million.

Ethnic Composition

The population of Myanmar is ethnically diverse. The politically and economically dominant Burmans constitute 68% of the population. Shan, Karen, Chinese, Mon, and other groups make up the other 32%. The Burmans live mainly in the central plains, while the minority groups live primarily in border regions. Burmese is the official language, although the ethnic minority groups use their indigenous languages domestically. About 90% of Burmese residents are Theravada Buddhists, and Muslims, who constitute about 4% of the population, are the only unified religious minority group.

Burmans number 32.3 million and tend to dominate all aspects of Myanmar life. Burmans migrated from southern China about 3,000 years ago and were the first rulers of the unified Burmese state established in 1044. Burmans speak Burmese and almost all are Theravada Buddhists, although their beliefs and practices differ in some ways from the Theravada Buddhism of nearby Thailand. Burmans are primarily wet-rice farmers. The city of Mandalay in central Myanmar remains the center of Burman culture. Although Burmans have always dominated Burmese life, their relative influence increased during the era of British rule. As leaders of the independence movement, they became the major force in political and economic affairs following independence in 1948. After a military coup in 1962, the ruling Burman leadership sought to centralize Burman control, weaken ethnic autonomy, and build the economy by exploiting both natural resources in ethnic minority regions (especially in the north) and minority labor. All ethnic minorities have resisted those efforts. The Burman government has responded with military campaigns, forced detentions, population relocations, and other repressive measures. Similar tactics have been used to control Burman political opponents. By 1995, violent ethnic conflict was largely controlled and the Burman military regime remained in power.

In addition to the Burmans, Myanmar is home to a number of other large ethnic groups, all of whom have been in the region for centuries. Most significant because of the current political situation in Myanmar are those groups involved in conflicts with the government—the Chin, Kachin, Karen, Mon, Rohingya, and Shan.

Chin peoples number 990,000 in India and Myanmar. The Chin include the Chin proper, who number anywhere from 200,000 to 400,000 in the Chin State in Myanmar, the Mizo or Lushai across the border in India, the Kuki and Hmar also in India, and the Asho in Myanmar. Present in the region since the 12th century, the Chin came under foreign rule during the British era and achieved some political autonomy following Indian and Burmese independence. However, the autonomy of the Chin has been threatened by their economic ties to neighboring peoples and by Burmese centralization policies. Some have fled to India or Thailand, while others have resisted Burman control through the Chin National Front, which seeks Chin independence. Others have entered Burmese politics and represent Chin interests in the national government.

Kachin live almost exclusively in Kachin State and northern Shan State in Myanmar, as well as in nearby regions of China, Thailand, and India. Although the majority of Kachin live in Myanmar, relocations due to the 1962 war with the Burmese government make it impossible to accurately enumerate the Kachin. They may number as many as one million in Myanmar. The Kachin have been a major participant in ethnic resistance to Burman rule in northern Myanmar (mainly through the Kachin Independence Organization) and have strongly pushed for an independent Kachin nation. In the 1980s and 1990s, this resistance produced thousands of casualties and the destruction of hundreds of Kachin villages. The conflict ended formally in 1994, but continued exploitation of Kachin labor is reported. Most Kachin are either Protestant or Catholic; a minority are Buddhist.

Karen is the general name for a number of related groups in eastern Myanmar and neighboring Thailand. About three million Karen live in Myanmar, and over 200,000 live in Thailand, including some 70,000 refugees. Major Karen subgroups are the **Sgaw, Pwo, Bwe, Pa-O, Kayah (Red),** and **White Karen.** There is much linguistic and cultural variation among these subgroups, and experts now agree that pan-Karen ethnic identity is based to a large extent on both self-identification as Karen and opposition to Burman rule. Although a majority of Karen are Buddhists, a significant minority, including many of the more assimilated Karen, are Christians. Since the mid-1960s, the Karen have been pitted against the Burmese government in an armed struggle for political autonomy. The conflict, centered in the highlands of eastern Myanmar, has also involved Karen living further west in the plains. About one dozen Karen organizations have been involved in the struggle, the Karen National Union being the largest and at times the most effective. Conflicts between Christian and Buddhist leaders have hindered pan-Karen resistance, and yet by 1995 all but one group had agreed to a cease-fire with the Myanmar government. By year's end, however, the agreements were unraveling amid charges of continuing exploitation of Karen labor. Return of the 70,000 Karen refugees from camps in Thailand is also a political issue in Thailand, because some fear that among these refugees are those most resistant to Burmese rule, and their return might threaten the peace process.

Mon number as many as 1.3 million in Myanmar and about 100,000 living as refugees across the border in Thailand. Mon live mainly in villages in the northern section of the narrow southern strip of Myanmar bordered by Thailand on the east and the Bay of Bengal on the west. The Mon have lived in this region for at least 1,000 years. They are Theravada Buddhists, many of whom are assimilated into Burmese society and have played a leading role in Burmese life. Since the 1960s, they have been excluded by the dominant Burmans, and as a result some have joined the multiethnic independence movement. The Mon region has suffered from Burmese military incursions and human rights violations. Some refugees were forcibly returned from Thailand in the 1990s. In 1995 a cease-fire formally ended hostilities.

Rohingya, also called **Arakanese** after the province where they live, are the Muslim people of western Myanmar, concentrated in the region near the border with Bangladesh. Muslims from what is now Bangladesh have come to Myanmar since the 7th century. Relations with neighboring Buddhist groups have always been tense, a situation made more complicated by the preferential treatment afforded the Rohingya by the British. In the period since independence, nearly 400,000 have been forced by the Burmese army to flee to Bangladesh. About one-half of these refugees had returned to the region by 1995. Estimates place their current population in Myanmar at about 1.5 million.

Shan is a generic label for Tai peoples of Southeast Asia outside of Thailand. In Myanmar, the Shan live in Shan State, formed after independence from Shan political units that had been present in Myanmar for 1,000 years. In the war between the Shan and the central Burmese government, which began in the 1950s, hundreds of Shan villages have been destroyed. As many as 500,000 Shan have been forced to relocate to other Shan communities or have fled across the border to Thailand. Shan goals range from complete independence from Myanmar to autonomous status within the nation. There are from three million to four million Shan in Myanmar. The Shan are mainly rice farmers and nearly all are Theravada Buddhists, although their incorporation of some indigenous beliefs distinguishes Shan Buddhism from that practiced elsewhere in Myanmar.

There are a number of other groups that have not been directly involved in the ethnic conflict in Myanmar, although some have been affected by it. The **Akha** (200,000) live mainly in villages in the mountainous eastern region bordering China, Laos, and Thailand. Akha live in these nations as well, including some 1.3 million in China, where they are called **Hani.** The Akha migrated into Myanmar and then Laos and Thailand in the 1800s, either from southern China or Tibet. They continue to practice their traditional religion, which focuses on the growing of rice and ancestor worship, although some have been converted to Christianity. As a small group, they live among the more numerous Shan and have suffered from the relocations and disruptions resulting from the Shan-Burmese conflict.

Chinese number about 700,000, making them the largest nonindigenous ethnic minority. Most emigrated from southern China and are businesspersons, traders, or small-shop owners. Few are assimilated into Burmese society and, while they speak the languages of the peoples among whom they live, most speak Chinese at home and maintain social relations only with other Chinese.

Lahu (about 150,000) live in villages throughout Shan State in eastern Myanmar near the border with China, where the majority of Lahu live.

Lisu number perhaps as many as 250,000 in Myanmar and live in the northeastern corner of the nation, near the border with China across which the majority of Lisu live. Lisu live in villages among the more populous Shan, their lives disrupted by the Shan-Burmese ethnic conflict in the region.

Nagas number several thousand in villages near the Indian border in northwestern Myanmar, and about 1,000 refugees are in India, where most Nagas live.

Palaung live in east-central and northeast Myanmar among the more numerous Shan and Kachin peoples. A small, dispersed group in a region dominated by the Shan and Kachin where ethnic conflict has reigned for over 30 years, little is known about the current status or population of the Palaung (probably about 200,000).

Wa live in villages in the mountainous region along the border with China. The number of Wa in Myanmar is unknown, although the majority of Wa live in China, where they number about 354,000.

Other groups include several thousand **Hmong** near the Chinese border, several hundred **Purum** near the Indian border, and an undetermined number of **Indians** and **Pakistanis.**

The **Moken,** also called **Sea Gypsies** or **Sea Nomads,** are a unique group. They were formerly a nomadic people who subsisted by living in boats and fishing in the waters off the coasts of Myanmar, Thailand, and Malaysia. Since the end of World War II, their way of life has changed drastically, and most now live in coastal villages and work as wage laborers. Due to the disruption of their traditional culture and their low status, social problems such as alcoholism and a high infant mortality rate are typical of many Moken communities. Moken off the coast of Myanmar have resisted assimilation more successfully than groups farther south. Some Moken still subsist by nomadic travel on outrigger canoes, living in settled villages only during part of the year. They number about 8,000.

Ethnic Relations

Myanmar (Burma) first became a sovereign nation in 1044, and since then has experienced periods of unified monarchical rule, division into independent states, incursions by neighboring nations, and British rule beginning in 1886. After independence in 1948, Myanmar became one of the most politically unstable nations in the world. Continuing attempts at both democracy and dictatorial rule have failed in the face of often violent resistance from Communists, minority ethnic groups, and protest parties. Since 1988, Myanmar has been ruled by the State Law and Order Restoration Council (SLORC), whose policy of military rule and severe repression of ethnic and religious minorities and Burman political opponents has led to widespread condemnation by other states, the United Nations, and human rights organizations such as Amnesty International and Human Rights Watch. Ethnic conflict has been a major component of the political unrest of the past 50 years and has included Burman repression of minority groups, as well as conflict between minority groups. Underlying all ethnic conflicts in Myanmar is Burman cultural, economic, and political control; Burman policies of forced labor, excessive taxation, and military rule; and Burman repression of political opponents, be they Burman or others. These ethnic conflicts have forced about 5% of Burmese to flee their homes and resettle elsewhere either in Myanmar or as refugees in neighboring China, Thailand, or Bangladesh.

Nauru

Nauru is a small, coral island located in southeast Micronesia in the Pacific Ocean. From 1896 until independence in 1968, the island was successively under German, Australian, Japanese, and United Nations administration. Foreign governments were attracted by the large phosphate deposits in the island's interior. The proceeds of phosphate sales have made Nauru one of the wealthiest nations in the region.

Ethnic Composition and Ethnic Relations

Despite the small population of 11,000, the island is a multiethnic nation composed of Nauruans, other Pacific Islanders, British, and Chinese inhabitants. Most are involved in phosphate mining or government services. Relations among the groups are peaceful, although the Nauruans, who control the political and economic system, are the only group privileged to own and inherit land.

Nauruans may be descended from Kiribati, who settled the island at some point in the past. They number approximately 6,400, or 58% of the population. About 60% are Protestant and 40% Catholic. Due to their involvement in the international phosphate market, much of traditional Nauruan culture has disappeared. Nauruans maintain close ties with New Zealand and Australia, where they travel to purchase material goods and where some of their children are sent to school. Most Nauruans are bilingual in Nauruan and English. **Britons** number about 900, or 8% of the population, and are primarily involved in the management of the phosphate facility. The **Chinese** number about 900, or 8% of the population, and are mainly shopkeepers.

Pacific Islanders, who number about 3,000, or 26% of the population, come from nearby Kiribati and Tuvalu and work in phosphate mining, fishing, and shopkeeping.

Nepal

The Kingdom of Nepal, located in northern South Asia, is bordered by the Tibet region of China on the north and India on the east, south, and west. It has a population of 22 million. Nepali is the official language, although over 20 other languages are also spoken. Nepali is related to Hindi and Sanskrit. Beginning in 1768, Nepal was inhabited by a mix of ethnic groups and divided into a number of politically autonomous principalities. From 1794 until the end of World War II, Nepal was aligned with Great Britain, and one of its best known functions was the supplying of soldiers—known as Gurkhas—to serve in the British military. The Gurkhas are not an ethnic group but are drawn from a number of different ethnic groups in Nepal. After World War II, Nepal struggled to form a stable government. Since 1990, it has been a constitutional monarchy, and the role of the king has been greatly reduced.

Ethnic Composition

The ethnic situation in Nepal involves variations in language, religion, ethnicity, caste status, and region among different groups. In addition, the last few decades have seen considerable migration by peoples within the country leading to a far greater mixing of groups than in the past. Because of these factors, census information about Nepal's ethnic groups is not considered reliable. Nepal's current ethnic composition reflects its location on the borders of China and India and the immigration of peoples from those two nations to Nepal over the centuries. The labels **Nepali** and **Nepalese** have two meanings in Nepal. First, in a general sense, the names refer to all citizens of Nepal regardless of their ethnic identity. Second, they refer more specifically to the original inhabitants of Nepal, such as the Newars, Limbu, and Khas. Nepal is often described as having three zones of occupation—north, central, and south—with different ethnic groups living in each region. Despite recent migrations from north to south, this pattern continues to exist.

The northern region of Nepal in the foothills of the Himalayas is occupied by a number of ethnic groups generically labeled **Bhote (Bhotia), Himalayan Highlanders,** or **Tibeto-Mongolians.** Specific groups are the **Sherpa** (25,000), who are well known as guides on mountain-climbing expeditions; **Gurung** (175,000); **Magars** (500,000); and

Nyinba (1,300). All of these groups speak languages related to Tibetan, and they are Buddhist or a mix of Buddhist and Hindu. They subsist through a combination of farming and herding, with herding being more important in the higher altitudes. The distinctive group identities are based largely on subregional location, with each group traditionally occupying a particular valley or region in the Himalayan foothills. In the 1990s, there has been considerable migration out of the foothills into the hill country of central Nepal and also to the plains in the south. Ties to the traditional homeland remain strong nevertheless.

The people inhabiting the highlands of the central region, where the capital city of Kathmandu is located, are mainly **Pahari.** The term Pahari in the general sense means people of Indian origin, as opposed to those who came from Tibet. The Pahari view themselves as distinctly superior to the Bhote of the north. Indian culture has had an enormous impact on Nepal. About 90% of the population is Hindu, although some adhere to syncretic belief systems that combine elements from Hinduism and Buddhism.

The Hindu caste system organizes village life in central and southern Nepal. The two most significant groups of Indian origin in Nepal, both in the central region and across the nation, are the **Brahmans** and **Chettris,** who own much of the land and occupy senior government positions. While castes and caste categories are not ethnic groups, the two do have some features in common, including the sharing of a common identity different from that of other groups and marriage within the group. At the same time, ethnic and caste identity often overlap, and in any single ethnic group the population is often subdivided into occupational castes.

Another major group in the central region is the **Newars,** one of the indigenous peoples of Nepal, who have been influenced by Hindu culture for over 1,000 years. The Newars are mainly farmers, traders, and crafts workers. Many are also employed by the government. Formerly Buddhists, some are now Hindus, and others combine beliefs and practices from the two religions. As with Hindu groups in Nepal and India, the Newars are divided into

a number of occupational castes—priests, silversmiths, farmers, barbers, fishers, and so on—and different castes serve the Buddhist and Hindu Newar communities.

Also located in the central region are a number of groups of Tibetan origin that have moved south and now form border populations between the central and northern zones. The two largest of these groups are the **Tamang** (about 500,000) and the **Limbu** (about 250,000), who live in the east. Both groups subsist primarily by farming and day labor and have come under the control of the Pahari, especially the Brahmans, who now control much of the land in the region.

The southern zone of Nepal is the tropical plain known as the Tarai. This region was settled by peoples from India, although it has been heavily populated only in the last 30 years following the eradication of malaria. The primary group in the region is the **Tharu,** who number about 500,000 and are wet-rice farmers. They rank near the bottom of the caste system. As the region has become more heavily settled, the Brahmans and Newars have achieved economic and political dominance.

In addition to these groups, Nepal also houses almost 100,000 refugees, including about 10,000 **Tibetans** in the north and about 80,000 **Nepalese** from Bhutan in camps in the south. The latter were exiled or forced to leave Bhutan by a Bhutanese government seeking to eradicate Nepalese influence there. The two governments are negotiating the return of the refugees to Bhutan.

Ethnic Relations

In the context of Nepal's transformation from a monarchy to a constitutional monarchy, the primary ethnic issue is the disproportionate power wielded by the Brahmans, Chettris, and Newars. Although these three groups form just over 50% of the population, they own most of the agricultural land, control trade, and occupy most senior- and lower-level government positions. For the other ethnic groups, especially groups such as the Limbu who have lost much of their land, land ownership and a greater role in government are major issues.

New Zealand

N ew Zealand, located in the southwest Pacific Ocean, is a nation composed of two main islands—North Island and South Island—and dozens of smaller islands. Although the European discovery of New Zealand dates to 1642 and British settlement to the 1790s, large-scale British colonization did not begin until 1840, and the British remained in control until 1947 when New Zealand became an autonomous nation. New Zealand has a population of 3,547,000, up from 3,435,000 in the 1991 census. About 85% of New Zealanders live in the country's major cities or towns. English and Maori, the language of New Zealand's indigenous people, are the official languages. Only about 50,000 Maori still use Maori as their primary language. Most people are Christian: 24% Anglican, 18% Presbyterian, and 15% Roman Catholic.

Ethnic Composition

Over the last two decades, New Zealand has become a more ethnically heterogeneous society, although two groups—British and Maori—constitute about 85% of the population. New Zealand was settled by the **British,** most of the early settlers being English and Scottish. Those of British ancestry continue to be the politically, economically, and socially dominant group. In fact, British New Zealanders have been described as more British than the British, with carefully designed and manicured parks, neat rows of houses, love of sports such as rugby and cricket, and an English-style education system. British New Zealand has also developed its own cultural traditions based in part on an appreciation for the rugged natural environment. Politically and economically, New Zealanders have been forging closer ties with Asian nations. About 74% of New Zealanders are of British descent, a recent decrease due both to an increase in the Maori population and to the arrival of immigrants from Asian nations. In addition to those of British ancestry, about 10% of New Zealand's population is of **European** ancestry, including **Dutch, Greeks, Germans, Croats,** and **Scandinavians.** Many of these people arrived between 1870 and 1926, when European immigration was encouraged to add to the labor force. These groups are all quite assimilated into New Zealand society.

The second largest ethnic group is the **Maori.** The Maori inhabited New Zealand at the time of British settlement. According to the 1991 census, they numbered 330,000 but some believe they now number over 500,000.

A Maori master woodcarver. The Maori are revitalizing their culture by teaching the Maori language and maintaining their distinctive dance, art, and craft traditions. Photo: Corel Corp.

In any case, the Maori population has increased since an 1890 estimate of 40,000. A good bit of the growth is based on a change in the official definition of Maori. Previously, at least 50% Maori ancestry was needed for an individual to be counted. Now, having some Maori ancestry and defining oneself as a Maori is enough. The Maori clearly distinguish between themselves and the British, whom they call **Pakeha.** The descendants of the modern Maori arrived on North Island in 1350 from Polynesian islands to the north. They eventually displaced and assimilated others already living on the islands, who had arrived earlier also from Polynesia. In the mid-19th century, the Maori numbered perhaps as many as 250,000 and were divided into about 50 tribes. At that time, the Maori were farmers and fishers, although today most live in towns and cities due to a shortage of land.

Because of New Zealand's strong economy, the possibility of education and employment, and a relatively liberal immigration policy, the composition of New Zealand society has changed since the 1970s. A significant number of **Pacific Islanders** and **Asians** have added to the **Chinese** and **Asian Indians** already in New Zealand. Pacific Islanders number about 130,000; Chinese about 35,000; Indians about 30,000; and Asians from Vietnam, Cambodia, Laos, Hong Kong, and Taiwan about 100,000. Pacific Islanders have come from territories in New Zealand's possession (Cook Islands, Tokelau, Niue), the residents of which are citizens, and from other Polynesian islands, including Western Samoa, Tonga, and Fiji.

Ethnic Relations

Ethnic relations in New Zealand concern people of British ancestry (or Europeans in general) and the Maori. Although relations between the groups are somewhat more harmonious than in the past, Europeans continue to describe the Maori in stereotypical terms. Thus, while the Maori see themselves as a distinct cultural group, the Pakeha (Europeans) view them as a race and use skin color as a marker of Maori identity. Regular association between the Maori and British dates from missionary activity in the early 19th century. In 1840, as a prelude to colonization, the British and many Maori tribal leaders signed the Treaty of Waitanga, which gave Britain sovereignty over the islands, afforded the Maori British protection, and also guaranteed Maori land rights. The British, however, immediately began taking Maori land, leading to two wars in 1845–48 and 1860–70. The Maori soon lost most of their land on North Island, and by the 1890s their population had decreased to 40,000. Slowly they began to agitate for their rights, and gradually the population increased. Finally, in 1989 the government agreed to investigate Maori land claims. In 1995, the North Island claims were settled, and the Maori received 39,000 acres of land and a compensation payment of $112,000,000. In 1996, the government formally apologized for taking Maori land and made a supplemental payment of $26,000,000. The Maori have also attempted to revitalize their culture through teaching the Maori language and reviving Maori dance, art, and crafts. The Maori have even achieved some political influence. Four of the 99 legislative seats are now reserved for Maori representatives, and three Maori were appointed to the cabinet in 1996.

North Korea

The Democratic People's Republic of Korea occupies the northern two-thirds of the Korean Peninsula in East Asia. Bordered by China on the north and South Korea on the south, North Korea is touched by the Yellow Sea on the west and the Sea of Japan on the east. North Korea has a population of 23.9 million. There is also a substantial overseas Korean population of about 4 million, the majority of which are in China, the former Soviet Union, the United States, and Japan. A basically rural, agricultural society until the middle of the 20th century, Korea experienced rapid industrialization and urbanization in the 20th century. Under the control of China during much of its history, Korea's language, religion, arts, traditional patriarchal social organization, and dynastic form of government were all borrowed from or influenced by Chinese civilization.

Ethnic Composition and Ethnic Relations

Like South Korea, North Korea is an ethnically homogeneous state, the entire society being **Korean.** Koreans trace their ancestry to the Chosen Bronze Age culture that existed from 2333–194 B.C. Large-scale conversion to Christianity took place in the 19th century through the efforts of European and American missionaries; Buddhism was brought earlier by the Chinese. Religion has been restricted by the Communist government and it is not known what percentages of North Koreans continue to adhere to Buddhism, the nation's traditional religion. Most Korean Christians fled to the south after 1945.

The major ethnic minority is the **Han Chinese** in the north. Chinese and Koreans live on both sides of the Korea-China border. In the past, the Chinese played a major role in the region as traders, and despite the state-controlled economy of both nations, the Chinese continue to play this role in many villages. The Chinese are freer to cross the border, and they bring goods from China into North Korea.

As an ethnically homogeneous society, ethnic conflict is absent in North Korea. Japan has conquered Korea at various times and from 1910 to 1945 ruled it as a colony. During that period the Japanese sought to destroy Korean culture and make "Japan and Korea as One." Although the effort ultimately failed, the Japanese banned the use of the Korean language in schools and publications, attempted to convert Koreans to Shinto, and made Koreans the subjects of the Japanese emperor. During World War II, Korean women were forced to serve as prostitutes for Japanese military forces, and only in the 1990s has Japan taken responsibility for this program. This history plus the second-class status of Koreans in Japan today continue to define Korean attitudes toward the Japanese. However, relations between Koreans in North Korea and North Koreans in Japan, who number about 250,000, are close, and money sent from those in Japan is an important source of income for some North Korean families.

Oman

The Sultanate of Oman is located on the southeast coast of the Arabian Peninsula. It is bordered on the north by the Strait of Hormuz, on the northeast by the Gulf of Oman, on the east and south by the Arabian Sea, on the southwest by Yemen, on the west by Saudi Arabia, and on the northwest by the United Arab Emirates. Oman has a population of 2.2 million. Arabic is the official language. Oman has been settled for some 5,000 years. Its strategic location has at times led to conflict with the United Arab Emirates and Saudi Arabia, although relations with these nations are now harmonious. Since the discovery of oil in 1964, Oman has developed economically and socially, although the majority of the population is still rural and lives by farming or herding.

Ethnic Composition and Ethnic Relations

Oman has an ethnically heterogeneous population, composed of Arabs, foreign workers from Asia, and a number of localized non-Arab groups. **Arabs** form the majority of the population. Arabs are an ethnic group indigenous to the Middle East. They are the majority population in 15 nations in the Middle East and North Africa. The history of the emergence of Arabs as a distinct group in the region is unclear, but as early as 853 B.C., the Arabic language was in use. Although being an "Arab" has different meanings in different nations, a shared Arab identity is based on a number of key elements. These include use of the Arabic language in its classical form (used in religion and literature) and the varieties of colloquial Arabic used in daily life; a personal identity with Arab culture, history, and the Arab community; a strong value placed on children and family life; a clear division of labor based on sex; and adherence to Islam. About 93% of Arabs around the world follow Islam. However, not all Muslims are Arabs, and the largest Muslim populations are found in the non-Arab nations of Bangladesh, Indonesia, and India.

The Arab population in Oman is divided into three religious sects. The majority of Arabs in Oman are adherents of the **Ibadi Muslim** sect, which developed following the death of Muhammad, the founder of Islam, in the 7th century. The relative isolation of Oman from the Islamic world allowed the sect to survive. Outside of Oman, there are only scattered Ibadi communities in North Africa, India, and Pakistan. Ibadis differ from other Muslims on a number of issues, including the question of who is qualified to lead the Islamic community. For this reason, they are not fully accepted as Arabs by the Sunnis, who constitute the majority of Arabs in the world. About 25% of Arabs in Oman are **Sunni Muslims,** and a small minority are **Shi'ite Muslims.** Unlike the situation all other Middle Eastern nations, where formerly nomadic Arabs (Bedouins) and rural farmers have been migrating to towns and cities, Arabs in Oman remain a largely rural people. About 90% subsist by farming, and about 5% continue to live a life centered around the herding of goats and camels.

Revenues generated by the oil industry, which have developed the economy and social system over the last 30 years, have also led to the recruitment of foreign workers to perform tasks not desired by Omanis. As elsewhere in the region, these workers are mainly **Asians (Indians, Pakistanis, Sri Lankans, Filipinos,** and **Bangladeshis).** Many are Muslims, but there are some Hindus from India as well. In the 1990s, concerns about the growing foreign population coupled with improved education for Omanis have led to a movement to curtail the recruitment of foreign workers.

Oman's location along the primary maritime trade route linking East Africa, the Middle East, and South and Southeast Asia has led to the establishment of small, ethnic communities in the coastal regions. These include **Baluch** from Pakistan and Iran, a community of Iranians known as **Shihuh** (who number about 20,000), the **Khoja** from India, and Swahili-speaking **East Africans.** Most of these peoples are Muslims and occupy specific economic niches in Oman—Africans in the police, Baluch in the military, and the Khoja in commerce.

Oman is relatively free of ethnic conflict, although it has experienced some internal problems in the last 30 years. From 1964 to 1975, some people in the Dhofar region organized as the Dhofar Liberation Front, and, aided by South Yemen, later allied with the Marxist Popular Front for the Liberation of Oman and the Arab Gulf in a failed effort to depose the sultan. In the 1990s, the major issue has been Islamic fundamentalism and efforts by fundamentalists to form opposition organizations. The government has responded by arresting organizers and forcing their groups to disband.

Pakistan

The Islamic Republic of Pakistan is located in the region where the Middle East, Central Asia, and South Asia come together. It is bordered by Iran on the west, Afghanistan on the north, India on the east, and the Arabian Sea on the south. The region of Pakistan was populated by Hindus and closely linked to India for 2,000 years, until Islam was introduced in the early 8th century. At that time, the population began converting to Islam, and ties were established with the Muslim world to the west. From 1526 until 1857, the area of Pakistan was ruled by the Muslim Mughal Empire and then came under British control. With the end of British rule in

1947, the state of Pakistan was created for the Muslim population and partitioned from India, a state that was to be home to Hindus. East Pakistan, or Bangladesh, became a separate nation in 1973. Pakistan has a population of 129,275,900. The official religion is Islam, and about 97% of the population is Muslim, the remainder being mainly Hindu. Urdu is the national language, although more people actually speak Punjabi and Sindhi. Some upper-class Pakistanis also speak English.

Ethnic Composition

Pakistan is politically divided into four provinces—Sindh, Baluchistan, Punjab, and the North-West Frontier Province—and the ethnic composition matches the four groups associated with these regions—Sind, Baluch, Punjabi, and Pashtun. While this scheme describes the situation in general terms, it is overly simplistic for it ignores the multiethnic composition of some provinces, the numerical dominance of the Punjabis (two-thirds of the national population), the multiethnic population of the major cities, the Muhajireen (post-1947 immigrants from India), and a number of smaller tribal groups in the interior.

The **Baluch (Baluchi)** live in Pakistan's western province of Baluchistan, in Iran, and in Afghanistan. In Pakistan, they also live in Sindh and Punjab. Estimates are unreliable, but the Baluch probably number about five million in Pakistan, Iran, and Afghanistan. The smallest of the four major ethnic groups in Pakistan, the Baluch are Sunni Muslims and trace their ancestry to Arab lineage and to Muhammad (the founder of Islam). It is likely, however, that some ancestors of the Baluch were resident in the region prior to the arrival of Islam. The Baluch live a seminomadic lifestyle based on farming and the herding of cattle, sheep, and goats. Three dialects of the Baluch language are spoken. Political organization is based on clans and tribes, and tribal leaders wield considerable authority and influence.

The **Sind** live primarily in Sindh Province in southeastern Pakistan and number about 16 million, or 13% of the national population. Sindh itself has an ethnically heterogeneous population. The two major groups are the Sind and the **Muhajireen.** The Sind are the traditional residents of the region, speak three dialects of the Sindhi language, and are relatively poor farmers who grow wheat, cotton, rice, and other crops in irrigated fields. About 80% are Muslims, and 20% are Hindus. Sindhi society is organized along caste lines, and the population is divided into hundreds of occupational castes, even though most Sinds are farmers. Hindus form the lowest castes. Prior to the separation of India and Pakistan in 1947, the region had several million more Hindus and **Sikhs.** Many of them fled to India while Sindh in India, who were mainly Muslims and spoke Urdu, immigrated to Pakistan. This population is known as the Muhajireen or **"new Sindhis,"** and they are mainly urban and middle class. In addition to these two groups, Sindh is also the home to Pashtuns, Baluch, Punjabis, and Shi'ite Muslims, most of whom live in the capital of Karachi.

Pashtuns (Pakhtuns, Pathan) live primarily in the North-West Frontier Province where they number about 11 million. There are also about 1.2 million Pashtun refugees from Afghanistan in the region and about 10 million Pashtuns in Afghanistan. The Pashtun live across a large region and in different administrative districts, and for those reasons there is considerable cultural diversity within the population. However, there is also considerable similarity and a strong sense of Pashtun identity, which rests on speaking the Pushto language, adherence to Sunni Islam, belief in descent from a common ancestor, and a strong sense of male honor. The Pashtun are a tribal society in the sense that the traditional primary social units were regional tribes composed of clans, which were in turn composed of lineages of related people who traced their family ties through their fathers' lines.

The Punjab is the fertile agricultural region that lies in both Pakistan and India. The **Punjabi** are the major ethnic group in the region and number about 85 million in Pakistan, or about 66% of the national population. Almost all Punjabis in Pakistan are Sunni Muslims, while those in India are Sikhs or Hindus. The Punjab region is fed by five major rivers, and for over 2,000 years has been one of the major agricultural centers of the world. Most Punjabis live in village farming communities. They are farmers and landowners, or are involved in occupations that support farming. Other Punjabis work in the professions and service industries in Pakistan's cities and have benefited from the economic development of the region in the last few decades. Rural Punjabis are organized into numerous occupational castes; the **Jats** (farmers) and **Rajputs** (landowners) are the two best known. Punjabis speak numerous dialects of the Punjabi language, and upper-class Punjabis in the cities speak Urdu.

In addition to these major groups, Pakistan is home to a number of smaller ethnic groups. The largest group is the **Brahui,** numbering about one million, who live in Baluchistan and Sindh. They are a Sunni Muslim, tribal people like the Baluch and subsist through farming and herding. Other groups include the **Burusho (Hunza)** and small groups who speak Dardic languages in the north; the **Kalasha (Hindus)** in the North-West Frontier; the **Khoja** trading caste of Ismaili Muslims; the **Kohistani** Muslim farmers, now much assimilated into Pashtun society; and the **Sidi,** former African slaves, who form a caste of religious specialists in Sindh.

Ethnic Relations

Ethnic relations in Pakistan are complex and marked by considerable conflict. Although adherence to Islam unifies the nation and distinguishes it from Hindu India, the presence of the five major ethnic groups has impeded the creation of a national Pakistani identity.

Most inhabitants continue to affiliate more closely with their tribe or ethnic group than with the Pakistani nation. This holds true both for those living in their home province and those living in other provinces or in ethnically mixed cities such as Karachi. The absence of a national language used by a majority of the population also contributes to ethnic division. Although Urdu is the national language and the primary literary language—it is foreign to most Pakistanis and is associated with the Muhajireen—most speak their ethnic language in daily life. Ethnic rivalries are also based on the unequal distribution of wealth and power. The Baluch and Pashtun, poor in comparison to the Punjabi, Sindh, and Muhajireen, blame Punjabi-inspired government policies for the wealth gap. The Punjabis dominate the government and military, the two most powerful institutions in Pakistani society. The Muhajireen, seen as outsiders by other Pakistanis, are especially resented for their wealth and economic influence. Some elements of the Muhajireen community have sought to establish a separate Muhajireen state in Sindh, a wish opposed by other Pakistanis.

Although there have been ethnic-motivated attacks and riots in the 1970s and 1980s, ethnic conflict has not torn Pakistan apart and there are no major separatist movements underway. At times, however, some Pashtun have advocated a Pashtun nation built with land to be taken from both Pakistan and Afghanistan. Ethnic conflict has been controlled by the continuing strong affiliation that people feel toward their tribe and ethnic group, the association of the major groups with different regions, adherence to Sunni Islam, and repressive governments that have used force or the threat of force to maintain order.

Palau

P alau is an archipelago in the western Caroline Islands in the western Pacific Ocean. The nearest large nations are the Philippines to the west and Papua New Guinea to the south. Formerly under Spanish, German, Japanese, and U.S. control, Palau became an independent nation in 1994. It has a population of about 17,000. The indigenous people of the islands are the **Belau,** who number about 14,600 in Palau, or 86% of the population. There are also Belau in the United States, Guam, and Hawaii, where they have immigrated in search of employment. The remaining 14% of the Palau population is composed of **Filipinos** (10%), other **Pacific Islanders** (2%), **Chinese** (1%), and **Europeans** and **Americans** (1%). These last groups are mainly involved in commerce, retail trade, and the service sector. Most Belau subsist through a combination of fishing and the growing of taro, a root crop. The government is the primary source of employment outside the home. Belau society is organized along kinship lines, with Belauans tracing their ancestry and affiliating with relatives through their mothers' lines. Belauans speak Belau, older people also speak Japanese (Japan ruled the islands from 1914 to 1944), and younger people speak English (the islands were administered by the United States from 1947 to 1994). Most Belauans are Roman Catholic, Seventh-Day Adventist, or Mormon, with elements of indigenous belief and practice mixed into these religions.

Papua New Guinea

T he Independent State of Papua New Guinea is located in the southwest Pacific Ocean, north of Australia. It comprises the eastern half of the island of New Guinea as well as 600 smaller islands. The western half of the island of New Guinea became Irian Jaya, a province of Indonesia, in 1963. The island of New Guinea was first settled by peoples migrating across what was then land and shallow water from Southeast Asia about 38,000 years ago. Most current Papua New Guineans are descended from peoples who arrived much later. European colonization brought a number of colonial powers to different sections of the island: the west was claimed by Spain in 1545, the Dutch and British later agreed to divide this claim, and the Dutch colonized the west (what is now part of Indonesia) while the British colonized the east and later the south. The Germans attempted to colonize the north in the 1850s, and in 1885 they took the north, and the British took the south. In 1902, the British-controlled section of New Guinea went to Australia, as did the German section after World War II. Reorganization and self-government schemes continued until New Guinea became an independent nation in 1975. Colonization had been confined mainly to the coasts, and copra (dried coconut meat for oil) was produced on plantations by local peoples and peoples forcibly imported from the Pacific Islands. The interior of New Guinea was only substantially penetrated beginning in the 1930s by the Australians, yet, even in the 1950s, some indigenous groups had not come into contact with outsiders. New Guinea's population numbers 4,394,537. English is the official language, although most people continue to speak one of the 700 or more indigenous languages. Tok Pisin and Hiri Motu, two pidgin languages originally developed for trade purposes, are still used for communication between different communities.

Ethnic Composition

Over 700 different languages are spoken in Papua New Guinea, although several hundred of these are related tongues spoken in the interior highlands. If language variation equals ethnic variation, Papua New Guinea probably has more indigenous ethnic groups than does any other nation in the world. To a large extent, this ethnic variation is the result of New Guinea's topography. The island has a long and high series of mountain ranges, known as the highlands, running through the interior, and another range along the north coast, as well as a number of major river systems and floodplains fed from the high central mountains. In addition, the north and south coastlines are dotted with hundreds of islands, many of them inhabited. A number of ethnic groups live in the central highlands. Some experts say that over every mountain, one encounters a new culture. Evidently, many of these groups share a common ancestry, but over the millennia, through isolation in different valleys, they have become distinct cultural groups.

Most of New Guinea's ethnic groups are small, numbering less than 10,000 people, although some, like the Chimbu, are larger, numbering about 60,000. In larger groups, and even to some extent in smaller groups, village and tribal affiliations tend to be more important than does any sense of a more general ethnic identity. In fact, many groups (speakers of the same languages living in the same region) had no name for themselves at the time of European colonization, and their names are ones assigned by Europeans. After independence, ethnic identity was viewed as a link to political power and control of land, making it more salient.

To make some sense of New Guinea's large number of groups, experts have developed various categorization systems. The most general and least informative one places all New Guinea peoples into two groups—**Papuans** and **Melanesians**—the latter defined as speakers of non-Papuan languages. The Melanesians tend to live near the coast, while the Papuans live inland, although this is not the case in all regions.

A second, somewhat finer, classification system divides the population into regional clusters based on major topographical features and cultural similarities. Although this system is commonly used by anthropologists, some question its accuracy, because it sacrifices cultural variations in regions for cultural similarities. This system delineates four major regions:

the highlands running across the center of the nation, the Sepik River region in the north, the southern lowlands and coast, and Papua and associated islands in the southeast. Regions such as the highlands can be further divided into subregions such as the Southern, Western, and Eastern Highlands, as can the Enga and Chimbu regions named after their major ethnic groups. To some extent, more cultural similarity exists among the cultures of the highlands than is the case for other regions.

In all regions where there are both inland and coastal groups, a significant difference can usually be found between the two in their subsistence system. Inland groups subsist mainly through horticulture, while coastal groups rely on fishing as well. Primary crops are root crops grown through shifting cultivation, in which fields are prepared for growing by the slash-and-burn method, used only for a few seasons, and then left for several years while the soil renews itself. In addition to horticulture of root crops, shared features of traditional New Guinea cultures include residence in small villages and social organization based on affiliation with clans and tribes governed by "big-men." A big-man is a man who achieves political leadership through personal qualities such as power of personality, prestige, or public-speaking ability. Since independence, many traditional patterns of life have been disrupted by economic development, centralized government, public education, and improved transportation and communication with the interior. Although some 90% of Papua New Guineans have been converted to Christianity (about one-third Protestant, two-thirds Roman Catholic), most traditional religions also survive, either through incorporation with Christianity or alongside it.

Some groups in the major regions are as follows.

Highlands
    Bena Bena
    Chimbu
    Huli
    Enga
    Fore
    Gadsup
    Gahuku Gama

Gainj
Gururumba
Kakoli
Kuma
Maring
Melpa
Mt. Hagen
Sambia
Siane
Tairoro
Wontoat
Wovan

Sepik River
Abelam
Arapesh
Boiken
Chambri
Gnau
Iatmul
Kwoma
Miyanim
Mundugumor
Murik
Telefolmin
Wape
Yanguro

Southern Lowlands and Coast
Boazi
Keraki
Kiwai
Gogodala
Namau
Orokolo

Papua
Dobu
Koiari
Mafulu
Mailu
Maisin
Mekeo
Motu
Orokaiva
Tauade
Wamira

In addition to these indigenous peoples, there are about 30,000 **Westerners** (mainly **Australians** and **British**) and **Chinese** (mainly traders in towns) in Papua New Guinea.

Ethnic Relations

When Papua New Guinea began moving toward independence in 1973, ethnic-based problems immediately emerged. People in the Papua region, formerly administered separately, agitated for a separate state, and people on the island of Bougainville requested (in 1975) separation and possible affiliation with the Solomon Islands to the north. These two movements evolved against a backdrop of major national issues, including land reform, writing of a national constitution to define citizenship, and a need to balance the authority of the national as against the provincial governments.

Although the secessionist movements died down, they reemerged in the 1980s. Papuans, the poorest people in the nation, continued to see separation as a viable solution to the region's problems, and in 1986 the debate over central versus provincial control led to riots in the highlands, which had emerged as a politically powerful region.

In 1990, the Bougainville Revolutionary Army (BRA) led a movement that declared independence. Bougainville, rich in copper, is desired by both Papua New Guinea and the Solomon Islands, whose government is accused of aiding the separatist movement. In 1992, government troops fought the BRA, and in 1993, troops of Papua New Guinea invaded the Solomon Islands as punishment for assisting the BRA. In January 1998, the conflict with the Bougainville rebels drew near an end as sides agreed to a cease-fire and a permanent end of the fighting to go into effect in May.

Despite the conflicts described above, ethnic relations in Papua New Guinea are generally peaceful. As the nation stabilizes, however, they are likely to become more visible in the political arena as rival blocs of regional groups vie for power.

Philippines

Located in Southeast Asia, the Republic of the Philippines is a nation made up of some 1,000 islands. The Philippines are surrounded by the Pacific Ocean on the north, the Philippine Sea on the east, the Celebes Sea on the south, and the South China Sea on the west. Although the islands have been continuously inhabited for over 25,000 years, the major events that have shaped ethnicity and ethnic relations in the 20th century began in the 15th century with the arrival of Islam in the southern islands from Indonesia and Malaysia, and the European discovery of the Philippines by Magellan in 1521. Spanish colonization accelerated later in the century and most of the population eventually converted to Roman Catholicism, the Philippines becoming the only predominately Catholic nation in Asia. Following its victory in the Spanish-American War, the United States took control of the Philippines in 1898 and has been a major influence ever since, save for the Japanese invasion during World War II. The Philippines became an independent nation in 1946. The population is 74.5 million. Pilipino, based on Tagalog, and English are the official languages.

Ethnic Composition

The Philippines are homogeneous in that about 90% of the population is Filipino, and 83% of the population is Roman Catholic, although regional variations exist in this general population. The Philippines are heterogeneous in that about 5% of the population is Muslim and another 5% is composed of indigenous peoples, including the Negritos, first inhabitants of the islands, and several dozen other groups collectively labeled uplanders, hill tribes, or highlanders.

The people today labeled **Negritos,** in reference to their darker skin, are the indigenous inhabitants of the Philippines. They arrived from Southeast Asia between 25,000 and 30,000 years ago. Traditionally they were hunter-gatherers, but with the arrival of the Malays 20,000 years later, the Negritos entered into a pattern of trade relations that persists to this day—one in which they trade meat and other forest products to the settled Malays in exchange for rice and vegetables. Since the arrival of the Spanish in the early 16th century, the Negritos have been pushed toward assimilation and extinction. In the 1990s there are only about 15,000 Negritos remaining, organized into some 25 groups on the islands of Luzon, Palawan, Panay, Negroes, Cebu, and Mindanao. Many have been converted to Roman Catholicism and work as wage laborers. The best known of the Negritos are the **Tasaday,** who were "discovered" as the last Stone Age people in 1974. Subsequent research suggests that they are a Negrito group, but their pattern of life much resembles that of other related groups.

About 90% of the population are classified as **Filipinos** (or **Filipinas,** the feminine form), and they are sometimes collectively labeled **Christian lowlanders** or **Christian Malays,** indicating that their religion and/or ethnic ancestry sets them apart from other Philippine ethnic groups. Filipinos are primarily of Malay descent, having come from what is now Malaysia and Indonesia over the past 5,000 years. Some intermarriage has occurred with other groups and with the Chinese. Most Filipinos speak Pilipino, the national language, and those in urban areas such as Manila also speak English. Many continue to speak their regional language as well. These regional languages are related, but are not mutually intelligible. Migration to other islands and to Manila, public education, easier communication and travel, and involvement in the global economy have all, during the 20th century, eroded regional and cultural variations and have created a strong, though not all-encompassing, identification with the Philippine national state. Frequent migration from one region to another and the loss of regional identities in cities make it difficult to estimate the population of the regional Filipino cultures. The largest groups are the **Cebuan, Tagalog,** and **Ilocano.** The nine major groups are distributed on the following islands, where they live mainly along the coasts and in the lowlands.

Nine Major Regional Filipino Cultures

Group	Location
Cebuan	Masbate, Leyte, Cebu, Bohol, Mindanao
Tagalog	Luzon, Calapan, Mindoro, Palawan
Ilocano	Luzon
Pangasinan	Luzon
Pampangan	Luzon
Bicolano	Luzon, Masbate
Ilongo	Negros, Panay
Waray-Waray	Leyte
Boholano	Cebu

Most Filipinos now speak Tagalog, at least as a second language. Employment opportunities and government relocation initiatives have led to considerable internal migration, and members of many formerly localized regional groups are now found throughout the Philippines. About 83% of Filipinos are Roman Catholic, and 7% are Protestant.

Muslim groups in the Philippines live primarily on western Mindanao, on the southern coast of Mindanao, on southern Palawan, and in the small southern islands known as the Sulu Archipelago. Islam was introduced to the Philippines by traders from Indonesia and Malay in the 15th century. **Muslims** number about 3.5 million, or 5% of the population. The Muslims are referred to collectively as **Moros** by the Christian Filipinos, a term some Muslims find derogatory. The Muslims are not a unified group either culturally or religiously. A number of distinct Muslim groups occupy specific regions of the southern Philippines. While all are Sunni Muslims, some groups are more orthodox. Groups on Mindanao converted to Islam later than did others in the Philippines and often retain elements of their indigenous religion, such as beliefs in magic and sorcery. Those in the interior subsist by farming, while those on the coast rely on fishing. Groups range in size from the Sangil (about 4,000) to the Maguindanao (over 500,000). The major groups in the Sulu Archipelago are the **Tausug, Samal Moro,** and **Bajau.** On Mindanao, the **Maguindanao** are the largest group followed by the **Yakan, Maranao, Ilanon,** and **Sangil.** The **Melabugan** and **Jama Mapun** are found on Palawan. Due to their religion and location

in the extreme south, the Muslim groups have lived outside mainstream Filipino-dominated society. Efforts to develop Mindanao since the 1950s led to widespread conflict, as discussed below.

In addition to the Filipinos and Muslims, the third major ethnic category is the **hill tribes** that live mainly on Luzon and Mindanao. Assimilation into mainstream society makes population estimates difficult. Estimates suggest that the hill tribes account for anywhere from 5% to 10% of the national population. As their generic label suggests, the hill tribes populate mountainous or hilly regions. They subsist primarily by growing rice. Some groups such as the **Ifugao** in the north are well-known for the elaborate stone terraces covering their mountainsides. Wet rice is grown in the shallow mud pools on the terraces. Although missionaries have been active among the hill tribes, most of them retain traditional religious and social organization based on families and small villages. If all subgroups are counted as distinct groups, there may be as many as 60 hill tribes in the Philippines. The major groups and their island locations are as follows:

Luzon
  Bontok
  Gaddang
  Ibaloi
  Ifugao
  Ilongot
  Isneg
  Itneg
  Kalinga
  Kankanai
  Sagada Igorot

Mindanao
  Babobo
  Bilaan
  Bukidnon
  Kalibugan
  Subanun

In addition, the **Palawan** and **Tagbanowa** live on Palawan, the **Sulod** on Panay, and the **Hanunóo** on Mindoro.

In addition to these three categories of ethnic groups, there are about 600,000 **Chinese** and 131,000 **U.S. Americans** in the Philippines. The proximity to China and Taiwan has led to emigration from China. The current Chinese population is descended from those who came earlier as laborers and traders and they are relatively poor. More recent arrivals are involved in industry and commerce and are wealthy. Although there has been considerable intermarriage between the Filipinos and Chinese, people stress their Filipino rather than Chinese ancestry.

Ethnic Relations

In ethnic relations between the Filipino majority and other groups, Filipinos, in general, consider themselves superior. The hill tribes and Muslims are stereotypically described as "ignorant" and "backward." The Chinese are seen as "too aggressive," especially recent Chinese emigrants from Taiwan, who are viewed as exploiters of Filipino labor and institutions. As with regional cultures, the general Filipino goal since independence in 1946 has been assimilation into Filipino society, especially through speaking Pilipino and being employed in the growing industrial and service sectors of the economy.

The major ethnic conflict has involved Filipinos and the Muslims in the south. From the early 1970s until a peace accord was signed in 1996, the two groups were involved in an often violent struggle for control of southern Mindanao. The Muslims feared national assimilation programs, the dominance of the Christian Filipinos, and economic development of the region. The government, while concerned about Muslim ties to Islamic communities in Indonesia and Malaysia, was also interested in exploiting natural resources such as timber on Mindanao. The clash over these

A fisherman from Zamboanga, on the island of Mindanao. Efforts by the national government to develop Mindanao have led to conflict with the region's Muslims. Photo: Corel Corp.

issues resulted in thousands of deaths and population relocations. It also destroyed hill tribe communities on Mindanao that were caught between the Muslims and Filipinos. In 1989, the conflict began to be resolved when Muslims were granted limited political autonomy in southern Mindanao, Palawan, and the Sulu Archipelago. In 1996, a peace treaty was signed creating an autonomous Muslim state in southern Mindanao. Not all Muslim rebel groups agreed to it, and some continued to seek complete separation from the Philippines.

Qatar

L ocated in the Middle East, Qatar is a peninsula extending northward from the east coast of Arabia into the Persian Gulf and includes numerous small islands. Qatar is bordered on the south by the United Arab Emirates and Saudi Arabia. It was first permanently settled by Bedouin Arabs in the 1700s. Qatar remained a lightly populated and poor region until 1940, when oil was discovered. The nation then became wealthy and prosperous, gaining independence in 1971. Qatar had previously been under Ottoman Turk control and then British rule in the 20th century. It has a population of 550,000. Arabic is the official language, and 95% of the population is Muslim.

Ethnic Composition and Ethnic Relations

As with other small, oil-rich nations in the Middle East, Qatar has an ethnically diverse population of foreign workers, indigenous **Qatari Arabs** being a numerical minority. They constitute about 20% of the population. **Asians (Indians, Pakistanis, Filipinos,** and **Bangladeshis)** constitute about 35%, **Arabs** (mainly **Egyptians**) and **Palestinians** 25%,

Iranians (Persians) 16%, and foreign workers about 4%. Guest workers comprise almost the entire workforce. Compared to the Qatari Arabs, these groups constitute a poor majority, who cannot become citizens and are in Qatar at the pleasure of the government. Most do expect to become permanent residents and are in Qatar to work at the jobs that provide considerably more income than those available in their homelands.

Saudi Arabia

T he Kingdom of Saudi Arabia, located in the Middle East, is bordered by Jordan on the north; Iraq on the northeast; Kuwait, the Persian Gulf, Qatar, and the United Arab Emirates on the east; Oman on the southeast; Yemen on the south and southwest; and the Red Sea on the west. Islam emerged in Saudi Arabia in the 7th century, and the holy cities of Medina and Mecca remain the most important spiritual sites for Muslims, two million of whom make an annual pilgrimage to Mecca. Economically, Saudi Arabia has benefited as a major producer and supplier of the world's oil. It maintains close ties to Western nations such as the United States and to other Arab nations in the Middle East. Saudi Arabia has a population of 19.5 million, although this figure does not include the millions of foreign workers who live there temporarily. Islam is the official religion and Arabic the official language.

Ethnic Composition and Ethnic Relations

On the surface, it appears that Saudi Arabia is a homogeneous nation, because 90% of the Saudis are **Arabs,** and 100% of the Saudi population are Muslims (85% Sunni and 15% Shi'ite). Islam is an especially powerful force in Saudi Arabia, as it was the birthplace of this world religion and the place from where it

spread to Asia, Africa, and southern Europe. Each year hundreds of thousands of Saudi pilgrims join other Muslims to undertake the annual pilgrimage to the holy sanctuary in Mecca, making Saudi Arabia the focus of Islam for Muslims around the world. Saudi Arabia is also among the most conservative of Muslim nations. Severe restrictions are placed on women's activities, entry into the nation by non-Muslims is carefully controlled, and visitors must follow strict guidelines in personal behavior and dress so as not to insult Islam. For example, foreign soldiers stationed in Saudi Arabia during the Gulf War were not allowed to display publicly any symbols of other religions, such as crosses. Despite the conservative nature of Islam in Saudi Arabia, Islamic fundamentalists have been active there and in other Middle Eastern countries. In Saudi Arabia their major concern has been the government's political and economic ties to the Western world and associated economic development. The government has responded by banning fundamentalist activities and has gone so far as to remove its traditional advisory body of religious-legal scholars and to replace it with a committee more loyal to the government.

Despite the centrality of Islam, Saudi Arabia displays considerable diversity, even though it is not ethnic in nature. Additionally, Saudi Arabia currently hosts between four and five million foreign workers and their families. Although they are neither permanent residents nor are they counted in the census, many of these are Arabs and Muslims, the rest being primarily from South and Southeast Asia.

Traditionally, the major diversity in the region that is now Saudi Arabia was based on occupation and wealth. Society was composed of three Arab groups—nomadic herders of sheep, goats, and camels called Bedouins; settled farmers who lived around oases; and merchants, crafts workers, and others who lived in villages and towns. Most of these peoples were Arab and Muslim and they converted to Islam in the 7th century.

Until the middle of the 20th century, **Bedouin Arabs** constituted about 50% of the Saudi population. Since then, a decline in the importance of camel trading, the availability of modern forms of transportation, and government programs to settle nomads have resulted in a sharp decline in the number of migrating Bedouins relying on herding for their livelihood. Most

Bedouins are now settled in towns like other Saudis and have access to generous government-supported health, education, and social programs made possible by the nation's oil wealth. At the same time, however, Bedouins continue to maintain their unique identity, and ties to family and tribes remain important.

These ties to family, clan, and tribe have always been important to Bedouins and to all Arabs in Saudi Arabia. **Saudi Arabs** trace their kinship ties patrilineally—through the father's line. Thus, fathers, brothers, uncles, and nephews linked in this way come to form important economic, political, and social units with obligations to assist one another and offer support in conflicts with other families. Groups of families that claim a common ancestor are organized into clans and the clans into tribes. Leadership at all levels rests with the eldest man. Family, clan, and tribal affiliations remain important to Saudi Arabs, and specific families that rule the nation, control the military, and manage the oil industry.

Another form of cultural variation is based on region of birth and residence. For example, Saudis in the south have for several thousand years had close ties to Arabs in Yemen and were much involved in the trade that flowed through Yemen north across the Arabian Peninsula. These ties remain important today. In the Hizaj region where Mecca is located, the population, although Muslim, also includes people of

Bedouin women preparing food in front of their tent. Such scenes are now rare as currently most Bedouin throughout the Middle East live settled lives. Photo: Corbis-Bettmann.

mixed ethnic ancestry whose parentage resulted from the intermarriage of Arabs with pilgrims from Turkey, Iran, Indonesia, Pakistan, Africa, and other non-Arab countries. In the northwest, there is a significant population (numbering close to two million) of people of African and Arab ancestry reflecting the long history of trade relations between Arabia and east Africa, as well as the importation of slaves, which lasted into the early 20th century.

A final source of diversity is status. Those families that can trace their ancestry to the first Arabs in the region or to the founders of Islam enjoy high prestige. Higher status is also associated with wealth. In the past, it was the traders and the rulers of the Islamic Empire who were wealthy; today it is the ruling family, their supporters, and those involved in the oil business. Saudi Arabia is one of the wealthiest nations in the world, and its citizens have access to a wide range of services and material goods.

Much of the labor in Saudi Arabia is performed by outsiders. It is estimated that between four and five million foreign workers, some with spouses and children, are resident in Saudi Arabia in the late 1990s. They work in construction, in the service industry (some as domestics), in the oil fields and refineries, and in business (as technicians and managers). The majority are **Muslim Arabs** from **Egypt, Jordan, Syria,** and **Kuwait,** and some are **Palestinians.** The 1 million workers from Yemen were expelled in 1991 after Yemen supported Iraq in the Gulf War. Other workers come from **Pakistan, India, the Philippines, Sri Lanka,** and **South Korea.** Many, but not all of these, are Muslims as well. There are also about 200,000 **Europeans, Americans,** and **Canadians** who fill technical and managerial positions. These workers are not citizens of Saudi Arabia and are subject to expulsion at any time. The lure of Saudi Arabia is steady employment and high wages, although these workers often live in government housing that is substandard, and they do not have access to all the social and educational programs available to the Saudis. The government's policy since the late 1980s has been to reduce the number of foreign workers and replace them with Saudis. For various reasons, this has not yet taken place. One major reason is that women in Saudi Arabia are discouraged from working, so the labor pool is quite small; a second reason is that Saudi education is not geared to training people for technical and managerial work; and a third reason is that few Saudis desire low-level manual and service-type employment.

Singapore

The Republic of Singapore is a small island nation located off the southern tip of the Malaysian Peninsula in Southeast Asia. Malaysia is located to the north and Indonesia to the south. Singapore was established as a trading colony by the British in 1819 and remained so until 1959. From 1963 to 1965, Singapore was part of Malaysia but then became an independent nation. A major global trade and commercial center, Singapore has a population of 3.4 million, yielding a population density of 13,753 persons per square mile, the highest of any nation. Most Singaporeans live in large high-rise apartment complexes that function as self-contained communities.

Ethnic Composition

An ethnically heterogeneous society, Singapore's citizens may be classified in three ethnic categories: (1) Chinese numbering 2.6 million, or 76% of the population; (2) Malays numbering 510,000, or 15% of the population; and Asian Indians numbering 221,000, or 6.5% of the population. The remainder of the population is composed of people from Europe, North America, the Middle East, and other Southeast Asian nations. This tripartite division of Singaporean society masks the considerable complexity that exists within each category.

Chinese have been involved in trade in Singapore for centuries and were present when the British established the colony in 1819. The current Chinese population represents at least seven different regional Chinese cultures— **Hokkien** from southern China, **Teochiu** also from southern China, **Hakka** from central China, **"Three Rivers People"** from central China, **people from Hainan Island** off the south China coast, **Cantonese,** and **Malay-speaking Chinese** long resident in Malaysia. These groups speak different regional varieties of Chinese. In Singapore some general overarching sense of Chinese identity has emerged partly because the Chinese are the largest group. The Chinese have traditionally stood in opposition to the Malays on the peninsula, and in recent years Mandarin Chinese has become the standard language. The Chinese also share a common religious history, and most follow a combination of Buddhism, Taoism, and Confucianism. Politically and economically dominant in Singapore, a few wealthy Chinese families continue to control some aspects of the economy, and kin-based international business networks remain important. At the same time, advanced education and the ability to conduct business in English are becoming important determinants of success in the business world.

Malays are the indigenous inhabitants of Singapore, although they are now a numerical minority. They are dominated politically and economically by the Chinese. The origin of the current Malay population is mixed. The majority (about 70%) do not actually come from Malaysia but rather from Indonesia, and most are Javanese, the dominant ethnic group there. Other Malays are from Malaysia and Indonesian islands to the south of Singapore. The unifying force for Muslim Malays is religion. Malays are found among the poor and the unemployed of Singaporean society. Many women work for low wages in factories and many men are unemployed. The community suffers from a high crime rate, much drug addiction, and a high dropout rate in schools. The government and private organizations have

developed special education and social service programs for the Malays in order to raise their status. In the 1990s, these programs began to show positive results, such as higher test scores by Malay students.

The term **Indians** in Singapore refers to people from South Asia—**Indians, Bangladeshis, Burmans,** and **Sri Lankans.** The majority of Indians are Tamils from Tamil Nadu State in southeastern India. Other significant Indian populations are Sikhs, Malayalis, and Gujaratis. Most Indians are Hindus or Sikhs; those from Myanmar and Bangladesh are Muslim. The commonality of Islam has led to considerable contact and intermarriage between the Muslim Indians and Malays. Although Indians were first brought to Singapore by the British, a flow of Indian immigrants continues in the 1990s, and many are men seeking employment. The four-level caste system of India has been revised in Singapore to reflect the make-up of the Singaporean Indian population. Brahmans (Hindu priestly caste) and wealthy merchants and bankers form the upper caste, people from midlevel castes in India form a middle caste, and people who were of low castes or from the Untouchables in India form the lowest caste. Intermarriage among the castes is limited.

Ethnic Relations

When Singapore became an independent nation in 1965, the government was faced with the problem of creating a unified national identity in a population that was ethnically diverse and where ethnic groups had lived in largely separate social worlds. Each ethnic group resided mainly in its own neighborhood, people tended to marry within their own groups, and the workforce was to some extent ethnically stratified. Chinese held most professional positions, the Malays were policemen and government employees, and the Indians worked as unskilled laborers. The government rejected the idea of creating a melting-pot society based on a combination of customs from different ethnic groups, as well as the notion of creating an assimilation society in which the minorities were forced to adopt a Chinese lifestyle. Instead, it advocated a policy in which Singapore was seen as an Asian society, in which each ethnic tradition was equally valid, and in which programs were designed to create an overarching sense of Singaporean identity. Although Singapore is tied to the Western world as a major global trading center, the government also rejected any movement toward Singapore becoming a culturally Western nation. Among the key elements of the new Singaporean national identity are a modern economy, improved education, bilingualism (English and native language facility), ethnic and religious freedom, decision-making through consensus and discussion, and a communal rather than individual orientation. Key elements of this approach have been promotion of the use of English and its adoption as the language of education, and promotion of Mandarin as the primary language for all Chinese. Among

young people, a creole version of English and Chinese called "Slinglish" has become common. The government has also attempted to end the spatial segregation of the ethnic groups by building apartment house complexes that require each new building to have a mix of Chinese, Malays, and Indians. This approach has been less than successful, and many people continue to interact mainly with co-ethnics. Some even sold their apartments and moved nearer to co-ethnics, recreating the very ethnic communities that the government sought to eradicate. A greater mixing of the ethnic groups has resulted from economic changes as the traditional ethnic-based occupational system disappeared. There is now opportunity for all people throughout the entire economy. Foreign firms now operating in Singapore tend not to consider ethnicity in hiring, and ethnically mixed workforces are common in these firms.

Solomon Islands

The Solomon Islands is a nation located in the South Pacific Ocean east of Papua New Guinea. Solomon territory consists of the main islands of Choiseul, New Georgia, San Isabel, Guadalcanal, Malaita, and San Cristobal plus smaller islands including Anuta, Tikopia, Rennell Island, and Ontong Java. The Solomon Islands became independent in 1978, following nearly 100 years of British control. During World War II, some islands were occupied by Japanese forces, and Guadalcanal experienced some of the most difficult fighting in the Pacific when the Allied forces invaded. The devastation caused by World War II, combined with earlier British exploitation, led to the postwar Maasina (Marching) Rule social movement that pushed for the end of colonial rule and a renewal of traditional customs. About 100 languages and dialects are spoken on the islands, although English is the official language. Pidgin English serves as the lingua franca for inter-island communication. The population of the Solomons is almost entirely Christian, the major denominations being Anglican (33%), Roman Catholic (19%), Evangelical (17%), and Methodist (11%). The population numbers 413,000.

Ethnic Composition and Ethnic Relations

The Solomon Islands has always been a society of small village communities. Each community tends to see itself as a distinct cultural entity, even if trade and kinship ties are maintained with nearby communities. Many of these communities—over 4,000 in the islands—form distinct cultural units with their

own language or dialect, system of government, and property ownership. The economy is based on the growing of root crops and on fishing. Copra (dried coconut meat) was produced for export on some islands during the colonial period, and many villagers were recruited as plantation laborers.

The Solomon Islands is an ethnically diverse nation. The major population centers are Malaita (about 100,000) and Guadalcanal (about 70,000). Cultural variations on Malaita occur between groups living in the interior and those on the coast.

Guadalcanal is home to a number of related groups, the largest being the **Kaoka.**

Other major groups are located on Choiseul, New Georgia, and San Cristobal. The peoples on these islands are classified culturally as **Melanesians.**

The Solomon Islands also has a small population of **Polynesians** (about 15,000) who live on Ontong Java, Rennell, Bellona, Anuta, and Tikopia islands.

In addition there are several hundred **Chinese,** traditionally involved in the copra trade; about 1,000 **Europeans;** and immigrants from Kiribati who come in search of land or employment. Since independence there has been considerable internal migration, especially movement to the capital city of Honiara.

Despite this cultural and linguistic diversity, general national cohesion is maintained by a number of factors. Nearly all Solomon Islanders are Christian. Emphasis is placed on the maintenance of traditional customs, called *kastom,* reflecting an ideology of cultural equality among the various groups. The belief in kastom persists despite the reality that some groups—and especially groups from Malaita—have more power and influence than do other groups.

South Korea

T he Republic of Korea occupies the southern section of the Korean Peninsula in East Asia. It is bordered by North Korea on the north, the Yellow Sea on the west, the East China Sea on the south, and the Sea of Japan on the east. South Korea has a population of 45.5 million. There is also a substantial overseas Korean population of about four million with the largest populations living in China, the former Soviet Union, the United States, and Japan. A basically rural, agricultural society until the middle of the 20th century, Korea has experienced rapid industrialization and urbanization in the last 50 years. Korea was under the control of China at various times in its history and its language, religions, arts, traditional patriarchal social organization, and dynastic form of government were all borrowed from or influenced by Chinese civilization.

Ethnic Composition and Ethnic Relations

Because the entire society is **Korean,** South Korea is an ethnically homogeneous state. Koreans trace their ancestry to the Chosen Bronze Age culture that existed from 2333–194 B.C.

South Koreans are not religiously homogeneous: about 49% are Christian (Protestant and Roman Catholic); 47% are Buddhist; and the remainder are Taoist and Confucianist. Large-scale conversion to Christianity took place in the 19th century through the efforts of European and American missionaries; Buddhism was brought by the Chinese.

Although ethnic conflict is absent in South Korea, relations with the Japanese across the Sea of Japan are difficult. Japan has conquered Korea at various times, and from 1910 to 1945,

they ruled it as a colony. During that period, the Japanese sought to destroy Korean culture and make "Japan and Korea as One." Although the effort ultimately failed, the Japanese banned the use of the Korean language in schools and publications, attempted to convert Koreans to Shinto, and made them subjects of the Japanese emperor. During World War II, Korean women were forced to serve as prostitutes for the Japanese military, and not until the 1990s did the Japanese take responsibility for this program. This history—plus the second-class status of Koreans in Japan—continues to define Korean attitudes toward the Japanese. However, relations have improved in the last decade as Japan and Korea, the two major industrial nations of Asia, have become trading partners.

Sri Lanka

S ri Lanka is a multiethnic island nation located off the southeast coast of India. It has a population of 18 million, the majority of which lives in rural villages. Sri Lanka was probably settled by peoples migrating from the South Asian continent.

Ethnic Composition and Ethnic Relations

Sri Lanka has an ethnically heterogeneous population. Although the Sinhalese form the majority of the population, there are three significant ethnic minorities as well as a remnant population of Veddas, the first inhabitants of the island. Sri Lanka has been the scene of one of the most violent ethnic separatist conflicts of the last decade, involving the dominant Sinhalese majority and the Sri Lanka Tamil minority, which seeks an independent Tamil state in the northeast. The conflict has involved assassinations, riots, looting, forced population relocations, intervention by Indian military forces, on-and-off negotiations, and at least 20,000 deaths. By 1997, the Sinhalese had become largely successful in controlling the Tamil independence movement, although Tamil resistance continues in the form of bombings and attacks on Sinhalese. In 1998, violence involving the Tamil rebels continues, with a suicide bombing at the nation's holiest Buddhist temple taking 13 lives and wounding 23 others in January.

Sinhalese, who are 70% Buddhist and 30% Roman Catholic, speak Sinhala and comprise 70% of the Sri Lankan population, dominating the southern two-thirds of the island. Sinhalese have lived on the island for over 2,000 years, and there are marked cultural differences between those inhabiting the interior highlands and those living near the coast. Under colonial domination from the early 1500s until independence in 1948, the Sinhalese began in the early 1960s to increase Sinhalese control of the government and business at the expense of the Sri Lankan Tamils.

Sri Lanka Tamils began coming to the island from southern India as long as 2,000 years ago. Today their culture is a mix of Tamil, Sinhalese, and south Indian elements. They speak a dialect of Tamil and comprise 11% of the Sri Lankan population. Nearly all Sri Lankan Tamils now live in the northeast region of the nation.

Indian Tamils are descendants of Tamils brought to Sri Lanka by the British in the 1800s. They make up 8.5% of the population and, while they speak Tamil, they are culturally and politically distinct from the Sri Lankan Tamil.

Moors (Muslims) comprise 7% of the population, and, while not directly involved in the Sinhalese-Sri Lankan Tamil conflict, several hundred thousand have been forced by Tamil violence and threats to relocate or flee the island.

Veddas are the indigenous inhabitants of the island. Today, they number less than 10,000. Assimilated into both Sinhalese and Tamil society, they speak either language. They are mainly either Hindu or Buddhist. Their traditional hunting-gathering way of life had largely disappeared by the early 20th century.

Syria

Syria, located in the Middle East, is bordered by Jordan on the south, Iraq on the east, Lebanon and Israel on the southeast, Turkey on the north, and the Mediterranean Sea on the west. Traditionally, Syria occupied a region larger than that of today's nation, including modern Lebanon and parts of Israel. During the Islamic era beginning in the 8th century, Damascus, the current capital of Syria, was the center of an Islamic Empire that spread from Central Asia across western Asia, North Africa, and parts of southern Europe. Since then Syria has been under the control of Mongols, Ottoman Turks, and, most recently, the French. Syria has a population of 15.6 million. It is an Arab Islamic nation in which Arabic is the official language.

Ethnic Composition and Ethnic Relations

An ethnically and religiously homogeneous society, 90.3% of Syria's population is Arab, and 90% is Muslim. There are important religious differences within the Arab population, however, and a number of distinct ethnic minorities exist as well. Syria is relatively free of ethnic disagreements, its primary foreign conflict being with Israel. An internal conflict involves the Sunni and Alawite Muslims.

Arabs number 14.1 million in Syria. Arabs are an ethnic group indigenous to the Middle East. They are the majority population in 15 nations in the Middle East and North Africa. The history of the emergence of Arabs as a distinct group in the region is unclear, but as early as 853 B.C., the Arabic language was in use. Although being an "Arab" has different meanings in different nations, a shared Arab identity is based on a number of key elements. These include use of the Arabic language in its classical form (used in religion and literature) as well as the varieties of colloquial Arabic used in daily life; a personal identity with Arab culture, history, and the Arab community; a strong value placed on children and family life; a clear division of labor based on sex; and adherence to Islam. About 93% of Arabs around the world follow Islam. However, not all Muslims are Arabs, and the largest Muslim populations are found in the non-Arab nations of Bangladesh, Indonesia, and India. In Syria, most Arabs adhere to Sunni Islam, as do a majority of Muslims in the Middle East. A minority are Alawite Shi'ites and Druze, two sects not recognized as fully Islamic by Sunni and Shi'ite Muslims.

The **Alawites** live mainly in the north and since the 1960s have been politically involved in the Ba'ath political party, which advocates a secular Syrian nation. President Assad and many other political leaders are Alawites.

The **Druze** live in the south, primarily along the border with Israel. Druze are a distinct Arab group that emerged in the 11th century as a Muslim religious minority, and through a combination of ways of adhering to their unique form of Islam—living in close-knit communities, fighting for autonomy, and accommodating (to a limited extent) the demands of the peoples among whom they have lived—have managed to survive as a distinct ethnoreligious minority. There are about 350,000 Druze in the world, about 70,000 of whom live in Israel and the Israel-occupied Golan Heights region of Syria. At various times they have been persecuted by Arab Christian groups and Muslims.

The major non-Arab ethnic groups are the Kurds, Armenians, and Circassians. **Kurds** are the largest ethnic minority and number about 1.3 million in Syria. Kurds are the indigenous people of the region known as Kurdistan, located in eastern Turkey, northern Syria, northeastern Iraq, and western Iran. Although Kurdistan has never been politically unified under Kurd control, the Kurds claim it as their homeland. Kurds number about 26 million, with 13.7 million in Turkey, 6.6 million in Iran, and 4.4 million in Iraq, in addition to those in Syria. Kurds speak dialects of Kurdish, a language related to the Persian spoken in neighboring Iran. Kurds are mainly Muslims of the Sunni sect. Traditionally, the Kurds were a mountain people who lived by herding and farming. Kurdish culture is today more varied, and several million Kurds live in cities. The Kurds have never been politically unified and are organized into a number of tribes and confederacies. Politically, they are now represented by a number of different political parties. Kurds in Syria are not involved in ethnic autonomy movements, as they are in Turkey and Iraq.

Circassians (numbering a few thousand) live in Damascus, where they moved from their villages following the Israeli capture of the Golan Heights in 1967. Many have since immigrated to the United States (*see* Russia).

Armenians are a remnant population formed from those who lived in Lebanon and those driven into Syria by the Turks in 1915. They are Christians, involved mainly in commerce and business.

Taiwan

T he Republic of China, as Taiwan is officially called, is an island nation located in the South China Sea off the coast of the People's Republic of China. Formerly under Dutch, British, and Japanese control, and at times a part of China, Taiwan became an independent nation in 1949 after the Communist Party came to power in China. Taiwan has a population of 21.5 million. Through its ties to the United States, Taiwan has become a highly industrialized nation, although many Taiwanese continue to be involved in farming. Mandarin Chinese is the official language, and 93% of the population adhere to various combinations of Buddhism, Taoism, Confucianism, and Chinese folk religion. About 4.5% of the population is Christian, and there is a small Muslim community.

Ethnic Composition and Ethnic Relations

Taiwan's population is mainly of Chinese origin, but some diversity exists, based on length of settlement on Taiwan and current political and economic status more than on ethnic or language differences. At the time the Chinese settled Taiwan, beginning in the 16th century, the island was home to a number of groups now collectively labeled **Yuanzhumin,** previously called **Taiwan Aboriginal Peoples** and **Gaosazhu.** They are descendants of peoples who migrated from Southeast Asia. While Taiwan was under Chinese control from 1683 to 1885, these indigenous groups were largely assimilated or driven into the mountains. In the 1990s, the Yuanzhumin number about 340,000. Seven groups retain a distinct identity (although the individuals themselves are assimilated into mainstream society): **Ami,** **Atayal, Bunun, Puyuma, Saisiat, Paiwan-Rukai,** and **Tsou.**

Taiwanese of **Chinese** origin fall into three categories. First are the speakers of Min dialects from southern China, who began settling on Taiwan in the 17th century, and whose modern descendants form the majority of the Taiwan population. Second are the Hakka, also mainly from southern China, who form a minority of the modern-day population. Although the governments in both mainland China and Taiwan classify Min and Hakka as dialects of Chinese, many experts consider them distinct languages. Today, Mandarin Chinese is the national language in Taiwan, and most people speak it as their primary language. Until the 20th century, most of the settlers from the mainland were farmers. Under Japanese rule and since independence in 1949, many Taiwanese have become a part of the large manufacturing sector of the economy. The final Chinese group (about two million in number) is those who arrived after 1949 from mainland China. Members of the military or the government fled with their families to Taiwan after the Communist victory in 1949. They ruled Taiwan and dominated the economy from 1949 until 1987, when political opposition broke into the open. While most of the post-1949 immigrants were Chinese, some members of national minorities immigrated as well, including the Hui, who are Muslims.

The use of the name **Taiwanese** is confusing. Outsiders label all residents of the island with this name to distinguish them from residents of mainland China, although the mainland government considers Taiwan a province. The Min and Hakka refer to themselves and the indigenous groups as Taiwanese and call the post-1949 immigrants **Mainlanders.** The Min and Hakka also call themselves **Formosans,** another name that does not apply to the post-1949 population.

Tajikistan

The Republic of Tajikistan is located in southern Central Asia. It is bordered by Uzbekistan on the west, Uzbekistan and Kyrgyzstan on the north, China on the east, and Afghanistan on the south. The population is 5.9 million. Throughout most of its history, the area that is now Tajikistan was not unified politically. Following the demise of the Soviet Union and the independence of Tajikistan in 1991, the nation became consumed by a violent civil war. To some extent the war involved rivalries between traditional groups and between Sunni and Shi'ite Muslims, but the three major factions were the Communists, the advocates of democratic rule, and the Islamic political parties. The latter two groups have been allied against the former, which is backed by Russia. In addition, regional clans, important in the past, have reemerged as potent political forces. Although a peace agreement was signed in late

Russian guards on the Tajikistan-Afghanistan border buying goods from a traveling merchant. Civil war has disrupted life in this nation since the early 1990s. Photo: Reuters/Corbis-Bettmann.

1996, violence continued, and in 1997, hundreds of thousands of people remained as refugees either within Tajikistan or in neighboring nations. Tajik is the official language, and very few Tajiks speak Russian. The majority of the population is Muslim.

Ethnic Composition

Discussions of the ethnic composition of Tajikistan are confused by different usages of the term "Tajik." Prior to 1929, there was no general sense of Tajik identity across the region. Rather, people in what is now Tajikistan and across the border in what is now Afghani-

stan identified themselves by the region where they lived and the dialect of the language they shared. The notion of a single Tajik identity was promulgated by the Russians during the Soviet era, as part of an attempt to create a Tajik republic within Soviet Central Asia. Since then, the term Tajik has been used in a number of ways: to mean ethnic Tajiks in Tajikistan, to mean all people in Tajikistan, or to mean all ethnic Tajiks in the region, with Dari-speakers in northern Afghanistan also being labeled Tajiks. In addition to ethnic Tajiks, Tajikistan has populations of other Central Asians, as well as Tatars, Russians, Jews, and Koreans.

Tajik (Sart) ethnic identity is based on speaking the Tajik language—a language consisting of a number of closely related dialects of Farsi (the Persian spoken in Iran)—on sharing a traditional way of life farming and living in permanent villages, and on adhering to Islam. Based on these three criteria, and ignoring some internal differences, the number of Tajiks in the world can be estimated to be about nine million. Of these, 3,168,000 live in Tajikistan, about 4 million reside in Afghanistan (where they are also called Dari-speakers), about 900,000 are found in Uzbekistan, and the remainder live in other Central Asian nations and China.

Tajikistan, located at the crossroads of Central and Western Asia, is part of region continuously occupied by humans for over 7,000 years. Tajiks are descended from a mix of Iranian peoples from the south and Turkic peoples from the north, who passed through or settled in the region thousands of years ago. Tajiks speak some 19 different dialects of the Tajik language. Most Tajiks are Sunni Muslims, although there is a Shi'ite minority in Tajikistan. Relations between these two groups are often strained.

In the Soviet era, traditional farming gave way to collective agriculture and cotton was the major crop. Most Tajiks have continued to farm because jobs in industry were controlled by the Russians.

Related to ethnic Tajiks in Tajikistan are the Pamir peoples of the Pamir Mountains to the south and east. Although classified as Tajiks by the Soviets, the Pamir prefer to label themselves **Pamirian Tajiks** to mark their distinctiveness from the Tajiks. There are about 120,000 Pamirian Tajiks to whom regional affiliations have traditionally been more important than any unified sense of Pamirian or Tajik identity. Regional groups such as the **Sarikoli, Wakhi,** and **Shugni** remain important in the 1990s. Pamirians speak dialects related to Tajik. Mainly farmers and herders,

their isolation in the high mountains of the region has kept them relatively free of Soviet influence. Pamirians are Islamic adherents of the Ismaili sect, which separates them from other Tajiks and Muslims. The Pamirians were badly affected by the civil war, and about 50% of the population fled into Afghanistan, although many have now returned home.

The two major Central Asian groups in Tajikistan are the **Uzbeks** (1,198,000) and the **Kyrgyz** (64,000). The presence of the large Uzbek community reflects Uzbek control of the region dating from the 16th century. Russia conquered the region in the 19th century, and the Soviet-determined borders were drawn in the 1920s. The Uzbeks and Tajiks have coexisted in Central Asia for centuries, dating back to a time when cities and towns were defined by a hybrid Turko-Iranian culture. The Kyrgyz live mainly in the east, an area with few Tajik inhabitants. The presence of these large ethnic groups concentrated in certain regions has inhibited the growth of a unified nation in the post-Soviet era. Both the Uzbeks and the Kyrgyz, like the 72,000 **Tatars** also in Tajikistan, are Muslims.

The major non-Asian, non-Muslim ethnic group is the **Russians,** who numbered 388,000 in 1989. Their numbers have rapidly dropped since Tajikistan became independent in 1991. In 1997, they may number less than 200,000 in Tajikistan. The Tajiks fiercely resisted Russian and Soviet rule. Russians remain outsiders in Tajik society, living mainly in cities and working in government and industry. Few Tajiks learned Russians and few Russians learned Tajik. Included with the Russians are much smaller numbers of **Armenians, Belarusians,** and **Ukrainians.**

In addition to these groups, Tajikistan has two other distinct urban minorities: the Bukharan Jews and the Koreans. **Koreans** are a small group in Tajikistan, 90% of whom live in cities. They arrived during World War II, deported from far eastern Russia by Stalin. Koreans work mainly in commerce and the professions.

Bukharan Jews, also called **Central Asian Jews,** are a distinct Jewish group claiming ancestry from one of the "10 lost tribes of Israel" and said to have settled in the region

2,500 years ago. An arrival in the 6th century seems more likely. Bukharan Jews live mainly in Uzbekistan and Tajikistan, numbering anywhere from 30,000 to 75,000. In the post-Soviet era some have immigrated to Kazakhstan, Russia, Israel, and the United States. Traditionally, Bukharan Jews were an urban group who specialized in the dying of yarn. Today, their economic activities are more varied, and many work in the professions or as crafts workers. The practice of Judaism was suppressed during the eras of Russian and Soviet control, but has rebounded in the post-Soviet era.

Ethnic Relations

Although the Russians sought to control Central Asia from the 19th century on, the Tajiks put up strong resistance and were able to preserve more of their traditional culture than other ethnic groups did under Soviet control. Their distance from Moscow and their ties to related peoples in Iran and Afghanistan aided the fight to preserve their cultural autonomy, as did their strong devotion to Islam. Less than 10% of Tajiks learned the Russian language, and few showed an inclination to serve the Communist Party. Most continued to maintain Tajik traditions in their homes while conforming to Soviet economic and political practice

in public. Despite Russian objections, all Tajiks returned to rural settlements for part of the year and lived the traditional lifestyle. In the late 1980s and early 1990s, anti-Russian sentiments were manifested in riots, motivating Russians and other Slavs to leave Tajikistan.

One other important ethnic issue is the nature of relations between Tajiks and Uzbeks. As noted above, the two groups were in consistent contact in the region for hundreds of years within a Turkic-Iranian culture that emerged in Central Asian towns and cities. In the 19th century these cities came under Russian control. The Soviet division of the region in the 1920s placed the largely Tajik cities of Bukhara and Samarkand within Uzbekistan. Tajiks resident in those cities and in Tajikistan believe that the cities should be part of Tajikistan. The large Uzbek population in Tajikistan (almost 20% but far greater in some districts) has made them a potent political bloc and has raised fears among Tajiks about Uzbek involvement in Tajik affairs. So far, these concerns have not been a major element of the civil war, although some of the regional factionalism does reflect underlying rivalries between Tajik and Uzbek for power and control of local economic resources.

Thailand

T he Kingdom of Thailand, located in Southeast Asia, is bordered by Myanmar on the west and northwest; Laos on the northeast and east; and Cambodia, the Gulf of Thailand, and Malaysia on the south. Thailand's southern peninsula also has a long western coastline on the Andaman Sea. Thailand has a population of 58.8 million. It is the only nation is Southeast Asia to have avoided European colonization, although trading ties with Europe have been important since the 1800s. Since the 1970s Thailand has experienced considerable political unrest. Thai is the official language and the Central Thai dialect the major form. Theravada Buddhism is the official religion.

Ethnic Composition

Thailand is an ethnically heterogeneous nation, in spite of Thais constituting 85% of the population. The Central Thai have been the dominant group for several centuries, and this

has produced a long-term pattern of other groups assimilating into Central Thai society. The ethnic groups of Thailand can be divided into three categories: (1) Thais; (2) Hill Peoples of the north; (3) other groups including the Chinese and minorities in the south.

In the most general sense, "Thai" refers to speakers of Thai (Tai) languages in Thailand or neighboring nations. It also refers specifically to the ethnic Thais who form four major regional groups in Thailand—Central Thai, Northeast Thai, Northern Thai, and Southern Thai. The Thai migrated to Thailand from southern China beginning in the 11th century. They are closely related to the neighboring Lao, the major ethnic group in Laos.

The **Central Thai** comprise about 32% of the population of Thailand. Since the late 1600s, when their dialect of Thai became the standard language, they have been dominant culturally, politically, and economically. Central Thai identity is based on being born in a Central Thai community and speaking the Central Thai dialect. Because Central Thai identity is prestigious, Central Thais retain their identity whether they live in the core Central Thai regions of central Thailand or elsewhere in the nation. In recent decades, there has been considerable migration to other regions of Thailand. Many Central Thai live in cities, but those who live in rural areas follow a traditional lifestyle based on wet-rice farming and Theravada Buddhism. About 85% of Central Thai men are ordained priests, although only a small minority actually join the priesthood.

The second largest Thai group is the **Northeast Thai,** also known as the **Thai Lao** or **Lao Isan,** indicating their similarity to the Lao across the border. Their presence in Thailand is largely the result of shifting political boundaries in the past. In language and some customs, the Northeast Thai are more like the Lao than like the Central Thai. The Northeast Thai constitute about 30% of the population and live mainly in the poor northeast region, where they subsist by growing rice and other crops and raising cattle and water buffalo for sale. For over 100 years, the northeast region has been run by Central Thai administrators reporting to the government in Bangkok. There is also a sizable Northeast Thai population in the Bangkok region who more closely associate with the Central Thai. The Northeast Thai are Theravada Buddhists, although they also celebrate regional festivals not celebrated by other Thais.

The two other major Thai-speaking groups are the **Northern Thai (Yuan)** and the **Southern (Pak) Thai**. Each group numbers about 6.5 million. Although the Northern Thai are often described as heavily assimilated into Central Thai society, they continue to see themselves as both a distinct group and the major Thai group across much of northern Thailand. Like the Northeast Thai, the Southern Thai are related to the Lao of Laos. In addition, they speak a distinct dialect of Thai, continue to use their own written language, and view the major northern city of Chiang Mai as their political and cultural center. Through trade relations, they have been influenced by southern Chinese culture over the centuries. The Southern Thai are the major Thai group in the rural south, a poor region that has been considerably influenced by the Malays of neighboring Malaysia. Unlike the rest of rural Thailand, which is composed mainly of small wet-rice farms, the south has been exploited for its rubber trees and tin mines and has become an area of considerable environmental degradation. In addition to working in these industries, the Southern Thai have also been fishers. Due to the declining economy, many Southern Thai have immigrated to other nations—especially those in the Middle East—in search of employment. While the majority are Buddhists, ties to the Malays have produced a small Muslim minority.

In addition to these four major Thai-speaking groups, there are also a number of much smaller Thai-speaking ethnic minority groups in the north and northeast, most of whom are

Theravada Buddhism is Thailand's official religion. A large proportion of Thai men are ordained priests, although only a small minority actually join the priesthood. Photo: Corel Corp.

either assimilated into the larger Thai population or retain ties to co-ethnics in Laos, Myanmar, or China. The major Thai minorities are the **Phuthai** (about 100,000), **Phuan, Saek, Khorat Thai, Shan,** and **Lue.**

The **Hill Peoples** of Thailand live in the northwest extension of Thailand that is bordered by Myanmar on the west and Laos on the east. The region, known as the Golden Triangle, was, and to some extent continues to be, a center for the growing of poppies for opium production. Some of the Hill Peoples were already resident in the region when the Thai migrated from China. Others have arrived more recently. Many of these groups live near the border, and there are often other communities across the border in Laos and Myanmar, even as far north as China. The total population of these groups is unknown, because some individuals or communities have assimilated into Thai society. Others, usually isolated in the hills, have avoided such assimilation. A reasonable estimate is probably about one million Hill People in the region. The major groups (with population estimates) are the **Akha** (35,000), **Hmong** (50,000), **Karen** (20,000), **Kui** (100,000), who are mostly assimilated, **Lahu** (65,000), **Lisu** (18,000), **T'in** (Htin) (30,000), **Yao** (36,000), and **Chong** (6,000). The **Chaobon,** who live south and east of the northwest territory number about 15,000 and are classified as a Hill People. The region is also the home of the **Yumbri,** indigenous hunter-gatherers who have been largely assimilated. Those communities not assimilated into Thai society continue to live primarily by simple farming on semipermanent plots with dry rice (rice grown with rainwater only) the major crop. Many communities also have maintained their traditional religions or combined them with Buddhism. In assimilated communities, wet-rice farming is the norm and most people are Buddhists.

Thailand has yet other ethnic minorities. Some of them are relatively small border groups whose major populations lie across the border in Myanmar (**Karen, Mon**), Malaysia (**Malays, Semang**), or Laos (**Kmhmu, So**). The Karen and Mon populations have increased in recent years due to the arrival of refugees fleeing the political conflict in Myanmar.

There are also a number of large national minority groups in Thailand. The most significant ethnic minority is the **Chinese,** who constitute about 11% of the population and live mainly in cities and towns in the central and southern regions. The Chinese have been in Thailand since the 14th century, first as traders, and then—during the period of French and British colonialism in the region—as intermediaries between Thais and Europeans, especially in the rubber and tin trade. To a large extent the Chinese are assimilated into Thai society. Most are Thai citizens, many have taken Thai names, and most speak Thai as well as Chinese languages. The Chinese still occupy an important role in the economy as traders and store owners, but they are also involved in a much wider range of occupations. They remain a distinct minority due to continued use of the Chinese language, membership in trading networks, and adherence to their traditional Buddhist-Taoist-Confucianist religion—all important markers of Chinese identity.

In addition to the Chinese, Thailand has significant populations of Vietnamese and Khmer from Cambodia. **Vietnamese** number about 70,000 and live mainly in the northeast. Almost all came to Thailand as refugees—one group in the mid-19th century running away from Vietnamese rulers, others later escaping the French, and still more after World War II fleeing the conflict there between France and the United States.

The **Khmer** numbered close to one million in Thailand in the 1980s, nearly all of whom were refugees from the civil war in Cambodia. At the end of the war, in the 1990s, nearly all were sent home. Descendants of a Khmer population that had come under Thai control in the 15th century are now assimilated into Thai society.

The final major Asian ethnic minority is the **South Asians** who number about 60,000 and come mainly from India with small populations from Bangladesh and Pakistan. The **Indians** are a diverse group of whom **Punjabis** (about 20,000) are the largest. South Asians are primarily Hindus or Sikhs. There is also a small number of Muslims. Most South Asians work in the service sector and in retail trade. A sense of group identity is maintained across the Indian population by participating in social and religious organizations and by sending children to Indian-language schools. At the same time, some Indians are being assimilated into Thai society through seeking citizenship, taking Thai names, speaking Thai, joining Thai social organizations, and most importantly, through intermarriage with Thais.

Ethnic Relations

From the late 17th century, ethnic relations in Thailand have amounted to the assimilation of other groups into Central Thai society. Enjoying the highest status in Thailand, the Central Thai emphasize their ethnic identity wherever they live, while people from other Thai groups who live in Central Thai regions seek to identify themselves as Central Thais, primarily by speaking the Central Thai dialect. In addition, the Chinese and South Asians have surrendered to assimilative pressure. Children born in Thailand can become citizens by birth, naturalization is relatively easy, and

the use of Central Thai is needed to be successful in education, business, and politics. Assimilation among the Hill Peoples takes the form of a shift from dry-rice to wet-rice farming, settlement in permanent villages, and conversion from traditional religions to Theravada Buddhism. In addition to having high social status, Central Thais also dominate the government bureaucracy. Their presence in both the northeast and south has led to conflict with the regional Thai populations, who resent Central Thai control. Ethnic tensions have been the most difficult in the poor southern region populated by over one million Muslim Malays and Southern Thai, some of whom are also Muslims. In the 1980s, the government sought to control a separatist movement by initiating sweeping economic and social reforms designed to raise the quality of life in the region. The government also began in the 1980s an ethnic revival initiative, across the nation, which stressed the unique cultures of regional Thai groups. Traditional arts and crafts were revived, regional languages (along with Central Thai) were taught in schools, and traditional forms of clothing were again allowed to be worn in public.

Tonga

The Kingdom of Tonga, located in the South Pacific Ocean, has been an independent nation since 1970. Tonga consists of three major coral island clusters having a total land area of only 646 square kilometers. Of the 150 islands, 36 are inhabited. The population of 96,000 represents a decline of about 10,000 from the 1980s, due to regular immigration to the United States, Australia, and New Zealand. Although under British protection from 1900 to 1970, Tonga was never a colonial conquest. Continuous Christian missionary activity beginning in 1797 has had a profound influence on the indigenous Tongan culture, and the establishment of Tonga as a constitutional monarchy in 1875 has afforded the islands considerable political stability. A more recent influence is that of Mormon missionaries, who assist Tongans in relocating to the United States.

Churchgoers in Tonga. Christian missionary activity in Tonga began in 1797 and has profoundly affected Tongan culture. Photo: Corel Corp.

Ethnic Composition and Ethnic Relations

Tonga is ethnically homogeneous; only small groups from other Polynesian islands such as Fiji, Samoa, and Tahiti regularly live on the islands in addition to the Tongans. Tourism is popular on the islands, and Americans and others involved in tourist businesses live in Tonga.

Tongans are descended from people who settled the main island grouping of Tongatapu about 3,000 years ago. Classified as part of Polynesian regional culture of the Pacific, Tongans are organized hierarchically into three classes: the king, a nobility of 33 families, and commoners. While this structure is still operative, the social order in Tonga is also now influenced by relations among kin groups, an urban middle class, and a large overseas population in the United States, New Zealand, and Australia, which contributes to the Tongan economy through remittances sent to relatives living on the islands. The overseas migration has been stimulated by a land shortage caused by the limited amount of agricultural land and a law that guarantees each male eight acres of land (although in fact many men do not own land). Wesleyan Methodism is the official religion, although nine other denominations now have followers on the islands. Tongans have a long history of contact with Fijians, Samoans, and Tahitians based on trade, warfare, and intermarriage.

Turkey

Turkey, located between southeastern Europe and southwestern Asia, is bordered on the north by Bulgaria, the Black Sea, and Georgia; on the east by Armenia and Iran; on the south by Iraq, Syria, and the Mediterranean Sea; and on the west by the Aegean Sea and Greece. Turkey has a population of 62.5 million. The official language is Turkish, but Arabic and Kurdish are also widely spoken. About 99% of the population is Muslim, although Turkey is a secular nation. The island of Cyprus off the southwest coast of Turkey has an almost exclusively Turkish population in the northern third of the island. Modern Turkey was established in 1922 as the successor to the defunct Ottoman Empire, which from the early 13th century until 1921 ruled various parts of the Middle East, North Africa, and Europe.

Ethnic Composition

Turkey is an ethnically heterogeneous nation in which the major ethnic groups are Turks (about 80%) and Kurds (nearly 20%). The remainder of the population is composed of some dozen Muslim groups from the Caucasus region in the former Soviet Union, a number of European minorities, and Arabs. Almost the entire population is Sunni Muslim, although there is some diversity among the Muslims. Muslims who prefer Turkey to remain a secular nation and those who prefer Turkey to become an Islamic state (like other Middle Eastern Muslim nations) account for one source of diversity in Turkey. A second source is found among small Muslim sects, such as the Shi'ite Alawites, and various groups among the Kurds. Although the ethnic composition of Turkey is known, population figures are not reliable, because the government does not systematically enumerate by ethnic categories.

Turks number about 50 million in Turkey, or about 80% of the population. The ethnic label, "Turk" refers to people descended from nomadic tribes that emerged in Central Asia (Mongols, Huns, and others). The Turks as a distinct group appeared about A.D. 500 in Mongolia. The Turkish empire subsequently spread west to the eastern part of Europe. After contact with Arab Muslims and service in Arab armies, the Turks converted to Islam in the 9th century and 10th century. They wrested control of much of what is modern Turkey from the Byzantine Empire and settled in the Middle East. The Turkish Ottoman Empire began in the 13th century and lasted until the end of World War I. Turks today are classified in three groups, of which **Anatolian Turks** make up nearly the entire Turkish population of Turkey. Traditionally, they were farmers and herders in the eastern region, but now are found throughout the nation. **Rumelian Turks** are those who settled in southern Europe when the region was under Ottoman control. Many have subsequently returned to Turkey from Romania, Bulgaria, and Greece, while the remaining Turkish population in those nations suffers discrimination as ethnic minorities. The third category of Turks is **Central Asian Turks,** who in Turkey are a small population consisting mainly of **Crimean Tatars** and Turkmen. Crimean Tatars are people of Turkish ancestry who settled in the Crimea region of Ukraine. About 10,000 live in Turkey. **Turkmen** are a Central Asian, Muslim ethnic group related to the inhabitants of Turkmenistan. A small number live in eastern Turkey. Another Turk group is the **Yörük,** who live along the Mediterranean coast of southwestern Turkey. Their number is unknown because they are considered Turks by the government, and many are assimilated into mainstream society. Although they speak Turkish, come from Central Asia, and practice Islam, Yörük consider themselves distinct from both the Turks and other ethnic minorities.

Kurds are the indigenous people of the region known as Kurdistan, located in southeastern Turkey, northern Syria, northeastern Iraq, and western Iran. Although Kurdistan has never been politically unified under Kurd control, the Kurds claim it as their homeland. Kurds number about 26 million with 13.7 million living in Turkey, 6.6 million in Iran, 4.4 million in Iraq, and 1.3 million in Syria. The Kurds in Turkey constitute 52% of the Kurd population. Kurds speak dialects of Kurdish, a language related to the Persian spoken in neighboring Iran. Kurds in Turkey, who speak the Kermanji and Zaza dialects, are mainly Sunni Muslims, although a significant minority there follow Sufi sects. Traditionally, Kurds were a mountain people who lived by herding and farming. Kurdish culture is today more varied and several million Kurds live in cities. The Kurds have never been politically unified

Iraqi Kurd women and children in a refugee camp across the border in Turkey. Photo: Reuters/Corbis-Bettmann.

and are organized into a number of tribes and confederacies. Politically, they are now represented by a number of different political parties. In Turkey, they have been at war for over 10 years with a government that has attempted to suppress Kurd identity. The Kurds seek either political autonomy or equality with the Turks. The population of Kurds in Turkey increased after the 1991 Gulf War when Kurds from northern Iraq fled across the border into Turkey.

Peoples of the Caucasus number about 1.2 million, virtually all of whom are descended from Muslim peoples who fled to Turkey following the Russo-Turkish wars of 1853–56 and 1877–78, and war in the Caucasus region in 1914–18. The largest group is comprised of **Circassians** (over 100,000), followed by **Georgians** (100,000), and **Laz** (50,000), the last being rapidly assimilated into Turkish society.

Other groups whose populations in Turkey number in the thousands or tens of thousands are the **Abkhazians, Chechens, Gagauz, Ingush, Nogay, Ossetes,** and **Yezidis.** All of these peoples are Muslims with a long history of ties to Turkey, and they fit into Turkish society relatively easily. After the fall of the Soviet Union in 1991, some of these groups renewed ties to co-ethnics in the former Soviet Union and have supported the attempts of the Chechens, Ossetes, and Abkhazians to gain cultural and political autonomy in Russia and Georgia.

Arabs, an ethnic group indigenous to the Middle East, are the majority population in 15 nations there and in North Africa. In Turkey, Arabs live mainly along the border with Syria, especially in Hatay Province, which had a large Arab population when it became part of Turkey in 1939. Arabs in this region were traditionally Bedouin nomadic herders, but under Turkish rule they have settled in towns and villages. Arabs from Egypt and other North African nations are also found in Turkey. They came as farm workers, and many are now involved in regional business and trade.

Despite Turkey's ties to Europe through the North Atlantic Treaty Organization, there are relatively few people of **European** ancestry in Turkey. The three major groups are the Armenians, Greeks, and Jews, most of whom live in Istanbul. **Armenians** now number less than 70,000, a sharp decrease from the 2.5 million in Turkey at the mid-19th century. In the Armenian genocide of 1915–16, about 1.5 million Armenians were killed by the Turkish government. The Armenian population in Turkey today is involved in commerce and maintain strong ties to Armenia. Members of the Armenian Apostolic Church, they have maintained their own religious and cultural institutions in Turkey.

Once the largest European minority, **Greeks** now number less than 25,000. Living mainly in Istanbul and on islands in the Aegean Sea, they are involved in commerce and are adherents of Greek Orthodoxy.

Jews have been a presence in Turkey since the late 15th century when they were welcomed following their expulsion from Spain in 1492. With the establishment of the State of Israel in 1948, many Turkish Jews emigrated, and their population in Turkey is now less than 20,000. Most are **Sephardic (Spanish) Jews,** although smaller communities of **Ashkenazi (Eastern European) Jews** and members of the **Karaite** and **Dönme** sects also live in Turkey. The Dönme are Jews who long ago converted to Islam but are not fully accepted by either religion.

In addition to these groups, there are small numbers of **Pomaks** (Bulgarians who converted to Islam during the era of Ottoman rule) and **Albanians,** some of whom also converted to Islam during Ottoman rule.

Ethnic Relations

Ethnic relations in modern Turkey are determined by four factors. First, centuries of Ottoman rule led to contact between Turks and other peoples in Europe, Africa, and Asia. Second, Turkey was located on the border of Europe and Asia. Third, the Turkish government attempted after 1922 to downplay the nation's ethnic differences and create a new "Turk" national identity. And fourth, a substantial portion of Kurdistan was located in eastern Turkey.

Although the Ottoman Empire disappeared following several centuries of decline and its defeat in World War I, relations between Turks and some neighboring peoples remain strongly influenced by the history of the Ottoman period. Relations with the Russians, Greeks, and Armenians are less than congenial. Conflict with the Greeks stems from the fate that Greeks suffered during Ottoman rule, the related treatment of Turks remaining in Greece, the flare-ups over ownership of small islands in the Aegean Sea, and the war between Turks and Greeks on Cyprus. Hostility between Armenians and Turks dates from the extermination of about 1.5 million Armenians by the Turks in 1915–16, an event for which the Turks refuse to take responsibility. Turkish-Russian relations are influenced by Turkish fears that Russia desires Turkish land for a Mediterranean seaport, and by Russian concerns about the loyalty of Muslims in the Caucasus.

Turkey's location on the border between Europe and the Middle East has created a culture that is in some ways European (NATO membership, use of the Latin script for written Turkish, Western-style clothing) and in some ways Middle Eastern (Islam, economic ties to Iraq and Iran). This dual identity has led to ethnic and religious conflict in the 1990s as Islamic fundamentalism has spread to Turkey, and Islamic political parties now compete with secular parties for political power. Islamic parties advocate an Islamic religious state in which the laws of Islam become the laws of the nation. Secular parties, backed by military leaders, prefer that Turkey remain a secular state with ties to both the West and to the Middle East. In 1998, the High Court banned the Islamic Welfare Party because of its alleged threat to the secular government. What effect this will have on relations between secular and fundamentalist Muslims is unclear, although it seems certain that the party will remain active in national affairs. Although this conflict is basically religious and not ethnic, there has been an increase in attacks on religious minorities such as Jews and Alawites in the 1990s.

Following the creation of the modern nation of Turkey in 1922, the new government instituted a policy designed to create a sense of Turkish unity among the population. Ethnic identities were legislated out of existence, and all residents were considered Turks, even the millions of Kurds who were labeled "Mountain Turks" or "Eastern Turks." Use of non-Turkish languages was banned, and all publications were printed in Turkish. Public education and military service brought many rural Turks into contact with mainstream Turkish society, and over the years there has been a gradual assimilation of all groups except the Kurds in the southeast.

The Kurds represent a special case in Turkey. Accounting for about 20% of the population, they constitute the major group in the southeast and have ethnic ties to other Kurd communities in neighboring Iraq, Iran, and Syria. The Kurds' desire for their own homeland—Kurdistan—to be carved in part out of Turkish territory has led to a fear of Kurdish separatism and continuing efforts by the government to both displace and assimilate the Kurds and to destroy their political leadership and unity. Since the mid-1980s, the government has used military force to control the Kurd region—killing resisters to Turkish rule, capturing political leaders, destroying villages, and generally displacing Kurds. So far, thousands of homes and hundreds of villages have been destroyed, and over 20,000 people have been killed. The Turkish military has even launched incursions into Iraq against Kurds who have fled there. The Kurds have responded with attacks on government facilities and personnel, both in Turkey and elsewhere.

Turkmenistan

The Republic of Turkmenistan, located in Central Asia, is bordered by Kazakhstan on the north, Uzbekistan on the north and northeast, Afghanistan on the southeast, Iran on the southwest, and the Caspian Sea on the west. Nearly 90% of Turkmenistan is composed of the Kara Kum Desert, which contains little arable land. The population of 4,149,000 lives almost exclusively on the edges of the desert, especially in the south and southeast. The major trade route between Europe and Asia runs through Turkmenistan, which came under Russian control in 1885. The Turkmen fiercely resisted Russian and later Soviet encroachment, but in the 1920s were finally pacified and their territory was made a republic within the Soviet Union. The economy was then transformed from one based on agriculture and herding to one devoted to the commercial growing of cotton. All other economic activity was secondary. Exploited by Moscow and the Communist Party for 70 years, Turkmenistan declared its independence upon the demise of the Soviet Union in 1991. Turkmen is the official language, although Russian continues to be used in government and business.

Ethnic Composition and Ethnic Relations

Turkmenistan is an ethnically heterogeneous nation. About 73% of the population is Turkmen, 9.5% is Uzbek, 9% is Russian, and the remainder consists of smaller numbers of Slavs and Central Asians.

Turkmen number 3,028,770 in Turkmenistan, and sizable numbers are also found in Uzbekistan, Tajikistan, Afghanistan, Iran, Iraq, and Turkey. The Turkmen are descended from the Oghuz people who migrated from Inner Asia to the region that is now the nation of Turkmenistan in the 9th century and 10th century. Modern Turkmen trace their ancestry to the Oghuz khan who first ruled this region. Traditionally farmers and nomadic herders, over 50% of Turkmen still live in rural communities where they are engaged mainly in cotton farming. Craft production, especially the weaving of carpets, is also an important economic activity. For the Turkmen—perhaps more so than for any other Central Asian people—loyalty to one's lineage (a family unit traced through the father's line) and to one's tribe remains a major feature of individual identity. The Turkmen are Sunni Muslims. A distinct Turkmen subgroup is the **Owland,** an in-marrying religious group who trace their ancestry to the earliest leaders of the Muslim Empire of the 7th century.

The other major Central Asian, Muslim groups in Turkmenistan are the **Uzbeks,** who number 394,000, and the **Kazakhs,** who number 88,000. There are also smaller populations of Islamic **Tatars** (39,000) and **Azerbaijanis.**

The primary non–Central Asian and non-Muslim groups are the **Slavs,** primarily the **Russians** who number about 334,000 and the **Ukrainians** who number 36,000. They are mainly an urban population that lives in the cities and works in government, business, and the manufacturing industry. Beginning in the 1920s, the Moscow government attempted to eradicate Turkmen religious culture. Islam was banned, the Russian language was put in place of Turkmen, and the population was forced to end its nomadic lifestyle and live on collective farms. The Turkmen resisted assimilation into the Russian-controlled society, and their relative isolation in rural areas allowed them to maintain much of their traditional culture, including Islam and the use of yurt housing. Despite the potential for ethnic conflict in the post-Soviet era, Turkmenistan has not experienced the problems of other Central Asian republics. In part this is the result of the authoritarian leadership maintained by the former head of the Communist Party (who is still in power) and by the discovery of oil and gas in Turkmen territory.

Tuvalu

Tuvalu is a small nation composed of nine islands in the southeastern Micronesian region of the Pacific Ocean. Formerly part of the Gilbert Islands (now Kiribati) and under British rule from 1892, it became an independent nation in 1978. Settlement of the islands dates back about 500 years to migrants coming from other islands, such as Samoa, Tonga, and Kiribati. It is possible that eight of the nine islands that are settled were each discovered by different people and that only under British rule did the islands as a group develop a single political and ethnic identity.

Tuvaluans number about 8,500 on the islands, and several thousand on New Zealand, Kiribati, Nauru, and Fiji. As noted above, Tuvaluan ethnic identity is a recent development, probably the result of British rule, Protestant missionary activity, and a resentment of the more numerous Kiribati. Different dialects of Tuvaluan are spoken on each island, and many islanders also speak English. Although Tuvalu is a modern nation in politics, economics, and religion, much of daily life revolves around traditional ties based on kinship, family, and village of residence. In addition to the Tuavaluans, there are small numbers of **Kiribati** and **Europeans** on the islands.

United Arab Emirates

T he United Arab Emirates (U.A.E.) is a federation composed of seven small states located along the coast of the eastern Arabian Peninsula, between the Persian Gulf and the Gulf of Oman. The constituent states are Abu Dhabi, Dubai, Sharjah, Ra's al-Khaimah, Fujairah, Umm al-Qaiwain, and Ajman. The U.A.E. is bordered on the north by the Persian Gulf, on the east by Oman, on the south and west by Saudi Arabia, and on the northwest by Qatar. The population of the U.A.E. is 3,057,337. Discovery of oil in the 1930s and the creation of the oil export industry in 1963 have made the U.A.E. one of the wealthiest nations in the world. It has also transformed the nation from one that was lightly populated (mainly by Arabs and Iranians) to one that has a highly urbanized (90%) population composed of foreign workers who live in the modern cities.

Ethnic Composition and Ethnic Relations

The U.A.E. is ethnically heterogeneous, 88% of the population being foreign workers who hold virtually all jobs throughout the economy, save for senior government, business, and some technical positions. The foreign worker population is diverse and includes **South Asians,** such as **Bangladeshis, Indians, Pakistanis,** and **Sri Lankans** (about 45% of the total population), **Arabs,** primarily **Egyptians** along with **Jordanians, Iraqis,** and **Palestinians** (13% of the population), **Iranians** (17%), and smaller populations from the **Philippines, Indonesia,** and **North Africa.** There is also a small group of **Europeans** employed in the oil industry.

The two largest minorities are the **Indians** and **Iranians.** The Indian population includes both Muslims and Hindus, many of whom speak Hindi or Urdu. The Iranians are Muslims who speak Farsi. Foreign workers are generally poor and do not enjoy any benefits of citizenship. Concern about the treatment afforded some workers became an international issue in 1995 when a Filipina maid was punished with 100 lashes for killing the employer who had raped her. Foreign workers are in the U.A.E. at the will of the government and the emirs who control each state, and they may be deported for any reason. Not planning to become permanent residents, they are there to earn wages higher than what they can earn in their homelands. They are normally permitted to establish their own cultural institutions, such as schools and places of worship to serve their communities.

The remaining 12% of the population is composed mainly of Arabs and some Iranians (Persians). Both groups are Muslim and speak Arabic, the official language of the U.A.E. Forming the nation's wealthy, urban minority, they control the government and oil industry. Nearly all jobs are performed by foreign workers, so most citizens do not have to work. The oil wealth has resulted in such a high standard of living that all social and health services are provided by the government.

Uzbekistan

The Republic of Uzbekistan, located in Central Asia, is bordered by Afghanistan and Turkmenistan on the south, Kazakhstan on the west and north, and Kyrgyzstan and Tajikistan on the east. A former republic of the Soviet Union having been under Russian control since the 19th century, Uzbekistan became an independent nation following the demise of the Soviet Union in 1991. Since then it has experienced ethnic, religious, political, and economic unrest as it undergoes major social, political, and economic reforms. Uzbekistan has a population of 23,418,381. Uzbek is the official language, and Sunni Islam is the majority religion.

Ethnic Composition

Uzebekistan has an ethnically heterogeneous population, of which Uzbeks and other Central Asian Muslim ethnic groups constitute over 95%. The ethnic minorities are the Slavic people—Russians, Ukrainians, and small numbers of Belarusians and Moldovans—and Koreans.

Uzbeks numbered 14,123, 626 in the 1989 census, but their population has increased since then because Uzbeks from other Central Asian republics have returned. Uzbeks now constitute over 70% of the population, also an increase since 1989, due to the emigration of ethnic groups. The Uzbeks emerged from the clans and tribes that vied for control of Central Asia from the 12th century through the 15th century. Although the Uzbeks are politically and culturally unified today as the nation of Uzbekistan, clan and tribal links continue to compete with national loyalty. More important in creating unity is adherence to Islam. Since independence from the Soviet state in 1991, the Communist Party of Uzbekistan has changed its name but not its lust for power. From the 1850s the Uzbeks have been forced to deal with Russian control of the region. Traditionally the two groups remained largely separate. Russians lived in the cities and worked in government and heavy industry; Uzbeks lived in the country and farmed, even under Soviet collectivized agriculture. In the post-Soviet period, the Uzbeks have revitalized their culture, especially public adherence to Islam, which had been discouraged by the Soviets.

In addition to the Uzbeks, Uzbekistan has a substantial population of other Central Asian peoples, primarily adherents of Sunni Islam like the Uzbeks. Four of these peoples form the major ethnic groups in other Central Asian nations and are described elsewhere in this volume. They have the following populations in Uzbekistan: **Kazakhs** (808,090), **Kyrgyz** (174,899), **Tajik** (931,547), and **Turkmen** (122,566). In addition, there are some 106,000 people labeled as **Turks** (with no specific group identity) and two other large Turkic groups, the Tatars and the Karakalpaks. **Tatars** number 467,676. Tatar is an imprecise label, in the most general sense referring to people of Turkic ancestry present in Russia since the 13th century. About 190,000 of the Tatars in Uzbekistan are **Crimean Tatars,** forcibly resettled in Central Asia during World War II. Their total population in the former Soviet Union is 6.7 million.

Karakalpaks number 396,000 in Uzbekistan, almost the entire population living in the north, in the Karakalpak republic to the west of the Aral Sea. The Karakalpaks are a Turkic, Muslim, Central Asian people and speak a language with dialects related to both Kazakh and Uzbek. They are a numerical minority in their republic, with Kazakhs and Uzbeks being the majority populations. Although isolated from Uzbek and Soviet political control, the Karakalpaks have had to alter their traditional economic system to accommodate the Soviet-mandated decision to change the economy from subsistence farming to commercial cotton production. This decision has led to critical environmental problems, the most serious of which is the drying-up of the Aral Sea. The relative isolation of the Karakalpak has allowed them to maintain much of their traditional family-based culture and to eat their own ethnic foods; wear ethnic attire; and practice their art, theater, and craft traditions.

Another Islamic group in Uzbekistan is the **Meskhetians,** most of whom have now left Central Asia. They come from the area of southern Georgia and northern Armenia, but had been deported to Kazakhstan, Uzbekistan, and Kyrgyzstan in 1944. The name is derived from the Meshki Turks, one of the deported groups. Only in the 1960s did they emerge as a united group, largely in reaction to their deportation to and virtual captivity in Central Asia. The object of discrimination and violence, including two murders in 1989, they are leaving Central Asia. Numbering 160,000–260,000 in Azerbaijan, 14,000 in central Russia, and an undetermined number in the Central Asian republics, their request to immigrate to Turkey or resettle in Georgia has been refused by the two governments.

The largest non-Uzbek ethnic group in 1989 was the **Russians,** who numbered 1,652,000. In addition, there were some 154,000 **Ukrainians,** a Slavic group closely related to Russians. The major long-term effect of Russian influence has been the massive destruction of the environment, especially in the regions adjacent to the Aral Sea. Large-scale cotton growing required irrigation and the use of water from rivers flowing into the Aral Sea, which caused a 40% decrease in its water level. Irrigation has salinated the soil, making farming difficult, and the widespread use of chemical fertilizers, pesticides, and herbicides has created major health problems such as high rates of cancer, anemia, and infant mortality.

The major non-Turkic and non-Slavic ethnic group in Uzbekistan is the **Koreans,** who number 183,000. They are descendants of Koreans who first settled in eastern Siberia in the 1860s and then in 1937 were forcibly relocated to Central Asia. The survivors of the relocation were for several decades farmers, but since then the Koreans have become mainly urban professionals, with a sizable number joining the Communist Party and speaking Russian. At the same time, a strong Korean identity is maintained through clubs, newspapers, language schools for children, and marriage within the group. Adherence to Confucianism, Buddhism, and Korean folk religions has eroded in Uzbekistan and most Koreans are nonbelievers. As a small group, the Koreans enjoy peaceful relations with the other groups.

Ethnic Relations

For the past 150 years, the main ethnic relationship in Uzbekistan has been that between the Russians and the Uzbeks. Under Russian and then Russian-dominated Soviet control, the Uzbeks suffered from the same Russification and Sovietization programs experienced by other non-Russians. Attempts were made to replace the Uzbek language with Russian, Uzbek history was rewritten to reflect Russian and Communist ideology, Russian Orthodoxy was promoted, and Islam was repressed. However, while the building of mosques and the training of religious leaders were banned, Islam was allowed to survive, once the Soviets decided to use Central Asian Islam to build relations with Islamic nations in the Middle East and Asia. After 1989, Islam rebounded, new mosques were built, open worship was encouraged, and closer ties evolved between the government and the Islamic leadership.

When the independence movement gained momentum in the late 1980s, resistance to Russian influence became more vocal, and in 1989 there were riots against the Russians in Tashkent, the capital city. Anti-Russian and Uzbek national sentiment was also seen in the reestablishment of Uzbek as the official language, in attempts by the new Uzbek government to form closer ties with Middle Eastern nations, and in a transformation of the workforce in which Uzbeks took jobs in industry formerly held by Russians. In the 1990s, ethnic unrest has led to attacks on Meskhetians, Crimean Tartars, and Kyrgyz. All of these groups, whose populations are now declining in Uzbekistan, are seen by Uzbeks as economic rivals who take jobs from Uzbeks, a serious issue in a nation with an unemployment rate as high as 10%.

Vanuatu

The Republic of Vanuatu is an island nation located in the South Pacific Ocean. It consists of over 80 volcanic and coral islands. The Solomon Islands lie to the north, Fiji to the east, New Caledonia to the south, and Australia to the west. The peoples of these islands came into regular contact with British and French colonists and missionaries in the 19th century and were jointly administered by the two nations as the New Hebrides from 1906 to 1980, when they became the independent nation of Vanuatu. Vanuatu is the home of a number of distinct cultural groups, each group linked to a specific island or section of an island. In the past, over 100 languages and dialects were spoken on the islands; on some islands, the people spoke as many as five different languages. Today, indigenous languages remain in use, although most Vanuatuans speak Bislama, the national language—a Creole language based on English and local languages. Many people also speak English and French, which are taught in the schools. The population of Vanuatu is about 177,000, and there is also a sizable overseas population of Vanuatuans, who have immigrated to Fiji, New Zealand, and the United States in search of employment and education. Vanuatuans were converted to Christianity (Protestantism or Roman Catholicism) in the 19th century, and most remain Christians, although indigenous beliefs and practices are sometimes combined with Christianity.

Ethnic Composition and Ethnic Relations

The five major cultural groups in Vanuatu are the **Ambae** (7,500), **Pentecost Islanders** (10,000), **Malekula** (1,000), **Nguna** (2,000), and **Tanna** (20,000). On many islands, the primary resource is the fertile volcanic soil, which supports an economic system based on horticulture and cash cropping. Common crops for home growing are taro, yams, and bananas, while coffee, cocoa, and coconuts are grown for sale. Most Vanuatuans live in small villages and are linked to others in the community or on the island through ties of kinship. People trace their kin through either their maternal or paternal line. Village life is managed by family leaders and local "big-men" who come from high-ranking families. The national government is involved in health care, education, and the settlement of major disputes at the local level. Many other local matters remain in the hands of village councils and big-men. The national government is advised by a council of chiefs representing the indigenous groups.

In addition to the islanders, a few thousand **British, French,** and other **Pacific Islanders** live in Vanuatu. Ethnic conflict is not a problem, because each island group continues to function as a self-sufficient unit. Prior to European colonization, conflict within island groups over land was evidently common but decreased under British and French control.

Vietnam

The Socialist Republic of Vietnam, located in Southeast Asia, is bordered by China on the north, the South China Sea on the east and south, and Cambodia and Laos on the west. It has a population of 73.4 million, making it the twelfth-largest nation in the world. Vietnam was settled by a mix of peoples who entered the region and settled there from 2000 to 500 B.C. These peoples came from what is now Indonesia, mainland Southeast Asia, and China. By about 300 B.C., a distinctive Vietnamese polity emerged. The region was under Han Chinese control from 11 B.C. to A.D. 939, and the Chinese influence continues to be felt in the Vietnamese language and religion. After centuries of expansion and contraction, Vietnam was ruled by the French from 1859 until defeated by the Vietnamese at Dienbienphu in 1955. The nation was then divided into North and South Vietnam. The 1965–1975 Vietnam War ended in victory for the Communist-ruled north, and in 1976 Vietnam was reunified. Vietnamese religion is a mix of traditional religions, Buddhism, Taoism, and Confucianism. About five million Vietnamese are Roman Catholics, having converted during the era of French rule, and about four million are adherents of indigenous religious move-

Fishermen unloading their catch at Thuan Phouoc beach. Fishing and farming are important economic activities in Vietnam. Photo: Agence France Presse/Corbis-Bettmann.

ments that have developed in the 20th century. Religion has been suppressed by the Communist government and plays a limited role in Vietnamese society.

Ethnic Composition

From the viewpoint of the Vietnamese government, there are two categories of ethnic groups in Vietnam—the Vietnamese, who account for about 87% of the population, and the National Minorities, who account for the other 13%.

Vietnamese number about 63 million. They trace their ancestry to the first Vietnamese state, which appeared in about 300 B.C. Most Vietnamese are rural farmers who live in small villages and grow rice as their primary crop. Fishing is an important economic activity along the coast. Vietnamese who live in cities are engaged in all occupations typical of urban life and dominate the political and economic sectors. The Vietnamese language, which was influenced by Chinese, is the national language. Most Vietnamese are Buddhists, with elements of traditional Vietnamese religions, Taoism, and Confucianism added to the Buddhist base. Those who practice Roman Catholicism no longer enjoy the high status they were afforded during the era of French rule. During the French period and the U.S. presence in the south from 1955 to 1975, various elements of Western culture, including a market economy and Western-style education, were adopted by the elite. Western ideas were eliminated by the Communist government after 1976, and Chinese influence lessened when relations between the two nations deteriorated in 1979.

The term "national minority" is an official government designation and was developed by the government in the post–Vietnam War era. It includes three major types of ethnic groups: (1) Chinese, (2) Highlanders or Hill Tribes, and (3) non-Highlanders. In developing this classification, the government lumped together various groups and ignored variation within groups. The government also standardized the spelling of the names of many groups.

Chinese in Vietnam numbered as many as two million in the early 1970s. They now number about 700,000. Chinese in the north were mainly rice farmers while those in the south, who formed the majority of the Chinese population in Vietnam, lived mainly in the eastern lowland cities and were heavily involved in business. Before the Communist victory in 1975, the Chinese controlled much of the retail, wholesale, and foreign trade in south Vietnam. Following the Communist victory and the abolishing of private commerce in 1978, many Chinese left Vietnam. Several hundred thousand returned to China, and hundreds of thousands of others formed the majority of Vietnamese "Boat People," who fled to Hong Kong and other Southeast Asian nations. Many eventually settled in the United States, Australia, Canada, Sweden, Norway, and Denmark.

The groups labeled as **Hill Tribes, Highlanders,** or **Montagnards** (meaning "mountaineers") form the bulk of the national minorities and live in the mountains that cover much of the western two-thirds of Vietnam. Many groups live in the central highlands of what was formerly South Vietnam. For most of their history, these groups lived outside Vietnamese society and were relatively unaffected by developments in the eastern plains. Although there were, of course, variations from group to group, including language, there were also some similarities. Most groups subsisted as horticulturists by growing rice, cassava, corn, beans, bananas, and other crops in large gardens cleared and made fertile by the slash-and-burn method. Horticulture was supplemented by hunting; gathering wild plants for food; fishing; and the keeping of pigs, chicken, and water buffalo. Some Hill Tribes were nomadic but the majority moved every few years when gardens needed to be slashed-and-burned. The primary social units were the family and the village. Each village had dwellings for the resident families as well as a men's house, where men gathered and single men might live. The material culture centered on the construction of goods from bamboo. Each village was governed by a headman, and in some groups there were a number of social categories based on wealth. During the period of French control that began in 1859 and ended in 1954, some of these groups were introduced to Roman Catholicism and to French administration, which undermined the role of the headman in some villages. Certain groups accepted French control, others resisted, and some were unaffected. During the Vietnam War from 1965–1975, many villages were drawn into the fighting and the region was devastated by bombings. Both the North Vietnamese and Americans sought the assistance of the peoples of the central highlands. Relatively little is known about the current status of most of these groups, because they have been little studied in the last 40 years.

The non-Highlander minorities are the **Cham, Hmong, Tay (Thai),** and **Khmer.** The Hmong, Tay, and Khmer are groups whose major populations are located in China, Thailand, and Cambodia, and they are discussed elsewhere in this volume. The Cham are descendants of the South Asian people who ruled the coastal region from 200 B.C. to A.D. 1471 when they were defeated by the Vietnamese. The Cham now number about 150,000 and live in south-central Vietnam and Cambodia. Since their defeat, the Cham have been under strong pressure to assimilate from the dominant Vietnamese, and they are now largely integrated into Vietnamese society as rice farmers. The most significant surviving feature of traditional Cham culture is religion—those in Vietnam are mainly Hindu and those in Cambodia mainly Muslim. Both religions reflect the Cham migration from South Asia into Vietnam.

National Minorities of Vietnam

Group	Population
Akha	10,000
Bahnar	137,000
Bru	50,000
Cham	150,000
Chrau	20,000
Co Sung (Lahu)	4,000
Duane	unknown
E Dé (Rhadé)	195,000
Halang Doan	2,000
Hmong	300,000
H. Rê (Hre)	94,000
Katu	37,000
Khua	5,000
Kmhmu	30,000
Ma	40,000
May	1,500
M.Nông (Mnong)	67,000
Monom	5,000
Muong	500,000
Pacoh	15,000
Rengao	15,000
Tau-Oi	26,000
Tay (Tai, Thai)	1,200,000
Xó dâng (Sedang)	97,000
X. Tiêng (Stieng)	51,000

Ethnic Relations

Ethnic relations in the 1990s focus on contacts between the Vietnamese and the national minorities. In the past, the Vietnamese viewed the Hill Tribes as inferior and commonly labeled them "savages." Thus, the two groups had relatively little to do with each other. The Vietnamese lived on the coast and on the lowland plains, and the minorities dwelled in the highlands. The highlands were not suitable for Vietnamese wet-rice farming, and the lowlanders had little reason to migrate into the interior. Non-highland minorities, such as the Tay and Hmong, were considered to be less backward than the highlanders, but still culturally inferior to the Vietnamese. Then, as now, the Vietnamese controlled the nation and their culture was dominant. In the Communist era, contact between the Vietnamese and highlanders has increased significantly through efforts to collectivize farming and settle nomadic highlanders. Government relocation programs have moved several million Vietnamese into the highlands to start new farms and to work in factories, and efforts are underway to replace the traditional village headmen with Communist Party officials. While not all of these programs have been successful, the overall effect has been to make highlanders a minority in their indigenous territory and to gradually assimilate them into mainstream society.

Western Samoa

The Independent State of Western Samoa is a nation located in the Polynesian cultural region of the South Pacific Ocean. Western Samoa consists of the large islands of Savai'i and Upolu, and several smaller islands. It is located about 12 degrees south of the equator and just east of the International Date Line. Western Samoa was settled by the ancestors of the contemporary Samoans about 3,000 years ago and came into contact with European explorers in the 1700s. From the mid-1800s to the early 20th century, the islands were under British, American, and German control, and from 1919 until independence in 1962, they were administered by New Zealand. Significant contact with the West began in 1830, upon the founding of the London Missionary Society and the subsequent conversion of virtually the entire Samoan population to Christianity.

Ethnic Composition and Ethnic Relations

Western Samoa has a population of 214,000. **Samoans** constitute about 92% of the population; Samoans of mixed Samoan and European or Chinese ancestry about 7% of the population; and **Chinese,** other **Pacific Islanders,** and **Europeans** the remaining 1%. A desire for university education and employment has prompted many Samoans to leave the islands; about 75,000 live in New Zealand, and others in American Samoa, the United States, and Australia. The islanders speak Samoan, although English is also an official language. Nearly all Samoans are Christian: about 50% are Congregationalist; 17% each are Roman Catholic and Methodist; and the remainder are Mormon, Seventh-Day Adventist, and Baha'i. Despite the long history of European contact, the Samoans remain in control of their land and the islands. Many Samoans are horticulturists, who grow root crops for their own use, and coconuts, cocoa, and bananas for export. Tourism is an important economic activity, and some Samoans own shops or work in the government. Social and political life is organized along kinship lines; groups of related individuals and families own and allocate land and select leaders. The Samoans, one of the largest Polynesian groups, make a clear social distinction between those of full Samoan ancestry and those of mixed ancestry. The small Chinese population, which was imported by the British, continues to grow bananas and other crops for export. Europeans are mainly involved in commerce.

Yemen

Y emen, located on the southwest corner of the Arabian Peninsula, is bordered by Saudi Arabia on the north, Oman on the east, the Arabian Sea on the south, and the Red Sea on the west. The region that is now Yemen has been inhabited for thousands of years and from the 10th century to the 2nd century B.C. was the home of the Kingdom of Sheba, a rich and powerful Arabian monarchy that controlled the trade route from Africa to South Asia. Arabs in the region were among the first converts to Islam in the 7th century and were much involved in spreading Islam across the Middle East and into Africa. After centuries of Ottoman Turk and then British control, Yemen in the 20th century has experienced much political instability. From 1962 to 1990 it was divided into two nations. Census information is not reliable; the population in the late 1990s probably ranges from 10 million to 13 million. At times there has been a large Yemeni population, composed of male workers, holding down jobs in other Middle East nations. The largest contingent, some 1.1 million in Saudi Arabia, was expelled from that nation in 1991, when Yemen supported Iraq in the Gulf War.

Ethnic Composition and Ethnic Relations

Yemen is an ethnically homogeneous nation; nearly 100% of the population is Arab and Muslim. In addition to **Yemenis,** there are small numbers of people of mixed African or Indian and Arab ancestry, which reflects Yemen's past as a center of regional trade. In the absence of ethnic diversity, variation in Yemen is primarily based on religion—Shi'ite Muslims in the north and Sunni Muslims in the south, affiliation with different tribes in some regions, and a complex system of hierarchical organization based on descent from nobility and occupation. Tribal leaders and legal scholars hold the highest positions while most menial work is given to Yemenis of partial African ancestry. Many of the latter are descendants of slaves brought to Arabia from Ethiopia.

PART FOUR
The Americas

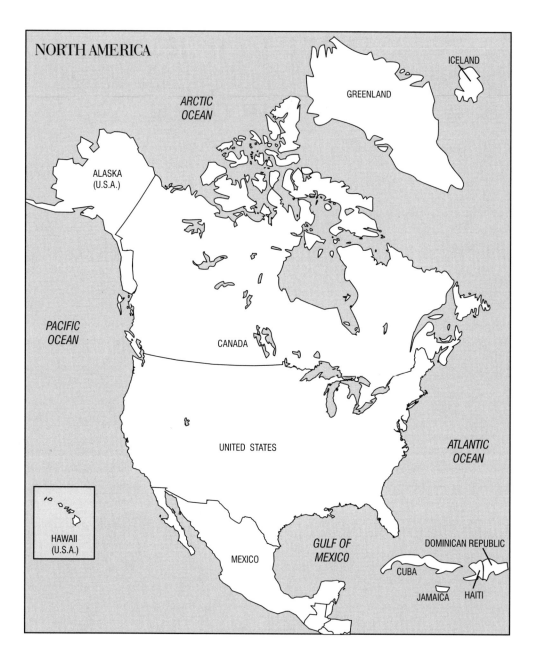

NORTH AMERICA

ICELAND

GREENLAND

ARCTIC
OCEAN

ALASKA
(U.S.A.)

PACIFIC
OCEAN

CANADA

UNITED STATES

ATLANTIC
OCEAN

HAWAII
(U.S.A.)

DOMINICAN REPUBLIC

MEXICO

GULF OF
MEXICO

CUBA

JAMAICA   HAITI

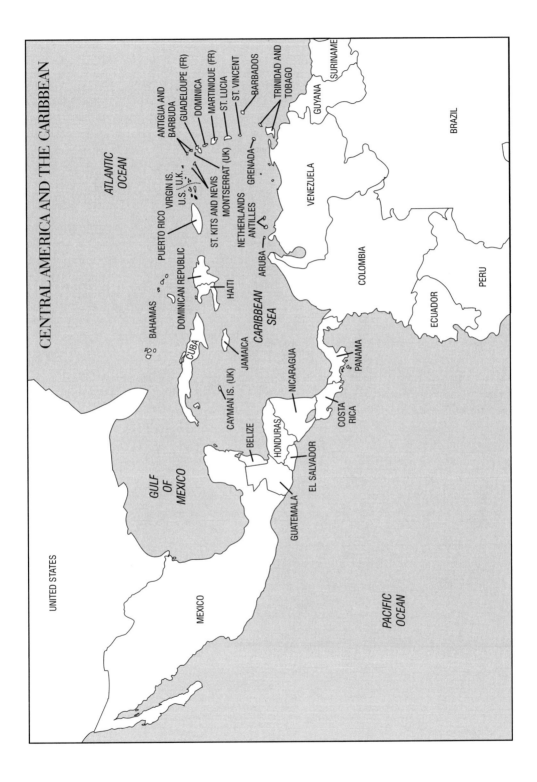

CENTRAL AMERICA AND THE CARIBBEAN

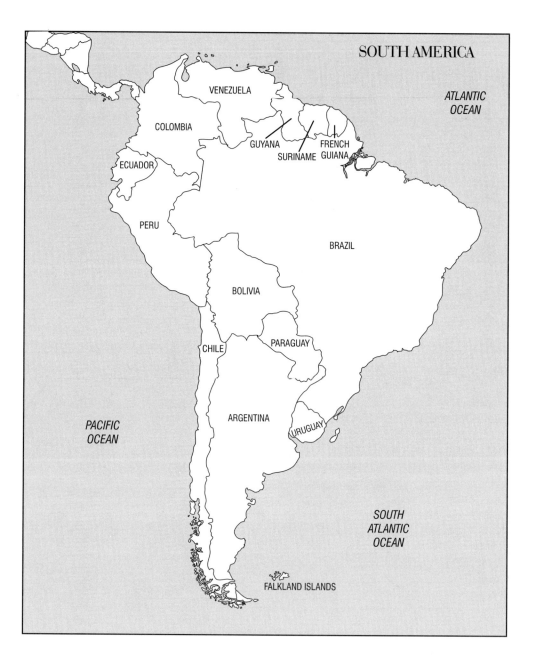

SOUTH AMERICA

ATLANTIC
OCEAN

VENEZUELA

COLOMBIA

GUYANA

SURINAME

FRENCH
GUIANA

ECUADOR

PERU

BRAZIL

BOLIVIA

PARAGUAY

CHILE

PACIFIC
OCEAN

ARGENTINA

URUGUAY

SOUTH
ATLANTIC
OCEAN

FALKLAND ISLANDS

THE AMERICAS
Introduction

There is no single pattern that can fully and accurately describe the varieties of ethnic composition or ethnic relations for all nations of the Americas. There are, however, a number of subregional patterns, which can be seen in the Spanish Americas, the British Americas, the French and Dutch Americas, and North America.

The Spanish Americas

The Spanish Americas are those nations colonized by Spain in which Spanish remains the primary language—countries such as Mexico, Peru, Colombia, and Ecuador. This label does not mean that these nations have remained culturally Spanish; all have developed their own national cultures and identities, and their closest relationships today are with other nations in the Americas, not with Spain. However, what enables us to delineate patterns of ethnic composition and relations is their shared Spanish colonial experience, which to some extent determined the ethnic composition and the nature of ethnic relations in these nations.

For the most part, the nations of Spanish America are composed of people from five ethnic categories, although there is some variation across these nations in the size of each of these categories and their role in society. The five categories are: (1) peoples of Spanish and other European ancestry; (2) Mestizos (Ladinos), peoples of mixed European-Indian or, in some nations, mixed European-Indian-African ancestry; (3) American Indians; (4) people of African ancestry, many with mixed African and European ancestry; and (5) people of Asian ancestry—mainly Koreans and Japanese, along with a smaller number of Chinese.

In the Spanish Americas, the pattern of ethnic relations established in the 16th century continues to hold, although with some modification. The small political and economic elite is made up of those of Spanish or other European descent or of Mestizos who identity closely with European culture—they live in cities, speak Spanish, and are Roman Catholic. The middle class, which has expanded during the 20th century in many nations, is composed of Mestizos and some people of African ancestry, especially if they identify with the mainstream national culture. American Indians and people of African ancestry, especially those living in rural areas, form the lowest class and continue to be discriminated against, despite new laws and policies designed to end inequality in employment, housing, and education. Asians in the Spanish Americas form a special class of people who are mainly involved in commerce and industry.

In the last several decades, a development common to many nations has been the emergence of African and Indian rights movements, which push for the revitalization of the traditional cultures of these peoples, the return of land, and political and economic rights.

The British Americas

The British Americas are mainly the islands in the Caribbean that were or still are British colonies along with coastal areas in Central and South America, most importantly, Belize and Guyana. These nations' Indian populations had been exterminated or removed by the 17th century, and millions of slaves were imported from Africa to work on the sugar cane plantations and in other kinds of agricultural. When slavery ended in the 1830s, the ethnic composition of the British Americas changed again, with Asians (mainly Asian Indians and Chinese) imported as indentured laborers to replace the slaves. In most nations, the Asian immigrants quickly abandoned farming and turned instead to the retail trade and later to commerce.

In most of these nations today, the pattern of ethnic composition remains the same—a small minority of people with European ancestry, a majority of people with African ancestry, and a minority of people who are descendants of Asian immigrants. Additionally, there are sometimes other groups such as Madeirans or Lebanese who are involved in retail trade. Europeans and white North Americans continue to dominate the economy. Politically, since independence—which came for most islands in the 1960s—the African-ancestry majority is dominant, although the situation is more complicated in nations with large Asian populations, as ethnicity and economic interests intersect and lead to various political alliances. By and large, the Asians and other small minorities continue to play specialized economic roles.

The French and Dutch Americas

The pattern in the former and current Dutch and French colonies—again, mainly islands in the Caribbean—is similar to, though also different from, the situation in the British Americas. The similarity is that the two main ethnic groupings are those of European ancestry (the minority) and peoples of African or mixed African-European ancestry (the major-

ity), with an absence of American Indians, who were killed or driven off in the 16th century. The difference is that in the French Americas, Africans were assimilated into French society and culture and, as a result, have strong ties to France. The major exception to this is Haiti, where separation from France occurred in the early 1700s. In the Dutch Caribbean, the major difference is the emergence of a distinct ethnic group composed of people of African or partial African ancestry whose culture is based on a mix of African, Dutch, and Spanish elements.

North America

The two North American nations of Canada and the United States have the most complex ethnic mix in the Americas and equally complex patterns of ethnic relations. Both nations have populations composed of Native American groups and immigrants from most other nations in the world. In both nations, the descendants of immigrants from Western Europe are the culturally dominant groups, while groups whose forebears came from other nations show considerable variation in their degree of assimilation to the general culture. In both nations, Native Americans form a poor and isolated population, although the last several decades have seen movement in the direction of Native peoples gaining lost rights and achieving greater economic and political stability. The United States and Canada, although displaying some similarities regarding ethnicity, also have important differences. First, the United States has large and complex African American and Hispanic (Latino) populations, while Canada does not. Second, the United States takes an officially assimilationist view toward ethnic relations, with all people expected to become "Americans." Canada, on the other hand, is an officially bilingual (English and French) and multicultural nation, where it is expected that immigrant groups will retain some features of the culture of their place of origin.

This summary of the four main regional patterns of ethnic composition and ethnic relations in the Americas is, of course, very general, and it ignores such nations such as Argentina and Brazil that deviate from the broad patterns in important ways. However, the summaries do highlight some major features of ethnicity in the Americas: the region is mainly populated by immigrants; American Indians are largely second-class citizens; African Americans continue to suffer from the slavery experience; and the descendants of European immigrants are politically and economically dominant.

The Americas Bibliography

Barrett, Leonard. *The Rastafarians: The Dreadlocks of Jamaica.* London: Heinemann, 1977.

Bratsberg, Bernt; and Dek Terrell. "Where Do Americans Live Abroad?" *International Migration Review* 30 (1996): 788–802.

Bremer, Philip, et al. *The Cuba Reader: The Making of a Revolutionary Society.* New York: Grove Press, 1989.

Chapin, Mac. *Indigenous Populations: The Coexistence of Indigenous Peoples and the Natural Environment of Central America.* Washington, DC: National Geographic Society, 1992.

Collingwood, Dean W.; and Steve Dodge, eds. *Modern Bahamian Society.* Parkesburg, IA: Caribbean Books, 1989.

Coniff, Michael L.; and Thomas J. Davis. *Africans in the Americas: A History of the Black Diaspora.* New York: St. Martin's Press, 1994.

Corradi, Juan E. *The Fitful Republic: Economy, Society, and Politics in Argentina.* Boulder, CO: Westview Press, 1985.

Cross, Malcolm. *The East Indians of Guyana and Trinidad.* London: Minority Rights Group, 1982.

Dann, Graham. *The Quality of Life in Barbados.* London: Macmillan, 1984.

Davis, Mary B., ed. *Native Americans in the Twentieth Century.* New York: Garland, 1994.

Degler, Carl N. *Neither Black nor White: Slavery and Race Relations in Brazil and the United States.* New York: Macmillan, 1971.

Dow, James W., ed. *Encyclopedia of World Cultures,* Volume 8, "Middle America and the Caribbean." New York: G. K. Hall/Macmillan, 1995.

Ferrell, Robert H.; and Joan Hoff, eds. *Dictionary of American History, Supplement.* New York: Charles Scribner's Sons, 1996.

Gabriel, John. "UNO…What Happened to Autonomy? Politics and Ethnicity on Nicaragua's Atlantic Coast." *Ethnic and Racial Studies* 19 (1996): 158–84.

García, Aníbal Cueva, ed. *Gran Atlas Geográfico del Peru y el Mundo.* Lima: 1991.

Grasmuck, Sherri; and Patricia A. Pessar. *Between Two Islands: Dominican International Migration.* Berkeley: University of California Press, 1991.

Greenfield, Sidney. *English Rustics in Black Skin.* New Haven, CT: College and Universities Press, 1966. (Caribbean)

Hanbury-Tenison, Robin. *A Question of Survival for the Indians of Brazil.* New York: Charles Scribner's Sons, 1971.

Harner, Michael J. *The Jívaro: People of the Sacred Waterfalls.* New York: Doubleday, 1973. (Ecuador)

Hirschfelder, Arlene; and Martha Kreipe de Montaño. *The Native American Almanac: A Portrait of Native America Today.* New York: Prentice Hall, 1993.

Ho, Christine G. T. "Hold the Chow Mein and Give Me Soca: Creolization of Chinese in Guyana, Trinidad, and Jamaica." *Amerasia Journal* 15 (1989): 3–25.

Hoxie, Frederick E., ed. *Encyclopedia of North American Indians*. Boston: Houghton Mifflin, 1996.

Key, Mary Ritchie. *The Grouping of South American Indian Languages*. Tübingen: Günter Narr, 1979.

Klein, Herbert S. *Bolivia: The Evolution of a Multi-Ethnic Society*, 2nd ed. New York: Oxford University Press, 1992.

Koulen, Ingrid; and Gert Oostindie. *The Netherlands Antilles and Aruba: A Research Guide*. Dordrecht: Foris Publications, 1987.

Kuper, Adam. *Changing Jamaica*. Boston: Routledge & Kegan Paul, 1976.

Laguerre, Michel S. *The Military and Society in Haiti*. Knoxville: University of Tennessee Press, 1993.

Layng, Anthony. *The Carib Reserve: Identity and Security in the West Indies*. Lanham, MD: University Press of America, 1983. (Dominica)

Lazarus-Black, Mindie. *Legitimate Acts and Illegal Encounters: Law and Society in Antigua and Barbuda*. Washington, DC: Smithsonian Institution Press, 1994.

Li, Peter S. *Race and Ethnic Relations in Canada*. Toronto: Oxford University Press, 1990.

Lipset, Seymour M. *Continental Divide: The Values and Institutions of the United States and Canada*. New York: Routledge, 1990.

Lizarralde, Manuel. *Indice y Mapa de Grupos Etnolingüísticos Autóctonos de America del Sur*. Caracas: Fundación La Salle de Ciencias Naturales, Instituto Caribe de Antropología y Sociología, 1993.

Maybury-Lewis, David; and James Howe. *The Indian Peoples of Paraguay: Their Plight and their Prospects*. Cambridge, MA: Cultural Survival, 1980.

Merrill, Tim, ed. *Guyana and Belize: Country Studies*. Washington, DC: Government Printing Office, 1993.

Miller, Marc S., ed. *State of the Peoples: A Global Human Rights Report on Societies in Danger*. Boston: Beacon Press, 1993.

O'Leary, Timothy J.; and David Levinson, eds. *Encyclopedia of World Cultures,* Volume I, "North America." Boston: G. K. Hall, 1991.

Page, Joseph A. *The Brazilians*. Reading, MA: Addison-Wesley, 1995.

Plant, Roger. *Sugar and Modern Slavery: Haitian Migrant Labor and the Dominican Republic*. Totowa, NJ: Biblio Distributors, 1986.

Poston, Dudley L., Jr.; and Mei-Yu Yu. "The Distribution of the Overseas Chinese in the Contemporary World." *International Migration Review* 24 (1990): 480–508.

Reddy, Marlita A. *Statistical Record of Native North Americans*. Detroit: Gale Research, 1993.

Reister, Jürgen. *Indians of Eastern Bolivia: Aspects of Their Present Situation*. Copenhagen: International Work Group for Indigenous Affairs, 1972.

Reitz, Jeffrey G.; and Raymond Breton. *The Illusion of Difference: Realities of Ethnicity in the United States and Canada*. Toronto: C. D. Howe Institute, 1994.

Root, Maria P. P. *Racially Mixed People in America*. Newbury Park, CA: Sage, 1992.

Ruiz, Ramón Eduardo. *Triumphs and Tragedy: A History of the Mexican People*. New York: W. W. Norton, 1992.

Rumbaut, Ruben G. "Origins and Destinies: Immigration to the United States since World War II." *Sociological Forum* 9: 583–621.

Statistics Canada. *Ethnic Origin*. Ottawa: Industry, Science and Technology Canada, 1993.

Statistics Canada. *Profile of Canada's Aboriginal Population*. Ottawa: Industry, Science and Technology Canada, 1995.

Steward, Julian H., ed. *Handbook of South American Indians*. 6 vols. Washington, DC: Smithsonian Institution, 1946–59.

Thernstrom, Stephan, ed. *Harvard Encyclopedia of American Ethnic Groups*. Cambridge: The Belknap Press, 1979.

U.S. Bureau of the Census. *Detailed Ancestry Groups for States*. Washington, DC: U.S. Bureau of the Census, 1992.

U.S. Bureau of the Census. *Statistical Abstract of the United States, 1992*. Washington, DC: U.S. Bureau of the Census, 1992.

U.S. Committee for Refugees. *1995 World Refugee Survey*. New York: U.S. Committee for Refugees, 1996.

Wade, Peter. *Blackness and Race Mixture: The Dynamics of Racial Identity in Colombia*. Baltimore: Johns Hopkins University Press, 1993.

Wagley, Charles. *An Introduction to Brazil*. New York: Columbia University Press, 1971.

Wauchope, Robert, ed. *Handbook of Middle American Indians*. 16 vols. Austin: University of Texas Press, 1964–76.

Whitten, Norman E., Jr. *Black Frontiersmen: Afro-Hispanic Culture of Ecuador and Colombia*. Prospect Heights, IL: Waveland Press, 1989.

Whitten, Norman E., Jr., ed. *Cultural Transformations and Ethnicity in Modern Ecuador*. Urbana: University of Illinois Press, 1981.

Wiarda, Howard J.; and Michael J. Kryzanek. *The Dominican Republic: A Caribbean Crucible*. 2nd ed. Boulder, CO: Westview Press, 1992.

Wilbert, Johannes, ed. *Encyclopedia of World Cultures,* Volume 7, "South America." New York: G. K. Hall/Macmillan, 1994.

Wiley, James. "Undocumented Aliens and Recognized Refugees: The Right to Work in Costa Rica." *International Migration Review* 29 (1995): 423–40.

Wilk, Richard R. *Ethnic Minorities in Belize: Mopan, Kekchí, and Garifuna*. Belize City: SPEAR, 1990.

Yelvington, Kevin, ed. *Trinidad Ethnicity*. London: Macmillan, 1992.

Antigua and Barbuda

A ntigua and Barbuda is a small nation located in the Leeward Islands of the Lesser Antilles, in the eastern Caribbean Sea. The nation consists of the islands of Antigua, Barbuda, and Redonda (which is uninhabited). Nearly the entire population of 65,000 lives on Antigua, with only about 1,500 people living on the smaller island of Barbuda. The islands were an English colony from 1632 until the nation achieved independence in 1981.

Ethnic Composition and Ethnic Relations

Antiguans and **Barbudans** number about 63,000—about 98% of the population. They are almost entirely people of African ancestry, descendants of slaves brought to work on the English sugar cane plantations. After slavery was ended in 1834, most former slaves became farmers, working land owned by a small number of British landowners. Nearly all live on the island of Antigua, where the traditional rural life, based on subsistence farming, is giving way to a more diversified economy based now mainly on tourism and government services. The 1,500 who live in Barbuda enjoyed somewhat greater freedom from English influence and continue to maintain a more traditional culture, including the communal ownership of farmland. Antiguans and Barbudans all speak English, although an English-African creole is spoken in rural areas, as well. Nearly all Antiguans and Barbudans are Christians, with the majority belonging to Protestant churches representing nearly a dozen denominations. Antigua and Barbuda is ethnically homogeneous, with only small numbers of **Syrian** and **Lebanese** shopkeepers, along with **Portuguese, Chinese,** and **Asian Indians,** all of whose ancestors were brought to the islands by the British. There are also a small number of wealthy **U.S. Americans** and **Britons** involved in economic ventures in the tourism industry.

As a homogeneous society, ethnic relations between the Antiguans and Barbudans and the small ethnic minorities are harmonious.

Argentina

A rgentina is a large nation that occupies most of the southern third of South America. It is bordered by Chile on the west, Bolivia and Paraguay on the north, Brazil and Uruguay on the northeast, and the south Atlantic Ocean on the east and south. It has a population of 34.3 million, with over 80% of the population living in urban areas, including Buenos Aires with over 12 million residents. Argentina, colonized beginning in the 1500s by the Spanish moving south from Bolivia, achieved independence in 1816. Government campaigns in the 1830s and 1880s resulted in much of the American Indian population being either killed, displaced, or removed, and Native Americans now number about 100,000. The removal of the Indians from the pampas and Patagonia regions opened these areas to settlement, farming, and ranching. The Argentinian government actively encouraged emigration from Europe beginning in the late 1880s, and by the early 20th century, Argentina was the "European" society it remains today. Spanish influence remains strong, as evidenced by the use of the Spanish language (although many words have been added from other languages), the large number of Spaniards in the economic and political elite, and the fact that 92% of Argentinians are Roman Catholic.

Ethnic Composition

Argentina is an ethnically heterogeneous society, the heterogeneity arising from the mix of Europeans who have settled there and who now constitute 85% of the population. Spaniards and Italians are the largest and most influential of the several dozen European ethnic groups in Argentina. The remaining 15% of the population is composed of Mestizos (mainly from neighboring nations), Asians, Native Americans, and Blacks. Some experts classify Mestizos as Europeans, increasing the figure for the European percentage of the population to about 97%. As a relatively wealthy nation, Argentina has attracted laborers from other nations in the region, and its population includes over 1.5 million other South Americans.

Spaniards were the first European inhabitants of Argentina and their descendants are currently the largest ethnic group. Although at a lower rate than in earlier centuries, emigration from Spain continues in the 1990s. Spanish colonization is evident in the primacy of the Spanish language, Roman Catholicism, and Spanish-style buildings in the many regions. The Spaniards initiated the Europeanization policy as a way of settling Argentina and have generally been willing to share economic gains and power with other European groups, all of whom stress their Argentinian identity. The Spaniards generally consider the remaining Native Americans and Africans to be socially inferior.

Italians are the second largest ethnic group, and with the Spanish, they constitute about 80% of the population. Italians, mainly farmers from southern Italy, began arriving in Argentina in the 1850s during the Europeanization program of 1852–80. Although about two-thirds eventually returned to Italy, many of those who stayed prospered as farmers and ranchers, and their children, grandchildren, and great-grandchildren—as well as Italians who arrived in the 20th century—form the Italian community today. While some Italians still farm and ranch, many are now urban professionals.

Europeans, other than the large Spanish and Italian communities, include **Britons, French, Poles, Germans, Russian Old Believers, Yugoslavians, Welsh, Bretons, Dutch, Basques, Finns, Russians,** and **Hungarians.** They came to Argentina in three major waves. The first group came during the Europeanization effort of 1852–80, although about 80% who arrived then were from Spain or Italy. Also in this early wave were French, Poles, Russians, and Germans, who settled in the west. A much larger and more diverse group of European immigrants came after the 1880s. They, too, settled in the pampas and Patagonia, where they raised grain, cattle, sheep, and fruit. Many prospered, and as a group they developed the open lands of western Argentina, making the Europeanization program a success. The last major wave of Europeans consisted mainly of refugees from Central and Eastern Europe who arrived after World War II and settled both in the west and in cities. Since then, European immigration has declined, save for Italians and Spaniards who now constitute about 90% of the recent European immigrant population. Each of these European immigrant groups has maintained its ethnic identity through ethnic associations, residential isolation, occupational specialization, and preservation of their language. However, they are also integrated into the social class–based society, and nearly all speak Spanish.

Other **South Americans** number over 1.5 million in Argentina. The major nationalities and their estimated numbers are: **Paraguayans** (600,000), **Bolivians** (500,000), **Chileans** (400,000), **Uruguayans** (150,000), and **Brazilians** (100,000). As a relatively wealthy nation with employment opportunities, Argentina has attracted people from neighboring nations as contract laborers since the early 1970s. Most originally worked on farms and ranches in the north and west, but many evenutally moved to cities and took low-level jobs not desired by Argentinians or European immigrants. The Uruguayans live mainly in Buenos Aires and are professionals.

Jews number about 212,000 and include both Ashkenazic Jews from Central and Eastern Europe and Sephardic Jews from Africa and the Middle East. Major Jewish presence dates to the 1800s when Jews, like other European immigrants, settled the plains. Their numbers increased after World War II when many refugees settled there, and they are now a mainly urban population. Jews have long feared anti-Semitism in Argentina, and in 1994 a terrorist bombing killed 100 people at the Jewish Cultural Center in Buenos Aires. The Jewish population in Argentina is declining through immigration to Israel and the United States.

Japanese number about 25,000 and are mainly immigrants or descendants of Japanese immigrants who originally settled in Brazil. They live mainly in Buenos Aires and most are involved in finance.

Afro-Argentinians number about 50,000, nearly all of whom now live in Buenos Aires. Argentina did not import large numbers of slaves, and the Afro-Argentinian population today is descended from freed slaves and slaves who escaped to Argentina from Bolivia, Paraguay, and Brazil. As part of the Europeanization program of the late 1880s, Afro-Argentinians were pushed off their land. African identity was defined as inferior, and warfare, disease, and intermarriage decimated the population. Although largely ignored and relegated to low-level jobs, the Afro-Argentinian community continues to function as a distinct community in Buenos Aires.

Araucanians (Mapuche), who number about 400,000 in Chile, have a population of approximately 40,000 in western Argentina. Araucanians are the indigenous inhabitants of Chile, and some migrated to Argentina in the 18th century during wars in Chile with the Spanish. In the then-uncolonized open areas of western Argentina, the Araucanians established settlements and soon dominated much of western and central Argentina. The Spanish campaigns of the 1830s and 1880s drove the Araucanians out, and the remaining population is now located near the border with Chile. Like other Native Americans in Argentina, they now live apart from mainstream society.

Mataco are an American Indian group who live in northwestern Argentina and southern Bolivia. Population estimates for the Mataco are unreliable, ranging from 14,000 to over 60,000, with most living in Argentina. The Mataco did not come into regular contact with outsiders until the 1930s and since then have resisted assimilation. Much of their land was lost to the government or developers, although some has now been returned to them. The Mataco have a subsistence economy based on hunting, gathering, farming, and fishing; the extended family; and their traditional religion, which has survived along with nominal adherence to Roman Catholicism.

Mocoví are an American Indian group numbering 3,500 in northeastern Argentina. Because of regular contact with the Spanish since the mid-1700s, their pre-contact culture has largely disappeared and they now live in villages and work as laborers for the neighboring Europeans.

Toba are an American Indian group native to northeastern Argentina. They number about 30,000, and all but about 3,000 who reside in cities live in their traditional territory. The Toba, along with neighboring peoples who have now mostly disappeared, have resisted Spanish control since their first contact with the Spaniards some 300 years ago. Today, the region is heavily settled by Europeans, and the Toba are a small minority subject to new programs and policies meant for the Europeans. To cope with this situation, which threatens Toba cultural survival, new laws have been enacted giving them control over their lands. Some Toba have combined traditional practices such as hunting with new ones such as wage labor, and others have migrated to the cities of Buenos Aires and Rosario, where they live in shantytowns.

Other Native Americans include a total of about 1,500 **Chulupí, Ava, Chorote,** and **Nivacle,** who live in the north. The indigenous inhabitants of the islands of Tierra del Fuego—the **Yahgan, Ona,** and **Tewelche**—are now culturally extinct, although about 100 individuals can trace their ancestry to these peoples. Other groups include Native peoples from Bolivia, Brazil, and Paraguay who have migrated to Argentina in search of work. The three largest groups are the **Aymara** (30,000), **Chiriguano** (21,000), and the **Quechua speakers** (12,000) from Bolivia.

Ethnic Relations

Save for anti-Semitism and continued discrimination against Native peoples, who live
in poor settlements in the north and south and
in urban slums, Argentina is relatively free of
ethnic conflict and violence. However, charges
in the 1990s that Argentina was a major haven
for former Nazi officials and army officers, as
well claims that Argentinian banks failed to
account for money taken from Jewish World
War II Holocaust victims, have raised new
concerns about the level of anti-Semitism in
Argentina.

Although ethnic identity is important for
the millions of second-, third-, and fourth-gen-
eration Europeans in Argentina, and allegiance
to one's group is strong (as reflected in the
thousands of ethnic organizations and dozens
of European-language newspapers), ethnic
identity is not a major organizing factor in
Argentinian society. Rather, most immigrants
publicly identify themselves as Argentinians,
and society is organized along social-class
lines. There is a small upper class composed
of the wealthy and influential ranchers, farmers, businesspatrons, government officials, investors, and military officers centered in
Buenos Aires. About 40% of the population—
regardless of ethnic identity—constitute the
middle class of small-business owners, professionals, and technicians, and the remainder
of the population forms a large working class.
Educational and employment opportunities
make upward mobility achievable for those of
European ancestry.

Aruba

Aruba is a small island nation about 16 miles north of Venezuela. Once politically
part of the Netherlands Antilles, it became an independent nation under Dutch control in
1988. The current population is about 75,000, including as many as 5,000 undocumented immigrants who have come to Aruba from other Caribbean islands and South America to work in the
tourism industry. In 1499, Aruba was visited by the Spaniards, who enslaved and deported the
Indian population. It was subsequently repopulated by Indians from South America. The Dutch
took control in 1636 but began settling on the island only in 1754.

Ethnic Composition

Despite its small size and population, Aruba
is a multicultural nation with problems of ethnic rivalry and conflict. In addition to the
Arubans, who form the majority of the population, there are residents from North America
and Europe, Indonesia, Portugal, northern
South America, and other Caribbean islands.
The multicultural composition of Aruban society is due to a number of factors including
Dutch colonialism, proximity to South
America, the oil refinery industry that began
in the 1920s, and the tourism industry that is
now the backbone of the economy.

Arubans form the majority population on
the island. People defined as native Arubans
are descended from the American Indian inhabitants at the time of Dutch settlement, the
Dutch settlers, and to a lesser extent, the few
African slaves brought to the island. A distinction is made between those of Dutch-Indian
and those of Dutch-Indian-African ancestry.
Because few slaves were needed on the island
(the soil is not rich enough to support agriculture), the Aruban population has far fewer
people of African ancestry than most other
Caribbean islands. Through contact with the
Dutch, Venezuelans, North Americans, and the
British, a new Aruban culture and identity
emerged over the 19th and 20th centuries.
Arubans play an active role in government and
some businesses, although the major tourism
businesses, such as hotels, are controlled
mainly by outsiders. A key marker of Aruban
identity is speaking Papiamento, a creole language based on a mix of Portuguese, Dutch,
Spanish, West African languages, and South

American Indian languages. Most Arubans also speak Dutch, the island's official language, along with English and Spanish.

Asians include four major groups, although they number only a few thousand individuals in all. **Lebanese** and **Chinese** are primarily shopkeepers, while **Indonesians** from the former Dutch colony in the East Indies are involved in the tourism industry. **Filipinos** have come recently to work as dishwashers, housekeepers, and maintenance workers in the expanding tourism industry.

Caribbeans and **South Americans** include islanders such as **Jamaicans, Venezuelans,** and **Colombians.** The men tend to work at low-level jobs in the tourism industry while the women work both in the tourism industry and as domestics for European or upper-class Aruban families. Their residence on Aruba is somewhat seasonal and increases during the winter tourist season.

Europeans include the **Dutch,** who are involved in government, own shops, and the oil industry, and the **Portuguese** both from Portugal and Madeira who came to Aruba beginning in the 1920s to work in the oil refinery industry. Also from Europe are a small number of **Jews** from the Netherlands who are generally shopkeepers.

Ethnic Relations

Although ethnic rivalry is an ever-present feature of Aruban life, overt conflict is prevented by attempts to have all groups represented in the government, residence in distinct ethnic communities, and ethnic occupational specialization. Current ethnic problems center on recent legal and illegal immigrants, mainly from South America and the Caribbean, who are alleged to be taking jobs from Arubans and driving down the pay scale.

Ethnicity and wealth, as reflected in social-class distinctions, are two important markers of identity in Aruba. In this regard, as well as in the relatively high standard of living and heavy involvement in the global economy, Aruba is more like many Western nations than other Caribbean island nations. In addition to its year-round residents, Aruba has numerous tourists. It is a major tourist destination, and in the winter months, its population is swelled by over a half-million visitors from Europe and North America.

Bahamas

The Commonwealth of the Bahamas is a string of islands located off the southeastern coast of Florida in the northeastern Caribbean Sea. The Bahamas includes some 700 islands, of which only 30 are inhabited. About two-thirds of the population of 259,000 live on the island of New Providence. The islands were settled by the British in 1647 and remained a British colony until full independence was achieved in 1973. Before independence, British officials dominated affairs on the islands. Since then, African Bahamians have played an increasingly central role in government and the economy, although wealthy Whites remain economically powerful.

Ethnic Composition

The current population is about 85% people of African or of African and European ancestry, and 15% people of European ancestry. The only significant minority is Haitians, many of whom are in the Bahamas illegally. There is also a small Greek community composed of the descendants of Greeks who came to fish for sponge in the 19th century.

African Bahamians are descendants of slaves imported from Africa in the 17th and early 18th centuries and slaves brought by British loyalists fleeing the United States in the 1780s. They number about 218,000 and constitute 85% of the population. There are also large numbers of Bahamians in the United States and Great Britain. Bahamians speak various local dialects, as well as standard English. Most are Christians, having been converted during British rule, although the Africa-based Obeah religion is strong in rural areas, the traditional Junkanoo carnival is celebrated in winter, and African-based goombay music is popular.

Haitians in the Bahamas are believed to number about 40,000. Despite efforts in the 1980s to control emigration from Haiti and to nationalize Haitians already in the Bahamas, the majority are illegal immigrants who have come in large numbers since political unrest began in Haiti in 1991. They are employed mainly in the tourism industry, in low-level service jobs generally considered undesirable by Bahamians.

White Bahamians, including small numbers of **Greeks** and **Jews,** number about 38,000, constituting 15% of the population. Most (about 25,000) are of British ancestry and are descended from British settlers in the United States who migrated to the Bahamas

voluntarily before the American Revolution and those who fled after the Revolution. Some of these are of mixed British and African ancestry. The remainder are mainly **U.S. Americans, Canadians,** and **Britons** who have chosen to settle in the Bahamas since the 1960s. Nearly all are Christian, most belonging to mainstream Protestant and Catholic churches and others to evangelical churches. All speak English and most live on the island of New Providence.

Ethnic Relations

Relations between the African Bahamians and White Bahamians are peaceful, with both groups in the 1990s focusing their attention on controlling the immigration of Haitians. In the 1990s, a decline in the tourism industry has made the Haitians a target of ethnic animosity, and the government has sought to reduce their presence through mass arrests and by increasing fees for residency and work permits. As a result, many Haitians who were living in the Bahamas have fled to the United States.

Barbados

B arbados is the easternmost island in the Caribbean Sea. It has a population of 257,000. The British ruled the island from 1627 until independence was achieved in 1966. Since the late 1600s, Barbados has been heavily populated. There is a long history of immigration to other islands such as Jamaica and Antigua, and to Guyana, the eastern United States, and Great Britain by those who could not obtain land for farming or jobs on the island. Barbadian society is divided into two classes: a small upper class of the wealthy includes both White and African Barbadians, and a very large middle class or working class encompasses almost all other Barbadians. Since the end of British rule, ethnicity and race have declined as major factors in socioeconomic mobility. Tourism is now a major industry, and the island is visited in the winter months by hundreds of thousands of tourists from the United States, Canada, and Great Britain.

Ethnic Composition and Ethnic Relations

About 90% of Barbadians are of African ancestry. The remaining 10% are split about equally between those of African and British ancestry and those of British ancestry.

Bajans is the name for African Barbadians who are descended from the slaves brought to the island in the 17th and 18th centuries to work on the sugar cane plantations. Today they number 230,000; about 90% of the population. Their dialect—Bajan, a creole language based on English and West African languages—is disappearing. The Barbadians were strongly influenced by the English, and much in the current legal, educational, and political systems is modeled on the British system. Similarly, the majority are Christians, with over half being Anglicans. Tensions regarding the low status of the Bajans have largely disappeared since independence. A distinct subgroup is people of mixed African and British ancestry.

People of **British** ancestry on Barbados, who number about 13,000, are descendants of the early British settlers. British domination of the island ended about 100 years earlier than on other islands, and many of the settlers chose to remain rather than return to Britain. Thus, Barbados has a much larger British population than many other Caribbean islands. Most British are in the economic elite or in the professions. A distinct subgroup are the "red legs," descendants of British laborers who were replaced by slaves and have since lived outside mainstream society as farmers and fishers.

Other groups include small numbers of **Indian Hindus, Jews, Rastafarians,** and **Muslims.**

Belize

F ormerly known as British Honduras, Belize is a small nation located in northeastern Central America. It is bordered by Mexico on the north, the Caribbean Sea on the east, and Guatemala on the south and west. Home of the Mayas, Belize was colonized by the British in 1638 and achieved independence in 1981. The population is 214,000.

Ethnic Composition

Belize is ethnically heterogeneous, with four major groups and a number of smaller ones. The largest groups are the Creoles, Mestizos, Mayans, and Garifuna, who together make up about 90% of the population. Shifting ethnic identities, particularly in the Creole and Mestizo categories, make exact population counts impossible. The remaining 10% of the population is composed of Mennonites, Chinese, Asian Indians, Arabs, and small numbers of **U.S. Americans** and **Europeans.** The population is mainly Christian; 62% are Protestants of various denominations and 30% are Roman Catholics. English is the official language, although in the north a majority of people speak Spanish as their domestic language, and many Creoles speak Belizean Creole (based on English and African languages) rather than standard English.

Arabs in Belize include **Syrians, Lebanese,** and **Palestinians** and number several thousand. They have been in Belize since the early 1900s and are primarily merchants in larger cities. Some are Christians and others follow Islam.

Chinese number several thousand, and the current population is composed of Chinese who arrived in the 1900s. Those who arrived earlier had already immigrated elsewhere. The population has increased in recent years as Chinese have arrived from Singapore and Hong Kong. As elsewhere in the Chinese diaspora, Chinese live in many towns where they often own small shops or restaurants. The largest community is in Belize City.

The term **Creoles** is the name used in Belize, and elsewhere in Central America, for people of mixed African and European or African and American Indian ancestry. They number about 64,000 or 30% of the population. Creoles differ widely in physical appearance, and European features such as straight hair and light skin color are still considered more prestigious, although African features are no longer the social barrier they were during British rule. Creoles are heavily concentrated in and around Belize City. They speak English or Belize Creole and most are Protestant, although a significant minority have converted to Roman Catholicism. The Creoles are often seen by outsiders as being in opposition to the

Mestizos, although ethnic relations are actually far more complicated and less conflict-ridden.

Garifuna number about 15,000 in Belize, constituting 7% of the population. They live primarily in small villages along the southern coast. Also known as the **Black Carib,** the Garifuna are descendants of the Carib Indians who inhabited many Caribbean islands when the Spaniards arrived in 1492. They intermarried with African slaves and many were relocated to Central America by the British in 1797. They are integrated into Belizean society as their economy is based on wage labor and most are Roman Catholics. About 500,000 Garifuna live in Central America, and there is also a large Garifuna community in the United States.

Asian Indians form two distinct groups, totaling no more than 2,000 people. First are the descendants of Indian laborers imported by the British in the 19th century to work on the sugar cane plantations. They have intermarried with other groups and are now assimilated into Belizean society. Second are Indians from Bombay who have arrived since the 1960s and who live in cities in the north. These Indians are unassimilated, are adherents of Hinduism, and maintain their own communities. They own many businesses and dominate the financial market.

Mayas are represented by two groups in Belize. About 4,000 of a total of about 350,000 **Kekchí (or Q'eqchi') Maya** live on the border with Guatemala, where most Kekchí live. The second group is the **Mopan Maya** who number about 5,000 in southeastern Belize where they live near the Kekchí. The Mopan migrated to Belize in the mid-1800s from Mexico to escape political unrest, and others have recently migrated from Guatemala for the same reason. Both groups speak Mayan languages and their small populations make them relatively unimportant in Belizean society.

Mennonites number about 5,500 and live in autonomous communities in northern Belize, which they established following migration from Mexico in 1958–62. They speak German and Spanish. Although they live outside mainstream society in some ways, such as not voting or standing for office, their highly productive farms have become major suppliers of produce, poultry, and furniture to other Belizeans.

Mestizos are people of mixed Spanish and Indian ancestry, although some have African ancestry as well. They number about 100,000, 46% of Belize's population, and are most heavily concentrated in the northern third of the country. As with the Creoles, there is considerable variety in physical appearance, with European features regarded as most desirable. Many Mestizos speak Spanish as their domestic language and others speak English. Along with the Mayas and Garifuna, the Mestizos share an adherence to Roman Catholicism that tends to distinguish them from the mainly Protestant Creoles and other groups.

Ethnic Relations

Ethnic identity is but one of a number of factors that interact in complicated and often shifting ways to define relations among the peoples of Belize. Skin color, place of residence, social-class status, language, religion, and political affiliation also play roles in shaping relations in contemporary Belize. The situation is further complicated by a long history of intermarriage, which further softens ethnic boundaries. Although there are animosities between certain groups, such as the Creoles and Garifuna, ethnic conflict is not typical of Belize society. Factors that make for relatively peaceful relations are intermarriage, the location of different groups in different regions, occupational specialization on the part of the small minorities, and a relatively open social-class structure that, while still favoring lighter-skinned Creoles and Mestizos, does provide the opportunity for upward social mobility for all.

Bolivia

B olivia, located in west-central South America, is bordered by Brazil on the north and east, Peru and Chile on the west, and Argentina and Paraguay on the south. It has a population of 7.9 million. About 95% of the population is Roman Catholic, with traditional Native American practices surviving alongside Roman Catholicism in many Aymara and Quechua communities, and in other Indian and Afro-Bolivian communities as well. Spaniards ruled from the 1530s to 1825. Spanish, Aymara, and Quechua are the three official languages, although knowledge of Spanish is needed for full participation in the national economy. About 40% of the population use Spanish as its first language, 37% speak Quechua, and 24% speak Aymara, with many Aymara and Quechua speakers also speaking Spanish.

Ethnic Composition

Bolivia is an ethnically heterogeneous nation, and the population is composed of four major sociocultural groupings: Blancos (people of European descent), Aymara, Quechua speakers, and Mestizos. There are also several hundred thousand Afro-Bolivians and several dozen other Native American groups with a total population of less than 100,000.

Blancos is the generic label used for Spanish-speaking "Whites," who number about 800,000 or about 10% of the population. Blanco or White is more a social-class designation than an ethnic one, as identification as a Blanco is based on a combination of having light skin color and European features, speaking Spanish, and possessing enough wealth or education to be classified as upper or middle class. Blancos form the ruling elite in Bolivia, and categorization as a Blanco is considered desirable by people of full or partial European descent. Blancos generally view all other groups as inferior and are, in turn, resented by others because of their Spanish ancestry and control of Bolivian society. However, wealth is the most important element of being a Blanco, and wealthy Mestizos or Indians can help their children become Blanco by marrying Blancos. A distinct Blanco subgroup is the **Germans,** who came during and following World War II and form distinct communities in La Paz and other cities. Also of European ancestry are the **Mennonites,** who number about 8,000 and live in independent agricultural communities.

Mestizos number about 2 million and constitute about 25% of the population. Mestizos are people of mixed American Indian and European ancestry, although classification as Mestizo has more to do with social-class status than ancestry. Depending on where they live and with whom they interact, Mestizos may speak Spanish, Quechua, or both. As in much of Latin America, Mestizos form the rural peasantry and work mainly as farmers on their own land or on land owned by others, in related occupations, and as low-level government agents. Mestizos in cities generally seek to move up the social-class ladder and self-identify as Blancos. Their relations with the Aymara and Quechua speakers are complex, as in rural communities there is frequent contact between the groups. Before the 1952 revolution, Mestizos were economically and politically dominant and viewed themselves as socially superior. After the revolution, their power declined, and the Indians are less willing to be as deferential as in the past, to the displeasure of some Mestizos. A distinct subgroup of Mestizos is the **Cholo.** Indians who seek to become Mestizos by speaking Spanish, dressing like Mestizos, and working in traditionally Mestizo occupations.

Bolivia has a diverse American Indian population. The two largest groupings are the Aymara and Quechua speakers. The **Aymara** number about 2.4 million in Bolivia, constituting 30% of the population. Smaller numbers of Aymara live in Ecuador and Peru. The Aymara are the indigenous inhabitants of the region and traditionally lived in the Andean region in the southeastern part of the nation. Since the reforms of 1952, there has been a large migration to cities, especially to La Paz.

Aymara Indians in reed fishing boats contrast with a modern hydrofoil on Lake Titicaca. The Aymara constitute about 30% of Bolivia's population. Photo: UPI/Corbis-Bettmann.

The 1952 revolution also ended the centuries-old pattern of absolute Spanish dominance, although the Aymara have yet to benefit greatly from new economic opportunities. Today, the Aymara find themselves in competition with the Mestizos, Afro-Bolivians, and Quechua speakers, and some seek to enhance their status by speaking Spanish although most continue to speak Aymara as well. The Aymara were converted to Roman Catholicism by the Spanish, but traditional beliefs and practices remain strong, as does affiliation with one's Aymara community.

Quechua speakers number about 2.4 million; about 30% of the population. They live mainly in central Bolivia in villages and towns where they may be the dominant group or they may be a minority in or near a Mestizo community. Quechua speakers and other Native Americans in Bolivia are identified by a number of labels including **Indígenes** and the insulting **Indios.** Quechua was the language of the Inca Empire, and it spread to other Native American peoples conquered by the Incas in what are now Colombia, Ecuador, Peru, Bolivia, and Argentina. As many as 11 million people now speak Quechua in these five nations. Contact with Spaniards for 500 years has produced a Quechua culture that is neither Indian nor Spanish but a mix of elements drawn from both, combined with specific cultural adaptations in different Quechua communities. Some Quechua speakers also speak Spanish or Aymara. The independence of some

Quechua groups has been threatened by the migration of Mestizos and by economic development and resource exploitation in their lands. Some groups have responded by forming political action groups and staging protests, which have been to some extent successful in protecting the territory of some communities. Some Quechua have also allied themselves with Indian groups for this same purpose.

In addition to the Aymara and Quechua speakers, who form about 60% of the national population, there are several other American Indian groups of significant size. The **Chiquitano** number about 40,000 in eastern Bolivia and Brazil. They were first exploited for their labor by the Spanish and converted to Roman Catholicism. Later exploitation occurred under Mestizos who moved into the region. Despite the fact that many Chiquitano now work as wage laborers for Mestizos, some continue to live as farmers in their own communities and stress their Chiquitano identity.

The **Chiriguano** number about 46,000, with 22,000 in Bolivia, 21,000 in Argentina, and 3,000 in Paraguay. The four subgroups are the **Ava, Izoceño, Simba,** and **Chane.** Dominance by the Spanish and a long history of labor migration have weakened the traditional culture and have left many communities dependent on governmental assistance.

The **Guarayu** number about 7,500 in northeastern Bolivia. They are not indigenous to the area but were brought there by Spanish explorers in the 1600s. Despite centuries of Spanish rule and conversion to Roman Catholicism, much of the traditional way of life survives, including subsistence agriculture and many religious beliefs and practices.

The **Mojo** number about 17,000 over a wide region in eastern Bolivia. Centuries of Spanish exploitation reduced the population and ultimately resulted in the Mojo settling in farming communities. About 30% continue to speak Mojo, the balance now speaking Spanish.

Finally, in addition to the Quechua speakers, the Aymara, and the other smaller American Indian groups noted above, there are other, even smaller groups in Bolivia. **Araona** number 65 individuals in north-central Bolivia. **Ayoreo** number about 3,500 in southeastern Bolivia and across the border in Paraguay. **Baure** number about 4,000 in northern Bolivia. **Chácobo** number about 300 in two communities in northeastern Bolivia. **Chimane** number about 2,500 in east-central Bolivia and have come under pressure from other Indian groups settling in the region. **Chipaya** number about 1,800 and live among the Aymara in southwestern Bolivia. **Chulupi** number about 100 and live in southeastern Bolivia. **Huaraya** number about 1,000 and live in northwest Bolivia and across the border in Peru. Some communities are assimilated while others are less so. **Ignaciano** number about 4,000 and live in north-central Bolivia. **Itonama** number about 4,750 and live in northwestern Bolivia where they are assimilated into Mestizo society. **Jaminawa** number about 150 in Bolivia, 360 in Brazil, and 500 in Peru. **Kanichana** number about 500 in northwestern Bolivia. **Kavinenya** number about 500 in northwestern Bolivia. **Kayavava** number about 50 in northern Bolivia. **Kayuvava** number about 40 in northern Bolivia. **Leko** number about 200 in north-central Bolivia. **Manhuy** number about 1,000 in southeastern Bolivia. **Mataco** number about 2,000 in southern Bolivia and over 12,000 across the border in Argentina (*see* Argentina). **Moré (Itene)** number about 140 and live in central Bolivia where they are on the verge of extinction through assimilation. **Movima** number about 1,500 in north-central Bolivia where they are assimilated into Mestizo society. **Pauserna** number about 14 people who live in north-central Bolivia. **Pawnaka** number about 180 and live in north-central Bolivia. **Reyesano** number about 1,000 and live in north-central Bolivia. **Sirionó** number about 1,800 and live in northeastern Bolivia. **Tacana** number about 5,000 and live in northwestern Bolivia among Quechua speakers. **Tapieté** number about 45 in southeastern Bolivia. **Uru** number about 750 in southern Bolivia. **Yuqui** number about 130 in west-central Bolivia. Once classified as a Sirionó subgroup, they are now considered to be a distinct cultural group. **Yuracaré** number about 2,000 in central Bolivia.

All of these groups are under intense assimilation pressures from developers, settlers, and the government. Major forces include the migration and settlement of Mestizos in territory that was formerly Indian; involvement of Indians in wage labor, including migration to cities or plantations; government incursions in the form of road building and the provision of school and health facilities; and Roman Catholic missionary activities. These forces have combined to replace the traditional American Indian subsistence economies with involvement at low levels in the market economy, to replace the traditional religion with Roman Catholicism (although some traditional beliefs and practices often survive), to alter the structure and nature of family relationships, and to place political leadership in the hands of young people. In some of these groups, some segment of the population seeks to avoid assimilation, sometimes by relocating and sometimes also by looking to regional indigenous rights organizations, such as the Confederación Indígena del Oriente Boliviano and the Confederación Indígena de la Cuenca Amazonia, for legal and political support.

Two other distinct ethnic minorities are the Afro-Bolivians and Japanese. **Afro-Bolivians** are people of full or partial African descent whose ancestors were brought to Bolivia as slaves in the 1600s and 1700s. The Spaniards imported few slaves directly to Bolivia; most were brought from Peru to work on Bolivian cocoa plantations. The number of Afro-Bolivians is probably about 100,000. They live both in agricultural communities in central Bolivia and in major cities. Afro-Bolivians have never been fully integrated into Bolivian society, and relations with Mestizos and the Aymara vary from region to region, with contacts so close in some that intermarriage is common and so distant in others (such as La Paz) that the groups are open rivals for political power and jobs. In these situations, the Afro-Bolivians see themselves as second-class citizens and complain about special favors afforded the Aymara. The Afro-Bolivians are mostly Roman Catholics, although traditional beliefs and practices remain important, especially in rural communities.

People of **Japanese** ancestry in Bolivia number about 10,000. Nearly all are immigrants from Brazil and Peru who came to Bolivia after 1952 in search of better employment opportunities.

Ethnic Relations

Of the four major groupings, only the Aymara are an ethnocultural group in the strict sense of the word. The other three represent a system of classification found throughout Latin America, in which people are classified into categories and these categories ranked on the basis of skin color; ancestry; place of residence (urban or rural); and social class, which is indicated by wealth, occupation, or level of education. There is some social mobility available to individuals, and people often do attempt to change their public identity in order to move up the social-class ladder. This ladder is arranged, in a very general sense, with small Native American groups and Afro-Bolivians being at the bottom, the Aymara and Quechua speakers coming next, followed by Mestizos, and finally with Blancos at the top. However, while across Bolivia Blancos are at the top and some Native Americans and Afro-Bolivians are at the bottom, the relative positions of the other groups vary from region to region and even from town to town.

Because of the dominance of the Blancos, relations among these groups are superficially harmonious, although there are tensions among the three groups in the middle, and Afro-Bolivians, Quechua speakers, and Native Americans continue to protest discrimination.

In general, the history of ethnic relations in Bolivia is one of Spanish exploitation of the native groups. With the labor and land reforms since 1952, this pattern has weakened, although the overall status hierarchy remains unchanged. There is still considerable competition among groups in the middle categories for power and wealth.

Brazil

The Federative Republic of Brazil is the largest nation in Latin America. Located in northeastern South America, it is bordered by Colombia on the northwest; Venezuela, Guyana, Suriname, and French Guiana on the north; the Atlantic Ocean on the east; Uruguay, Argentina, Paraguay, and Bolivia on the south; and Peru and Colombia on the west. At the time of European discovery by Pedro Cabral of Portugal in 1500, Brazil was the home of dozens of small Indian groups. The region was colonized by Portugal and gained independence in 1822.

Brazil has enormous mineral and forest resources, as well as land suitable for farming and ranching. The development of the interior has long been a major goal—but it is also a controversial issue that, in the 1980s and 1990s, has drawn international attention from environmentalists and human rights advocates. Brazil has a population of 163 million, the second largest in the Americas and the fifth largest in the world. Portuguese is the official language. German, Italian, Spanish, and Polish continue to be spoken in some of the nation's immigrant communities, and various indigenous languages are used by American Indians. About 88% of the population is Roman Catholic, 6% are Protestants, and the remaining 6% are adherents of other religions, including Eastern Orthodoxy, Buddhism, Judaism, and African-based religions.

Ethnic Composition

Brazil is an ethnically diverse nation, with the population falling into five general categories: (1) people of Portuguese and other European ancestry (mainly German, Spanish, Italian, and Polish); (2) Afro-Brazilians; (3) Mulattos; (4) people of Japanese ancestry; and (5) American Indians.

Despite this ethnic diversity, it is important to note that most Brazilians—regardless of ethnic identity—share a strong sense of Brazilian identity. That identity is based on speaking the Brazilian dialect of Portuguese; recognizing a Brazilian culture based on a mix of Portuguese, African, and Indian elements (with the Portuguese ones being the most important across the entire nation); pride in the vast natural resources of the nation; a government-controlled education system; far-reaching economic institutions; Roman Catholicism; strong Brazilian literary, cinema, television, music, and dance traditions; and support for and identification with the national sport of soccer.

Existing alongside this sense of national identity is also a strong sense of regional identity, although experts do not agree on how many cultural regions there are in Brazil. These cultural regions developed as a result of geography and environment, Portuguese colonial administrative units, the composition of the population, and the region's major economic activities. One widely accepted scheme suggests six major regions: Northeast Coast, the *Sertao*, Eastern Highlands, South, Amazon Basin, and Far West. In terms of social relations, an important aspect of the Brazilian view of these regions is the stereotypes of the people who live in each region. These stereotypes—such as the Southern cowboy or superficial Northeasterner—are important elements of the Brazilian social order and help people manage social relations in the large and diverse society.

At the time of Portuguese arrival, it is estimated that there were anywhere from one to four million **American Indians** in what is now Brazil. They lived in hundreds of groups, with the local village being the primary unit of affiliation. Groups of villages were linked through a common language and intermarriage although they rarely formed unified political units with a single leader. These hundreds of groups, some of whose ways of life have persisted into the late 20th century, are generally classified by anthropologists into two general categories—(1) tropical forest horticulturists,

and (2) the marginal or semi-marginal hunter-gatherers. The tropical forest horticulturists, a category that includes most of the Indian population, live in the rain forest in small, semi-permanent villages and subsist mainly by fishing and by slash-and-burn horticulture. Their primary crops are manioc (cassava, tapi-

Indians in Brazil building an Amazonian-style hut to house meeting delegates from abroad. Brazil's Indians have gained international support from human rights and environmental groups in their efforts to protect their lands and cultures. Photo: Reuters/Corbis Bettmann.

oca), maize, beans, tobacco, squash, and various nuts and fruits. Horticulture is usually supplemented by hunting, gathering, and fishing. Historically, the most important of these groups were speakers of Tupi-Guarani language, which became the basis of the contact language, called *lingua geral*, that was used by missionaries and Portuguese agents. The language continued to be widely used into the early 20th century in rural Brazil but has now been supplanted by Portuguese. Most of the marginal and semi-marginal peoples lived on the plains or on plateaus and subsisted mainly by hunting and gathering. Some also practiced horticulture, but not on the scale of the tropical forest peoples.

Although protected at first by the Jesuit missionaries, Brazilian Indians did not fare well under Portuguese colonialism. European diseases such as smallpox, measles, and diphtheria killed many and the rubber boom of the late 19th and early 20th centuries, which brought rubber-extracting enterprises onto Indian lands, caused much death and dislocation. Beginning in the 1960s, intense exploitation of the rain forest—including logging, road building, mining, and industrial development—has led to more loss of lives and

Large American Indian Groups in Brazil

Group	Population
Apurina	3,000
Atiku	1,300
Curripaco	4,700
Desana	960
Fulnió	4,000
Gorotire	1,000
Guajarara	6,700
Hupda	1,400
Kaimbé	1,400
Kaingang	10,500
Kamba	2,000
Karajá	1,200
Kashinawa	2,000
Kiriri	1,800
Kulina	2,500
Macushi	15,000
Maku	2,200
Mawé	3,000
Mbüá	2,200
Mundurucu	1,500
Mura	1,300
Nyandeva	4,900
Pai Taivera	7,000
Pankararé	1,800
Pankararú	4,000
Patasho	1,700
Potiguára	4,000
Satere	4,000
Shakriabá	3,500
Shavante	4,400
Shukurú	3,000
Tariana	1,600
Terena	9,800
Tikuna	18,000
Tukano	2,600
Wapishana	5,100
Wari	1,100
Wasu	1,300
Yanomamo	8,000

displacement from traditional territories. The Indian population is currently estimated to be about 250,000 people in some 257 groups, although some of these groups may be extinct, others number a few dozen or less, and some may be subdivisions rather than separate groups. Under government programs, some groups have been placed on Indian reserves where they are allowed to continue their traditional way of life while being provided with modern health, social, and education services.

People of **European** ancestry in Brazil are estimated to make up between 55% and 58% of the population. The major groups are those of **Portuguese, Italian, German, Spanish,** and **Polish** ancestry, although many other European nations are represented as well. The **Portuguese (Luso-Brazilians)** colonizers left their mark on Brazil in the form of the Portuguese language, Roman Catholicism, Portuguese political and legal institutions, the patriarchal family, and what is known as the "gentleman complex." Cited by some writers as a key Portuguese-based element of Brazilian culture, the gentleman complex is the idea that people of European ancestry should engage in professional work and that manual labor should be performed by others—Indians and people of African ancestry. The question of Portuguese influence has long been debated by experts. Some see Portuguese culture as the basis of Brazilian culture; others see its influence mixed with Indian, African, and other European traditions; and still others point out that many Brazilians distance themselves from Portugal and see themselves as culturally distinct.

In addition to the Portuguese, colonial Brazil had sizable populations of **French** and **Dutch** settlers who controlled the north for some years. These peoples were absorbed into Portuguese-dominated colonial Brazil, and it is the European immigrants who arrived in the late 19th and early 20th centuries, along with those who came after World War II, who form the basis for the contemporary non-Portuguese ethnic groups in Brazil. A major factor encouraging immigration to Brazil at the end of the 1800s was the abolition of slavery in 1888, which created a need for agricultural laborers on the coffee plantations in the northeast. This flow of immigrants, which was as high as 100,000 people in some years and rarely lower than 50,000, included people from many European nations and the Middle East, the majority from Portugal, Spain, Italy, and Germany. Restrictive immigration laws limited the arrival of people from Africa and Asia.

The more recent Portuguese immigrants have settled mainly in major cities and are employed primarily in lower-level service occupations, such as driving taxis, and a substantial number have opened retail stores.

The **Italians** were recruited mainly to replace the freed slaves on the coffee plantations. They often earned their freedom from indentured servitude in three or four years, at which time many became farmers or set up their own businesses. Those who settled in cities became an important segment of the growing industrial business class.

The **Germans,** like other immigrants, came to Brazil because of the economic opportunities, especially the promise of land and free transportation. German settlers became involved in industry, cattle ranching, and farming. To a greater extent than other German immigrant groups, those in the south maintained a distinct German identity until after World War II. Although they have become more assimilated since then, German-speaking farming communities are still to be found in southern Brazil.

The **Japanese** in Brazil number about 1.5 million, forming the largest Japanese-ancestry population in any nation other than Japan. In the last several decades, there has been considerable intermarriage between Japanese Brazilians and European Brazilians, and in the 1990s about 50% of Japanese Brazilians are actually of mixed ancestry, although most continue to be identified as Japanese Brazilians. Japanese immigration to Brazil was heaviest from 1908 until the 1930s, when government restrictions went into effect. The Japanese were encouraged to settle in Brazil as agricultural workers and came there in large numbers because of restrictions on immigration to the United States and Canada. Once mainly rural farmers, about 90% of Japanese Brazilians now live in cities. The majority speak either Japanese or Japanese and Portuguese, although the number of those who speak only Portuguese is increasing. Most Japanese Brazilians are employed in professional positions in commerce, industry, and technology. Japanese Brazilians are structurally assimilated into Brazilian society but also retain a strong sense of Japanese ethnic identity and identification with the Japanese Brazilian community.

The term **Afro-Brazilian** is an ambiguous label: In the most general sense, it applies to some 45% of the population, 6% of whom are classified as Afro-Brazilians (**Black Brazilians**) and 39% as Mulattos—people of mixed European and African ancestry. If this general definition is used, Brazil has the largest African-ancestry population of any nation except for Nigeria. However, there is far more variety in Afro-Brazilians than classification into these two categories suggests. First, Africans were imported to Brazil as slaves—slavery was a basic institution of colonial society, with virtually every Portuguese family owning them. African slaves came from virtually every nation in West Africa, as well as from the Portuguese colonies in southern Africa. Thus, they brought with them many different languages, religions, and customs. Relations between European men and African women were common, and a new category of people was produced—**Mulattos**—who often served in an intermediary position between the slave owners and slaves. Although concentrated in the Northeast and major cities, Afro-Brazilians live throughout Brazil. They adhere to a wide range of religions, with perhaps only a minority following syncretic African-Roman Catholic religions such as *Xango* and *Candomblé*. Although Afro-Brazilians are employed at all levels of the economic system, they are heavily concentrated in the low-paying occupations.

Brazilians do not make a simple distinction between **Whites** and **Blacks;** that is, between people of European ancestry and people of African ancestry. In fact, the idea that people can be classified into these fixed categories seems strange to a Brazilian. Instead, there is a continuum of color categories, and in the recent census, people used over 100 different words to classify themselves and different members of the same family are often labeled with the different terms. Thus, there is no consensus in Brazil about a given individual's identity, although lighter skin color is associated with higher social status and greater economic opportunity. At the same time, it has been suggested by some observers that wealth outweighs skin color. Thus, darker-skinned people can elevate their status by accumulating wealth.

Ethnic Relations

Ethnic relations in Brazil focus on Black-White relations, although the status of American Indians has become a major issue in the last two decades. Up until the 1960s, Brazil was often described as a nation free of racial discrimination and racial tensions between Blacks and Whites. Despite centuries of slavery nationwide in Brazil and its abolition only in 1888 (Brazil was the last nation in the Americas to ban it), this view of comparative racial harmony and Black participation in Brazilian life was supported by the ethnic heterogeneity of many Brazilian communities; the widespread distribution of Afro-Brazilians; the incorporation of African-based music, dance, and literary themes in Brazilian culture; the popularity of the Afro-Brazilian soccer star Pelé; the ambiguous nature of "Black" identity; and the perceived ability of at least some Afro-Brazilians to climb the socioeconomic ladder. Since the 1960s, perhaps in response to the civil rights movement in the United States, this view has been challenged by some in the Afro-Brazilian community, as well as by outsiders who note that Afro-Brazilians have had limited political influence, are heavily concentrated in the Northeast, are poorer than Whites, hold a disproportionately high percentage of low-paying jobs and a disproportionately low percentage of high-paying jobs, are kept largely outside the political process, are less likely to intermarry with high-status Whites, and are often stereotyped as lazy and ignorant. In addition, some observers pointed out that given their large population, wide distribution, variation in African homelands, and adherence to different religions, the Afro-Brazilian population forms a number of distinct communities rather than one culturally monolithic population. This revision in thinking about the role and status of Afro-Brazilians has led to—or perhaps was part of—an Afro-Brazilian movement that has called attention to racism in Brazilian society and has, with some success, pushed for greater participation by Afro-Brazilians in the political process, greater public recognition of Brazilian cultural institutions of African origin, and greater recognition of cultural diversity within the Afro-Brazilian population.

As pointed out above, Indians in Brazil suffered loss of life and land during the colonial era, and this pattern continues in the 1990s. The surviving Indian groups constitute less than .001% of the population and live primarily in the interior, a region now coveted by the government, investors, and developers, who seek to exploit the rich forest, mineral, and other resources of the rain forest. The economic exploitation of the interior is broadly supported by the Brazilian population, as economic growth has long been a unifying theme in Brazilian society. Indian peoples in Brazil are badly outnumbered and outgunned. Their rights are often ignored by the government, and contact between developers and Indians has often resulted in Indians being killed or displaced from their land. The government has sought to offer protection by creating reserves for some Indian groups, although even these are sometimes invaded by loggers and miners. The Indians have gained international support from human rights and indigenous rights groups, as well as environmental groups whose desire to protect the rain forest coincides with the Indians' desire to protect their land. To what extent these efforts have been helpful to Brazil's Indians is unclear, and outside organizations sometimes differ among themselves as to the best tactics, proposing wide-ranging strategies that include converting Indians to Christianity, promoting assimilation, protecting Indian groups by establishing reserves, and encouraging Indian participation in the global economy by providing forest resources to Western markets.

Canada

C anada is in North America, bordered by the United States on the south and northwest (Alaska). According to the 1991 census, it had a population of 26,994,000. It is a heavily urbanized society, with 77% of the population living in cities. Both English and French are the official languages, although French is spoken commonly only in the province of Québec.

At the time of European arrival, Canada was settled by the Inuit in the north and American Indian groups spread across much of the rest of Canada. Although Vikings established a short-lived settlement on the coast of Newfoundland in about A.D. 1000, extensive European settlement did not begin until the arrival of French explorer Jacques Cartier in 1534. The French were became an independent dominion in the British Empire in 1931 and became entirely free of British administration in 1982.

Much to the displeasure of many Canadians, their nation's culture is often discussed in terms of, or compared to, U.S. culture to the south. Although there is extensive contact between Canada and the United States, and some aspects of Canadian life have been influenced by the United States, Canada is unique. Canadians tend to have a stronger sense of identification with their provincial governments than with the national government, tend to see the government as an agent of positive social change, value neatness and orderliness, and, unlike Americans, do not emphasize the absolute separation of church and state.

Ethnic Composition

Canada is an ethnically heterogeneous nation. In ethnic terms, the population can be classified into three categories: (1) Aboriginal peoples, which includes Native Americans, Métis, and Inuit; (2) charter groups, meaning people of French and British ancestry; and (3) newcomers or immigrants.

Aboriginal Peoples

According to the 1991 census, there were 1,002,670 Aboriginal or indigenous people in Canada. This figure includes people who claim Aboriginal origins alone or have mixed ancestry, but it does not include some 13,000 people who are registered as American Indians but do not claim Aboriginal ancestry; that is, although they are classified as American Indians, they may not have such ancestry. In including people who claim either single or multiethnic ancestry, the Aboriginal population breaks down as follows: 783,980 American Indians, 49,260 Inuit, and 212,650 Métis. In terms of religion and language, a substantial number are assimilated into Canadian society. Some 457,225 are Roman Catholic, 356,725 are Prot-

estant, 9,905 follow their native religion, 6,570 adhere to other religions, and 172,259 profess no religious affiliation. As to mother tongue—the first language one learns as a child and continues to speak as an adult—688,685 speak English, 121,420 French, 171,360 a non-official language, and 171,340 their native language. The native languages with the most speakers are Cree (73,140) in the midwest, Inukitut (24,005) in the north, and Ojibway (21,800) in the south-central region. Despite assimilation into Canadian society, the Aboriginal Peoples are second-class citizens. A five-year government study released in 1996 makes it clear that Aboriginal Peoples have benefited least from the advances of Canadian society. The life expectancy of men and women is six years less than that of the general population, the tuberculosis rate is almost 30% higher, 20% more need public assistance to avoid living in poverty, and 12% live in housing without heat. Similarly, Aboriginal Peoples have less education, double-digit unemployment rates, and are more likely to be victims of violent crimes.

Classification as a **Native American** in Canada is complicated, as it involves classification both of individuals and of groups. At the individual level, to be officially recognized as an Indian, an individual must register with the government. Such Indians, who constitute about 75% of the Indian population, are called "status" or "registered" Indians, while the others are called "non-status" Indians. Most status Indians live on reserves, land held in trust by the government. Most reserves and most status Indians live in the provinces of Ontario, British Columbia, Saskatchewan, and Manitoba. At the group level, Native Americans in Canada are classified into cultural groups—called First Nations—and political units called bands. There are 47 First Nations and 601 named bands in Canada.

First Nations Groups in Canada

Group	Population
Cree	117,195
Ojibway (Chippewa)	73,350
Micmac	13,650
Montagnais-Naskapi	11,500
Blackfeet	11,470
Dakota	9,755
Halkomelem (Cowichan)	8,885
Chipewyan	9,210
Mohawk	8,130
Carrier	6,520
Algonquin	5,270
Slave	5,070
Shuswap	4,745
Gitksan	4,395
Coast Tsimshian	4,285
Nootka	4,100
Kwakiutl	3,890
Ntlakapamux (Thompson)	3,750
Nishga	3,470
Attikamek	3,400
Dogrib	2,830
Lillooet	2,500
Okanagan	2,185
Haida	2,165
Squamish	1,970
Kutchin (Louchaux)	1,810
Chilcotin	1,650
Tutchone	1,575
Heiltsuk (Bella Bella)	1,520
Straits Salish	1,510
Beaver	1,365
Tahltan	1,275
Huron	1,200
Hare	1,175
Tlingit	1,105
Bella Coola	960
Haisla	915
Abenaki	810
Sarcese (Sarsi)	785
Comox	765
Kaska	670
Sekani	615
Delaware	560
Kutenai (Kootenay)	525
Sechelt	515
Han	480
Potawatomi	80

Each of these groups is politically subdivided into one or more bands, with most bands having less than 500 members. For example, the Beaver are divided into seven bands: Beaver, First Nation, Blueberry River, Dog River, Halfway River, Horse Lake, and West Moberly Lake. The larger the First Nation, the more bands it will likely have, and thus the Sekani have only 3 bands while the Nootka have 15 and the Cree have 137.

Prior to French and English influence, most Native Americans lived in the forested regions of the east and west and had a nomadic or seminomadic lifestyle based on hunting, gathering, fishing, and some farming. Other groups who lived on the west coast lived in large villages and subsisted through fishing. The Great Plains extends into southern Canada and groups in this region, such as the Blackfeet and Dakota, lived a nomadic lifestyle based on the hunting of buffalo. In the 1600s, and 1700s many Indian groups were drawn into the fur trade by the French and British, and trapping and selling furs markedly altered their traditional ways of life. Indians settled near White settlements or trading posts, became dependent on Whites for supplies and food, and were drawn into the money-based economy. The continuing economic, social, and health problems of some communities date to this period.

The **Inuit** live in northern Canada, north of the Arctic Circle. Inuit arrived in the Americas later than, and separately from, people labeled Indians, and they speak different languages. Traditionally, most lived in small, nomadic bands and subsisted by fishing and hunting sea mammals and caribou. The major, named groups are the MacKenzie Inuit, Copper Inuit, Caribou Inuit, Netsilik Inuit, Ingulik, Southampton Inuit, Baffinland Inuit, and Labrador Inuit. Inuit culture began to change shortly after continual contact with Europeans began in the 1700s, but government programs in the last half of the 20th century have led to the greatest changes, including living in settled communities; wage labor; and the use of government education, medical, and social services.

In the most general sense, the term **Métis** can refer to people of mixed Indian and European (primarily French, British, or Scottish) ancestry. More specifically, however, it refers to people of mixed ancestry whose ancestors were involved in the fur trade and lived in fur-trading communities. Indians of mixed ancestry who affiliate with Indian bands are not considered to be Métis. The people now called Métis were distinct from both the Indians and European traders. Most Métis today live in the western provinces of Manitoba, Saskatchewan, and Alberta. The group is classified by the government as a distinct ethnic category. As such, the Métis have obtained reserve land and have entered into various economic and political relationships with the provincial governments. In the United States, however, they are not recognized as a distinct group and they tend to associate with nearby American Indian groups.

Charter Groups

The term **charter groups** is the somewhat outdated label given to the British and French, the first European colonizers of Canada. People of British ancestry constitute about 40% of the Canadian population, and people of French ancestry constitute about 27% (about 90% in the Province of Québec). English and

French are both official languages in Canada, although French is not spoken widely outside Québec.

The **French** Canadian population falls into two groups—the **Québécois** who live in Québec, and the **Francophones** who are dispersed among the general population or in small French Canadian communities elsewhere in Canada. A key marker of French Canadian identity is speaking French. Adherence to Roman Catholicism is no longer as important to French Canadian identity as it was in the past. Although French Canadians are in many ways integrated into Canadian society, they maintain strong ties to French culture and identify with French communities outside Canada.

As in Great Britain, the label **British** in Canada is based on geography and politics and masks much ethnic diversity. British in Canada number about 10.8 million. About 6.7 million are of English, 2 million of Scot, 2 million of Irish, and 100,000 of Welsh ancestry. These figures should be taken only as rough estimates, as many people identified as British are of mixed ancestry. In addition, it is also important to note that for many people, assimilation into Canadian society and Canadian identity is more important than ethnic ancestry. Early British settlers were mainly English and Scots, with Highland Scots from the Orkney Islands playing a major role in the Hudson's Bay Company, which spread British culture into the north and the interior of Canada. Most Irish and Welsh came after 1850. As these peoples spoke English, were already affiliated with England, and stood in opposition to the French, assimilation into British Canadian society was often rapid. Ethnic identity (which for the Scots also meant Lowland versus Highland, and for the Irish also meant Catholic versus Protestant) was and continues to be maintained through membership in ethnic associations and the continuation of ethnic arts, crafts, music, and dance. Paradoxically, the Scots, who have enjoyed the greatest political and economic success in Canada, have also maintained a stronger sense of ethnic identity than have the Irish and Welsh.

Canada is a British nation in that English is the primary language, the legal and government systems are based on British models, a sizable portion of the population is Protestant, it remains part of the British Commonwealth of Nations, and many immigrants come to Canada from nations that were British colonies. Thus, a Canadian version of British culture is what other groups assimilate into in Canadian society, and British Canadians consider themselves the true Canadians.

Immigrant Groups

People classified as members of immigrant groups or as newcomers are all those who are not classified as Aboriginal or as members of the French Canadian and British Canadian communities. For a nation with a small population, Canada has an extremely diverse immigrant population: government policies have, at times, made Canada a welcoming place for immigrants from many places.

People of African ancestry, usually labeled **Blacks,** are a relatively small population in Canada and fall into two general categories: those from the Caribbean and those from Africa. The major groups from the Caribbean are as follows:

West Indians in Canada

Group	Population
Barbadian	33,178
Guyanese	16,755
Haitian	22,885
Jamaican	20,910
West Indian	18,820
Trinidadian/Tobagonian	8,930

Blacks from the West Indies live primarily in major cities such as Montréal, Toronto, and Vancouver, with a substantial percentage of the population having settled in Canada in the latter decades of the 20th century. There is a clear distinction between Caribbean Blacks who arrived before World War II and those who arrived since the 1960s. Individuals in the former group more closely identify with Canadian society, are more completely assimilated, and tend to be highly educated and work in the professions and business. The more re-

cent immigrants maintain closer ties to their ethnic communities and are found working mainly in low-level service and labor occupations. With the exception of the Haitians (who are from what was a French colony), they come mainly from former British colonies and thus most speak English and are Protestants.

Blacks from Africa number only about 36,000 in Canada, and they are mainly refugees from Ethiopia and Somalia.

Europeans

Substantial emigration from European nations other than France and Great Britain began in the late 1800s when the Canadian government actively recruited farmers from Europe to come and settle in the western provinces, which had been linked to the east by the cross-continental railroad. Most of these immigrants came from central and northern Europe, and today people of **German, Ukrainian,** and **Scandinavian** ancestry continue to be major population groups in the rural western provinces. Immigrants from southern and eastern Europe began arriving in substantial numbers after 1914, when the government sought factory workers. Unlike the northern Europeans who came earlier, these later immigrants were the victims of considerable ethnic prejudice, and in the cities, patterns of segregation—with ethnic groups living in their own neighborhoods—persist in the 1990s. The Canadian policy of multiculturalism has encouraged all groups to preserve their cultural traditions through ethnic associations, native-language schools and publications, dance and music groups, and ethnic festivals.

In addition to the major national groups listed below, there are also a number of distinct European religious minorities. The largest such group is the **Jews,** who number 245,800. They live mainly in Montréal and Toronto in distinctively Jewish neighborhoods. Most, however, are integrated into the mainstream economy and hold professional and management positions. Other religiously distinct European-origin groups are the **Doukhobors, Hutterites,** and **Russian Old Believers.**

Canadians of European Ancestry

Region/Group	Population (*estimate)
Europeans—Northern and Western	
Austrian	27,131
Belgian	31,475
Danish	40,640
Dutch	358,180
English	*6,700,000
Flemish	3,010
German	911,560
Icelandic	14,555
Irish	*2,000,000
Luxembourger	515
Norwegian	63,030
Scandinavian	12,805
Scot	*2,000,000
Swedish	43,345
Swiss	23,610
Welsh	*100,000
Europeans—Eastern	
Albanian	1,555
Armenian	26,005
Belarusian	1,015
Bulgar	4,750
Croatian	41,550
Czech	21,190
Estonian	12,940
Hungarian	100,725
Latvian	11,490
Lithuanian	15,180
Macedonian	14,030
Polish	272,810
Romanian	28,650
Russian	38,220
Serbian	13,085
Slovak	15,945
Slovenian	8,050
Ukrainian	406,645
Yugoslavian	48,420
Europeans—Southern	
Basque	495
Cypriot	1,300
Greek	151,150
Italian	750,050
Maltese	15,525
Portuguese	246,890
Spanish	82,675

Peoples from Asia and the Pacific

People of Asian ancestry in Canada are a highly diverse group and come from at least 18 different Asian nations, although 3 nations—China, India, and the Philippines—account for the majority. Immigration prior to the 1960s was restricted primarily to the **Chinese, Japanese,** and **Sikhs** from India, who settled in the west and worked in mining, building railroads, and farming; all were subjected to considerable discrimination. Restrictive immigration laws slowed or ended Asian immigration from the 1920s until after World War II. Since the 1960s, there has been considerable immigration from Asia, most notably from China and Hong Kong, Korea,

Canadians of Asian Ancestry

Region/Group	Population
Asians—Eastern	
Chinese	586,645
Japanese	48,595
Korean	44,095
Asians—Southern	
Bangladeshi	4,790
Bengali	1,200
Burmese	580
East Indian	324,840
Pakistani	35,680
Punjabi	20,960
Singhalese	980
Sri Lankan	23,150
Tamil	8,695
Asians—Southeastern	
Cambodian	16,940
Indonesian	2,210
Filipino	157,250
Laotian	13,365
Malay	1,715
Thai	1,640
Vietnamese	84,005

the Philippines, India, and Vietnam. The majority of immigrants arrive speaking English, settle mainly in cities in the east, and are employed in a wide range of occupations. Although the overt discrimination of earlier in the century has ended, there continues to be resentment against Asians who are seen as taking jobs and university positions from Canadians (of European ancestry). The Asian immigrants in Canada adhere to a wide range of religions: Protestantism, Roman Catholicism (Filipinos), Buddhism (Vietnamese), Sikhism, Islam, and Hinduism.

The smallest Asian-Pacific ethnic category is composed of **Pacific Islanders** and includes some 6,700 Fijians and 500 people classified as Polynesian. The Fijians are primarily Indo-Fijians who, because of the history of British rule in Fiji, speak English. They are in Canada having fled the ethnic conflict in their homeland.

Caribbeans and South and Central Americans

Because of the long distance between Canada and the Caribbean and South America, and because of few colonial ties, the number of people in Canada from these regions is small.

Canadians of Caribbean, Central American, and South American Ancestry

Group	Population
Argentinian	3,090
Brazilian	2,525
Chilean	12,795
Colombian	3,110
Cuban	660
Ecuadorian	2,700
Guatemalan	3,855
Mexican	8,015
Nicaraguan	3,210
Peruvian	4,935
Salvadoran	12,445
Uruguayan	1,470
Other Central/South American	21,740
No National Designation	5,655

Most have settled in Canada for business or education, or they are fleeing conflict in their homelands, as is the case with the Salvadorans, one of the largest groups.

Peoples from the Middle East and North America

Immigrants from the Middle East and North Africa are mostly Muslims, of whom many are Arabs. Like other non-European groups, they have arrived mainly since the 1960s and live in cities in the east. The two largest groups—who form a majority of the non-European population—are Iranians and Lebanese who have fled conflict and repression in their homelands. The Iranians are Muslims while the Lebanese are Muslims and Christians.

Canadians of Middle Eastern and North African Ancestry

Group	Population
Afghan	5,875
Arab	27,270
Iranian	38,915
Iraqi	3,520
Israeli	755
Kurdish	1,170
Lebanese	74,250
Palestinian	4,050
Syrian	7,080
Egyptian	18,950
Moroccan	5,005
West Asian	410

Ethnic Relations

In 1971, Canada began moving toward establishing itself as a multicultural society, and in 1988 the Multiculturalism Act was passed. The Act sets forth what this means for Canadian society.

- Multiculturalism is the official government policy.
- Multiculturalism reflects the racial and ethnic diversity of Canada.

- All members of society should fully participate in Canadian society.
- Members of all communities have made a contribution to Canada.
- All individuals have a right to equal treatment and equal protection.
- The government will assist in the preservation and use of languages other than English and French.
- The government will assist in the expression of cultural variation.

Prior to the 1970s, Canada was better described as a bilingual nation, with most attention being paid to the large French and British populations and little attention to the Aboriginal Peoples or to the immigrants. The multicultural policy was supported by the government for a number of reasons, including a fear that racial violence (like that in the United States in the 1960s) would occur in Canada; the reality that over the 20th century, the ethnic composition of Canadian society has become much more diverse; Canada's growing involvement in the world community, which brought with it contact with many African and Asian nations; and the need to create a framework to balance the needs of the three major ethnic group categories.

The multicultural societal model was set forth as an alternative to an assimilation model, in which people in Canada would be expected to assimilate into either French Canadian or British Canadian society. However, since English and French are the national languages, the ability to read and write in one of these languages remains an important requirement for success in Canadian society.

The multicultural model is not without its critics, among both Canadian citizens and experts on ethnic relations. For example, many French Canadians in Québec continue to prefer separation from Canada, and many Canadians of British ancestry in the west see few advantages in forcing Québec to remain part of Canada. And, despite recent government reports pointing to the disadvantaged conditions in which Aboriginal Peoples live and blaming government policies for the situation, many Canadians do not support more government spending to assist these communities. Some

experts question whether the official multicultural policy actually reflects Canadian attitudes about multiculturalism. Some research suggests that despite very different public models of ethnic relations—assimilation and multiculturalism—U.S. citizens and Canadians actually have quite similar attitudes about ethnicity. The White population in both nations generally considers Whites superior, with other groups regarded as less American or less Canadian, and Blacks as seen as inferior.

The two most pressing ethnic-based issues facing Canada are the problem of French Canadian separatism and the status and role of Aboriginal Peoples in Canadian society. Difficulties between the British and French date to rivalries and wars between the two nations in Europe and rivalry and wars in Canada. The Québec Act of 1774 created two Canadas—British and French— and gave French Canadians the right to continue to speak French, to practice Roman Catholicism, and to follow French laws and customs. Since then, Québec has been a French enclave in what eventually became British Canada, and relations between the French and British were generally peaceful. In 1945, a separatism movement began in Québec, fueled mainly by an increase in the power and role of the national, British-dominated government, a change that threatened provincial independence and the influence of the Catholic Church. By the mid-1960s, the influence of the Church had declined, but Québec autonomy remained an issue, with French Canadians and Canadians in general divided on the issue. When efforts by the national government in the 1980s to ensure Québec's cultural autonomy failed to gain general support across Canada, the separatism movement gained strength. In a referendum on separation in 1995, opponents of separatism were victorious by less than 1% of the vote.

As noted above, Aboriginal Canadians are largely second-class citizens who live outside mainstream society socially, politically, and economically. Even though a substantial number of Indians live in major cities such as Toronto, Montréal, and Vancouver, they often live outside the fabric of urban life. The 1996 government report by the Commission on

Aboriginal Peoples lays the blame for this situation on non-Aboriginal Canadians: "The legacy of Canada's treatment of aboriginal people is one of waste: wasted potential, wasted money, and wasted lives." The Commission's recommendations to improve the lives of Aboriginal Canadians have not been unanimously accepted across Canada. Opponents object on various grounds: Aboriginal Peoples already get too much aid, other government programs should not be cut to fund Aboriginal programs, and some programs, such as creating an Aboriginal Parliament, are unrealistic. However, Aboriginal peoples generally see the report and its recommendations as an opportunity to bring real change to their communities.

In late 1997, Indians made headway in their efforts to regain control of aboriginal land: the Canadian Supreme Court ruled that claims to land could be based on tribal history, even when there are no titles or treaties governing its ownership. This decision has caused concern among Whites in western Canada, as much land they now own or control might be contested by Indians in the future.

For Aboriginal Canadians, the primary issues are those facing Aboriginal peoples elsewhere in the world: self-government, land rights, educational opportunity, and economic development.

Chile

C hile is located along the Pacific coast of southwestern South America. It is bordered by Peru on the north, Bolivia on the northeast, and Argentina on the east. Before the European colonization of South America, the region that now constitutes Chile evidently had a smaller and much more dispersed Indian population than the territories of other Latin American nations. Spaniards settled Chile in the 16th century, mainly in the center portion of the nation. As Chile lacked mineral wealth, major colonial enterprises were not established, and with a climate similar to that in Europe, many settlers established farms. With little need for labor, few Indians were enslaved and few slaves were imported from Africa. Chile thus developed with a distinct European flavor, although the Indian cultural presence was obvious as well. Chile won independence in 1818. Today, Chile has a population of 14.3 million. About 90% of the population is Roman Catholic, the remainder being mainly Protestant.

Ethnic Composition

As a product of its unique colonial and social history, Chile is an ethnically homogeneous society. Nearly all Chileans self-identify as Chileans, rather than as members of any specific ethnic group, even though many are descendants of people from different European countries and cultures. This is indicative of the long history of assimilation into Chilean society. During the colonial era, intermarriage of Indians and the Spanish settlers produced a majority population of **Mestizos.** However, the Mestizo population was mainly Spanish in cultural orientation, speaking Spanish and adhering to Roman Catholicism. Other

Europeans began arriving in the mid-19th century. The largest group was **Germans,** followed in size by the **British,** although **Italians, French,** and **Croats,** and later **Jews, Palestinians,** and Christian **Lebanese** and **Syrians** also arrived. To a large extent, all rapidly assimilated into the existing Mestizo society, and by the second generation, these immigrants saw themselves as Chilean. The only significant minorities are the Mapuche Indians (Araucanians) in the south, the Aymara in the north, and the Easter Islanders (Rapa Nui) on an island in the Pacific.

Aymara number about 70,000 in northern Chile, with the majority living in Peru and Bolivia.

Easter Islanders, also known by their Polynesian name, **Rapa Nui,** are the indigenous people of Easter Island, located 2,500 miles off the Chilean coast in the Pacific Ocean. The island was taken by Chile in 1888 and is now a dependency, and the Rapa Nui are Chilean citizens. The island population is about 2,500, about 2,000 of whom are Rapa Nui, the remainder being Chilean government officials and military personnel. Easter Island has drawn considerable attention because of the large stone monuments created by the Rapa Nui, as well as because of Thor Heyerdahl's *Kon-Tiki* expedition, which suggested the possibility that Easter Island was settled from South America. However, most experts classify the Rapa Nui as Polynesian in origin, not South American. At the time of European contact, Easter Island's population and culture were declining. In the late 1800s, the Rapa Nui were converted to Roman Catholicism and were drawn into the agricultural/sheep-raising economy created by Chile. As their culture was already disappearing, they were rapidly assimilated into Chilean society. In the 1990s, some aspects of the indigenous culture—primarily craft items—have been revived for the tourist trade.

Mapuche, also known as **Araucanians,** are the largest and only significant minority. These American Indians number about 400,000 and live mainly in the central region. There are also about 40,000 Araucanians in Argentina. Prior to Spanish settlement, the Mapuche were divided into three regional groups: north, central, and south. Those in the north came under Inca control in the early 1500s and were decimated by the Spaniards. Those in the center and south resisted Spanish rule, although there was much Mapuche-Spanish intermarriage. In the 1860s, as the Spaniards and Germans settled the central region, the Mapuche lost much of their land, and in 1894, they were placed on small reservations. Government policies in the 20th century have led to a breakup of some reservations, although most Mapuche still live on them. Reservation life put them in regular contact with non-Indians, and the majority now live in Western-style homes and live a Chilean lifestyle, with their communities organized both by family ties and social-class distinctions. Only about 10% continue to speak Mapuche as their daily language, with 40% speaking only Spanish and 50% speaking both languages. One aspect of their traditional culture that has survived is religion, which stresses ancestor worship and dream interpretation.

Ethnic Relations

With the long history of immigrant assimilation into Chilean society and the subjugation of the Mapuche in the late 1880s, ethnic relations in Chile have been peaceful in the 20th century. The main issue concerns the Mapuche and competition for their land. While the Mapuche prefer to maintain their reservations, they face pressures to divide their communally held land and allocate it to individuals, a change that will also make some of it available to outsiders.

Colombia

Colombia is located in northern South America and is bordered by the Pacific Ocean and Panama on the west, the Caribbean Sea on the north, Venezuela and Brazil on the east, and Peru and Ecuador on the south. It has a population of 36.8 million. Spanish is the national language and Roman Catholicism the national religion (95% of the population is Roman Catholic), although freedom of religion is guaranteed.

Colombia was colonized by Spaniards in the 1530s and achieved independence in 1819. The Spanish colonial influence remains strong in Colombia—perhaps stronger than in most other former Spanish American colonies—as indicated by the prominence of the Spanish language, Roman Catholicism, and a social-class structure dominated by people of Spanish descent. Since the late 1940s, Colombian society has experienced considerable unrest and violence. Among major issues facing the nation are poverty, rural-to-urban migration, a high birth rate, violence related to the illegal narcotics trade, political corruption, and social tensions causes by large race- and ethnicity-based differences in wealth and access to political influence. Colombia also has a more sizable urban population (about 60% of the populace) than many other Latin American nations, with Barranquilla, Cali, Medellín, and Bogotá all now being major metropolitan regions with diverse populations.

Ethnic Composition

Colombia is an ethnically heterogeneous society composed of five major ethnic categories: Afro-Colombians, Europeans (mainly of Spanish descent), Indians, Mestizos (people of mixed Indian and Spanish ancestry), and Mulattos (people of mixed African and European ancestry) and Zambos (people of mixed African and Indian ancestry). As there has been no reasonably accurate census by ethnicity since 1912—and the government has not attempted such a census since 1918—the number of people in each category is unknown. A recent estimate suggests that about 50% of the population is Mestizo, 25% European, 24% of full or partial African ancestry, and less than 1% American Indian. In addition to ethnicity, region is also an important organizing principle in Colombian society. The rugged and mountainous landscape of Colombia has produced a number of different regional traditions within the general Spanish model. Although these differences have lessened over time, Colombians continue to stress their regional identity: Costeno from the northern Atlantic coast, Valluno from the Cali region, Paisa from the Medellín region, Cachaco from the Bogotá region, and Chocoano from the Chocó region. The last designation is also used for Afro-Colombians, as the majority of the Chocó population is of African ancestry.

Afro-Colombians

Afro-Colombians are people of African or partial African ancestry. Their number is unknown, with estimates ranging from 4% (1.4 million) to 24% (8.8 million) of the population. Africans were brought to Colombia by the Spaniards beginning in the 1520s to work in gold mines, on sugar cane plantations, and as household workers. Unlike in some other Spanish colonies, Africans in Colombia did not form their own communities; most were assimilated into colonial society, although they were socially separate from Spaniards and many Mestizos. Thus, Afro-Colombians speak Spanish and nearly all are Roman Catholic. In addition, there is a small population of Afro-Colombians on the islands of San Andrés, Providencia, and Santa Catalina off the coast of Nicaragua. These islands are also claimed by Nicaragua but are now under Colombian control. The African population speaks English and is Protestant.

Despite the social isolation of Africans in Colombia, contact with other groups occurred. The children of African Spanish and African Indian unions have produced subgroups of Afro-Colombians labeled **Zambos** and **Mulattos.**

Afro-Colombians are concentrated in three regions, with large populations in major cities as well: Afro-Colombians account for as much as 90% of the population in the Pacific region; they are mixed with the largely Mestizo population along the Caribbean coast; they and are also concentrated in the Cauca Valley near Cali. When slavery ended in 1851, many Afro-Colombians continued in the same work they had done as slaves (mining, ranching, and farming), a pattern that continues in rural areas in the 1990s. Those in cities are wage laborers or are unemployed. Through assimilation into Spanish society, most African customs disappeared, although the African influence remains in religion, with traditional beliefs being integrated with Roman Catholicism, and in music, especially the "salsa" style that has become popular around the world.

Europeans

Europeans in Colombia are mainly of **Spanish** descent, speak Spanish, are Roman Catholic, and live in the major cities. They form the upper class and the core of the middle class. Europeans stress education and European traditions in art and literature, and they view manual labor as more suitable for Mestizos, Afro-Colombians, and Indians. At the top of the social hierarchy are those who trace their ancestry to the original Spanish colonists, although a distinct wealthy class composed of those who have made their wealth through commerce and industry in the last several decades now rivals the old elite. The European category also includes Mestizos who—through a combination of physical appearance, education, occupation, and lifestyle—are classified socially as European.

Indians

Indians in Colombia in the 1990s number about 250,000, although the absence of recent and accurate census information means that any estimate of the Indian population is open to dispute. Advocates of Indian rights argue that the population is considerably higher than this figure. In any case, Indians in Colombia today represent only a small percentage of the Indian population of some 1.5 to 2 million at the time the Spaniards arrived in the early 1500s. Indians in Colombia are a marginal population—geographically, socially, economically, and politically. Geographically, they are concentrated in border regions, with the largest concentrations living in the highlands of the southwest and the lowlands of the east. Indians in the highlands have been in contact with the Spanish since the 16th century and many are assimilated in the surrounding Mestizo society, while the large number of Mestizos in the region attests to the earlier and frequent contact between Spanish men and Indian women. In the western Amazon region, contact came later, and integration into Colombian society is more a 20th-century phenomenon. Culturally, it is impossible to describe Colombia's Indians in any general terms, as there are large variations across groups, and even within groups, in their degree of assimilation into Colombian society. In comparison to the other Colombian groups, Indians are poor, rural, and have limited access to political influence.

American Indians of Colombia

Group	Location	Population
Achawa	Southeast	80
Andoke	Southeast	103
Awá Kwaiker (Koakir)	Southwest	5,000
Bará	Southeast	300
Barasana	Southeast	300
Barí	North	450
Bintukua	North	3,000
Bora	West	400
Chami	East	5,000
Chimila	North	300
Chocó	West	18,000–30,000
Cubeo (Kobewa)	Southeast	4,500
Cuiva	East	540
Cuna (Kuna) (*see* Panama)	North	2,500
Desana	Southeast	1,000
Emberá (*see* Panama)	West	2,000
Guajiro (*see* Venezuela)	North	60,000
Guambiano	Southwest	10,000
Hitnu	Northeast	230
Hiwi	Northeast	11,000
Hupda	Southeast	500
Kamsá	South	3,000
Karihona	Southeast	100
Ka'wiari	Southeast	100
Kogi (Cagaba)	North	4,000
Korewahe	South	500
Macuna	Southeast	400
Malayo	North	4,000
Noanamá	Southwest	1,000
Paéz	Southwest	60,000–80,000
Piapoco	East	450
Piaroa	East	280
Puinave	East	2,500
Quechua (*see* Ecuador)	Southwest	9,000
Saliva	East	750

Siona	Southwest	250
Tadó	Center	1,000
Tanumuku	Southeast	300
Tatuyo	Southeast	400
Ticuna	Southeast	1,000
Tucano	Southeast	2,000
Tunebo	North	3,000
Wakuenai	East	400
Wambiano	South	7,000
Wanano	Southeast	800
Witoto	Southeast	700
Yagua	Southeast	3,250
Yukpa	North	2,500
Yukuna	Southeast	425

Awá Kwaiker (Koakir) number about 5,000 and live in the tropical rain forest along the border with Ecuador. Strictly speaking, they are not one group but rather a mix of groups that coalesced following the Spanish conquest. Through contact with Catholic missionaries, Mestizos, and landowners, some have been drawn into Colombian society while others have retreated deeper into the forest to retain their traditional way of life based on slash-and-burn horticulture. It is estimated that about 65% are assimilated or being assimilated while about 35% still live the traditional lifestyle.

Barí are a small group numbering about 1,600 in eastern Colombia and western Venezuela. Those in Colombia have lived on reserves since the 1970s, where they subsist by cattle ranching and growing crops for sale in regional markets. In the 20th century, their relations with outsiders have been difficult: early in the century, oil prospectors displaced the Barí, and more recently, their territory has been used by guerrilla movements revolting against the government.

Chocó is the name for a number of groups on the border with Panama. About 18,000–30,000 live in Colombia, with a smaller number residing across the border in Panama where they are called the **Embera**. Although the groups labeled Chocó have been in contact with the Spanish for 400 years, they have been able to maintain use of their traditional languages and their "slash-and-mulch" form of horticulture by frequently migrating to new locales and creating new villages beyond Mestizo and Spanish influence. However, in the late 20th century, they are losing land to Mestizo settlers and are organizing politically to protect their land.

Cubeo number about 4,500 in the Amazon region of southeastern Colombia. Like many groups in the region, their remote location and the undesirability of the region for agriculture enabled them to avoid regular contact with the Spaniards for several centuries. It was not until the late 19th century, when rubber tappers entered the region, that they came into regular contact with non-Indians. This contact escalated in the 20th century when gold miners arrived and also as the region became a center for the processing of coca. The Cubeo live on the large Vaupés Reserve created by the government for them and other groups. While the reserve ensures the Cubeo use of their traditional territory and allows for a continuation of some traditional customs, they have also been integrated into the national education system and trade networks, and many have converted to Roman Catholicism.

Guambiano live in the southwest, in the foothills of the Central Cordillera range. Estimates place their population at from 10,000 to 18,000. As is the case with some other groups in the highlands, the Spaniards created reserves (called *reguardos*) for their exclusive use in the early 1700s. The land on the reserves was for Indian use, although the Indians did not have the right to sell it. However, Indian ownership was routinely ignored by Spanish and Mestizo settlers who simply took the land and established haciendas, with the Guambiano and other Indians reduced to the status of peasants who worked the hacienda land. As peasants, the Guambiano were drawn into the wider society, with Spanish replacing their indigenous language and many converting to Roman Catholicism. In the 1990s, the Guambiano have organized to fight to retain remaining land and to reacquire some that has been lost. An important force in this fight is local village councils—once centers of the indigenous communities—which are being revitalized as political-action groups.

Kogi (Cagaba) number about 4,000 and live on the northeastern peninsula. The Kogi originally lived in the valleys but moved up the mountain slopes to avoid the Mestizos who were settling in the region. Their relative isolation led to the survival of many elements of their traditional culture, including the Kogi language, slash-and-burn horticulture, and the central role played by the Kogi religious specialist who is the religious leader, healer, and political leader of the community.

Paéz number anywhere from 60,000 to 80,000 and are the largest Indian group in Colombia. They live in the southwestern highlands, and—like the Guambiano and others in the region—at first benefited from the reserves created for them in the early 1700s. Since then, however, they have lost much of their reserve land to Spanish and Mestizo landowners and farmers, and nearly all now live in Spanish-style villages with central plazas, a Catholic church, stores, and a school. Most are farmers, although there has also been significant migration to cities by those in search of work, and some men work as contract laborers on coffee plantations. Although they are significantly assimilated into Colombian society, throughout the 1900s they have sought to regain some of their land.

Yagua number about 3,250 and live in the Amazon rainforest in Colombia, Brazil, and Peru. Like other groups in the region, they did not come into regular and destructive contact with outsiders until the late 19th century when rubber extractors entered the region and displaced and enslaved them. The traditional hunter-gatherer way of life was largely destroyed, and the Yagua became farmers and settled in villages. Although some elements of the traditional culture survive, they are to a large extent assimilated into the surrounding Mestizo society.

Mestizos

Mestizos are estimated to constitute about half of the population, or about 18 million people. Mestizos populations began in the highlands where the Spanish colonists mixed with Indian women. Mestizos were a largely rural population of farmers until the 1940s, when many began moving to the major cities in search of better jobs and education. In many cities they now constitute the majority of the working and poor classes. Despite the racial basis of Mestizo identity, Mestizo in Colombia—as elsewhere in Latin America—is a social category, not a racial one. Mestizos who are wealthy, educated, and live in cities are often classified as European rather than as Mestizo. For a Mestizo, European physical appearance, education, a job that does not require manual labor, and living a European lifestyle all can lead to upward social mobility.

Other Groups

Unlike some other nations such as Argentina, Chile, and Brazil, Colombia has long resisted foreign immigrants, and there are relatively few non-Spanish Europeans and Asians. The largest groups are the **Germans** and **Italians,** who were involved in business and trade and rapidly assimilated into the upper class, primarily through intermarriage with the Spanish. The population of **Jews** has decreased in the 1990s to less than 10,000 as many have fled to the United States to avoid the continuing violence in Colombia. Another distinctive minority early in the 20th century are the **Lebanese** (often called **Turks** because they came from the Ottoman Empire), who are also involved in commerce and are associated with the European upper class.

Ethnic Relations

Colombian society is stratified on the basis of both skin color and ethnic background. High social status, wealth, and urban residence are associated with being White and living a Spanish lifestyle: specifically, speaking Spanish, adhering to Roman Catholicism, working in business or owning property, and living in a major city. In the colonial era and today, Mestizos are classified as inferior to Europeans but superior to Afro-Colombians and Indians. However, considerable mixing of the Spaniards, Indians, and Afro-Colombians from early colonial times has made ethnic identity an ambiguous concept in modern Colombia. Afro-Colombians and Indians occupy the lowest rung of the social-class ladder. However, as with Mestizos, Afro-Colombians of mixed ancestry can enhance their social status if they appear to be European and live a European lifestyle. In general, Mestizos have an easier time moving up the social ladder than do Afro-Colombians, whose African ancestry tends to more readily differentiate them from the dominant Spanish population.

Since the 1980s, Indian and Afro-Colombian rights have been a major issue in Colombian society. Both groups are largely rural and subsist by farming, and when roads were cut into their regions (especially into the Afro-Colombian Pacific region and the Indian Ama-zon region), both groups began to politically and legally resist attempts to take their land and to settle other Colombians into the regions. Both groups have been successful in having the government set aside land for their exclusive use. Success on the political front has stimulated a "Black consciousness" movement, in which the histories of Afro-Colombian communities are stressed, relations are established with other Afro-Caribbean organizations, and distinctively Afro-Colombian festivals are staged.

Costa Rica

Costa Rica is in southern Central America. It is bordered by Nicaragua on the north, the Caribbean Sea on the east, Panama on the south, and the southern Pacific Ocean on the west. The population is 3,463,000, Spanish is the official language, and Roman Catholicism the major religion. It was colonized by Spaniards in 1502 and became independent in 1821. Costa Rica is unique among former Spanish colonies in Latin America in that the majority of its population is of European (Spanish) ancestry; the number of Mestizos is small; the Black population does not have its origin in Costa Rican slavery; the nation has had a long history of stable, democratic rule; and the economy is generally healthy.

Ethnic Composition

Costa Rica is an ethnically homogeneous nation, with 96% of the population classified as Costa Rican, or Ticos as they are sometimes called. The remainder of the population consists of Blacks (3%), American Indians, and people of Chinese ancestry. Ticos and Chinese are found across the nation, while Blacks and Indians are regionally localized in the east and south. Almost the entire population is Roman Catholic and Spanish-speaking. In the 1980s and 1990s, Costa Rica provided shelter for several hundred thousand refugees from the civil wars and domestic turmoil in Guatemala, El Salvador, Nicaragua, and Panama. The end of these conflicts in 1994 and 1995 led many of those refugees to return home, although as many as 100,000 may still remain in Costa Rica.

Blacks number about 104,000, constituting 3% of the population. Although Blacks live in all of Costa Rica's larger cities, they are heavily concentrated in the province of Limón on the Caribbean coast. Unlike most other European colonies, Costa Rica was not reliant on plantation agriculture. Therefore, few slaves were imported to Costa Rica from Africa. The current Black population is descended from Jamaicans who immigrated to Costa Rica in the late 1800s to work on building a railway across the nation. When this work ended, many stayed on and took work on the banana plantations established by American companies. Seen as competitors for jobs desired by other Costa Ricans and as physically and culturally different, Blacks were discriminated against and denied citizenship until 1948. Although Blacks are required to learn Spanish in the schools, assimilation into Costa Rican society has progressed slowly, and most Blacks continue to speak Jamaican creole English, to marry other Blacks, and to live in mainly Black communities.

People of **Chinese** ancestry number about 7,000, and in the 1990s, they form three distinct communities: (1) those from southern China who are descended from the Chinese who arrived in the late 1800s to work on building the railroad; (2) Taiwanese who have arrived in a small but steady stream since the 1950s; and (3) Chinese from Hong Kong, who have also arrived since the 1950s. A fourth group with Chinese ancestry is the **Cruzados,** people of mixed Chinese and Costa Rican ancestry, most of whom are affiliated with the first group—those descended from southern Chinese immigrants of the 19th century. They are the largest and the most assimilated of the Chinese groups. Nearly all speak only Spanish; identify themselves as Costa Ricans; and work in the retail trade, commerce, professions, and politics. They are a highly visible and active component of Costa Rican society. The second and third groups are smaller, and as recent arrivals, many speak Chinese and affiliate more strongly with their communities than with Costa Rican society.

Costa Ricans (Ticos) constitute 96% of the population. Although they are homogeneous in religion and language, there are cultural differences based on both social class and region. As Spanish settlement and rule were mainly in the central valley, the other regions were settled by Spanish settlers not tied to the ruling class. Since then, individual ownership of land and of one's house have been important Costa Rican values. Costa Ricans also value democracy, compromise, family, community, and education. Additionally, many vestiges of Spanish society still found in other Latin American nations are now less obvious in Costa Rica. Thus, male and female status tends to be relatively equal, divorce is more common, and there is more opportunity for upward social mobility whether through education or employment in the expanding economy.

Indians number about 20,000 and fall into five different groups—**Maleku** in the north, who number about 200; **Teribe** in the south, who number a few hundred in Costa Rica, with a larger population across the border in Panama; the **Boruca,** who number about 2,700 in the south; the **Bribri,** who number about 7,000 in the south; and the **Cabécar,** who number about 8,500 in the south. Most members of the last three groups live on reserves. Nearly all Indians in Costa Rica are Roman Catholic, speak Spanish as their first or primary language, and are assimilated into Costa Rican society. Their identity as Indians is maintained by self-identification as such, by government classification, and by residence in Indian communities. As elsewhere in the Americas, control of their land is a major issue for Costa Rican Indians, and their reserves are held in trust for them by the government. The traditional hunting-gathering-fishing way of life has virtually disappeared, and Indians in Costa Rica now work as wage laborers, in the government service, and in the professions.

Ethnic Relations

Ethnic relations are peaceful, although there are clear social barriers between Blacks and other Costa Ricans. A key element in ethnic relations is the belief that all people should assimilate into the Costa Rican way of life, with middle- and upper-class Costa Ricans seen as the most desirable models. Blacks are still seen as outsiders, in part because of their skin color and in part because of their British cultural heritage and the continuing use of English in Black communities. Nonetheless, there has been a slow movement toward assimilation over the last 50 years, with the number of Black-Tico marriages increasing and Blacks moving to cities in search of employment.

There is also discrimination against the refugees from the other Central American nations: and even those with official refugee status—despite laws barring discrimination in hiring—are often denied jobs.

Because of their small numbers and assimilation, American Indians in Costa Rica find themselves in the precarious position of disappearing as distinct cultural groups and thereby losing rights to their land. Both the government Indian agency and Indian organizations have been working to preserve Indian rights.

Cuba

C uba is the largest island nation in the Caribbean Sea and has a population of 10,951,000. Cuba was colonized by the Spanish in the early 16th century. In the colonial era, Cuba was a major Spanish colony and provided an administrative center; fortresses; a hub of trade; and plantations that grew sugar cane, tobacco, and other crops. Its proximity to the United States (90 miles south of the south Florida coast) led to contact between the two nations, and the United States took the island from Spain in the Spanish-American War of 1898. From then until the Cuban revolution of 1959, there were close economic and political ties between the United States and Cuba, with Cuban affairs often dominated by U.S. interests.

Ethnic Composition

Prior to the 1959 revolution that brought Fidel Castro to power and converted Cuba to a Communist society, the Cuban population was ethnically heterogeneous: White, Afro-Cuban, Mulatto, and Chinese. While it is still possible to characterize Cuban society as composed of these groups, it is now much more difficult to categorize individuals. Group differences have disappeared to some extent, and a Cuban ethnic identity is most salient today. The difficulty in assigning ethnic identity is indicated by the variation in recent estimates of the ethnic composition of the population—37%–66% White, 22%–51% Mulatto, 11%–12% Afro-Cuban, and 1% Chinese.

The **White** category is composed of people of European ancestry—mainly **Spanish,** with a small number of **Germans** and **British.** Prior to the 1959 revolution, there was a sizable population of U.S. citizens involved in commerce, trade, and the tourism industry. Nearly all left Cuba at the time of the revolution. Following the revolution, Cuba was allied with the Soviet Union, and technicians, government officials, and others from Russia and Eastern Europe lived and worked in Cuba. Most departed following the demise of the Communist governments in Eastern Europe and the disintegration of the Soviet Union between 1989 and 1991.

Afro-Cubans are descended from slaves who were imported from Africa to work on the plantations. **Mulattos** are people of mixed European and African ancestry; those with lighter skin color and European features are often classified as White. Those of **Chinese** ancestry are descended from indentured workers imported to replace the freed slaves in the late 1800s. They are assimilated into Cuban society and are now mainly involved in trade and commerce.

Today, nearly all Cubans are native born and there are virtually no immigrants. The 1959 revolution led to a large exodus of people in the upper and middle classes, most of whom settled in the United States. They number about 800,000, residing mostly in East Coast cities, with about 500,000 in Miami, Florida. Most Cubans are Roman Catholic, with a minority of Protestants. The Santería religion, a mix of Roman Catholicism and African religions, has many adherents in the Afro-Cuban and Mulatto communities and enjoys an equal status with Christian denominations.

Ethnic Relations

During the Spanish colonial era, Cuban society was dominated by a small upper class of people of Spanish descent. The large African and Mulatto populations were poor and rural. This pattern continued until 1959, with people from the United States joining the small economic and political elite. Afro-Cubans formed a distinct minority who were excluded from mainstream society. Since the 1959 revolution, the Castro government has worked to weaken people's sense of ethnic identity, to end discrimination against Afro-Cubans, and to build a strong sense of Cuban identity. Economic reform has been effective in reducing large-scale differences in wealth and in increasing the quality of life for Afro-Cubans and Mulattos by making education, health care, employment, and housing available to all. Politically, the White elite has been eliminated and has been replaced by a government that better represents all segments of society. In terms of ethnic identity, considerable effort has been given to developing a strong sense of Cuban identity that is more important than other identities. Cuban cultural identity is reflected in being born in Cuba; speaking the Cuban form of Spanish; participation in Cuban Communist political, social, and economic institutions;

and Afro-Cuban music and dance. Cuban identity is also tied to Cuban success in international sports competitions, especially in baseball, volleyball, track, and boxing. Exactly how effective the government has been in creating this shared Cuban identity and in ending racial discrimination is not clear. And in the post-Soviet era, as Cuba begins to initiate some free-market reforms to deal with economic problems, it also not clear whether old ethnic divisions will reemerge.

Dominica

D ominica is the northernmost of the Windward Islands in the eastern Caribbean Sea. It has a population of about 82,000, nearly all of whom are of African or partial African ancestry. Control of the island was contested by the French and English for nearly two centuries, with the English ruling from 1805 until Dominica became an independent nation in 1978.

Ethnic Composition and Ethnic Relations

Although French and English cultural influences were considerable, Dominica was never heavily settled by Europeans, and the contemporary population is composed almost entirely of descendants of African slaves, along with a small, remnant population of Carib Indians.

The **Caribs** are a native South American group who, at the time of Columbus's arrival in the New World in 1492, occupied many islands of the Caribbean. Within 100 years, the Caribs had virtually disappeared from the Caribbean islands because of diseases introduced by the Europeans, enslavement, and forced relocations to other islands. Caribs are found in greater numbers in northern South America and eastern Central America. Caribs in Dominica number about 3,500 and live in the Carib territory on the east side of the island,

which was established by the British in 1900 as a means of protecting the small Carib population from complete assimilation. The Caribs of Dominica are the only remaining Carib group in the eastern Caribbean. Carib identity is based on having at least one Carib parent and residing in Carib territory. Culturally, the Carib of Dominica are assimilated into Dominican society.

Dominicans number about 79,000 and are of either African, African-European, or African-Carib ancestry. As a small population on a small island, the African slaves from whom Dominicans are descended were rapidly assimilated into French and then British Dominican society, and little of the traditional African culture remains. All Dominicans speak English and French creole, and nearly all are Christians, with about 85% adhering to Roman Catholicism. Relations with the Caribs are harmonious.

Dominican Republic

The Dominican Republic is an island nation in the Caribbean Sea, occupying the eastern two-thirds of the island of Hispaniola (the western third of which is Haiti). Between 1492 and 1697, Spaniards colonized the island, exterminated the Taino and Carib Indian populations, established plantations and mines, imported African slaves, and then abandoned the island because it was no longer economically useful. Since then, the island has been controlled by France, Haiti, and Spain again; it became fully independent in 1843; and it was occupied by the United States from 1916 to 1924 and in 1965. Through all of this, the Spanish influence has remained dominant, and today Spanish is the official language and nearly the entire population is Roman Catholic.

Ethnic Composition

The population of 8 million is ethnically heterogeneous, with about 70% of the population of mixed African and Spanish ancestry (Mulattos), 15% of Spanish ancestry (Whites), 10% of African ancestry (Blacks), and 5% made up of more recent immigrants, the largest group of which is Haitians. There is also a large population of immigrants from the Dominican Republic in the United States, estimated to be as a large as one million and centered in the Bronx borough of New York City, and about 200,000 others in Puerto Rico.

Blacks are descendants of African slaves whose ancestry is exclusively African or whose skin color is too dark to allow them to be classified as Mulatto. They number about 800,000, making up 10% of the population. With the Haitians, they form the lower class and are the poorest segment of Dominican society. Relations with other groups are distant. While most are Roman Catholics, some African religious beliefs and practices are still followed, and evangelical Christianity has won converts in recent years.

Haitians are estimated to number anywhere from 200,000 to 1 million in the Dominican Republic. Many came following the political unrest in Haiti in the 1990s, and it is likely that the majority are illegal immigrants. Haitians began coming to the western part of the Dominican Republic around the turn of the 20th century to work as cane cutters on the sugar plantations—work that Dominicans did not want to do. In the 1930s, they were sent back to Haiti, and as many as 20,000 were killed by Dominican government forces. Since the 1950s, agreements between the two countries establish the number of Haitian contract cane cutters to be allowed into the Dominican Republic. Since the 1970s the Haitians have also been performing other, higher-paying plantation work, and also have been working on coffee and rice farms. Still, they are paid less than Dominicans performing the same work, are subject to expulsion, and are relegated to the lowest rung of Dominican society.

Mulattos are people of mixed African and Spanish ancestry; descendants of the Spanish colonists and African slaves they imported. Some Mulattos claim Spanish and Indian ancestry to enhance their social status, although there was actually little Spanish-Indian intermarriage in early colonial times. Mulattos number about 5.6 million. Internally, the group is stratified on the basis of skin color, European features, and wealth (which is closely tied to physical appearance). Mulattos form the large middle class and some manage to move up into the upper class.

Whites are descendants of the Spanish colonists or are Mulattos whose appearance and wealth allow them to be categorized as White. They number about 1.3 million and most are middle class, with a relatively small number of families forming the core of the Republic's upper class.

Other groups include **Sephardic Jews** and **German Jews; Chinese,** who came in both the 19th and 20th centuries and who now own restaurants and hotels; **Arabs (Lebanese, Syrians,** and **Palestinians),** who are mainly merchants; and small numbers of descendants of **British, Dutch, Canarian, Danish,** and **Hungarian** workers. The Northern Europeans are primarily Protestant and many are professionals.

Ethnic Relations

Dominican social organization is based mainly on skin color. Europeans and light-skinned Mulattos control the economic and political systems, most Mulattos fall into the middle class, and poor Blacks and Haitians form the lower class. The effect of skin color can be modified to some extent by government service and education. Class differences are apparent in family structure, with the upper-class families dominated by the oldest men, middle-class families more often following a nuclear family model, and lower-class families often headed by a woman. Ethnic tensions focus on the Haitians who enter legally and illegally to work on the sugar cane plantations. Most Dominicans resent their presence but tolerate it so that the low-level work is performed.

Ecuador

E cuador is located in the northwest part of South America. It is bounded by Colombia on the north, Peru on the east and south, and the Pacific Ocean on the west. It has a population of 10.9 million. Ecuador's current ethnic composition and ethnic relations are a product of the nearly 300 years of Spanish rule, from the 16th to the 19th centuries. Ecuador became independent in 1833. Spanish is the country's official language, and 95% of Ecuadorians are Roman Catholics.

Ethnic Composition

Ecuador contains three major sociocultural groupings: Blancos (people of European descent), Quechua speakers, and Mestizos. There are also several hundred thousand Afro-Hispanics, and less than 100,000 Native Americans.

Afro-Ecuadorians or **Afro-Hispanics** are people of full or partial African ancestry who are part of the Afro-Hispanic cultural tradition found in villages, towns, and cities in the lowlands of Ecuador and Colombia. In the two nations, they number about 500,000, with significant internal differentiations made on the basis of darkness of skin color and social class. Escaped slaves began arriving in Ecuador in 1533 and mixed with local indigenous peoples. Under Spanish rule, some Africans were enslaved while others were free, although considered inferior to Spaniards. Most speak Spanish-African creole languages, and their religions combine elements from traditional African religions and Roman Catholicism.

The term **Blancos** is the generic label used for Spanish-speaking Whites who number about 1.6 million and constitute about 15% of the population. Blanco or White is more a social-class designation than an ethnic one, as identification as a Blanco is based on a combination of light skin color, European features, speaking Spanish, residence in the western part of the nation (especially in a city), and enough wealth or education to be classified as upper or middle class. However, in some rural regions, Mestizos refer to themselves as Blancos to distinguish themselves from Native Americans and Quechua speakers. Blancos form the ruling elite in Ecuador, and categorization as a Blanco is considered desirable by people of full or partial European descent. Blancos generally view all other groups as inferior and are, in turn, resented by others because of their Spanish ancestry and control of Ecuadorian society.

Mestizos number about 4.4 million and constitute about 40% of the population. Mestizos are people of mixed Indian and European ancestry, although classification as a Mestizo has more to do with social-class status than ancestry. Depending on where they live and with whom they interact, Mestizos may speak Spanish, Quechua, or both. As in much of Latin America, Mestizos form the rural peasantry and work mainly as farmers on their own land (or on land owned by others) and in related occupations. Mestizos in cities generally seek to move up the social-class ladder and self-identify as Blancos. They are seen as socially inferior by Blancos, who refer to them as **Cholos,** an insulting term. However, in rural communities, Mestizos often refer to themselves as Blancos to distinguish themselves from Quechua speakers.

Quechua speakers number about 4.4 million and constitute about 40% of the population. They are heavily concentrated in the Andes region in villages and towns where they may be the dominant group or, as Mestizos move west, in or near Mestizo communities. Quechua speakers and Native Americans are identified by a number of labels, including **Indígenes, Runas,** and the insulting terms **Indio** and **Chinita.** Quechua was the language of the Inca Empire and it spread to Native American peoples that the Incas conquered in what are now Colombia, Ecuador, Peru, Bolivia, and Argentina. As many as 11 million people now speak Quechua in these five nations. Quechua is the name given to the related forms of the language spoken (in a number of different dialects) in Ecuador. Contact with the Spanish for 500 years has produced a Quechua culture that is neither Indian nor Spanish but a mix of elements drawn from both, combined with specific cultural adaptations of different Quechua communities. Some Quechua speakers also speak Spanish or the language of nearby Indian groups. Quechua regional groupings or communities are sometimes identified by specific names such as **Canelos Quechua, Cotopaxi Quechua, Otavalo, Salasaka,** and **Saraguro.** However, residents of these regions or communities do not necessarily self-identify with these names. The independence of some Quechua groups has been threatened by migration of Mestizos and government- and business-inspired economic development and resource exploitation.

Some groups have responded by forming political action groups and staging protests that have been, to an extent, successful in protecting the territory of some communities. Some Quechua have also allied themselves with Indian groups for this same purpose.

Native Americans in Ecuador (other than Quechua speakers) are now a small minority, numbering less than 100,000 in total and confined to a number of small territories and reservations. **Jivaro (Shuara)** are a Native American group numbering about 31,500 who live in the Andes foothills of Ecuador. There are four major subgroups: **Antipa, Aguaruna, Huambiza,** and **Achuale,** with the last sometimes considered a distinct group. The Jivaro have fought for centuries against incursions into their territory by the Inca, Spanish, and 20th-century gold miners. Most now live on reservations, raise their own food, and work as wage laborers, but continue many indigenous customs and retain much of their traditional religion. While some are assimilated, others remain among the least assimilated of Ecuadorian Native Americans. **Waorani (Wao)** are an indigenous Native American group of the tropical forest of the Andes foothills and number about 1,000. They have been in regular contact with other groups for less than 50 years. Incursions by the government, missionaries, and loggers substantially reduced their territory and most now live in a small protected area or in the Yasuní National Park. Contact with Whites and Mestizos and involvement in the market economy have altered much of their traditional culture, although aspects of the indigenous religion, settlement patterns, and family relationships survive. Other Native Americans also live in Ecuador, in small groups, all of which are being rapidly assimilated into Ecuadorian society. **Andoa** number only 6 individuals in Ecuador, with about 100 more across the border in Peru. **Awá Kwaiker** number about 7,000, of which about 2,000 live in northwest Ecuador and 5,000 across the border in Colombia. **Colorado (Tsátchela)** number about 1,500 and live in western Ecuador. Although placement on reservations was meant to stem assimilation, their population has declined steadily over the century, and they work now mainly as wage laborers and compete for jobs with Afro-Hispanics who have moved into the region. **Kayapa (Cayapa)** number about 3,000 and live in western Ecuador. **Kofán** number about 600 and live in northeast Ecuador. **Secoya** number about 450 with about 300 in northeast Ecuador and about 150 across the border in Peru. **Siona** number about 350 with about 100 in Ecuador and 250 in Colombia.

Ethnic Relations

The three major "ethnic" groupings in Ecuador are not ethnic groups in the strict sense of the word. They represent instead a system of classification found throughout Latin America in which people are classified into categories, and these categories are ranked on the basis of skin color; ancestry; place of residence (urban or rural); and social class, which is indicated by wealth, occupation, or level of education. There is some mobility available to individuals, and people often attempt to change their public identity in order to move up the social ladder, which in a very general sense is arranged with Native Americans at the bottom, then Afro-Hispanics, then Quechua speakers, then Mestizos, and finally, Whites. However, while Whites are at the top and Native Americans are at the bottom all across Ecuador, the relative positions of the other groups vary from region to region and even from town to town. Because of the dominance of the Whites, relations among the other groups are superficially harmonious, although there are tensions among the three groups in the middle, and at times Afro-Hispanics, Quechua speakers, and Native Americans have protested against discrimination. In general, the history of ethnic relations in Ecuador is one of Spanish exploitation of the other groups. About 95% of the population is Roman Catholic, with traditional practices surviving alongside Catholicism in some Indian and Afro-Hispanic communities. With the labor and land reforms of the last several decades, this pattern has weakened, although the overall status hierarchy remains unchanged, with considerable competition among groups in the middle categories for power and wealth.

Relations between Mestizos and Quechua speakers are complex, as in rural communities there is frequent contact between the groups and in some communities Quechua speakers are numerically dominant and perhaps wealthier, as well. In general, Mestizo-Quechua relations are marked by superficial cooperation and an often hidden distrust on the part of the Quechua speakers and a sense of superiority on the part of the Mestizos.

Since the 16th century, the relationship between the Afro-Ecuadorians and the Quechua speakers and Indians has been one of Afro-Ecuadorians replacing the Native peoples as they are forced off their land by descendants of the Spanish. In villages, towns, and cities, descendants of Africans are considered socially inferior to Whites and many are employed as migrant wage laborers.

Over the centuries, Native Americans' territory has been reduced and their cultures destroyed by the Inca, Spaniards, Mestizos, and Afro-Hispanics. Some segments of a few groups continue to maintain some major elements of their indigenous culture, while others are being rapidly assimilated into Ecuadorian society, although they exist only on its margins. The major assimilation forces are the migration and settlement of

A healer distributing amulets to a crowd in Tabacundo. Although Ecuador is 95% Roman Catholic, traditional beliefs and practices have also survived. Photo: Agence France Presse/Corbis-Bettmann.

Mestizos in territory that was formerly Indian; involvement of Indians in wage labor including migration to cities or plantations, government incursions in the form of road building, and the provision of school and health facilities; and Catholic missionary activities. These forces have combined to replace the traditional subsistence economies with involvement at low levels in the market economy, to replace the traditional religion with Roman Catholicism (although some traditional beliefs and practices often survive), to alter the structure and nature of family relationships, and to place political leadership in the hands of young people. In some of these groups, a segment of the population seeks to avoid assimilation, often by relocating to more remote areas higher in the mountains or deeper in the rain forest, depending on the locale of the group.

El Salvador

El Salvador is a small nation located on the Pacific coast of Central America. It is bordered by Honduras on the north and Guatemala on the northwest. It has a population of about 5.8 million. It was colonized by the Spanish and became an independent nation in 1821. Spanish rule has had a continuing legacy in El Salvador—Spanish is the primary and official language, most of the population is Roman Catholic, and at least 95% of the population is of mixed Spanish and Indian ancestry.

Ethnic Composition and Ethnic Relations

El Salvador is an ethnically homogeneous society. Almost all Salvadorans are **Ladinos (Mestizos),** of mixed Spanish and Indian ancestry. However, for Salvadorans, it is the Spanish heritage—not the Indian—that is meaningful for their sense of ethnic identity.

At the time of the Spanish conquest in the early 16th century, western El Salvador was the home of the **Pipil** Indians who had migrated there from Mexico. European colonization decimated the Pipil, although some survived. The population was essentially eradicated in a military massacre in 1932, when some 300,000 peasants and Indians were killed after they protested working conditions. Although as many as 2,000 people continue to be identified as Pipil in western El Salvador in the 1990s, they are assimilated into Salvadoran society and do not constitute a distinct Indian culture of the type found in most other nations in the Americas.

The descendants of a small number of **Africans** imported as slaves in the colonial era have also been assimilated and do not form a distinct ethnic group.

The primary ethnic minorities are **Lebanese, Palestinians,** and **Jews.** All of these are recent arrivals who form a merchant class. They are lumped under the insulting label **Turcos** by the Salvadoran upper class.

As El Salvador is ethnically homogeneous, ethnic relations do not play a role in structuring society. Rather, the key distinctions are ones based on wealth and power, as reflected in the three-level social-class hierarchy. About 2% of the population forms the upper class, which consists of the old, moneyed families who own much of the agricultural land; those involved in banking and finance; and those involved in retail sales and manufacturing. A small middle class comprising about 8% of the population is made up of shopkeepers, professionals, and government employees. The remainder of the population constitutes the large working class. They are mainly workers or poor farmers who either work on estates owned by the wealthy or work their own small farms.

French Dependencies
(French Guiana, Guadeloupe, and Martinique)

France continues to rule three political units in the Americas, all of which are officially considered to be overseas "departments" (territories or colonies) of France:

- French Guiana on the north coast of South America, bordered by Suriname on the west and Brazil on the south and east, with a population of about 151,000
- Guadeloupe, composed of a number of islands in the Leeward Islands of the Caribbean Sea with a population of 408,000
- Martinique in the Windward Islands of the Caribbean Sea, with a population of 399,000

These departments were colonized by the French, and a plantation-based colonial society emerged with the growing and processing of sugar cane being the primary industry. African slaves were imported, Catholic missionaries worked to convert them, and the colonies were managed by the French government. Unlike the Spanish and British, the French, though they abused their slaves, also pushed slaves to become "French," as the French tended to see their colonies as part of France. Slavery was abolished in the late 18th century, was restored in 1808 when the sugar industry declined, and then was banned for good in 1848. The French colonial approach has created overseas dependencies that are basically French in culture and world view, and ties to France are strong.

Ethnic Composition

In terms of ethnic composition, French Guiana, Guadeloupe, and Martinique all are ethnically homogeneous, as over 90% of the population is of full or partial African ancestry. The three departments also show religious homogeneity, as over 95% of their populations are Roman Catholic and all speak French (or French creole, which is more common in rural areas). However, in terms of ethnic relations, the departments are heterogeneous, as there are a number of distinct social categories within the general African category, and the ethnic minorities play a significant role in internal affairs.

Arabs are mainly **Lebanese** and **Syrians** who came in the early 1900s and established small businesses and shops, activities with which they are still associated. Some are Christians and others are Muslims, and they remain a distinct group in society.

Asian Indians were imported by the French as indentured workers to replace the slaves on plantations when slavery ended in 1848. Most quickly left the plantations and entered the retail trade as shopkeepers and gro-

cers. Some converted to Roman Catholicism, while others have maintained their Hindu beliefs.

Blacks are descended from the African slaves imported by the French. They form 90% or more of the population in all three departments, and most are Roman Catholic, although since the 1980s, some have been drawn to Protestantism by missionaries. Blacks in French Guiana, Guadeloupe, and Martinique strongly identify with French culture and speak French or French creole, based on French and West African languages. At the same time, African culture survives in the arts, music, and religion. Blacks live both in cities and rural areas and are found at all levels of society. Many are employed by the government and most political officials, including representatives to France, are Black.

Individuals of **Chinese** ancestry in the three French dependencies are part of the larger Chinese diaspora throughout the Caribbean. Never a large population in the French colonies, they are mainly involved in retail trade and are largely assimilated.

Indians who inhabited Guadeloupe and Martinique were exterminated by the French and other nations attempting to settle the islands. In French Guiana, some Indian groups survived, four of which are still in existence: the Emerillion, Maroni Carib, Palikur, and the Wayâpi. The **Emerillion** number only 100 in southern French Guiana near both Suriname and Brazil. In the mid-20th century their region and culture were destroyed by prospectors. Their small population and its poor health make assimilation and/or complete extinction likely. The **Maroni Carib** number about 2,400 and live along the border with Suriname. They were largely left alone by the Dutch in Suriname and, with the exception of conversion to Roman Catholicism, continue to practice much of their slash-and-burn farming way of life in their villages on both sides of the Maroni River. The **Palikur** number about 1,000, with about 60% living in Brazil and 40% in French Guiana. However, they form one cultural unit, and contact between the communities is regular. Their region in French Guiana was the object of a Portuguese-French dispute, and after the Portuguese took the region, many Palikur preferred to maintain their connection with the French Guiana Blacks, who had treated them better than the Portuguese had. In the last 25 years, the Brazilian government has made an effort to assist the Palikur people, to provide them with education and other services, and to reserve land for their use. In both Brazil and French Guiana, the Palikur continue to maintain some aspects of their culture, based on fishing and horticulture, but they are also being influenced by mainstream society. Palikur in French Guiana speak their native language and French creole. The **Wayâpi** number 525 in French Guiana and 310 in Brazil. They are divided into a number of communities, some of which are integrated into the mainstream societies through wage labor, others of which maintain their traditional horticultural way of life, and still others that have no contact with outsiders. Their religion has been largely uninfluenced by Christianity. As with other Indians, they fear encroachment by outsiders, and in both Brazil and French Guiana, they are pushing to have land set aside for their exclusive use.

Ethnic Relations

Because of considerable mixing by the ethnic groups since the earliest days of slavery, the populations of the three departments show considerable physical diversity. People are often classified by their ancestry: Black, White, Black-White, White-Mulatto, Black-Chinese, and so on. This classification scheme is hierarchical: social status, education, and wealth are all closely related to skin color and physical features. Light skin color and "White" features are considered the most desirable; thus, the White (French) minority controls much of the wealth, and light-skinned Blacks control local government. In general, darker skin color and African features relegate an individual to a lower rung on the social and economic ladder. Therefore, many people seek to marry or to have children with individuals who have "Whiter" features and lighter skin, which will give them greater access to education and economic opportunities.

Grenada

G renada is a small island nation located at the southernmost extreme of the Windward Islands in the eastern Caribbean Sea. In addition to the main island, the islands of Carriacou and Petit Martinique are also populated. Grenada has a population of 94,500, 91% of whom are of African or mixed African European or African Asian ancestry. The island was settled by the French in 1650 and then contested with the British until Britain took control in 1784 and ruled until Grenada achieved independence in 1974. The indigenous Arawak and Carib Indian populations were exterminated through disease and enslavement. Although the French have long departed, their influence is still obvious in French surnames and place names, the continued use of French creole (although English is the primary language), and adherence to Roman Catholicism by 65% of the population. For over 100 years, large numbers of Grenadians have been leaving the island for employment in Great Britain, other Caribbean islands, and North America. Ethnic conflict is minimal to nonexistent.

Ethnic Composition and Ethnic Relations

Afro-Grenadians number 86,000, constituting 91% of the population. African slaves were brought to Grenada by both the French and British to work as field hands on plantations. Although a homogenous group culturally and in religion (Christianity), Afro-Grenadians are of varied ancestry. Those on Carriacou, who have been isolated from the majority of the Grenadian population, are of mainly African ancestry, while those on the main island of Grenada reflect both African and a mix of African Asian and African European ancestry. Lighter skin color and partial British or French ancestry are associated with higher social status, and lighter-skinned Afro-Grenadians and Europeans form the economic and political ruling class.

Europeans number about 2,000 and are mainly of **British** and **French** ancestry. They form the economic elite of the nation and have been actively involved in the economic expansion of the 1980s and 1990s that has emphasized tourism and foreign investment. **Maltese** and **Portuguese** workers who were brought to Grenada by the British to replace the freed slaves after 1854 have been assimilated into the general population.

Asian Indians from Madras and Calcutta were brought to Grenada after the slaves were freed in 1834 to work as indentured laborers. Never numbering more than a few thousand, they were rapidly assimilated into the African community. Some Grenadians mark their Indian heritage by classifying themselves as of mixed African and Asian descent, rather than as African.

Guatemala

G uatemala is located in northern Central America and is bordered by Mexico on the north and west, Belize and the Caribbean Sea on the northeast, Honduras and El Salvador on the southeast, and the Pacific Ocean on the south. It has a population of 11.3 million. At the time of the Spanish conquest in the early 16th century, Guatemala was the home of several dozen Maya Indian groups who had either settled in the region several thousand years earlier or had arrived more recently. The Spanish conquest disrupted the relations among these groups, and since the 16th century, most Indians have been living in small farming communities. The Spanish influence continues to be evident in the widespread use of Spanish and in that about 80% of the population is Roman Catholic. From the 1960s until 1994, Guatemala experienced a destructive civil war that pitted rural peasants and some Indians against the repressive national government.

Ethnic Composition

Guatemala is often described as a nation with two major ethnic populations: Indians and Ladinos. The actual situation is somewhat more complex, as there are some 20 different Maya Indian groups in Guatemala that vary greatly in size, culture, and current circumstances. In addition, as discussed below, the Ladino population is not homogeneous either. Along with these two major groupings, there are small numbers of people of **European** and/or **African** ancestry. There are few people of African ancestry in Guatemala because the large indigenous Indian population provided an ample supply of laborers for the Spanish colonialists, and thus few Africans were imported as slaves.

Indians in Guatemala are a diverse population, although all speak Mayan languages and in a very general sense can be classified as Maya. Indians are labeled **Indígenas** and individual Indians are called Indígena. The Indian population is estimated at from 44% to 53% of the national population. Due to disruptions caused by the civil war, several hundred thousand Indians fled to the United States, Mexico, Belize, and Honduras. Indian groups in Guatemala are not closely related culturally, and they do not form one political entity. Most Indians live in small, rural communities called municipos that exist, to some extent, outside of mainstream Guatemalan society. Many of these municipos are farming communities with corn, beans, and squash being the most important crops. In others, farming has declined when Ladinos have moved in and taken land, and Indian men often migrate elsewhere in search of work. Many communities mark their identity by the unique designs woven into blankets and clothing. Although the

Indians of Guatemala

Group	Location	Population
Awakateko	West	about 3,000
Ch'orti'	East	50,000
Chuj	Northwest	30,000
Itza'	North	2,000–4,000
Ixil	Central	50,000–80,000
Jakalteco	West	16,000–2,000
Kaqchikel	Southwest	450,000
K'iche'	West	750,000
Mam	West	550,000
Mopan	Northeast	5,000
Poqomam	Central	50,000
Poqomchi'	Central	60,000
Q'anjob'al (Kanjobal)	West	70,000
Q'eqchi' (Kekchí)	East	350,000
Sipakapense	West	5,000
Tojolab'al	Northwest	unknown— most in Mexico
Tz'utujil	Central	70,000
Uspantec	Central	2,000
Xinca	Southeast	3,500

majority of Indians are nominally Roman Catholic and speak Spanish, the traditional religions and languages survive in most communities. Similarly, while under the control of the federal government, the traditional political and legal systems remain in place in most communities.

Chuj Maya, who number about 30,000, live in western Guatemala in a region heavily populated by a number of Indian groups. Having lived in the region for about 4,000 years, the Chuj now live in three communities and identify with their villages rather than with the Chuj entity as a whole. For many years, the Chuj derived considerable income from the salt mines in their territory. However, in the 1960s the salt trade declined when roads were cut into the region and the resulting deforestation disrupted the underground salt deposits, while the roads also made it easier to obtain salt from outside the region. Most Chuj now subsist by growing corn.

Ixil number between about 50,000 and 80,000 and live in central Guatemala. They are a highland group who were conquered by the neighboring K'iche' before the Spaniards arrived, won their freedom, and then were conquered by the Spaniards in the 1540s. Although they continue to live by growing corn and other crops, Ixil culture has been adversely affected by Spanish and then Ladino rule. Most Ixil converted to Roman Catholicism; many men became laborers on haciendas while others were sent to the Pacific region to work on plantations; they lost most of their land in the land reform of 1871; and many fled the ravages of civil war and settled in the United States.

K'iche' number about 750,000 and are the largest Indian group in Guatemala and one of the largest Maya groups in the Americas. The K'iche' encountered by the Spanish colonizers had a culture that had developed through a merging of the region's indigenous K'iche' with the Toltecs, who moved into the region from western Mexico in the 13th century. Like other Maya groups in Guatemala, the K'iche' live in autonomous villages, lost much of their land in the late 19th century, and today are mainly farmers and wage laborers. Many K'iche' communities were actively involved in the civil war and suffered government reprisals. As a large group with many communities, the K'iche' display considerable cultural diversity, with some communities being mainly Roman Catholic and Spanish-speaking and others living a much more traditional lifestyle.

Mam number about 550,000 and are the second largest Indian group in Guatemala. Like many other Indian groups, the Mam do not share any general sense of Mam identity. Rather, their identity is based on residence in or near one of the 56 villages that have a large or exclusively Mam population. The Mam were relatively free of Spanish influence until the late 19th century when coffee plantations were built in western Guatemala and their lives were disrupted by the plantations and the arrival of Ladinos. Since then, they have been under pressure from Ladinos in the region and have reacted by moving to more remote villages further up in the mountains. Most Mam are farmers and wage laborers. The mix of Mam and Ladino culture in the region is reflected in the complex religious situation, with some Mam adhering to their traditional beliefs, others practicing Roman Catholicism, others being Protestant, and still others being recent converts to evangelical Christianity.

Ladino is a term used for people in some Central American nations and southern Mexico who are of mixed European (Spanish) and Indian ancestry but have rejected their Indian ancestry and stress only their Spanish ancestry.

Thus, from the viewpoint of ancestry, Ladinos are the same as Mestizos. However, they differ culturally in that Ladinos strongly associate with a Spanish, urban lifestyle; speak Spanish; are Roman Catholic; and stress their Guatemalan identity. Mestizos also commonly reject their Indian heritage, but they tend to be rural and poor in comparison to Ladinos. The confusion over who is a Ladino, Mestizo, or Indian in Guatemala is reflected in the figures given for Ladinos in the general population—estimates range from 45% to 56%.

Ethnic Relations

The major ethnic relations issue in Guatemala is the relationship between Ladinos and Indians. From the time of the Spanish conquest in the 1530s, Guatemala's Indians have been, at best, second-class citizens, despite their population being approximately 50% (or more) of the national population. Although there were some exceptions, most Indians were converted to Roman Catholicism, were forced to work on colonial haciendas, and generally were excluded from participation in national affairs. In the late 19th century, new land-tenure laws ended communal ownership of land, and much land that had been used by Indian communities but not owned by individual Indians was taken by Ladinos. While some Indians were able to continue subsistence farming, many were forced to turn to wage labor as farm workers or to migrate elsewhere in search of work. Education that was provided by the government stressed Ladino culture and values and purposely denigrated Indian culture and values.

It is not clear yet what long-term effect the civil war that raged for 35 years from the 1960s until 1994 has had on relations between Indians and Ladinos. The war was basically a peasant uprising in which the rural poor sought to overthrow the repressive government. Some Indian groups sided with the rebels and others attempted to avoid the con-

In Guatemala, where many people are of mixed European and Indian ancestry, ethnic identity is often determined by a person's life style, language, and religious affiliation. Photo: Corel Corp.

flict. Nonetheless, many groups were affected, especially those perceived by the government as supporting the rebels. Some of these Indians were deported from their villages and forced to live in government camps under military rule. Many were indoctrinated in government programs, and some men were forced to serve in the Guatemalan army. Very conservative estimates indicate that at least 200,000 Indians fled Guatemala, especially in the 1980s, and settled in the United States,

Mexico, Honduras, and Belize. It is believed that as many as 25% of the populations of some groups such as the Ch'orti' and Q'eqchi' may have settled in the United States. Although some Indian groups and Ladinos saw themselves as allies during the war, previously there was often conflict between the groups as Ladinos continued to settle near Indian villages and Indians resisted losing more of their land and coming under the influence of Ladino culture.

Guyana

G uyana is located on the north coast of South America and is bordered by Venezuela on the west, the Atlantic Ocean on the north, Suriname on the east, and Brazil on the south. This region was contested in the colonial era by the British, French, and Dutch, and was divided among them in 1815, with the British getting the region that became the nation of Guyana. The current ethnic composition and the nature of ethnic relations in Guyana are largely a product of British colonialism. All ethnic groups on the island share the common historical experience of British rule. The British imported African slaves to work on the sugar cane plantations, and after slavery ended in 1838, they replaced the slaves with indentured workers, mainly from India. In order to maintain control, the British often played the two groups off against each other, and some of that antagonism continues into the 1990s. Despite the ethnic diversity, Guyana remains a "British" nation in the cultural sense. English is the national language, with most people speaking creole English; the legal, government, and educational systems reflect their British origins; and association with Britain is still a marker of high social status. The population is 712,000.

Ethnic Composition

As a result of British colonialism, Guyana is an ethnically diverse nation. About 51% of the population is of Asian Indian ancestry, 43% is of African or mixed African and European ancestry, and the remaining 6% is of Chinese, Portuguese, European, or American Indian ancestry. In addition, Guyana is also religiously diverse. The Christian population is about 60% Protestant and 40% Roman Catholic. There are also evangelical Christians, Seventh-Day Adventists, Moravians, and Jehovah's Witnesses. Most Asian Indians are Hindus, with a minority of Muslims. And in some Afro-Guyanese communities, traditional African religious beliefs and practices are integrated with Christianity.

Afro-Guyanese are descendants of the slaves imported from Africa by the British to

work on the sugar cane plantations. They were the majority population during the colonial era, although they are now outnumbered by the Asian Indians (Indo-Guyanese). They speak English and nearly all are Christians. The category of Afro-Guyanese also includes those of mixed African and European (British) ancestry. Following emancipation from slavery in 1838, some continued to work their own farms, while other moved to towns where they worked for the British government and as low-level professionals such as teachers and nurses. In the 1990s, the Afro-Guyanese and the Indo-Guyanese form the two major ethnic and political groups in Guyana.

Chinese people in Guyana number about 4,800—less than 1% of the population. Most Chinese immigrants arrived after the end of slavery in 1838 as indentured workers. Most planned to move into retail trade, but the Portuguese, with British support, monopolized this niche until the early 20th century. Thus, many Chinese left Guyana for better economic opportunities in Trinidad and Jamaica. Of those who stayed, many did eventually move into retail trade, government employment, and later, into the restaurant business. They also rapidly assimilated into Guyanese society, with the Chinese language and family structure and ties to China virtually disappearing. In the late 1990s, the Chinese in Guyana are divided into two groups—the assimilated Guyana-born, who see themselves as Guyanese, and a smaller group of recent arrivals who maintain ties to China. The two groups tend not to intermarry, and both also discourage marriage with Afro- and Indo-Guyanese. The native-born, however, frown less on marriages to Europeans or to people of mixed European and other ancestry.

Indians number about 20,000, or 3% of the population. The groups in the north—**Carib, Arawak, Akawaio, Pemon,** and **Warao**—are largely assimilated into Guyanese society. Those in the south, due to their more isolated location and the opportunity to move across the border into Brazil, have been drawn into Guyanese society only in the 20th century. A combination of mining, cattle ranching, missionary activity, and government programs has

Indians of Guyana

Group	Population
Akawaio	3,500
Arawak	5,000
Carib	600
Cariña	475
Makushi	1,300
Patamona	3,500
Pemon	450
Waiwai	300
Wapisiana (Wapishana)	4,900
Warao	2,500

led many Indian communities to relocate near government services, mission stations, or commercial centers and has also involved many Indians in the economy as wage laborers.

Indo-Guyanese number about 363,000 for 51% of the population. The modern Indo-Guyanese population is descended from the nearly 240,000 Asian Indians brought to Guyana by the British between 1838 and 1917. They came mainly from northern India and were both Hindus and Muslims, and from a range of different castes. As with the other ethnic groups in Guyana, initial work in agriculture was followed by work in the retail sector and government. The British labor system, which lumped all workers together, undermined the caste system, although the Hindu-Muslim distinction survived. Both the Hindu and Muslim communities are divided into traditionalists and the modernists, with the latter pushing for closer ties to other religious communities in Guyana. Relations between Hindus and Muslims are harmonious.

Portuguese from Madeira were the first indentured laborers brought by the British to replace slave labor. In the mid-1800s Madeira experienced a labor glut, so many came in search of jobs. Relatively few in number, they were soon replaced by the Asian Indians and they moved to towns where many found jobs in the service sector and opened small businesses.

Ethnic Relations

Ethnic relations in Guyana concern relations between the Afro- and Indo-Guyanese. Animosity and competition between the groups date to the late 1800s when the British began a policy that favored the Asian Indians. Indian workers who had completed their service as indentured laborers were given land to farm on their own, although freed African slaves had often been denied land some 50 years earlier. Animosity grew in the 1930s when Indo-Guyanese began to give up farming and move to the towns, where they competed with the Afro-Guyanese for government jobs. In addition, although the British had made little effort to allow slaves to keep their families and communities intact, the Asian Indians were left largely alone. Similarly, while the Africans were subjected to continual missionary activity, the Indians were allowed to practice Hinduism or Islam. In addition, the British—both consciously and unconsciously—stereotyped the two groups and treated them in accord with those stereotypes. Afro-Guyanese were seen as strong but lazy, and the Indo-Guyanese as industrious but greedy. To some extent, these two groups also adopted the stereotypes of the other, although these stereotypes have largely disappeared in contemporary Guyana.

In modern Guyana, social class has emerged alongside ethnic identity as a major marker of social status, and people from all ethnic groups, except for the indigenous American Indians, are found in all social categories. Social class and ethnic identity tend to be most important in politics. Afro-Guyanese and Indo-Guyanese affiliate with different political parties. However, this affiliation is not absolute, and economic and social issues matter more than ethnic identity to some voters. In the 1960s, there was a brief period of political unrest by Afro-Guyanese who objected to what they perceived to be the pro–Asian Indian policies of the Indo-Guyanese party government. Since then, however, differences have been worked out through elections.

Haiti

Haiti is a small nation on the western third of the island of Hispaniola in the Caribbean Sea. The Dominican Republic occupies the eastern two-thirds of the island. Haiti's population is estimated at 7.3 million, although political unrest since 1987 and massive emigration since then make an accurate enumeration impossible. The island was colonized in 1697 by the French. The indigenous Indian population was exterminated through disease and enslavement and was replaced with slaves imported from West Africa to work on the sugar cane plantations. A slave revolt in 1791 ended French rule, and the nation has been independent since—although the United States has influenced internal affairs since the early 1900s. Twenty-six years of dictatorial rule by the Duvalier family ended in 1986. Since then, Haiti has been torn by political violence, and the nation has experienced extreme poverty and massive emigration. There are large numbers of Haitians in the United States, Canada, and the Dominican Republic.

Ethnic Composition and Ethnic Relations

The current population is ethnically homogenous and free of ethnic conflict. At least 95% of Haiti's people are of African ancestry. The primary minority groups are small numbers of **French, Americans,** and **Lebanese,** who are involved in commerce and trade. The current size and status of these minority groups are unclear, although it is likely that many of their members have fled since the mid-1980s. The primary division in Haitian society is between poor farmers, who are the majority of the population, and a small elite, who are of French and African ancestry, speak French, are Roman Catholic, and live in the capital city of Port-au-Prince.

Haitians number about seven million in Haiti and more than one million in North

A Haitian family in Port au Prince. Most Haitians are descended from African slaves brought to work on sugar cane plantations. Photo: UPI/Corbis-Bettmann.

America. While the educated elite speak French, over 90% of the population speaks Haitian creole, a language based on French and African languages. At least 75% of Haitians live on small farms where the primary focus of life is the large, extended families whose members interact with one another on a daily basis. While 80% of Haitians are Ro-

man Catholic, having been converted by French missionaries, most are also adherents of the Vodun (also called Voudou or Voodoo) religion, which developed on Haiti through a mix of elements drawn from Roman Catholicism and African religions brought by the slaves.

Honduras

Honduras is a nation in Central America bordered on the north and east by the Caribbean Sea, on the west by Guatemala, and on the south by El Salvador and the Pacific Ocean. It has a population of 6.5 million. Honduras was colonized by the Spanish, and Spanish is now the national language. About 97% of the population is Roman Catholic. Honduras became free of Spanish control in 1821 in alliance with other Central American nations, and then an independent nation in 1838. In the 20th century, U.S. business firms and the U.S. government have been heavily involved in Honduran affairs, especially in the banana industry.

Ethnic Composition

Honduras is ethnically homogeneous. **Mestizos,** people of mixed Indian and Spanish ancestry, form 90% of the population and dominate the social, economic, and political affairs of the nation. They are often labeled **Ladinos,** rather than Mestizos, to indicate that it is their Spanish ancestry that is important. They are nearly all Spanish-speaking and Roman Catholic and have dominated Honduran life for three centuries. Ladinos are found at all social-class levels in Honduran society and form the majority of the middle class.

The remaining 10% of the population is ethnically heterogenous and is composed of people of partial African ancestry, three American Indian groups, and a distinct population of Arabs.

The three American Indian groups are the Lenca, Jicaque, and Ch'orti'. To what extent these groups continue to maintain their indigenous cultures is a matter of debate among experts, as all are heavily assimilated into Honduran society. The **Lenca** are the largest group, with a population estimated at between 50,000 and 100,000. They live in the moun-

tainous region of western Honduras. They have been in contact with the Spanish since colonial times and have a long history of working in mines and on coffee and banana plantations. The loss of some of their land has resulted in most, if not all, living an essentially Mestizo lifestyle. All now speak Spanish, and it is likely that the Lenca language is extinct. The majority are also Roman Catholics, although some Precolumbian beliefs survive. The **Jicaque** number about 9,000, although only a few hundred who live on a reserve in the northwest can be considered culturally Jicaque. The remainder were assimilated into Mestizo society beginning in the 19th century. The **Ch'orti'** number about 4,000 in the west with over 50,000 across the border in Guatemala (*see* Guatemala). In addition, there are small communities of **Maya** and **Pipil** in border regions.

People of mixed African and other ancestry live mainly on the Caribbean coast. Unlike the Indians who were in contact with the Spanish, these groups were in contact with the British, who colonized parts of the Caribbean coast of Central America. The two major groups are the Garifuna and the Miskito. **Garifuna (Black Caribs)** is the name given people of

Carib Indian and African descent in the Caribbean and Central America. Garifuna are descended from the Carib Indians who intermixed with African slaves and escaped slaves on the Caribbean islands. The Garifuna came to Central America when they were deported there in 1797 by the British, who feared their revolts might disrupt British rule on the island of St. Vincent. They live along the coast from Belize through Nicaragua. Their population is unknown, although there may be as many as 500,000 Garifuna in Central America. In Nicaragua, they sided with the Spanish in conflicts with the British, and most were converted to Roman Catholicism. Garifuna live in their own communities and many are employed in low-paying, unskilled jobs. They play a small role in regional or national affairs, and since the 1960s there has been a pattern of migration of men and more recently women to other nations, including the United States, in search of better-paying employment.

Miskitos number about 75,000 in Nicaragua and Honduras. They live mainly in a series of villages along the strip known as the Miskito Coast. The Miskitos developed as a distinct group in the late 1600s through a mix of Indians indigenous to the region and Africans brought there as slaves. The Indian tribe that became the Miskitos likely migrated to the region from South America as they spoke a South American Indian language that, over the centuries, has been modified by words added from English, Spanish, and West African languages. Their distinctive language continues to serve as a marker of ethnic identity in the region. The Miskitos allied with the British, who supplied them with guns and established a Miskito monarchy that ruled parts of the region until the British left in the early

1800s. The Sandinista Revolution in the 1980s disrupted their communities in Nicaragua and forced many Miskitos to flee to Honduras. They began returning in 1985, but the settlement of many Mestizos in the region has made resettlement difficult. In addition, there is a small African-ancestry population in the Islas de la Bahía off the coast. They are descended from British and Africans who came to the islands in the 19th century from Belize and the Cayman Islands.

Arabs form another distinct group in Honduran society. They arrived mainly from Palestine and Lebanon in the early 20th century when those nations were under Ottoman rule. They are collectively labeled **Turcos** in Honduras, as they were so identified when they arrived with Ottoman Turk passports. The label is now considered insulting and also masks the group's actual heterogeneity, based on place of birth and religion (Christianity or Islam). Initially traders and storekeepers in the banana region, they have since formed a class of wealthy manufacturers and businesspeople.

Ethnic Relations

Ethnic relations are peaceful, given the numerical and political dominance of the Mestizos and the assimilation of the Indians into Mestizo society. Unlike in some other nations in the Americas, there is no well-organized or influential Indian rights movement in Honduras. Hondurans of partial African ancestry and those of Arab heritage continue to retain a separate ethnic identity, although even they are subject to assimilation through intermarriage, education, and involvement in the expanding Honduran economy.

Jamaica

Jamaica is an island nation located south of Cuba in the Caribbean Sea. The population is 2.6 million, of whom about 95% are of African or mixed African and other ancestry. The island was controlled by the Spanish from 1509 until it was taken over by the British in 1655. Independence was achieved in 1962. The indigenous Arawak Indian population was exterminated by the Spaniards, and the English imported nearly one million Africans to work as slaves on the sugar cane plantations. Many slaves resisted British rule and escaped, fleeing into the mountains where they established all-African communities. Slavery ended in 1838 and the African slave labor on plantations was replaced first by Asian Indians and then by Chinese. The escape from slavery by large numbers of Africans has meant that many West African cultural features have survived in Jamaica, although they have merged with British cultural features to produce a Jamaican culture. The economic, legal, political and educational systems all reflect British influence, while African traditions are most evident in religion, festivals, arts, music, and folk medicine. Up until the middle of the 20th century, skin color was a primary marker of social status, with light-colored skin being more desirable. This is no longer the case, but a social hierarchy based (in part) on skin color still exists.

Ethnic Composition

Afro-Jamaicans are people of African or of mixed African and other ancestry. Those of African ancestry number almost two million, making up 76% of the population. Those of mixed African and European (mainly British) ancestry number 390,000 or 15% of the population. **Afro-Chinese** and people of mixed African and Asian Indian ancestry number about 100,000, constituting 4% of the population. In terms of ethnic relations, people of mixed ancestry may affiliate with the African community, the community of their other ancestry, or both. As nearly all Jamaicans were born on the island, all associate themselves with the national culture. Most Jamaicans are Protestants, with a wide range of denominations being represented. Religion is an important element of Jamaican life, and many religious sects and movements began there, including the Rastafarian Movement (with about 130,000 followers in Jamaica) and Zion Revival.

Because of limited employment opportunities, since the 1960s many Jamaicans have left the island. In the 1960s, Great Britain was the preferred destination, with greater numbers having come to the United States and Canada since the early 1980s. There are more than one million Jamaican immigrants in these three nations.

Chinese number about 26,000 or 1% of the population, not counting those of mixed Chinese and African ancestry. The Haitians of Chinese ancestry are mainly Hakka Chinese who were imported as indentured laborers by the British between 1853 and 1879. Many quickly opened small shops, and most remain merchants and restaurant owners. In many ways they are assimilated into Jamaican society—they speak English or creole, are Protestant, and marry Africans and Indians. At the same time, their specialized economic role and greater wealth keep them apart from the majority of African Jamaicans.

Asian Indians number about 52,000 or 2% of the population, not counting those of mixed Indian and African ancestry. Like the Chinese, they were imported after the end of slavery in 1838 to work on the sugar cane plantations and now are largely assimilated into Jamaican society.

Other groups include **Whites** (**U.S. Americans**, **Canadians**, and **British**) and **Arabs** (primarily **Lebanese**), who number about 50,000 or 2% of the population. The Lebanese are mainly merchants, and Whites include businesspersons, expatriates, and retirees, most of whom are financially well-off.

Ethnic Relations

Although political and other violence is not uncommon, ethnic conflict is not a serious problem. All residents—African and non-African—are to some extent integrated into Jamaican society, and non-Africans such as the Chinese and Asian Indians occupy clearly defined economic niches that determine their role in society. Jamaicans speak English and Jamaican creole, based on English and West African languages. Language use is a marker of social status: the educated elite and middle class speak standard English, while the majority of the population, which is poor, speaks regional dialects of Jamaican creole.

Mexico

M exico is in northern Central America. It is bordered by the United States on the north, the Gulf of Mexico on the east, Belize and Guatemala on the south, and the north Pacific Ocean on the west. It has a population of 94 million, making it the second most heavily populated nation in the Americas, following the United States. Mexico is a rapidly modernizing nation with significant income inequality, a large rural peasantry, a mobile population that is migrating to the major cities, and considerable economic and political unrest and corruption. Prior to Spanish colonization and settlement in 1521, Mexico was the location of a number of

major Precolumbian civilizations, including the Maya, Toltec, Olmec, Tarascan, and Aztec. These past civilizations form an important component of present-day Mexican identity and are stressed by the government as a major factor in Mexican history. In this sense, Mexico today can be thought of as reflecting a mix of three cultural heritages—Precolumbian Indian, post-Columbian Indian, and Spanish. Mexico is also greatly influenced by United States culture.

Mexico was colonized by Spaniards beginning in 1521 and achieved independence in 1821, although the following

Roman Catholicism is a key element in Mexican identity. The nation's historic ties to Spain can also be seen in this church's architecture. Photo: Barbara Flaxman.

100 years were marked by political turmoil and social unrest, which culminated in the revolution of 1917. Political stability returned in 1929. Throughout the 20th century, there has been a powerful and successful movement—initiated by intellectuals and then taken up by the government—to create a strong Mexican identity, in which people formerly classified as Mestizo are labeled Mexican. Mexican identity, now widely subscribed to across the country, is based on a veneration of the Precolumbian Indian civilizations, pride in Mexican national independence, the absence of a Spanish ruling elite, an open social-class system, Spanish as the national language, and adherence to Roman Catholicism. The social-class system consists of a small upper class of the wealthy and powerful and much larger middle and working classes. Unlike in many Latin American nations, the upper class in Mexico is not dominated by Spaniards or other people of European descent but is made up of Mexicans. A key social distinction is made between those who work with their hands (the working class, which is both rural and urban) and those who do not (the middle and upper classes). Education, friendships, and kin-based social networks are the major means for climbing the social-class ladder in modern Mexico.

Ethnic Composition

Mexican society is conventionally classified into two major ethnic groups: Indian and Mestizo. However, the use of these two general categories masks the considerable diversity within each group. In addition, the labels Mestizo and Ladino (which is used in southern Mexico) are no longer commonly used in Mexico, having been replaced by Mexican.

Mexicans number about 66 million and comprise anywhere from 70% to 95% of the population, depending on who is considered an Indian or a Mexican. As elsewhere in Latin America, a Mestizo is a person of mixed American Indian and Spanish ancestry, and the category emerged shortly after Spanish settlement when regular contact with the Indians began. Today, identity as a Mexican is far more important than identity as a Mestizo, although it is understood that most Mexicans are of Mestizo heritage. Although it is correct to say that Mexicans are the dominant group in Mexico, they are not an ethnic group, but rather members of a national culture (like Americans or Canadians).

American Indians in Mexico constitute anywhere from 7.9% to 30% of the population, depending on who is defined as an Indian. If we use the 7.9% figure, which is based on anthropological criteria such as use of the indigenous language, adherence to some traditional religious beliefs, and living an Indian lifestyle, Indians number about seven million in Mexico today.

Following the Spanish conquest, the Indian population in Mexico was reduced by disease and warfare, and many Indians took refuge in small settlements that were relatively isolated from the Spaniards and the growing Mestizo population. Spanish missionaries often assisted the Indians, and conversion to Roman Catholicism occurred quickly for many groups. During the centuries of political unrest, Indians lived largely outside Mexican society, subsisting mainly by hunting and by farming beans, corn, and squash.

Many Indians identify most strongly with these communities that developed after the Spanish conquest, rather than with a specific Indian group or with the Indian population in general. While many continue to live in all-Indian or mainly Indian communities, there also has been migration to cities, especially to Mexico City, in the last two decades. In the urban environment, some Indians retain their Indian identity while others choose to live a Mexican lifestyle. Most Indians speak Spanish and their native language, and about 15% continue to speak their native language in their homes. Nearly all are Roman Catholics, although indigenous beliefs and practices are salient in many communities, and Pentecostal Christianity is winning converts in the poorer Indian communities in the south.

Indians can be classified into three general regional groupings: Indians of central Mexico, Indians of northern Mexico, and Indians of southern Mexico.

Indians of northern Mexico are concentrated heavily along the coast and inland from the Gulf of California. Groups in this region are the **Cahita** (about 60,000), which is composed of the **Mayo** and **Yaqui,** who live in small agricultural communities; **Guarijio** (1,600); **Opata** (600); **Pima Bajo** (2,000–4,000); **Seri** (800), who are much involved in the tourist trade; **Tarahumara** (65,000), who have maintained much of their traditional culture and live in an uneasy peace with Mexican neighbors; and the **Northern Tepehuan.** In the far north near the U.S. border are the **Kikapu (Kickapoo),** who also live in the United States, and small numbers of **Apache**, **Tohono O'odham**, **Pima,** and **Papago,** the majority of whom live north of the border. Finally, a small population of about 2,000 Indians lives in Baja California. Early missionary activity led to their almost complete assimilation into the regional farming society.

The Indians of central Mexico include a number of the groups who were most affected by the Spanish conquest and the fall of the Aztec Empire. Most of these peoples now live in small communities populated by Indians, although the regional population is mostly Mexican. The major groups in central Mexico, heavily concentrated in the central and eastern regions and near Mexico City, are the **Huastec (Wasteko),** a Maya group of 120,000 who have lived apart from other Maya groups for some 2,000 years; **Nahua speakers (Mexicano)** who, with a population of 1.2 million, are the largest Indian group and are direct ancestors of people who were part of the Aztec Empire; **Otomí** (180,000), who are now divided into highland and lowland communities; and the **Totonac** (208,000), who assisted the Spaniards in defeating the Aztecs but suffered like all other Indians afterward. Further west are the **Mazahua** (130,000) and **Tarascans** (170,000), who are integrated into the nation economically but maintain a stronger ethnic identity than do many other groups. Further north near the Pacific Coast are the **Cora** (12,000), **Huichol** (25,000), and **Southern Tepehuan** (16,000). Settlement by Mexicans and loss of land have led to conflicts over land among these three groups and with the Mexicans. Finally, the **Pame** (6,000) live in relative isolation in the deserts and mountains of the north-central region of central Mexico.

Southern Mexico, including the Yucatán Peninsula, contains several dozen Indian groups, some of which are speakers of Mayan languages. Some of these peoples in Chiapas, the poorest state in Mexico, are involved in the Zapatista Movement that began on January 1, 1994, to protest mistreatment of Indians in Chiapas and to fight for the economic and political rights of peasants in the region. The revolt was repressed by the Mexican army, although the protest continues and the government is negotiating with the rebels.

Moving from north to south and east through the region are the **Nahua speakers, Otomí,** and **Mazahua,** who are also in Central Mexico; the **Popoloca** (26,000); **Mazatec** (170,000); **Mixtec** (330,000); **Triqui** (15,000); **Amuzgo** (33,000); **Chocho** (1,200); **Chinantec** (70,000); **Cuicatec** (12,000); **Zapotec** (400,000); **Tequistlatec** (14,000); **Mixe** (76,000); **Popoluca** (30,000); **Zoque** (44,000); **Chol** (100,000); **Tzeltal** (50,000); **Tzotzil** (14,000); **Tojolab'al** (40,000); **Mam,** who number a few thousand, with over 500,000 in Guatemala; **Jakalteko** (1,000); **Chuj Maya,** who number a few thousand with the majority in Guatemala; **Lakanadon** (300); and the **Yucatán Maya** (500,000) on the Yucatán Peninsula.

In addition to Mexicans and American Indians, Mexico hosts a number of distinct **European** groups, Africans, people from the United States, and others. Mexico has also had a relatively lenient policy regarding political refugees and asylum-seekers, and in 1995 received 49,000 **Guatemalans,** including **Maya Indians;** 3,300 **Salvadorans;** and several hundred each **Chileans, Nicaraguans, Hondurans, Colombians, Somalians,** and **Iranians.** In addition, there are probably 200,000 or more undocumented refugees from other Central American nations in Mexico.

There is a large Mexican population estimated at about 15 million in the United States. While concentrated in the Southwest and California, Mexicans now live in nearly all regions of the United States. The issue of Mexican immigration to the United States—both legal and illegal—has become highly politicized in both countries in the 1990s. Efforts in California and at the national level to limit immigration and to curtail services to both legal and illegal immigrants in the United States have been criticized in Mexico.

African Mexicans live in cities on both coasts but are most heavily concentrated in a number of predominantly African Mexican communities on the southern west coast. People of African ancestry in Mexico are descendants of slaves imported by the Spaniards to replace Indian labor. Those on the west coast are descended from slaves who escaped and established communities there. Africans elsewhere in Mexico were more likely to intermarry with Indians, Spaniards, and Mestizos. It is believed by some experts that as many as three million Mexicans have some African ancestry, although only several hundred thousand acknowledge it. On the west coast, relations between African Mexicans and Mexicans are distant and marked by distrust.

U.S. Americans living in Mexico number 522,600, the largest number of U.S. citizens living in any foreign nation. The group is diverse and includes students, workers, business owners, investors, and retirees (who form the largest group). Attractions of Mexico include the climate, low prices, and proximity to the United States.

Mexican president Ernesto Zedillo (right) listening to a Tzotzil Indian as Chiapas governor Julio Cesar Ruiz Ferro looks on.
Photo: Agence France Presse/Corbis-Bettmann.

Spaniards were the first European settlers of Mexico, and communities of Spaniards, as well as individual Spaniards, continue to live in Mexico. The Spanish heritage in Mexico is evident in the speaking of Spanish, Roman Catholicism, and architecture, although Spanish culture and identity have been largely been replaced by the Mexican national culture that developed in the 20th century.

Other groups include **Chinese, Arabs, Gypsies,** and **Mennonites,** who number several thousand each and generally provide specialized services such as restaurants, small shops, and produce for the Mexican population. There are also about 30,000 people of **Italian** ancestry in Mexico, most descended from immigrants who arrived in the late 1880s. Most are now fully assimilated, although a number of distinctly Italian farming communities survive.

Ethnic Relations

Despite the ethnic diversity, ethnic relations in Mexico are generally peaceful, save for the current Zapatista Revolution in southern Mexico discussed above. However, in rural areas there are often disagreements between Mexicans and Indians over ownership and access to land and, in general, Mexicans look upon the Indians as inferior, while Indians have little trust in Mexicans and the national government. Throughout Mexico, all Indian cultures have changed through contact with the Spaniards and Mexicans, and the survival of the indigenous Indian cultures and communities is threatened by the in-migration of Mexicans; tourism; use of Indian land for farms, ranches, factories, and logging; and the provision of health and educational services by the Mexican government.

Netherlands Antilles

The Netherlands Antilles are two island groups in the Caribbean that are dependencies of the Netherlands. They are the Windward Island groups of Curaçao and Bonaire (Aruba, a former member is now politically separate) and the Leeward Island group of Saba, the southern half of Saint Martin, and Saint Eustatius. Although these islands were contested by European powers during the European colonial era in the 1600s, they eventually came under Dutch control. The entire population is 209,000. Dutch is the official language, although Papiemento (a creole language based on Portuguese, Spanish, African languages, and English) is the primary language for Afro-Antilleans in the Windward Islands, while English and Spanish are also spoken in the Leeward Islands. Reflecting the early Spanish influence, Roman Catholicism is the primary religion in the Leeward Islands, while Protestantism is the primary religion in the Windward Islands.

Ethnic Composition and Ethnic Relations

All of the island populations are ethnically heterogeneous. **Afro-Antilleans,** including people of both African and mixed African and European ancestry, form 85% of the population and are the majority population on all the islands. The modern population is descended from African slaves imported by the Spanish, British, and Dutch when they ruled the islands. Because the islands are small and some environments are not suitable for farming, large-scale plantation agriculture did not develop on these islands during the European colonial era. Instead the islands were primarily trade and commercial centers, and the Africans who were imported worked in the shipping industry, for the colonial government, and as household help for the European ruling class. Some were also farmers. Because the colonial societies lacked the rigid European/African social dichotomy typical of plantation societies, contact between Africans and Europeans was more frequent and somewhat more relaxed, although there was (and remains) a clear social differentiation, with Euro-Antilleans at the top and Afro-Antilleans beneath them. Afro-Antilleans are excluded from the economic and political ruling class on the islands and are the poorest segment of the population. However, because of the generally profitable tourism industry and support from the Netherlands, poverty is not a major social problem. Because of limited economic opportunities, a substantial portion of Afro-Antillean men migrate to other islands, North America, South America, and the Netherlands in search of better-paying jobs; consequently, many Afro-Antillean families are headed by women. Although Afro-Antilleans are assimi-lated into the European-based island societies, elements of their African heritage remain in music, dance, and religion.

The remaining 15% of the population of the islands is composed of **Euro-Antilleans** (of **Dutch** and **British** ancestry), **North Americans, South Americans,** and **Chinese.** Dutch Europeans and, to a lesser extent, British and Americans, form the economic elite and control commerce, trade, and the tourism industry. The Dutch occupy the high positions of government. There is also a small **Jewish** community on Curaçao, descended from the **Sephardic Jews** who formed the trading class during the colonial era. The largest immigrant group is the **Surinamese,** an ethnically mixed group of people of African, Javanese, Chinese, and Asian Indian ancestry. They are drawn to the islands (especially to the Leeward Islands) because Suriname was formerly a Dutch colony and because of the better-paying jobs.

Nicaragua

Nicaragua, the largest nation in Central America south of Mexico, is bordered by Honduras on the north and by Costa Rica on the south, with coasts on both the Caribbean Sea and the Pacific Ocean. Its capital city, Managua, is located in the southwestern part of the country. The Caribbean coast of Nicaragua is a low, tropical rain forest that rises to a plateau covering one-third of the country. This plateau is interrupted by mountain ranges that divide Nicaragua into western and eastern zones. The western zone (on the Pacific Ocean) was colonized by the Spanish moving south from Mexico. The east was inhabited by various Indian groups and controlled by the British. Today, ethnic divisions between the regions remain, with the west being mainly Mestizo, Spanish-speaking, and Roman Catholic and the east containing six distinct ethnic groups, being mainly English-speaking, and Protestant. The western region is politically and economically dominant—all of Nicaragua's major cities are there, as is most of the population.

Ethnic Composition

Because no reliable census has been taken since 1971, and because of the population shifts caused by the civil war in the 1980s, there are no up-to-date counts of Nicaragua's ethnic populations. One authority estimates a population of 4.1 million, of which about 90% are Mestizo (people of mixed European and American Indian ancestry), with the remaining 10% being Miskito, Creoles, Sumu, Garifuna, and Rama, all of whom live in the east. These peoples are collectively labeled *costeños.*

Creoles are people of African ancestry and number about 25,000 in Nicaragua. They live mainly on the Caribbean coast with about half the population living around the town of Bluefields. Creoles are descended from the African slaves imported by the British in the 17th and 18th centuries, runaway slaves, and freed slaves who came to Nicaragua from Caribbean islands. Creoles speak Miskito Coast

Creole, a language based on English and African languages, and many also speak English and Spanish. The Creoles are Moravian and Anglican Protestants, although elements of their ancestors' African religions are still followed. Religion is a major feature of Creole communities, with church leaders being respected members of the community, and the church itself serving as a primary focus of community activity. Once a majority population in some regions of the east, in the last half of the 20th century, Creoles have become a minority as Mestizos from the west have moved to the east. Still, as a well-educated group with a long history of professional and skilled occupations, most remain in the middle or near the top of the east coast social hierarchy.

Garifuna is the name given to people of Carib Indian and African descent in the Caribbean and in Central America. The Garifuna are descendants of Carib Indians and African slaves and escaped slaves on the Caribbean islands. The Garifuna came to Central America when they were deported there in 1797 by the British, who feared their revolts might disrupt British rule on the island of St. Vincent. They live along the coast from Belize through Nicaragua. Their population is unknown, although there may be as many as 500,000 Garifuna in Central America. In Nicaragua, they sided with the Spanish in conflicts with the British and most were converted to Roman Catholicism. Garifuna live in their own communities and many are employed in low-paying, unskilled jobs. They play little or no part in regional or national affairs, and since the 1960s there has been a pattern of migration of men (and more recently, women) to other nations, including the United States, in search of better-paying employment.

Mestizos, who form 90% of the population of Nicaragua, are people of mixed American Indian and Spanish ancestry. They are nearly all Spanish-speaking and Roman Catholic and have dominated Nicaraguan life for three centuries. Until the mid-1900s, Nicaragua's Mestizos lived mainly in the west; since then, many have moved across the mountains to the east, where in towns they have become the middle class and in rural areas they have established farms.

Miskitos number about 75,000 in Nicaragua and Honduras. They live mainly in a series of villages along the strip known as the Miskito Coast. The Miskitos developed as a distinct group in the late 1600s, descendants of Indians who were indigenous to the region and Africans brought there as slaves. The Miskitos' Indian forebears likely migrated to the region from South America, as today they speak a South American Indian language that has been modified over the centuries by words added from English, Spanish, and African languages. Their distinctive language continues to serve as a marker of ethnic identity in the region. The Miskitos allied with the British, who supplied them with guns and established a Miskito monarchy that ruled parts of the east until the British left in the early 1800s. They lived in relative isolation until the Sandinista Revolution in the 1980s, which disrupted their communities and forced many Miskitos to flee to Honduras. They began returning in 1985, but the settlement of many Mestizos in the region has made resettlement difficult.

Rama number only about 700 and are nearly extinct as a distinct cultural group. Only a dozen or so people continue to speak the Rama language. The Rama are not an indigenous group but developed through the merging of various Indian tribes decimated by the Spanish in the 17th century. Subsequently, the Rama were conquered by the Miskitos, and in the 1980s their settlements were destroyed during the civil war.

Sumu number about 15,000 in Nicaragua and about 1,000 across the border in Honduras. The Sumu were the largest Indian group in the region when the Spaniards arrived but were quickly decimated by disease. When the region came under British rule, the British enlisted the help of the Miskitos in controlling the Sumu, who were either killed, driven to the interior, or enslaved. In 1894, a reservation was created for exclusive Sumu use, and since then, many have lived there outside mainstream Nicaraguan society. Most are Moravians (a Protestant sect), having been converted in the early 1900s. During the civil war of the 1980s, Sumu communities were destroyed and most Sumu fled to Honduras or were killed. Survivors returned to Nicaragua in 1985, and since then have been attempting to regain rights to their lands.

Ethnic Relations

Ethnic relations in Nicaragua are complicated, both on the national level and in the east. For much of its history, Nicaragua has been accurately described as two Nicaraguas—Mestizo in the west, multiethnic in the east. In the west, the population is nearly all Mestizo, and social class—rather than ethnicity—determines access to wealth and power. In the east, animosity and warfare were the rule among the ethnic groups in the colonial era, with the Miskitos, who enjoyed British support, being the dominant group. Since independence, and especially in the 20th century after a road linked the east and west, the Mestizos have exerted more and more influence in the east. It is likely that in the 1990s they have become the majority population in the east, and other groups have been assimilating into Mestizo society by speaking Spanish, working for Mestizo businesses, and being represented in government by Mestizo politicians. In the east,

a social hierarchy has emerged with the Mestizos at the top; Creoles forming the middle class; poor Mestizos forming a working class; and the Garifuna, Rama, Sumu, and Miskitos forming the lowest class.

The Sandinista Revolution of the 1980s disrupted life in Indian communities in the east. The Sumu and Rama, and some Miskito and Garifuna communities, were effectively destroyed by Sandinista and government forces and by the policy of both groups of trying to force Indian men to fight in their army. Over 200,000 Indian people fled to Honduras and the United States during the revolution, but they have been returning since 1985. Efforts to rebuild their communities have been hampered by the large number of Mestizos who have moved into the region and their desire for land. In the 1990s the government has become more responsive to Indian land claims. Unlike the other groups, the Creoles, long suspicious of the Mestizo government in the west, tended to support the Sandinistas. Creoles continue to maintain distance from other groups, although intermarriage with Mestizos has ended the open antagonism of the past. Creoles, however, continue to see other groups as inferior and see themselves as superior.

Panama

P anama is located in southern Central America and is bordered by Colombia on the east, the Pacific Ocean on the south, Costa Rica on the west, and the Caribbean Sea on the north. It has a population of 2.65 million. Spanish is the national language and the majority of people are Roman Catholic. Panama was a Spanish colony and a part of Colombia until it became independent in 1903. Since then it has been strongly influenced by the United States.

Ethnic Composition

In general terms, Panamanian society can be divided into three categories: (1) Mestizos of mixed Spanish and American Indian ancestry, who form about 80% of the population; (2) Indians who fall into a number of distinct groups and constitute about 5% of the population; and (3) Afro-Panamanians who form

about 8% of the population. In addition, there are perhaps as many as 100,000 Chinese and far smaller numbers of Greeks, Asian Indians, Christian Lebanese, West Europeans, and North Americans.

Afro-Panamanians number about 215,000, or about 8% of the population. Although Panama imported tens of thousands of slaves from Africa during the Spanish colonial era, most modern Afro-Panamanians are descendants of the over 50,000 Black West Indians who were recruited mainly from British islands in the Caribbean to work on building the Panama Canal in the first decades of the 20th century. They are often labeled **Antillean Blacks.** They arrived in Panama as an English-speaking and Protestant group, and remain largely so in the 1990s. These two characteristics, plus their dark skin color, distinguish them from the other ethnic groups in Panama. Despite their efforts to assimilate into Panamanian society through education and military service, Afro-Panamanians remain a distinct ethnic group, with many continuing to live near the Canal Zone.

Indians number about 170,000, with the two largest groups, the Kuna and Ngawbe, accounting for nearly the entire Indian population. The figure of 170,000 is only an estimate as "Indian" is an elusive concept in Panama: some people who speak Spanish and live a rural Mestizo lifestyle identify themselves as Indians, while others who speak Indian languages do not self-identify as Indians. Most Indians live in rural areas that only recently have come into regular contact with mainstream Panamanian society. Thus, at least some communities have been able to maintain their traditional ways of life into the 20th century.

The **Kuna (Cuna)** live on the northeast coast and on offshore islands. They number about 30,000 with about 10,000 living in the cities of Panama City and Colón. Most live in the San Blas region. The Kuna settled in Panama after being driven out of Colombia in the 16th century by the Spanish. Since 1925, the Kuna have had some degree of political control of the San Blas region, and since 1945 they have owned the land in their region. This has afforded them considerable autonomy from the Panamanian government, as well as a say in the economic development of the region. It has also enabled them to maintain much of their traditional culture, including the Kuna language, horticulture, voluntary work groups, and much of their indigenous religion, although many are nominal Catholics or Protestants. At the same time, Kunas have become involved in the national and regional economy

through work on the Canal, the coconut trade with Colombia, and the sale of their distinctive sewn fabric panels, known as *molas*.

The **Ngawbe,** who are commonly known as the **Guaymi,** number about 126,000 and live in the mountains of western Panama. Unlike the Kuna, they do not control their land and much of their traditional territory is now occupied by Mestizos. Roads were cut into the region only in 1970, so they have been able to live in relative isolation and maintain much of their traditional culture, including their language, which is still widely spoken. They live by farming fruits and vegetables for their own use and for sale, and through wage labor on plantations. As with many American Indian groups, contact with mainstream society has led to the development of internal conflicts that pit traditionalists against modernists.

The three smaller Indian groups are the Bugle, Teribe, and Embera. The **Bugle** number about 1,500 and live in northwestern Panama. They are closely related to the Ngawbe and live on land claimed by them. The **Embera (Chocó)** and closely related **Wounaan** live in Colombia and Panama, with about 20,000 in the former and 12,000 in the latter. In Panama, they have been influenced by the Kuna and the two groups are politically aligned. The **Teribe** number about 1,000 and live in western Panama.

Mestizos—or **Ladinos,** as they are sometimes labeled in Central America—are the majority of the Panamanian population and the carriers of the national culture. Mestizos are people of mixed American Indian and Spanish ancestry. However, they ignore their Indian heritage and instead stress the Spanish ancestry and their Panamanian national identity. Speaking Spanish, living in Mestizo communities or cities, and being employed in non-Indian types of work, including owning small stores and working for the government, are major markers of Mestizo identity.

As with other nations in the region, Panama also has a small minority population of people of **Greek, Asian, Indian, Chinese, Christian Lebanese, North American,** and **European** ancestry. They are engaged mainly in trade and commerce.

Ethnic Relations

Panama is stratified by social class and ethnicity. Those of European ancestry, who traditionally owned much of the land and now control much of the economy, form the elite. They are joined by a small number of Mestizos, although Mestizos form the large middle and working classes. Other groups such as the Chinese and Lebanese, who are often shop and business owners, also fall into the middle class. Beneath these are the Indians and Afro-Panamanians. The status of Indians is somewhat ambiguous as they live outside mainstream society. Some, such as the Kuna, exercise considerable economic and political power in their regions. Others, such as the Ngawbe, do not hold legal title to their land and thus are much more vulnerable than the Kuna. For the Ngawbe, gaining title their land is a high priority, and they have staged protests toward this end. Many Ngawbe are also exploited as low-paid laborers on banana plantations. Indians now have some representation in the National Assembly, although all see land ownership and the resulting right to control settlement and development by non-Indians as the only way to maintain independence. The history of Africans in Panama is one of slavery and discrimination.

Discrimination remains an issue and focuses on Black West Indians who arrived in the early 1900s to work on the Panama Canal. Those who remained were seen as taking jobs desired by other Panamanians. In 1941 they were stripped of citizenship, although it was restored in 1946. Since then, though the largest minority, they have been discriminated against in education, housing, and employment and have no real political influence.

Paraguay

P araguay is a small, landlocked country in south-central South America. It is bordered by Bolivia on the west and north, Brazil on the north and east, and Argentina on the south. Paraguay was colonized by the Spanish in the 1530s, and Asunción became a major regional center of Spanish rule. The rest of the nation, occupied by a number of Indian groups, came under the influence of Jesuit missionaries who established Indian communities and helped forge mostly peaceful relations between the Indians and Spaniards. There was considerable interaction between the Spaniards and Indians in Paraguay, and though Spanish is the official language today, many people also speak Guarani, the Indian language used as the contact language by the Jesuits. As a landlocked nation, Paraguay has long had conflicts with Argentina and Brazil regarding access to the ocean. Paraguay has a population of 5,504,000 and 90% of the people are Roman Catholics.

Ethnic Composition and Ethnic Relations

Paraguay is an ethnically and culturally homogenous nation. About 95% of Paraguayans are Mestizos—of mixed Spanish and Indian ancestry. The Spanish cultural tradition is dominant and preferred, with the exception of the speaking of Guarani. The other 5% of the population are Indians, Asians, Brazilians, and Mennonites. Because of economic and political instability, Paraguay has suffered from heavy emigration of its people to other nations, especially to its more prosperous neighbors, Argentina and Brazil. Most of those who have left are Mestizos, and since the 1950s the government has sought to replace them by recruiting educated, skilled workers from Asia.

Asians in Paraguay number about 50,000, although their exact population is unknown, and there is a pattern of frequent emigration from Paraguay to Brazil, Canada, and the United States. Asian immigrants have been actively recruited by the Paraguayan government since the 1950s in order to form the core of an educated, skilled labor force and also to help build the economic and trade sectors.

Japanese began arriving in the early 1950s, although only about 9,500 have arrived since then, a far smaller number than recruited by the government. They formed agricultural colonies. At first, they sought to maintain use of the Japanese language and culture and to resist assimilation. However, by the second generation, assimilation in the form of speaking Spanish and Guarani had begun.

Koreans began arriving in 1875 and by the early 1900s some 120,000 had come to Paraguay. However, many moved on to Brazil or North America and they number only about 30,000 in Paraguay in the late 1990s. Like other Asians in Paraguay, they live in cities and are involved in managing factories and the sale of electronics products manufactured in the factories. Koreans in Paraguay are often involved in extensive international kinship networks.

The **Chinese** were the last Asian group to arrive and are the smallest. Like the Koreans, they are involved in manufacturing and trade.

Brazilians number as many as 400,000 in Paraguay and live almost exclusively in the agricultural region along the Paraguay-Brazil border. They began arriving in substantial numbers in the 1970s when land in the region became available for sale. The parcels were larger and far less costly than land in Brazil. Thus, many Brazilian farmers sold or abandoned their land and moved across the border. They are the dominant population in the region, and some Paraguayan farmers have sold their land to Brazilians and moved elsewhere. The Brazilians speak Portuguese and do business using Brazilian currency.

Indians number about 35,000 and thus form only a very small percentage of the population. They live mainly in the north and south. Indians in Paraguay have a unique history of contact with the colonizing Spaniards. Because much of what is now Paraguay was not desired by the Spanish colonists, the Jesuit missionaries were free to establish self-sustaining Indian settlements in much of Paraguay, in which the Indians were shown how to live in Spanish society but also were protected from enslavement and exploitation. The villages were called *reducciones*. This system lasted from the mid-1500s until 1767, when the Je-

suits were expelled by the Spanish authorities, who had become interested in the Indians' land. The villages collapsed without Jesuit support, and because settlers were moving in, the Indians fled into the country's interior regions. At that time, there were about 100,000 Indians in Paraguay. In the 20th century, the Indians in the northwest were caught in the Chaco War of 1932–35 between Paraguay and Bolivia, in which many were killed or displaced from the land. Later in the century, the cutting of roads into the region opened it to logging, ranching, and settlement that further disrupted Indian life. With a few exceptions, most Paraguayan Indians are assimilated into mainstream society, although they constitute the poorest segment.

Ache (Guayaki) number about 600 and live in eastern Paraguay. A hunting-gathering people, they were not brought under complete government control until the 1970s, and all now live on four reservations where farming and wage labor has largely replaced hunting and gathering.

Angaite number about 2,400 and live in the highly developed eastern region, where many work on ranches, on farms, and in factories. In the 20th century, they have had frequent contact with Paraguayans, Argentinians, and other Indian groups, and much of the traditional Angaite culture has disappeared.

Ayoreo number about 3,500 and live in northern Paraguay and across the border in Bolivia. They live mainly by farming and gathering wild plant foods. Their often hostile attitude toward others in the region—Indians and non-Indians—has helped them to maintain much of their traditional kin-based culture and also to withstand missionary efforts (since the 1690s) to convert them to Christianity.

Chamacoco number about 1,000 in northeastern Paraguay. They have been in regular contact with the Spanish since 1800 and are now largely assimilated into Paraguayan society. Wage labor in logging and ranching, farming, craft production for tourists, and government support have replaced hunting and gathering as the major forms of subsistence. In the 1980s, many converted to evangelical Christianity under the influence of missionaries in the region.

Chorote (Choroti) number about 400 in Paraguay and 800 in Argentina. Settlement by Whites, the Chaco War of 1932–35 between Paraguay and Bolivia, and Christian missionary activity have largely destroyed the traditional hunting-gathering culture. It has been replaced with one based on farming, fishing, wage labor, and new a religion based on elements from the traditional religion and evangelical Christianity.

Chiriguano number 3,000 in Paraguay, 22,000 in Bolivia, and 21,000 in Argentina (*see* Bolivia).

Lengua number 10,000 in the Chaco Region of northern Paraguay. From the time of Spanish arrival in the 16th century and continuing through today they have been the largest Indian group in the region. However, like other groups, their territory was overrun by Spanish settlers and they were displaced by the Chaco War of 1932–35. Missionary activity also restricted the practice of their traditional religion, and today the Lengua are dispersed over the region as wage laborers, ranch hands, and farm workers.

Maká number 600. Formerly a hunting-gathering people of the northern Chaco region, they now all live in Asunción. Before and during the Chaco War of 1932–35, the Maká assisted Paraguay, and as a reward, they were given land on the edge of Asunción, where most have lived since 1940. In this new location, they have gradually assimilated into Paraguayan society and their numbers have decreased.

Nivaclé number about 7,000 and live in the Chaco region of northwestern Paraguay. The Chaco War disrupted their indigenous way of life and many became migrants. In the 1940s they began settling near the then-new Mennonite agricultural colonies, and many have become farmers, either working for the Mennonites or on collective farms established under Mennonite direction. Although they have resisted complete assimilation, the culture is strained by increasing mainstream influence, activity by competing missionaries, and periodic efforts by some to revive the traditional culture and to resist outside influence.

Paï-Tavytera number between 8,000 and 10,000 in Paraguay and 6,000 in Brazil, where they are called the **Kaiowa.** In Paraguay, they are one of the largest and the least assimilated of the Indian groups. Although many were placed on the Jesuit *reducciones*, after the departure of the Jesuits in 1767, many also were able to avoid the activities of loggers and others who exploited the region. Today, many communities own their land, and slash-and-burn farming remains the principal economic activity, with corn being the major crop. In addition to their Guarani language, many other indigenous customs continue including the initiation ceremony for boys, pottery and basketmaking, extended families, self-government, and the entire indigenous religion based on a pantheon of gods and spirits and a belief in paradise. In Brazil, the situation is essentially the opposite, and little of the indigenous culture survives, although the Kaiowa have been given a small reservation to live on.

Mennonites are a German-speaking, Anabaptist communal group that emerged in Europe in the 1520s. Persecuted there, some ultimately immigrated to the Americas and established farming communities. In Paraguay, most settled in the Chaco region and established the Menno colony in 1926 and Fernheim and Neuland colonies in 1930 and 1947. They number about 15,000 in Paraguay—the largest number in any Latin American nation—and have been a major economic and political force in the region. They have been especially influential with the Indians of the Chaco and have employed many as laborers, have helped others establish farm communities, and have sought to convert them to Christianity. Mennonite influence on the Indians has been controversial, as some Indian advocates see them as exploiting the Indians for their labor and destroying indigenous Indian customs and beliefs, while others argue that the Mennonites have helped make some Indians self-sufficient and have eased their integration into Paraguayan society. In addition to the Mennonites, who were originally from Germany, there is also a **German** population of unknown size in Paraguay, composed in part of former German officials and military officers who fled to Paraguay after World War II, and their descendants.

Peru

P eru is located on the Pacific coast of western South America and is bordered by the Pacific
Ocean on the west, Ecuador and Colombia on the north, Brazil and Bolivia on the east, and
Bolivia and Chile on the south. It has a population of 24,523,000, which is heavily concentrated
in the eastern coastal region. Peru was colonized by Spain, and the Spanish influence remains
strong in the form of the continuing political dominance of people of Spanish ancestry, the
widespread use of the Spanish language, and 90% adherence to Roman Catholicism. In 1975,
Quechua, the language of millions of Peruvian Indians, was made an official language alongside
Spanish. About 72% of Peruvians speak Spanish as their primary language, 27% speak Quechua,
and the remaining 1% speak Aymara and other Indian languages.

Ethnic Composition

The arrival of Spaniards in western South
America in the early 16th century and the
implementation of Spanish colonial policies
created a nation that was divided into three
distinct ethnic zones. The lowland coastal region was the home of the Spanish landowners
and ruling class and the African slaves imported to work on the plantations. The central
highlands were the home of Indians who spoke
Quechua languages, and later the Mestizos—
farmers of mixed Spanish and Indian ancestry.
The interior Amazon region was the home of
dozens of small Indian groups who lived by
slash-and-burn horticulture and hunting and
gathering. To some extent, this pattern continues into the late 20th century, although there
has been a spread of Mestizos eastward into
the Amazon region, and Asians now form a
significant minority in the coastal region.

As this history suggests, modern Peru is a
multicultural nation, with the population classified into four major groupings: Spaniards and
other Europeans, Mestizos, Indians, and
Asians. Estimates of the percentage of the
population in each grouping are difficult, with
one estimate suggesting 15% for Europeans,
45% for Indians, 37% for Mestizos, and 3%
for Asians and Afro-Peruvians.

In addition to ethnicity, region of birth also
plays a role in a Peruvian's social identity. To
some extent, these overlap with ethnic identity, although not absolutely. People from the
west coastal region are called *costeños*, those
from the central highlands are called *serranos*,
those from the Lima region are called
mazamorreros, and those from the Amazon
region are called *sharapas*.

Afro-Peruvians are fewer in number and
a less visible minority than people of African
descent in some other Latin American nations
such as Brazil and Colombia. Because of considerable mixing with Europeans and Indians
over the centuries, the number of Afro-Peruvians is impossible to determine. African
slaves were brought to Peru by the earliest
Spanish conquistadors as soldiers, and later by
Spanish landowners to work the sugar, grape,
and cereal plantations of the coastal region.
Africans were thought to be more reliable
workers than the Native Americans and they
often supervised Indian work crews. Africans
were also employed in crafts and in domestic
work, and this mix of economic roles led to
considerable interaction with both the Spaniards and Indians. After slavery ended in 1854,
Afro-Peruvians largely disappeared as a distinct group. At the individual level, however,
awareness of African ancestry remains a factor in modern Peruvian society, as individuals
with "African" physical features are socially
inferior to those with "European" features.

Asians number about 150,000, with about
60% being of **Japanese** ancestry and 40% of
Chinese ancestry. The Chinese arrived first,
when the Peruvian government began importing Chinese contract laborers from southern
China in 1848. Over the next 25 years, some
81,000 Chinese were brought to Peru from
China and also from the large Chinese community in San Francisco, California. They
worked mainly on plantations in the northwest
and also in building the railway into the Andes.

Chinese involvement in these activities was short-lived, however, and within several decades most had moved to cities or towns in the coastal region and had become involved in retail trade. Many people in Peru of Chinese ancestry are still shopkeepers; many others are involved in manufacturing. They speak Spanish and are mainly Roman Catholic. Japanese immigrants began arriving in 1899, and despite periods of immigration restriction, some 36,000 had settled in Peru by 1976. Since then, a secondary migration has occurred, which has resulted in a Japanese population composed of those assimilated into Peruvian society and those who still maintain ties to Japan. With a population of about 90,000, the Japanese are the largest immigrant minority in Peru. The original Japanese immigrants were contract laborers who worked on cotton plantations. At the end of their five-year contracts, most moved to cities, and 85% of Japanese Peruvians today live in cities, mostly in Lima. Many Japanese are involved in commerce and business. Although the Peruvian president, Alberto Fujimori, is of Japanese descent, Japanese involvement in government remains limited and Peruvians of European ancestry resist marriage with Japanese Peruvians.

Europeans in Peru, who number about 3.7 million, are mainly people of **Spanish** ancestry who trace their heritage to the early Spanish colonists. Also included in the European group are **Mestizos** who have completely shed their partial Indian ancestry and are identified as "White." People of Spanish ancestry are Roman Catholic, speak Spanish, and live mainly in cities. They form the economic, political, and social elite and tend to marry within the group. Also within the European category are small numbers of **Germans, Italians,** and **Swiss** who also live in cities. While these other Europeans do not rival the Spaniards politically or socially, they are often wealthy and are involved in commerce in industry. Compared with other South American nations, European immigration to Peru was quite low, which is another reason that Asian immigration was encouraged.

Indian is a somewhat ambiguous category in Peru. Individuals and communities who live an "Indian" lifestyle—wear Indian style clothing, eat Indian foods, adhere to Indian religious beliefs, and associate with other Indians —are considered to be Indian, even if they are of mixed ancestry. Mestizos who live a White lifestyle are not considered to be Indian. The number of Indian groups in Peru is enumerated at anywhere from a low of 20 to a high of 80. This wide range is a result of two factors. First, 27 of these groups are quite small, with populations of less than 200, and some of them are disappearing as distinct groups or represent only a small percentage of the entire group, the majority of which lives across the border in Brazil, Colombia, or Bolivia. Second, some groups identified as a single group are actually conglomerations of several related groups who, because of similarity of language and culture, are classified by outsiders as one group, while they may see themselves as members of different groups. For example, there are 6 "Campa" groups and at least 14 regional "Quechua" groups in Peru. Estimates of the number of Indians in Peru range from 8 to 11 million or from about 33% to 45% of the population. In the last several decades, as government programs have sought to assimilate Indians into mainstream society, the number of reported Indians has declined. Whether this represents a government bias or an actual decrease in the number of people identifying themselves as Indians is not clear.

Indians in Peru can be classified into two very broad categories—those of the central highlands, who are mainly Quechua speakers, and those of the Amazon region of the east. **Quechua speakers** number about 7.25 million, constituting the majority of the Indian population and about 30% of the national population. They live mainly in the highlands of central Peru and reside in farming villages (where they may be the dominant group) or in or near Mestizo communities. Quechua speakers and Indians in general are identified by a number of labels including **Indígenes** and the insulting **Indios**. Quechua, the language of the Inca Empire, spread to Native American peoples whom the Incas conquered in what are now Colombia, Ecuador, Peru, Bolivia, and Argentina. As many as 11 million people now speak Quechua in these five nations. Contact with the Spanish for 500 years has produced a

Quechua-speaking Indians in Peru number about 7.25 million, constituting about 30% of the national population. Photo: Corel Corp.

Quechua culture that is neither Indian nor Spanish but a mix of elements drawn from both, combined with specific cultural adaptations of different Quechua communities. Although Quechua has been an official national language since 1975, some Quechua speakers also speak Spanish. The independence of some Quechua groups has been threatened by migration of Mestizos and government- and business-inspired economic development and resource exploitation. Some groups have responded by forming political action groups and staging protests, which have been, to some extent, successful in protecting the territory of some communities. Some Quechua have also allied themselves with Indian groups for this same purpose, while others have moved east, in the process, threatening other, smaller groups already settled there. The major regional Quechua groupings are the **Ancash** (125,000), **Arequipa** (1.5 million), **Ayacucho** (1 million), **Cajamarca** (35,000), **Cusco** (1.25

million), and **Huanuco** (120,000). Smaller groups are the **Chachapya, Junín, Lambayeque,** and **Yauyos.**

The Indians of the Amazon region in eastern Peru are mainly of the tropical forest cultural type, a type of culture characteristic of many Indian groups in the Amazon region of South America. The **Aymara,** the second largest Indian group in Peru, are of this culture type. Although there are variations across groups, there are also many similarities:

- The groups tend to be small—numbering from a few hundred to a few thousand individuals.
- They live in kin-based groups in semipermanent circular villages.
- They subsist through slash-and-burn horticulture, with manioc (cassava) being a major crop. Produce from gardening is often supplemented by fishing, hunting, and gathering wild plant foods.
- They maintain alliances between villages through kinship ties based on either the mother's or father's line.
- A central role is played by the shaman as healer and religious specialist.
- They adhere to a religious belief system in which the universe in divided into the sky, earth, and underworld.

Because of their relative isolation and the unsuitability of the region for plantation agriculture and ranching, the Indians in this region experienced less contact with the Spanish settlers than did those in the highlands. Thus, their traditional cultures survived into the 20th century, even though some people were converted to Roman Catholicism earlier. In the late 20th century, roads cut into the region have opened it to settlement by Mestizos and Quechua speakers and to economic development. Thus, control of their traditional lands and maintenance of their traditional ways of life are now major concerns for these groups.

The following list covers the major Indian groups in Peru.

Indian Groups of Peru

Group	Location	Population
Aguaruna	Northwest	25,000–30,000
Amahuaca	Southeast	500–1,500
Amuesha	Central	5,000–7,500
Aymara	South	400,000–500,000
Campa (Kampa)	South-Central	31,000–40,000
Candoshi	Northwest	2,250–3,000
Cashibo	Central	1,000–2,500
Cocoma	Northeast	10,000–18,000
Culina	Southeast	350–500
Chayahuita	Northwest	6,000
Huaraya	South	600
Jamináwa	Southeast	400–2,000
Jebero (Hevero)	North-Central	3,000
Kashinawa	Southeast	1,000–12,000
Marinahua	Southeast	150
Mashco	South	6,000
Matsigenka	South	7,000–12,000
Mayoruna	Northeast	350
Piro	South	1,500
Quechua	Central	7,425,000
Sharanahua	Southeast	500–2,000
Shipibo	Central	9,000–30,000
Ticuna	Northeast	1,500–26,000
Witoto	Northeast	1,000
Yagua	Northeast	3,500

Of these groups, a number also have populations across the border in neighboring nations: Amahuaca (Brazil), Aymara (Bolivia), Campa (Brazil), Culina (Brazil), Jaminawa (Brazil and Bolivia), Kashinawa (Brazil), Mayoruna (Brazil), Ticuna (Brazil and Colombia), Witoto (Brazil and Colombia).

Mestizos number about nine million and are the second largest ethnic category following the Indians. As elsewhere in South America, a Mestizo in Peru is a person of mixed Spanish (or other European) and Indian ancestry. However, Mestizo is far more a social than a racial categorization, as Mestizos emphasize their European ancestry and downplay their Indian ancestry. Their acceptance in "European" Peruvian society depends on their becoming "White." This can be achieved by marrying non-Mestizos or Mestizos with "White" features, obtaining education and professional employment, or acquiring wealth. Mestizos are distributed socially and geographically across the full range of Peruvian society. They speak Spanish and are almost all Roman Catholics.

Ethnic Relations

Peru is an ethnically and racially stratified society. At the top are people of Spanish ancestry who continue to control much of the nation's wealth and also occupy most major governmental positions. They also constitute the social elite and tend to marry within their own group. Aligned with those of Spanish ancestry are the others of European ancestry. Beneath the Europeans socially and politically, although not always economically, are Asians. Although their economic status is secure, Asians are not considered the social equals of Europeans in Peru. Japanese enjoy somewhat higher status than the Chinese, in part because other Peruvians see economic benefits from closer ties to Japan. Also beneath the Europeans are the Mestizos, although Mestizos who are "European"—those with White features and a European lifestyle—may be classified and treated as European. The majority of Mestizos, however, are middle class or poor. At the bottom of the social hierarchy are the Indians.

Indians remain a disadvantaged group in Peru, despite their large population. The peoples of the Amazon are especially at risk as their limited contact with Europeans until the 20th century leaves them susceptible to European diseases, to which they have no natural immunity. In addition, exploration for oil, gold, and the massive clearing of the rain forest to permit farming and ranching in the region have badly eroded the environmental base on which their traditional ways of life depend. In response to attempts by outsiders to take their land, some groups such as the Shipibo have been successful in gaining legal control of their land. However, the dominant ideology is that of individual ownership of land, which makes communal land—if divided up—susceptible to acquisition by outsiders. In the Quechua regions, Indians were forced to labor under the *encomienda* system in colonial times and as poor peasant farmers under the debt peonage system after independence and into the 20th century. Thus, most Quechua are farmers and are seen as inferior by their Mestizo neighbors. For Indians in general, the only way to increase social status and to gain greater economic opportunity is to renounce their Indian identity and become a Mestizo—that is, stop speaking their native language and speak Spanish instead, live a "White" lifestyle, and reside in "White" communities. Also desirable, for those who choose this course, is to marry—or to have one's children marry—a non-Indian.

Puerto Rico

P uerto Rico is an island located in the Caribbean Sea, to the east of the Dominican Republic. It is a commonwealth of the United States, and Puerto Ricans are citizens of the United States. The population of Puerto Rico is about 3.8 million, with an estimated 3 million Puerto Ricans living in the United States, primarily in New York City and other East Coast cities, but also in Chicago, Houston, and Miami.

Puerto Rico was colonized in the 1500s by the Spaniards, who imported African slaves to work on the farms and plantations. In 1898, the island was taken from Spain by the United States in the Spanish-American War, and it has been closely tied to the United States ever since. In 1917, Puerto Ricans were given U.S. citizenship, mainly so that Puerto Rican men could be drafted into the armed forces, and shortly thereafter a pattern of large-scale migration back and forth between the United States and Puerto Rico developed. In addition, tax breaks offered to companies building factories in Puerto Rico, and the island's relatively low-paid and nonunion work force, have led to the establishment of a number of American industrial enterprises, such as pharmaceutical and electronics plants.

Ethnic Composition and Ethnic Relations

Puerto Rico is an ethnically homogeneous society, as nearly the entire population is culturally **Puerto Rican.** The Spaniards who colonized Puerto Rico established an agricultural plantation colony, with Africans imported as slaves to work in the sugar cane fields and cane-processing facilities. Contemporary Puerto Ricans trace their ancestry to these Spaniards and the Africans who arrived during the colonial period. Over the course of its history, Puerto Rico developed a distinctive culture based on a combination of Spanish, African, and later, U.S. beliefs and customs. Among key features of modern Puerto Rican culture are the use of the Spanish language (spoken in a form different from that in most other Spanish-speaking nations in the Americas); Roman Catholicism; Spanish-style town planning and architecture; frequent migration in search of work both on the island and to and from the United States; the idealization of the *jibaro*—the independent farmer; Puerto Rican cuisine; *machismo* in male-female relations; and distinctive Puerto Rican theater, dance, music, literature, and poetry. In the United States, Puerto Ricans have developed stable neighborhoods that have continued over long periods of time. Many Puerto Ricans resist assimilation to U.S. culture and instead transfer customs such as outdoor meeting houses and family-based childcare to the United States. Most eventually return to Puerto Rico, and even those who have lived and worked in the United States for many years express a desire to retire in Puerto Rico.

While Puerto Rico is ethnically homogeneous, there is cultural variation within the Puerto Rican population. One distinction is based on physical appearance: the north coast has a number of towns whose residents are dark-skinned and are seen as more African than other Puerto Ricans. A second distinction is based on wealth and education; as in the United States, Puerto Rican society is divided into three broad classes—upper, middle, and lower. A third distinction is urban-rural, with those in the island's interior continuing to live a more traditional rural way of life. A fourth distinction is based on contact with the United States. People living around San Juan on the north coast and working for American businesses are more likely to speak English, to travel to the United States, and to desire American material goods. Those on the south side, where there is less contact with the United States, live a more Spanish style of life, as reflected in the architecture, pace of life, cuisine, and almost exclusive use of Spanish. A fifth distinction is between Puerto Ricans in Puerto Rico and those living in the United States. Puerto Ricans born in the United States are called **Nuyoricans,** reflecting the view of those in Puerto Rico that those in the United States live a bicultural lifestyle combining traditional rural Puerto Rican values with urban, American ones.

The major minority group in Puerto Rico is the **Dominicans,** who number as many as 200,000. Many are in Puerto Rico illegally and are drawn there by its relative wealth, job opportunities in the tourism industry, the proximity to the Dominican Republic, and the opportunity to migrate from Puerto Rico to the United States. Puerto Rico is also considered a desirable place for Dominicans because of cultural similarities between the two islands and because similar versions of Spanish are spoken.

In addition to Dominicans, Puerto Rico has a small population of **U.S. Americans,** most of whom are involved in managing American businesses on the island.

Ethnic relations are harmonious, although there is resentment of the Dominicans, especially when they are perceived as taking jobs desired by Puerto Ricans.

Saint Kitts and Nevis

The Federation of Saint Kitts and Nevis is in the Caribbean Sea in the Lesser Antilles Leeward Islands. St. Kitts is also known by the more formal name of St. Christopher, which is the name given it by Christopher Columbus in 1493. The island of Nevis is about two miles southeast of St. Kitts. The islands were contested by the British and French in the 17th and 18th centuries, with the British gaining control in 1713. The British developed an agricultural colony with sugar cane being the major crop. Slaves were imported from Africa to work on the plantations. When slavery was abolished in 1834, many British land owners left, and the former slaves took over the land, becoming peasant farmers. The islands became an independent nation in 1983. In the 1990s, the economy has diversified and tourism and offshore banking have become major economic activities, along with the sugar industry and cotton growing on Nevis. St. Kitts and Nevis have a combined population of about 41,000.

Ethnic Composition and Ethnic Relations

Over 90% of the population is of African ancestry. The remainder is made up of those of mixed African and European (**British** and **French**) ancestry, **Europeans** who are involved in banking and commerce, and **Asian Indians** and **Pakistanis** who constitute about 3% of the population. There are also immigrants from other islands such as St. Vincent, who work on the sugar cane and cotton farms. East Asians and Pakistanis were imported by the British during the colonial era and are now mainly involved in local commerce and trade.

The African-ancestry population is known as **Kittsians** or **Nevisians,** depending on the island of residence and birth. The majority of people are Anglicans, having been converted during the British colonial era, with other Protestant sects and Roman Catholicism represented as well.

Beginning in the 1950s, there has been regular immigration to the United States, especially by women, who seek higher-paying work, especially in nursing. However, since independence in 1983, as employment opportunities in government and business have opened up on the islands, out-migration has declined. With Africans forming the majority of the population and controlling the government, and other groups filling specific economic roles, ethnic relations are harmonious.

Saint Lucia

S aint Lucia is a small island in the Lesser Antilles chain of the eastern Caribbean. It has a population of 145,000, over 90% of whom are of African or partial African ancestry. The island was colonized by the French in 1674, followed by 150 years of French and British influence, and British rule from 1714 until independence in 1979. The current population is mainly descended from African slaves imported to work on the sugar cane plantations. There are also several thousand Whites, including business owners and retirees. The indigenous inhabitants of the island at the time of French colonization, the Caribs, have disappeared through assimilation.

Ethnic Composition and Ethnic Relations

African Saint Lucians number about 135,000 and consist of three groups—**Melates** (those of African and European descent), **Doglas** (those of African and Asian Indian descent), and **Chabeans** (those of African, Asian Indian, and Carib descent). The culture is a mix of African, French, and English—people speak both English and a French creole language called Patwah; they are adherents of both Roman Catholicism and Obeah, an African-based religion; and Great Britain is the country's primary trading partner. Saint Lucian society is divided along class lines, with a small, urban, English-speaking, light-complected upper class and a much larger, Patwah-speaking, darker-complected, rural lower class of agricultural and tourism workers.

Asian Indians number about 7,000, imported by the English to serve as low-level government employees. There has been much intermarriage with the African population and relations between the groups are harmonious.

Saint Vincent and the Grenadines

S aint Vincent and the Grenadines are an island nation located in the Windward Island group of the Lesser Antilles, in the eastern Caribbean Sea. The capital city, Kingstown, is located on the southeastern coast of the island of St. Vincent. The nation has a population of 117,580, of whom 100,000 live on St. Vincent, the rest on the Grenadines. In the 18th century, the islands were contested by the British and French, finally coming under British control in 1783. They remained a British colony until independence in 1979. The official language of St. Vincent and the Grenadines is English. Some islanders speak a French-based language that is a mixture of African languages, French, English, and Spanish. A very small minority of people speak French as their first language. The population was converted to Christianity during the period of British rule, and nearly half are members of the Anglican Church. About 28% are Methodist, 13% Roman Catholic, and the remainder are Asian Indians who are Hindus or Muslims.

Ethnic Composition

Its colonial history has made the modern nation a multiethnic society. About 65% are of African ancestry, descendants of African slaves imported by the British; 19% are of mixed African and European ancestry; and the remaining 16% are of European, Asian Indian, and North American ancestry.

A distinct ethnic group called the **Black Carib** developed in the early 18th century through a mixing of escaped slaves and the indigenous Carib Indians. In 1795, the British deported the Black Caribs to British Honduras (now Belize), where they became a large population throughout Central America known as the **Garifuna.**

Afro-St. Vincentians are descendants of African slaves imported by the British to work on the plantations. Including people who claim pure African ancestry or mixed African and other ancestry, Afro-St. Vincentians number about 99,000, or 84% of the population. They are a largely rural population, with most continuing to subsist as small farmers. They also constitute almost the entire lower class on the islands, although many have risen to the middle class since independence. Lack of employment has led to considerable immigration to other islands, including Trinidad and Martinique, as well as to Guyana, Great Britain, and Canada.

This frequent migration by men has led to many families on the islands being headed by women.

People of **Asian** ancestry number about 6,400 or 5.5% of the population. The group includes both Hindus and Muslims. They are descended from the 2,200 Asian Indians who were imported as indentured laborers in the last half of the 19th century to replace Africans who had been freed from slavery in 1834. Today, people of Asian ancestry in St. Vincent are involved mainly in commercial activities.

People of **European** descent make up about 6% of the population and include **Britons,** who form the upper class and dominate the economy, and **Madeirans,** whose ancestors immigrated to St. Vincent in 1848 because of the lack of jobs in the Madeira Islands.

North Americans are mainly wealthy people from the United States who have retired to homes built on St. Vincent or on small islands in the Grenadines.

Ethnic Relations

Ethnic relations are harmonious on the islands, due largely to the presence of the large African majority and the occupational specialization characteristic of the small minorities.

Suriname

S uriname is a small nation located in northern South America. It is bordered by Guyana on the west, the Atlantic Ocean on the north, French Guiana on the east, and Brazil on the south. The northeast region of South America was contested by the British, French, and Dutch colonizers, and in 1667, what is now Suriname was awarded to the Dutch. It developed as a Dutch colony, but there is considerable ethnic diversity because the population is made up of the descendants of the various peoples imported by the Dutch to work on the plantations. The population is 436,000, and the official language is Dutch.

Ethnic Composition

Despite its small size and small population, Suriname is an ethnically heterogenous nation. In addition to a small Dutch minority, about 37% of the population are Asian Indians, 30% are Creoles, 16% are Javanese, 12% are Maroons, 2% are Indians, and the remainder are Chinese, Portuguese, and Lebanese. The nation is also religiously diverse—about 48% Christian, 27% Hindu, and 20% Muslim. While many people speak Dutch, English is also spoken in the north, and a creole language (Sranan-tongo)—based on English, Dutch, Portuguese, and African languages—is spoken as well, along with Hindi and Javanese.

Asian Indians, also called **Hindustanis,** number about 161,000, and at 37% of the population, they are the largest ethnic group. Their forebears were imported by the Dutch as indentured laborers to work on the plantations after slavery ended in 1863. Between 1874 and 1930, some 34,000 Asian Indians were imported. The Indians who came to Suriname came from a number of different castes in India. As elsewhere in the Caribbean, these caste distinctions quickly disappeared in Suriname, the major internal distinction being between those who are Hindus (80%) and those who are Muslims (20%). While many Asian Indians are farmers, with rice and dairy farming being the primary activities, Indians are now found in all occupations including commerce and trade.

Chinese number about 10,000 in Suriname, or about 2% of the population. They are descended from the Chinese brought to British Guiana (now Guyana) by the British in the late 1800s and early 1900s. These Chinese people then migrated to Suriname. In Suriname they live mainly in the north and are involved in retail trade. Some are also involved in rice farming. As elsewhere in the region, the traditional Chinese culture has essentially disappeared, and the Chinese in Suriname are closely tied to the Creoles.

Creoles are people of mixed African and White ancestry, and in Suriname they are descendants of the African slaves imported in the 18th and 19th centuries and Dutch and British slaveholders. Numbering 131,000, they are second largest ethnic group after the Asian Indians. In Suriname, Creoles are distinct from the Maroons, who are also of African ancestry. Creoles live mainly in the north, many in cities, where they are of middle- or upper-class status. Creoles closely identify with European culture, value education, and most are Roman Catholic.

Indians, the indigenous inhabitants of Suriname, number about 8,000, or about 2% of the population. They can be divided into northern and southern groups. In the north are the **Cari'a** (2,400, with the majority in Venezuela) and the **Lokono** (2,000, with the majority in Guyana). In the south are the **Akurio** (45), **Galibí** (2,400, with the majority in Brazil and French Guiana), **Trio** (800), and **Wyana** (170). Until the 1950s, the groups in the south were largely unassimilated. Since then, however, the arrival of missionaries and government efforts to control the region have disrupted traditional life. Many Indians have been settled in permanent villages where they now have become reliant on food and material goods purchased from non-Indians.

Javanese are from the Southeast Asian island of Java in Indonesia, which at one time was a Dutch colony like Suriname. They number about 70,000 in Suriname. Like the Asian Indians, they were brought to Suriname after 1863 to replace the African slaves freed that year. Between 1873 and 1930, some 33,000 Javanese were imported as indentured laborers. At the end of their five-year period of indenture, many turned to rice farming. Having been wet-rice farmers in Java, they were ideally suited to this activity, and they were notably successful in the early 1900s, when rice farming became a major economic activity. Although a few have converted to Christianity, most Javanese are Muslims.

Maroons are people of African ancestry. Their forebears escaped from slavery and fled south into the rain forest, where they formed communities outside Dutch colonial control. Some communities entered into treaties with the Dutch in the late 1700s that granted them political autonomy. The Maroons number about 52,000 and are divided into six distinct groups: **Saramaka, Djuka, Matawai, Paramaka, Aluku,** and **Kwinti.** The

Saramaka and Djuka, each numbering about 22,000, are the largest groups. The Maroons are sometimes referred to collectively as **Bush Negroes**. They all speak creole languages closely related to the Sranan-tongo creole spoken elsewhere in Suriname. Until the 1950s, when government contact intensified, the Maroons were able to maintain self-sufficient communities based on slash-and-burn horticulture, fishing, hunting, and gathering wild foods. Community organization was, and to a large extent still is, based on kinship groups that trace their ties through the female line. The internal war that began in 1986 and pitted the Djuka and Saramaka against government forces disrupted community life for the Maroons.

Other groups, whose populations number less than 10,000, include descendants of the **Dutch** colonists, **Britons, North Americans, Madeirans,** and **Lebanese Christians.**

Ethnic Relations

The ethnic diversity in Suriname is reflected in the different constituencies represented by different political parties. The National Party is mainly Creole, the Progressive Reform Party is mainly Asian Indian, and the Indonesian Peasant's Party is mainly Javanese. In 1991, these three major parties formed a coalition to defeat the ruling National Democratic Party, which also has a Creole base. However, ethnic identity and political party affiliation do not always coincide, and there are a number of smaller parties whose membership crosses ethnic boundaries and whose positions represent the interests of the middle class or the professions.

The most recent and serious ethnic conflict in Suriname was the internal conflict involving the Maroons and the national government, which began in 1986. The conflict was caused by government attempts to gain greater control of the sparsely inhabited interior and southern regions and the stationing of government troops there. The Maroons, accustomed for centuries to political independence, saw their traditional way of life threatened by governmental control and reliance on the national economy. They resisted, and warfare resulted. Many Maroons were killed, villages were destroyed, and about 12,000 fled to safety across the border in French Guiana.

Maroons are especially concerned about disruptions caused by planned logging and mining operations in their region. The Maroon resistance is known as the Surinamese Liberation Army (also called the Bush Negro Insurgency and the Jungle Commandos). The conflict ended in 1992 through a peace treaty with the government that ensured Maroon autonomy but allowed logging in the region.

Trinidad and Tobago

Trinidad and Tobago is an island nation off the coast of northeastern Venezuela consisting of the larger island of Trinidad and the smaller island of Tobago. The islands were first settled by the Spanish in 1592, then after a period of shifting control between the British and French, they became a British colony in 1802. The two islands became a single administrative unit in 1889 and an independent nation in 1962. The mix of Spanish, British, and French colonists; African slaves; and Asian Indian laborers, with the later addition of American (U.S.) cultural influence, has left Trinidad and Tobago an ethnically diverse nation that has produced its own distinctive culture. Among the most visible markers of Trinidadian culture are its unique forms of music, art, and literature. In addition to the arrival of Africans and East Indians after European settlement, migration has also played a large role in the nation's settlement history. Because the islands provided employment opportunities in the post-colonial decades, in the late 1800s over 60,000 people immigrated there, mostly freed slaves from other British colonies in the Caribbean. Additionally, in the late 1900s, a pattern of transmigration developed, with many people migrating back and forth between the United States and Trinidad and Tobago. Ninety-six percent of Trinidadians are literate and many are professionals or skilled workers, making it easy for them to find employment off the islands. The population is about 1.3 million. Trinidadians and Tobagonians speak English, with various local and social class–based dialects used.

Ethnic Composition

Trinidad and Tobago is an ethnically heterogeneous society, with 43% of African ancestry, 40% of East Indian ancestry, 14% of mixed African-European and African–East Indian ancestry, 1% of European ancestry, 1% Syrian and Lebanese, and 1% Chinese. The population is also diverse in religious beliefs, with 32% being Roman Catholic (having been converted by the Spanish and French), 25% Hindu, 15% Anglican (having been converted by the British), 6% Muslim, and the remainder other Protestant sects.

Afro-Trinidadians and Tobagonians number about 600,000, or 43% of the population. Nearly 96% live on the island of Trinidad. They are descended from African slaves brought to the islands by the Spanish, French, and British colonists and also from other West Indians who migrated to the islands in the late 1800s. Afro-Trinidadians have been associated with the People's National Movement, the nation's first political party, which has been in power for much of the time since independence. Afro-Trinidadians are a largely urban group, with many people employed as professionals and in skilled occupations. They are also well represented in the civil service, as their political party has long controlled the government. A distinct subgroup is the **Afro-Trinidadian Muslims** that is composed mainly of the urban poor.

The term **East Indians** is the generic label for people from South Asia and their descendants. They are mainly from India and include both Muslims and Hindus and peoples from various castes. Numbering about 520,000, they are mainly a rural group, although some have left farming to work in the oil refineries and to open small businesses. Hindus form about 34% of the group and Muslims about 6%. The Muslims tend to support the People's National Movement, while the Hindus support various opposition parties. East Indians speak English although Sanskrit continues to be used for religious purposes. While the caste system—which organizes social relations in India—has disappeared in Trinidad, Hinduism has undergone a revival in the last several decades.

Other groups include about 12,000 each of **Europeans** (including a **Portuguese** community), **Syrians, Lebanese,** and **Chinese.** All tend to be small-business owners, with the Chinese dominating the small-grocery business in the rural areas, and the other groups operating in more urban areas.

Ethnic Relations

Although a clear social-class hierarchy is identifiable, ethnic identity is a more salient determinant of social status in Trinidadian society. In all socioeconomic classes, people of African ancestry are of the highest status, although light-complected Afro-Trinidadians generally have higher status than do darker-skinned people. East Indians consider themselves socially superior to Afro-Trinidadians and look down upon mixed marriages. However, East Indians tend to be rural and concentrated in the working class, while most professionals and skilled workers are Afro-Trinidadians. The other ethnic groups are small and occupy specific economic niches, and therefore they do not play a major role in ethnic relations. While it is rare for ethnic conflict to be openly public, it is played out in the political arena, with the dominant People's National Movement enjoying the support of most Afro-Trinidadians and some East Indians. This joint support has generally given the party a majority, making it difficult for parties supported primarily by the East Indians to gain power.

United Kingdom Dependencies

The United Kingdom dependencies in the Americas are the following islands or island groups, listed with their populations:

- Montserrat (12,800)
- British Virgin Islands (13,000)
- Cayman Islands (34,600)
- Turks and Caicos Islands (14,300)
- Bermuda (62,100)
- Anguilla (7,000)
- Falkland Islands (2,300)

All are located in the Caribbean, except for Bermuda (which is off the coast of North Carolina) and the Falklands (which are off the coast of Argentina). These islands are under British control, although some enjoy a degree of self-government.

The islands were colonized by the British in the 17th and 18th centuries and most were developed as agricultural colonies with sugar cane being the major crop. Work was performed by African slaves. Most islands have a dual cultural identity. The official language (English), majority religion (various denominations of Protestantism), form of government, and educational system are all British. At the same time, the culture of the majority population—people of African ancestry—conforms to the general Afro-Caribbean model, with Creole versions of English spoken as the daily language; elements of traditional African religions merged with Christianity; a mix of marital and quasi-marital relationships; local markets for the exchange of food and information, and traditional forms of music, dance, and art that may reflect early influences of the Native American populations.

Ethnic Composition and Ethnic Relations

All of the islands today, except for the Falklands, have a majority **African**-ancestry population. The only island with a sizable non-African minority is Bermuda, with about 31% of the population being of **European** ancestry (mainly **British** but also **Canadian** and **Portuguese**). The Cayman Islands have a large mixed European-African population (about 55% of the population), reflecting mixing that dates to colonial times. As the Caymans did not have a large agricultural sector, the social structure was less rigid than on other islands, leading to a greater mixing of Whites and Blacks. The Caymans also have a large number of temporary workers from other Caribbean islands, the United States, Canada, and Great Britain who work in the tourism and finance industries. Unlike elsewhere in the region, many of these workers are professionals such as accountants, lawyers, and teachers who can be supported by the lucrative tourism and overseas banking industries.

In addition to people of European and African ancestry, many islands have small populations of **Chinese** and **Asian Indians** who are active in retail trade, and **North Americans** who have retired to the islands. On islands with a large tourist trade such as the Caymans, immigrants from other Caribbean islands such as Haiti and the Dominican Republic may be found in low-paying jobs in the tourism industry.

The only island with a significant ethnic relations problem is Bermuda. Tensions between the European and African communities date to the early 1970s and center on the wealth and political power of the minority European community and the poverty of the African community.

United States

The United States is located in North America. Its 48 contiguous states are bordered by Canada on the north, the Atlantic Ocean on the east, the Caribbean Sea and Mexico on the south, and the Pacific Ocean on the west. The other two states are Hawaii, a group of islands in the Pacific Ocean, and Alaska, in northwestern North America. The population counted by the 1990 census was 248.7 million. In 1996, it was estimated to be 264.6 million.

Ethnic Composition

The United States has one of the most complex ethnic populations and perhaps the most complex set of ethnic relations of any nation in the world. This is partly due to the belief—perhaps unique to the United States and Canada—that the nation will benefit and prosper because it has an ethnically diverse population. In all other nations, the reverse philosophy has generally been the rule. This American belief, while not always reflected in actual behavior, is reflected in the settlement history of the United States. The nation's original inhabitants, now collectively called Native Americans, were a diverse group who spoke over 250 different languages and had developed a wide range of cultural adaptations to the varied environments of what is now the United States. To this existing ethnic diversity was soon added the diversity that existed among settlers from Europe and then all other regions of the world. Following Christopher Columbus's European discovery of the New World in 1492, people from every nation in the world settled in the United States in the centuries that followed. Depending on whether the person counting is a "lumper" or a "splitter," the number of ethnic groups represented by these settlers and their ancestors ranges from 125 to nearly 200.

In addition, there is often considerable cultural diversity within groups that are identified as a single group, either by outsiders or by government census criteria. For example, Filipinos in the United States are a heterogeneous group made up of subgroups formed by immigrants from different geographical and cultural regions of the Philippines. Similarly, Jews are not a homogeneous group. There are considerable differences in the regions and nations Jews emigrated from, their degree of assimilation into American society, and their degree of adherence to Judaism. The German ethnic group provides an example of another form of internal variation. The majority of German Americans, whose ancestors came to the United States generations ago, are fully assimilated into American society. However, there are communities of people of German ancestry in New York City, the Midwest, and Texas who remain culturally German—they speak German as their domestic language, associate mainly with others like themselves, read German newspapers and books, live in German-style houses and communities, and strongly identify with German history and culture. And, there are still others of German ancestry—Mennonites, Amish, and Hutterites—who maintain their traditional rural cultures in their own self-supporting communities outside mainstream American society.

In addition to being ethnically diverse, the population of the United States is highly diverse in other ways. First, unlike many other nations, there is no official American religion, and religious freedom is guaranteed by law. Although the majority of Americans are Christians, all major branches of Christianity are represented, as are dozens of Christian sects and many non-Christian religions.

In the United States, religion and ethnicity do not necessarily coincide. For example, Roman Catholics of Irish, Italian, Polish, and Filipino ethnicity are considered to be distinct ethnic groups both by themselves, by each other, and by other Americans. Their religious practices tend to reflect their cultures rather than vice-versa. On the other hand, some religious groups are distinct cultural groups, such as the Mormons (Latter-day Saints), ultra-Orthodox (Hassidic) Jews, Amish, Hutterites, and Mennonites.

Major U.S. Religions

Group	Population
Adventist	808,000
Baha'i	300,000
Baptist	36,481,000
Buddhism	780,000
Churches of Christ	2,700,000
Eastern Orthodox	5,301,000
Episcopal	2,500,000
Hinduism	900,000
Islam	5,000,000
Jehovah's Witnesses	945,000
Judaism	4,300,000
Latter-day Saints	4,765,000
Lutheran	8,344,000
Methodist	13,531,000
Pentecostal	10,602,000
Presbyterian	4,193,000
Reformed	2,040,000
Roman Catholic	60,190,600

Second, there is also considerable linguistic diversity in the United States, both in regional and localized dialects of English—such as Southern English and Black English—and in the continued use of many native languages by immigrants. Although English is the standard language, and there is a political movement to make it the official language, Spanish in various forms, Chinese, Japanese, Navajo, Hindi, and dozens of other languages are commonly spoken in many communities, where some people do not speak English at all. Additionally, some Americans are bilingual—they speak and write English in public, but use another language at home or when speaking to other members of their ethnic community. Unlike religion, however, language use and ethnic identity are closely related, and those who speak languages other than English generally have a stronger sense of ethnic identity than do those who now use English as their domestic language and are more fully assimilated into American society.

A third form of diversity is that based on observable physical differences in appearance, or in what are commonly called racial differences. Americans often look quite different from one another, and physical appearance, most importantly skin color, is a major public marker of ethnic identity, even though physical differences often do not reflect cultural differences. For example, nearly all peoples with black or brown skin color are categorized by many Americans (mainly non-Blacks) as Blacks or African Americans. This broad classification, based on superficial features, masks considerable diversity among peoples of African ancestry: there are African Americans descended from slaves in the rural South, Haitians, and Jamaicans, as well as other groups of African ancestry who—though they may look like other African Americans—consider themselves separate and distinct ethnic groups.

A fourth source of diversity results from the historical emergence of regional cultures in the United States. These regional cultures reflect both the influence of the indigenous cultures of the immigrants who first settled there, as well as adaptation to different environmental circumstances. They include New England, the South, the Midwest, the Southwest, California, the Plains, and the Northwest Coast. While mass communication and travel have diluted regional differences in the 20th century, many Americans continue to identify with a specific region and regional differences are reflected in speech variations, values, style of dress, and food preferences.

The fifth and final major source of diversity is that based on social-class distinctions. American society is stratified into a number of distinct, although fluid, social-class categories. While neither average Americans nor experts can clearly define or delineate the "American" class structure, all agree that social class is a key component of the American social order. To some extent, class status is based on wealth. As with religion and race, social-class status does not necessarily coincide with ethnic identity, although patterns of ethnic and racial discrimination have limited the possibility of upward movement for some groups, resulting in disproportionately large percentages of people from certain ethnic groups in certain class categories. For example, African Americans and Latinos are overrepresented in the working class and poor categories. All of these factors interact with ethnic identity in ways that make for complex patterns of ethnic identification and equally complex patterns of ethnic relations.

The large number of ethnic groups in the United States and the significant cultural variation within groups make it difficult to fully account for the diversity of ethnicity in American life, both across and within groups. A number of classification schemes have been developed to organize groups into a more useful framework. One such scheme is especially useful for discussions of contemporary ethnic relations. With this scheme, all groups in the United States can be divided into two general categories, both with a number of subcategories: (1) *Native Americans*—peoples already resident in what is now the United States at the time of European settlement; and (2) *Immigrants*—peoples who arrived and settled in what is now the United States beginning in 1492.

In addition to these two categories, there is also a very large number of Americans of mixed ethnic and racial ancestry who do not fit neatly in the ethnic categories commonly used by Americans. Unlike in other nations in the Americas, people of mixed ancestry in the United States are almost always classified as members of only one of their ancestry groups. There is no category equivalent to the Mestizos of Latin America, nor any gradation of ethnic categories based on differences in skin color, as found in Brazil. Thus, all African Africans in the United States, if they have dark skin and "Black" features, are considered Black, even though it is estimated that from 30% to 70% of African Americans have some European ancestry. Similarly, people from Central and South America, who are mainly Mestizos (of mixed Indian and European ancestry), are considered in the United States to be Latin Americans, not Indians and not Eu-

ropeans. Somewhat more ambiguous in the United States are Amerasians and Eurasians, who number about 23,000; it is often not clear whether they fit into the White or the Asian category.

The classification of U.S. ethnic groups, and the description of ethnic relations that follows, is based on this system, with further categorization used for Native Americans and Immigrants. This classification scheme makes it easier to identify and discuss general patterns of ethnic relations in the United States.

Native Americans

As noted above the term Native American is an all-encompassing label for people whose ancestors already inhabited the Americas at the time of European arrival in 1492. In what is now U.S. territory, there are four major Native American subcategories: Hawaiians, Aleuts, Eskimos, and American Indians.

Hawaiians are the indigenous inhabitants of the Hawaiian Islands. Their ancestors migrated to the Hawaiian Islands from the Marquesas Islands in about A.D. 300. In the 1990 U.S. census, 205,800 people identified themselves as of native Hawaiian ancestry, about 20% of Hawaii's population. Most of Hawaii's residents are of mixed ancestry (Chinese, Japanese, Filipino, and Hawaiian), and the number of people with two Hawaiian parents is only about 9,000. The development of American agricultural plantations in the 1800s and the importation of Asians to work on the plantations reduced the native Hawaiians to a poor underclass in their homeland. Missionary activity ended the traditional religion, and most Hawaiians are now Protestant or Roman Catholic. Despite efforts to make land available to Hawaiians and to afford them a greater role in Hawaiian society, they continue to be the main ethnic group in the working class.

Eskimos are the indigenous peoples of Alaska and are closely related to the Asiatic Eskimos of Siberia and the Inuit of Canada and Greenland. Eskimos of the United States numbered 57,000 in the 1990 census and fall into three general geographic-cultural groups: **Alutiiq (South Alaskan Eskimos), Iñupiat (Pacific Eskimos),** and **Yup'ik (North Alas-**

kan Eskimos). Largely because of their isolation, Eskimos have been able to preserve much of their traditional culture into the 20th century. However, the rich mineral deposits in their region brought in outsiders, and the Eskimos were drawn into White society, mainly through the use of White technology and White encroachment on their traditional hunting and fishing lands. In 1971, in order to settle Eskimo land claims, the U.S. Congress passed the Alaska Native Claims Settlement Act, which divided Alaska into 12 geographic regions, with 9 of the regions being occupied by Eskimos. The regions were also incorporated as for-profit corporations, with the Eskimos owning and controlling them. The corporations were free to exploit mineral and other resources, provide employment for Eskimos and others, and invest in economic ventures in Alaska and elsewhere. Although non-Eskimos often played a role in developing and running the corporations, the income provided economic stability for many communities. The Alutiiq are affiliated with the Chugach, Alaska Corporation, Koniag Inc., and the Bristol Bay Native Corporation; the Yup'ik with Ahtna, Inc., the Cook Inlet Region Inc., and the Calista Corporation; and the Iñupiat with the Bering Straits Native Corporation, the Nana Regional Corporation, and the Arctic Slope Regional Corporation.

Aleuts are the indigenous people of the Aleutian Islands and adjacent areas of mainland Alaska. They are of the same ethnic group as the Aleuts of the Commander and Pribilof Islands in Russia. They number about 3,500. The Aleuts migrated into the region from Asia around 2000 B.C. Since contact began with Russian traders and missionaries in the mid-1700s, the Aleuts have been assimilated first into a Russian-style and then a White North American–style culture. Most are adherents of Russian Orthodoxy and derive much of their income from wage labor. Under the Alaska Native Claims Settlement Act of 1971, each of the 13 Aleut villages was given land and the Aleut Corporation was created. In 1990, it had assets worth over $17 million and 198 employees.

A Navajo woman sells jewelry at a roadside stop in the Southwest. The Navajo are the most populous Native American tribe in the United States. Photo: Corel Corp.

American Indians in the United States were and remain an extremely diverse group in comparison with both the other categories of Native Americans and immigrant Americans. There has never been any agreement among experts as to the number of American Indian groups present in the United States, either in the past or today. Traditionally, experts have dealt with this diversity by classifying Native American groups into 16 regional groupings, based on environmental and cultural similarities among the cultures in each region: Greenland, Arctic Coast, Mackenzie-Yukon, Northwest Coast, Plateau, Oregon Seaboard, California, Basin, Peninsula, Southwest, Gulf, Plains, Eastern Canada, Midwest, Northeast, and Southeast. All but the first two groupings were regions occupied by peoples now classified as American Indians. Whether or not these grouping were ever valid, it is clear that American Indians cannot now be lumped into these regional categories. While control of their indigenous territory and their indigenous languages and cultures remain important markers of ethnic identity for many Indian groups, today, organization and recognition as distinct political entities (nations) are perhaps equally important, or even more important, in terms of relations with non-Indians and with the state and federal governments. Thus, the listing below is of American Indian peoples that have been recognized as political units by state governments, the federal government, or are currently seeking federal recognition.

According to the 1990 census, there were 1,878,000 American Indians in the United States. In 1995, the federal government recognized over 300 tribes as distinct political units, with over 100 other tribes seeking such recognition. Recognition as a political unit—a tribe—does not always correspond to traditional cultural identity. Thus, some groups such as the Cherokee or Chippewa are divided into a number of tribes, and some tribes are formed from two or more previously independent cultures. About 66% of American Indians are members of a specific tribe. About 25% of American Indians live on the 287 Indian reservations or on land near reservations. Americans Indians as a group are the poorest ethnic population in the United States, with 31% living below the poverty line. In addition, social problems such as unemployment, alcoholism, and violent crime are serious issues in some Indian communities. At the same time, since the American Indian Movement began in 1968, many Indian communities have become politically involved in seeking redress for past wrongs, have taken control of their local economies, and have become self-governing. While the majority of American Indians are nominally Christian, many are also adherents of their traditional religions, including the Native American Church, the Handsome Lake religion, and the kiva-based religions of the Southwest.

American Indian Groups by State with Population

Alabama, 17,000

Cherokee	Creek
Choctaw	

Alaska, 86,000

Ahtna	Athabaskan
Tsimshian	Chugach
Eskimo	Tlingit
Calista	Haida

Arizona, 204,000

Chemehuevi	Pima
Cocopah	Quechan
Havasupai	San Carlos Apache
Hopi	Tohono O'odham
Hualapai	Tonto Apache
Maricopa	White Mountain Apache
Mohave	Yaqui
Navajo	Yavapai
Paiute	

Arkansas, 13,000

Cherokee	Ouachita

California, 242,000

Achomawi	Mattole
Cahto	Miwok
Cahuilla	Mission
Chemehuevi	Mohave
Choinumni	Mono
Chukchansi	Nom-Laka
Chumash	Paiute
Costanoan	Pomo
Diegueño	Shasta
Hoopa	Shoshone
Karok	Tolowa
Klamath	Tule River
Konkau	Wailaki
Little Lake	Washoe
Luiseño	Wintun
Lumbee	Yuki
Maidu	Yurok

Colorado, 28,000

Delaware	Ute

Connecticut, 7,000

Mohegan	Pautucket
Golden Hill Paugusset	Mashantucket Pequot
Golden Hill Pequot	Schaghitcoke

Delaware, less than 500

Nanticoke

Florida, 36,000

Cherokee	Miccosukee
Creek	Seminole

Georgia, 13,000

Cherokee	Creek

Idaho, 14,000

Bannock	Kootenai
Coeur d'Alene	Nez Percé
Delaware	Shoshone

Indiana, 13,000

Miami

Iowa, 12,000

Fox	Sac

Kansas, 22,000

Delaware	Fox
Iowa	
Kickapoo	Potawatomi
Muncie	Sac

Louisiana, 19,000

Biloxi	Coushatta
Choctaw	Houma
Chitimacha	Tunica

Maine, 12,000

Maliseet	Passamaquoddy
Micmac	Penobscot

Maryland, 13,000

Conoy	Piscataway

Massachusetts, less than 500

Mashpee	Wampanoag
Nipmuc	

Michigan, 56,000

Chippewa	Ottawa
Mackinac	Potawatomi
Ojibwa	Shawnee

Minnesota, 50,000

Chippewa	Sioux
Odawa	

Mississippi, 9,000

Choctaw

Missouri, 20,000

Cherokee

Montana, 48,000

Assiniboine	Crow
Blackfeet	Gros Ventre
Cheyenne	Kootenai
Chippewa	Salish
Cree	Sioux

Nebraska, 12,000

Fox	Sac
Iowa	Santee Sioux
Omaha	Winnebago

Nevada, 20,000

Goshute	Shoshone
Paiute	Washoe

New Jersey, 15,000

Nanticoke Leni-Lenape

New Mexico, 134,000

Acoma	San Ildefonso
Cochiti	San Juan
Isleta	Sandia
Jemez	Santa Ana
Jicarilla Apache	Santa Clara
Laguna	Santo Domingo
Mescalero Apache	Taos
Nambe	Tesuque
Navajo	Tiwa
Picuris	Ute
Pojoaque	Zia
San Felipe	Zuni

New York, 63,000

Cayuga	Seneca
Mohawk	Tuscarora
Oneida	Shinnecock
Onondaga	

North Carolina, 80,000

Cherokee	Lumbee
Coree	Meherrin
Haliwa	Tuscarora
Hattadare	

North Dakota, 26,000

Arikara	Mandan
Chippewa	Sioux
Hidatsa	

Ohio, 20,000

Allegheny	Shawnee
Miami	

Oklahoma, 252,000

Apache	Modoc
Arapaho	Osage
Caddo	Oto
Cayuga	Ottawa
Cherokee	Pawnee
Cheyenne	Peoria
Chicasaw	Ponca
Choctaw	Potawatomi
Comanche	Quapaw
Creek	Sac
Delaware	Seminole
Fox	Seneca
Iowa	Shawnee
Kaw	Tonkawa

Kickapoo	Wichita
Kiowa	Wyandotte
Miami	Yuchi

Oregon, 38,000

Cayuse	Paiute
Cherokee	Siletz
Coos	Siuslaw
Coquille	Umatilla
Klamath	Wallawalla
Lower Umpqua	Warm Springs
Northern Paiute	Wasco

Rhode Island, 4,000

Narragansett

South Carolina, 8,000

Santee

South Dakota, 51,000

Cheyenne River Sioux	Santee Sioux
Crow Creek Sioux	Sisseton-Wahpeton Sioux
Lower Brulé Sioux	Standing Rock Sioux
Oglala Sioux	Yankton Sioux
Rosebud Sioux	

Tennessee, 10,000

Cherokee

Texas, 66,000

Alabama	Kickapoo
Coushatta	Tigua

Utah, 24,000

Goshute	Shoshoni
Navajo	Ute
Paiute	

Vermont, 2,000

Abenaki

Virginia, 15,000

Mattaponi	Rappahannock

Washington, 81,000

Chinook	Palouse
Colville	Quileute
Cowlitz	Quinault
Duwamish	Puyallup
Entiat	Sanpoil
Hoh	Sauk-Suiettle
Kalispel	Skokomish
Klallam	Snohomish
Lakes	Snoqualmie
Lummi	Spokane
Makah	Squaxin
Methow	Steilacoom
Moses	Stillaquamish
Muckleshoot	Suquamish
Nespelem	Swinomish
Nez Percé	Upper Skagit
Nisqually	Wenatchee
Nooksack	Yakima
Okanagon	

Wisconsin, 39,000

Brotherton	Mohican
Chippewa	Potawatomi
Menominee	Winnebago

Wyoming, 9,000

Arapaho	Shoshone

Immigrant Groups

The United States is a nation of immigrants, as over 99% of Americans were either born elsewhere or are descended from people born elsewhere. American immigrants can be divided into seven general categories, based on an ancestor's place of birth—Africa, Asia, Americas, Europe, Pacific Islands, Middle East, and North Africa. The statistical information that follows is based on the 1990 census, and specifically on people's responses to questions about their ancestry. The numbers reported here are for people's reports of their first or primary ancestry or what one would assume is the ancestry most important to them. Of course, through intermarriage, many Americans are of mixed ethnic ancestry.

One of the more significant features of this information is the number of Americans who did not identify themselves in terms of a particular ethnic ancestry. Of a total of 224,788,502 people counted, 17% were non-specific about their ethnic background and reported their primary ancestry as follows:

Americans Claiming No Specific Ethnic Ancestry

Identity	Population
American	12,395,999
None Reported	23,921,371
United States	634,561
White	1,799,711

African Ancestry People of African ancestry in the United States are a culturally diverse population, although differences within the group are masked by the prevailing view that anyone with observable "African" physical features is, simply, African American or Black. Unlike the situation in many Latin American nations, where there is a gradation of being Black based on a number of factors including skin color, wealth, education, and lifestyle, from the perspective of White people in the United States, one is either Black or not. People of African ancestry in the United States fall into three general categories. The largest is African Americans, composed of people descended from Africans brought to the United States as slaves. They numbered 23,541,280 in 1990, or about 10% of the population. The second category, also composed of descendants of African slaves, is Blacks from the West Indies (the Caribbean islands), as follows:

West Indians in the United States

Origin	Population
Bahamian	18,752
Barbadian	33,178
Bermudian	4,007
British West Indian	35,446
Guyanese	75,765
Haitian	280,874
Jamaican	410,933
Trinidadian/Tobagonian	71,720
U.S. Virgin Islander	6,831
West Indian	138,521
Other West Indian	3,405

West Indians are a diverse population, and despite the practice of outsiders lumping them with other African Americans, West Indians tend to affiliate with their island homeland and marry within their group. Most are Christians, although in some groups syncretic religions based on African religions and Christianity, such as Voudou (Voodoo), are followed as well.

The third major African group is Africans who have arrived recently from Africa:

Africans in the United States

Origin	Population
Eritrean	4,231
Ethiopian	29,637
Ghanaian	19,695
Kenyan	4,460
Liberian	8,309
Nigerian	86,875
Sierra Leonean	4,441
South African	15,347
Ugandan	2,475
Other	28,407

Again, this is a diverse group, with ties to the homeland remaining strong. The largest group is those from Nigeria, with most being either from the Igbo or Yoruba ethnic groups. Many Africans come for education and employment opportunities and to escape conflict, famine, and other problems in Africa.

African Americans were once a largely rural population, but following Reconstruction in the South in 1870, a mass migration to the North began, and the majority of African Americans now live in the North and in cities. From the 1960s on, as Whites left the cities for the suburbs, the percentage of African Americans in cities increased, and in many cities today, African Americans are the largest ethnic group. They are heavily concentrated in inner-city neighborhoods, often labeled ghettos, and over 66% of African American children attend schools with a majority of African American students. The history of African Americans in the United States is one of racism, segregation, and discrimination. Despite the civil rights movement, which gained momentum beginning in the late 1950s, and numerous new laws and court decisions, African Americans are the poorest ethnic group in the nation, with 33% living below the poverty line, compared with 14% of Whites. Although the number of African Americans in the middle class has grown, the average African American annual income is $21,609, in contrast to $27,325 for Whites. In education, employment, and most other areas of life, discrimination against African Americans remains a problem. Perhaps the two arenas in which African Americans have faced the least discrimination are in the military and in politics, although most African American elected officials represent African American constituencies. African Americans also have a strong presence in sports and in entertainment, but mainly as performers—they are underrepresented at the management level.

In addition to differences based on place of birth, U.S. residents of African ancestry are diverse in other ways. One is residence: the South versus the North, and the related distinction of rural versus urban. There is also significant social-class diversity, produced in large part by the recent increase in the number of middle-class African Americans. Middle-class African Americans tend more often to live in the suburbs, to be college educated, and to hold professional jobs. A third source of diversity is religion. While most African Americans are Christians, some attend mainstream White churches while others belong to African American churches. In many communities, the church is the center of social and political life, and the minister is an important community leader. A small number of African Americans are Jewish, and there is a community of Blacks who are Muslims.

European Ancestry   The United States is often classified as a European society, in part because the most powerful segment of society is of European ancestry, and in part because the major American institutions—the economic, legal, and political systems; the major religions; and the language are of European origin. As the following list shows, Americans come from every European nation.

To a large extent, Americans of European ancestry are assimilated into American society. In fact, they form the cultural core of modern American society, with the cultures of Great Britain and Northern Europe being the most important in this regard. Americans of European ancestry are represented across the entire social-class spectrum, and they dominate the economic and political system. Most Americans of European ancestry are Christians, with Roman Catholicism, various branches of Eastern Orthodoxy, and all branches of Protestantism being represented. Most Jews first came to the United States from Europe.

Americans of European Ancestry

Origin	Population
General	444,107
Gypsy (Rom)	3,353
Europeans—Northern and Western	
Alsatian	9,683
Austrian	542,138
Bavarian	2,833
Belgian	239,439
British	867,255
Celtic	22,966
Central European	5,434
Cornish	2,237
Danish	980,868
Dutch	3,475,410
English	21,834,160
Finnish	465,070
Flemish	8,636
French	6,194,501
German	45,555,748
German from Russia	9,833
Icelandic	27,171
Irish	22,695,454
Luxembourger	28,846
Manx	3,806
Northern European	64,758
Northern Irish	2,832
Norwegian	2,517,760
Other Western European	1,328
Pennsylvanian German	246,461
Prussian	19,184
Saxon	2,658
Scandinavian	480,646
Scots	3,315,306
Scots-Irish	4,334,197
Swedes	2,881,950
Swiss	607,833
Tirolean	3,718
Welsh	1,038,603
Wend	1,935
West German	3,509
Western European	41,664
Europeans—Eastern	
Albanian	38,361
Armenian	267,975

Belarusian	3,471
Bulgarian	20,894
Carpatho-Rusyn	6,927
Croat	409,458
Czech	769,427
Czechoslovakian	240,489
Estonian	20,996
Hungarian	997,545
Latvian	75,747
Lithuanian	526,089
Macedonian	16,113
Moravian	2,660
Other Eastern European	123,717
Polish	6,542,844
Romanian	235,774
Russian	2,115,232
Ruthenian	3,010
Serbian	89,583
Slavic	43,301
Slovak	1,210,652
Slovene	87,500
Soviet Union	6,080
Ukrainian	514,085
Yugoslavian	184,952

Europeans—Southern

Basque	37,842
Cape Verdean	46,552
Cypriot	4,678
Greek	921,782
Italian	11,246,781
Maltese	30,292
Portuguese	900,060
Sicilian	40,034
Spaniard/Spanish	1,938,731

A street in Chinatown in New York City. Some businesses cater to outsiders, others to the local Chinese community. Photo: Jake Goldberg.

Asian Ancestry Asians are the fastest-growing immigrant group in the United States, largely due to the Immigration of Act of 1965, which effectively ended restrictions on emigration from Asia that had been in place for much of the 20th century. Asian Americans constitute about 2.8% of the U.S. population. While those who came in the late 19th and early 20th centuries were poor and settled in the rural West or in "Asian towns" in cities, those who have arrived in the last few decades are a more mixed population, including some who are poor, many who are middle class, and some who are wealthy. They live in communities throughout the United States, and those in the middle and upper classes often settle in suburbs. Japanese, Koreans, East Indians, and Filipinos are heavily represented in the middle class, while many Vietnamese, Lao, and Cambodians are poor. As a group, Asian Americans have a higher income than Whites by 3%, and over 40% are college educated—the highest percentage for any group in the United States other than Mormons or Jews. In the 1990s, Asian Americans have developed a reputation for being the "model minority"—ambitious, educated, with close-knit families, and with communities free of problems such as drug use and violence. Some Asian Americans see this as more of a stereotype than reality, and point out that it ignores the considerable poverty in some groups and subtle forms of discrimination experienced by many Asian Americans, and problems of illegal immigration, sweat shops, and drug trafficking in some urban communities.

Americans of Asian Ancestry

Origin	Population
General	100,663
Asians—East	
Cantonese	24,926
Chinese	1,404,634
Hong Kong	4,541
Japanese	908,599
Korean	798,595
Mongolian	2,554
Okinawan	8,498
Taiwanese	187,012
Asians—South	
Bangladeshi	11,901
Burmese	7,196
Indian	549,669
Nepali	2,369
Other	116
Pakistani	95,301
Sri Lankan	13,541
Tibetans	1,970
Asians—Southeast	
Cambodian	132,157
Hmong	89,194
Indonesian	27,936
Filipino	1,333,521
Khmer	2,979
Lao	142,640
Malaysian	25,317
Singaporean	2,230
Thai	102,941
Vietnamese	519,200

Pacific Islander Ancestry   The smallest ethnic category is composed of people from the Pacific Islands. They have come to the United States mainly since the end of World War II, which had put many Pacific Islanders in contact with American forces. For many of these immigrants, life in the United States is expected to be temporary—a means to obtain education and higher-paying and more varied employment. Money sent home to the islands in what are called remittances is a major component of some island economies. Having been converted by missionaries, most Pacific Island-

ers are Christians, most arrive already speaking English, and most have settled on the West Coast.

Americans of Pacific Island Ancestry

Origin	Population
Australian	36,290
Chamorro	4,065
Fijian	6,928
Guamanian	33,053
Micronesian	3,171
New Zealander	5,997
Pacific Islander	17,547
Polynesian	8,303
Samoan	49,503
Tongan	14,971

Caribbean, Central American, and South American Ancestry   Following African Americans, immigrants of non-African ancestry from the Caribbean, Central America, and South America form the largest non-European immigrant population. In 1990, they made up 9% of the U.S. population. In addition, there are at least three million undocumented (illegal) immigrants from these regions in the United States. Language and location are the primary criteria that are used in placing people in this category—nearly all speak Spanish and all are from the Americas. The two most common labels for this category are Hispanic, which stresses the Spanish heritage, and Latino/Latina, which stresses the Latin American heritage. Many people now prefer the latter, as they see their cultures as having evolved in the Americas and as being considerably more complex in origin (including African and Indian heritage) than just Spanish.

All Caribbean, Central American, and South American groups speak Spanish (except Brazilians, who speak Portuguese). These groups speak a number of different varieties of Spanish, however, with (for example) quite different vocabulary and pronunciation in the Spanish spoken in Argentina, El Salvador, and Puerto Rico. In addition, for each national group, its own version of Spanish is an important marker of cultural identity and serves to differentiate that national group from other Latinos. Also as a result of Spanish colonization of the region, most Latinos are Roman Catholic, although in the last two decades a significant minority, especially among the poor, has converted to evangelical Christianity. Hidden within the Latino category and its national groups are about 200,000 Indians, mainly Mayas from Mexico and Guatemala and Garifuna from Central America, who have immigrated to the United States to escape the civil wars and conflicts in their homelands.

Latinos in the United States are a diverse group and are not unified culturally, economically, or politically. The largest group is Mexicans, and while concentrated in California, Texas, Arizona, and New Mexico, Mexicans now live in every state, where they often work on farms or in factories. Two other large groups, the Puerto Ricans and Dominicans, live mainly in New York City and other northeast cities, while the majority of Cubans live in Miami, Florida.

Americans of Caribbean, Central American, and South American Ancestry

Origin	Population
Argentinian	54,324
Belizean	21,205
Bolivian	31,035
Brazilian	57,108
Central American	9,755
Chilean	54,842
Colombian	329,160
Costa Rican	45,601
Cuban	805,204
Dominican	484,893
Dutch West Indian	33,473
Ecuadorian	182,904
Guatemalan	229,479
Hispanic	1,059,910
Honduran	108,364
Latin American	39,446
Mexican	11,165,939
Nicaraguan	167,395
Other Central/South American	5,018
Panamanian	76,829
Paraguayan	4,916
Peruvian	147,504
Puerto Rican	1,813,122
Salvadoran	479,977
South American	9,075
Uruguayan	13,418
Venezuelan	40,331

Middle Eastern and North African Ancestry

People who have immigrated to the U.S. from the Middle East and North Africa are mainly Arabs, with Persians (Iranians), Jews from Israel, and Copts from Egypt being the major non-Arab groups. However, not all Arabs are Muslims, and there are significant minorities of Syrian Christians, Lebanese Christians, and Palestinian Christians. Although Arabs have been coming to the United States since the late 1800s, many have arrived since the Immigration Act of 1965 ended restrictions on immigration by non-Europeans. Arab Americans live mainly in or around Dearborn, Michigan; New York City; and Southern California. As a group, they are rela-

Americans of Middle Eastern and North African Ancestry

Origin	Population
Afghan	30,600
Arab	112,411
Assyrian	46,099
Iranian	220,714
Iraqi	20,657
Israeli	69,018
Jordanian	19,657
Lebanese	309,578
Middle Eastern	6,654
Palestinian	44,651
Saudi Arabian	4,257
Syrian	95,515
Turk	66,492
Yemeni	3,497
Algerian	2,537
Egyptian	73,097
Moroccan	15,015
Sudanese	3,341

tively well-educated, and the average family income exceeds the American average.

North American Ancestry   In addition to several hundred groups listed above, there are also some two million people of Canadian ancestry living in the United States. The majority of these are Acadians of Louisiana and Texas.

Americans of Canadian Ancestry

Origin	Population
Canadian	354,656
French Canadian	1,698,394
Newfoundlander	3,636
North American	12,618
Nova Scotian	3,320
Other	185

Ethnic Relations

As with ethnic composition, ethnic relations in the United States are exceedingly complex. Any discussion of ethnic relations in the United States must proceed from the reality that the basis of American culture is "Mainstream European American Culture." Mainstream European American Culture is based on cultural institutions such as the English language and British educational principles brought by the British colonists and core American values that developed in the United States. These include English as the national language, religious tolerance, individualism, majority rule, equality, a free-market economy, and a commitment to—and the idealization of—progress. It is likely that the majority of Americans—and certainly most Americans of European ancestry—believe that all Americans, including immigrants, should assimilate to this set of core institutions and values.

Although the United States is a nation of immigrants, Americans have long had an ambivalent attitude about immigration. While millions of immigrants have found freedom and prosperity in the United States, the history of immigration is considerably more complex. From the beginning, the preferred immigrants have been those from northern Europe—British, Irish, Germans, Dutch, and Scandinavians—who could easily assimilate into mainstream American culture. Although immigration by peoples from eastern and southern Europe was considerable from the 1880s until the 1920s, many of these ethnic groups, such as the Poles, Hungarians, and Italians, faced discrimination in employment and housing, and it took two or more generations for economic assimilation to take place. While all of these groups are now assimilated into American society, they have also contributed to American culture by adding new religious traditions, food, and words to the English language. Despite assimilation, for many members of these groups, a sense of ethnic solidarity remains salient.

The history of Asian immigration is different. Chinese and Japanese workers were brought to the United States as laborers in the mid-19th century. When some did not return to their homelands after they were no longer needed on the railroads and in the mines in the West, laws were enacted effectively ending Asian immigration and denying many Asians full rights as American citizens. The immigration law of 1925 sharply reduced immigration for all except northern Europeans, as immigration quotas were based on the percentage of an immigrant group's population already in the United States. Immigration was made easier when the law was changed in 1965, and Asians and Latin Americans then became the largest immigrant streams. In the 1990s, concerns about immigration in the face of high unemployment have led to new restrictions on immigration, aimed mainly at Latin Americans and poor immigrants.

In addition, major ethnic relations issues in the contemporary United States concern Black-White relations, Native American–White relations, and relations among specific ethnic groups. In this discussion, "White" means mainstream European American culture. Despite the economic and political gains achieved by the civil rights movement, the United States remains a nation divided by race. African Americans and White Americans, to a large extent, live in different social and economic worlds. Compared with Whites and many Asian Americans, African Americans are second-class citizens—they have lower incomes, less education, less employment opportunity, a lower life expectancy, more health problems, and are more likely to be the victims of crime. Many African Americans believe that the criminal justice system is biased against them. There are also continuing tensions between Blacks and Jews, as well as between Blacks and some Asians, especially Koreans. In some African American urban communities, Jews and Koreans own or owned many businesses, and their presence is resented by those who advocate African American business ownership in their communities.

Relations between Native Americans and White Americans have been characterized, from the first encounters in the early 16th century, by racism, genocide, forced assimilation, and widespread sickness and death from European diseases to which Native peoples had no natural immunity. The effect of these policies and developments was so great that by 1900, the Native American population had decreased from perhaps as many as 8 million to 250,000, almost all Native Americans were confined to reservations, and many Indian nations had disappeared or ceased to function as political and economic entities. Over the 20th century, the Native American population has gradually increased, and in the last 30 years, an effective Indian rights movement has emerged that has used legal, political, economic, and moral means to begin restoring Native American rights. These include the right to determine who is a member of a Native American nation, the right to own and control indigenous territory, the right to control resources on Native American lands, the right to practice Native American religions, and the right to participate in the public display of Native American cultures. Especially important to American Indians has been the image of Indians created through movies, museum exhibits, and school textbooks. To a large ex-

tent, Indians continue to be portrayed in an idealized and romanticized way, shown as they are believed to have existed prior to European settlement. Although Indians want their past and their history recognized, they also want modern Indian cultures to be regarded as equally valid.

A final major issue affecting ethnic relations in the United States in the 1990s is illegal immigration. In early 1997, the Immigration and Naturalization Service estimated that there are five million immigrants in the United States who have entered the country illegally. Of this number, 54% are from Mexico and at least another 20% are from other nations in the Americas. Of the countries with significant numbers of illegal immigrants in the United States, only the Philippines (1.9%) and Poland (1.4%) are non-American nations. In the United States, illegal immigrants are heavily concentrated in California (40%), as well as in Texas (14.1%), New York (10.8%), and Florida (7%). Illegal immigrants come to the United States for jobs, and they are preferred by some employers because they can be paid low wages, and fired easily, and they cannot unionize. They also come for a better life for their children, as anyone born in the United States is a U.S. citizen, regardless of the citizenship of his or her parents. In the 1990s, in California and elsewhere in the nation, there has been a movement to control illegal immigration. New laws were enacted in 1996 that make it easier to deport illegal immigrants and that limit their and their children's access to education, health care, and public assistance.

In addition to these patterns of ethnic relations, there is also continuing anti-Semitism—although surveys suggest it is decreasing and is less common in younger people—and anti-Arab sentiment fueled by terrorist attacks or the threat of such attacks.

Uruguay

U ruguay is a small nation in southeastern South America. It is bordered by Brazil on the
north, the Atlantic Ocean on the east, and Argentina on the south and west. It has a population of 3,239,000 and is one of the more urbanized nations in the world with about 87% of the
population living in cities and 40% in or around the capital of Montevideo. During the colonial
era, Uruguay was controlled by the Spanish colony of Buenos Aires (which later became part of
Argentina). It became an independent nation in 1828. Uruguay has long been a prosperous
nation and generally free of the political conflict experienced by many other nations in Latin
America.

Ethnic Composition and Ethnic Relations

Uruguay is unique among the nations of Latin
America in that its population is predominantly
of European ancestry, with virtually no indigenous Indian population. The Indians present
at the time of Spanish settlement were quickly
killed or dispersed to the interior. About 88%
of the population is of European ancestry; primarily **Spaniards** and **Italians,** with smaller
populations of people of **Portuguese** and **British** ancestry. Many Uruguayans of European
ancestry speak Spanish, although Uruguayan
Spanish has been influenced by Italian. The
majority are Roman Catholic.

The other 12% of Uruguay's population is
either Mestizo (8%) or Afro-Uruguayan (4%).
Mestizos, of mixed European and American
Indian ancestry, live mainly in the interior and
are marked as inferior by their darker skin
color.

Although many **Afro-Uruguayans** are assimilated into Uruguayan society, they continue to form a distinct population and are
considered socially inferior. Economically,
they have fewer opportunities than Uruguayans of European ancestry. Many work as mu-
sicians and entertainers, and Afro-Uruguayan
women dominate the domestic worker economic niche.

In addition to these groups, there is a small
Jewish population that has decreased to less
than 20,000 as many have left for Israel or the
United States due to anti-Semitism.

Social class status, as indicated by occupation, wealth, and place of residence, is far more
important than ethnic identity in Uruguayan
society.

Venezuela

V enezuela is in northern South America. It is bordered by Colombia on the west, the Caribbean Sea on the north, Guyana on the east, and Brazil on the south. It has a population of
21.9 million. Due to its oil industry, Venezuela is one of the wealthiest nations in the region. It
also has enjoyed a stable democratic form of government for several decades, although economic problems have led to some political instability in the 1990s.

Venezuela was colonized by Spaniards, but a distinctive Venezuelan society and identity have
developed from a mix of Spanish, African, and American Indian traditions. One example of this
unique Venezuelan culture is the cult of Maria Lionza, which incorporates images based on a
Roman Catholic saint, an African hero, and an Indian chief. The official language of Venezuela is
Spanish, and 96% of the population is Roman Catholic.

Ethnic Composition

Venezuela has not attempted to classify its population on the basis of ethnicity since the 1920s. This reflects, in part, the relative unimportance of ethnicity in Venezuelan society. The important markers of group identity in Venezuelan society are skin color and social status. The question of ethnicity is further complicated by a long history of mixing among those of Spanish, African, and Indian ancestry. Thus, "Mestizo" in Venezuela means a person of any mixed ancestry—African-Spanish, Indian-Spanish, and African-Indian—not just Indian-Spanish, as elsewhere in Latin America. With these caveats in mind, it is possible to say that Venezuela's population is about 68% Mestizo, 21% people of European ancestry (mainly Spanish), 10% Afro-Venezuelan, and 1% American Indian.

Afro-Venezuelan is an ambiguous concept for a number of reasons. First, in its most restricted sense, the term refers only to people who identity themselves as Afro-Venezuelan and who live in or associate with Afro-Venezuelan communities. These people number about 2.2 million, or 10% of the population. Another 50% of Venezuelans have some African ancestry but are labeled as Mestizos. The second reason that the term is ambiguous is that all of modern Venezuelan culture has been influenced by Afro-Venezuelan music and art, and by the promotion the use of Afro-Venezuelan culture in tourism. Thus, the African experience is not separate from the Venezuelan experience. Third, the Afro-Venezuelan category is composed of a number of very different groups—people descended from the African slaves imported by the Spanish in the 16th and 17th centuries, people descended from Black West Indians who immigrated to Venezuela in the late 1800s, people of African ancestry who have immigrated from neighboring Guyana and who speak English, and since the Cuban Revolution of 1959, Afro-Cubans.

Afro-Venezuelans tend to live in their own communities, both in rural areas where they are primarily farmers and in cities where they live in their own neighborhoods (barrios) or in makeshift communities on the outskirts of cities. Three important elements of Afro-Venezuelan culture are *conucos*, *cofradías*, and the syncretic religion. Conucos are the small farms that form the basis of rural Afro-Venezuelan society. Cofradías are communal organizations that take religious, economic, and social forms and are a key ordering mechanism in Afro-Venezuelan communities. Although most Afro-Venezuelans are Roman Catholic, Roman Catholicism in Venezuela has been influenced by the indigenous religions of Afro-Venezuelans as reflected in belief in spirits and patron saints.

People of **European** ancestry constitute about 21% of the population. Most are of Spanish heritage, but others of European ancestry live in Venezuela, as well, attracted by the growing economy of the 1970s and 1980s and the stable government. In the 1990s, Venezuela has been actively involved in recruiting Eastern European technicians to work in Venezuelan industries. Once forming the elite of wealthy landowners, those of Spanish ancestry still occupy many high-status positions in Venezuela, although access to top government, military, and business positions is also available to others. Venezuelans of Spanish ancestry are seen as the carriers of Spanish culture including the Spanish language, Roman Catholicism, and Spanish styles of art and literature.

Indians constitute about 1% of the population, though they occupy about 33% of the land. Nearly all Indian groups are located in border regions with Colombia, Brazil, and Guyana, and many have communities on both sides of the border. Counts of the number of groups vary, depending on whether some groups are classified as subgroups of larger groups or as distinct cultures. A conservative estimate is that there are 21 major groups in Venezuela, plus a number of smaller ones such as the **Makushi, Tunebo, Arawak,** and **Saliva,** whose major population is across the border in one of the neighboring nations. The following table lists the name, location, and population of the major groups and is followed by more detailed descriptions of the largest groups.

Indian Groups of Venezuela

Group	Location	Population
Baniwa	West	1,200
Baré	West	1,300
Barí	Northwest	1,000
Cariña	West	7,000
Cuiva	Northeast	300
Curripaco	West	1,600
Guahibo	West	30,000
Guajiro (Wayuu)	Northwest	60,000
Hiwi	West	7,300
Hoti	South	400
Panare (E'ñapa)	South	2,400
Paraujano	Northwest	2,600
Pemon	Southeast	11,600
Piaroa	West	7,000
Puinave	West	500
Pume (Yaruro)	Northwest	3,900
Sanema	Northeast	2,400
Warao	Northeast	20,000
Yanomamo	South	12,500
Yekuana (Yekwana)	South	3,000
Yukpa	Northwest	3,000

Guahibo is a label that covers a number of related groups that live in the Guahibo culture area of eastern Venezuela and western Colombia. The four groups lumped together under the Guahibo label are the **Sikuani, Cuiva (Cuiba), Hitnu,** and **Guayabero.** The total population is about 30,000 with the majority (about 70%) living in Venezuela. The Guahibo groups have been in contact with the Spaniards since the 16th century, and the establishment of cattle ranches in their region began a long process of assimilation into Venezuelan society. Since the 1970s, most have lived on reserves.

Guajiro (Wayuu) are the largest indigenous group in Venezuela. They numbered 100,000 in 1982, with 60,000 in Venezuela and 40,000 in Colombia. They live on the Peninsula de la Guajira and in and near the city of Maracaibo. Following the arrival of the Spaniards in the early 16th century, the Guajiro adopted the herding of horses and cattle as their primary economic activity. Most continue to herd and graze cattle, sheep, and goats. Horses have almost disappeared, having been replaced by pickup trucks. Although in regular contact with outsiders, Guajiro society continues to be organized around clans, whose members trace their descent from common female ancestors.

Pemon numbered 11,600 in the 1982 census and live in southeastern Venezuela. Their traditional livelihood was based on a combination of slash-and-burn farming, hunting, fishing, and gathering wild foods. All of these activities remain important, although some Pemon now earn money by working as wage laborers in the local diamond mines. Although missionaries have worked among the Pemon since the 1920s, Venezuelan society began to influence their way of life only since the 1970s, when roads were cut into their territory and mining operations began.

Warao are the second largest Indian group, numbering 19,600 in 1982 and over 20,000 in the 1990s. They live near the coast and along waterways in the northeast. Their economy is based on fishing, slash-and-burn farming, and in recent years, wage labor in the regional logging and mining industries. Despite missionary activity dating to the 1920s and their more recent involvement in the economy as wage laborers, much of the traditional culture survives, and the Warao enjoy some protection from outside influence through their control of a sizable percentage of land in the region.

Yanomamo (Yanomamö, Yanamami, Yanomama) number about 21,000, with 12,500 in southern Venezuela and 8,500 across the border in Brazil. Culturally, the populations in the two nations are quite similar, with life centered around the semipermanent circular villages, slash-and-burn farming, and a pattern of continual warfare and alliances among the villages. However, the two national populations vary markedly in their experience with outsiders. The Venezuelan Yanomamo have lived in relative isolation, with most of their contact with outsiders being with missionaries, traders, and other Indians. For the Yanomamo in Brazil, the situation is much different. Their territory contains mineral wealth that has attracted Brazilian miners who in recent years have raided Yanomamo villages and driven off or killed dozens of Yanomamo. The presence of these outsiders has also spread disease among the Yanomamo of Brazil, causing additional problems. The situation faced by the Yanomamo received international attention as advocates for indigenous rights and human rights have criticized the Brazilian government for failing to protect the Yanomamo and their territory.

Ethnic Relations

The distribution of people from different ethnic groups across social-class lines in Venezuelan society has changed dramatically in the last half of the 20th century. Prior to 1950, those of European ancestry formed the political, economic, and social elite, with Mestizos forming a small middle class, and other Mestizos, Afro-Venezuelans, and Indians forming the very large class of rural poor. Since the 1960s, Venezuela has enacted democratic and social reforms that have expanded economic opportunity and encouraged relocation to cities. The social-class system is now much more fluid, and Mestizos and Afro-Caribbeans have considerably more opportunity for movement into the middle and upper classes. Some experts believe that opportunities for people of African ancestry are greater in Venezuela than anywhere else in Latin America.

The only ethnic group that remains outside mainstream society is Venezuela's Indians. Relations between the Indian groups and other Venezuelans, as well as between Indians and the Venezuelan government, are major issues. The status of the Indians was boosted by the 1982–83 Venezuelan Indian Census, which brought them to national attention, and a governmental agency—the Venezuelan Office of Indian Affairs—is responsible for supplying technical, health, social, and educational assistance to Indian communities. Missionaries have been active in some Indian communities for centuries, and Roman Catholic, Seventh-Day Adventist, and evangelical missionaries continue to play a major role in mediating relations between Indians and the non-Indian world. In many groups, missionary activity has been a force for assimilation into mainstream society. However, not all groups have undergone assimilation to the same extent: some remain relatively isolated, others live on reservations, and still others have experienced a significant amount of assimilation through intermarriage with non-Indians.

A unifying issue for all Indian groups is land ownership. Some groups own no land, others live on reserves with the land being controlled by the government, and others own their land. All groups would prefer absolute ownership as a means of controlling access, resources, and settlement of their territory by outsiders. This wish is opposed by those who seek to develop natural resources on Indian land.

INDEX

by Virgil Diodato